THE GREAT GAME
1856–1907

THE GREAT GAME
1856–1907

*Russo-British Relations in
Central and East Asia*

EVGENY SERGEEV

Woodrow Wilson Center Press

WASHINGTON, D.C.

Johns Hopkins University Press

BALTIMORE

EDITORIAL OFFICES
Woodrow Wilson Center Press
One Woodrow Wilson Plaza
1300 Pennsylvania Avenue, N.W.
Washington, DC 20004-3027
Telephone: 202-691-4029
www.wilsoncenter.org

ORDER FROM
Johns Hopkins University Press
Hampden Station
P.O. Box 50370
Baltimore, Maryland 21211
Telephone: 1-800-537-5487
www.press.jhu.edu/books/

The Library of Congress has cataloged the hardcover edition of this book as follows:

Sergeev, E. IU. (Evgenii IUrevich), 1959–
[Bolshaia igra, 1856–1907. English]
The Great Game, 1857–1907 : Russo-British relations in Central and
East Asia / Evgeny Sergeev.
pages : maps ; cm
Includes bibliographical references and index.
ISBN 978-1-4214-0809-5 (cloth)
1. Russia—Relations—Great Britain. 2. Great Britain—Relations—Russia. 3. Asia,
Central—Foreign relations. 4. Asia, Central—History. 5. East Asia—Foreign relations.
6. East Asia—History. I. Title.
DK67.5.G7S4413 2012
958'.03–dc23   2012037090

ISBN 978-1-4214-1557-4 (paperback)

For my mother, Eleonora Sergeeva

CONTENTS

ACKNOWLEDGMENTS

To study the history of the Great Game called for a great amount of work with archival records, published collections of documents, memoirs of eyewitnesses, and an extensive bibliography. This undertaking was made easier by the sympathy of many people whose aid was of great importance to the author. I am therefore very grateful to all my colleagues, who provided much advice in writing this book. Special thanks must go to my coworkers at the Institute of World History of the Russian Academy of Sciences for reading and commenting on draft chapters.

The book could not have been completed without the assistance of the staff of the Russian federal archives and national libraries in Moscow and Saint Petersburg. To the experts working at the British Library and the National Archives of the United Kingdom, I also owe a heavy debt of gratitude. The research was carried out thanks to grants given to me by the British Academy. My sincere and earnest thanks must be tendered, therefore, to Francine Danaher and Samantha Jordan. I am also grateful to those anonymous expert readers who reviewed my manuscript and offered critical remarks and reasonable comments. And I must express my heartfelt thanks to Joseph Brinley, director of the Woodrow Wilson Center Press, for his skillful guidance during the publication process.

I owe special thanks to my mother, Eleonora Sergeeva, my wife, Irina, and our sons, Dennis and Oleg, for their constant support and immense patience, which made this book possible after six years of intensive work.

SELECTED CHRONOLOGY

1856

The Paris Peace Treaty ends the Crimean War and begins the Great Game; March.
The Second Opium War breaks out between Britain, France, and China; October.
Alexander Gorchakov becomes Russian foreign minister; April.
Herat falls to the Persians; October.
A British military force captures Bushire on the Persian Gulf, causing Nasir-u-Din, the
   shah of Persia, to withdraw from Herat and abandon his claims to it; December.

1857

The world economic crisis breaks out for the first time in history.
The Indian Mutiny threatens British rule in India; May.

1858

Nikolai Khanykov, a Russian political agent, attempts to make contact with the emir
   of Afghanistan, Dost Mohamed, but is rebuffed by him; spring.
The Indian Mutiny is finally suppressed; spring.
The India Act abolishes the right of the East India Company to rule in India and
   transfers all authority to the British Crown; August.
Colonel Nikolai Ignatiev heads up a Russian mission to Khiva and Bokhara to
   discover how far the British have penetrated Central Asia; summer.

1859

Major General Ignatiev heads up a mission to Peking to get the Qing government
   to formally cede to Russia the territories it has captured following the Second
   Opium War (spring)

1860

After the British and French leave Peking, Ignatiev negotiates the Treaty of Peking
   with the Chinese, giving Russia a large territory north of the Amur River and the
   right to open embassies in Xinjiang and Mongolia; November.

1861

The Russians, under Colonel Nikolai Verevkin, capture Yengi Kurgan, a Khokandian boundary town; November.

1863

Herat is reconquered by Dost Mohamed Khan.

1864

The Russians advance on Central Asia, consolidating their southern frontier by capturing Yesse, Chimkent, and other towns and forts in the northern domains of the Khan of Khokand; summer–autumn.

Arminius Vambery travels through Central Asia.

Gorchakov distributes a memorandum to the European powers to explain Russian advances into Central Asia; December.

1865

Yakub Beg arrives in Kashgar from Khokand and goes about consolidating his power in Kashgaria; January.

The new Turkestan Province is established on the steppes between the Lake of Issyk-Kul and the Aral Sea; February.

The Russians, under Major General Mikhail Cherniaev, capture Tashkent; June.

1866

Russian troops, under Major General Dmitry Romanovsky, badly defeat the Bokharian forces at Irjar; May.

1867

Alexander II establishes the governorship of Turkestan at the initiative of his adjutant general, Konstantin Kaufman; July.

1868

The Russians, under Kaufman, capture Samarkand and force the Emir of Bokhara to agree to make Bokhara a Russian protectorate; May–July.

Robert Shaw and George Hayward travel, separately, from Ladakh to Kashgar to establish contact with Yakub Beg for trade and geographical survey purposes, respectively; September–December.

Russian forces temporarily invade Kuldja; autumn.

1869

The Russians build a permanent fortress in Transcaspia at Krasnovodsk; January–March.

1870

George Hayward embarks on a journey to the Pamirs and is murdered by tribesmen near Darkot, between Chitral and Gilgit; July.

Captain Nikolai Przhevalsky's first Inner Asian expedition begins; until 1873.

1871

The Russians, under General Kaufman, invade the Ili Valley, annexing it for ten years; June.

The British establish a direct submarine cable link between London and India.

1872

The Russians dispatch a mission led by Captain Kaulbars to Yakub Beg to discuss trade terms designed to favor Russian over British goods; spring.

1873

Russia acknowledges that Afghanistan lies within the British sphere of influence in the agreement between Gorchakov and Clarendon; January.

The Russians, under Kaufman, capture Khiva and turn the Khanate of Khiva into the Russian protectorate; May.

British trade mission to the city of Kashgar, headed up by Douglas Forsyth; summer.

Sher Ali, the Afghan emir, approaches the Indian government with a proposal for a defense treaty against the Russians, but is refused by the British; autumn.

1874

Lieutenant Colonel Thomas Gordon and a small British party explore the Pamirs; spring.

A commercial agreement is signed between the Russians and Yakub Beg of Kashgaria; summer.

1875

The Russians, under General Kaufman, capture Khokand, after an uprising against the Russians and the puppet khan they had installed there previously; August.

The khan of Khelat permanently leases the Bolan Pass and Quetta to the British; autumn.

The khan of Khokand cedes all territories on the right bank of the Syr Daria to Russia; October.

Captain Frederick Burnaby departs from Britain on his journey across Russian Central Asia; November.

1876

All Khokandian territories are annexed by the Russians after the uprising is suppressed; February.

Colonel Nikolai Przhevalsky's second Inner Asian expedition begins; until 1878.

1877

The Russo-Turkish War breaks out; April.

Death of Yakub Beg in the city of Kashgar; May.

The Chinese recapture Kashgar; December.

1878

Queen Victoria is proclaimed the Empress of India; January.

The Russians, under General Kaufman, prepare a march against India from Turkestan; May–June.

Major General Nikolai Stolietov's mission to Kabul results in the signing of a treaty of friendship between Russia and Afghanistan; August.

The British inform Sher Ali that they intend to send a mission to Kabul and ask for a safe passage; August.

After Sher Ali rebuffs the British request for a safe passage, the British march on Kabul begins the Second Afghan War; November.

1879

The British and the Afghans sign the Treaty of Gandamak, ending the war and granting significant concessions to Britain, including control of Afghan foreign policy; May.

The British mission, under Major Louis Cavagnari, reaches Kabul; July.

The Russians attempt to capture the Turkmen stronghold of Geok Tepe but are defeated; September.

The British mission in Kabul is attacked by an Afghan mob, and all are killed; September.

A British punitive force, under General Frederick Roberts, reaches Kabul; October.

Colonel Nikolai Przhevalsky's third Inner-Asian expedition begins; until 1880.

1880

Abdur Rahman, the nephew of Sher Ali, returns from exile in Samarkand to claim the Afghan throne; February.

The Chinese threaten to take back Kuldja, in the Ili Valley, by force; spring.

The British garrison at Kandahar is defeated in the battle of Maiwand, near Kandahar, by Ayub Khan, the ruler of Herat and Abdur Rahman's rival for the throne; June.

The British agree to leave Kabul and let Abdur Rahman have the throne, in exchange for his promise to have relations with no other power but Britain; July.

Roberts' forces from Kabul defeat Ayub Khan, who is later driven out of Afghanistan by Abdur Rahman, who captures Herat; autumn.

The Russians begin to extend the Trans-Caspian Railway east from the Caspian port of Krasnovodsk to Tashkent.

1881

The Russians, under Lieutenant General Mikhail Skobelev, capture Geok Tepe,
    slaughtering those who flee from the fallen fortress; January.
The Treaty of Saint Petersburg results in Russia's retrocession of Kuldja to China; June.
A treaty is signed between Russia and Persia concerning the boundary line in
    Turkmenia; December.

1882

Lieutenant Alikhanov arrives in Merv to spy out the Turkmen defenses of the city and
    prepare for its annexation by Russia; February.
Nikolai Petrovsky, the Russian consul, arrives in the city of Kashgar.

1883

Major General Nikolai Przhevalsky's fourth Inner Asian expedition begins; until 1885.

1884

Merv agrees to come under Russian protection; February.
The Chinese establish the new Province of Xinjiang in Eastern Turkestan; November.

1885

The Russians, under Major General Alexander Komarov, capture the Afghan town of
    Penjdeh, halfway between Merv and Herat; March.
A British military survey party, under William Lockhart, is dispatched to map Chitral
    and Hunza; summer.
The Joint Anglo-Russian Boundary Commission begins to demarcate the Afghan
    boundary; September–October, until the next summer.

1887

Dulip Singh, an Indian maharajah in exile, appeals to Russia for support; March–April.
Lieutenant Francis Younghusband travels across China from Peking to India;
    April–December.

1888

George Curzon travels through Central Asia.

1889

Lieutenant Younghusband leads an expedition to Hunza to warn the ruler against
    raiding British traders; August–December.

1890

Lieutenant Younghusband and George Macartney survey the Pamirs and travel to the city of Kashgar, where Macartney becomes the British consul.

1891

Reports reach London that the Russians are planning to annex the Pamirs; July.

Captain Younghusband encounters a Russian detachment, under Colonel Mikhail Ionov, in the Pamirs who have claimed Afghan and Chinese territory for the tsar; August.

The British and Kashmiris march against Hunza, resulting in its capture and incorporation into British India; November.

1893

The Russians clash with the Afghans and Chinese in the Pamirs; summer.

Peter Badmayev, a Buriat Mongol, submits a plan to the tsar for bringing Tibet under Russian rule.

1894

The Sino-Japanese War breaks out; August.

1895

The British, under Major General George Robertson, march on Chitral, placing their own choice of ruler on the throne; February.

The Russians and the British settle the Pamirs question; March.

Umra Khan, ruler of Swat, lays siege to the British troops in the palace in Chitral; March.

A British relief force, under Colonel James Kelly, delivers the British in Chitral, ending the siege; April.

The Sino-Japanese War ends in China's defeat; April.

1897

Germany leases Kiaochow on the Shantung Peninsula; November.

1898

Russia diplomatically gains the warm-water naval base of Port Arthur from the Chinese; March.

Britain also diplomatically gains the naval base of Weihaiwei from the Chinese; April–June.

Agvan Dorzhiev, the Dalai-Lama's Special Envoy, sets up for his first mission to Saint Petersburg; summer.

Lord Curzon becomes viceroy of India; December.

1899

Russo-British agreement on Chinese railways is signed; April.

Captain Peter Kozlov sets up for a mission to Inner Asia; summer.

The Boer War begins in South Africa; October.

1900

The Boxer Uprising in China leads to the occupation of Peking by the European
powers, including Russia and Britain; August.

1902

Anglo-Japanese Alliance is signed in London; January.

The Boer War ends; May.

1903

A British mission to Lhasa, led by Younghusband, is turned back by the Tibetans; April.

A second mission, led by Younghusband, starts to Lhasa; December.

1904

Tibetan troops are massacred by the British en route to Lhasa; January.

The Japanese unexpectedly attack the Russian fleet at Port Arthur, initiating the
Russo-Japanese War; February.

Britain and France sign an entente treaty; April.

The British mission enters Lhasa; August.

The Dogger Bank (Hull) incident brings Russia and Britain to the verge of war;
October.

1905

Port Arthur falls to the Japanese; January.

The Japanese destroy the Russian Baltic Fleet in the Tsushima Straits; May.

Russia and Japan sign the Peace Treaty of Portsmouth, ending the war; September.

The British mission leaves Lhasa after the Anglo-Tibetan Convention is signed; September.

1906

Anglo-Russian negotiations on delimitation of spheres of influence begin in Saint
Petersburg; May–June.

1907

The Russians and the Japanese sign an entente treaty in the Far East; June.

The Anglo-Russian Convention officially brings the Great Game to an end; Britain
abandons the policy of "splendid isolation"; August.

THE GREAT GAME
1856–1907

RECONSIDERING ANGLO-RUSSIAN RELATIONS IN ASIA

We are on the eve of stirring times; but if we play the great game that is before us, the events will be incalculably beneficial to us and to the tribes whose destinies may change from turmoil, violence, ignorance, and poverty to peace, enlightenment and varied happiness.

—Arthur Conolly, in a private letter to Henry Rawlinson in London, 1840

Since obscure prehistoric times, humankind has known countless conflicts that have divided people. Yet, along with bloody clashes, there developed cooperation between individuals, social groups, and states in general. This intermixture of mutual revulsion and tolerance, hatred and affection has been accompanying human beings for more than five thousand years of recorded history. And it often forms a kind of "game"—or, in other words, a competition of two, or rarely three or more, participants for domination over territories, resources, and residents.

Being a paragon of this dialectical circulation, the "Great Game" played by both the European great powers and local potentates in Central and East Asia in the second half of the nineteenth century must be reexamined by historians from temporal, geographical, sociopolitical, economic, and cultural perspectives. The need for unbiased, rigorous interdisciplinary research on this historical phenomenon seems multi-faceted, for three main reasons. First, the end of the Cold War epoch in the early 1990s symbolized a break from obscurant, ideological, "black-and-white" mental stereotypes, especially those related to a distorted image of Russia in the West and also to an imprecise perception of the Occidental countries by many Russians. Second, a vacuum of power in the contact zones of civilizations where different ethnic and religious communities live, which have been so thoroughly analyzed by Samuel Huntington, accentuated the need for a more scrupulous study of modern conflicts along with their origins and mainsprings. And third, because scholars have recently gained access to archival collections in Britain, Russia, India, Iran, and the post-Soviet Central Asian republics, they could enjoy an opportunity to use unique, previously unknown sources, and in this way reconsider the Great Game through the lens of comparative approach.[1]

If an ordinary reader, eager to understand the "hidden agenda" of historical events, were asked to explain how he or she views the Great Game, the answer could easily be predicted. Most probably, the reader would say that this definition refers to the geostrategic rivalry, primarily between the British Empire and the Russian Empire, for the control of Central Asia in the nineteenth century, when, facing the challenge launched by the latter against the supremacy of the former, London had to combine both diplomatic and military means to attain a three-faceted goal: to keep the balance of power in Europe, to expand its possessions in India, and to secure its commercial routes from the Mediterranean to the Indian and Pacific oceans.

However, this response indicates too narrow an explanation of the problem. Despite an array of publications by scholars, former military staff members, journalists, and freelancers, who have traveled intensively in Oriental countries for the last few decades, the genesis of the Great Game, its own dynamics and the effect it had on international relations, remain understudied or misinterpreted. We still lack a broader panorama of the multisided intercourse that the big powers maintained with each other and traditional Asiatic societies in the age of industrial modernization. Hence, this book aims to fill this gap in the study of the process carried on by many Great Game players, whether they were statesmen, public figures, military thinkers, travelers, or native scouts. More important, the book takes an in-depth look at the Great Game in connection with the development of Russo-British relations throughout the Victorian and post-Victorian periods. Its purpose is to shatter myths and correct evident inaccuracies in our understanding of how preindustrial states and peoples were incorporated into modern civilization owing to the great powers' competition for supremacy in Asia.

Yet the initial obstacle that confronts any scholar in undertaking this research remains the lack of a clear definition of the "Great Game" itself. Therefore, to accurately describe this phenomenon means, above all, to identify the personality who articulated it for the first time, and next, expound its connotation, geographical coordinates, and successive stages.

It is a well-established fact that Captain Arthur Conolly of the Sixth Bengal Native Light Cavalry Regiment, a "daring, resourceful, and ambitious" subaltern in the service of the East India Company, was the first to scribble the combination of the three words "the Great Game" in an annotation on a copy of a letter from the British envoy in Kabul to the governor of Bombay in 1840.[2] That same year, Conolly reproduced this word combination in a private message to Major Henry Rawlinson, then a military officer, and later to become a diplomat of the minister rank, and then president of the Royal Geographical and Asiatic Societies, a founder of the Assyriology, and a leading expert on Russia's policy in Asia: "You have a great game, a noble one, before you." As historians have noted, Conolly also used a slightly modified form of this expression—the "grand game"—in his correspondence with fellow officers and relations.[3]

But why did Conolly regard his mission to be a "game," though his epistles and diaries contained reminiscences of a spiritual, antislavery, liberatory crusade in Central Asia? Some authors, like Peter Hopkirk, have argued that Conolly did have in mind the actual game of rugby, which was invented by William Ellis at the famous Rugby School in the early 1820s.[4] Yet this deduction seems neither convincing nor accurate. Alexander Burnes, another famous explorer and sometime British political resident in Central Asia, offered a more adequate explanation during his travels. On making acquaintance with the younger subaltern, Burnes observed that

> he [Conolly] is a flighty, though a very nice fellow. He is to regenerate Turkestan, dismiss all the slaves, and looks upon our advent as a design of Providence to spread Christianity.[5]

According to Sir John Kaye, the secretary of the Political and Secret Department of the India Office and a renowned British historian of the First Anglo-Afghan War who had discovered the reference to the Great (or Grand) Game in Conolly's papers,[6] the latter even plotted to mold an Anti-Slavery Confederation in 1838, including the khanates of Bokhara, Khiva, and Khokand as "buffer states," under the guidance of the British, who were expected to contribute to the liberalization of the feudal regimes as "champions of humanity and pioneers of civilization." Thus, the British would anticipate the Russian advance and reshape the Orient according to their own vision, predicated upon the ideas of European Enlightenment.[7]

Consequently, the propaganda for such a notion among Muslims dominated Captain Conolly's belief system, whereas he fatalistically regarded himself as a tool of Providence "playing" the Game, which surpassed human understanding, with himself and his colleagues. Apart from a pure theological interpretation, another, more secularized version may be suggested as well. During Conolly's service for the East India Company, it continued to be, at least de jure, a private joint venture, though it was supervised by the London Cabinet. However, the majority of clandestine reconnaissance missions conducted by gentlemen explorers and surveyors for the benefit of the company in distant no-man's-lands were looked upon as expeditions taken at their own risk without any reaffirmed official support from governmental bodies. In Conolly's case, for example, despite the fact that the British envoy to Tehran encouraged his trip and the East India Company even reimbursed him for his expenses, Sir Robert Peel, then the foreign secretary, denied his employment upon public service during the mission, when interrogated in the House of Commons on August 24, 1843.[8]

Doubtless, the "greatness" of the civilizing mission carried on by Arthur Conolly and similar protagonists of Great Britain's colonial expansion impressed the Victorians. In fact, the reformation of traditional societies, on the one hand, and the prevention of their domination by the "semibarbarous Muscovites," on the other, motivated many contemporaries, including those in the British Isles. As Edward Said metaphorically put it in his famous book *Orientalism*, explorers and missioners were considered in Victorian times as heroes "rescuing the Orient from obscurity, alienation, and strangeness."[9]

Finally, one should bear in mind a third possible dimension of the Great Game—the competition for goods and capital investments in preindustrial Asian markets where European companies could test the water at low political risk. "Britain's rulers took it for granted that the international world was one of competing powers and that their duty was to make the most of whatever assets were available to them," commented the historian Max Beloff on the position of the liberal British Empire in the global economy.[10]

Yet with the escalation of the diplomatic struggle between the great powers in the 1870s and 1880s, the very perception of the Great Game underwent a transformation. Characteristically, an anonymous pamphlet titled *The Great Game. A Plea for a British Imperial Policy* came out in Britain in 1875. Oddly enough, the author advocated an offensive policy on the periphery of Europe, particularly in Central and South Asia, where Britain and Russia would have every chance to unite their efforts, in order "to keep more than half of the world in peace and security from all attacks launched" by other countries, not excluding China.[11]

This and similar publications notwithstanding, one could hardly anticipate any sympathy from the British public for the Russian policy in Asia in the 1870s and 1880s, when the two empires balanced on the brink of open hostilities. It was small wonder, therefore, that Rudyard Kipling, a brilliant storyteller and poet of British India—"the Raj," as the local Indian population and British colonial officers called it, "visualized the Great Game in the terms of an Anglo-Indian boy, *Kim* [a famous character created by Kipling], and his Afghan mentor who was foiling Russian intrigues along the highways to Hindustan," in the words of an American scholar.[12] Although Kipling caught the epoch's tenor, his depiction of the widespread and effective British intelligence-gathering network beyond India's frontiers reflected merely one aspect of the Game, and besides, did not sufficiently portray it.[13] Yet it was Kipling's interpretation of the struggle for supremacy in Asia as a secret war against the Russians, and later also against the Frenchmen who allied with the tsar in the early 1890s, that brought fame and publicity to the phenomenon of the Great Game.[14]

Interestingly, the Great Game's vocabulary gradually seeped into the lexicon of politicians, diplomats, and travelers at the beginning of the 1900s. For example, the prominent explorer and later colonial officer Francis Younghusband wrote about meetings with Tsarist military administrators in Inner Asia:

> We and the Russians are rivals, but I am sure that individual Russian and English officers like each other a great deal better than they do the individuals of nations, with which they are not in rivalry. We are both playing at a big game, and we should not be one jot better off trying to conceal the fact.[15]

Another "player" of the Great Game, Henry Whigham, commented on the Russo-British contest in Persia in the following typical manner:

> Our danger lies not so much in our failure to recognize the importance of the Shah's kingdom as a piece on the check-board of Asia, as in the apparent inability of our rulers in Downing Street to grasp the fact that the game is already in progress, and that without an immediate move on our part, the denouement cannot long be delayed. And it is imperative that the move should be in the right direction. We are playing against an opponent who thought out his plan of campaign long ago, and has never lost an opportunity of carrying that plan into effect. His game is masterly and consistent because he knows all the time what is his final aim.[16]

Apart from a varied series of descriptive works—particularly those by George Curzon, an intrepid traveler and statesman who dealt with various aspects of this competition, such as frontiers, buffer states, and India's defense[17]—the founders of geopolitical theory, Halford Mackinder and Karl Haushofer, used the Great Game to elucidate geographical motives in the struggle for world leadership.[18] Later, in the 1950s, Morton Kaplan further analyzed these motives in devising his famous classification of international state systems.[19]

Yet it was Henry Davis, a professor of history at Oxford University, who reviewed the Game's origins for the first time in a Raleigh Lecture delivered in 1924. Davis characterized the Game as a synonym for a series of reconnaissance missions conducted by Europeans in disguise—primarily the British, Russians, French, and Germans—on the fringes of their possessions.[20] Two decades later, another British historian, Guy Wint, while reflecting on how the British and Russians had competed with each other in Asia, correctly remarked that "on each side the government gave license to its agents to plot and counterplot to the limit of causing an actual explosion, and a kind of game grew up with recognized though unadmitted convention."[21]

A new, more comprehensive, and objective consideration of the meaning of the Great Game was pursued in the 1970s and 1980s by such prominent British and American historians as Michael Edwardes, David Gillard, Gerald Morgan, and, particularly, Edward Ingram. According to Edwardes, the Game, being a contest for political ascendancy in Central Asia between democratic Britain and autocratic Russia, fitted in very well with the Victorian model of "the romance of empire." Symptomatically, the historian quoted the phrase used by the Russian chancellor, Count Karl Nesselrode, who described it in the 1850s as a "tournament of shadows."[22] For David Gillard, Great Britain and Russia, the empires that replaced France and China as the hegemonic states in the race for supremacy in Asia, radically transformed the traditional balance of power on the Eurasian land mass. It was telling that the Crimean War of 1853–56 moved the epicenter of the struggle for domination from the Caucasus to the Pacific.[23] In turn, Gerald Morgan argued that the Game had been a nickname for development, being in nature more imaginary than real. His study highlighted the necessity of cross-verifying the intelligence collected on the spot by either British or Russian military and political agents, who had missed no opportunity to exaggerate or even fabricate sinister plots of adversaries. Doubtful of Davis's argument regarding the espionage web created by British and Russian military intelligence agents, Morgan maintained that the "tournament of shadows" was nothing but a myth created by a few enthusiastic subalterns to promote their military careers in the entourages of bloody Muslim fanatics.[24]

Edward Ingram, who thoroughly investigated the origins and early flaws of the Great Game, substantially contributed to the multilevel research on this unprecedented competition. "Between 1828 and 1907," wrote Ingram in the book that initiated his thematic series of publications on the subject under consideration, "the Great Game in Asia was Britain's search for a method of preventing the power of Russia from endangering British India." Moreover, he focused upon its genesis: "A fact of geography, that the British had a frontier to defend, and a fact of politics, that they could find no one to defend it for them, were the origins of the Great Game in Asia."[25] While extending the period of his study back to the French Revolution of 1789, he supposed that "the Great Game had been rehearsed in Egypt and Baghdad during the war of the second anti-Napoleonic coalition in the very end of the eighteenth century."[26] Thus, for Ingram, the Anglo-French competition for domination in Europe actually signified the end of the Columbian Era and simultaneously triggered the Great Game, whereas Russia had replaced France as a key "player" by the 1820s.[27] In his final study of the period, covering the years from before the French Revolution to the aftermath of the Napoleonic Wars, he arrived at the somewhat bizarre inference that the Game "was an attempt made by the British in the 1830s to impose a view on the world and, afterwards, to escape the consequences of their failure."[28] To supplement this interpretation, he defined the Game "as a British invention, played in Asia in cooperation with the Turks, Persians, Afghans, and Sikhs, against the Russians."[29]

To all appearances, all these historians and thinkers reduced the Great Game to one or two basic aspects, whether political or economic.

A more balanced approach may be found in an article written by David Fromkin in 1980, in which he tried to delineate a difference between narrow scholarly treatments of the Great Game and wider readings of its significance. In the former case, researchers have usually focused on espionage; in the latter, they have tended to see the Game through the prism of the general Russo-British imperial contest. It should be noted that Fromkin devoted much attention to the Game's geostrategic features, at the same time portraying its major players.[30]

The collapse of the Soviet Union in the 1980s and early 1990s engendered a reexamination of the Great Game. Ex-diplomats, former intelligence agents, and journalists joined in the research and publication process. For example, Gordon Whitteridge, the U.K. ambassador to Kabul in the years 1965–68, classified the Great Game as a series of "tentative moves by the British and Russian empires on the Central Asian stage to find a satisfactory defensive frontier."[31] Peter Hopkirk, whom I mentioned above, publicized "a shadowy struggle for political ascendancy in Asia" in lengthy, albeit sometimes superficial, essays based on a selection of British archival documents.[32]

Apart from Hopkirk's works, which revived public interest in the Great Game, two American journalists, the married couple Karl Meyer and Shareen Brysac, offered a lucid but not always accurate picture of "the Victorian prologue to the Cold War," following David Gillard's earlier comparison of the Great Game with the confrontation between the Soviet Union and the United States after 1945.[33] Similarly, Lawrence James, a modern British historian, viewed the origins of the conflict in terms of a dramatic difference between Russian and Western belief systems, which he also inaccurately compared with the ideological divergence of capitalism and communism in the Cold War epoch. "The personal, political and legal freedoms which characterized Britain and, according to many, gave it strength and greatness, were totally absent in Russia," he wrote in his authoritative treatise on the rise and fall of the British Empire.[34] From another vantage point, Peter Brobst, the American biographer of Sir Olaf Caroe, a brilliant explorer and high-ranking administrator in British India before it achieved independence, contended that "the Great Game was largely an economic contest, but commercial profit was not the measure of victory."[35] However, the political interpretation of the Russo-British rivalry still remains more accepted by modern historians, like Charles Allen, who treats the Great Game as a "dangerous high-altitude contest of bluff and counter-bluff," or, in other words, as "the long-range struggle between Britain and Russia for the political control of the great open space of Central Asia."[36]

Regrettably, current scholarship on the Great Game, with Robert Johnson and Jules Stewart as typical representatives, still tends to look at the Game primarily through the prism of either military planning or espionage.[37] Frederick Hitz, a retired officer of the U.S. Central Intelligence Agency, views the Game within the paradigm of global competition for the control of the Hindu Kush and the adjacent territories of Afghanistan, Pakistan, and India. "Ironically," he remarks, "the religious terrorist threat will require a reversion to the tradecraft and technique of an earlier espionage era—that of the Great Game, before the gadgetry and sophistication of overhead photography and instant wireless communication."[38]

To complete this picture of the Great Game's interpretations, a gender-based explication of the phenomenon is also worthy of note. Elaine Showalter, a feminist writer, believes that the Game was an extension of so-called clubland, or the network of men's clubs that reinforced the spatial and social barriers separating the sexes. Furthermore, she sees the Game as forming a unique world created by younger, adventurous male volunteers, who preferred dangerous travels across faraway no-man's-lands in High Asia to tedious and boring life in the Victorian society of the nineteenth century.[39]

Before the October Revolution in 1917, Tsarist military analysts described the Anglo-Russian contest in Eurasia as inevitable and exhausting for both empires. The treatises written by Konstantin Abaza, Mikhail Veniukov, Nikolai Grodekov, Mikhail Grulev, Lev Kostenko, Aleksei Kuropatkin, Dimitry Romanovsky, Andrei Snesarev, and Mikhail Terentiev, to mention just a few, contain valuable data on the Russian conquest of Central Asia, along with frequent invectives against those in British leadership circles who allegedly schemed to counteract the Russian civilizing mission in the Orient by any means.[40]

For example, the General Staff colonel Mikhail Grulev compared the natural origins of Russian progress in Central Asia with the somewhat artificial British advent in India. As he saw it, the Russians' honorable civilizing mission in "the barbaric Asian states" differed from British colonial policy, which in his opinion resembled the repressive methods applied by the Spanish conquistadors to subjugate aboriginal peoples in South America.[41]

The first thing that strikes any reader of the Soviet historiography of the Great Game is the rigorous ideological clichés that dominated scholars under the totalitarian regime. Although Soviet historians had never formulated any special definition of the Russo-British rivalry, it was analyzed in a number of works published both before and after World War II, when they created two theories describing the reasons for and consequences of Tsarist colonial rule. In the 1920s and 1930s, it was stigmatized by Stalinist scholars, even though later, in the 1950s and 1960s, the champions of the so-called concept of the lesser evil advocated the Russian penetration of Central Asia as a progressive development aimed at the reformation of preindustrial societies.[42] Yet despite these differences, all Soviet scholars shared the opinion that Britain had always been an aggressive imperialistic power in the Orient and that British colonial rule should be considered as far crueler and less acceptable to indigenous ethnicities than that inaugurated by Tsarist civil and military authorities—for example, in Turkestan. Admittedly, Britain's encroachments upon Central Asia were also interpreted in the light of its ambitions to set up a coalition of local Muslim khanates in order to stop the Russian march to the Indian Ocean.

It is not an exaggeration to say that Soviet historians focused upon the exposure of "devious imperialistic plots against national-liberation forces." Notions of this kind may be found in the publications by Aleksander Popov, Evgeny Steinberg, Goga Khidoiatov, Nina Kiniapina, Olga Zhigalina, and others that came out from the 1920s to the 1980s.[43] But the concept that Russian imperialism in Asia was the "least evil" in comparison with British rule dominated Soviet historiography in the long run. On the basis of authentic records in the archives of Tashkent, the former capital of Russian Turkestan, Naftula Khalfin, a renowned historian from Uzbekistan, drew attention to the "economic war" launched by "perfidious Albion" against Tsarist Russia in the second half of the nineteenth century.[44]

Regrettably, Russia's transition to a relatively democratic state order at the turn of new millennium has not yet led to any unbiased reappraisal of Russo-British relations with regard to the Great Game. Although modern historians in the post-Soviet Commonwealth of Independent States devote much attention to the colonial history of the Caucasus and Central Asia, many of the Game's episodes are still studied through the lens of "British imperialistic, aggressive policy." Because they are obsessed with Anglophobia, some modern Russian historians continue to write about the "mortal combat" in which the Russians had been embroiled against British invaders in defense of their mother state for the last several centuries.[45] At the same time, they reanimate out-of-date, often fabulous theories, according to which the Great Game is viewed as a prelude to the Cold War from the 1950s to the 1980s, or as a never-ending rivalry of the United States, China, and even Pakistan and Turkey for mastery in Asia.[46] Characteristically, in 2008, a Russian television channel broadcast a documentary movie about the Great Game, which was interpreted by the commentators as a permanent Cold War between Slavdom and the West.[47]

Given the resurgence of Muslim extremism and the emergence of conflicts along the so-called Arc of Instability stretching from the Middle East and Inner Asia through Xinjiang, Tibet, and North India to Southeast Asia, scholars from Asian countries have also contributed to the latest studies of the Great Game. Although many of their works, published from the 1950s to the 1970s, reflected pro-British sympathies along with condemnation of Tsarist despotic rule in Turkestan, in the closing years of the Cold War, Asian historians began to sharply criticize Britain for settling disputed issues with Russia in 1907 at the expense of Persia, Afghanistan, or China.[48]

A characteristic recent interpretation of the Great Game is presented by Memet Yetisgin in his doctoral thesis. This young Turkish researcher analyzed Britain's drift to continental commitments:

The British decided to resist Russia by seeking alliances with European big powers and helping decadent states, such as the Ottoman Empire, Persia, Afghanistan, and China. These states also feared Russia's unsatisfied appetite for expansion. Thus, under the so-called Eastern Question, Central Asian Question and the Far Eastern Question, a "great game" and a "cold war" [sic] determined the course of history.[49]

Even this brief review reveals the fact that the narration of adventures and risky covert operations by intelligence agents in exotic remote countries, along with "black and white" ideological stereotypes, prevents the reader from gaining a proper understanding of Anglo-Russian intercourse in the Victorian age. Therefore, it is important to assemble the results of fragmentary case studies in a single "jigsaw" representing an overall panorama of the Great Game in three interrelated dimensions:

- as a competition between different models of early globalization suggested by Britain and Russia to non-European decadent societies;
- as a complex, multilevel decisionmaking and decision-implementing activity directed by their ruling elites; and
- as a crucial period in the development of the Russo-British relationship in Asia that precipitated their consequent rapprochement and military alliance in World War I.[50]

With regard to the chronological frame of the Great Game, scholars like Ingram, Morgan, Edwardes, Hopkirk, Meyer and Brysac, and Chavda have expressed their belief that it started in the second half of the eighteenth century. For example, Robert Johnson dated its beginning to 1757, and his colleagues found its starting point in the Napoleonic Wars. Edwardes specified that it began in July 1807, when Alexander I and Napoleon I met in the boundary town of Tilsit on the Neman River to discuss the plan for a combined offensive against British India.[51] A few comparable fixations of the Game's initial period were suggested by Ingram, who indicated 1798, 1828–34, or 1828–42 as possible dates for its beginning.[52] Curiously, in his final study of British policymaking in the Middle East, he even pointed to December 29, 1829, because it was on that very day when Lord Ellenborough, the president of the East India Company's Board of Control and an ardent Russophobe, told the governor-general, Lord William Bentinck, to open up a new trade route to Bokhara. According to Ingram, the goal of the government, headed by the duke of Wellington, was to respond to the Russo-Persian and Russo-Turkish treaties of Turkmanchai and Adrianople in 1828–29. In Ingram's view, those in British leadership circles regarded these agreements as consistent steps toward the eventual conversion of Persia and Turkey into Russian protectorates.[53] However, the most incredible version was suggested by the Russian television journalist Mikhail Leontiev, who attributed the commencement of the Great Game to a Russophobe speech delivered by the prime minister, William Pitt the Younger, to the House of Commons in 1791, after Tsarist troops had seized the Ottoman fortress of Ochakov.[54]

In reality, researchers have often neglected the particular period of the Russo-British long-term geostrategic rivalry, which began right after the Swedish defeat in the Northern War of 1700–1721.[55] Despite controversial opinions about the advances made by Napoleon to Tsar Alexander I before 1812 or the divergence of views on the British allegedly plotting a coup d'état in Saint Petersburg during the reign of Tsar Paul I, many contemporaries observed friendly relations between the United Kingdom and the Tsarist Empire in the first quarter of the nineteenth century. Commented a Russian historian:

> After the victory over Napoleon, Alexander I hoped to arrange the work of state and economic apparatus of his empire according to the British model, and to educate his subjects in the British way. The Russian public opinion seemed to favor these plans. However, soon the emperor began to consider this idea as a complete utopia.[56]

In the opinion of the author of the present volume, the starting point of the Great Game must be postponed until the late 1850s, when a combination of six key driving forces put this process in motion. First, the end of the Caucasus War in 1859 meant the release of Tsarist expeditionary troops eager to wage further military campaigns. Second was the outburst of the Sepoy Mutiny and its suppression by reinforced Anglo-Indian detachments in 1857–58, a tragedy that had greatly vexed the British authorities both in Calcutta and in London, making the home Cabinet modify the administration of the Raj. Third, the Second Opium War of 1856–60 led to the first partition of the spheres of influence in China between the great European powers. Fourth, the Anglo-Persian struggle for Herat in 1856–57 destabilized the general configuration of affairs in the Middle East and Inner Asia. Fifth was the culmination of the expansion of Britain's free trade toward Asian markets, which almost coincided with Russia's embarking on rapid industrial modernization prompted by liberal reforms in the reign of Tsar Alexander II. Sixth and last, the American Civil War of 1861–65 severely hampered the United States' raw cotton exports to Europe and compelled both Britain and Russia to hunt for raw cotton resources in Asia. Additionally, the outburst of the first world economic crisis of 1857–58 resulted in the penetration by British manufacturers and traders into Oriental consumer markets in order to compensate for Britain's deficit in its balance of payments with continental Europe and America.[57] Contrary to these developments, the traditional despotic regimes in Central and East Asia, with the exception of Japan, had been lagging far behind the European countries throughout the period in question, and thus they were doomed to be subjugated by the more dynamic non-Asian powers.

While the major European states concentrated on the Ottoman Empire as a pivot of their geostrategic struggle in the Great Game at the end of the eighteenth and the first half of the nineteenth centuries, the alignment of forces suffered mutation after the end of the Crimean War. Although access to Constantinople and the Eastern Mediterranean through the Aegean Sea remained a bone of discord between London and Saint Petersburg for a few more decades, the focus of Anglo-Russian relations in the post-Crimean epoch shifted toward other Asian regions.[58] One could be led to believe, therefore, that the two empires inaugurated a new round of their competition/ collaboration in Persia, Afghanistan, and the khanates of Central Asia, whereas they later "exported" the Game to Tibet and the Far East. Yet for the fact that the Ottoman Empire in the west and later the Japanese Empire in the east occupied the flanking positions, acting as marginal "playfields," their additional roles deserve special study. That is why this book touches upon them merely in connection with the Russo-Turkish War of 1877–78 and the Russo-Japanese War of 1904–5, when Constantinople and Tokyo were in the focus of realpolitik.

Conceding for a moment that Russia had lost the war against the Ottoman Empire in 1878, London and Saint Petersburg would have continued playing the Great Game in the territories mentioned above, perhaps even more intensively. Although the stakes in the Russo-Turkish struggle were the Balkans and the Near East, the two imperial powers, Russia and Britain, sought to reshape Eurasia according to their own vision of the world order. This vision was predicated primarily upon national interests that contradicted the chimerical aspirations to monarchical solidarity cherished by Alexander I and the other sovereigns who were part of the Holy Alliance in the first quarter of the nineteenth century. It was not coincidental, therefore, that Alexander Gorchakov, the new Russian foreign minister, wrote to Alexander II in 1856: "Russia is not facing great challenges in Europe while she has a vast field of political activity in Asia." The emperor annotated Gorchakov's report: "I completely agree with this."[59]

In the same way, a key aspect of the Great Game—the adaptation of Asian nations to the modern network of political, economic, and cultural connections promoted by Britain and Russia—needs further profound examination. Moreover, some scholars have erroneously prolonged the Great Game's epoch to 1917–18, when the Bolshevik turnover in Saint Petersburg caused a repudiation of all the Russian Empire's previous international obligations. For example, the American historian Jennifer Siegel disagrees with the interpretation of the Anglo-Russian Convention, signed in 1907, as the document that put an end to the Game. She points to the dissatisfaction with which British and Russian ruling elites, especially the high-ranking military, received this convention. In her view, "for both Britain and Russia, the 1907 agreement proved to be not a solution, but a temporary bridge over the gaping divide that separated British and Russian aims and desires in Central Asia." Characteristically, a chapter title in her book is "The Death of the Anglo-Russian Agreement in 1914."[60] A slightly modified version of this approach is taken by the British scholar Alastair Lamb, who maintains that after 1907 "the Game was, if not ended, at least reduced to a minor league in the British diplomatic calendar."[61]

Still another group of academicians argues that the Great Game did not evaporate until the second half of the 1940s, when the British granted independence to the countries on the Hindustan Peninsula.[62] Gerald Morgan proposed an even more exotic chronology. He specified the Russo-British détente in the Pamirs in 1895 as the end of the Game.[63] Finally, a minority of modern historians still believe that the Game continued throughout the twentieth century. "The Great Game did not end with British rule in August 1947. Nor did officials of the late Raj expect that it would," writes, for example, Peter Brobst.[64]

The present study reveals, however, that the so-called diplomatic revolution in the early twentieth century might be regarded as the real closing date of the Game. To corroborate this conclusion, two epochal events need to be taken into account: the end of Britain's "splendid isolation" in 1902–7; and the failure of the continental coalition under the aegis of Germany to oppose the maritime nations in 1905–6, which really marked a turning point in the policy of Britain and Russia, the two empires that counteracted various unprecedented challenges in the nineteenth century. As Francis Younghusband later asserted in his reminiscences, it was not territorial expansion that Britain had to fear henceforth, so much as the expansion of ideas.[65]

Significantly, in the opinion of the author of the present volume, the period of the Great Game itself encompassed five successive stages—beginning with 1856–64 as its initial phase; followed by 1864–73, a period of the Russians' full-scale offensive against the khanates of Central Asia and the British defense in the context of so-called masterly inactivity; then coming to the climax of the Russo-British race for domination, accompanied by the intensive "forward" policy that both sides pursued during the years 1874–85; almost ending initially in a deadlock, when both London and Saint Petersburg did their utmost to settle their frontier dispute in spite of sporadic crises in bilateral relations during the years 1886–1905; and finally, reaching détente as a result of the secret negotiations in 1906–7.

While bearing in mind the Game's specification as a spacious "chessboard" stretching "from the snow-capped Caucasus in the west, across the great deserts and mountain ranges of Central Asia, to Chinese Turkestan and Tibet in the east,"[66] the author of the present volume offers, nevertheless, his own understanding of these geographical frames. This understanding is predicated upon a broader view of its playfield corresponding to "the Southern British World that runs from Cape Town through Cairo, Baghdad and Calcutta to Sydney and Wellington," mentioned by Leopold Amery, a respected journalist and public figure, in a letter to David Lloyd George on June 8, 1918.[67] Besides, the consequences of Russia's three-pronged penetration of Asia—through Western Siberia toward Chinese Turkestan, across Eastern Siberia to the Far East, and through Central Asia to the Persian Gulf—also need to be taken into account, because the advance in each direction proceeded hand in hand with the construction of defense lines, the establishment of military-administrative outposts on remote frontiers, and the colonization of fertile agricultural areas under Russian control.[68]

According to UNESCO's definition of Central Asia as a terrain "protracting from Mongolia to North-East Iran, and from taiga in the north to deserts and arid steppes in the south,"[69] the geographical coordinates of the Great Game may correspond to a spacious region lying between 50°–20° northern latitude and 50°–130° eastern longitude. Conversely, from the perspective of comparative frontier studies, a conventional line of delimitation between Central and Eastern Asia may be drawn along the administrative border of Xinjiang and Tibet. As to the definition of Inner or High Asia, it was usually applied by contemporaries to Eastern (Chinese) Turkestan and the Tibetan mountain range. Consequently, the author of the present volume regards the Far East as a part of Eastern Asia adjacent to the Pacific Ocean.

The landscapes of this playfield varied from the highest, thinly populated mountain terraces of Tien Shan, the Hindu Kush, and Tibet to the
densely inhabited oases of Turkestan. It is also known for the colossal
deserts stretching with intervals from Persia to Mongolia. The amalga-
mation of multiethnic, multireligious nomadic tribes and settled rural
communities that have adapted to the subtropical or arid continental
climate also typify this region. Another important quality is the paucity
of great waterways or lakes, with the exception of the Caspian Sea
and Aral Sea, and the River Amu Daria (Oxus) and River Syr Daria
(Yaxartes). Under severe climatic conditions, with the temperature fluc-
tuations from −30° C in the winter to +40° C in the summer, adventurous pathfinders from European countries used to sustain regular attacks
of poisonous vermin that infected people with contagious diseases, such
as malaria, cholera, and plagues. So it was small wonder that their travel
diaries were filled with stories of natural horrors and even mystical
incidents that they had survived in the heart of Eurasia.[70]

To clarify the political situation, it is useful to unite the territories
of the Great Game along the Great Silk Road into three main clusters:

- large, ancient states, such as China, Persia, and Afghanistan;
- medieval khanates and emirates, such as Khiva, Bokhara,
  Khokand, Kashmir, and Punjab; and
- proto-state tribes and communities occupying the so-called no-
  man's-lands.

In the case of the proto-state tribes and communities, minor hill principalities succeeded in retaining their independence primarily due to
their isolated geographical positions and the scarcity of natural mineral
resources. These "lost worlds"—surrounded by the highest mountain
ranges and immense sandy deserts, deficient in passages, and inaccessible
to strangers—seemed to be territories free from any real dependence
on either local despotic rulers or the European great powers.

This introduction would be incomplete without mentioning this
book's sources, which the author studied intensively for five years.
They were both archival and published collections of documents,

parliamentary papers, political pamphlets, memoirs, diaries, and private epistles, along with contemporary newspaper articles and guidebooks. Most of the unpublished records—reports; memoranda; and notes and minutes by statesmen, diplomats, and military officers—are deposited in national archives and library manuscript divisions both in the Russian Federation and the United Kingdom. To verify the most valuable nuggets of information, the author additionally studied separately published documents from Indian and Uzbek republican depositories. These materials are presented in the list of selected archival sources and bibliography.

A reflective analysis of archival holdings was supplemented with a thorough study of written testimonies by some of the players of the Great Game. It should be noted that the vast majority of them appeared to the author of the present volume as both brilliant intellectuals and heroic explorers. As Milan Hauner correctly wrote:

Another [apart from historians] strong intellectual impulse for expansion into Asia came from the Russian Geographical Society, founded in St Petersburg in 1845. Its talented members, spearheaded by a group of enterprising military geographers, played the Great Game of Central Asia with their British counterparts.[71]

Along with voluminous documentary publications, a great bulk of data in British parliamentary blue books related to Persia, Afghanistan, Central Asia, the Pamirs, Tibet, and the Far East also needed to be taken into consideration.[72] Another direction of inquiry was the examination of geographical, topographical, and statistical materials on Asia in eighty volumes published by the Russian General Staff. In fact, this publication is a potpourri of staff studies, personal papers, and generalized briefings about different states, regions, or cities—supplemented with translations of the most valuable papers from European languages into Russian. Although military staff members usually voiced individual opinions in their memoranda, the inferences they drew after trips to Asian countries somehow prejudiced decisions by governmental cabinets.[73]

At the same time, the study rests on collections of documents edited by Russian, Uzbek, and Turkmen historians both before and after the collapse of the Tsarist regime. Apart from the famous multivolume publication of official correspondence on the conquest of Turkestan collated by Lieutenant Colonel A. G. Serebrennikov and some thematic issues of the *Krasnyi Archiv*, the leading journal of archivists in the Soviet Union during the period 1920–30, the author of the present volume also looked through recent documentary surveys by Russian historians.[74] Finally, he devoted necessary attention to maps and charts by the military topographers and secret intelligence agents who operated on the playfields of the Anglo-Russian competition.[75]

This book aims neither to reproduce the notorious "tournament of shadows" in all details nor to replicate intelligence missions undertaken by servicemen or freelancers. The author believes, however, that any reassessment of the Great Game as a polyphonic, multifaceted process implies the disclosure of myths and the presentation of realities concerning the development of Russo-British intercourse in Asia.

To realize this intention, this monograph contains six chapters that cover the origins, crucial stages, and ending of the Great Game. A brief epilogue presents the author's distilled findings about this phenomenon. The context is supplemented with an appendix, which consists of a chronological listing and a nominal roll of the prominent persons whose activities affected the Great Game.

All the dates are rendered according to the Gregorian calendar, which is known to be ahead of the Julian one, in use by Russia before February 1918, by twelve days in the nineteenth century and thirteen days in the twentieth century. The book regularly refers to the metric system, with some exceptions. The correlation between Oriental and Russian currencies is given for 1911 in the following proportions: a Persian toman was equivalent to 3.30 rubles; a Chinese tael, to 2.21 rubles; an Indian rupee, to 0.60 ruble; and £1, to 9.45 rubles. Transliteration from the Cyrillic alphabet meets the requirements of the Library of Congress system without special diacritic marks, and common spellings are given to the generality of proper names, except for Chinese lexical units, which are used according to the Pinyin system, save such frequently used names as Peking. Finally, throughout, many sources from the period being described refer to "England" when they mean "Britain," that is, the whole of the United Kingdom; this discrepancy has of course been left in quotations.

CHAPTER 1

THE PROLOGUE OF THE GREAT GAME

Hurrah, hurrah, it's north by west we go!
Hurrah, hurrah, the chance we wanted so!
Let 'em hear the chorus from Umballa to Moscow:
As we go marching to the Kremlin.

—Rudyard Kipling, "The Sacred War Song of the Mavericks"

This chapter delineates Russia's and Britain's motives in their nineteenth-century advances into Asia, which were marked by strong differences, in spite of the "white man's burden" theory proclaimed by both powers. There is every evidence to argue that the quest for natural, or "scientific," frontiers above all spawned the great powers' geopolitical aspirations, especially outside Europe. The chapter also considers profiles of the Great Game's players, who fell into three main categories—the first group comprising monarchs and high-standing bureaucrats, the second consisting of military and diplomatic agents in the state's service, and the third embracing explorers, journalists, and other freelancers, who often acted at their own risk. Finally, the chapter investigates the roles of Asian countries in the prologue of the Game, which aimed at incorporating decadent Oriental states into the global system of relations.

RUSSIAN AND BRITISH MOTIVES IN THEIR
ADVANCES INTO ASIA

It is common knowledge that the conflict between the two worlds of Christianity and Islam dates back to the time of the Arab invasion of the Middle East, North Africa, and the Iberian Peninsula. This armed confrontation continued for centuries in the epoch of the Christians' Crusades to the Holy Land—Palestine—and later during their Spanish Reconquista. However, the Muslims retaliated by establishing the Ottoman Empire from the fourteenth to the sixteenth centuries. The Muslims' capture of Constantinople in 1453 and the siege of Vienna in 1529 symbolized the culminations of this new wave of aggression from the Orient. Thus, nearly every social stratum of Christian Europe—nobility, clergy, townsfolk, and peasantry—perceived this peril as a reality at the dawn of the Modern Age.

The great geographical discoveries of the sixteenth through eighteenth centuries spurred the advance of industrial modernization. Following the rapid development of Europe, the balance of power between the West and the East changed to the benefit of the former. Big European nation-states set about pressing their political influence upon Arab territories in West Asia and North Africa. According to Samuel Huntington, there were ninety-two seizures of Muslim territories by non-Islamic powers between 1757 and 1919, and every second conflict from 1820 to 1929 took place between the hostile Christian and Islamic civilizations.[1]

But what were the real motives of the great powers, Russia and Britain in particular, for these invasions of Oriental countries? In the view of the author of the present volume, the quest for natural, or "scientific," frontiers above all spawned the great powers' geopolitical aspirations, both within and outside Europe.[2] Moreover, the high prestige of sovereigns traditionally depended on the extent of their territorial possessions and the wealth of resources under their domination, Russia and Britain being no exception. In the light of external policy, all the tsars, beginning with Peter I, allegedly proclaimed the attainment of access to warm-water ports in the Atlantic, Pacific, and Indian oceans as their principal goal.[3]

Looking back to Russia's permanent yearning to conquer vast steppes, endless deserts, and sky-high mountain ranges in order to get hold of outlets to the most important sea routes, the *Times of London* wrote on January 29, 1873:

> As the great highways of Western commerce are the Mediterranean, the Atlantic, and the Indian Ocean, and as she [Russia] possesses very inadequate means of reaching any of them, the great problem of Russian statesmanship must continue to be, as it has been for the last two hundred years, how to obtain for her a Southern seaboard.[4]

Hence, Russia aspired to establish or capture key strongholds, such as Murmansk and Archangelsk in the north, Constantinople in the Turkish Straits, Libava and Riga in the Baltic, and Vladivostok and Port Arthur in the Pacific.[5] The institution of control over territories abutting Russian lands factually meant a conversion of continental supremacy into sea power, an increase in geostrategic potential, and safe land boundaries. It is characteristic that Alfred Mahan, the United States' prominent naval strategist, compared Russia's advance toward the Persian Gulf with that by Britain to Egypt:

> Russia is in a disadvantageous position for the accumulation of wealth; which is but another way of saying that she is deficient in means for advancing the welfare of her people, of which wealth is at once the instruments and the exponent. This being so, it is natural and proper that she should be dissatisfied, and the dissatisfaction readily takes the form of aggression—the word most in favor with those of us who dislike all forward movement in nations.[6]

Any Russian move to Central or East Asia stood in need of heavy military spending for the construction of outposts that formed extended defensive lines and also for the colonization of vast, yet scarcely populated, territories. It was thus necessary for Russia to survey the various natural borders that separated the areas with indigenous ethnic groups differing from one another in dialect, confession, or culture; to pacify warlike nomadic tribes; and secure trade routes, especially in the Middle East and Inner Asia.[7]

On the other side, Britain was engaged in building up the "second empire" after it had lost its American colonies, except Canada. Contrary to the doctrine of mercantilism, this new version of empire rested on the principles of the free trade economy formulated by Adam Smith, David Ricardo, and John Stuart Mill. If the "first empire" attracted traders and planters, who left London and Liverpool for Philadelphia and New York in order to earn their fortunes in the far-flung corners of the imperial domains, "its later incarnation is alleged to have appealed to investors who upheld entrepreneurs in their attempts to open new markets for the products of British industry and who organized new sources of raw materials for the factories at home."[8]

Accordingly, hereditary aristocrats, primarily landlords, still represented national interests in both the Russian and British empires throughout the nineteenth century, not occasionally to the detriment of the industrial classes. As a Cambridge historian has rightfully maintained, "The British elite, drawn in part from the aristocracy for a long period of time, and mostly with an Oxbridge education overwhelmingly classical …in its emphasis, was frequently disdainful of business interests."[9] However, the aspiration for adventures in faraway exotic places, typically aristocratic in origin, began to evaporate by the turn of the next century. Instead, there emerged the cold pragmatism of merchants and industrialists in their quest for economic expansion to Asian countries.

Another exemplary feature of both Russian and British colonial administrations was the comparative autonomy of military and civic officials in the "far pavilions"—an expression used by some contemporary Victorian journalists regarding those administrators recruited from the middle classes who did not hesitate to serve on the outskirts of empire. These men, who were ambitious in their career making, epitomized a curious breed of romantic individuals, who "guarded the frontier marches" and strongly "believed themselves engaged in a struggle of cosmic significance." Their activities found a response not only in the press but also in novels and poems by many European beletrists.[10]

Despite obvious similarities, at least three main distinctions may be discerned between the Russian Empire and British Empire. Whereas Russia had been slowly progressing for decades as a continental state, Britain had always remained a sea power, which had revived after an interim decline in the late eighteenth century and undergone the Industrial Revolution from 1780 to the 1850s.[11] Contrary to the autocratic regime in Tsarist Russia, for Imperial Britain the necessity of harmonizing the liberal underpinnings of its nascent representative parliamentary democracy at home with the authoritarian style of governing on its colonial periphery became urgent, "the white" dominions making a few exceptions. Any unbiased observer might describe Britain's "second" empire as Protestant, maritime, and free, guided by the motto of the three Cs—commerce, Christianity, and civilization.[12] Besides, unlike Russia, Britain preferred to establish its supremacy over dependent territories primarily through the informal means of *sanads* (i.e., title deeds given to native rulers establishing them in their states, in return for their fealty), subsidies, or personal alliances with local rulers, though the home Cabinet would resort to the armed forces if Oriental rulers of a different caliber tried to distort this "harmony." Bearing in mind their apparent and overwhelming leadership in maritime logistics and world trade, the vast majority of the British regarded commercial profits as far more essential than any kind of a tough political control over remote Asiatic regions.

This is why economic motivations should be also taken into consideration. First of all, many experts have pointed to a basic incongruity between British and Russian commerce in their methods. According to various data, Britain earned a considerable surplus on its trade with Asia, in particular China and India. Thanks to this positive balance of trade, it managed to settle the deficits it owed on its transactions with commercial partners in America and Europe, including Russia, which ranked second after France from the 1860s to the 1880s. As some historians have maintained, this surplus in trade with India prevented the British Empire from introducing preferential tariffs against the United States and European countries. It was small wonder, therefore, that the empire's expansion seemed to Lord Curzon and other "true imperialists" "an inevitable necessity and majestic obligation" in the preservation of Britain's world leadership, as he wrote in a letter to John Morley, the India Office secretary, in the late 1890s.[13]

Russian industry, presenting a striking contrast, was susceptible to lagging behind its most advanced foreign rivals on world markets. However, aggregate demand for Russian consumer goods, both within imperial borders and in neighboring Asian territories, might also be secured by political means. A memorandum by Thomas Michell, the attaché to the British Embassy in Saint Petersburg, on Anglo-Russian trade in 1865 held that

> the object for which so much revenue is annually sacrificed, so much fraud and demoralization tolerated, for which international, commercial relations are permitted to suffer neglect, and to which, it should be remembered, the most important interests of Russia have been made subject, is the protection of native industry from ruinous foreign competition.[14]

Significantly, Russian merchants intended to monopolize local markets with the aid of Tsarist military administrators. Otherwise, the majority of merchants who delivered goods from the Russian Empire to Central and East Asia might be ruined to the point of bankruptcy, because few manufactures could compete with commodities from British India or China. Such articles as calico, hardware and other metal products, leather, sugar, paraffin, wheat, and rye flour accounted for 80 percent of annual Russian exports to the East.[15] That was why merchants from the Romanovs' Empire regularly accused British traders of unfair rivalry, while experts in their memoranda to governmental officials urged them to take strong protectionist measures against the commodities retailed by Western companies. A typical commentator criticized Great Britain for its desire to oust Russian products from the market in Central Asia:

> England has got all the chances to draw Ameer of Bokhara to her side and convert him into a true collaborator. In other words, England is at ease to grasp the essence of the Central Asian Question.

To resolve it profitably, a British merchant should arrive in Bokhara. Done so, afterwards, everything is in England's power.[16]

Peter the Great was the first Russian emperor to put a protective customs tariff into operation. Thus, from 1717 onward, the Tsarist government conducted a policy of mercantilism for many decades. In 1850, a new customs tariff replaced that of Peter I. Although it symbolized a somewhat moderate alternative to protectionism, the government retained high tariffs on imported goods until the 1890s.[17]

Interestingly, mainstream Russian commerce with Asia changed direction several times throughout the first half of the nineteenth century, following the cycles of ups and downs in domestic and international politics. Although, in the 1820s, Russian business with Persia was prospering, later Russian exports to that country decreased, but commerce with Afghanistan and the khanates of Central Asia—Khiva, Bokhara, and Khokand—began to develop. "The Persian brought word of intense Russian trading activity," maintained a British researcher, "with gigantic caravans of 4,000 to 5,000 camels making the four-month journey between Bokhara and the tsar's dominions once a year."[18]

Afterward, there came a period of Russo-Chinese rapprochement, progressing hand in hand with an intensification of bilateral trade relations during the 1840s and the 1850s. At the same time, annual trade turnover between Russia and the khanates of Khiva and Bokhara temporarily declined. By 1856, Russia's imports across its Asiatic frontiers amounted to approximately 14 percent of all commodities brought in, while exports exceeded 60 percent of commodities sold. The regions, which were involved in this process, shared in the trade turnover with Russia according to the following proportions: the Qing Empire, 58.2 percent; the Kazakhs, 20 percent; Persia and Afghanistan, 14.8 percent; and the khanates of Central Asia, 7 percent.[19] Under these circumstances, new Russian commercial enterprises emerged in the 1850s, like mushrooms after heavy showers. For example, V. A. Kokorev, a capitalist and merchant, established the Trans-Caspian Trading Company, sponsored by the Caucasus governor-general, Prince Alexander Bariatinsky. This company was exporting Russian commodities to Persia, Afghanistan, and the Turkmen lands in exchange for various types of raw materials, gold, and crude precious stones.[20]

In 1881, these protectionist policies resulted in the Tsarist government's adoption of the Interim Regulations for Imports. According to these regulations, all the caravans of merchants traveling from Bokhara and Khiva to the Russian provinces were to be examined at the border by customs offices in order to arrest the uncontrolled transit of European products through these khanates. The regulations revealed the adherence of the Tsarist colonial administration to the preservation of a prohibitive tax system in Central Asia, which had already been conquered by that time. Its establishment was completed in the mid-1890s, when customs officers were commissioned to all frontier outposts in the empire.[21]

World politics furthermore modified international trade contacts. After the outbreak of the American Civil War in 1861, the delivery of raw cotton from the United States to Russian markets fell to a negligible quantity. Many Russian textile manufacturers were forced to import cotton, primarily from Central Asia (in spite of poor quality). To secure the delivery of this strategic raw material, the Tsarist government attempted to monopolize overland trade with Persia, Bokhara, Khiva, and China. Doubtless, the original purpose of railway construction in Turkestan was military and not economic; yet an inappropriate cargo fleet likewise motivated Russian engineers to construct railroads linking European Russia to Southern Siberia and Central Asia. According to the available data, more than 5,000 kilometers of railways were built in Central Asia alone between 1872 and 1915, not to mention the branch lines to the Volga region and the Urals.[22]

As was noted earlier in this chapter, British commercial turnover with India and neighboring minor states substantially underpinned its positive overall trade balance in the nineteenth century. However, India also played a key role as an intermediate base on long-distance routes from the Atlantic Ocean to the Pacific Ocean. The statistics for the 1860s demonstrated that the proportion of British goods in Chinese imports amounted to 90 percent, whereas the quotas of Great Britain and India in Chinese exports respectively equaled 33.4 and 35.6 percent.[23] "We must safeguard India as a cornerstone of the British prosperity"—such was the incantation repeated by all British cabinets, irrespective of party affiliation, in the Victorian and Edwardian epochs. As a *New York Times* journalist described the state of affairs,

> Not only on the Black Sea and in the direction of Turkey and the Mediterranean have the Russian movements been jealously watched, but her advances along the eastern shore of the Caspian and into Turkestan and Bokhara have been looked at with much uneasiness by Great Britain, as being dangerous military approaches toward the northwestern boundary of her Indian Empire, and the line of the Hindu Kush, the great bulwark of that boundary, had been sedulously guarded.[24]

Therefore it was small wonder that British expeditionary troops conducted never-ending frontier wars against turbulent Sikhs and Pashtun tribes in the period from 1839 to 1849 to subjugate and later consolidate the motley ethnic, religious, and social groups in the northwest corner of the Hindustan Peninsula.

The reader would draw a false conclusion, however, in supposing that merchants from British India controlled Asian markets for consumer goods in the mid-1850s.[25] Although Britain ranked first among other nation-states on the list of Russia's commercial partners at that time, the balance of Russo-British trade inclined to the benefit of Saint Petersburg. And it was China, not Britain, that acted as the major commercial rival to Russia in Central Asia, Kashgaria, the Pamirs, and the Hindu Kush, at least in the first half of the nineteenth century.[26]

Following the political and economic origins of the Great Game, certain sociocultural and civilizational factors should also be taken into consideration. Even Karl Marx, the founder of the theory of Communism, who worked as a part-time correspondent for the *New York Daily Tribune* until the mid-1850s, once wrote that "England is destined to fulfill a two-fold mission in India—devastating, which means annihilation of old Asiatic society, and creative, which intends the organization of social structure in Asia according to Western pattern."[27] Reciprocally, a Russian expert proudly commented on the progressive role of the Tsarist Empire in the Orient:

> The Russians have contributed much to local civilizations; they
> put an end to the predatory regime and gave an initial impetus to
> the assimilation of people whose domestic economies differ from
> a progressive mode. Owing to our efforts, traditional trade routes
> became safe.[28]

In fact, many Europeans, including representatives of the political elite,
were supposed to view the expansion of colonial powers to Central and
East Asia as the replacement of despotic regimes—with their groveling
superstitions, cruelty, immorality, and total misery—with a state order
based upon standards of humanity. Even the local environment corresponded with decadent social structures in Asia, as the reader could find
in the writings of travelers. For example, on coming back from his secret
mission to Kashgaria in the late 1850s, Captain Chokan Valikhanov, an
ethnic Kazakh in the Russian service, reported to the Main Staff:

> Central Asia, in today's stage of social organization, presents a truly
> mournful scene; her current stage of development being, so to say,
> a sort of pathological crisis. The whole country, without exagger-
> ation, is nothing but one vast waste, intersected here and there by
> abandoned aqueducts, canals, and wells. The desolate sandy plains,
> dotted occasionally with ruins and overgrown with ugly prickly
> shrubs and tamarisks, are wandered over by herds of wild asses,
> and hardly less shy and timid *saigaks* [i.e., saiga antelopes, which
> originally inhabited a vast area of the Eurasian steppe zone from
> the foothills of the Carpathians and the Caucasus into Dzungaria
> and Mongolia]. In the midst of this "Sahara," along the banks of
> the rivers were located several small oases, shaded by poplar, elm,
> and mulberry plantations; while nothing intervenes to break the
> monotony of view, save rice fields and bushes of cotton here and
> there, which are badly cultivated and diversified with occasional
> vineyards and orchards, left by lazy and improvident population to
> the care of Allah. In the center of these oases, constructed above

numerous ruins of ancient cities, long since moldering beneath the soil, stand the miserable mud hovels of a wild and barbarous race, demoralized by Islamism, and reduced almost to idiocy by political and religious despotism of their native rulers.[29]

The European governments agreed on an understanding that Christian civilization—whether Catholic, Protestant (including Anglican), or Orthodox—was far more progressive than that of the Muslims, Buddhists, or the adepts of Confucian ethics in an age of industrial modernization. The British foreign secretary, Lord John Russell, expressed his opinion on this subject to Baron Phillip Brunnov, the Russian ambassador to the United Kingdom from the 1830s to the 1870s, in the following way:

I recognize the aims of the Russian government as quite legal; and on the whole, I have always sided with any civilized power against a barbarous country. We [Britain] ourselves proceeded in India according to imperative force of circumstances, which frequently involved us further than we initially wished to go.[30]

Although we may suspect that Russell's allegation aimed to provide a smokescreen for any real intentions of Whitehall, many high-ranking Russian and British officials were enthusiastic about the tremendous role their mother states were destined to play in the Orient. For example, Lord Augustus Loftus, another British representative in Saint Petersburg, shared the opinion that Britain and Russia "ought to have common interests in the promotion of civilization and in the development of industry and commerce in our extended spheres, without jealousy and without seeking aggrandizement."[31] Similarly, Alexander Gorchakov, the foreign minister, formulated the purpose of inculcating universal Christian values in the minds of the Asiatics:

The position of Russia in Central Asia is that of all civilized states which are brought into contact with half-savage nomadic populations, deficient in any fixed social organization. Under such circumstances, it always happens that the more civilized state is forced, in the interest of the security of its frontier and commercial relations, to exercise a certain ascendancy over those whose turbulent and unsettled character make them undesirable neighbors.[32]

On this reading, using the metaphor by Edward Said, "the Occident was seen as a hero rescuing the Orient from obscurity, alienation, and strangeness."[33] Thus, the Russian and British advance into Asia was marked with conflicting differences, in spite of the "white man's burden" theory proclaimed by both powers in the nineteenth century. Unlike the British, who were imbued with the principles of Protestant ethics,[34] many Russians cultivated the opinion that they were the sole real champions of European liberties and human rights in Asia, because it was the mighty Russian Empire that had defended the borders of the Old World against numerous "hordes of ogres" invading it from the depths of Inner Asia. Thus, an observer of *The Economic Journal*, a Saint Petersburg monthly, metaphorically argued that

> Russia's role as the vanguard force of Europe, when the former saved the latter from destruction many times, means her right to submit territories wherefrom hordes of barbarians used to flow out for looting and murdering to hamper Russia's state development. The possession of neighboring Central Asian regions is required by geographic and historical needs, and partly reimburses the lasting struggle against the Asiatic hydra.[35]

The Russians, who were revengeful toward nomadic nations in the opinion of some Western political observers, sought to accomplish their great destiny in the East—to defeat and subjugate the descendants of Genghis Khan or Timur in retaliation for the prior humiliation of their Slavic forefathers. Conversely, the slave markets in big Asian cities had never been so overcrowded with human beings of all races and nationalities for sale as in the mid-1850s. This is why the government had to check mounted bandit gangs making forays into Russian settlements and capturing subjects of the tsar to make them slave laborers in Asian khanates and emirates.[36]

At the same time, the majority of British ruling elites cherished a so-called Peter Pan theory, regarding the autochthonic population of Oriental countries as adolescents who would never become adults. They needed, therefore, permanent patronage and guidance from progressive nations, including the Russians—who, according to European public opinion, were bound to assist Britain and France in civilizing the medieval East.[37]

Hence, a hypothesis may be offered that political ambitions, in combination with sociocultural factors, overshadowed economic expediency at the initial stages of Russo-British competition in Asia, because the latter was a priority of neither central governments nor military administrators on the spot.[38] Yet much also depended on the caliber and individual aspirations of those "players" themselves and the unwritten "rules" of the Great Game spawned by its own dynamics.

PROFILES OF THE GAME'S PLAYERS

The advance of European nations to Oriental lands was prepared, instigated, and executed by personalities both in the capitals and in the field. Although the first category comprised monarchs and high-standing bureaucrats, the second group consisted of military and diplomatic agents in the state's service, whereas the explorers, journalists, and other freelancers in the third category often acted at their own risk with little or no assistance from government bodies.

Above all, certain attention should be devoted to those decisionmakers in ruling circles who outlined a mainstream of foreign policy. Apart from sovereigns and prime ministers, their foreign, war, and colonial secretaries traditionally exercised functions of this kind in London. The India Office secretary (starting in 1858) and high-profile Admiralty officers also contributed to formulating a political course in Asia.

Historians have scrupulously investigated Queen Victoria's role in British foreign policy throughout her long-lasting reign, particularly in the aftermath of the Crimean War.[39] We need not, therefore, dwell upon this topic. According to Her Majesty's correspondence, she strongly believed that any expansion of Russia would dramatically shift the balance of power and result in its control over the whole of Eurasia. Whereas the queen kept on maintaining family contacts with the Romanovs, being charmed by the impeccable manners and good temper of Nicholas I and Alexander II, she strongly recommended that her cabinets pursue power politics vis-à-vis Saint Petersburg.[40]

Edward VII, who succeeded the queen on the throne, altered the focus of his diplomatic voyages to European countries in an attempt to contribute to the regrouping of great powers in the early 1900s. But the first violin in the decisionmaking process during the Edwardian epoch was surely played by the foreign secretaries—the Conservative Lord Lansdowne and the Liberal Sir Edward Grey.

In comparison with British monarchs, Russian tsars had always considered foreign affairs as a domain of their personal authority. Thus Alexander Rediger, the war minister in the reign of Nicholas II, wrote in his memoirs,

> All the questions of external policy belonged to the competence of His Majesty, and the ministers, apart from the Secretary for Foreign Affairs, were informed or enlisted to join the discussion only at special requests of the Emperor.[41]

An exemplary reference may be found in the correspondence between Alexander II and Prince Bariatinsky, the commander in chief of the Caucasian Corps, who was later to become the viceroy of the Russian Caucasus. Speculating upon current affairs in Persia, the tsar instructed his general: "The time has not come yet for the Russian Empire to commence a general advance into the Asian khanates, and into the Trans-Caspian region in particular. Only after Russia has subjugated the Caucasian nations and established her preponderance in the Amur Basin, she would be able to go ahead in Central Asia."[42]

Significantly, many Tsarist officials sought to inculcate in the minds of their sovereigns an idea of the legacy that the great Asian potentates of the past had allegedly left to Russian emperors. To illustrate this notion, it is sufficient to quote Mikhail Przhevalsky, the most respected Russian military explorer, who opined at the sunset of his life that

> the nomad Mongols, the Dungans, or the Moslem Chinese, and the inhabitants of Eastern [Chinese] Turkestan, especially the latter, are all more or less possessed with the idea of becoming subjects of the White Tsar, whose name, equal to that of the Dalai Lama, appears in the eyes of Asiatic masses as surrounded with a halo of mystic might. These poor Asiatics look at the advance of the Russian power with the strong conviction that its advent is synonymous with the commencement of a happier era meaning to them greater security of life.[43]

Yet nearly all Russian monarchs, Nicholas II being a paragon, suffered pressure from aristocratic factions at the Court of Saint Petersburg, when, as Lord Salisbury, then the British foreign secretary, once remarked in an epistle to Robert Morier, the ambassador to Russia, "each influential person, military or civil, snatches from him [the tsar] as opportunity offers the decisions which such person at the moment wants, and that the mutual effect of these decisions on each other is determined almost exclusively by chance."[44]

Ministers and other high-ranking bureaucrats, especially those dealing with foreign affairs and military politics, often acted as the mouthpieces of such cliques. That is why Alexander Gorchakov, Dimitry Miluitin, Sergei Witte, and Alexei Kuropatkin, the key Russian statesmen in the epoch of the Great Game, may also be regarded as its participants. According to David Mackenzie's argument, "consideration of power and prestige appears to have played for them an even greater part in causing the Russian advance" than any economic, cultural, or religious motive.[45] Because of permanent interdepartmental rivalry, for example, between the Foreign Ministry and the War Ministry, the general course of Russian policy in Asia fluctuated from an application of "hard" to "soft" power, depending on the current intentions of the sovereign.

In the British case, however, prime ministers' activity included the duties of foreign secretaries on a regular basis. Such outstanding national leaders as Henry Palmerston, William Gladstone, Benjamin Disraeli, and Lord Salisbury decisively promoted the British advance into Asia. For example, a study of Palmerston's correspondence along with reminiscences written by his contemporaries demonstrates that the prime minister, a man of strong character and intellect, believed that Britain, being strategically unassailable on sea, was predestined to act as an arbiter in the so-called Concert of Europe—a constellation of the great powers of the time. That is why he sturdily opposed any challenge to Britain's role as a beacon of progress and a major driving mechanism for the renovation of the Orient, according to the traditional paradigm of the European liberalism. Commenting on the contingency of the Russo-British struggle on the outskirts of the two empires, Palmerston remarked as early as in July 1840,

> It seems pretty clear that, sooner or later, the Cossack and the Sepoy, the man from the Baltic and he from the British Islands will meet in the centre of Asia. It should be our business to take care that the meeting should take place as far off from our Indian possessions as may be convenient and advantageous to us. But the meeting will not be avoided by our staying at home to receive the visit.[46]

More important, Palmerston's vision of external policy rested upon two fundamental principles—preservation of the balance of power in Europe, and prevention of any encroachment upon Britain's commercial interests all over the world. The well-known incident with Don Pacifico, a British subject protected by Palmerston in the House of Commons after his mansion in Athens had been plundered by Greek marauders, testified to these principles.[47] Although Palmerston might have differed with Gladstone, Disraeli, or Salisbury in the understanding of Russian intentions in various regions, all of them surmised that Russia constantly sought to become a hegemonic empire in Eurasia only to eventually demolish the "Concert of Europe" and destroy British rule in India. "If the Russians had Constantinople," replied Disraeli to an interpellation of a certain member of Parliament in October 1876, "they could at any time march their army through Syria to the mouth of the Nile," thus threatening British India.[48] Likewise, Lord Salisbury was convinced that Britain ought to collaborate with the other European powers without any commitment on its side to long-term continental alliances. He regarded the policy of Russia as a cocktail of idealism, intrigue, and power; but being a realist in international relations, he believed that there was still enough room in Asia for both empires—continental and maritime—to develop their strengths on the foundations of laissez-faire and free trade.[49]

The ultimate need to correlate British political and economic activity in the East with the ambitions of the Tsardom often compelled Whitehall to issue "general cautions combined with concessions," both in Europe and Asia.[50] Besides, such pragmatic statesmen as Lord Salisbury were well informed that Britain's presence in India rested primarily on its coercion of the national liberation movement, though it had never repudiated moral obligations of the white race to Indian nations. In Salisbury's case, it is not an exaggeration to infer that the Great Sepoy Mutiny of 1857–58 definitely affected the belief system of young Robert.[51]

One could be led to believe that British foreign secretaries, together with the chiefs of the War, Colonial, and India offices, may be added to the Great Game's participants, as capable to mold the foreign affairs of Albion. But unlike their Russian counterparts, they were answerable to Parliament and British public opinion for their decisions and actions in external policy.[52]

The colonial reformers—such as Edward Wakefield, Charles Buller, Lord Durham, and Sir William Molesworth—proposed overseas emigration and colonial investments on a massive scale as appropriate remedies to consolidate British possessions in Asia. All of them were obsessed with the idea that war might have a disastrous effect upon business, whereas the decline of trade, heavy material losses, and inevitable downfall of credit that would accompany hostilities might pave the way for civil unrest in the mother state, resulting in a general destabilization of the "second" empire. To avoid such negative consequences, this group of statesmen and public figures regarded methods of indirect, or "soft," colonial rule as more appropriate for the empire than violence and repression.[53]

As for such "masterly inactivists," or supporters of nonintervention in the affairs of Asian states, as Richard Montgomery, William Muir, or George Campbell, who held positions in British diplomatic missions and political agencies in the Orient, their invectives for the stationing of expeditionary forces, primarily on the northwest frontier of India, stemmed from the belief that all expenditures on enduring petty wars and punitive expeditions aimed to pacify restless tribes and retaliate for bandit forays were useless. Besides, in the event of occasional misfortunes, Britain's position there might be destabilized and its world prestige might be undermined. Hence, they feverishly supported a policy of compromises with the Tsarist government to defeat the Russians economically and culturally. In other words, they regarded "an active intervention [in Asian countries] so hazardous as to be justified only by the avoidance of still greater risks."[54]

Simultaneously, their opponents, protagonists of the "forward" policy, favored the usage of "hard" power for the subjugation of Asian nations. Supported by the majority of colonial administrators, especially by those who had made their careers in India, such "forwardists" as David Urquhart, Henry Rawlinson, and Arminius Vambery insisted on resolute measures to be taken on Indian frontiers against bellicose khanates or warlike tribes to frustrate their alliances with Russian military governors in the "far pavilions." According to Lord Roberts, who occupied the post of the commander in chief in India during the late 1870s and early 1890s, the "forward" policy implied an extension of influence and an establishment of legal order on the territories, where anarchy, murder, and robbery had reigned supreme up to the time of the British conquest.[55] The proponents of this political course were eager, according to William Dawson, "to anticipate a development of events already assumed to be inevitable, and at once bind all the frontier rulers and chiefs to the British government by means of alliances, missions and, where necessary, subsidies in the form of money and material of war."[56] A typical example was John Kaye, first a distinguished bureaucrat in the

India Office and later a historian, who brought the problem of Central Asia into the focus of public opinion in the British Isles.[57]

Certainly, the so-called forwardists should not be labeled as steady Russophobes, and, vice versa, those champions of "masterly inactivity" should not be labeled as diehard Russophiles. The difference between them seemed not so great, because many personalities from both camps were often next of kin, engaged in the same business transactions or public interactions. It should also be borne in mind that, according to Lawrence James, who investigated all this thoroughly in his book *The Rise and Fall of the British Empire*, "Russophobia infected the minds of nearly every nineteenth-century British statesman, diplomat and strategist, and was strongly felt among all classes and shades of political opinion," when the majority of British people looked upon Russia as a state "irretrievably bent on acquisition, enlarging itself to provide living space for its growing population."[58] Nikolai Yerofeev, a pioneering Soviet researcher on Russophobia in the United Kingdom, also argued that no particular social groups in Britain were obsessed with it, but he found that certain groups of military strategists, colonial administrators, and overseas traders, disappointed by Russia's authoritarian regime and its protectionism in commerce, might have cherished Russophobia as a sort of psychological compensation for infelicities in dealing with some Tsarist administrators.[59] Besides, as maintained by Anthony Cross, a prominent expert on the history of Russo-British cultural intercourse, the Russian victory over the Ottoman Turks at Ochakov in 1791 or the three divisions of Poland in the second half of the eighteenth century might have shaped a negative image of Russia in the public opinion of Britain.[60]

Yet John Gleason, an American historian, offers a somewhat different explanation of the genesis of anti-Russian feelings. In his view, "English Russophobia was primarily a product of the forces which determined events in England and upon the Continent in the years after Waterloo." According to Gleason, the British public distrusted any official diplomatic statements, because a gap had always existed between them and realpolitik of any Tsarist government. It was this very skepticism that spawned Russophobia in the Victorian age. Gleason considered British foreign policy even more aggressive than Russian, but hypocritical and better camouflaged to disseminate humane values to Asian nations.[61]

In the opinion of the majority of contemporaries, the problem of Indian defense had been always on the mind of British politicians and public activists throughout the nineteenth century. Before the Sepoy Mutiny of 1857–58, the possessions of the East India Company consisted of the Bengal, Madras, and Bombay presidencies, each with its own civil administration and military forces but under the supreme control of a governor-general, his commander in chief, and a Council. They used to be stationed in the colonial capital, Calcutta, from October to March, moving each year to Simla, a remote hill village in the Himalayan foothills some 1,200 miles from Calcutta, to better survive the hot season from March to October. Traditionally, each governor-general was responsible to the members of the East India Company's Board of Control, who held regular sessions in the City of London, though the Mogul emperor, as a nominal suzerain of numerous vassal maharajas, continued to symbolize the supreme authority.[62]

Since the adoption of the India Act in 1858, which put an end to the East India Company's autonomy, the system had undergone reorganization. Henceforward, British India, or the Raj, comprised territories of three kinds: presidencies, provinces, and more than six hundred princely states; the latter occupied 60 percent of Hindustan and were ruled by hereditary potentates, with British political residents attached to their courts. Viceroys combined supreme legislative and executive power, retaining, at the same time, responsibility to the newly established India Office. As a rule, their tenure of five years allowed no prolongation, with few exceptions, Lord Curzon being one.[63]

More important, until the very end of colonial rule, British India possessed a full-scale and largely independent military establishment. As a Canadian historian pictured it,

The Viceregal court and the local courts of the Presidencies blazed with the splendor of military uniforms, and the cantonments of the Indian Army, even more than the growing commercial centers of Bombay, Calcutta, and Madras, were the centers of British society in India, since the army rather than the civil service or trade, attracted to the continent many younger members of the landed aristocracy, which until the end of the nineteenth century was the effective ruling class of Britain.[64]

The autonomy of the viceroy and his administration from London may be illustrated by the fact that special import tariffs and custom duties were granted to the Indian Empire by the queen. In contrast to a system of representative democracy, the Viceregal Council, established after the Sepoy Mutiny to replace the legislative and administrative bodies of the East India Company, might act both as the Cabinet of Ministers and the Legislative Assembly. The India Act authorized the viceroy to summon his Council whenever he wished. It also regulated the viceroy's prerogatives—for example, the right to impose a veto on any decision approved by the members of his Council.[65]

Lord Canning, the acting governor-general, was the first to procure the appointment of the viceroy of India in 1858. A British historian commented on the significance of the Viceroyalty in Indian political life: "Only the Autocrat of All the Russians and the President of the United States can really be compared with Viceroys as rulers; and while they both ruled larger territories than he did and enjoyed considerably more power, they fell far behind him in the number of subjects."[66] It needs to be mentioned that there were a few outstanding figures in the line of British viceroys before 1914—such as Sir John Lawrence (1864–69), Lord Lytton (1876–80), and Lord Curzon (1899–1905)—whose role in the transformation of the amorphous constellation of feudal possessions into modern India could hardly be overestimated.[67]

Looking back to the history of this institution, which was abolished by the Indian republican government in 1947, historians are able to document the great contribution that the viceroys definitely made to the conduct of imperial policy in Asia. Suffice it to say that British diplomatic missions and political agencies in Tehran and in the Persian Gulf were supervised by the viceroys of India. Symptomatically, most viceroys in the nineteenth century shared Russophobic views. For example,

Lord Ripon described his attitude toward the Romanovs' Empire in the following way:

> That great, grim, shadowy power, which sits brooding over Europe and Asia, and of which no man knows really whether it be strong or weak, whether its people be a young race yet to play a great part in the world's history, or men, as Diderot describes them, rotten before they are ripe; that dark, silent Russian Czar, the hater of freedom, the foe of every people struggling to cast off oppression, the proponent of Austrian rottenness, whose image recalls the visions which old Hebrew prophets saw of the Babylonian power as it advanced stride by stride to swallow up Jerusalem.[68]

Hundreds of officials in the Victorian period shared this stereotypical image of Russia. Additionally, they usually perceived political developments in Central or East Asia through the prism of European problems and believed that a "cordon of buffer states" on Russia's frontiers would check its advance into Asia. Scared by the monstrous "Russian Bear," Russophobes stubbornly urged Whitehall to curb any messianic activity by Tsarist emissaries in Oriental countries, especially with regard to their support for authoritarian regimes instead of the values of liberal democracy.

It needs to be mentioned, however, that the scope of functions exercised by colonial officers on the spot often exceeded their competence and the limits of the assignments they were committed to fulfill in remote countries. Their ambitions rested, moreover, on the sympathies of the Victorian public, with strong-willed individuals motivated by a sense of duty and guided by the highest moral principles. To characterize, so to say, the predecessors of some of the Great Game's key figures, Charles Allen narrated the life story of a certain John Nicholson, who served in India from 1839 until he was killed by Sepoy rebels. "Although anything but a team player," contended Allen, "Nicholson was an extricable part of a small bond of military officers–cum–civil administrators—the *Soldier Sahibs* of my title—who between them shaped what is still to this day known in Pakistan as the North-West Frontier Province—the NWFP, for short."[69]

Most of these young subalterns remained underpaid, badly coordinated, and often critically short of maps, especially at the Great Game's onset. On May 19, 1864, Horace Rumbold, the British chargé d'affaires in Saint Petersburg, portrayed them in a letter to Lord Clarendon, the foreign secretary:

> There were in the field numerous "unquiet spirits," of whom some were actuated by an honorable desire to distinguish themselves by brilliant achievements, while others were adventurers, or men bankrupt in fortune or reputation, sent to those distant regions in disgrace.[70]

However, one could not overestimate the contribution of such audacious travelers as Arthur Conolly, Henry Rawlinson, Alexander Burnes, Arminius Vambery, Ney Elias, and Francis Younghusband, to mention but a few, to the reconnaissance of no-man's lands, the mapping of their natural resources, and the processing of information on their ethnoreligious composition. Characteristically, as Robert Johnson remarked, "None of the British officers involved in the Great Game wanted the stigma of 'spy' and tended to describe their activities as adventurous expeditions which would add to the stock of geographical knowledge of the world."[71]

In a very similar fashion, Russian emperors appointed governors-general to occupy the highest administrative positions in the frontier territories. Vasily Perovsky, Konstantin Kaufman, Dimitry Romanovsky, Mikhail Cherniaev, and other commanders did their utmost to free their sovereigns "from dependency on ministers in Saint Petersburg," acting as mediators between autocrats and regional elites—the relations somehow resembling the dealings of British military representatives on the colonial periphery with the Crown and home Cabinet.[72]

At the level of "ordinary players," comparable ethnic naïveté, topographical ignorance, uncritical enthusiasm, and career ambitions were inherent in the characters of Nikolai Przhevalsky, Petr Pashino, Bronislav Grombchevsky, Nikolai Notovich, Petr Kozlov, Karl Mannerheim, and others.[73] Like their British counterparts, all of them manifested the progress and enlightenment that the Tsarist Empire was bringing to the Orient. "In case the conflict with England occurs," wrote Nikolai Ignatiev, one of the "architects" of the Great Game, "it is only in Asia that we shall be able to struggle with her with a chance to reduce British world power."[74] Aged in their twenties or thirties, well educated (most of them had graduated from the Academy of the General Staff), extremely courageous, and imbued with loyalty to the sovereign, they restlessly hunted for decorations and higher ranks in military campaigns against nomadic tribes and Asiatic rulers.[75] It is not an exaggeration, therefore, to depict them in the manner used by the war minister, Dimitry Miliutin, to portray Mikhail Skobelev, a victorious commander in the Russo-Turkish War of 1877–78 and the conqueror of the Turkmens' fortress of Geok Tepe in 1881. According to Miliutin, Skobelev "was accurate in service, industrious, and capable, albeit sometimes unscrupulous. Excessive ambitions, the desire to upstart and outstrip the others, induce him to shake heaven and earth."[76]

To complete the picture, it would seem appropriate to quote from the travel diary of Colonel Frederick Burnaby, a British officer who, when on furlough, made a long trip across Central Asia to Khiva in the mid-1870s:

> We can not wonder at the tsar's officers in Turkestan being so eager to continue in their line of conquest. Taken for the most part from poor but well-born families, having no inheritance but the sword, no prospect save promotion, their thirst for war as the only means at hand for rapidly rising in service.[77]

In corroboration of Burnaby's opinion, Russian analysts themselves recognized personal ambitions as a main driving force of the Great Game. As one of them remarked, "A positive fever for further conquest raged among our troops—an ailment to cure which no method of treatment was effective, especially as the correctives applied were freely interspersed with such stimulants as honors and decorations."[78]

Hence, the dilemma of insubordination by frontier officers to central administrative bodies needs a thorough discussion, because some historians argue that military commanders in the field used to take separate actions, imposing their vision of current affairs upon superiors and conceiving petty wars behind the backs of the Russian or British ruling leaders, who sought to curb these aggressive aspirations. Many researchers maintain, moreover, that territorial expansion, whether continental or across a sea, spawned the so-called colonial generality ("admiralty"), who elaborated their own strategy and tactics in Asia.[79] Thus, though local civil and military administrators allegedly intensified tension on Asian frontiers, central governments reacted to their activity spontaneously, without any adequate understanding of the situation there. If a successful commander won a battle or captured an enemy's city, his superiors awarded him with decorations and promoted him to a higher rank, because "the Game's unspoken rule was that the alchemy of success could always turn mutiny into initiative."[80] Otherwise, a loser was usually impeached by some higher-ranking chiefs for exceeding his commissions and was even stigmatized by the press as a nonprofessional troublemaker.[81]

It should be noted that this common practice led to the mutual accusations of "double standards" practiced by both sides. For example, in Palmerston's view, the information about some higher-level Tsarist bureaucrats surreptitiously encouraging military commanders in the field to punish Asian rulers at their own risk overshadowed official condemnation of these campaigns by Russian diplomats.[82] Analogously, the Unionist Cabinet in London laid the blame for the famous Tibet expedition of 1903–4 upon Francis Younghusband and partly on Viceroy Lord Curzon (see chapter 5), though the viceroy countenanced the invasion of this inaccessible region only after intensive consultations with Prime Minister Arthur Balfour and Secretary of State for India George Hamilton.[83]

A notorious "double standard" approach may be, however, excused on some grounds, which Dimitry Miliutin outlined in his memoirs:

While demanding strict adherence to instructions and fulfillment of orders from local military commanders, I regarded it was wrong, at the same time, to take initiative fully away from them. The fear of responsibility for any deviation from instructions may kill enthusiasm and enterprise. Under certain circumstances, a commander ought to assume responsibility for action, not envisaged in the scheme beforehand. The fact was that such divergences from the agenda in details did not contradict general objectives and meet urgencies.[84]

In a broader sense, despite their sometime insubordinate aggressiveness, most victorious generals, who served on Asian frontiers for years, knew how to deal with local populations, acting not as seasoned officers but as shrewd administrators, able to implement regulations in the territories occupied by Russian or British troops. Besides, such military administrators contributed to the abolition of slavery markets and medieval punishments in public prisons, the commutation of sentences, and the protection of caravan routes from the forays of bandit gangs. Conversely, they did not interfere with the domestic affairs of local communities and aspired to adjust their government to the manners and customs of Asian countries.

Occasionally, however, they expressed scorn for the indigenous population in their reports and minutes to their superiors. For example, Colonel Nikolai Grodekov, who was later to become the governor-general of Turkestan, reported to the Main Staff after his trip across Persia and Afghanistan that "the Turkmen as a nation is a black hole on the Earth; they are the shame of mankind which tolerates them."[85] In the account of his travels through Chinese Turkestan, Nikolai Przhevalsky likewise contended that "there are many scores to settle with our haughty neighbor [the Qing Empire], and we are obliged to demonstrate to it that Russia's spirit and Russian courage know no match, whether at home or in the Far East." The traveler cited a prominent Russian jurist, Feodor Martens, who explained the European annexation of Asian states by a maxim: "International law does not apply to savages."[86]

In the same vein, the Cabinet of Saint James aimed to control the Great Game's players in the field by means of administrative regulations and budget subsidies. A system of cross-verifications of intelligence from different secret agencies was established in the latter part of the nineteenth century by the Russian Main Staff and the British

Committee of Colonial (later Imperial) Defence to supervise the semi-official activities of military commanders, explorers, and adventurers of various kinds.

Apart from Europeans, Asiatic nationals also participated in the Great Game as surveyors, scouts, and secret informants ("newswriters"). They were employed by British and Russian military spymasters to collect information on current developments in their countries and the intentions of the opposite side.[87] Having received grants from different financial sources, most of them reconnoitered frontier areas disguised as traders, pilgrims, or beggars. According to an Indian scholar, the main criterion for the selection of the so-called pundits by British military authorities was their good rapport with northerly neighbors in Tibet and knowledge of their way of life. The trainees were drilled in the basics of route surveys; the usage of elementary topographical instruments, such as a compass, sextant, and thermometer; and the maintenance of field books.[88]

ASIAN COUNTRIES IN THE PROLOGUE OF THE GAME

The first thing about the participation of Asian countries in the Great Game that should be taken under consideration is the position of the Black Sea and the Caucasus as a bridgehead for Russo-British geostrategic rivalry, because both London and Saint Petersburg considered this region as linking Europe to Middle East and Inner Asia. According to Prince Bariatinsky,

> If the Sovereign desires to exploit favorable state of affairs (the Sepoy Mutiny in India, decline of Turkey, amicable attitude of France and Persia to Russia), the first thing we ought to do is the establishment of our mastery over the Caucasus. On attaining this goal, we would be able to dominate the East.[89]

Few scholars have devoted attention to the fact that Russia could hardly implement an active policy in the aftermath of the Crimean War unless it completed the conquest of the bellicose mountain tribes that inhabited the Northern Caucasus. Not coincidentally, the Caucasus War being in full swing, British and American observers recommended to Whitehall to deploy an expeditionary corps of 40,000 to 50,000 infantrymen and cavalrymen to support Chechen and Circassian guerrillas in their struggle against Tsarist troops. A British journalist raised arguments for such a gamble:

> Having swept the Caucasian isthmus clean of Muscovite intruders, a large force of splendid chivalrous cavalry will be at our service to strike a heavy blow on enemy at once. Russia lies open to our army and we can threaten Moscow, Sebastopol, Odessa, and the rear of the Russian Danube army all simultaneously.[90]

It was impossible for Nicholas I and his ministers to set about conducting any military operations in Central or East Asia without previous reconnaissance expeditions. Yet, doubtless, one may discover the origins of the Great Game in the results of the Russo-Turkish War and Russo-Persian War of 1827–28 and 1828–29, on the one hand, and in the aftermath of the Anglo-Afghan War of 1839–42, on the other. Symptomatically, David Urquhart, an ardent opponent of Tsarist colonial policy in this area and active supporter of the guerrilla struggle in Circussia, described the domestic situation in the Ottoman Empire and Persia by the 1850s in the following way:

> A small population, without the leading of the nations of the West, and unaided by the wise counsels of their governments, has rendered service to humanity. A new struggle indeed is opening, but it commences at this point.[91]

While making urgent preparations for further progress in Asia, both the Russians and the British, however, spontaneously sought to furnish the frontier zones with necessary logistical infrastructure—they constructed high roads, fortified military outposts, installed depots for ammunition, and surveyed appropriate routes for the advance of troops.

The allied Anglo-French intervention of the Black and Azov seas during the Crimean War precipitated the course of the Caucasian campaign. The attempts of some adventurous British subjects to deliver arms to Muslim insurgents in the region and subsidize local guerrilla chieftains made the eventual subjugation of this area a sine qua non for Russian policy in West Asia.[92]

A series of reforms and innovations pursued by Bariatinsky and Miliutin in the Caucasus Army Corps led to the final defeat of the insurgents, who were headed by the legendary Imam Shamil. By the years 1863–64, their last strongholds had ceased to resist the offensive of Tsarist troops on the northern slope of the Caucasus Mountains. The time had come to move the victorious regiments further into Central Asia.

Therefore, Persia assumed particular strategic significance as a base for the conquest of Central Asia and a key transit state on the ancient Great Silk Road. According to the treaties of Gulistan (1813) and Turkmanchai (1829), Russia was granted the privilege to establish consulates in boundary Persian settlements. In response to this diplomatic success, Britain did its utmost to ally with the shah's empire with the Treaty of Tehran in 1814 to frustrate Afghan rulers' encroachments on northwest principalities in India. Two decades later, a bogey of the anti-Russian coalition—including the Ottoman Empire, Persia, and Britain—emerged on the horizon of international relations in Asia. The London Cabinet might have taken an opportunity to arrest Russian progress there using Russophobic hysteria instigated in the British press by George de Lacy Evans, David Urquart, and other journalists who were hostile to the Tsarist authorities.[93]

By the middle of the nineteenth century, the Russians had nearly completed the conversion of the Caspian Sea into their inner lake. With the beginning of the Crimean War, Tsarist diplomats worked intensively to coerce Tehran to sign a treaty of mutual military assistance between Russia and Persia, offering the shah annual subsidies of 2 million Persian tomans. Although these negotiations ended in a stalemate, they led to the conclusion of the convention on September 29, 1854. Pursuant to the document, the shah's government was obliged to remain neutral during the Crimean War.[94]

Mindful of the British troops being sent to strengthen their position in Arabia, the new Persian sovereign, Shah Nasir-u-Din, even applied to the American president for assistance in defense of the Persian Gulf. But Washington renounced this plea.[95] In October 1856, a sudden attack launched by the shah's army against Herat, a major stronghold in the north of Afghanistan, received Russian approval. Yet Britain, in its turn, inflicted upon the Qajar Dynasty a retaliatory blow—the expeditionary troops, sent from India, landed on Bahrain, Keshm, Harg, and other islands of strategic importance in the Gulf. The war came to an end only after the Anglo-Indian soldiers occupied the seaport of Bushire in the same year. Colonel Nikolai Ignatiev, a Russian military attaché, reported from London to Saint Petersburg on January 23, 1857:

> There is a diversity of opinions upon this war in England. Many people dislike it for fears of eventual involvement in a new tour of struggle against Russia.... England feels that the past war [the Crimean War] has not consolidated, but weakened British influence in Asia; that is why, seeing the need to reestablish it, they believe that the time has come to do this, while Russia remains humiliated after her defeat.... The latest news of the Amur area, the Syr Daria region and the coast of the Caspian Sea alarmed profoundly the East India Company and British traders. Everybody is concerned with Russia's shifting attention from western states to Asian territories, where there is an ample room for her political, moral, and commercial activity.[96]

The Anglo-Persian Treaty, signed in Paris on March 4, 1857, fixed the role of London as an established mediator between Tehran and Kabul in case of a dispute on the borders between them.[97] The East India Company, for its part, wished to maintain the status quo ante bellum. This meant Herat's autonomy from Kabul, where the ruler, Emir Dost Mohamed, yearned to bring together the semi-independent Afghan principalities.[98] At the same time, in spite of the victory gained by Britain in the Persian War of 1856–57, the approaches to India, in the opinion of the empire's ruling circles, including the government of

India, lacked protection from any attack that might be launched by a potential adversary.[99] Moreover, in the aftermath of the Anglo-Persian hostilities, London was bogged down in two other broad-scale armed conflicts—the Sepoy Mutiny; and the Second Opium War, which required extra budgeted spending on military campaigns. Meanwhile, Russian economic influence over Persia was increasing year by year. Besides, Nasir-u-Din, humiliated by the clauses of the Paris Peace Treaty with Britain, made overtures to the Russian emperor, Alexander II. According to a British historian,

> The ambitions of the Shah, which took the direction of military conquest and territorial aggrandizement, met with greater indulgence from the Russians, who wanted both to keep Persia weak and to divert the Shah from thoughts of recovering the lost Caucasian provinces, than they did from the British, who wanted him to concentrate upon internal reform.[100]

Political analysts in Britain realized the threat of the eventual Russo-Persian rapprochement in close proximity to India. As early as in 1836, John McNeill cautioned the government against underestimating Persia's military potential in combination with Russia's strategic projects:

> Fifty thousand Persian infantry, composed of what are perhaps the finest material in the world for service in those countries, and disciplined by Russian officers, with about fifty guns of Persian artillery, in a high state of efficiency, and an almost unlimited number of irregular force, could be put in motion by Russia, in any direction, within twelve months after the resources of the kingdom were at her disposal; and the acquisition of such an influence as would enable her, in the event of a war with England, to induce Persia to take part with her against us, would at once give her a complete control of the military resources of that country.[101]

In fact, by the 1850s, Russia had replaced France as Britain's principal opponent in the East, though some astute journalists had anticipated this scenario long before it revealed itself on the scene of world politics. For example, as early as 1800, a British commentator argued that "unless the progress of Russia was stopped, Persia, Turkey and India would become preys of her devouring ambition."[102]

However, what alarmed Whitehall most of all were the permanent internal feuds in Afghanistan—"a wall of the Indian garden," as Lieutenant Richmond Shakespear, a British traveler to Inner Asia, once remarked,[103] and a decline of the Turkic khanates in Central Asia. Regarding the former threat, it appeared critically important for Britain to keep a close eye on the districts adjacent to India's northwest frontier because a European power, almost certainly Russia, might have used disorder to establish its suzerainty over local chieftains. As to the latter peril, it was unclear to analysts what effect the decay of the khanates would have on the position of the Raj. Under these troublesome circumstances, British cabinets focused upon the situation in Afghanistan, because London faced a dilemma in that country: either to uphold a cluster of feeble, decadent emirates; or to stimulate someone among the local rulers to assemble different ethnopolitical and religious groups in a strong united kingdom under the aegis of the emir of Kabul, who was designated by military writers as either a guarantor of that country's transformation into a buffer state or a leader of an eventual Islamic renaissance in the Middle East and Inner Asia.

A man of cleverness and strong will, Dost Mohamed Khan, who was descended from the Barakzais tribe, proclaimed Afghanistan an emirate and one by one began to subdue the minor principalities neighboring his own hereditary domain of Kabul. This state of affairs seemed far from tranquil, for Dost Mohamed's brothers ruled Kandahar; Herat remained under the control of Kamran-mirza, who was descended from the Sadorzais tribe competing with the Barakzais; and Peshawar was occupied by the army of Ranjit Singh, the ruler of Punjab and Kashmir.[104] In this situation, the British had to choose between Shah Shuja-u-Mulk, who was susceptible of control but weak, and the authoritative but far less manageable Dost Mohamed, taking into account their strategic interests and, above all, the Russian threat to India. As Malcolm Yapp argued in his foundational study of the policy of British India,

A strong Afghanistan under the tough British control was to be the centre-piece of the new British policy in Central Asia. Afghanistan was not to be either another Iran, subsidized but uncontrolled, or an Assam, garrisoned and controlled; it was to be a new type of buffer state. Shah Shuja was to have full internal independence, although continually prompted to introduce reforms which would make his government popular, his army efficient, his revenues productive, and his commerce free and abundant.[105]

The aspirations of Russia to get an upper hand in Central Asia by forwarding Lieutenant Ian Vitkevich, adjutant of the governor of Orenburg, to Dost Mohamed's court in December 1837 ended in a failure, for Britain had outwitted Russia in a preventive mission conducted by Alexander Burnes, the subaltern of the Third Regiment Bombay Native Infantry.[106] At the same time, the First Anglo-Afghan War of 1839–42, in which Britain suffered heavy casualties and matériel losses, demonstrated the impotence of the East India Company to secure the borders of the Raj through direct interference in the feuds of claimants to the throne in Kabul.[107]

As in the cases of Persia and Afghanistan, Saint Petersburg and London were nervous about current instability in the states that remained in the medieval empire of Timur the Conqueror. The khanates of Khiva and Khokand, together with the Emirate of Bokhara, were regarded by contemporaries as the last three independent principalities in Central Asia. According to approximate calculations by European journalists in the mid-1850s, the overall local population might be estimated at 8 million, including the Uzbeks, who dominated a mixture of nations, such as the Turks, Iranians, Jews, Armenians, and others. Russian statistics demonstrated that the Turkic ethnos amounted to 85 to 90 percent of the inhabitants who could speak at least two languages.[108] For example, the urban population of Bokhara was bilingual, though official records were kept in Farsi.[109] Rural dwellers were partly engaged in cattle breeding, migrating with flocks of sheep or camels from one hill pasture to another, while other groups of the indigenous population settled in villages (*kishlaks*) and towns (*shakhers*) along the principal rivers. As to trade and domestic industries, they were concentrated in the big cities of Bokhara, Tashkent, Samarkand, and Khiva.

Interestingly, as early as 1700, the envoys of the khan of Khiva visited Moscow and submitted to the consideration of Peter the Great an appeal of their sovereign, who begged the tsar to take his country under the aegis of Russia. But the war against Sweden prevented the emperor from devoting proper attention to Central Asia.[110] Nevertheless, in 1716, the Russians embarked on the construction of the so-called Orenburg-Siberian defensive line—a cordon of fortified Cossack outposts that stretched for 3,500 kilometers, protecting the southern frontier of the Russian Empire. It threaded its way from the fortress of Guriev at the mouth of the Ural River along its left bank to Orenburg and farther to Orsk, where, crossed by the headwaters of the Tobol River, the line reached the stronghold of Troitska. From there it followed through Petropavlovsk and Omsk to Semipalatinsk on the Chinese border. However, nomadic tribes regularly raided the frontier area during the eighteenth and the first half of the nineteenth centuries—as, for example, they did under the command of the self-proclaimed Kazakh "sultan" Kenessary Kasimov in 1841–47. Numerous gangs of mounted bandits frequently broke through defensive lines of cordon posts, looted settlements of Russian colonists, captured many people, and sold them as white slaves on the markets of Khiva and Bokhara, while frontier guards were enlisted mostly to garrison service. The ignorance of local specialties, inadequate mobility, and a scarcity of the means of offensive prevented frontier guards from conducting effective punitive expeditions on a regular basis.[111]

Regrettably, relations in the triangle of Central Asian khanates also seemed far from harmonious. The khans and emirs constantly intervened in each other's domestic affairs, waging exhausting wars in attempts to seize neighboring territories. Thus, in 1810 the khan of Khokand devastated Tashkent and annexed it. Shortly afterward, Khokand subdued the nomadic Kyrgyz tribes to the north of the Syr Daria. Meanwhile, the emir of Bokhara regularly encroached upon the territory of Khokand in the 1850s and 1860s, and the khan of

Khiva waged endless wars against the Turkmen tribes to the south of the Amu Daria.[112]

To secure the southeastern frontier, the government of Nicholas I determined to construct a new line of military outposts, this time along the Syr Daria. A fruitless reconnaissance expedition to Khiva in 1839, undertaken by the Orenburg military governor, Vasily Perovsky, a close confidant of the emperor himself, aimed to establish Russian control to the south of this cordon, eliminate banditry and slavery in Central Asia, and, in this way, counterbalance the British offensive from India against Afghanistan.[113] After failing to achieve Khiva because of the unbearable weather conditions (severe winter), Perovsky, nevertheless, impelled Alla Kuli Khan to seek Turkish aid. Meanwhile, the Russians proceeded with the renovation of existing medieval fortifications and the building of new outposts along the Irgiz and Turgay rivers. In addition, they erected naval bases on the Aral Sea and arranged for navigation in the mouth of the Syr Daria in the years 1847–50.[114] Furthermore, several Russian diplomatic missions visited Bokhara between 1836 and 1843, in order to reach an accord with Nasrulla, the ruler of Bokhara, regarding customs duties, the protection of Russian merchants from encroachment upon their property, the liberation of slaves, and the establishment of relations with Saint Petersburg.

In the years 1842–43, Nicholas I asked Emir Nasrulla, though in vain, to set free two British emissaries, Colonel Stoddart and Captain Conolly, who had been imprisoned in Bokhara and were finally executed by the order of the emir as British spies in June 1842.[115] The request was conveyed to Nasrulla through Colonel Butenev, a special envoy committed to Bokhara and accompanied by a prominent expert in Oriental studies, Nikolai Khanykov.[116] The next year, Karl Nesselrode, the Russian chancellor and foreign minister, proposed to his British counterpart, Lord Aberdeen, "to preserve the khanates of Central Asia as a neutral zone interposed between the empires, so as to prevent them from any dangerous contact."[117] They were to fill in the vacuum of influence upon problem areas between the domains of the two empires. According to this notion, any buffer state might be regarded as territory that separated two rival or potentially hostile great powers for the preclusion of armed conflicts. Although the emergence of this very definition as an integral part of the theory of the balance of power dated to the seventeenth century, it was in the course of the Great Game that Britain and Russia attempted to apply it to non-European countries for the first time in the history of international relations.[118]

As for an alternative route for Russian intrusion into Trans-Caspia from the Caucasus region, many military observers believed that the Tsarist armies were insufficiently prepared for a full-scale offensive against the khanates from this very direction, because the territory of the Turkmen tribes first needed to be reconnoitered and mapped before any concrete plan for invasion could be adopted. One should also bear in mind that a few clans declared themselves vassals of the Muscovite Kingdom in 1677, whereas other tribes followed their example in 1745, 1802, and 1811. Interestingly, a greater part of the Yomud Turkmen voluntarily allied with Russian armies in the war of 1826–28 against Persia. On this reading, by 1850 about 115,000 Turkmen had already become Russian subjects by their own will.[119]

On the eve of the Crimean War, Vasily Perovsky achieved new success in Central Asia—the troops under his command captured Ak Mescid, a key stronghold of the Khokand khanate, just in the center of a new projected cordon of Russian military outposts. After the failure of all attempts to regain the fortress by the khan of Khiva, then a nominal vassal of the shah,[120] the Russians erected two more fortresses on the frontier between Ak Mescid and Aralsk to advance the line of defense further along the Syr Daria. Thereafter, they took under control of the Kyrgyz steppes, threatening to inflict a new blow upon Khokand. As a result of the uprising and internal feuds, the Khokand ruler, Mohamed Khudayar Khan, was dethroned in 1858 and escaped the country, while the Russians began to close a gap in the defensive cordon linking the coast of the Aral Sea to southern Siberia. As *The Times* reported on December 29, 1854,

It is perfectly palpable that Russia has been gradually working her way down to our frontier, never making a startling move, but steadily advancing her pawns. Her object is to establish her paramount influence throughout the various tribes of Central Asia, to inspire them with awe of her power, and to impress on their minds that the Russians are far more powerful than the English, though they have conquered Hindustan.[121]

However, it appears a misleading argument to solely accuse the Tsarist government and Russian military commanders in the "far pavilions" of nurturing sinister designs against local Turkic khanates. There is a good reason to turn to a more balanced approach, because British planners drew up projects of expansion similar to those of their Russian counterparts. Yet the rumors of the Cossacks approaching the "gates of India" and the necessity of regaining free access to new markets instigated the British advance into Central Asia.[122] Whereas traders from the Russian Empire simply bartered one kind of goods for another on Asian markets, their British, mostly Anglo-Indian, commercial rivals sold products in exchange for precious metals. Conversely, there were rumors in the khanates of an impending British attack against Bokhara via Afghanistan as revenge for the First Anglo-Afghan War and the execution of Stoddart and Conolly by Emir Nasrulla.[123] Nevertheless, in 1856 the British diplomatic mission arrived in Bokhara to negotiate a defensive alliance. According to the Russian military expert, Lieutenant Colonel A. Serebrennikov,

> In order to dominate the Bokharian markets and establish commercial relations with the khanate, the members of the mission expressed the willingness of British merchants to sell commodities at lower prices than Russian commercial agents did. They also appealed to the Emir to authorize British cargo shipping along the Amu Daria River. Finally, the emissaries proposed to him to arrange for a dispatch of British military instructors to drill the Emir's army as well as to supply it with arms, ammunition, and artillery.[124]

Regrettably, the author of the present volume lacks information about the reaction of the emir to these advances. Yet the appeal of the Khokand potentate, Mohamed Khudayar Khan, to the Anglo-Indian government for military and economic support after the Russian capture of Ak Mescid resulted in the dispatching of three Punjab officers to Khokand in 1854.[125] Significantly, the Khan alleged the Khokandians' friendly attitude toward Britain as a reason for the Russian occupation of Ak Mescid.[126]

A series of preventive measures taken by Britain and Russia in the Caucasus, Persia, Afghanistan, and the khanates of Central Asia may be regarded as a prelude to the Great Game. Conversely, also on the international agenda, these military-diplomatic operations led to the institution of spheres of influence in the Chinese Empire, which was declining under the reign of the Manchu Qing Dynasty. Friedrich von Hellwald, a prominent Austrian geographer, revealed the strategic importance of Inner Asia in view of the inevitable Russo-British "scramble for China":

By holding Turkestan, Russia will be able to penetrate into China through Southern Mongolia and link her domains on the Amur directly to Central Asia. This would strengthen Russian influence, which scares the British very much, while the British themselves subjugate China and gain unprecedented profits there, yet regard Russian rapprochement with the East as a flagrant capture of new territories.[127]

Most European analysts, like von Hellwald, pointed to the areas of eventual geopolitical rivalry between London and Saint Petersburg in China: Eastern Turkestan and Manchuria. As to the former region—known also as Chinese Turkestan, Chinese Tartary, or High Asia until the Qing authorities renamed it Xinjiang ("New Frontier" in Chinese) in the mid-1880s[128]—it had always played a key role as "a traffic corridor" between Europe and the Far East, known as the Great Silk Road since ancient times. Besides, this region was considered extremely rich in mineral resources, according to reports by Russian and European explorers.[129] It is more important, however, that the Russo-Chinese frontier remained flexible in this part of Eurasia, because it was demarcated as early as the end of the eighteenth century, when nomadic hordes on the Kyrgyz steppes became the vassals of the Russian tsar. At the same time, native merchants began to deliver British products to the markets of Chuguchak and Kuldja, albeit indirectly through the western provinces of China. The information on Britain's commercial expansion to High (or Inner) Asia, received by the Tsarist administration of the Siberian and Syr Darian defensive lines from secret agents and scouts, precipitated the negotiations for the Treaty of Kuldja with the Qing government in June 1851. Pursuant to this diplomatic act, Russian traders were granted the privilege of paying lower customs duties to the Qing officials on Russo-Chinese borders, and restrictions on non-Muslim merchants were abolished. Nevertheless, commercial transactions in frontier zones continued to be extremely risky for merchants of all races and nations because of gangster forays and corruption running rampant at boundary outposts.[130]

Although the British attempted to arrange for joint diplomatic pressure from the great powers upon the Qing government to ensure that European—in reality, British—products would pass freely via open ports in the Pacific after the First Opium War,[131] the Tsarist government sent one expedition after another to obtain information about the Priamur territories and Britain's intentions regarding them. The nuggets of intelligence that Nicholas I got from his emissaries annoyed the emperor. For example, one traveler reported to Saint Petersburg in the mid-1840s that

> an Englishman, named Austen, ostensibly a geologist, gathers intelligence of all kinds in Siberia. He has learned about the Giliaks in the Amur Delta, and that they considered themselves non-tribute bearers to the Chinese. As an independent group, they could be useful to the British and could cede them a strip of land to set up a trade factory at the mouth of the Amur.[132]

That was why the Tsarist government sent Commodore Gennady Nevel'skoi, who was later to become a rear admiral, to explore the Amur Delta and Sakhalin Island in the late 1840s and early 1850s. As a result, the new port of Nikolaevsk, the first Russian outpost in the region, was founded on the estuary of the great Far Eastern river. To add to the erection of trade offices, some British strategists urged Whitehall to declare the outlet of the Amur under Britain's protection, with the subsequent opening of steamer navigation along this Siberian river. The Foreign Office, however, turned down these projects, because Russia was regarded as a "paper tiger" in the Pacific in comparison with its key role in the Middle East and Inner Asia. Besides, most political liberals gave the cold shoulder to proposals of this kind, because the commercial interests of "the old China hands"—the staff members of a cluster of trading enterprises that had been operating in the Far East since the early nineteenth century—were concentrated primarily in the Yangtze River Basin.[133] The general concept of the home Cabinet before the Crimean War was given a thorough analysis in a book about the Russian expansion to East Asia:

> From first to last the attitude of Britain was completely, though unintentionally, conducive to the success of Russian aggrandizement. There is a kind of fatality about the way in which Her Majesty's government, knowing little and caring scarcely more about the Amur and Ussuri region, conveniently did everything at the right moment to facilitate the occupation and legal acquisition of the territory by Russia.[134]

The Second Opium War of 1856–60 and the Taiping Rebellion of 1850–64 encouraged such industrious statesmen as the governor-general of East Siberia, Nikolai Muraviev, nicknamed "Amursky" for his activity in the acculturation of Amur Province, to launch a new diplomatic offensive against the Qing Empire. As this leading statesman declared in May 1854,

> The Amur should belong to the Russians; we shall arrange regular navigation along this river, which is of need both for trade and military activity in our relations with China, Europe, and America.[135]

Owing to Muraviev's diplomatic and administrative talents, Russia managed to establish its position on the Amur estuary and, what was even more strategically important, on Sakhalin Island, which served as a natural barrier to any intrusion in the mouth of the great river. Imbued with Anglophobia and being extremely annoyed with alleged British secret activity, the governor-general regarded it unfair that "this small island [Britain] may write its own laws in all parts of the globe excluding America." Moreover, he recommended to the tsar "a close alliance between the USA and Russia." This, he was assured, would cause the collapse of British trade and prestige as a world power. Furthermore, Muraviev contended that Britain's main objective in the North Pacific was "either to possess Kamchatka or raze Russian seaports there to the ground and then cut off Russia from the Far East." In case this scenario was realized, Britain would be able to control the coasts of China and Japan in order to ship commodities along the Amur up to the Russian town of Chita, while Sakhalin and the delta of this Far Eastern water artery would be turned into a colony of Britain.[136]

On learning about the situation in the main playfields of the Great Game, one could be led to believe that geostrategic motives mostly shaped both Russian and British foreign policy in the Game's prologue, though the ideals of the civilizational mission of Christian nations, along with economic motives, also affected their Asian policy. Not coincidentally, as a modern British historian argues, "until the Crimean War Britain had been able to maintain her international position on the cheap."[137]

The Crimean War drew the line for the prologue of the Great Game. By 1853, the gap between the Russian and British cordons in the Middle East and Inner Asia had shrunk to 1,000 kilometers, five times smaller than in the early eighteenth century.[138] When the hostilities in the Crimea had ended, Saint Petersburg and London decided to rush into a struggle for domination in Asia, which meant incorporating decadent Oriental states into the global system of relations—though each of them saw the mode of this incorporation in a different light.

CHAPTER 2

RUSSIA'S CHALLENGE AND BRITAIN'S RESPONSE, 1856–1864

Russia is not sulking. Russia is simply withdrawing within herself.

—Alexander Gorchakov, in a circular to the Russian embassies in European countries, 1856

England, England, England,
Girdled by ocean and skies,
And the power of a world,
And the heart of a race,
And a hope that never dies.

—Wilfred Campbell, from "England"

This chapter initially explains the Russian menace to India as a trigger of the Great Game. The context for this triggering was the fact that the emergence and later implementation of Russia's plans to subjugate the khanates of Central Asia, along with other regions adjacent to British India, influenced public opinion in both London and Calcutta—because Britain appeared much more susceptible to pressure in the Middle East and Inner Asia, standing there alone, than in Europe, where the other great powers were also involved. This marked the real beginning of the Great Game, in which the two imperial powers struggled to impose their different visions for modernization on the preindustrial, decadent Oriental states.

The chapter further describes Russian diplomatic missions to Khiva, Bokhara, Kabul, and Peking, which aroused tensions with the British that in turn afflicted bilateral Russo-British relations in the aftermath of the Crimean War and Caucasian War to such an extent that they led to quite a new stage in their evolution. In addition, the great revolts that shook British India and China—along with the internal feuds that undermined medieval regimes in Persia, Afghanistan, and the khanates of Central Asia—spawned the illusion among the Russians that they could be subjugated at minimal risk, especially by military means. Finally, the chapter argues that though Britain and Russia had an opportunity to make a new, peaceful start in their relationship after the Crimean War, and despite the fact that Russia's social reforms were welcomed by Britain in the early 1860s as a possible harbinger of dialogue between London and Saint Petersburg on all the burning international issues, the Great Game in Asia was given a start by the military party at the Tsarist court and the so-called forwardists among the British ruling elite.

THE RUSSIAN MENACE TO INDIA: A TRIGGER OF THE GREAT GAME

It is a well-established fact that scores of Britons greatly contributed to the creation and later development of the Russian navy throughout the eighteenth century. The Tsarist government did not hesitate to employ British sailors, naval officers, and even admirals in the active service of the state. At that time, the majority of Europeans regarded the Royal Navy as a paragon of the sea fleet. However, Russian expeditions to faraway oceans were given support by the British Admiralty, as in the case of the squadron of battleships that made their route from the Baltic Sea to the Mediterranean Sea to fight the Turks in the 1770s.[1]

Unfortunately, a century later, respect for the United Kingdom as the maritime superpower did not prevent some Russian military strategists from plotting a war against British India, both on land and sea, which in their opinion represented the "most vulnerable point" and "a sensitive nerve" of Great Britain. The majority of Tsarist analysts were fully convinced that "even a single touch upon this nerve may easily compel Her Majesty's government to alter its hostile policy toward Russia and compromise on the points, whereon our…interests collide."[2]

The economic, but more often geostrategic, importance of India was a favorite topic in the never-ending discussions by politicians, diplomats, generals, and journalists. Since the Seven Years' War of 1756–63, when the foundations of the future Indian Empire had been laid by the British, the East India Company had gradually developed from a purely commercial enterprise into a political and administrative agent of the Crown. The wars with the Sikhs and the Pashtuns, waged by the Anglo-Indian army under the company's direct guidance during the period 1839–49, resulted in the consolidation of the British possession on the peninsula, later to become a principal underpinning of the new pattern of social order in the Indian Empire.

The British rule of the Raj seemed also to be carried out in accordance with the laws of nature in the view of Her Majesty's subjects, who looked upon India as strategic base for Britain's further advances into Asia, along with seeing it as a boundless market for textile products and a financial reservoir to offset Britain's balance of payments. Finally, the control over Hindustan symbolized Britain's prestige as a great power, whereas the native army, drilled by the British, proved to be a significant agent for enforcing imperial policy. "Admittedly, the defence of India was itself a heavy strategic burden upon the British Empire," wrote Ronald Robinson and John Gallagher, the Cambridge historians, "but to Victorian statesmen it seemed the essential supplement to British sea-power."[3]

So it was small wonder that any interference from outside or even a hint of it looked like a nightmare for the British ruling elites, whereas the defense of Hindustan from any potential aggressor became a real idée fixe for British statesmen. That was why Russian ambitions and undertakings in all the adjacent regions influenced public opinion in both London and Calcutta, acting as a trigger of the Great Game, because Britain appeared much more susceptible to pressure of any kind in Central and South Asia, standing there alone, than it actually did in European affairs, where the other great powers were involved and temporary alliances might be established in case of emergency.[4]

Amazingly, the first recorded project of the Russian march into India, in 1791, was given for the consideration of Empress Catherine II not by a Russian strategist but by the Prince of Nassau. A certain French staff officer, the creator of this plot, suggested launching a sudden attack against the British possessions via Bokhara and Kashmir. Yet Prince Potemkin, who had the ear of the empress, mocked the draft as an incredible and impracticable adventure.[5]

The Russian Court reconsidered the idea ten years later, when, on January 24, 1801, Paul I ordered General Orlov, the chief (*ataman*) of the Cossacks of Don Province, to begin military preparations for a march toward India. The emperor argued that

> Englishmen possess their commercial enterprises in India, which they had gained with subsidies or by armed force; hence, our goal is to devastate these enterprises and liberate the oppressed nationals, in order to lead them under the similar protection as that of the English, and to modify trade to our benefit.[6]

However, the assassination of venturesome Paul in a coup d'état staved off the expedition in the very beginning. Yet this Russian bogey matured to become a main excuse for those politicians who propagated the "forward" policy in the second half of the nineteenth century and whose activity was commented on by Alexander III in an interview with his confidant, Prince Vladimir Metscherskii:

> The Englishmen, as individuals, are very sympathetic but as a nation, they instinctively dislike us because of scares of our invasion of India. This is their idée fixe, which is impossible to knock out of them. And it was introduced in their mentality

by Paul Petrovich [Paul I]. Since the time he had dropped the phrase of "a march toward India," these words settled in the Englishmen for ever.[7]

Strange as it may seem, but Tsar Alexander I, who had inherited the throne from his father, Paul I, disliked the idea of an Indian campaign, though he listened attentively to the alluring proposals made to him by Napoleon during their historic Tilsit rendezvous in 1807. Twenty years later, the growing international tension in the Turkish Straits and the Near East led Colonel George de Lacy Evans to publish a series of Russophobic pamphlets. He was fully convinced that the Russians were plotting to seize Constantinople and rush into an offensive against India. According to Evans, such natural obstacles as the deserts between the Urals and the Caspian Sea would not be insurmountable barriers to Cossacks on their way to the prosperous oases of Bokhara, Samarkand, and Herat. To prevent this incursion, Evans recommended that the British government arrange a blockade of the principal Russian seaports and send expeditionary troops to the Black Sea in a coalition with Persia.[8]

In fact, most diplomats shared this view. Typically, Sir John McNeill, an envoy to Tehran, published anonymously a pamphlet in 1836 focusing on a hypothetical invasion of Hindustan through Persia. McNeill regarded the latter as a key country in the perimeter for the imperial defenses, because "the entire command of the resources of Persia would disturb the whole system of the government in India." According to his forecast, Russia's progress in the East would demand a substantial increase in military spending:

From the moment that she [Russia] occupies this position, it will become necessary so to augment our army in India, especially the European part of it, as to be prepared for the contingencies that may arise out of her proximity. This would be a large addition to our national expenditure, which would become permanent, because, if Russia were at Herat, we would no longer send our troops by sea as quickly as she could march them by land.[9]

In the same way, another leading spirit of the "forwardists," David Urquhart, the publisher and chief editor of *The Portfolio* magazine, issued countless articles to expose Russia's aggressive encroachments upon India. He sharply criticized the home Cabinet and even nicknamed the redoubtable Palmerston "a Russian agent."[10] Meanwhile, in 1838 an anonymous essay came out under the title *India, Great Britain, and Russia*. The author stigmatized "an unprecedented Russian aggression in all directions," claiming that the Tsarist statesmen were obsessed with the idea of India's conquest and were only looking for a better chance to bring their sinister desire to life. He further contended that Russia threatened India from the boundaries of Persia and Afghanistan, urging Whitehall "not to wait for the foe to appear at the fortress's [India's] gates" but to divest it of this chance.[11]

However, the present volume reveals that these Tsarist strategists, while engaged in the planning of war operations in the Caucasus, had ignored the Indian direction until the outbreak of the Crimean War. It was only in the course of hostilities that the military capacity of the Anglo-Indian army, which by that time numbered 300,000, drew the attention of Russian leadership circles. As Ivan Vernadskii, a professor of statistics at Moscow University, pointed out in his pamphlet *Political Equilibrium and England*, if Russia did not launch a preventive attack against India to undermine Great Britain's prestige, London would "overcome China as well, as it had subdued India." According to his estimations, by 1855 British colonial possessions were, respectively, twenty-seven and thirty-four times larger than those of Russia and France.[12]

The onset of the Crimean War had an effect upon this discussion. Much later, in the 1880s, Nikolai Giers, the foreign minister, confided to Baron Morenheim, the Tsarist ambassador to London, that

> the Crimean War signified a decisive turn in our relations with Britain and compelled Russia to look for weapons to fight England, or to seek an antidote to her policy, which was inimical to Russia. These kinds of weapons, moreover, would have been efficient in case she [Britain] had concluded an alliance with any

other power and, in this way, endeavored to involve the latter in the struggle against Russia.[13]

In 1854 Alexander Duhamel, a former Russian envoy to Tehran and then governor-general of Omsk, and Platon Chikhachev, a geographer and traveler, were the first Russian officers to report on the schemes of attack against India to Nicholas I, supplementing their papers with the skeleton maps of the possible march routes to India. They regarded both Persia and Afghanistan as of critical strategic significance for a military campaign of this kind. Whereas Duhamel argued that Russia ought to ensure the friendship of the Afghan tribes in order to facilitate Russia's invasion of India through their territory, Chikhachev projected two consequent stages of operation: first, the conquest of Herat by 15,000 troops; and second, the assembling of a corps of 30,000 infantry and cavalrymen to march via Kandahar toward Lahore.[14]

But this was only the beginning of the flow of draft plans, which deluged the offices of higher Tsarist military chiefs. In 1856, four top administrators sent memoranda for the consideration of the war and foreign ministers. Lieutenant General Stepan Khrulev, a veteran of the Russian campaigns against the Ottoman Empire, outlined the most detailed project. He dwelt upon the necessity to pass through Afghanistan in order to invade the Raj. Later in this chapter, his plan is considered in connection with a more comprehensive program for Russian expansion into India.[15]

With regard to other projects, a report by the topographer General Lieutenant Ivan Blaramberg, who had allegedly elaborated a strategy for a Persian attack upon Herat in the course of the Anglo-Persian War of 1856–57, attracted the interest of Prince Dolgorukov, the war minister, and the emperor himself. Blaramberg stipulated reasons for Russia's steadfast progress in Asia. "The conquest of India is a chimera, not worth thinking about," he wrote in the note, "but Russia disposes of all means to shake Great Britain's power there." Like his colleagues, the general reassessed two interrelated prerequisites for final success: assistance by the Persians; and assurance of friendly support from the Afghans, who in his view hated the British after the war of 1839–42.[16]

Shortly afterward, Alexander Bariatinsky, the viceroy of the Caucasus described in chapter 1, and Wilhelm Liven, the quartermaster-general of the Main Staff, penned two memoranda, the latter in coauthorship with Major General Alexander Neverovsky, the chief of the Caucasus Section of the General Staff. It is interesting to compare their proposals, which varied as to the practicability of war against British India. Bariatinsky recommended that the tsar undertake a set of protective measures in order to counteract a forthcoming British assault upon the southern and southeastern coasts of the Caspian Sea adjacent to the Caucasus, and Liven and Neverovsky concurred in the opinion that Russia's subjugation of India would require colossal resources, both material and human, of which the empire had been deprived as a result of the Crimean catastrophe. High-ranking military officers were convinced that the British "would seek to secretly undermine Russia's position in her Muslim provinces and the prestige of empire in the eyes of the Caucasus people by the intervention in the affairs of neighboring states." Yet if Russia had won a victory over Britain, the attack against India would have aroused the jealousy of the other big powers, spurring their counteractions, which would have had results that could hardly have been anticipated.[17]

Significantly, the perceptions of these notes by the emperor and Alexander Gorchakov, the foreign minister, also differed. Alexander II approved the measures to be implemented in conformity with the scenario drafted by Prince Bariatinsky. But Gorchakov, eager to occupy an intermediate position between the "forward" and "inactive" factions at the Court of Saint Petersburg, felt far less enthusiastic about the occupation of Hindustan.[18]

In the meantime, the newly appointed war minister, Nikolai Sukhozanet, analyzed the effect of India's conquest by the Russians:

Panic over the growing power of Great Britain in Central Asia has been recently raised and has spawned many projects, pursued both by the Russians and foreigners; they concentrated on the argument that this power may be easily demolished by the march of a Russian army or corps to India. According to many travelers, the coming of Russian bayonets to the banks of the Indus or even to Herat would instigate a general revolt of the indigenous Indian nationals, who strongly hate their oppressors, and crush a shaky constituency of British politics. Yet, other persons suppose the like opinions to be shallow, exaggerated, one-sided, or biased. We are absolutely aware of the great hatred of the Englishmen felt by Asian nationals; but what is more evident, the Indian population still relies upon Britain's power, the invincibility of her navy, and the superiority of her perfidious but competent and consistent policy. The control over more than 100 million subjects that the army holds, being recruited from natives with the negligible assistance of British troops, must not be called unstable; and such a state of affairs reveals that the British government has succeeded in linking the interests of local elites to their own ambitions.[19]

In this connection, a question may be proposed: What was the real attitude of the Indian people toward Russia in the period under consideration? It appears most probable that the vast majority of natives, excluding princes and other landowners, ignored the menace of a potential Russian advance onto the peninsula before the Crimean War. According to one Indian historian, "the few vernacular papers that were being published under great financial and technical difficulties did not pay any attention to politics."[20]

The Sepoy Mutiny of 1857–58 seems to have modified the state of mind in India. There emerged for the first time a perspective on the coalescence of Asian states under Russia's patronage to renounce a British civilizing mission.[21] The mutiny, which is considered in the Republic of India as the first war for national liberation, motivated the upper crust of Indian society, whether followers of Islam or Hinduism, to embark on a political struggle against colonial rule. Although the British did not hesitate any longer to pursue immediate reforms in the Anglo-Indian civil service and military government, some native princelings galvanized their interest in a Russian alternative for modernization. They began to dispatch secret missions to the Great White Sovereign in order to apply for both financial and moral support, promising in return to pass under his suzerainty. The missions by Prince Rao Raja Tula Singh of Marwar to Russia during the years 1858–60 vindicated this tendency, which continued until the late 1880s.[22]

Yet many historians arrived at the conclusion that the Tsarist Foreign Ministry tended to have only a cautious appreciation of these advances, though the "hawks" on the Main Staff and military commanders in the "far pavilions" persisted in patronizing native chieftains in frontier areas. Conversely, all attempts by military intelligence agents and journalists to trace any sign of Russia's involvement in the Sepoy Mutiny had failed. There is much evidence for believing that the Russians set about dispatching their emissaries to India no sooner than they had subjugated the khanates of Central Asia in the 1870s.[23]

The Indian uprising shocked the ruling elites, military circles, and public all over the British Empire to such an extent that skepticism reigned among observers with regard to India's geostrategic value. "The internal concerns of both the Indian government and the Indian military authorities," maintained one British historian, "did much to debilitate India's usefulness as a strategic asset, if such it was."[24] "What Crimea was to Russia," stated another author, "the Great Mutiny was to British India: an analogous blow to a complacent ancient regime."[25] As one scholar remarked, "something sour had gone into the empire."[26] What was more important, Nikolai Giers assessed the state of affairs in a similar way in a letter to Morenheim:

> The dreadful uprising of 1857 revealed the significance of India to us, while the hatred Treaty of 1856 [concluded in Paris after the Crimean War] in its most burdensome items increased the importance of Central Asia in our Sovereign's mind.[27]

It should be noted that the mutiny coincided with the beginning of the first world industrial crisis, which burst out quite unexpectedly in 1857–58 and accelerated commercial rivalry between the industrial powers, especially in the peripheral markets for commodities. Whereas the whole model of British strategic thinking focused upon overseas commerce, the ruling elites, according to Lord Randolph Churchill, took "an enormous vested interest in naval supremacy."[28]

At the same time, many Victorians strongly believed that any bloody disorder similar to the Sepoy Mutiny would inevitably decrease revenue collection, distort the mentality of local nationals, and destabilize the Asian frontiers, especially in northwestern India. As the officials at the Russian Foreign Ministry's Asian Department maintained in their annual report for 1857, this uprising "enabled Russia to establish a coalition of Asian countries in order to blow up British rule."[29]

One may assume, therefore, that Russian military experts perfectly realized the challenges with which Britain was confronted in the aftermath of the Great Indian Revolt. For example, Major General Yegor Chirikov, the high commissar on the staff of the Russo-Turkish Boundary Commission in 1858, revealed the interrelation of strategy and commerce. He argued, in particular, that Britain's "political involvement in the affairs of Afghanistan intensified her pressure upon Persia by the policy of encirclement, and in this way opened alternative trade routes, brought Britain closer to the Caspian Sea, and worried Russia—though also, perhaps, consolidated British rule in India to a certain extent."[30]

After the suppression of the Sepoy Mutiny, it became clear to most Russian strategists that an invasion of India might not merely distract Britain's attention from the European theater of military operations but also act as a means to instigate Indian rulers to restore their sovereignty. The newly appointed military attaché to London, Captain Nikolai Ignatiev, one of the most ardent champions of a Russian advance into Asia, meticulously collected intelligence on the Anglo-Indian troops— their matériel, drills, and preparedness for warfare against European or Asian armies. He even kept a special journal to record data concerning military plants, arsenals, and shipyards during his regular working trips around the British Isles.[31] As one contemporary observer sarcastically depicted Ignatiev's activity,

He consecrated himself to meticulously reporting on England's military position in India to the emperor, who was so satisfied with reports by Ignatiev that His Majesty called the writer to Warsaw for a personal interview. It would be interesting to know whether Captain Ignatiev already foresaw the probability of the Mutiny so soon afterwards to break out, and whether it was the method and style of reports or the substance and views enunciated therein, which commended it to the attention of Alexander II.[32]

By the fall of 1857, Ignatiev informed the Main Staff that Great Britain's strategic potential had been depleted by the Sepoy Mutiny, and that its aftermath appeared to him the most appropriate time for Russia to embark upon bringing Central and East Asia under the scepter of the Romanovs.[33] On returning to Saint Petersburg from a diplomatic mission to Khiva and Bokhara in 1859, Ignatiev submitted to the tsar a verbose memorandum titled "The Suggestions on the Military Diversion against India in Case of the Rupture with England," which contained his assessments of the resources needed to launch an assault upon India supported by the Persian army and irregular Afghan combatants. The overall number of troops needed to operate against the Raj would come to between 35,000 and 50,000 infantrymen and cavalrymen. The strategist outlined the three aspects of the offensive: (1) the main Russian contingent of 27,500 infantry and cavalry was to march to Kabul and Balkh; (2) a supplementary corps of 10,500 Cossacks was to move from Western Siberia through Chinese Turkestan to Kashmir; and (3) auxiliary Persian armed forces, attached to offensive Cossack detachments, were to occupy Kandahar. Next, Ignatiev analyzed a detailed scheme of logistics and eventual consequences for the campaign in offing. He emphasized that it aimed to involve Britain as deeply as possible in military spending, along with instigating disorder in the Raj to coerce London to revise the Paris Treaty of 1856 to Russia's benefit.[34]

The aggravation of tensions in Central and East Asia as a result of the Anglo-Persian War, the Sepoy Mutiny, and the Taiping Movement, and also the Second Opium War, necessitated the Tsarist Main Staff's elaborating plans for a limited war against Britain both within and outside Europe. The Polish national uprising in 1863 against the Tsardom led to a further destabilization of the situation in Eurasia. Russian punitive operations in Poland aroused overall antipathy from European elites and the ordinary public. The press, especially the British liberal dailies, stigmatized Russia as a regular gendarme among the autocratic regimes. Under these circumstances, Dimitry Miliutin, who succeeded Sukhozanet as war minister, directed Lieutenant General Nikolai Zalesov, the chief quartermaster of the Orenburg Military District, and Colonel Mikhail Cherniaev, later to become a victorious conqueror of Tashkent and the first military governor of Turkestan Province, to design a scheme for a three-pronged attack upon India along the Caspian coast, through Kashgaria and from the Valley of the Syr Daria.[35] According to Miliutin's memoirs,

> We acknowledged the instability of our position on the outskirts of empire—we even failed to fix our state border there. The Kyrgyz hordes, being nominally under Russian suzerainty, suffered from constant hostile incursions of the gangs raiding the area between Khiva and Khokand and also from internal petty wars that will never end; hence, the ancient caravan route from Bokhara to Orenburg remains in permanent jeopardy.[36]

Meanwhile, Nikolai Ignatiev, who was promoted to the rank of major general and appointed head of the Asian Department of the Foreign Ministry, notified Gorchakov that,

> in case of a break with England, the state of affairs seems intolerant to us principally because we are doomed to inactive defense. We ought immediately mobilize a huge mass of troops and strengthen all coastal strongholds, spending millions of rubles on it, in anticipation of hostilities; our sea trade may be annihilated in no time without much effort. The Englishmen are capable of endangering us along our coastline, exhausting us with impunity, or, finally, opting for a weak point to launch a resolute attack upon it.[37]

In Ignatiev's view, Saint Petersburg had to intimidate London with a possible charge, which the Russians were to rush, if a new war were to break out. He proposed to enlarge and reinforce the Pacific Squadron and rearm all the land troops, especially those stationed along the cordons in Central Asia.[38] He believed that the government needed to bring constant military-diplomatic pressure upon Whitehall. He wrote, therefore, that

> the British statesmen should not indulge in pleasant illusions of their colonies being secured, of impossibility for Russia to apply aggressive measures or of the deficiency of adventurous spirits as well as of inaccessibility of routes through Central Asia.[39]

Referring to a projected attack against India, Ignatiev pointed to Trans-Caspia and the Kazakh steppes as the main routes for an offensive. So it was small wonder that the Main Staff and the governors-general of Turkestan laid some of his ideas in the foundation of military campaigns against the khanates of Central Asia.[40]

Concurrently, Stepan Khrulev, the above-mentioned general on special commissions at the headquarters of the Caucasian Corps, suggested his own plan for an invasion to the tsar and Miliutin. This plan, which aimed at the complete extraction of the Britons from Hindustan and the restoration of the Mogul Empire, stipulated two fundamentals for the campaign—a new general insurrection, similar to the Sepoy Mutiny; and a friendly attitude of predatory Afghan tribes for Cossack squadrons during the offensive. Interestingly, Khrulev's plan relied upon a few local Armenian communities living in India, which were expected to accord a warm welcome and assistance to the invaders. Moreover, he proposed the reanimation of an anti-British continental alliance to divert the British Cabinet and public opinion away from Russian atrocities in the Polish provinces. He was convinced that Napoleon III, the emperor of France, being jealous of Britain's purpose to dominate Asia, would eventually side with Russia. Hence, Khrulev suggested to the war minister to concentrate 35,000 infantry combatants and Cossacks in order to start off on a 109-day march from the Caspian Sea's southeastern coastline to Peshawar. The second scenario for an invasion envisaged an advance from Astrakhan through the Khanate of Khiva toward the Kashmiri frontier. The total costs of the expedition, as calculated by Khrulev, should not exceed 25 million golden rubles, and thankful Indian princelings were expected to reimburse the Russians for this military spending after the evacuation of the British from Hindustan.[41]

Thus, an initial idea for Russia to blackmail Britain was transformed into detailed plans for a full-scale invasion leading to the establishment of several vassal states, either under the aegis of Persia backed by Russia or under Russia's direct political control. Apart from such notorious hawks as Bariatinsky, Ignatiev, and Khrulev, even the advocates of a more cautious politics in Asia—for example, Mikhail Veniukov—regarded a military expedition to India as "a demonstration of power, with the object to intimidate the enemy and divert his attention away from other regions, mainly Europe."[42]

The author of the present volume disagrees, therefore, with the dogmatic Soviet scholars who claimed that the Tsarist generals were planning an invasion merely as an act of diversion that was not intended to draw the British out of Hindustan.[43] Although some officers of the Russian General Staff did not exclude the possibility of such a limited military campaign on the northwestern frontier of India, the fact that troops were ill prepared or ill equipped to march into India in the early 1860s did not imply that "the Slav peril" to the British Raj might be looked upon simply as a sheer "myth" or "bogey."[44] Interestingly, Friedrich Engels, who at this time worked as a part-time military observer and correspondent for the *New York Daily Tribune*, likewise viewed Russia's initial acquisitions in Central Asia through the lens of an eventual assault upon the "Indian fortress":

> In the military point of view, a nucleus of operative base for offensive against India was created by this conquest; and, as a matter of fact, after such a deep penetration committed by the Russians in the heart of Asia the project of attack upon India from the north has already abandoned the state of vague speculations and assumed somewhat definite contours.[45]

Thus, Russia's plans to invade British India in the late 1850s and early 1860s marked the real beginning of the Great Game in Asia. Although unjustified fears and mutual misapprehensions contributed to the process, the two imperial powers actually struggled to impose their different visions for modernization upon the preindustrial decadent Oriental states. To clarify the state of internal affairs and curb British influence, in the late 1850s and early 1860s the tsar's government dispatched diplomatic and reconnaissance missions to some of the Game's principal "playfields"—Khorasan, the eastern province of Persia; Herat in the north of Afghanistan; Eastern Turkestan; and Peking.

RUSSIAN POLITICAL MISSIONS TO ASIAN COUNTRIES

It would appear probable that the Russians had learned a great deal about Central and East Asia through their diplomatic representatives, merchants, travelers, and pathfinders by the onset of the Great Game. Yet the political configuration of the regions in question were rapidly transformed during the 1850s, thanks to permanent internecine feuds among local rulers and warlords, the activities of predatory tribes, and, to a lesser extent, penetration of the region by the European powers. In addition, Saint Petersburg needed more topographical information to prepare its advance into Inner Asia. Finally, there was a group of statesmen at the Court who shared the concept of coming on friendly terms with feudal lords in Persia, Afghanistan, and Kashgaria, regarding it as a sine qua non for taking the upper hand in the contest with Britain. As current scholarship asserts, Tsarist generals stood little chance of success to win a regional military campaign against their British counterparts on the frontiers of the Raj unless they were backed by the majority of native rulers and chieftains.[46]

At the same time, many high-ranking administrators on the spot reported on the infiltration of British secret agents into Central Asia. Such were the cases with the Orenburg and West Siberian governors-general, who repeatedly urged the Cabinet of Saint Petersburg to accelerate war preparations against the khanates in order to eliminate the "Turkic menace" to the empire's southern frontiers.[47] With regard to British intrigues, a report by Commodore Butakov, the chief of the

Russian Aral Sea Flotilla, was a typical instance. In his overview of the alleged British designs to constitute their control over the Amu Daria River Basin, the naval officer proponed the following arguments:

> Thus, before drafting an attack in the basin of the Amu Daria, we are to anticipate an active rebuff from England, principally by indirect means, which imply intrigues, bribes, arms supply, financial subsidies, etcetera, but partly by direct ones as well, which entail sending military instructors, engineers, and artillery officers to the khanates.[48]

Referring to economic motivations, one should bear in mind the Tsarist government's intention to compensate for the balance of payments in its trade with the khanates, especially with Bokhara and Khiva. Although some British observers estimated total Russian exports to Asia at £1.8 million (including those to China of £865,000) and imports at £3 million (including those from China of £1.1 million),[49] Russia's annual deficit in commerce with Bokhara amounted to 300,000 silver rubles; and likewise, in dealing with Khiva, to 100,000 silver rubles.[50] As one Tsarist administrator described the state of commercial affairs in 1859:

> There is an inclination to regard our influence through the prism of opposition to the British. I do not believe, however, that this opposition would presume an armed counterattack, because it appears incredible that English and Russian military forces will collide in the deserts of Central Asia or on the outskirts of the existing British possessions in Asia. If, on the other side, we assume a risk for this event, we shall avoid any act of hostilities to England in view of the disadvantageous outcome of such a clash to us. Hence, the essence of our contest may be interpreted as a commercial rivalry. Yet for the fact that our trade with Central Asia remains unprofitable to us, the urgency to waste tremendous sums of money on such a competition seems far less justified.

Significantly, when Alexander II perused this report, he noted in the margin "Very true to life."[51]

The appearance of the Khivian and Bokharian envoys in Saint Petersburg to celebrate the coronation of Alexander II provided an opportunity for the Cabinet to dispatch a reciprocal mission to the courts of the khans—accordingly, Said Mohamed Khan and Nasrulla Khan. As a result, the tsar appointed Major General Nikolai Ignatiev, the former military attaché in London, as an envoy extraordinary and plenipotentiary to the khanates, being escorted by a group of military and diplomatic experts together with a convoy party. Although Lord Wodehouse, the ambassador to Russia, reported that three hundred persons had set out for Central Asia with Ignatiev, this seems an obvious exaggeration, for the real number in Ignatiev's group was eighty-three persons.[52]

Having reached Khiva by the summer of 1858, Ignatiev urged the khan to cease the blockade of the Amu Daria's upper flow in order to let Russian merchant vessels freely navigate up and down the river from the Aral Sea. He also applied to Said Mohamed with a suggestion to allow those traders coming from the Russian Empire to conduct commercial operations in the markets of the khanate. Oddly enough, the envoy was surprised to learn that a street organ that he had presented to Said Mohamed as a gift had become a favorite plaything of the potentate (similar to a rubber pillow that Ignatiev gave to Nasrulla Khan shortly afterward). However, Peter Hopkirk erroneously wrote in his book that "the Russians borrowed a Great Game subterfuge from the British, who had charted the River Indus in somewhat similar manner nearly thirty years prior to the attempt by Colonel [in fact, Major General] Ignatiev to map the Amu Daria River, or the Oxus."[53] In reality, the practice of presenting luxurious gifts to sovereigns of various kinds originated in medieval Europe long before the onset of the Great Game. But if European diplomats preferred to desist from utilizing this procedure in the period under consideration, any kind of rapprochement with Oriental potentates meant doing it on a wider scale.

Though the Khivian khan suspected the Russian envoy of having instigated one of the numerous Turkmen tribes—the Yomuds, nomads on the southern borders of the khanate—to go to war against Khiva, Ignatiev succeeded in gathering valuable nuggets of intelligence that corroborated the concerns of many Tsarist strategists regarding the deterioration of the situation on the frontier in Central Asia. For example, Colonel Mikhail Cherniaev reported to Adjutant General Alexander Bezak, the commander of the Orenburg Corps, that

> in accordance with its geographic position, the Khanate of Khiva may be of significance as an "observatory point" to monitor nomadic tribes in the delta of the Amu Daria. Whereas in the commercial aspect, Khiva continues to act as a market for people living in the suburbs of the capital, it has not yet assumed importance as a center of trade between Russia and Central Asia and will hardly do in the future, because it lies outside the commercial routes leading to Russia.[54]

In Bokhara, Ignatiev was confronted with, probably, a far more difficult challenge—he had to find a reasonable solution for a couple of diplomatic issues: first, to stave off any attempt on the part of the khan to form a united anti-Russian coalition of the Central Asian khanates supported by the Ottoman Empire; and second, to mediate routine feuds between local rulers in such a way as Russia would benefit.[55]

Judging from the envoy's concluding report to the tsar, Nasrulla promised to Ignatiev to set free all slaves, protect those commercial travelers who arrived in his country from the Romanovs' Empire, grant to Russian merchant vessels free access to the upper reaches of the Amu Daria, and reduce the customs duties imposed on products imported by Bokharian tradesmen. The most impressive results of the mission were, however, the assurances given to Ignatiev by the khan not to receive any official emissary from Europe and also not to permit any European to cross the Amu Daria and penetrate the khanate from Afghan territory. Significantly, Nasrulla even invited Russia to side with Bokhara against the khan's personal foe, the khan of Khokand. In turn, Ignatiev strictly forbade the members of his escort to ramble about Bokhara or leave the city on their own recognizance, in order to evade the slightest chance of provoking the displeasure of the local authorities and the ruler himself.

Despite the fact that Ignatiev was rather aware of the perfidious and even treacherous character of both Central Asian potentates, Said Mohamed and Nasrulla, he discovered the military weakness and incapability of Khiva and Bokhara to oppose Russian military advances.[56] The envoy inferred that "negotiations should give way to war action that will extend Russia's frontiers into Central Asia and open native markets to Russian commerce."[57]

Later, when he was retired from active service, he summarized the reverberations of his extraordinary ambassadorial mission to the khanates in the following way:

> The most significant and palpable effect of the mission to Central Asia in 1858 was that of dispelling a smokescreen which had prevented the Russian government from the knowledge of the real state of local affairs; it began to see clearly at last and learned the true price of "diplomatic intercourse" with the Khans of Khiva and Bokhara. The intelligence gathered by our mission, together with diligent nullification of previous "mirages," led to a cardinal modification of our relations with these unscrupulous and treacherous neighbors, and stimulated the establishment of a more correct view of the meaning and foundations of their power and also of their real strength, especially on the position that Russia ought to and could occupy in Central Asia with regard to her dignity and under the pressure of urgency.[58]

In Ignatiev's view, the Russian government should encourage Persia's aspiration to take Afghanistan under its protection and make the Central Asian rulers withdraw all British agents from the khanates in order to secure there the interests of Russia.[59] Later in this chapter, attention is given to the further diplomatic activity of Nikolai Ignatiev in the Far East during the Second Opium War.

Almost simultaneously, a Russian expedition headed by Nikolai Khanykov, a scientific explorer and founder of the Caucasian Branch of the Imperial Russian Geographical Society, set off for Khorasan and Afghanistan. His appointment as the chief of the mission was due to his experience traveling across Central Asia and excellent knowledge of Oriental languages.[60]

According to routine correspondence between the Russian diplomatic mission in Tehran and the foreign minister, Gorchakov, in 1857–58, Herat, as a key stronghold on the route to the Indus, remained a bone of contention between Persia and Afghanistan. Regarding the period in question, Russia was particularly worried about regular attempts by the Anglo-Indian government to act as an arbiter in the controversy between Tehran and Kabul. In December 1858, the annual report of the Asian Department to the Russian foreign minister took a pessimistic view of the contemporary state of affairs in Persia:

This weak country should be regarded neither as a reliable ally nor as a hazardous foe. Yet her independence prevents us from approaching to England's domains as well as from a conflict with this power. At the same time, the well-being of Persia is a key for success in our commercial expansion, while domestic order guarantees tranquillity on our borders.[61]

Interestingly, a secret agent in the service of the Tsarist Consulate in Persia even managed to intercept and make copies of the ciphered messages that Murray, the envoy to Tehran, dispatched to London.[62]

Strange as it may seem, most Western scholars devoted little attention to Khanykov's collection of geographical, ethnic, and military intelligence in the Trans-Caspian region.[63] Yet military staff members, including Miliutin himself, regarded this particular mission as extremely important for the purpose of political reconnaissance. To fulfill the task, the expedition commanded by Khanykov passed through Tiflis (Tbilisi), crossed the Caspian Sea on board a Russian merchant vessel, and proceeded via Herat to Kabul—the communication juncture and strategic bridgehead from Trans-Caspia to India. The Russian emissary was instructed to hand to Dost Mohamed Khan a message from Grand Duke Konstantin Nikolaevich, one of the tsar's closest assistants. "We had agreed with him on the manner of corresponding to each other during his trip," recalled Miliutin. "Thus, we invented a specific code for secret mails, looking like a sort of calculations summed up in various meteorological tables in order to avoid their interception by British code breakers."[64]

However, the government of India very soon became aware of the mission. On March 22, 1859, the head of the Foreign Department, Peacock, informed Lord Stanley, the secretary of state for India, about Khanykov's trip to Herat to meet the Afghan potentate.[65] Although Dost Mohamed did not hesitate to use any chance for the instigation of Russo-British discord in the Middle East and Inner Asia, he abstained from granting a personal audience to Khanykov. According to Hopkirk, at least four main reasons motivated the ruler's restrained attitude toward the emissary: Russia's defeat in the Crimean War, the failure of the previous mission to Kabul by Captain Ian Vitkevich in the years 1837–38, Great Britain's support for Dost Mohamed during the siege of Herat by the Persian troops, and the pressure of uncompromising Islamic fundamentalists upon the khan.[66] Although these arguments may be regarded as correct, two more factors should be added. First, the Afghan potentate did not support Russian plans to employ some Turkmen tribes to intimidate both Khiva and Kabul. And second, Dost Mohamed aspired for the unification of his country in order to conduct a more independent policy toward Britain and Russia, whereas, as he believed, the European powers were more inclined to deal with a cluster of semi-independent principalities in the Afghan territory. Nevertheless, the information gathered by Khanykov and his colleagues in the course of their travel to Kabul testified to the small chance that any anti-Russian Islamic coalition could be established in the Middle East in the near future.[67]

At this point, it is necessary to shift the focus of this study to the district of Ili on the border of Chinese Turkestan as the third starting point for the Russian march into India. As early as August 1857, a certain Zakharov, the consul in Kuldja (Inin), an administrative center and trade midpoint in the foothills of the Tien Shan Mountains, weighed the pros and cons of Russian advances into that region in a note sent to the Foreign Ministry. He described it as a vast province with a population of 1 million that was rich in mineral resources, especially polymetallic ores. "If we have to fight China, a war will certainly cause some clashes on a broader scale and inevitable military spending that were compensated by impressive acquisitions in Chinese Turkestan," asserted Zakharov.[68] Yet Ignatiev and other alarmists in the Foreign Ministry's Asian Department suggested exploiting the favorable position of Kashgaria as the crossroads of strategic routes from China to India and from Central Asia to Persia. They advocated a short, victorious campaign against the impotent Qing authorities of Eastern Turkestan where there were frequent Uighur uprisings, because there Russia would be able to establish a vassal khanate under its protection.[69]

To reconnoiter the routes to Kashgaria and procure intelligence on the state of affairs in this desolate part of the Qing Empire, twenty-one-year-old Lieutenant Chokan Valikhanov made a journey to these remote territories at his own risk disguised as a caravan merchandiser nicknamed Alimbai. His trip appeared, however, to be much more exhaustive than a pleasant stroll in the mountains. Valikhanov and his fellow travelers endured several snowstorms while crawling through high passes and crossing enormous mountain glaciers. Apart from the whims of weather and natural barriers, they had to rebuff attacks launched by the bandit gangs that plundered caravans marching in mountain ravines. Yet Valikhanov's trip to Kashgaria did not solely aim to collect intelligence about the economic situation, climate conditions, and natural resources of Altyshar, or the Country of Six Towns, as the local population called Kashgaria. According to the instructions he was given by the Main Staff, he was authorized to scout and map appropriate routes for an invasion of the Khanate of Khokand and British India through Eastern Turkestan.[70]

On returning to Russia, Valikhanov was decorated with the Military Order of Saint Vladimir and promoted to the rank of staff captain. His lecture at the plenary meeting of the Imperial Russian Geographical Society in 1860 aroused great interest in the audience and was highly appreciated by both military topographers and academic geographers. Shortly afterward, he made a short voyage to London to familiarize

British colleagues with the results of his unique mission, because he was only the fifth European since Marco Polo who had managed to make a successful expedition to this section of Inner Asia. The British edition of the official account of his trip came out in 1865, but the intrepid traveler did not see it because of his premature demise that same year.[71]

Meanwhile, on January 2 and 9, 1859, the tsar convened two special interministerial conferences to consider the prospects for Russian policy in Asia, given the results of the political missions conducted by Ignatiev, Khanykov, and Valikhanov. The conferences decided to bridge the gap of about 750 kilometers in the line of cordon outposts between Pishpek and Yany-Kurgan on the frontier with Khokand and Khiva. The governor-general of Orenburg and Samara, Alexander Katenin, proposed straightening out the existing Syr Darian line in order to reduce military spending, while the viceroy of the Caucasus, Prince Bariatinsky, again focused upon British progress in Persia, Trans-Caspia, and the Khanate of Khokand. Nonetheless, the participants agreed to postpone any further military advances into Central Asia and to continue to monitor any new steps that the British side might take in the Middle East and Inner Asia.[72]

It appears most probable that one of the main reasons for Russia's vigilant policy in the aftermath of the Crimean War was its intention to split up the Anglo-French coalition. Symptomatically, in 1859, Tsarist experts reviewed all the secret conventions that Russia had signed by that time. They decided to take advantage of the complications surrounding the so-called Sardinian question between France and Austria, in order to obtain from Napoleon III a promise not to support Britain in Asia in exchange for Russia's benevolent neutrality toward the Second Empire in the forthcoming war against the Austrians.[73] At the same time, Alexander II and his ministers regarded the internal disorder in China and the onset of the Second Opium War as a good opportunity "to fish in troubled waters," because the Qing Empire was balancing on the verge of decay, similar to how the other Asian states were doing in the mid-1860s. It is small wonder, therefore, that many journalists in Europe juxtaposed the British involvement in the Anglo-Persian armed conflict with the war launched by London and Paris to coerce Peking to open Chinese maritime provinces to European entrepreneurs and traders.[74]

As a response to these plans, Yegor Kovalevsky, then the director of the Foreign Ministry's Asian Department, exposed the far-reaching aspirations of the Tsarist government to occupy a harbor in the Far East. As this highly qualified diplomat stated in a dispatch to Gorchakov regarding the Second Opium War:

Things are moving very rapidly; the squadron of the Western powers has already reached the Chinese waters. The destruction of Canton signaled the beginning of the warfare in China, and European troops are expected to march to Peking. Their coming and the influence they have on the Chinese government will definitely be unfavourable to Russian interests on the Amur and, therefore, a question will inevitably arise: What should we do in view of the Chinese crisis? Should we collaborate with European states to gain similar privileges as they require of China? But our interests, the answer is, differ from the ambitions of other big powers, and, certainly, we can not rely upon their support of our policies in the Amur Basin.[75]

Shortly afterward, Kovalevsky referred to the additional arguments in favor of his opinion:

Our interests in China are too different from those of other powers…. The capture of Peking by the Europeans, like the British occupation of Herat, will be equally sensitive to us and will not let us remain indolent observers in any case; the first action will torpedo all our initiatives in the Far East, while the second one will bring the whole of Central Asia under the aegis of the Englishmen.[76]

Foreign Office officials were convinced that Russia intended to act as a mediator between Peking and the Western powers as well as a pacific influence in the Far East in order to consolidate its military presence in the Pacific region.[77] A dispatch from Count Efim Putiatin—an experienced naval officer and diplomat, who had married a daughter of a British admiral, Marie Nouls, and had signed the Treaty of Shimoda with Japan in 1855—to China underlay such deduction. In a private letter to Grand Duke Konstantin Nikolaevich, Alexander II stressed that "if the Chinese do not agree on our amicable proposals, then we shall have the free hand and need no more ceremonies; the left bank of the Amur will be ours at any rate."[78]

To bolster territorial claims on the Qings, the Russian Amur Flotilla—which consisted of a frigate, three corvettes, and three clippers—undertook a military demonstration in the proximity of the Chinese coast just at the climax of negotiations with the Manchu government, when vice admiral Count Efim Putiatin, the envoy extraordinary and plenipotentiary, offered military aid to Peking in exchange for territorial compensations favoring Russia in the basins of the Amur and Ussuri rivers. Because they were engaged in the suppression of the Taiping Rebellion, the Qing authorities yielded to these demands in view of Russia's eventual alliance with the Anglo-French coalition.[79]

However, an absolute diminution of Qing rule threatened the interests of the European powers, not excluding Britain and Russia, because the breakup of China might spark a total war for its geostrategic legacy, with unexpected reverberations for the world order. Conversely, the Tsarist government was annoyed by the Anglo-French intention to subdue the Peking government under the pretext of imposing on it a regime of financial capitulations and free trade. That was why Putiatin alarmingly reported to Gorchakov on July 6, 1858:

It was prescribed to China to unblock all political, social, and commercial relations with other nations entirely and without delay as well as to acknowledge the advantage of European power and lore. However, the faster such a transition will be, the more dangerous China's submission to English influence and even total dependence on Britain will be set up…. In order to prevent other states from exercising acts of aggression, China needs to reorganize its armed forces as soon as possible, and in this view, I did not give up insisting upon the invitation of our military instructors to Peking to drill Chinese regular troops on a regular basis.[80]

The members of the Special Committee for the Far East, which the tsar constituted to coordinate the empire's Far Eastern policies, recommended that the War Ministry send 10,000 rifles, 50 high-caliber artillery guns, and 5 military officers to China. Yet when they arrived in Kiachta, a Russian checkpoint on the Chinese border, in the fall of 1861, the Qing imperial armies had already suffered a total defeat at the hands of the Anglo-French expeditionary corps. Meanwhile, Putiatin signed the Treaty of Aigun with Peking in May 1858. This document laid foundations for the later partition of the Celestial Empire—as China referred to itself—by the European powers into their spheres of influence. Pursuant to the treaty's clauses, China ceded the Amur Basin to Russia, but further negotiations on the status of Ussuri Province were postponed until the Second Opium War came to an end.[81]

That was why the second Russian diplomatic mission, headed by the same Nikolai Ignatiev, set out for Peking in 1859. The tsar himself had instructed the envoy to work with the Peking government to accomplish the territorial delimitation of the estuaries of the Ussuri and the Amur rivers and, simultaneously, diminish Britain's suspicion of Russia's direct involvement in the defense of Chinese seaports and fortresses. Suffice it to say that Admiral James Pounds, the commander in chief of the British Pacific Squadron, urged London "to create a maritime empire with all appropriate attributes—naval positions, postage communications, hydrographic service, shipyards and dockyards." He drafted various operational plans that envisaged taking control over China, Japan, and the Russian possessions in the Pacific. Standing up for the occupation of Manchuria, which he called "a key to Pacific trade," he grounded the contingency of this step upon "a necessity to defend China and India from Russia's encroachment, using Japan as a rear base in the Far East."[82] Conversely, the Anglophile newspapers in Shanghai published the accounts of certain eyewitnesses who had allegedly met Russian military officers directing the firing of the Chinese artillery against British and French troops after they had landed near the sea Fortress of Dagu.[83]

The story of how Major General Ignatiev extracted agreement from the Peking government on territorial concessions that benefited Russia, while acting as an "honest mediator" between them and the envoys of Britain and France to China, falls outside the scope of this book.[84] It needs to be stressed, however, that Ignatiev most frequently contacted the British representative, Lord Elgin, in the course of the diplomatic mission. At the latter's request, Ignatiev even gave him a copy of a city map of Peking charted by Russian military staff members, which Elgin used during the negotiations with Chinese delegates on the readmission to the British and French headquarters of all European prisoners of war detained in Peking. Later, Ignatiev exposed his tactics in his reminiscences on his diplomatic career:

> It was necessary for us, the Russians, that the Western allies would undertake decisive actions, frighten the Chinese completely, eliminate their snobbism and doggedness, force them to think about us [the Russians], and, finally, capture if only a part of the city wall, however, not entering the capital immediately. Just in this case, I would have had a chance to get into Peking in time, gain any importance in the eyes of the Chinese, take an active part in subsequent events when they [the Chinese] were in danger, and settle a boundary question with them to the benefit of Russia.[85]

At their last rendezvous, Elgin told Ignatiev that he highly appreciated "Russian delicacy" and believed that Britain should cooperate with Russia in the Far East, because the British and Russians were the only nations that perfectly realized what kind of politics ought to be conducted in Asia. In response, Ignatiev assured his counterpart that his country took no special interest in the Orient and would not want to curtail British trade with Asian markets. "We compete exclusively on the questions of frontiers," emphasized the tsar's emissary, "which are very significant to Russia as the sole neighbor of China on land but are not of any importance to England or to any other power. Because the national interests of our two states nowhere connect, there are no reasons to prevent a combined attack of the Russo-British joint armed forces against the foe [China]."[86]

The negotiations between Russian, British, and French envoys to coordinate their diplomatic pressure upon Peking made it possible for Ignatiev to validate the secession of Priamur Province to Russia and delineate the territories of both empires in the basin of the Ussuri River. Besides, he succeeded in correcting the Russo-Chinese border on the Kazakh steppes and in the Tien Shan Mountains. As a result, in November 1860 the contacting sides concluded the Treaty of Peking, which further strengthened Russia's strategic position in the Pacific, secured its Asian borders, and prevented any attack from being launched against Russian settlements in the delta of the Amur. To add to this list of benefits, Ignatiev's mission instigated a kind of discord in the Anglo-French coalition. Finally, in spite of the assurances given to Lord Elgin that Russia was not interested in the development of its exports to China, the Peking Treaty of 1860 enabled Russian merchants to expand their trade with the northern and western provinces of the Qing Empire, because all the commodities were imported from Russia to China under the customs-free regulations.

Thanks to these transformations, the Central Asian question assumed a top priority on the agenda of Russian and British foreign policy, because the shortest way from the Caspian Sea to the Pacific Ocean threaded via the Middle East and Inner Asia. In other words, a master of Central Asia would control both major strategic and commercial continental routes. That was why the significance of Ignatiev's diplomatic mission to Peking could be hardly overestimated, for "not since 1815 had Russia concluded such an advantageous treaty, and probably never before had such a feat been carried off by so young a Russian diplomat." A British scholar was correct in his commentary when he deduced that "the successes of 1860 went far to obliterate the bitter memories of the Crimean defeat, the more especially as they had been achieved in good measure by hoodwinking the English."[87]

Summing up the results of the Russian political missions to Asian countries introduced above, it is not difficult to acknowledge that tensions in Central and East Asia afflicted bilateral Russo-British relations in the aftermath of the Crimean War and Caucasian War to an extent that marked the beginning of quite a new stage in their evolution. In addition, the great revolts that shook British India and China—along with the internal feuds that undermined medieval regimes in Persia, Afghanistan, and the khanates of Central Asia—spawned the illusion among the Russians that they could be subjugated at minimal risk, especially by military means. Therefore, Tsarist generals in the field—imbued with a spirit of adventure, along with a thirst for decorations and higher ranks—were ready to rush into immediate campaigns to conquer the khanates and no-man's-lands.

THE BEGINNING OF RUSSIA'S CONQUESTS IN THE REGION AND THE BRITISH REACTION

Thus far, this chapter has argued that the necessity for the autocratic regime to maintain Russia's great-power status—in connection with its geopolitical interests and prestige, as they understood it—finally overruled the cautious policy that Saint Petersburg had pursued in Central Asia during the Caucasian War and Crimean War in the first half of the nineteenth century. By the early 1860s, Russia's preparations for an overall absorption of the khanates came to their culmination: The scouts and pathfinders working in the service of the War Ministry had surveyed and mapped a theater of operations; the troops seasoned in the Caucasian War had been removed to the cordon outposts on the frontiers with Khiva, Khokand, and Bokhara; new country and high roads had linked the European provinces to Southern Siberia; and the Aral Sea Flotilla of the Russian men-of-war had been put into operation in the estuaries of the Amu and Syr Daria.[88]

Tensions in Russo-Khokandian relations continued to afflict the Tsarist government because it aimed to integrate the Kazakh and Kyrgyz tribes into the empire, while the khan of Khokand attempted to preserve his control over the steppes. Besides, Miliutin and the governors-general of Orenburg and Omsk pleaded with the emperor for a sanction to connect the Siberian cordon with that of the Syr Daria by annexing a rather wide strip of Khokandian territory. A high-ranking member of the Tsarist military, Lieutenant General

Zimmerman, implied in 1861 that "another little Caucasus"—the Khanate of Khokand, backed by the British—would emerge on the Russian southern frontier unless the government did not to take urgent steps there. According to Zimmerman, the only way out of the deadlock might be a sudden assault upon the Khanate of Khokand "in order to crush them completely and place them under the scepter of Russia." Referring to the fact that "England's aggrandizement and power were created by a policy of conquest and caused by a desire to expand her overseas trade," Zimmerman also argued that the export of Russian goods would definitely increase as a result of "a large expedition to Khokand," similar to the way in which British and French overseas trade had grown in the aftermath of the Second Opium War.[89]

General Adjutant Alexander Bezak, the governor of Orenburg, sent a memo to the tsar in which he assessed all the pros and cons of expansion toward Central Asia in 1861. One conclusion at which he arrived went like this:

> If the Englishmen succeed in taking Tashkent under their control before us and connect Khokand with Chinese Turkestan, they will become masters of Central Asia and have the upper hand in local trade.[90]

Curiously, although Bezak expressed doubts about British commercial expansion to the khanates in his later reports to Miliutin, because of the population's low living standards, he proposed a total occupation of the delta of the Amu Daria on the Aral Sea and stationing there a flotilla of steamers on a permanent basis to navigate up the river.[91]

Some lower-ranking military officers on the spot advocated this concept in the same manner. One of them, Lieutenant Colonel Nikolai Kazakov, who commanded a regiment of mounted frontier guards in the Orenburg Military District, presented his analysis of the situation to the tsar on June 14, 1862:

> There are plenty of the Englishmen in Tashkent, Khokand, and particularly in Bokhara, drilling native troops according to European

patterns. They [the British] sold rifled artillery guns, gunpowder, sidearms, calico, and even silk materials fabricated in Britain. I myself met the Englishmen in disguise on our Kyrgyz steppes; this fact evidently marks the desire of this nation to control Central Asia....The Englishmen carefully watch our progress in the region; they sought to deprive us of the rich natural resources of Central Asia, and they are satisfied with our inactivity.[92]

Two principal interpretations may be taken in account with regard to the perception of current affairs in Asia that underlay this point of view: the Polish uprising of 1863, mentioned earlier in the chapter; and the situation in Persia.

As to the interference of the great powers, not excluding Great Britain, with the Russian policy in the Polish provinces, Alexander II and Gorchakov bullied European leadership circles with a new wave of revolution, allegedly threatening pan-European stability. The official Saint Petersburg, therefore, was inclined to interpret London's intrigues in Eastern Europe as a plot to arrest Russian progress in Central Asia, so to say, with the hands of the rebellious Poles.[93]

With regard to the second factor, Shah Nasir-u-Din obdurately attempted either to oust the nomadic Turkmen tribes from his domains or to form an alliance with them against the Europeans. The punitive expeditions conducted by Persian troops compelled the Turkmen to redirect their inroads from the territory of Persia to the lands of the khan of Khokand, whose regime had deteriorated because of mass social unrest, facilitating its conquest by the Tsarist armies.[94]

Conversely, Russian strategists proposed to open hostilities against the khanate before it became easy prey for other Asian rulers or Britain itself. On July 4, 1863, Ignatiev, while still in charge of the Foreign Ministry's Asian Department, argued to Miliutin: "If the Englishmen learn that we shall launch an offensive by ourselves and reach India sooner or later, they will apprehend friendly relations with us."[95] Reciprocally, two weeks later, Ignatiev reported to the Main Staff on the interrelated factors of the Russian advance into Khokand: control over sea routes; and an alliance with Persia, Afghanistan, and several native princelings of the Raj.[96]

To defend themselves from both nomadic forays and regular Russian troops, the Khokandians established a line of fortified outposts along the perimeter of the steppes between Suzak and Pishpek. Moreover, they intensified their contacts with the Anglo-Indian government. As Major General Ivan Babkov, a well-informed senior quartermaster of the Orenburg Corps, reported to Miliutin early in January 1864,

> The English agents are rumored to have visited Khokand, and these rumors are not false, according to the Bokharians. Certain Englishmen are said to have been in contact with the Khokandians for a long time and even requested a portion of land in Khokand to be leased to them, but the ruler answered that they are permitted to hold it on a lease at the distance of not farther than 300 kilometers from the capital of the khanate.[97]

In the meantime, a correspondent for *The Times* compared the Russian military activity on the khanate's northern frontier with that of "a mole underground," who was working hard to undermine local regimes. The journalist dwelt upon the reasons for a Russian attack upon the khanates:

> These semi-barbarous states, ever at feud with one another, and in themselves weak, are yet highly fertile and attractive to an invader. That they must be so is clear from the fact that 300,000 Russian troops are stationed along the frontier lying between the Caspian Sea and the Balkhash Lake—forces that are not required for a defensive purpose alone.[98]

However, it seems very important to distinguish between the general proposals of military planners and the real political measures adopted by the Tsarist government. According to the official and private correspondence of contemporaries, the tsar and Gorchakov approved a large-scale advance in the mid-1860s on the initiative of Miliutin and the generals in the field, though they often carried out sporadic military campaigns "without a definite plan or pattern, and with little constructive direction from St Petersburg," as Barbara Jelavich, a respected American historian, remarked in her monograph on Russian foreign policy.[99] Not coincidentally, three decades later, Andrei Snesarev, a celebrated Russian military expert on Oriental affairs, repudiated the impulsive policy conducted by the tsar and his ministers in Central Asia, whereas the renowned diplomat and historian Roman Rosen recalled that the government and army waged even the Russo-Turkish War of 1877–78 "without understanding clearly what they desired to achieve by the force of arms." The Russian conquest of the khanates corroborated this view, with a few exceptions: the accurately plotted attack against Khiva in 1873; and the offensive against the Turkmen oases in 1880–84, which was planned long before it actually occurred.[100]

To reconcile the "hawks," headed by Miliutin and Ignatiev, with the "doves," represented in the ruling elite by Alexander Gorchakov and Mikhail Reitern, the finance minister, a series of conferences was held in the early 1860s. Such prominent military thinkers as Nikolai Obruchev, the chief of the Main Staff, and diplomats—for example, Major General Alexander Vlangali, the envoy to Peking—took the position that "the Cabinet should not make difficult Russia's position in Asia, but to the contrary, it ought to relieve the existing anxiety" in order to give the initiative to the Foreign Ministry in dealing with European affairs.[101] But in spite of the recommendations by Gorchakov and Obruchev to the tsar that no future changes of the Asian frontier might be regarded as urgent,[102] the champions of the armed offensive against the khanates managed to procure the highest endorsement for a more aggressive course to be taken in relations with Khokand, Khiva, and Bokhara. In a special memorandum, Miliutin insisted that the occupation of the khanates would be the only really satisfactory instrument at the disposal of Russia for bargaining with Britain in Europe. If Russia were to begin a war against Britain, he contended,

> we ought to particularly value the control of that region [Central Asia], for it would bring us to the northern borders of India and make easy our access to that country. By ruling in Khokand, we can constantly threaten England's East Indian possessions.[103]

As a result of this "under the carpet" struggle, military officers on the frontier were able to have a free hand in the armed conflicts against native rulers, while the tsar and his ministers usually presented new conquests to Western governments as a fait accompli.[104] In this way, Russia's diplomats seemed to have their hand merely in setting a smokescreen for military operations on its Asian frontiers, along with keeping a straight face at the invectives that the European mass media hurled at the Cabinet of Saint Petersburg with every new annexation of territories in Central Asia.[105]

Characteristically, on December 2, 1864, Gorchakov and Miliutin submitted to Alexander II a coauthored note on the strategic objectives for further Russian advances toward the Indian Ocean. The authors were in accord with the concept of fixed borders, which should replace the present unstable frontiers with a scheme for the invasion of the khanates that would put an end to the spontaneous campaigns by military commanders in the field that meant huge budgeted spending. These two leading statesmen claimed that

> by 1854, we [the Russians] have reached the Lake of Issyk Kul and the River Chu from West Siberia; we have erected, like-wise, strongholds in the lower flow of the Syr Daria. With our domains extending further, we find ourselves in close proxim-ity to the khanates of Central Asia, Khiva, and Khokand, which looked upon the Kyrgyz as their subjects. At present, we ought to establish a natural mountain border of the Russian Empire in the south, which is regarded as a frontier between the settled popula-tion and nomadic tribes, by the incorporation of Khokand in it.[106]

Reading this, one could be led to believe that Gorchakov and Miliutin formulated an idea of the so-called scientific frontiers long before George Curzon grounded it in the late 1880s. Factually, they pointed to natural barriers (mountains, deserts, lakes, and rivers), along with the areas inhabited by small ethnic groups, that ought to be taken into consideration by any strategist who elaborated geopolitical plans. All in all, their arguments seemed to have convinced the tsar to approve

Russia's aggressive advance into Central Asia "in the stages of acquisition, military control, and assimilation."[107]

The next day, Gorchakov explained this new strategy for Russia's diplomatic representatives abroad in his famous circular memorandum. This signified a new epoch in Russian policymaking, when national interests had definitely replaced ideals of dynastic solidarity, according to the dogmas of the Holy Alliance of the European sovereigns. Encouraged by the compromise with the war minister, Gorchakov opposed any further territorial extension of the empire, "meeting, as it would, no longer with unstable social groups, such as nomadic tribes, but with more regularly governed states."[108] Instead, he proclaimed Russia's great civilizing mission in Asia, along with offering a justification for its current territorial acquisitions there. This mission meant an impediment against forays committed by mounted gangs of natives, an abolition of slavery, and enlightenment of local inhabitants. To Gorchakov's mind, these sacred and righteous goals excused the Tsardom for the intention, as a contemporary Anglo-Indian journalist contended, "to exercise certain ascendancy over those whom their turbulent and unsettled character made most undesirable neighbours."[109]

While diplomats exerted themselves to find reasonable arguments for the Russian conquests already in progress, the Tsarist generals deployed Cossack hosts and infantry regiments in the offensive against the Khanate of Khokand as the key state in the region. As early as November 1861, they seized Yany-Kurgan, and then Suzak and Aulie-Ataors, and in 1864 they captured Yesse and Chimkent, though the latter surrendered only after repeated attacks.[110] Hence, a question may arise: What was the reaction of the British leadership circles and public opinion to this military campaign?

The conclusion of the Crimean War gave Britain and Russia an opportunity to make a kind of new start in their relationship. In fact, the ruling elites perfectly realized that the geostrategic potentials of both states, though higher in industrialized Britain than in stagnant Russia, might not be sufficient to achieve decisive success in their global competition. Besides, a decline in bilateral trade, an expected result of hostilities, contradicted their national interests. That was why the social reforms implemented by Alexander II in Russia were welcomed by the British establishment in anticipation of a possible dialogue between London and Saint Petersburg on all the burning international issues.[111]

In this connection, there were policymakers in both empires who shared the view of the Great Game's "playfield" as a military-diplomatic polygon suitable for the application of various means of pressure upon the opposite side. At the same time, scarcely anyone could ignore the vulnerability of India to foreign invasion, as was mentioned earlier in this chapter. The commercial expansion of the European great powers seemed to act as the third motivation they had to consider at the beginning of the Russian industrial boom of the 1860s and 1870s.

On January 16, 1858, Lord Clarendon, the foreign secretary, agreed on the reappointment of Baron (since 1871, Count) Phillip Brunnov as the Russian ambassador to London. This gesture of goodwill symbolized a strong desire on the part of the British ruling elite to return to the previous level of diplomatic contacts that Brunnov had managed to maintain during his fourteen years' tenure in the same office before the Crimean War.[112]

Moreover, Britain attempted to relate Clarendon's policies to a new balance of power as well as to those offensive tendencies in the policies of the other great powers, namely Russia and France, in Asia.[113] Significantly, Lord John Russell, who succeeded Lord Clarendon at the head of the Foreign Office, emphasized this "pacifist" attitude toward Russia in his instructions to Sir John Crampton, the ambassador to Saint Petersburg, on March 31, 1860:

> Great Britain had no wish to enter into a struggle with Russia for influence in Central Asia, but what we aim at is that Russia shall not take advantage of her relations with Persia and her means of pressure on the states of Central Asia to encroach upon countries [the emirates of Kabul, Kandahar and Herat], which...should remain in the possession of native rulers and be undisturbed by foreign intrigues.[114]

According to this concept, in the political sense, the territory of British India ought to be confined to the area under direct British control; and geographically, it should be extended as far as the proper defense of Britain's domains would require. In Ben Hopkins's study of the Anglo-Sikh alliance as seen through the lens of Russo-British rivalry, he discusses the dilemma that London faced vis-à-vis the northwestern frontier of India: either to secure it against Russian invasion and to promote the establishment of the consolidated state of Afghanistan, or to safeguard the borders of the Raj by depriving the Sikhs of their traditional area of expansion—Afghan lands, "where their ambition and opportunity converged."[115]

It would appear most probable that the proponents of the former approach had taken the upper hand among leading British analysts by the mid-1860s. In this respect, the renowned explorer Arminius Vambery recalled his interviews with Palmerston and Clarendon after his return from traveling to the Middle East. From his point of view, both statesmen's perceptions of the Russian attacks against the Khokandian strongholds were almost indifferent. They explained to Vambery that

> Russia's policy in Central Asia is framed in the same way as ours in India; she is compelled to move gradually from the north to the south, just as we were obliged to do in our march from the south to the north. She is doing services to civilization, and we do not care much even if she takes Bokhara.[116]

Though the apologists of a cautious policy in Asia, or "masterly inactivity," were supposed to be prevalent among British policymakers, some historians have also pointed to radical changes in the organization of the Anglo-Indian armed forces after the suppression of the Sepoy Mutiny. With the dissolution of the East India Company, British military officers and native rank-and-file soldiers were enlisted in the newly molded Anglo-Indian army under the direct supervision of the War Office, whereas many professional military men, who had made their careers in the Crimean War and the Second Opium War, were promoted to commanding positions in India.[117]

However, it was the secret service that suffered the most radical reformation. Although the first structure of the British home intelligence service had existed since 1803 as the Depot of Military Knowledge, followed by the Topographical Department in 1815, its tiny staff being engaged in collecting data from the foreign press and mapping unexplored territories,[118] the East India Company established a parallel Political Service to monitor the situation in the territory of the Raj in 1820.[119] Nearly ten years later, Lord Ellenborough, the president of the Board of Control for India, contributed to the setting up of a spy network in the regions adjacent to Hindustan.[120] Yet the recruitment of these "newswriters" from the local population was initiated by the next governor-general at the request of the East India Company no sooner than in 1832.[121] The scandals inside the anti-Russian coalition during the Crimean War along with the inability of intelligence agents to avert the Sepoy Mutiny resulted in the reorganization of the Topographical Department into the Topographical and Statistical Department of the War Office in 1855, and the assignment of special officials—military attachés—to the capitals of the great powers, including Russia.[122] As Christopher Bayly has noted, "Much of the British system of espionage and control was swept away in a matter of days and had to be reconstructed from scratch."[123] This "perestroika" resulted in the constitution of the renovated Topographical and Statistical Department, which capably drafted 237,519 copies of 2,000 charters, skeleton maps, and schemes from 1857 to 1870.[124]

At the same time, the government continued to carry on the Great Trigonometrical Survey (GTS) of India, which had been launched by the staff of the East India Company in the early nineteenth century. After the terrible experience of the Sepoy Mutiny, Captain (later Colonel) Thomas George Montgomerie, the first assistant on the staff of the GTS, hit "upon the idea of training native surveyors who could penetrate the porous borders of the Himalayas in disguise."[125] As was mentioned in chapter 1, they were known as "pundits," with the connotation of "adept experts" stemming from the word's original meaning of "men learned in Sanskrit lore." A selected group of natives was recruited by British spymasters in the villages located at the foot of the Hindu Kush and in East Turkestan to explore the hilly terrains to the north of India, especially the mountain passes controlled by the Chinese and Russian military outposts. Not coincidentally, it was Montgomerie who brought several pundits to the GTS Headquarters at the settlement of Dehra Dun and trained them as scouts on a regular basis in the years 1861–62. "By 1865," writes Jules Stewart in his recent study of pundits, "Nain and Mani Singh had passed out as fully qualified operatives of the Raj intelligence service and were now ready to embark on their first trans-Himalayan mission." But another scholar, Derek Waller, points to the summer of 1863 as the starting date of their initial travels across Tibet toward Yarkand, a big trade center in Chinese Turkestan.[126]

Historians still discuss the results of the pundits' intelligence-gathering activity in Asia. And many scholars highly appreciate their contribution to the scouting and mapping of desolate, almost inaccessible areas in the long course of the GTS.[127] Robert Johnson, for example, puts an emphasis on the combination of explorations with their spy tradecraft:

> Their achievements have hitherto been seen only in terms of geography, but there can be little doubt that the real purpose of their topographical work had less to do with extending knowledge for some academic purpose than acquiring intelligence that had a specific military or political objective.[128]

Unlike the pundits, far less is known about the reconnaissance practices of Muslim scouts who worked in the Russian service. Therefore, a memorandum by Mikhail Veniukov is worth mentioning, because it sheds light on the Turkic and Persian nationals who were in the service of the Russian Main Staff. In his comparative study of the most important topographical expeditions carried out during the period 1856–71, Veniukov regarded the missions undertaken by two Muslims—Abdul Mejid, in 1860; and Mohamed (Abdul) Hamid, in 1863—as the most important. According to Veniukov, the former had scouted the route from Peshawar to Khokand, whereas the latter had reconnoitered the road from Kashmir to Yarkand. Significantly, the expert meticulously compared the results of the trips taken by the natives in the Anglo-Indian secret service with those undertaken by the secret agents employed by the Russian Main Staff.[129]

CHAPTER 3

THE ROAD TO THE OXUS, 1864–1873

In no instance is a friendly glance directed to the white man's carriage.
Oh, that language of the eye. It is by it that I have learned that our race
is not even feared at times by many, and that by all it is disliked.

—A letter to *The Times*, quoted by Guy Wint in *The British in Asia*

This chapter explores the period that included the Russian assault on Khokand, the conquest of the khanates, the formation of the Turkestan governor-generalship, and the defeat of Khiva, the last independent Turkic state. With these events, both Russian and British empires tried to play for time while devising more effective methods to pursue their Asian policies. The chapter further considers various views of Britain's approach to its overseas endeavors—which advocates characterized as "masterly inactivity" and opponents labeled "imbecility." Whereas the former preferred a peaceful way of consolidating the Raj and other colonial possessions, the latter ironically saw cautious politics in Asia as imbecility. Those who were skeptical of both these approaches argued that a combination of "soft" and "hard" power should be applied to Russia and its satellite states.

The chapter also examines the role of Eastern Turkestan, which became one of the most significant "playfields" of the Great Game in the 1860s. Here, key roles were taken by risk takers like Yakub Beg, an adventurous and charismatic military commander but brutal and unscrupulous person, who persistently crushed one rival ruler after another under the green banner of Islam. Finally, the chapter describes the annexation of another Central Asian principality—the Khanate of Khiva—and debates on policy toward India. Although the conquest of this last independent khanate made it absolutely unrealistic to imagine a positive scenario for bringing the Great Game to an end, the first, fragile seeds of future collaboration had been implanted in the Russo-British relationship—as symbolized by the Gorchakov-Granville compromise, which anticipated the forthcoming end of the two empires' rivalry for the domination in Asia.

THE GREAT GAME AND THE ESTABLISHMENT OF RUSSIAN TURKESTAN

Major General Dimitry Romanovsky, one of the most active Turkestan commanders, regarded the interval between 1854 and 1867 as a crucial stage in the realization of Russia's ambitions for the subjugation of Central Asia.[1] Yet his reading needs a slight correction, because, as this study reveals, it was in the decade of 1864–73 when the conquest of the khanates really took place, beginning with the Russian assault on Khokand, and then culminating in the formation of the Turkestan governor-generalship and ending with the defeat of the last independent Turkic state—Khiva.

The Russian assault on Khokand annoyed both London and Calcutta. The functionaries of the Indian government would cable to Sir Charles Wood, the secretary of state for India, one ciphered message after another, expressing their concern about the perspective of the Cossacks to cross the Indus and rush to the plains of Hindustan. Simultaneously, some prominent public spirits issued many pamphlets about Russian armies standing at the gates of the Raj. Despite the Tsarist troops' initial failure to capture Tashkent, Viceroy Lord Lawrence and his ministers were panicky, and cabled to London from Fort William on November 22, 1864, that the envoys from Khokand, at an interview given them at Lahore, pressed upon our attention the advances which the Russian power was making in Central Asia and the threatening aspect of affairs which regard to the state of Khokand, by itself unable to cope with the armed forces which jeopardize its independence, if not existence. The envoys emphasized the necessity in which their country was deficient in assistance, and asked especially for the deputation of British officers and subordinate staff for the arrangement of military means disposed by Khokand.[2]

Regardless of the viceregal repudiation of any large-scale military assistance for the Khokandians, the envoys were requested "to select young men of intelligence and influence" to be delegated to India while Calcutta took responsibility for their drill "in different branches of military service, for which facilities would be afforded, if the Khokand government adopted such a course."[3]

The Foreign Office caught up the alarmist tune played in Calcutta when Lord Russell asked Phillip Brunnov about the current state of affairs in Khokand. The Russian ambassador in turn articulated the official opinion of his government concerning the necessity to check the never-ending forays of steppe bandits from Khokandian territory, along with the tasks of protecting commercial routes from attacks by predatory tribes on trade caravans and securing extended frontiers. He also asserted that the British faced similar challenges in Asian countries, for example, in "the belt of semi-independent minor mountain principalities to the northwest of the British Raj." Yet he abstained from any concretization of the goals that Russia would like to attain in Asia.[4]

It is worthy of note, in this connection, that as early as in January 1863, Robert Davies, the secretary of the British political representative in Punjab, summarized the information about trade between European states, China, and Central Asia. Later, the military attaché in London, Colonel Nikolai Novitsky, managed to intercept the report by Davies and submitted it as a supplement to his weekly report to the Main Staff. Comparing Russia's objectives in commerce with those of its British counterparts, Davies maintained that "the products and manufactures of

Europe ought and do, to the great extent, already find a readier access to the Central Asian mart from the frontiers of India than from the frontiers of Russia." The inference he drew from the statistical data at his disposal was the following:

We have seen, then, that a considerable trade with the countries of Central Asia does exist, and that there is a considerable demand for European and Indian goods; we have seen also that taking Yarkand, Bokhara and Herat as the foe of commerce in Central Asia, we are practically nearer those markets than Russia is; we should therefore lose no endeavour to stimulate the development of that trade, and do all in our power to remove any difficulties which may exist.[5]

Perfectly corresponding with this opinion was the strong evidence that the Russian assault on Tashkent, the biggest retail center on the former Great Silk Road, distressed London and Calcutta. Yet, conversely, Alexander Gorchakov's circular letter, dated December 3, 1864, envisaged incorporation of the backward, less-developed khanates into modern industrial civilization, which would obviously serve the interests of all the European nations, not excluding Britain.[6]

That was why British politicians were confronted with a dilemma—they either had to reconcile with a civilizing mission of Russia or assertively oppose its aggrandizement as a rival great power. The editorials in *The Times* may be regarded as the most striking instance of this ambivalent perception. When the Tsarist troops under Major General Mikhail Cherniaev attacked the fortress of Tashkent for the second time in May 1865, the Russians were rumored to have lost more than 4,000 men in the battle, which ended in their complete defeat. Referring to the intelligence that came from Tashkent, later to be proved untrue, a correspondent of *The Times* expressed his regret about the numerous casualties, while conversely manifesting his general support for Russia's efforts to bring the values of European civilization to Central Asia:

It may or may not be true that the policy of Russia is of a traditional and aggressive character, and that there still exist at St Petersburg vague projects of absorbing the East in one great Empire. But for generations yet to come any such project must be a wild and unpractical dream, and, amid the ever-changing political elements of dominion, speculations as to such a faraway future will not influence the action of a reasonable statesman.[7]

Although a number of authoritative studies have covered the Russian military campaigns against the Turkic khanates, the principal motives for these hostilities remain disputable.[8] It appears most probable that the conquest of these Asian territories gave a tremendous boost to the prestige of the Russian Empire as a world power. Obviously, this was achieved by a combination of tough treatment by the colonial authorities of nationalists, their religious tolerance for Muslim mullahs, and granting regular financial subsidies to various chieftains. The seizure of any Khokandian or later Bokharian stronghold was accompanied by the massacre of not merely armed defenders but also noncombatant townsfolk, including elderly people, women, and children. Many eyewitnesses of these hostilities, especially journalists from Europe, reported on the dreadful scenes of atrocities committed by Tsarist troops. Even Russian observers, such as Petr Pashino, an explorer and agent in the secret service of the Main Staff, disclosed these vicious practices in his diary:

Chimkent [a fortress at the approaches of Tashkent] fell into Russian hands on September 20 [October 2], 1864, owing to the assault upon it launched by General Cherniaev. The massacre was dreadful; having plundered the city bazaar, the soldiers rushed into the houses of peaceful townsfolk and killed them all; many women and children suffered badly from the acts of violence executed against them.[9]

Another typical case was the well-known order by the governor-general of Turkestan, Konstantin Kaufman, to his officers in the field to perpetrate the wholesale slaughter of the Youmud Turkmen in order to arrest their forays to the rear of troops besieging the stronghold of Khiva during 1873.[10] Characteristically, their brutality was usually mingled with persuasion when Tsarist generals propagated a legend of the Great White Sovereign from the north who was ostensibly predestined to oust other European nations, especially the British, from Asia. "The dissemination of prophesies like these among nomadic tribes, the sedentary population, and even local aristocratic families and rulers like the emir of Bokhara or the khan of Khiva," stated Veniukov, "will lay the foundation for Russia's progressive movement toward Khorasan and the Hindu Kush Mountains."[11]

However, Russian experts pointed to the threat of a Muslim holy war against infidels—jihad—in revenge for the large-scale massacre and plunder of peaceful cattle breeders and artisans. And the majority of British statesmen believed that the sparks of such a holy war might well inflame India and also cause social disorder in other British domains. That is why the Foreign Office sought to persuade the tsar and his ministers to abstain from using a "hard power" policy as a major underpinning of Russia's relations with Central Asian potentates.[12] Nonetheless, some Russian military writers stipulated a "hidden agenda" for British foreign policy. According to Veniukov, if even *The Times* encouraged Russian progress in Central Asia, it meant, in reality, that London aimed to induce Russia to occupy the infertile, arid steppes and sandy deserts with an unsettled, turbulent population in order to exhaust bellicose potential and to involve Russia in enduring military campaigns against Muslim rebellions. As Lord Lawrence asserted in his correspondence with Wood and Ripon in the years 1865–66:

> There could never be any Russian menace to India from the north-eastern areas of Central Asia. If ever India were invaded by a Russian army, it would only be via Herat. So it would be to British advantage to involve Russia in Yarkand and Bokhara. This would absorb her energies, deplete her resources, lessen the danger of her inciting the border tribes and promote anti-Russian sentiment among the Muslims of India.[13]

At the same time, Lawrence confessed to Lord Northcote on September 3, 1867, that "the further Russia extends her power, the greater area she must occupy, the more vulnerable points she must expose, the greater danger she must incur of insurrection, and the larger must be her expenditures."[14]

In the subjugated khanates, restraint and tolerance might be regarded as essentials for the new Russian political strategy toward merchants, artisans, and the other swaths of townsfolk, who ensured permanent commercial contacts with Russia in an atmosphere of state order and social stability. This was especially true with regard to non-Turkic and non-Muslim natives—Persians, Armenians, and Jews—who might be called Russia's "fifth column" in the Middle East and Inner Asia. Mikhail Terentiev, a contemporary eyewitness of the Turkestan campaign, later recalled that

> the Jews and the Persians were those town dwellers who welcomed our entry into Samarkand [May 1868] most of all; the former as outcasts who were granted Russian citizenship after the conquest and the latter as slaves or descendants of slaves who hoped to return to Persia.[15]

According to information shared by other participants, at the initial stage of the conquest the Russian military authorities treated the Bokharian Jews far better than the local Muslims. Until 1889, the Jews had enjoyed equal rights of citizenship with other nations in the Russian Empire, including suspension of the pale of settlement, which meant that they did not need any special permission to enter its European provinces.[16] So it was small wonder that many of them anticipated the coming of Tsarist troops, while a minority of them even assisted the assailants during attacks upon Bokharian footholds. The family members of the wealthiest and most respectable merchants in Chimkent, Tashkent, and other big city centers often acted as pathfinders for the Cossacks and opened the city gates for advancing Russian battalions. Apart from the sedentary population, the members of many Kyrgyz and Kazakh nomadic clans, who disliked the power of Khokand, acted as scouts or informants for the Russians during hostilities.[17]

Russian military administrators in the field frequently got in touch with non-Muslim nationals and gave regular monetary subsidies to those collaborators who were eager to take part in the adaptation of traditional governing structures to new realities. For instance, a certain secret agent in Bokhara informed his British patron on May 14, 1865, that the Russians had freed 12,000 Persian slaves, who had been captured by the Turkmen in 1859 and sold to Bokhara. Admittedly, they were invited to join the Russian service in auxiliary detachments, and nearly 10,000 men were recruited for irregular military service by the officers of the Turkestan governor-general.[18]

The second aspect of the systematic takeover of Central Asia by Imperial Russia was a desire to remodel the administration of Asian countries according to an autocratic vision, though one that had some common features with British rule in India. As one traveler correctly stated, "the role of the fear of England in the course of regular annexations must not be underestimated," for some improvident claimants to the thrones in khanates often appealed to the government of India or directly to British political residents and agents for assistance against "Russian aggressors." Typically, Abdul-Melik Khan, the eldest son of Said Muzaffar-u-Din, escaped from Bokhara to the Raj after he had suffered defeat in the uprising against his father-collaborationist and the Russian occupational administration. While hosted and subsidized by the government of India, he continued to insist on his rights as a legitimate heir to the khan's position for a prolonged period.[19]

This case illustrates the perception by Russian military-political elites that British Asian policy was the real obstacle to the consolidation of the southern frontiers of the Romanovs' Empire. To crush this policy, some Russian planners proposed to the emperor to propagate the values and principles of Holy Orthodox Russia in the Orient. "Because England remains our most powerful foe, who menaces us in the East to the largest degree," admitted Mikhail Veniukov in a review of Russian boundary territories in Asia, "we must concentrate efforts to maintain friendly, or at least neutral, relations with two great Asian neighbors [Persia and China], should we launch hostilities against Britain."[20]

In view of the horrific military campaigns that Russia waged against Khokand and particularly Bokhara, the annihilation of the former paved the way for the eventual penetration of Chinese Turkestan, whereas the establishment of protectorates instead of emirates and khanates would mean the spread of Russian control to a prominent confessional center of Islam—ancient Bokhara. Not coincidentally, the khan of Bokhara was regarded by some Muslims as a new "Timur," who thus was capable of reconquering Afghanistan and Chinese Turkestan, on the one hand, and rebuffing the Russian offensive, on the other.[21]

Furthermore, Tsarist diplomats depicted British fears of Russian expansionism as absolutely void, as Gorchakov did in an interview with Sir Andrew Buchanan on September 12, 1865. The foreign minister assured the British ambassador that the Tsarist government was going to set up governor-generalships in Asia, similar to the way in which the British had constituted the Viceroyalty of India in the aftermath of the Sepoy Mutiny.[22] Thus, he exposed a principal dilemma of Russian policy in Asia to Buchanan: either to colonize the conquered territories or to turn them into buffer states with the status of protectorates. In Gorchakov's view, the competition between these conceptions could decide the future of Russian and British colonial possessions.[23] As Mary Holdsworth aptly remarks in her book,

The system of buffer states and more or less openly acknowledged spheres of influence, which became the modus vivendi between Great Britain and Russia in Central Asia, was something which both Gorchakov and Giers sought to establish throughout the latter half of the century. This precarious balance was inevitably threatened with every step of Russia's advance, and it was this kind of consideration which restrained and postponed the more aggressive plans of the soldier-administrators, not only those in responsible posts in Turkestan and Western Siberia, but also those in the Caucasus.[24]

Chapter 1 mentioned the idea of the buffer states promoted by Karl Nesselrode, the Russian foreign minister in the first half of the nineteenth century. Later, some higher-ranking military administrators in the "far pavilions" attempted to bring this idea to life. For example, Nikolai Kryzhanovsky, the Orenburg governor-general, proposed to Gorchakov to restore the khanate of Tashkent, which had existed as an independent principality up to the 1810s.[25] Moreover, there were ardent proponents of Pan-Slavism among the Russian ruling elites, such as Nikolai Ignatiev and Mikhail Cherniaev, who were annoyed by each British step in Asia and competed with pro-European statesmen like Gorchakov or Brunnov for the benevolent attention of the tsar. In the end, these divergent approaches combined with personal ambitions and interdepartmental feuds to substantially reduce the effectiveness of the decisionmaking process at the Court of Saint Petersburg, relegating it to dealing with immediate measures to be carried out in the region.[26]

The cost of a systematic conquest, apart from regarding Central Asia as "the great military school of the Empire,"[27] remained another bone of contention in Russian public opinion. This was because some politicians considered sporadic punitive expeditions against warlike tribes or khanates to be far more expensive than the ultimate annexation of Central Asia.[28] The tsar's decision to replace the temporary occupation of the Khokandian territories with a permanent military administration led to an edict to organize a new province in the territory stretching from the Lake of Issyk-Kul to the Aral Sea. On February 6, 1865, Major General Mikhail Cherniaev, nicknamed "the Lion of Tashkent" by his contemporaries, was appointed military governor, under the governor-general of Orenburg, Adjutant General Kryzhanovsky. Cherniaev became known as a military commander who acted on his own will in the manner he considered most suitable for current circumstances—like a Tsarist conquistador. Thus, he distorted the real canvas of events in his alarmist reports to Kryzhanovsky and Miliutin on the activities of British agents in Central Asia and the khan of Bokhara's aggression against the rival Khanate of Khokand. Cherniaev was heedless of instructions from Saint Petersburg and Orenburg to abstain from spontaneous military attacks, and justified his assault upon Tashkent and subsequent invasion of the Bokharian territories as retaliations for the sinister British intrigues against Russians in the khanates.[29] Yet despite this victorious military campaign, shortly afterward the tsar and Miliutin were compelled to call back the obstinate general to Saint Petersburg for insubordination—though in 1882–84, under the reign of Alexander III, a new autocrat, Cherniaev was reappointed to the post of Turkestan's governor-general.

The war against Bokhara, conducted by the Russians in the years 1864–68, initially as part of the offensive against Khokand, predetermined the next edict by Alexander II, who augmented the status of Turkestan to the governor-generalship.[30] The former head of the War Ministry Chancellery, Adjutant General Konstantin Kaufman, was assigned to this post on July 23, 1867. His plenary powers were so formidable—the tsar delegated to him full political, military, and financial authority for the conquered territories—that local nationals called him the "semi-tsar" and some wits among the officers of the General Staff gave him the sobriquet "the merchant from Miliutin's boutique."[31] Commented the war minister himself:

> General Kaufman received instructions both from the Ministry of Foreign Affairs and Ministry of War, as well as from the Sovereign himself, to stop any further conquest, any expansion of imperial borders, regardless of how it would appear inducing and easy. Our policy in that distant region ought to be aimed to civilize the khanates in a moral way, develop peaceful commercial relations with them, and arrest any acts of pillaging our territory.[32]

The establishment of Russian Turkestan symbolized the coming of a new epoch. As one Russian historian metaphorically wrote, "To some extent Central Asia may be thought to act as Russia's overseas colony, the great sandy waste of desert assuming."[33]

It should be stressed that open criticism was given by a minor group of Russian political observers with regard to the pattern of military rule in Turkestan propagated by the central government and Kaufman himself. Some opponents commented on the poor knowledge of

Turkestan's geographical, political, and economic situation demonstrated by officials on the frontier. For example, Veniukov wondered if the government had enough information about the countries and nations which with Russia was dealing in Central Asia to enforce any assertive political course there. The military expert mocked the geographical ignorance revealed even by the foreign minister, Gorchakov, in 1873, when he instructed Kaufman "not to enter Kashgaria on his route of advance from Tashkent to Khiva in order to avert any disapproval of the British side." Cherniaev also testified to the systematic misunderstanding of many Central Asian realities by Russian high-ranking bureaucrats.[34] And Major General Swistunov, the head of the staff of the Caucasian Military District, even composed a special memorandum on the possible negative consequences of extending the Russian protectorate to Trans-Caspia. Drawing parallels between the conquest of the Caucasus region and the systematic annexation of Central Asia, Swistunov claimed that any new territorial acquisition there would inevitably remove Russia's political pivot to the east, reducing the integral links from the nucleus of the empire to its western outskirts, which in turn would lead to their impending secession. In his judgment,

If Central Asia means to us [the Russians] a bridgehead alone to assail English possessions in case of war; if we can find the Achilles' heel of the British power only in this way, then a proposed system of policies in Trans-Caspia meets our interests incomparably easier than the domination of the whole territory up to the sources of the Amu Daria and the spurs of the Hindu Kush Mountains. After the subjugation of Central Asia and in case of hostilities against Britain and Central Asian people, instigated by her and her ally Turkey, we would have either to concentrate a mass of troops within our possessions, while these troops, due to the incredible efforts to keep peace, would be incapable to conduct any offensive operations against British India; or to withdraw our armies completely from Trans-Caspia, leaving it to the mercy of fate in order to endeavor to reconquer it with far more exertion afterward.[35]

It was small wonder, then, that Russian ruling elites focused on a discussion of the Administrative Regulations of Turkestan—a quasi-constitution of the Viceroyalty proposed by Kaufman in 1871. Inasmuch as his antagonists argued that the regulations ran contrary to imperial interests by imposing an extra financial burden on the national budget, the regulations spawned a new tidal wave of criticism inside the governing bureaucracy.[36] With regard to the pacification of Turkestan, Russian staff members received information about the influence of the Bokharian and Khokandian diasporas in the Ottoman Empire upon the policies of the Turkish sultan as a spiritual leader of Islam, who was reported to play "the Central Asian card" in relationships with both Russia and Britain. Symptomatically, the ideas of Pan-Islamism began to penetrate into the khanates just at the time of their systematic annexation by Tsarist troops, when the frightened potentates of Khokand, Bokhara, and Khiva embarked on sending their emissaries to Constantinople on a regular basis. On this reading, most political observers and military writers in Europe interpreted these missions in light of the ambitions of the emir of Afghanistan. Although the sultan's government, occupied with domestic problems, preferred to abstain from giving any kind of massive military aid to the khanates in 1867–68, the Tsarist military authorities worried about the probable emergence of a Pan-Islamic coalition as retaliation for the establishment of Russian Turkestan.

To explain this situation, it is sufficient to quote an abstract from the analytical review by the General Staff colonel Leonid Sobolev, who stayed on active service during the conquest of Bokhara. His depiction of the Russian movement into Central Asia illustrated how Tsarist military planners evaluated the new challenge they faced in the late 1860s:

Influenced by the Anglo-Indian government, Sher Ali Khan [the new emir of Afghanistan] resolved, as rumors reached Bokhara, Samarkand, and other centers in Turkestan, to form a powerful alliance between the Muslim states, spearheaded against Russia. The Bokharian population became agitated; the people in the Khanate of Khiva got restless and the troops advanced to the borders; the steppes of Orenburg were set ablaze with the turmoil of nomadic tribes. This state of matters began to threaten our interests in Central Asia. What we needed was to torpedo the formation of any coalition of Muslim states, to separate the bellicose Turkmen from the Khan of Khiva, and to launch an offensive against the latter as soon as possible.[37]

Accordingly, in July 1868 Kaufman prohibited any independent relations between the Central Asian rulers and foreign representatives.[38] And along with imposing these restrictions, he hatched a plan for a Russian invasion of the lands inhabited by bellicose Turkmen tribes that recognized only nominal suzerainty, mostly either that of the shah of Persia or of the khan of Khiva, and a few that of the emir of Afghanistan. Because all these suzerains sometimes attached mounted Turkmen fighters to their regular troops as auxiliary contingents to make inroads (*alamans*) on Russian or Persian territories, they did not pay taxes to any potentate and had a traditional, primarily nomadic, way of life—though there was also a sedentary population among them in the few Trans-Caspian oases, such as Merv.[39]

In December 1864, Peter Stremoukhov, a newly appointed patron of the Foreign Ministry's Asian Department, outlined a memorandum on the Russian occupation of the Caspian eastern coast. He presented a cluster of convincing arguments for the urgent establishment of a Russian foothold in the western sector of Turkmenistan in order to secure this area from eventual encroachments by any European or regional power, to the detriment of the Russian plan to eventually bring the Caspian Sea under Russia's full protection.[40]

However, this memorandum was given the cold shoulder in the Cabinet of Saint Petersburg, inasmuch as the tsar and his generals concentrated on the military campaign against Khokand and Bokhara. Thus the project of how to subdue the Turkmen was relegated to the back burner until a more favorable contingency occurred. Yet this did not mean that the Tsarist government had fully abandoned its encroachments upon Turkmenistan, as later developments were to show.

After the conclusion of the interim peace agreements with Khokand and Bokhara, the Russians had their hands free for a new strategic move in Central Asia. According to a carefully elaborated plan, the foremost infantry detachments headed by Colonel Nikolai Stoletov, a future prominent figure on the Great Game's "chessboard," landed on the eastern coast of the Caspian Sea at the ancient mouth of the Oxus on November 5, 1869. Stoletov's principal objective was to construct the fortress of Krasnovodsk as a rearguard base for military logistics in Trans-Caspia. In fact, the Tsarist government's design was to cut that region off from Persia and Afghanistan, encircle the khanate of Khiva, and incorporate all the Turkmen tribes into the Russian sphere of influence.[41]

However, General Kaufman and his staff were confronted with the problem of how to convince the central government and Russian public of the profitability of the pattern of rule that was set up by military commanders in Turkestan. Responding to remarks critical of their opponents in the governing leadership with a memorandum dated December 12, 1868, Kaufman calculated the budget of the viceroyalty. Instead of a deficit of 3.3 million rubles, which emerged as the difference between the receipts (1.7 million rubles) and expenditures (5 million rubles) in 1872,[42] Kaufman proposed dividing all costs into three categories—one for the supply of Turkestan troops with foodstuffs and war matériel, one for the conduct of military operations, and one for the implementation of regulations of public order by the civil authorities. Although the first category of costs, argued Kaufman, would hardly increase in the future, the second one would be substantially reduced after the conquest was finally over. But what seemed even more important was that the third category was expected to be reimbursed with the progressively increasing tax payments from Asiatic subjects of the tsar.[43]

At the same time, the proponents of Kaufman's policy—for example, the military observer Lev Kostenko—asserted that, regardless of the payment deficit, Russia would reorganize Central Asia because the central government would benefit more from this part of the empire than from any other province in the long run, owing to the exploitation of Turkestan's mineral resources. As Adjutant General Kryzhanovsky told the finance minister, Mikhail Reitern, Central Asia would surely play an outstanding role in the future development of Russian commerce and industry.[44]

It would definitely be an error to surmise that Russian policies in Central Asia took the London Cabinet by surprise. Doubtless, the British governing elites persistently monitored the Russian advance to Turkestan, though one historian wrote that Whitehall allegedly "registered no great concern over the progress of Russian arms and influence in Central Asia prior to 1869.[45] Such an inference may be drawn from the following note by the foreign secretary, Lord Russell, to Brunnov in September 1865:

> We [the British] can not take any part in the fate of the emir of Bokhara who executes British subjects [Stoddart and Conolly], yet it is desirable that Afghanistan will remain as an independent, inviolable state and that Persia will be accorded assistance both from Russia and England.[46]

The overtures made by the shah of Persia to the Anglo-Indian government ended in Viceroy Lord Lawrence's refusal to provide any kind of military support to the khanates.[47] In response to the requirements of the Foreign Office on the possible limits of Russian systematic expansion in the Middle East and Inner Asia, Brunnov repeated the "magic formula" of the Russian policy in these regions:

> As a matter of fact, the Imperial Government would prefer to set up a kind of structure administered by local inhabitants under the protection of Russia. Yet the absence of reliable social strata which is necessary for the constitution of a permanent authoritative body of administration, has compelled the townsfolk of Tashkent to desire that the public order will be maintained under the sovereignty of the emperor [Alexander II].[48]

With recognition of the progressive mission that Russia pursued in Central Asia, a larger section of British ruling elites had to succumb to such a clarification given to them by the Russian diplomatic representatives, because the imperative of the Great Game was that both the British and Russian sides "not lose face" in Asia, even when challenged by the force of unfavorable circumstances.[49] This situation suggested that it was useless for Britain to be involved in the affairs of the khanates. The best thing that London and Calcutta could do was to be reconciled to Saint Petersburg's role as guarantor of social stability and order in the region, when the principles of a fair commercial rivalry and reduction in military spending guided the policy of so-called masterly inactivity in the Middle East and Inner Asia. Because its advocates considered chimerical nearly all the threats to British overseas possessions, a peaceful way of consolidating the Raj as well as that of other colonial possessions underlay this political course. As Lord Granville argued:

> We do not advance because we think the best way of preserving our enormous Indian Empire is to remain where we are. The Russians rightly or wrongly yield to the apparent necessity of protecting each new acquisition which they make, in the same way as we did at an earlier period of our Indian history.[50]

Likewise, Lord Northbrook, the next viceroy of India, shared the opinion of the duke of Argyll, the state secretary for India, on the uselessness of any active counteractions by the home Cabinet in Central Asia to counteract Russian progress in the khanates. On March 28, 1873, the viceroy wrote to the state secretary that

> I agree entirely with you upon the unnecessary trouble people have been giving themselves in England about Central Asian affairs. My view may seem paradoxical, but it is that the more Russia extends her possessions in those parts, the more open she is to injury from us, which she has no more power to injure us than she had before.... The nearer she comes, the less her interposition in India is likely to be looked forward to as a blessing by the Indian Muslims who are our most dangerous class.[51]

Oddly enough, the opponents of "masterly inactivity" were inspired by the brilliant military victories of Prussia in Europe that led to the emergence of the Second German Empire in 1871. Mindful of the pattern of unchecked Russian expansionism in Central Asia, and comparing the situation on the borders of Prussia with that on the India frontier, some British colonial officers on the spot—for example, Sir William Mansfield, the commander in chief, and Sir Henry Durand, the military member of the government of India—"strongly urged a closer but uncritical approximation of Indian defence to Prussian methods, strategies and organization."[52]

Meanwhile, tensions increased in Russo-British relations because of the decision of the Tsarist government to annul the clauses of the ill-fated Paris Peace Treaty concerning the Black Sea's neutralization, at the risk of a war with Britain as its principal guarantor.[53] Mindful of this diplomatic demarche of November 21, 1870, as a certain deviation from "the concert of Europe" in international relations, Prime Minister William Gladstone, however, admitted that "a spark of war lighted up in Central Asia would spread all over the globe, wherever England and Russia have possessions, and involve other nations in the conflagration."[54] Interestingly, some historians contend that this very statement had initiated an "appeasement tradition" in British foreign policy, extrapolating its repercussions to the late 1930s.[55]

Yet even "inactivists" in British leadership circles strongly believed that the Amu Daria should act as the last natural frontier of the Russian advance in the region. Typically, the earl of Mayo, another viceroy of India, stated in a private letter of 1869:

If Russia could only be brought to act cordially with us, to say that she would not obstruct our trade, that she would not encourage any hostile aggression or intrigue against Afghanistan, Yarkand, or the territories lying on our frontiers, and that she would stop with a strong hand the internecine feuds among those nations over whom she possesses influence, she would find that her mission in Asia would be facilitated, and that the civilization of the wide districts of Central Asia and the complete establishment of her power would be greatly hastened.[56]

The existing fundamental disagreement on the principles of the British strategy reflected the wide spectrum of interests that politicians, military, entrepreneurs, and ordinary public took in British policy with regard to the Oriental countries. "We have been constantly extending our lines of frontier in India by the force of circumstances," one military writer stated in 1869, "notwithstanding our natural anxiety to keep as much as possible within reasonable bounds."[57] Yet those who opposed this "close border" policy, arguing for a resolute stance in the relationship with Russia, were nicknamed "forwardists" by the media. Sir Henry Rawlinson—the former military officer, diplomat, explorer and strategist—became one of the charismatic propagandists of "forwardism." For thirty years, in public lectures, newspaper articles, and secret memoranda, Rawlinson preached the same essential doctrine: "Russia was hostile, Russia was expansionist, and Russia had designs on India, judgments for which he provided ample evidence."[58]

The most striking illustration of Rawlinson's approach was his memorial dated July 20, 1868. He reproached the British ruling class for its inactive position with regard to Muslim guerrillas in the Caucasus during the Crimean War, while Russia, for its part, "gradually worked her way from the Sea of Aral through the saline marshes of the lower Jaxartes, to the confines of the alluvial valley, above the desert." He exposed Russia's civilizing mission as a principal motivation of its progress in Asia, which, in his opinion, was just a smokescreen behind which military "hawks" drafted a geostrategic breakthrough to the Indian Ocean. In spite of promises to the contrary, he emphasized, Russia was steadily advancing toward Afghanistan. He pointed out that Russia's spearheaded position in Central Asia after the occupation of Khokand and Bokhara would become a pretext for interfering with the internal Afghan feuds. He alerted, furthermore, on the danger that Britain would face in the near future:

That if Russia once assumes a position which in virtue either of an imposing military force on the Oxus, or of a dominant political influence in Afghanistan, entitles her, in native estimation, to challenge our Asian supremacy, the disquieting effect will be prodigious.[59]

According to Rawlinson, a clique of high-ranking alarmists around Alexander II kept on intimidating their sovereign with tales of the fabulous anti-Russian alliance of the Muslim states under the aegis of Britain. He drew parallels between the protracted, though imminent, Russian advance toward Inner Asia and the regular siege of the British "fortress"—Hindustan. So that Russia would not lose the world competition of the two empires, he contended, it was essential to intensify war preparations on the frontiers of the British Raj and take under control the external affairs of Afghanistan as soon as possible. He proposed delegating a special political resident to Kabul, occupying Herat and Kandahar, and, finally, constructing a network of telegraph and railway lines toward the Indian northwest frontier.[60]

Many contemporaries admitted that Rawlinson's ideas matched the mentality of the British ruling elites—at least that of the majority of statesmen in the Cabinet. A similar inference was true with regard to some military experts and public opinion in Britain and India. Even Mayo, a regular opponent of Rawlinson and other "forward-ists," stated in December 1870: "As for Russia, if that country was demented enough to attack India, a handful of British agents and a few hundred thousand pounds in gold raise the whole Central Asia against her in a holy war. I could make a hotplate for our friend the Bear to dance on."[61]

If we were to concede for a moment that the governor-generalship of Turkestan had not been established in 1867 and the Russians had not landed their troops in Trans-Caspia two years later, it would hardly be possible to imagine that the Foreign Office would have proposed to Saint Petersburg a round of diplomatic talks on the question of Central Asia. In turn, the Tsarist government—challenged with the Muslim uprising in Chinese Turkestan (Kashgaria) in close proximity to Russian territory, and also annoyed by the vague prospect of appeasing the Khanate of Khiva—decided to take a respite from the conquest by arriving at a kind of interim compromise with London on the status quo in Central Asia. Just at that time, Adjutant General Kaufman confessed to Miliutin that

I would consider it a great victory if I manage to deal with Khiva and Kashgaria peacefully. Until the present time, we have failed to undertake any action in a noncombatant manner; each new step in our diplomacy, each success in trade, has been achieved with blood. Our triumph in Asia will be complete when we cease to take up arms to make neighboring states fulfill our modest, albeit rightful, demands.[62]

One could be led to believe, therefore, that the leadership circles of both empires intended to play for time in their attempts to suggest more effective methods to pursue their Asian policies.

"MASTERLY INACTIVITY" OR "IMBECILITY"?

A study of diplomatic correspondence reveals the eagerness of the British Cabinet to initiate diplomatic overtures to Saint Petersburg concerning the maintenance of the modus vivendi in Central Asia in view of the emergence of Russian Turkestan in close proximity to India. For instance, on August 21, 1868, the duke of Argyll, the secretary of state for India, received a cable from Calcutta:

We [the members of the Indian government] think that endeavors might be made to come to some clear understanding with the Court of St Petersburg as to its projects and designs in Central Asia, and that it might be given to understand, in firm but courteous language, that it cannot be permitted to interfere in the affairs of Afghanistan, or in those of any state which lies contiguous to our frontier.... The truth appears to us to be, that the advances of Russia, coupled with the constant allusions made in the newspapers to her progress as compared with what is called the inaction of the British government, have produced, in the minds of Europeans and natives, what we believe to be an exaggerated opinion of her resources and power. A mutual good understanding between these powers, though difficult of attachment, would enable us to take means to counteract unfounded rumours and to prevent unnecessary alarms.[63]

Bearing this opinion in mind, the foreign secretary, Lord Clarendon, proposed to Brunnov to recognize "some territories as neutral between the possessions of England and Russia which should be the limit of those possessions and should be scrupulously respected by both powers." Gorchakov responded to this initiative with a proposal to agree on "a zone that would restrain the empires from any direct contact with each other."[64]

In the meantime, Viceroy Mayo outlined basic guidelines for future negotiations with Tsarist diplomats. He was convinced that Asia should be looked upon as a natural and legitimate "field" for Russian activities, but that the home Cabinet ought not to let Tsarist strategists transform it into a means for anti-British policy in Europe. He admitted that the time had come to conclude an agreement between Russia and Britain to fix their borders in Asia. Yet he argued that Russia was militarily far less capable in the East than Britain, and thus the latter should not fear the former. "As regards population, revenue, and facilities for maintaining it within the intermediate states, Russia has not reached the point which we passed three quarters of a century ago," he asserted in an 1869 memo.[65]

Mayo's ambivalent attitude toward the Russian advance in Central Asia, so characteristic of British statesmen and the public in the Victorian period, may be also found in his private correspondence. For example, he wrote to Argyll on July 1, 1869:

Nothing would grieve me more than if during my term of office any misunderstanding should arise with Russia—I believe it can never take place, unless she willfully misunderstands our policy and ends. But, at the same time, if her objects are really those stated by *The Moscow Gazette* of the 5th of April, i.e., to make Central Asia a strong strategic point against England in the event of the Eastern War—then she cannot expect a British government to view her proceeding with apathy or indifference.[66]

Significantly, the critics of Rawlinson's "forward" concept advocated closer cooperation with Russia on issues of current politics in Asia. For example, David Macleod, the lieutenant governor of Punjab, stated in a note on October 10, 1868, that

the civility and confidence shown to our officers everywhere in Russia, the willingness with which the geographical and topographical information obtained by its officers is communicated to us; and the freedom with which the Russian newspapers discuss the events occurring in Central Asia, all seem to indicate that she has no wish to conceal her movements from us. And, however desirous she may be to secure an entrance and safe conduct for her trade with those regions, I am unwilling to believe that she would attempt or desire to exclude our trade seeking to find its way into the same countries. There is, I believe, abundant room for both. In many ways each might benefit the other. And I believe that a friendly rivalry, avowed and encouraged on both sides, would be productive of most beneficial results.[67]

At Mayo's initiative, Sir Thomas Forsyth, the commissioner at Peshawar, a stronghold on the border of Afghanistan, departed to Saint Petersburg in the second half of 1869. "On October 30 [1869] he [Forsyth] gave to Prince Gorchakov for perusal a letter from Lord Mayo, expressing his earnest desire that the most complete *entente cordiale* [*sic*] should be maintained between Russia and England in Asia," wrote Lord Tenderden in a review of Forsyth's mission ten years later.[68]

The British emissary held talks with the key Tsarist ministers and an interview with the tsar himself. For their part, the high-ranking Tsarist administrators, who were willing to consolidate the conquered territories and eliminate even a minor chance that any coalition of states in the Middle East and Inner Asia would threaten the interests of Russia, favored the commencement of a diplomatic dialogue with London. Back on March 7, 1869, Gorchakov had instructed Brunnov: "You may, my dear Baron, reassure the Prime Minister [Gladstone] that we regard Afghanistan as lying outside the sphere wherein Russia exercise her influence. Any intervention or encroaches upon the independence of this state is inconsistent with Russia's interests."[69] Significantly, in the following years until the final agreement on the delimitation of Afghanistan was reached, the Tsarist diplomats continued to assure the Foreign Office that this "gentleman's promise" remained in force.[70]

Judging from Russian diplomatic correspondence, the official contacts between Saint Petersburg and London assumed positive dynamics in the years 1869–72. For example, on March 30, 1870, Gorchakov wrote to the viceroy of Russian Turkestan, General Kaufman:

The recurrent dispatches from the Foreign Ministry keep Your Excellence fully aware of the friendly consultations going on between the Russian and the British governments on the affairs in Central Asia. We have already benefited from the frank exchange of opinions with the London Cabinet, inasmuch as we see that, on the one side, the English public modifies its apprehension of Russian intentions, while, on the other, the higher administrators in India apparently are inclined to share our point of view upon certain political and commercial aspects of the current developments in Central Asia and have abandoned, to a greater extent, the previous disbelief and suspicions they had about our activities there.[71]

The mass media reflected a sort of détente that began to reign in bilateral relations during the period under consideration. Russian and British national dailies, such as *The Moscow Gazette* and *The Times*, evidently curbed their castigation of the other side in their commentaries on the steps taken by their governments to defend national interests in Central Asia. Symptomatically, on March 16, 1869, *The Times* even published a complimentary estimation of a book by General Dimitry Romanovsky, *The Central Asian Question*. In turn, some Russian military commentators called upon Tsarist naval officers to follow the example of the British in rearming the Russian navy.[72]

The relaxation of tension between Saint Petersburg and London also facilitated Russo-British diplomatic cooperation in Persia. Above all, the British plenipotentiary minister to Tehran persuaded the shah not to be opposed to the Russian occupation of Krasnovodsk on the Caspian Sea, inasmuch as it was situated far to the north of the Persian border.[73] Then the Russo-British arbitration of a boundary dispute between the Ottoman Empire and Persia reached a successful conclusion with a bilateral agreement following an exchange of topographical maps of all the disputed areas in 1870.[74] Moreover, British and Russian emissaries arrived at the courts of, respectively, the emir of Afghanistan and the emir of Bokhara to inform them about their diplomatic consultations on the limits of their advance in the Middle East.[75]

It especially needs to be noted that a rendezvous of Clarendon with Gorchakov in the German town of Heidelberg early in September 1869 made it possible to define general guidelines for discussion. When they touched upon the problem of Central Asia during their talk, the British state secretary proposed to his counterpart to configure this region as a sort of Belgium by civilizing the khanates under consideration and incorporating them into the sphere of international law. According to Gorchakov's humble report to the tsar, Lord Clarendon grounded his suggestion with this argument: "We [the British] do not fear your government's designs on Central Asia.... We are concerned, however, that the ambitions of certain secondary administrators in the field may come true," because "they won't pay much heed to instructions of the central government."[76]

Obviously, the Liberal Cabinet showed signs of nervousness regarding unrestricted activity by Russian or British officers in remote Asian areas. Besides, the members of the Anglo-Indian government included "old Persian, Indian, or China hands" who influenced foreign policy and had their own business interests in these countries.[77] So it was small wonder that Ambassador Andrew Buchanan admitted to Gorchakov in 1869 that

a powerful neighbour like Russia might render it necessary for India's government to keep much larger military establishments on the north-west frontier than were now required, and if they would consider how many persons in England were interested in the financial prosperity of India, he would understand how sensitive public opinion might become respecting events that will probably compromise this prosperity, and how early the feelings of the public might eventually be brought to influence the measures of the government.[78]

The same impression might be attributed to those Anglophobes among the Russian ruling elites who opposed any idea of neutral Afghanistan as a buffer state between two empires. In fact, they continued to propagate a "hard power" strategy in Central Asia, opposing a more restrained and cautious approach to the Anglo-Russian discord there. A report by Colonel Pavel Kutaisov, the military attaché in London, testified to the fact that the post-Crimean illusions of a military revenge dominated the mentality of some high-ranking Russian bureaucrats and military officers throughout the second half of the nineteenth century. From his point of view,

England doggedly hinders all the Russian activities, while it is well known that Britain, as Russia's bitterest foe, has always defended her own interests and aspired to bring into life perfidious desires, feeling herself free from any moral restrictions or humane obligations.[79]

Yet his note made the reader believe that Britain's influence was a fable, though a couple of fundamentals underlay it: world naval supremacy and the rule of India. To undermine and completely crush the latter, one was bound to launch a simultaneous combined attack against the metropolis and key seaports by squadrons of battleships cruising in the Atlantic, Pacific, and Indian oceans. According to Kutaisov, the resurgence of privateering in case of war would confuse Britain's trade and put an end to its maritime domination. Interestingly, Russian naval planners brought about a strategy for controlling major ocean routes with a flotilla of speedy cruisers. Impressed with these designs, in 1872 Tsar Alexander II even ordered the removal of the Pacific naval headquarters from the port of Nikolaevsk, which was icebound for six months and fogbound for several months more, to the ice-free seaport of Vladivostok.[80]

The Franco-Prussian War, which destabilized the general state of political affairs in Europe, happened together with the initiation of steamer navigation through the Suez Canal. Although the role of France as a great power diminished, the redirection of maritime routes caused an increase in the strategic significance of the Middle East to Britain. Besides, an anti-Qing riot by the Muslim population burst out in Western Turkestan, which led Saint Petersburg to strengthen the Russo-Chinese frontier. Under such circumstances, an aggrandizement of the Russian Empire in Asia seemed inevitable, which might lead to the failure of British geostrategic headship and the triumph of an autocratic pattern for incorporating Asian countries into the world's undergoing industrial modernization.

Whereas British strategic and commercial ambitions focused upon the territories in the basin of the Amu Daria, further Russian advances meant, as Adrian Preston put it correctly,

> the danger of Russian ascendancy among the Afghans, of border raids on the northwest frontier, of sparks being thrown into the combustible material of northern India, of some Afghan attack perhaps stiffened by Russian detachments, arms and money and followed by a penetration into the plains of Punjab and a widespread revolt—the danger of ignition or explosion, rather than of direct invasion of India.[81]

That is why the government of India, backed by Whitehall, called for the Cabinet of Saint Petersburg to recognize that Bokhara, a Russian protectorate since 1868, "has lost all influence, jurisdiction or possession, south of the Oxus, except Charjui and Kerbi."[82] Meanwhile, Badakshan—as a part of North Afghanistan, rich in gold and precious stones, with the caravan routes crossing the space of land between Persia and India or China—began to be another bone of discord between London and Saint Petersburg. Although the British argued for Sher Ali Khan's legitimate right to add Badakshan to his possessions, the Russians referred to the vassal dependence of this territory on the emir of Bokhara, and ipso facto on Russia as his protector.[83]

The officially proclaimed noninterference with the affairs of Afghanistan notwithstanding, some authoritative politicians in both London and Calcutta defended a "forward" concept of policy for the Middle East and Inner Asia. Thus, Rawlinson and the members of the consultative group at the India Council sent Sher Ali an annual subsidy of £60,000 along with a regular supply of war matériel. They also encouraged the emir's patronage over the elder son of the Bokharian ruler, Abdul Malik, who had fled to Kabul after the defeat of an anti-Russian uprising in November 1868.[84] According to Frederick Roberts, who had been in the service of the government of India for more than forty years, the "forwardists" in reality had merely renovated the political doctrine of the governor-general, Lord Auckland, who had proclaimed as early as the 1830s the urgent necessity "to establish a strong and friendly power on the Indian northwest frontier," meaning Afghanistan.[85]

These ideas met British expectations in the region under consideration. For instance, Edward Eastwick, an expert in Persian affairs, submitted a memo to Lord Granville, the foreign secretary, in the spring of 1871. While stigmatizing "masterly inactivity" or "imbecility," as some opponents ironically called the cautious politics in Asia, Eastwick strongly argued in favor of a combination of "soft" and "hard" power to be applied to Russia and its satellite states. He asserted, above all, that Britain's firm stance enabled it to check the Persian advance to Herat in 1856–57 backed by the Russians. Now, wrote Eastwick, London faced the problem of how to transform Persia into "a secure external defence of India, inaccessible for Russia or any other power." He advocated that the Cabinet should therefore occupy a more benevolent position toward Persia—specifically, allocate financial subsidies to the shah, dispatch military instructors and ship war matériel to his troops, and even encourage his desires for Herat and Merv, albeit under the strict guidance of the Foreign Office.[86]

To expand the British position in Persia, business circles hurriedly invested capital in the development of the regional infrastructure—a process that had been stimulated by the Liberal government since the mid-1860s. The "old Persian hands," such as Baron Julius Reiter, rushed into the construction of telegraph lines, high roads, bridges, warehouses, and dockyards. Slowly but surely, Britain was taking the upper hand in commercial navigation across the Persian Gulf. Its engineers drafted plans for projects for meridian railway lines from the seaports of Bushire and Bender-Abbas to Tehran and along the coastline of the Caspian Sea. In other words, though the Liberal Cabinet pursued a strategy of "peace at any price," preferring not to infuriate the Russian Bear, a greater part of British leadership circles continued to regard the "forwardist" approach to the burning issues of Asian policy as a kind of insurance against the aggressive plots designed by Tsarist strategists.[87]

THE ROLE OF EASTERN TURKESTAN IN THE GREAT GAME

At this point, it is necessary to return to the problem of Eastern, or Chinese Turkestan, which became one of the most significant "playfields" of the Great Game in the 1860s. Geographically, the Tien Shan mountain range divided Turkestan's territory in two historical regions—Dzungaria to the north, with Kuldja as its administrative center; and Kashgaria to the south, with Kashgar as its capital.[88] As early as 1771, the Qing emperor Qianlun subjugated Eastern Turkestan, which henceforth was named Chinese Turkestan. Although Dzungaria had been totally devastated and its indigenous population of Mongol origin had been massacred by conquerors, the people who spoke Turkic languages in Kashgaria, such as the Uighurs, managed to conserve their traditional way of life under the yoke of the Qings. Curiously enough, a minor ethnic group of the Chinese, the so-called Dungans, adopted Islam and later joined Muslim insurgents in their struggle against the Qings.[89]

The four big cities, four medium-size cities, and twenty-three small towns of Chinese Turkestan were surrounded by deserts, arid steppes, and higher mountain ranges that constituted the natural barriers protecting it from foreign invasion, with the exception of the Ili Valley—an innate gap in the Tien Shan. This valley was a region abundant in iron, copper, oil, and gold mineral resources. The sedentary population of the Ili Basin produced grain and raw cotton, and trade statistics indicated a doubling in the exports of Ili Province to Russia for the period 1852–56.[90]

In 1861, Robert Davies, who was mentioned earlier in this chapter, drafted a note on the prospects of Britain's trade with the countries lying to the north of the Raj. Davies drew the attention of the Indian government to the strategic meaning of Chinese Turkestan as a foothold in the center of Inner Asia, a market for products, an apple of discord between Russia and China and, finally, a kind of bridle to curb Russia's ambitions, with the menace of the flame of Muslim rebellion spreading to the territory of Russian Turkestan. The document envisaged both the commercial and political expansion of the big powers, Russia in particular, to one of the most inaccessible regions in the world.[91]

According to Chinese historical records, antigovernment uprisings by local inhabitants were not rare in Eastern Turkestan, with four outbreaks in the first half of the nineteenth century alone. Nor should one ignore the effect that the Great Taiping Rebellion of 1850–64 had upon the alignment of forces in the region. The penetration of the Taiping rebels through Turkestan's outer borders in 1862 sparked a conflict among many wealthy Turkic and Chinese families.[92] Soon afterward, this confrontation triggered an uprising of Chinese Muslims, the Uighurs, the Dungans, and so on against the Qing authorities.[93] The rebels massacred many Han townsfolk, while the survivors escaped from the province to Russian territory as rapidly as they could. The following epistle illustrated how the Russian war minister, Miliutin, regarded the consequences of disturbances in Chinese Turkestan in September 1866:

The Dungans' occupation of Kuldja and Chuguchak, as far as the Foreign Ministry can judge, has put a section of Semirechie bordering China in rather an unfavorable position. The ultimate chaos that is reigning now in the provinces of Tarbagatai and Ili induces our Kyrgyz subjects to cross the frontier and get into plundering the Dungans, who responded with forays which even more instigated the Kyrgyz nomads to looting on a massive scale. These constant transfrontier escapades by Chinese subjects couple with a general tension increasing on the borders day by day, which adds displeasing components to the state of affairs on the outskirts of the Empire. Thus, there are grounds to anticipate the Dungans, imbued with the strongest Muslim fanaticism and abated in their struggle against the Chinese, being in a position to endanger even our rule in the steppes, since the attacks, they dared to rush into, were inflicted not upon the Kyrgyz alone, but on our troops as well.[94]

In addition, the Russian conquest of Khokand and Bokhara provoked the migration of townsfolk and rural dwellers to Chinese Turkestan on a massive scale. They escaped from the khanates in search of the protection of a new Muslim leader in the region—Yakub Beg. Originated from a wealthy Tajik family, he stayed in the service of different Turkic khans and emirs for more than twenty years, until the early 1860s.[95]

When Chinese supremacy over Eastern Turkestan had been shaken to its foundations thanks to the Taiping Rebellion and the liberation movement of the Muslim population, the former Qing province decayed into seven independent principalities, which were concentrated around fortified commercial centers. The time had come for risk takers like Yakub Beg to appear in the forefront of the Great Game. On leaving his former patron, the khan of Khokand, this adventurous and charismatic military commander, though a brutal and unscrupulous person by nature, set off for Kashgaria to escape from the Russian troops. Having arrived in Western Turkestan, he persistently crushed one rival ruler after another in the course of three years under the green banner of Islam. After 1867, he even attempted to "export" the Muslim revolution to the provinces of Shansi and Gansu. By 1870, he had drawn away the Qing regular troops and mandarins from Kashgaria, suppressed nearly all internecine feuds, and united five quasi-independent khanates into the Emirate of Yettishar (or the Country of Seven Cities), which was officially recognized in December 1873.[96] "His rule was theocratic and puritanical in nature, resembling the politico-religious system of the early caliphates. Strict observance of the Koran was enforced," commented a British researcher.[97]

It should be pointed out in this connection that before Yakub Beg embarked on the conquest of Kashgaria, in 1862 Tsarist and Qing diplomats had signed the Protocol of Chuguchak, which stipulated the clauses of the Peking Treaty signed in 1860 concerning transit trade across the Russo-Chinese borderline.[98] As the forwardist Arminius Vambery maintained in his publications,

> Still it must not be forgotten that the matter in question here is not the possession of a thousand square miles and some millions of inhabitants, but rather a revival of the great old commercial highway from the interior China to the west, which was in a flourishing condition up to the end of the middle ages; and the formation of it into a powerful and fruitful channel, carrying blessing and fertility through the great body of the Russian Empire.[99]

However, the establishment of a new, formidable Muslim state threatened to distort the status quo in Inner Asia where three empires met—the Chinese, Russian, and British. All of them disliked the probable proliferation of their rivals' influence upon Yettishar. While the Qing authorities sought to regain their control over Eastern Turkestan in the aftermath of the Taiping Uprising, the Tsarist planners were about to secure Semirechie, a province abutting Dzungaria, and the Anglo-Indian government could not tolerate Yakub Beg being egged on by Russian agents to outflank the Raj and cut off the lines of communication between China and India. It also needs to be noted that the chambers and associations of commerce in the British industrial centers—such as Manchester, Leeds, Bradford, Liverpool, Bristol, and Glasgow—consistently petitioned the India Office for a policy of free access of merchants and entrepreneurs to the markets in Chinese Turkestan. That is why Russia and Britain, frightened by an eventual breakup of the Celestial Empire, initially acted in support of the Manchu rulers engaged in the suppression of the Muslim uprising there, similarly to how they had aided the Peking government to mitigate the Taiping insurgents a decade earlier.[100]

Conversely, however, neither London nor Saint Petersburg refrained from attempts to outplay the opposite side in Eastern Turkestan. To have an objective view of current developments, various reconnaissance missions made their way to Kashgaria in the second half of the 1860s. On January 6, 1866, Lieutenant General Khrutschov, the chief of the West Siberian Military District, reported to Miliutin:

> According to the intelligence received from Namangan and Uch-Turfan, the Englishmen have dispatched a scientific expedition from Kashgar to the borders of Eastern Turkestan. The expedition has already penetrated through Badakshan to the Lake of Sarikul, surveying the country on its route and investigating mountain passes.[101]

The next year, Konstantin Pavlinov, the Russian consul in Kuldja, wrote to Stremoukhov, the head of the Asian Department, about British agents' arrival in Chinese Turkestan:

> Many Englishmen, allegedly amounting to 600, have come from Kashmir to Kashgaria to negotiate with Yakub Beg the problem of commerce. They have concluded an agreement on this subject and promised to Yakub Beg their aid against Burkha-u-Din, the ruler of Aksu, Kuch, and some of Turfan. The scouts informed me that the Englishmen had extended a railroad from Hindustan to the Hindu Kush mountains; and that they had constructed a telegraph line and compelled the ruler of Hotan to set up seventeen depots for their needs on the way from the spur of the hills up to the town of Iltsy, a principal foothold in the territory of the province.[102]

Referring to the establishment of the British trade office in Hotan, Pavlinov surmised that disturbances in Turkestan would probably not stave off the plans of the British to take over the trade of Eastern Turkestan and Central Asia with Western China, as they had done in Central China during the Taiping Rebellion.

A memo from Major General Vorontsov-Dashkov, one of the top dignitaries at the Court of Saint Petersburg, exposed the elites' concern about eventual British preponderance in Kashgaria and Dzungaria, which would have distressing repercussions in Russian Turkestan. If

Britain were to gain control of Yakub Beg, claimed the author in 1867, the trade markets in Western China would be lost to Russian merchants, while industrialists from Europe would exploit tremendous mineral resources there.[103]

Russian anxiety about British intrigues in the region was justified, given both the reconnaissance missions sponsored by the Royal Geographical Society and the official visits of political emissaries from Calcutta to Yettishar during the 1860s and 1870s. In the former case, Robert Shaw, who was interested in the "commercial possibilities" of Kashgaria, took a trip to Yarkand and was accorded an audience at the Court of Yakub Beg in 1869.[104] "He hopes that the Queen will permit him 'to warm himself in the rays of her glory,'" wrote Shaw shortly afterward, "and he would like to keep good relations with the Englishmen, because he is surrounded by adversaries and envious authorities.... He calls the Russians genies and devils."[105] Almost simultaneously, another explorer, George Hayward, disguised as a Pathan, surreptitiously crossed the frontier of British India in order to survey and map a vast mountain area. On returning to Britain, he was awarded the Gold Medal of the Royal Geographical Society for his contribution to the exploration of the Western Himalayas.[106]

Meanwhile, Robert Michell, a political officer in the service of the British Raj, composed a review of the situation in Chinese Turkestan, bringing into the focus of his study the eventual reverberations of the Dungans' rebellion and the emergence of Yakub Beg as an independent ruler. Michell recommended to the India Office to send a special envoy to Kashgar in order to sound out the position and intentions of the lord of Yettishar.[107]

This memo, and the intelligence collected by a number of pathfinders, paved the way for an official visit by Sir Thomas Forsyth to Kashgaria. Contrary to Shaw and Hayward, Forsyth's trip was authorized by the India Office and the viceroy himself in 1870.[108] According to a secret Russian agent who managed to obtain nuggets of information about Forsyth's meeting with chieftains and wealthy merchants in Ladakh (Kashmir) before his departure to Yettishar, Yakub Beg was allegedly inclined to sponsor his subjects to trade with British India. Yet the potentate of Yettishar dreaded the Russian occupation of his state as a kind of military assistance to the Qings. The attempts of Tsarist troops to invade Kashgaria in 1859 and 1867, when Russian delegates proposed to Yakub Beg to hack a way from Vernyi in Semirechie to Kashgar through the Tien Shan, worried him very much. But what was even more important, the Russians became aware of Yakub Beg concocting a favorable excuse to assume the status of a "buffer state ruler" similar to that of the emir of Afghanistan.[109]

To avoid any sort of Russian interference with the affairs of Yettishar, Forsyth was directed to convince Yakub Beg to conduct a more cautious policy toward Russia, because the British were concerned about any opportunity that Kaufman might take to invade Kashgaria.[110] Although Forsyth omitted this episode in his report to London, the scouts in the Russian service informed their spymasters about a battery of mountain canons and 10,000 rifles that Forsyth proposed to deliver to Yakub Beg free of charge.[111]

At the same time, nearly all emissaries—Captain Reinal in 1868 and 1875, Captain Kaulbars in 1872, and Captain Kuropatkin two years later—failed to prevent the consolidation of his state in proximity to Russian Turkestan. Though the envoys from Yettishar paid several visits to Saint Petersburg in the period 1869–73 in order to assure the tsar of their master's desire to remain on friendly terms, Alexander II gave the cold shoulder to these overtures.[112] The Russians simply used Yakub Beg as a pawn on the chessboard of the Great Game in order to force both the Chinese and British to agree to their presence in this part of Asia on a permanent basis. In addition, it appeared extremely urgent to Saint Petersburg to confer the influence of the Ottoman Empire upon Yakub Beg, inasmuch as the sultan proclaimed Yettishar under his supremacy and sent military instructors to Kashgaria to transform irregular combatants into modern soldiers.[113]

The emergence of Yettishar on the Asian political map that followed the Dungans' insurrection induced Tsarist military administrators of Siberia and Turkestan to urge the central government to take a more active role in Kashgaria. "The time has come to abandon a prudent policy toward Eastern Turkestan," claimed the governor-general of Eastern Siberia, Count Nikolai Muraviev-Amursky, at a conference held by Miliutin in September 1870. He reiterated this opinion in a memorial to the war minister on December 23 that same year.[114] So it was small wonder, as John Le Donne argued, that "the possibility of Yakub Beg's invasion of the Ili Valley under British sponsorship triggered Kaufman's preventive strike." Another argument for the outbreak of the Ili crisis, according to the historian, was a design to strategically encircle Mongolia with Russian possessions.[115]

The devastation of the Russian trading station in Kuldja by a gang of the rebel Dungans in the summer of 1871 gave an immediate pretext for Major General Kolpakovsky's commitment to action by Kaufman, who was ordered to occupy the Upper Ili Valley and the Tien Shan mountain passes with Russian troops. Although the Ili problem spawned a new round of discussion on the further Russian policies in Turkestan between military and diplomatic minds, the Qings were finally invited to cooperate with Kaufman in the restoration of tranquillity on the Russo-Chinese border.[116] If the status quo were to be reinstated, insisted the Russian ambassador in his interviews with Chinese mandarins, the occupational forces would be immediately withdrawn from Kuldja and the whole district would be given back to the Qings on condition they could control it by their own power.[117]

Russian pressure upon Yettishar resulted in the signing of the trade and consular treaty by the governor-general of Turkestan and Yakub Beg in 1872. The above-mentioned mission of Kaulbars to Kashgar inaugurated the establishment of a Russian consulate with the functions of a political agency, but it did not mean the recognition of Yakub Beg as a sovereign ruler de jure.[118] Suffice it to quote the tenth article of the instructions to Russian consul in the city of Kashgar:

> As to the relations between Yettishar and the British government, our political agent ought to devote attention to how far the Anglo-Indian administration supports Yakub Beg in the development of his power and military potential and to what extent he is submitted to the British, regarding it as a guideline of his anti-Russian policy.[119]

To camouflage the real goals of the Tsarist government, a legend was invented by some military writers. The majority of local Muslims were expected "to relocate from the Qing supremacy under the protective hand of the White Sovereign."[120] Yet the Manchu ruling elites apparently did not share these illusions. For example, General Tso Tsungtang reported to the Manchu emperor on April 12, 1875:

> The occupation of Ili by the Russians happened when we were involved in domestic disturbances. They claimed that they were coming to save the city [Kuldja] for the Chinese, but their real motivation was booty. They knew that the area of Ili was unusually rich, and it was close to their southern border, so they could come and go without much trouble.[121]

The Russian occupation of the Ili District of 1,400 square miles and 130,000 inhabitants compelled the Cabinet of Saint James to dispatch a second ambassadorial mission headed by Forsyth to Kashgaria from September 1873 to April 1874. This time the staff of the mission numbered more than 350 diplomatic, military, and intelligence officers, escorted by a battalion of armed cavalrymen. Having been accorded a hearty welcome, the British emissary managed to sign an agreement with Yakub Beg inaugurating Robert Shaw as the consul in Yarkand. Significantly, the members of the mission, who were responsible for reconnaissance, traversed and mapped less-explored and practically unknown passes through the Hindu Kush.[122]

This reciprocal diplomatic move by the British in the Great Game for Eastern Turkestan infuriated the tsar. Although Yakub Beg, according to Forsyth's recommendation, sought to abstain from anti-Russian policies, Saint Petersburg and Tashkent—the new capital of Russian Central Asia—observed his overtures to Britain with increasing jealousy and suspicion. The Asian Department's annual report of 1874 noted that

> in comparison with us, the Englishmen were granted a more friendly receipt in Kashgaria, they enjoyed full freedom of action and affected the potentate greatly.... The British Envoy, Forsyth,

who visited Kashgar last year, brought 2,000 rifles, ten artillery guns, a crown of the Sovereign, and a suit embroidered with pearl to him as gifts from the Viceroy of India. A few military instructors who accompanied Forsyth began to train the Kashgarian soldiers and supervise the construction of defensive fortifications. They are in charge of the production of guns and rifles. The mission staff members also brought a great amount of English products with them, which will doubtlessly undermine our commerce there. At the suggestion of the Englishmen, Yakub Beg took the title of Emir and started minting coins with the engraved names of himself and the Turkish Sultan, Abdul Aziz.[123]

Thus, implicitly, the political crisis in Chinese Turkestan contributed to the general deterioration of not only Russo-Chinese but also Russo-British relations.[124] Yet it was Russia's annexation of another Central Asian principality—the Khanate of Khiva—that made the positive scenario of bringing the Great Game to an end in the period under consideration absolutely unrealistic. As a British historian rightly remarked: "If any specific incident could be isolated as compelling a fundamental rethinking of the implications of India's defence posture, it would undoubtedly be the Russian conquest of Khiva in 1873, and the war 'scare' it generated, with more or less intensity, for the next thirty years."[125]

THE ANNEXATION OF KHIVA AND DEBATES ON THE POLICY TOWARD INDIA

Russia and Britain concluded their agreement on the delimitation of the territories located in the upper flow of the Amu Daria with notable reservations. As Granville mentioned to Lord Loftus, the British ambassador to Saint Petersburg, on January 23, 1873:

Her Majesty's Government cannot however but feel that, if Badakshan and Wakhan, which they consider the Emir justly to deem to be part of his territories, be assumed by England or

Russia, or by one or either of them, to be wholly independent of his authority, the Emir might be tempted to assert his claims by arms; that perhaps in that case Bokhara might seek an opportunity of acquiring districts too weak of themselves to resist the Afghan state; and that thus the peace of Central Asia would be disturbed, and occasion given for questions between Great Britain and Russia, which it is on every account so desirable to avoid, and which Her Majesty's Government feel sure would be as distasteful to the Imperial Government as to themselves.[126]

On February 12, 1873, Gorchakov replied to Granville, asserting the Russian government's strong and sincere desire to reinforce Russian policy in Asia with the principles predicated by the London Cabinet.[127] On April 22, Gladstone declared in the House of Commons that the Gorchakov-Granville agreement did not abrogate Britain's "right" to act in Afghanistan as she thought best, provided that the latter being excluded from the Russian sphere of influence and its borders being demarcated in a proper way, while the emir of Kabul pledged the British not to commit any acts of aggression against Bokhara as the vassal state of the tsar.[128] However, if "inactivists," primarily Gladstonian liberals, believed this "gentleman's agreement" would put an end to the race for supremacy in the Middle East and Inner Asia, the "forwardists" in London and Calcutta considered it useless in view of Britain's evident incapability to arrest effectively and with less spending the Russian expansion in Central Asia. Instantly, John Michell, the above-mentioned vice consul in Saint Petersburg, who also shared the concept of the "forward" policy, characterized the tsar's abrogation of the Paris Treaty of 1856 as the height of Russian perfidy and ambiguity, exposing the Russian officer corps' designs on Persia—a bridgehead for the offensive against India.[129]

In spite of the fact that the Tsarist governing elites had agreed on a compromise regarding the acculturation of Central Asia as a pivot for the political course to be pursued on the southern frontier of the empire, the "war party" at the Russian court, along with provincial military administrators, hurriedly nicknamed the Gorchakov-Granville accord *un pain à cacheter sur une voie d'eau* (a puny stopper of water in the hole),[130] yet again drafting an attack against Khiva for a few reasons: first, because this khanate remained a final barrier preventing the Russians from taking the lower Oxus under control; second, because Said Mohamed Khan was openly hostile to the Tsarist emissaries delegated to Khiva by Gorchakov and Miliutin; third, because Yakub Beg of Kashgaria sought to unite with the Khivans in intrigues against the Russians; and fourth, because the tsar was allied with Germany and Austria-Hungary, thus frustrating any possible negative reaction by Britain, isolated in Europe, to further Russia's conquest of Central Asia. Arguing in favor of new aggression there, the leading Russian newspapers and magazines pointed to "constant depredations on our territory, enormous taxes levied on our subjects, rebellions fomented in the boundary steppe against the Russian rule," the episodes that "compelled the government to determine upon retributive measures."[131] Simultaneously, many journalists commented on the dreadful conditions under which Russians slaves allegedly survived in the khanate.[132]

Indeed, the propaganda campaign in the Russian media impressed the European public, including the British people, in the spring and summer of 1873. Even such national periodicals as *The Times* and *The Quarterly Review* shifted their attention to the denunciation of the atrocities perpetrated by the khan and his satraps. "Plundering caravans and inciting the Kyrgyz to commit similar forays were, however, among the lesser crimes laid at the door of the khanate," wrote a British observer. "The traffic in kidnapped Russian fishermen carried on by the Khivan government with the pirates of the Caspian Sea was a more serious matter."[133]

In February 1873, when the ink on the Gorchakov-Granville document was not yet dry, the Russian Main Staff laid out a detailed plan for the campaign against the khanate, though some renowned commanders, such as Mikhail Skobelev, had much earlier sketched various scenarios for an assault, in 1870–72.[134] Meanwhile, the khan of Khiva desperately appealed for military aid to the Ottoman Empire, British India, and Persia, while ignoring the Russian ultimatums.[135] As Dimitry Miliutin recalled in his old age,

This time again the Khan devaluated the claims we had put in, and forwarded an emissary to Calcutta with a request to the Queen to stand up for Khiva against Russia. The Viceroy [Lord Northbrook] recommended to the Khivan emissaries to establish friendly relations with the Russian boundary authorities and release Russian prisoners of war. Nor had the Khan of Khiva, however, followed this advice.[136]

Thus the well-prepared assault upon Khiva by the three marching columns of troops from the west, north, and east under Kaufman's supreme command became imminent. So it was small wonder that the regular Russian battalions, seasoned from previous hostilities and now far better equipped, easily crushed the irregular Khivan detachments and seized the capital of the khanate in mid-June 1873.[137] Preliminarily, the expedition was a success owing to the effective reconnaissance of the theater of operations before the campaign, and especially to the accurate topographic maps of the khanate.[138] It seems also significant that some Turkmen tribes sided with the invaders, while the emir of Bokhara and the khan of Khokand supplied the Cossacks with food provisions and secured their free passage through the territories under their rule.[139]

The subjugation of Khiva enabled Russia to take the whole of Central Asia under its patronage, except Trans-Caspia. Commenting on the capture of Khiva by Tsarist troops, an editorial in *The Times* gloomily stated: "So perishes…the last relic of independence in Central Asia."[140] More important, the stronger was the position of Russia in Central Asia, the higher was the tone it would be able to assume in any conflict of European powers.[141] Although feeble voices of protest were heard in London and other capitals, the ordinary public in European countries believed that the Russian victory had finally imposed tranquillity in Turkestan, abolished the slave trade, and put an end to the forays of savage nomads. Not coincidentally, *The Map of Central Asia* came out in London in July 1874 complete with the new boundaries of the current Russian territorial acquisitions.[142]

Yet the alarmists amid the British governing elite could not but point to the military campaign against Khiva as an excuse for intensifying their bitter criticism of the vulnerability of India. For example, Vambery meticulously enumerated all the reasons for an expected advance of the Russians to Hindustan:

Russia wants India first of all in order to set so rich a pearl in the splendid diamond of her Asian possessions; a pearl for whose attainment she has so long, at so heavy a cost, been leveling the way through the most barren steppes in the world; next, in order to lend the greatest possible force to her influence over the whole world of Islam (whose greatest and most dangerous foe she has now become), because the masters of India have reached, in Mohammedan eyes, the ne plus ultra of might and greatness; and lastly, by taming the British Lion on the other side of the Hindu Kush, to work out with great ease her designs on the Bosporus, in the Mediterranean, indeed all over Europe.[143]

As Colonel Francis Wellesley, the military attaché in Saint Petersburg, recalled later in his memoirs:

That the invasion of India has occupied the thoughts of many Russian soldiers and statesmen, especially the former, is not of course to be denied, and to lead a victorious army a Muscovite general, as it was the ambition of Admiral Popov to sail a victorious squadron up the waters of the Thames.[144]

The recurrent visits of the secret delegates sent by some Indian maharajas to Tashkent, Orenburg, and other Russian strongholds in 1865, 1866, and 1870 only corroborated these concerns. Thus, Rambir Singh, the ruler of Kashmir, repeatedly dispatched his representatives to the governors-general of Orenburg and Turkestan. Although the Russian authorities usually discouraged these advances and delayed any concrete answer or replied rather evasively to pleas for military support, the London Cabinet and the Indian government were very annoyed by the rumors of the Cossacks allegedly crossing the Oxus and moving into the towns of Balh, Herat, and Kabul.[145] In Clarendon's view, which he shared with Buchanan on March 27, 1869, "unless stringent precautions were adopted, we should find, before long, that some aspiring Russian general had entered into communication with some restless or malcontent Indian prince, and that intrigues were rife, disturbing the Indian population on the frontiers."[146]

On the other side, the proponents of "masterly inactivity," like Lawrence, Northbrook, and Argyll, argued for the impossibility of any aggressive moves against India, while Kaufman and his staffers were engaged in the acculturation of Turkestan. "If a Russian army did venture to advance directly upon India without the impediments which experience has shown to be necessary to the successful conduct of a campaign in modern warfare," maintained Captain Francis Trench in his book on the defense of India, "its destruction, whenever it came into contact with an English force equipped with all requisite implements of war, would be inevitable."[147] Besides, the nonalarmists sharply criticized any reverse movement of British troops through Afghanistan to meet Tsarist armies at the distant approaches to India.[148]

Yet both camps of forwardists and inactivists concurred in the further rapid adaptation of the Indian secret service to the needs of a more effective defense of India. "The prime gain, however, which we look for from a permanent agency," wrote Vambery, "is that England, being accurately informed of proceedings in Central Asia, of the military and political movements of Russia, will no longer be exposed to the danger of finding herself suddenly surprised on one point or another, and, through the continual uncertainty in which she wavers touching the true state of things, of being disabled from taking the right precautions."[149]

The reforms in the military administration of the British Empire, promoted by Edward Cardwell in the early 1870s, also contributed to the improvement of political and military intelligence. It is well known that the secretary of war delivered a speech to the House of Commons on February 24, 1873, right after the conclusion of the Gorchakov-Granville agreement, whereby he announced the Cabinet's desire to establish the Intelligence Branch under the direction of Major General Patrick Macdougall assisted by twenty-seven officers on the staff. It was designated to replace the former Topographic and Statistical Department.[150]

Interestingly, Salisbury and Hartington—who then occupied, respectively, the posts of foreign secretary and India secretary—devoted more attention to the reform of intelligence than did military thinkers, because, as they surmised, an "intelligence screen" would become another significant means of security on the Indian frontier.[151]

Some historians maintained that Cardwell had thoroughly studied the experience of the British secret service in India.[152] It should be added, however, that the Russian General Staff, Foreign Ministry, and military commanders on the spot proved to be ahead of the British in the reorganization of intelligence agencies, for they had instituted a special Asian Division of the Main Staff and a Military Topographical Section at the headquarters of the Turkestan Military District as early as in 1866–67.[153]

Taken together, these tendencies—with the admixture of power, politics, commerce, and ambitions of major "players"—were to typify the apogee of the Great Game, which Russia and Britain had attained by the mid-1870s in spite of the sedative declarations heralded by Saint Petersburg and London. Yet the first, though fragile, seeds of future collaboration had been implanted in the Russo-British relationship, symbolized by the Gorchakov-Granville compromise, which anticipated the forthcoming end of the two empires' rivalry for the domination of Asia.

CHAPTER 4

THE CLIMAX OF THE GREAT GAME, 1874–1885

We prefer the English scheme of civilization, which has at this moment such splendid and surprising results to show in India, and wherever else it deals with Asiatics.

—Arminius Vambery, *Sketches of Central Asia*

This chapter first elucidates how, as the Great Game went on in the mid-1870s, the Russian Empire's autocratic model of colonial rule seemed more politically and economically adapted to Asian nations, whereas the modern features of the British Empire and most European states—especially a free market economy and liberal democracy—contrasted sharply with the predominantly vertical social links in preindustrial Asian societies. Second, the chapter reveals that both leaders and ordinary people in the two empires were very skeptical about a final victory for each competing side in the Game. Although Europe saw the annexation of Khokand by the Russians as a lesser evil than the chaos under the khanate, the British feared that Russia would take Khokand's liquidation as a pretext to activate the Great Game in Kashgaria, bordering the provinces that had been incorporated into the Russian Empire. The Afghan knot proved a real fulcrum for Russo-British relations during the late 1870s and early 1880s. The pages that follow seek to explain the core of this situation and how it contributed to the culmination of the Great Game, focusing on the abortive Russian march to India. Third, and finally, the chapter examines the complex Turkmen problem in the Great Game. By the end of the 1870s, Turkmenia was the only remaining independent region in Central Asia beyond the Russian and British spheres of influence. Of course, a struggle ensued between the two empires, and by 1884 both sides had agreed to establish a commission to set boundaries for the region's territories.

THE GAME MUST GO ON

By the mid-1870s, both the Russians and British had already left behind a larger part of their way to the River Oxus, or the Amu Daria—"the only river of any importance which intervenes between the Russian frontier and the Indus, except the Helmund on the road to Kandahar," according to Demetrius Boulger, a contemporary journalist, explorer, and member of the Royal Asiatic Society.[1] The subjugation of Khiva and the occupation of the Ili Valley in Eastern Turkestan by Tsarist troops infuriated British "forwardists" and those statesmen who sympathized with them, not excluding Prime Minister Benjamin Disraeli and the majority of the Tory Cabinet. In their evaluation, the Gorchakov-Granville agreement proved nothing more than a concession made by Saint Petersburg to London in view of the current international tension, specifically in Europe.

Yet the general contour of world politics also underwent substantial changes in the 1870s. Germany and Italy, as reunited national states with unsatisfied ambitions, joined in the world scramble for colonial possessions, while France, humiliated and devastated after the war against Prussia, became a second-rank power—albeit for the time being. Besides, the economic depression of 1873–96 afflicted international trade, especially those branches of Britain's industries that were involved in producing commodities for export to its overseas dominions. On reaching its nadir of £250 million in 1872, the value of British exports began to stagnate and even decrease in the last quarter of the century.[2]

While at the apogee of "masterly inactivity," the Liberal government in Britain sought to legitimize its cautious policy in the East, denying any immediate Russian threat that faced Britain's interests and advertising Russia as a pioneer of civilization, the Conservative Cabinet embarked on a staunch offensive course of policy, imperial at its core and free from any long-term continental commitments, later to be called a policy of "splendid isolation."[3]

For the fact that Germany assumed a new status in Europe, substantial attention of the British ruling circles was devoted to the problem of how to curb the growing strength of the Second Reich. As Disraeli formulated the strategic foreign policy objectives of his Cabinet, it was of essential importance to Great Britain to use Germany against Russia, blackmailing Berlin with the "sword of Damocles" of an eventual Russian occupation of the Turkish Straits. Robert Blake, a biographer of the great Tory leader, alluded to the episode of how, when being interrogated as to "why Britain should not follow the advice of those who wanted her to forget about Constantinople and secure the route to India by annexing Egypt," Disraeli replied:

> But the answer is obvious. If the Russians had Constantinople, they could at any time march their army through Syria to the mouth of the Nile and then what would be the use of our holding Egypt? Not even the command of the sea could help us under such circumstances. People who talk in this manner must be utterly ignorant of geography. Our strength is on the sea. Constantinople is the key of India, and not Egypt and the Suez Canal.[4]

It was no wonder, then, that the European media viewed the prime minister's sympathy with the Ottoman Empire through a lens of the "uncompromising defence against Russian aggression of the sovereign power of the Sultan and the integrity of his empire."[5] As a Russian political scientist later commented on this opinion,

> The only possible excuse for the British conservatives of Disraeli's camp, shivering with fear for their Asiatic possessions, was their

absolute lack of lore of Russia and the Russians; they knew no more about them than the ancient history of the Aztecs or Peruvians; the Russian nation remained a regular riddle to them, still unsolved to the end of the century.[6]

Yet, conversely, Disraeli and his proponents looked upon the Tsardom as a formidable conservative power in Europe, capable of checking the revolutionary mania of France or the boundless aggrandizement of Germany. Mindful of the often uncompromised, snobbish manner in which the Tory government under Disraeli dealt with international problems, even some high-ranking statesmen, let alone Liberal oppositionists, criticized him for the extremism and adventurism that overwhelmed Whitehall in the second half of the 1870s.[7] The verity would seem to hold that the Tory Cabinet drafted a military campaign that envisaged a three-pronged advance in Central Asia and the Near East, accompanied by anti-Russian revolts of the native population instigated by British spymasters.[8] Characteristically, Nikolai Tcharykov, the Russian political agent in Bokhara, recalled that Governor-General Kaufman had planned to build up fortifications around Samarkand in view of a potential attack by unfriendly warlike tribes with Britain standing behind them just at that time.[9]

Undoubtedly, a new book by Henry Rawlinson, *England and Russia in the East*, impressed Disraeli and many of those politicians who identified their interests with the "forward" policy. In his chapter on British relations with Persia, Rawlinson maintained that

> what she [Russia] would naturally desire, and we have especially to guard against, is a domination of the country by means of moral and political pressure, which would enable her to use Persia as a lever against contiguous nationalities, against the Turks on one side, against the Turkmen and Afghans on the other.[10]

This concept especially matched the aspirations of those industrialists and traders who were nicknamed "old Persian and Indian hands." Thus, the Russian military attaché, Colonel Pavel Kutaisov (see chapter 3), reported to Miliutin on his meeting with Lieutenant General Robertson, the commander in chief of the Anglo-Indian army, in March 1873. During this interview, they agreed that there was a deficit of communication lines in the region and about the hatred that local Muslim people felt toward all "infidels" who made journeys to Oriental countries. The British military were aware of the barriers that seriously hampered Russo-British cooperation on Asian frontiers, implied Kutaisov.[11]

The opinion of Major General Edward Cazalet, another respected veteran of the India service, dovetailed with the testimony of the Russian "shoulder-strapped diplomat" (an epithet for a military attaché):

> The accession of political strength and commercial activity which would accrue to us from uniting the Mediterranean with the Persian Gulf by a line of railway would place us in so strong a position of vantage that we could deal in a liberal spirit with the interests of Russia. Gibraltar, Malta, Cyprus, Syria and Mesopotamia would then complete our chain of communication with India by the shortest route which it is possible for us to retain under our own control.[12]

Significantly, this military expert also pointed to Russian designs on the establishment of modern logistics in Central Asia that, in his view, endangered either the geostrategic or commercial interests of Britain:

> These regions [the Middle East and Inner Asia] must be made accessible by railways, and by diverting the River Oxus into the Caspian Sea, thus connecting them with the water system of Central Russia. This undertaking should be (for Russia) a national one. The construction of these routes will be a most fatal and conclusive blow to England on the part of Russia. No railroads through Asia Minor to the Euphrates and the Gulf of Persia will be in a position to compete with this water route, leading from the Baltic Sea to the frontiers of Afghanistan, and the whole of Northern India must involuntarily and passively fall under the influence of Russia.[13]

Strong evidence that Tsarist ministers brooded over a scheme of how to modify a flow of the Amu Daria vindicated Cazalet's surmise. According to Miliutin, they discussed the scheme on January 3, 1875. Although all the members of the audience at the conference, except Kaufman, reacted negatively to a scheme for a railway network in Central Asia proposed by the famous French engineer Ferdinand de Lesseps, the chief engineer of the Suez Canal, some of the top Tsarist dignitaries favored the idea of diverting the Oxus into the Caspian Sea via the old riverbed.[14]

On this reading, both Britain's and Russia's patterns of colonial rule in their Asian possessions deserved a lively public discussion in the press and political pamphlets of various tenors. For example, a member of the Royal Asiatic Society commented that "the policy of Russia in Central Asia has been less magnanimous and noble so far than ours in India, but it has been more politic. It has not conferred any remarkable benefit upon its new subjects, but it has rendered its own rule practically safe and assured."[15] According to a contemporary observer, "a particular concern which exercised the minds of some of the British rulers was that they should not seem to be using the methods of the Russian Empire, which many of them held to be a model of despotism."[16] Hence, London conducted a policy of averting "unification of 'inner' and 'outer' ethnic groups" by, as the American scholar Owen Lattimore correctly noted, "favoring different tribes in different degrees, while evading the unprofitable expense of outright conquest and administration."[17] Yet Lattimore opined that such tactics were risky enough, inasmuch as English administrators might be easily entrapped by chieftains, whereas their ordinary tribesmen perceived the implicit British presence as interference by an overlord power in the internal life of a certain ethnic group. Coupled with preferences that the British rendered to social communities living on the frontiers of buffer states, these politics might provoke turbulent mountain clans to revolt against their rulers, which in turn would require the government of India to spearhead costly punitive expeditions to faraway areas.[18]

Mindful of the British achievements in India—such as the incorporation of various minor feudal states into the Raj, the construction of railways and telegraph lines, and the introduction of modern European systems of education and public health—Tsarist military thinkers contrasted, however, "the moral authority" of the Russian rule in the khanates with "the violence and perfidy" of their British counterparts.[19] Even some non-Russian commentators adhered to this opinion. A typical case was an interpretation of the British system of domination by a prominent Austrian geographer, Friedrich von Hellwald, who pointed out the contradictions between declarations and practice in India. Following some Russian political observers, von Hellwald contended, moreover, that British rule in the Raj rested primarily on high poll taxes and military suppression of even feeble discontent among local residents.[20]

A deeper insight into this problem led many authors, however, to conjecture that a certain semblance of the methods that the British and Russian colonial administrations applied in Asia could not repeal such evident dissimilarities.[21] It should be stressed, above all, that though Great Britain had basically completed its industrialization by the 1870s, Tsarist Russia had merely embarked on the way toward modernization. Also, if Britain was a maritime empire, Russia remained the largest continental realm in the world, occupying one-third of Eurasia. And finally, though the United Kingdom and the Russian Empire were both ruled by hereditary monarchs, the discrepancies between their regimes stipulated the polar character of policy in Asia.

In a narrow sense, taking Russian Central Asia and British India as paragons, it was not a problem for contemporary experts to find even more differences. Although, in the former case, a deficit of local residents hampered the acculturation of steppes and deserts, in the latter, the British colonial administration was bound to command territories with a high density of sedentary population. If Russia had no competition from any European power in Turkestan except the United Kingdom, London had subdued the Indian states in the course of a bitter, long-term struggle against Portugal and France. Finally, India's commercial significance to the metropolis, as the previous chapters have argued, far exceeded the role of Central Asia in the industrial development of Russia, at least in the initial stages of the Great Game.

Summing up what has been said, it is not difficult to acknowledge that the Russian "model" of colonial rule appeared to be more adapted to Asian nations in political and economic spheres. This was especially true with regard to the despotic regimes to which the local population was accustomed and that corresponded perfectly to the autocratic political structure of the Romanovs' Empire. Conversely, many more modern features, such as a free market economy and liberal democracy, that were typical of most European states in the second half of the nineteenth century, sharply contrasted with the primarily vertical social links in preindustrial Asian societies. As an American Sinologist correctly depicted the posture toward economic affairs among the despotic monarchies of the East,

> Commerce in the ports of trade in Inner Asia or along the China coast was administered, at least theoretically, in accord with regulations that implicitly denied the possible development of a supply-demand market mechanism. Such a mechanism could not exist in the presence of regulations controlling access to the market and the rate, or "price," at which exchanges were to take place.[22]

Nevertheless, apart from mutual critical commentaries, voices in support of Russo-British cooperation in Asia were also heard on the banks of both the Neva and the Thames. For example, Feodor Martens, a prominent Russian jurist, asked a question: "Who will benefit from a constant struggle of Russia and Great Britain in Asia?" In his answer, Martens predicated a future rapprochement of the empires, arguing that

> the more England and Russia will harmonize their mutual interests, the more they will be aware that collaboration for the sake of nations is a distinguished feature of civilization, the more substantial and effective will be the foundations of their domination of Asiatic people and the guarantees of universal peace in Europe and Asia.[23]

Equally, the anonymous author of a brochure on British imperial policy urged London and Saint Petersburg to unite their efforts to civilize remote Asian states. He foretold that

> Russia and Britain are two great powers who can do most good and most harm to each other, and therefore, they have every reason to be friendly. They have everything to gain by mutual friendship and nothing whatever to lose. United they will be strong enough to keep more than half of the world in peace, and in security from all attack, even when the rowdy colossus of the West has grown up to his full belligerent stature. If Russia is with us, who will dare to be against us, or against her. Alliance with her is the condition of our imperial success in the vital matters of guarding against Chinese and Egyptian dangers to India. Let Englishmen, therefore, not be too fastidious. Russian culture and morality are indeed not up to the German level, and in some respects below the French or American. But Russia's faults are those of raw youth, not of old corruption. She is conscious of her deficiencies, and willing to learn from her elders. She is eminently the most progressive of continental European countries. And above all, she tends more than any other country to progress on English lines and learn from English examples.[24]

Yet the realities of the uncompromising struggle for supremacy definitely prevailed in the minds of contemporary policymakers, if, for example, the correspondence between Lord Northbrook, the Indian viceroy in 1872–76, and Lord Salisbury, then the secretary of state for India, was taken into consideration. The latter believed that the tsar was unable to efficiently charge his generals in Central Asia, while, on the other side, Salisbury discredited both the emir of Afghanistan and the shah of Persia. Therefore, he recommended that the viceroy "be ready for a march to Herat, as the Prussians were for a march to Paris," meaning the blitzkrieg offensive taken by the Germans in the latest war against the French.[25]

Having arrived in London on a state visit in May 1874, Alexander II and Gorchakov "flooded" Whitehall with peaceful proposals, complaining at the same time of Britain's subversive activity in Kashgaria, North Persia, and the Central Asian khanates.[26] Reciprocally, Disraeli and Lord Derby, the foreign secretary, accused Russia of perpetual outright violations of all the existing bilateral arrangements, including that of Gorchakov with Granville. On June 2, Disraeli corresponded to Lord Salisbury: "I am not assured of a possible attainment of any effective agreement with Russia."[27] Similarly, Salisbury shared his view on Russia's policy in a letter to Northbrook late in 1874:

> It may be quite true that Russia cannot invade India, and that the Afghans, if Russia induced them to move, would be beaten. But the real fear is that if Russia occupies either materially, or diplomatically, Afghanistan, she will require to be watched by a large force; in other words, she will hold in check an important fraction of our scanty British Army.[28]

The majority of the British public concurred in the pessimistic opinion that the Russians sought "to besiege Constantinople from the heights above Peshawar." Boulger reflected these emotions five years later:

> We are therefore compelled to recognize the stern fact that no faith can be reposed in the guarantee of Russia not to do such and such a thing. In Central Asia, where there is no court of Great Powers to maintain the standard of international equity, Russia is supreme, and she guides her political action regardless of those scruples which mar the effect of the policy of less happily constituted governments and peoples.[29]

That is why both the leadership circles and ordinary people in the two empires proved to be extremely skeptical about a final victory for each competing side in the Great Game. Moreover, they favored its geographical displacement from the khanates of Khokand, Khiva, and Bokhara to Kashgaria, Afghanistan, and Trans-Caspia.

THE ANNEXATION OF KHOKAND AND THE
GAME IN KASHGARIA

After Russia had taken Bokhara and Khiva under its protection, the Khanate of Khokand, despite the initial defeat, remained a hotbed of anti-Russian intrigues in the basin of the River Oxus and the last barrier of strategic significance to Tsarist armies in the establishment of a Russian sphere of influence, though the Khokandian townsfolk, along with the Kyrgyz and Kipchak tribes, were reported not to oppose their admittance as subjects to the Romanovs' Empire.[30]

In 1873, the heavy direct taxes that Mohamed Khudayar Khan imposed on his subjects provoked a mass revolt, following by long-lasting internal feuds. The unrest forced the ill-fated potentate to escape abroad. The insurgents seized the city of Khokand and proclaimed the eldest son of the khan, Said Nasir-u-din, as their new ruler.[31] Yet dissipations between nomadic elements, primarily the Kyrgyz, and sedentary population, chiefly the Tajik, continued to destabilize the social order. Moreover, they threatened Russian interests in Central Asia, inasmuch as the rebels declared a holy war against all "infidels" and embarked on "exporting" hostilities to the territory of the Turkestan governor-generalship. A careful observer, Demetrius Boulger, alluded to an amazing abstract from the declaration of insurgents, who urged the Russians living in the area under consideration either to convert to Islam or withdraw from the khanate.[32] To complete this gloomy picture, Kaufman suspected that Yakub Beg, the ruler of Kashgaria, had his hand in this anti-Russian movement. According to Aleksei Kuropatkin, who made a trip to the city of Kashgar in 1876,

the immense personal successes of Yakub Beg,...and his boundless power over the vast country has surrounded his person with a halo not wholly undeserved. Suffice it to say that, due to his ambitions, many people look at him as a second Tamerlane. The resources of this ruler were likewise greatly exaggerated. The authentic information regarding the purchase of a large consignment of quick-shooting rifles in Constantinople by the emissaries of Yakub Beg, as it was supposed, through the agency of Englishmen, gave the foundation to these allusions.[33]

Mindful of a perspective for Yettishar to turn into a rallying place for coreligionists all over Central Asia, Kaufman, Skobelev, and other high-ranking military commanders on the "pavilions" convinced the tsar and Gorchakov of the necessity of inflicting a decisive blow upon Khokand. This attack resulted in the ultimate defeat of the insurgents and the devastation of the capital on September 11, 1875. In compliance with a treaty that was signed a month later, a new puppet khan, Said Nasir-u-din, ceded to Russia all the territories located on the right bank of the Syr Daria, along with the lands sandwiched between it and the Marin River. The newly conquered lands were immediately proclaimed a new district of Namanghan under the Russian government. After a last desperate attempt by Said Nasir-u-din to rebuff the Russian offensive by obtaining war matériel and financial subsidies from Punjab ended in failure, because the British colonial authorities ignored all his pleas for immediate support, the khan was dethroned by Kaufman and the territory of the khanate became the Russian province of Ferghana in February 1876.[34]

Although the European public regarded such an outcome as a lesser evil in comparison with the chaos and disorder that had reigned in the khanate before the Russian occupation, the British ruling elites feared that Russia would take the liquidation of Khokand as a pretext to activate the Great Game in Kashgaria, bordering the provinces that had been incorporated into the Romanovs' Empire by that time. The aggravation of international tension in the Balkans intensified these concerns, inasmuch as the Tory Cabinet, which was involved diplomatically in the Russo-Turkish conflict, sought to find some appropriate means of response both in Europe and at the far approaches to India.[35]

For their part, some Russian observers—for example, Vasily Vasiliev, a professor of Sinology at the University of Saint Petersburg—again pointed to the eventual British intrigues in the hinterland of Central Asia, if a new Russo-Turkish war were to break out. In a memo to Miliutin, he wrote:

On entering the war against us, the Englishmen certainly will not miss a single means to trouble us; they will probably make an attempt to equip our petty foes, the Turkmen; they will instigate Khiva, Bokhara, the state of Yakub Beg and the Emir of Afghanistan; they will dispatch emissaries to our Muslim subjects and socialist revolutionaries [*sic*].[36]

Significantly, Vasiliev proposed to the war minister to make a defensive alliance with China in order to coerce Peking to dispatch military contingents to Burma, Nepal, and Kashgaria with the purpose of diverting the attention of the Tory Cabinet from the northwest Indian frontier. It would be then possible for Russia, in Vasiliev's view, to draw the British away from Hindustan and twist the arms of the rulers of Kashmir and Afghanistan.[37]

In this connection, Mikhail Veniukov even suggested a political transformation of Eurasia. He maintained that Russia and China, as the largest continental empires, ought to unite in efforts to oppose their common foes—Britain, its puppet Islamic states, and the warlike nomadic tribes, who had been incited by the puppet states against Russia. Veniukov was certain that a breakup of China would afflict the Russian Empire, and vice versa.[38] Though regarding proposals to interpose a belt of buffer states between the Russian and British possessions in Central Asia as utterly unreal, he believed that such a neutral zone would leave the Russian frontiers unprotected and doom Russia, like the Ottoman Empire, to perpetual military conflicts on its borders.[39]

However, the Tsarist government vacillated between application of "hard" and "soft" power in dealing with Yakub Beg of Kashgaria. On the one hand, Kaufman, an advocate of a buffer state policy, albeit according to his own understanding, sought to bolster him as a quasi-independent ruler under the aegis of the Russian Empire, for such tactics would ensure Russia's geopolitical and trade interests in Eastern Turkestan with less budgeted spending.[40] Not coincidentally, he continued to be in correspondence with the potentate and his elder son—a claimant to the throne, Beg Kuli Beg. One could be led to believe that Kaufman sounded them out on the possibility of a gradual transformation of

Yettishar into a third Russian protectorate, following the example of Bokhara and Khiva. Peter Stremoukhov, the director of the Foreign Ministry's Asian Department, also sympathized with this scenario.[41]

The annihilation of Khokand and the events in the Balkans compelled the Tsarist authorities to dispatch an extraordinary political mission to Yettishar in May 1876. Captain Aleksei Kuropatkin, as its head, was instructed by Kaufman to negotiate amendments to be made in the boundary regulations, whereas a hidden agenda for the trip envisaged the collection of intelligence about Yakub Beg's genuine intentions. Shortly afterward, Kuropatkin reported on his impressions to the Main Staff:

> The knowledge of Kashgaria that we possessed at the time was not merely incomplete, but it, to a considerable degree, exaggerated the real power of the ruler of the country and the importance of the state, which he had founded. We saw in Kashgaria a powerful Muslim state, to which, as to a centre would be drawn the sympathy of the population, not only of the weak Muslims which had preserved their independence but also that of the population of the provinces which we have conquered. The significance of Kashgaria in our eyes was, moreover, increased in consequence of the attempts of the English to draw this country to their side, so as to incorporate it, first, in a neutral zone of countries, which was to separate Russia from India; and, second, to acquire in Kashgaria a fresh market for the sale of their manufactured goods.[42]

Some contemporaries and later historians juxtaposed this mission with the earlier trips to Yettishar undertaken by the aforementioned T. Forsyth.[43] However, there is every evidence to believe that in spite of all nuances, the notorious Muslim ruler preferred to avoid taking either the British or Russian side in an attempt to retain his independence and power at any cost.[44] But the imminent Russo-Chinese collaboration, along with money grants and a supply of war ammunition from Calcutta, determined his final choice in favor of the British. The secret contacts with the delegates from Constantinople and the mass migration of the Dungans to Russian Turkestan also contributed to the emir's pro-British and pro-Turkish orientation. In fact, the visits of his closest adviser, Seid Yakub Khan, to Constantinople, Calcutta, and even London coincided with the British viceroy Lord Lytton's conduct of the buffer state policy, including his project to reconcile Yakub Beg with the Peking government.[45] Apparently, the impending Russo-Turkish War became the "last drop," which motivated the Kashgarian ruler to rely not upon the Russians but the British in the strengthening of his regime.[46] As Kaufman analyzed the hidden underpinnings of the rapprochement between Yakub Beg and Lytton as early as in June 1870:

> There is reason to believe that the excited feeling which prevails throughout these countries [in the Middle East and Inner Asia], and more especially among the Afghans, that owing to an implacable hatred of one another the Russian and English must sooner or later come to blows in Asia.[47]

Thus it was small wonder that the "military party" at the Court of Saint Petersburg strongly disapproved of any diplomatic contacts with Kashgaria. Even Gorchakov and Kaufman, who were annoyed by the intensification of political dialogue between Yakub Beg and the government of India, succumbed to plans to overthrow the newly established potentate. Thus, the extraordinary conference that was convoked by Tsar Alexander II to elaborate the necessary arrangements to be made to protect Russian Turkestan from any invasion from abroad viewed the traditional Qing Empire as a more desirable neighbor state for Russia than Yettishar. Finally, the tsar countenanced the resolution of the conference to render no assistance to Yakub Beg in anticipation of the advancing punitive armed forces sent to Kashgaria by the Qings. Moreover, the Cabinet of Saint Petersburg decided to provision the Manchu troops under the command of General Tso Tsungtang with forage and grains.[48]

On the whole, a combination of a high poll tax on merchants and peasants imposed by the emir, the bloody repressions against non-Islamic dissidents committed by his satraps, the offensive launched by the Chinese, and the diplomatic pressure brought by the Russians upon the ruler destabilized the regime of Yakub Beg. The sudden death of the emir on May 29, 1877, added to all misfortunes that had fallen upon Yettishar, bringing the state to the point of collapse after the victorious Chinese troops suppressed the last hotbeds of resistance and captured the city of Kashgar early the next year.[49] Characteristically, Adjutant General Kaufman wrote to a correspondent on December 27, 1877:

A piece of news has been received that the khanate of Kashgaria, this favourite creation of the Englishmen, this powerful Muslim state, in their opinion, the state, which, they believed, would arrest our progressive movement to India, has collapsed.[50]

The reconquest of Kashgaria by the Qing Empire corresponded with two armed conflicts that afflicted the Great Game in the long run: the Russo-Turkish War and the Anglo-Afghan War. Because the Tsarist government was engaged in warlike preparations, Peking stepped up its plan to regain the Ili District, which had been occupied by Russian troops in 1871. Nor was that all; the Chinese government applied to London for diplomatic backing in the period when the Foreign Office embarked on putting together a coalition of European powers, including France and Germany, to oppose Russian ambitions not solely in the Balkans but also in Asian regions, the Middle East being a typical paragon.[51]

According to the American historian Immanuel Hsue, whose study covered the Ili crisis in Sino-Russian relations, the British plenipotentiary minister to Peking "inquired London about the possibility of Chinese employment of British officers and that the Foreign Office, the War Office and the Admiralty in the Disraeli's ministry agreed to allow British officers to enter the Chinese army before the war [Russo-Chinese] broke out."[52] The lobbying groups in Parliament supported this plea. It should be noted that the diplomatic staff of the British Embassy in Saint Petersburg acted as confidential advisers to the Chinese delegation on its arrival in Russia to negotiate the problem of the Ili with Gorchakov and Miliutin, while Sir George Macartney, later to become the first British consul to Kashgaria, assumed the duties of the secretary of Chung Hou—the envoy extraordinary and plenipotentiary to the Court of Alexander II.[53]

Most Russian scholars put the blame for this crisis upon the British, who had allegedly provoked tension in Russo-Chinese relations in order to tie the hands of Tsarist generals in the Balkans and Afghanistan. For example, Aleksei Voskresensky argues that Disraeli and his Cabinet were disappointed with the conclusion of the Russo-Chinese Treaty of 1879, because it could diminish the British sphere of influence in Central Asia.[54]

The diplomatic correspondence illustrates Russian efforts to boost preparations for a war against China after the Peking government disavowed the treaty signed by Chung Hou, obviously an easygoing Mandarin, on October 2, 1879. In compliance with its provisions, the Qing Empire was obliged to pay 5 million rubles to reimburse the damage that the Russians had suffered during the occupation of Kuldja by the Muslim rebels as well as to open a new caravan route for Russian brick-tea traders. The Peking government, furthermore, had to leave Russia in possession of 70 percent of the province of Kuldja, along with strategic passes in the Tien Shan Mountains.[55]

There is strong evidence for believing that Tsarist strategists anticipated a war against China, both in Eastern Turkestan and in the Far East. To compel the Qings to agree to the conditions of a draft treaty, Kaufman outlined a short-term scheme for the offensive military campaign in Chinese Turkestan. Simultaneously, Russian vanguard troops were reinforced, rearmed, and reorganized along the Far Eastern section of the Russo-Chinese border in order to efficiently resist an eventual counteroffensive that the Peking government might launch in the Far Eastern Priamur and Ussuri provinces.[56] At the same time, a squadron of battleships was directed to sail off to the Pacific, because, as the Russian military attaché to London, Major General Alexander Gorlov, reported to Miliutin in November 1877, various scenarios for a naval war in the Pacific were being actively discussed by the staff at the Admiralty. That is why Gorlov suggested a series of reciprocal actions, including the recruitment of a gang of saboteurs from the Irish living in San Francisco to organize a terrorist attack on the harbor of Vancouver in British Canada. According to Gorlov, a number of leaders of the Irish nationalist movement were even about to initiate the formation of a special Irish brigade of volunteers as a separate detachment to join Russian troops fighting the Anglo-Indian army in Central Asia. Another proposal of the military attaché was to employ Chinese subjects in Hong Kong to commit acts of sabotage against the local British naval authorities.[57]

It should be reiterated that Russia's War Ministry and Foreign Ministry received the memoranda submitted by military experts, diplomatic staff members, public leaders, and even academic scholars, who suggested how to defend the Russian positions in Asia. In March 1878, for example, a certain Captain Lieutenant Semechkin called for arrangements to be made for a "cruise war" against the British Empire on maritime communications.[58] Almost simultaneously, in January 1878, the Naval Ministry ordered the chief of the Russian squadron in the Pacific, Adjutant General Lesovsky, to collect intelligence at Russian consulates on the organization of the naval defenses in British overseas settlements.[59]

Five years later, a memorandum from British naval experts interpreted the risks of a war at sea against the Russian Empire in the following way:

> In 1878, when our relations with Russia were strained, it was generally believed that, in the event of war between the two countries, Russia's objectives in a naval campaign would have been the capture and destruction of our commerce on the high seas, and the attack of our then almost unprotected colonies.[60]

Appendix D to this memorandum contained the Russian schemes of war in 1877–78 intercepted by the British intelligence agents. For example, Colonel Bodisco argued for a simultaneous naval attack upon Newcastle in the Atlantic, Hong Kong and Singapore in the Pacific, and the major seaports of Australia. His fantastic project, nevertheless, was adopted by Admiral Lesovsky, who delegated five naval officers on a reconnaissance mission to Melbourne and Sydney.[61]

The more the diplomatic crisis deepened in the winter 1879–80, the more intensified became the critical campaign in China against Russia. Some statesmen accused the Romanovs' Empire of ominous designs to annex those Qing provinces that adjoined its frontier zone. Sir Robert Hart, the long-term inspector-general of the Chinese Maritime Customs—whose strong, sometimes even overwhelming, influence upon the Peking government was recognized by many his contemporaries[62]—wrote to a friend that the outlook in China seemed very serious: "If Russia attempts coercion, China will fight, and, if not materially aided by foreigners, will be thrashed. The settlement to be made after such a thrashing will wipe a large slice out of Chinese territory: The customs will probably come to grief in scrimmage."[63]

The exchange of correspondence between Tsarist diplomats, political agents, and military commanders testified to the critical situation in Russo-Chinese relations, which were on the brink of an open rupture. On June 24, 1880, two more senior General Staff officers were temporarily assigned to the Far East to find out both the intentions of the Peking government and the situation in the North Pacific.[64] Shortly afterward, Admiral Lesovsky suggested that the naval and war ministers carry out a landing operation against China, taking the Anglo-French invasion of the Qing Empire from the seacoast in 1860 as a pattern. According to his meticulous calculations, in case of war, military spending alone would amount to 6,000,000 rubles and require 25,000 men, 100 cannons, and about 90 ocean vessels to transfer the expeditionary corps from Odessa to the shores of the Yellow Sea.[65]

Yet Russia's internal disorder, which culminated in the assassination of Alexander II by leftist terrorists—coupled with a budget deficit after the Russo-Turkish War and the pressure of the great powers, not excluding Great Britain, upon the Cabinet of Saint Petersburg—made it abstain, albeit only temporarily, from bringing about aggressive designs against China. Conversely, a group of Qing dignitaries, including the governor of the capital province, Li Hungzhang, perceived a high risk for China, even backed by Britain, in entering an open armed confrontation with Russia, also taking into consideration the existing tension in Sino-Japanese relations caused by a conflict over the territorial integrity of the Ryukyu

Islands.[66] That is why both Russia and China preferred to sit at the negotiating table that was set up in Saint Petersburg late in 1880.

The Russo-Chinese Treaty of February 24, 1881, drew a line under the Ili crisis. It resulted in the setting up of a special commission for the delimitation of the boundary between Russian and Chinese Turkestan three months later. As for the local, non-Han Islamic population, about 50 percent had to escape from the Ili District to Russian Turkestan, following the withdrawal of occupying troops from Kuldja in 1883. The next year, the Peking government declared the establishment of a new province—Xinjiang (New Frontier).[67]

Historians have ranked the Ili conflict in different ways; some have pointed to the diplomatic success gained by Peking owing to the Chinese patriots like Marquis Tseng, the Qing representative at the second round of diplomatic consultations; others have been more inclined to focus on the compromise that the two empires reached in the final settlement.[68] However, in this author's opinion, though the Tsarist government had always controlled the situation on the Chinese border, its lenience in the territorial arrangement was due in no small measure to the pressure brought by London upon Saint Petersburg and the lack of international stability in Europe.[69] And even more important, the consideration of the privileges obtained as a ransom for Kuldja seemed more valuable to the Tsardom than acquiring a few thousand square miles of mountain and desert.[70]

Not coincidentally, an eyewitness account in 1886 noted that "at present, the markets of Kashgaria are flooded with Russian fabricates, and it would not an exaggeration to say that all the Kashgarian trade is monopolized by the Russian subjects, who are named the Andijans [after the city of Andijan] here."[71] The appointment of Colonel Nikolai Petrovsky, a former financial adviser to the governor-general of Turkestan, to the post of the Russian consul in Kashgaria in 1882 aimed to further promote Russian commerce in the region. Having served in Eastern Turkestan for more than twenty years (after 1895, as the consul-general), Petrovsky received the cognomen of the "real ruler" of Kashgaria. Some contemporaries characterized him as "a man of strong ambition and dominating personality, temperamental and vain, he was capable of preposterous rudeness and bitter enmity, but he could also, when he wished, be a charming and witty host, urbane and astonishingly well informed about the world's affairs."[72]

Soon after Petrovsky, accompanied by his wife, son, private secretary, and an escort of forty-five Cossacks, arrived in the capital of Chinese Turkestan, he assumed such influence upon the provincial Qing chief administrator (the *amban*) that the latter began to regularly borrow money from the Russian consul to pay monthly salaries to the soldiers and officers in the local military garrison, who were short of regular subsidies from the Peking government.[73] It should be noted that apart from his official functions, Petrovsky was famous for owning a very valuable collection of ancient manuscripts in different Oriental languages of more than 1,500 copies, which is now in the State Hermitage in Saint Petersburg. Characteristically, George Macartney, the special assistant for Chinese affairs to the resident in Kashmir, later also to become consul in Xinjiang, and a son of Halliday Macartney, who had accompanied the Qing delegates to Saint Petersburg during the Ili crisis of 1879–81, evaluated the role of Petrovsky in the formulation of the Russian policy toward China. Such respected and experienced explorers as Francis Younghusband and Ralph Cobbold, who repeatedly made their way via Kashgar to High Asia in the late 1880s and 1890s, used to confer with Petrovsky in order to find out his opinion on the current situation in the region.[74] As some modern British scholars maintain, when Cobbold arrived in Kashgar in 1898, he found the consul-general to be one of the best-informed officials he had ever met, whereas Younghusband was particularly fascinated by Petrovsky's collection of topographic instruments and his interest in astronomy and earthquakes—though, on the other side, the traveler noticed such negative features of Petrovsky's personality as supreme egoism, vengefulness, and a lack of ability to speak Chinese.[75] Even Lord Kimberley, the secretary of state for India, pointed to the significance of the Russian consular position in Kashgaria being designated to act as an observatory point at the gates of Afghanistan, India, and China, when he commented on December 5, 1884, that a British Consul ought to be as safe at Kashgar as a Russian [Petrovsky], and the position seems to me to be one of some importance for the observation of Russian movements on the northern frontier of Afghanistan and Chitral, and for the promotion of our trade.[76]

In reality, Consul Petrovsky set up an ample spy network to collect intelligence about not only Chinese Turkestan but also the Pamirs. He was a Russian pioneer in recruiting natives to serve as secret agents in Asian countries and British India, according to a scheme that he proposed to the foreign minister in February 1887. Interestingly, he even sketched a kind of instructive circular letter containing the issues of interest to Russian military intelligence in Inner Asia.[77] Though this initiative was cast into a dustbin, Nikolai Notovich, an experienced diplomatic official on the staff of the Turkestan governor-general, nonetheless appreciated Petrovsky's contribution to the establishment of a modern intelligence service on the outskirts of the Russian Empire.[78] Cobbold, who traversed the Pamirs in 1897–98, was especially struck by Russian Turkestan officers' lore about the region. "This I put down as being due to the extensive system of espionage which is encouraged by the Russian government along the Indian frontier," wrote the explorer in his book.[79]

Consequently, Russian and British perceptions of the stalemate in Chinese Turkestan differed. For example, Colonel Beliavsky of the General Staff depicted Russian progress there in a secret brochure submitted for the consideration of the war minister on December 5, 1884:

This part of the Qing Empire is looked upon as a vulnerable one, because the Muslim people, hostile to the Chinese and often rebellious in the past, inhabit it. The natural environment of Chinese Turkestan, which is separated by the vast deserts from other populated and productive territories of the Celestial Empire, severely hampers its defense and the deployment of troops by the Chinese. But at the same time, the environment deprives our offensive in this direction of significance.... That is why an opinion prevails that this theater of military operations should be ranked as the secondary one in case of war with China.[80]

Some Tsarist military thinkers believed, moreover, that Kashgaria would inevitably fall into Russia's hands like a ripe fruit because of its predominant influence upon Chinese Turkestan and the hatred of the Muslim population for the local Chinese authorities.[81]

On the other side, a severe deterioration in Russo-British relations by the mid-1880s due to events in Turkmenia, which are examined below, also instigated some Anglo-Indian newspapers to reanimate the problem of Kashgaria. For example, *The Pioneer Mail* published an article titled "The Anglo-Chinese Alliance" on July 26, 1885. Its key idea was a canalization of China's activity to Xinjiang in order to counteract Russian aggression with the aid of local Muslims backed financially by the British. "On condition we are in the Chinese government's good books and enjoy the favour of Islamic people in Asia," maintained the author of the article, "we would be able to convert the Tien Shan Range into a unsurpassable hindrance for the Russians, at least up to Kashgar in the west; we would be also in a position to set up military settlements in Kashgaria and in this way to strengthen our power in Afghanistan. Hence, on concluding an alliance with Persia and Turkey, we would have every reason to hope to repulse the Russians from Turkestan and Armenia [*sic*]."[82]

Although such pathfinders as Nikolai Przhevalsky, Bronislav Grombchevsky, Peter Kozlov, Ney Elias, Alexander Hosie, and Francis Younghusband, not to mention many other adventurous spirits, continued to ramble about the mountains and deserts of Eastern Turkestan,[83] it had ceased to be one of major "playfields" of the Great Game after the end of the Ili crisis. The attention of the European public was again attracted to the situation in Xinjiang not earlier than in the 1930s, when a new, massive uprising of Chinese Muslims led to the establishment of the self-governing Uighur Republic under informal Soviet protection. This was, however, quite another episode, which needs a separate study.

THE AFGHAN KNOT AND THE ABORTIVE
RUSSIAN MARCH TO INDIA

Throughout the second half of the 1870s and the first half of the 1880s, the Afghan knot proved a real fulcrum for Russo-British relations. The question may be asked, What was its core, and how did it contribute to the culmination of the Great Game?

To give an exhaustive survey of the Afghan problem, one should bear in mind the developments in the Balkans and the Near East, where the great powers scrambled for supremacy at that time. In addition, the decline of the Ottoman Empire and the liberation movement of the Slavonic nations led to the escalation of tension in the Turkish Straits. Regrettably—as the head of the Main Staff's Asian Division, Colonel Aleksei Kuropatkin, postulated in a note dated March 18, 1879—in general, Russia was "a means for the European Slavs, but not an objective." Kuropatkin definitely foresaw that "on gaining an autonomous status or even independence with the help of Russia, the Slavonic countries will ignore her, if being compelled to alienate her; they may, moreover, side with our foes on a free basis." To exclude this alternative and become unassailable to any foreign power in the Black Sea Basin, according to Kuropatkin, Russia was bound to capture at least the Strait of Bosporus.[84]

The beginning of hostilities between Russia and Turkey on April 24, 1877, and the subsequent avalanche movement of Tsarist troops across the Balkans to Constantinople, shocked public opinion in Europe, though many ordinary people sympathized with aspirations to draw the Turks away from the Balkan Peninsula. "If the Russians reach Constantinople, the Queen would be so humiliated that she thinks she would immediately abdicate," wrote Her Majesty to Disraeli, urging him to "be bold" in the confrontation with Russia.[85] British leadership circles anticipated the consolidation of Russia in the Eastern Mediterranean and the degeneration of Turkish power there, which would have a "domino" effect upon Persia, on Afghanistan, and, in the final account, on British India. As early as April 1875, Lord Loftus, the ambassador to Saint Petersburg, communicated to Lord Derby, then the foreign secretary, his concerns about a probable shift of accent in Middle Eastern and Asian politics:

> From private information which has reached me, I am inclined to think that the Russian government have some notion of forming a separate independent state of the province of Herat detached from the sovereignty of Afghanistan, and charged, in common understanding with Persia and Russia, to keep under subjection the Teke Turkmen; or that, if the constitution of an independent state should be impracticable, they [the Russians] may seek to gain the entire support of Persia by holding out to the Shah the hopes of requiring Herat and the surrounding district as a tributary state under the government of Abdur Rahman Khan, now enjoying the protection of the Russian government at Samarkand.[86]

To augment the prestige of Britain in Asia, Queen Victoria officially took the title of the empress of India at the strong recommendation of Disraeli on April 26, 1876. The prime minister repeatedly avowed his antipathy for Russia in his regular correspondence with the queen, who, as he wrote, "should order Her armies to clear Central Asia of the Muscovites and drive them into the Caspian."[87] Under these circumstances, Russian military intelligence agents reported to the Main Staff that the British War Office had already worked out an annual plan for a military campaign against Russia, which called for the transportation of 60,000 Anglo-Indian troops to Asia Minor via Afghanistan in compliance with a secret agreement allegedly signed with the emir.[88] Not coincidentally, on November 10, 1876, Miliutin informed Baron Fredericks, the governor-general of Eastern Siberia, that because the Cabinet of Saint Petersburg expected a sudden rupture of diplomatic relations with Britain in the near future, he was committed to outline a plan of defensive arrangements to be made in case hostilities broke out.[89]

It should be noted, however, that pacifist voices were also heard in British ruling circles at that time. For example, Salisbury, though not a "dove" himself, attempted to mollify the reaction to Russian expansionism among the ardent proponents of the "forward" policy at any risk, like Disraeli and Lytton, by opining that

> Russia, mined by revolution, on the very brink of bankruptcy, without one commander of any note, and having to contend even in the defence of her own frontiers against the difficulties of economy, distances and scanty population, was powerless for a distant blow.[90]

Yet, in his reply, Lytton juxtaposed Russia's progress in Asia with the subversive activity in the Great Game's "playfields":

> Now in Central Asia the success of Russia's diplomacy is entirely due to the fact that her diplomatic agents, however unofficial, are everywhere regarded as the scouts and *avant-couriers* of her armies; and that both are perceived to be steadily advancing; that rightly or wrongly, all her Asiatic neighbors believe her to be utterly unscrupulous in her recourse to the sword; and that she both menaces and promises, as against us, more than we can, as against her.[91]

It is not surprising, therefore, that most contemporaries drew attention to the boom in intelligence missions that London and Saint Petersburg repeatedly dispatched to the Middle East and Inner Asia in the course of their uncompromising struggle for supremacy.[92] According to numerous reports submitted by military experts to the India Office Political and Secret Department, the British and Russians meticulously prepared such trips, while, at the same time, drafting counterintelligence measures to prevent foreign spies from penetrating the territories contiguous to their frontier areas.[93] Taking Miliutin's prohibition of Captain Frederick Burnaby's right to enter British India via Russian Turkestan in 1875–76 as a striking instance, it is interesting to consider the arguments of Tsarist bureaucrats: first, insecure routes on land; and second, regular preclusive steps by the government of India to permit Russian military officers to travel to the Raj. As Miliutin wrote to Kaufman,

Apart from the English government's unfavourable attitude to our travelers on the north-west frontier of India, compelling us to act in the same manner with regard to the so-called English tourists in Central Asia, one can not but draw attention to very frequent visits of Great Britain's officers to our borders on the Atrek River [between Turkmenia and Persia] as well as to their contacts with the Teke Turkmen living in the neighborhood of our domains.[94]

Referring to the clandestine activity of both empires, one may call the period of the 1870s and 1880s a benchmark in the history of their intelligence structures. The military reforms promulgated by Miliutin and Cardwell at the apogee of the Great Game spawned several modern intelligence institutions, such as the Military Academic Committee of the Main Staff and the Naval Military Academic Section of the Main Naval Staff in Russia, along with the Intelligence Branch and the Foreign Intelligence Committee in Britain.[95] In addition, the Colonial Defence Committee was inaugurated to meet the new challenges in foreign affairs in 1878–79.[96] Although it functioned episodically, Salisbury, who was convinced that Russian intelligence obtained information about the meetings of the Cabinet through a certain informant on the staff,[97] urged the secretary for war to reestablish it on new grounds during the Turkmen crisis (see the next section). Soon, this coordinative board became the embryo of the Committee of Imperial Defence, which was renowned for its contribution to strategic planning and decisionmaking processes in the twentieth century.[98] Simultaneously, the reorganization of the Intelligence Department was set in motion by the Anglo-Indian government.[99]

On arriving in Calcutta in 1876, Lord Lytton suggested undertaking countermeasures not merely to strengthen Indian defenses but also to increase British influence upon Afghanistan. According to Johnson, "already on appointment, Lytton had drawn up a new agreement with the khan of Khelat and took Quetta as a forward base from which to strike upon Kandahar. Lytton also considered Salisbury's idea of delegating a British political resident to Kabul 'to be worthy of implementation as soon as possible.'"[100] The viceroy decided, therefore, to forward a special diplomatic mission headed by his representative, Louis Pelly, to the emir of Afghanistan. The mission aimed to inform Sher Ali Khan of Lytton's inauguration as the new viceroy in Calcutta and, what was more important, to sound out the political situation in the country.

Yet the emir refused to accept the delegates. The Anglo-Afghan negotiations, spurred by simultaneous Russian progress in Turkmenia, recommenced at the Peshawar conference held in January–March 1877. But any attempts by Lytton to get written permission from the emir to station British political agents in several towns along the northern Afghan frontier in order keep abreast of all current developments in Russian Turkestan, Persia, and Turkmenia proved abortive. On paper, Britain's influence on Afghanistan appeared to be of paramount importance, because the emir was subsidized by the Indian government on a regular basis; in reality, however, the British preferred to stand aloof from internal feuds and settle them only to uphold a particular claimant to the throne or to curb the ruler's encroachments upon neighboring states.[101]

The stalemate at the Peshawar conference because of the unexpected demise of the emir's plenipotentiary envoy at the end of March 1877 slowed down the Anglo-Afghan diplomatic dialogue. The verity would seem to hold that the Cabinet of Saint James was entrapped by the conflict between controversial tendencies in Middle Eastern and Asian policy. On the one hand, they were alarmed by Russian intrigues on the northern frontiers of Afghanistan and Persia, be they real or imaginative. Yet on the other hand, some "forward-ists" in London and Calcutta still cherished the idea of a coalition of "buffer states," like Afghanistan, with a handful of minor frontier khanates in the Russophobe Muslim League, though this scenario would threaten the position of Britain itself.[102] That is why the policy of both the Cabinet of Saint James and the Anglo-Indian government under Lytton needed justifying arguments in order to apply military means to the Afghan problem. In their view, Russia's war victories in the Balkans and Transcaucasia, along with its military preparations in Turkestan, might be considered as such arguments.

On the Russian side, the bellicose Pan-Slavic Party at the Court also saw a good opportunity to kill two birds with one stone: first, to realize their age-old dream of a Tsarist banner fluttering above Saint Sophia Cathedral in Constantinople; and, second, to use Afghanistan as a springboard for a campaign against the British Raj. In the latter case, Tsarist military planners set about elaborating a detailed scheme for an invasion while bearing in mind all preceding projects. As Veniukov assessed the state of matters,

> The continental lands of British Asia may and should be regarded as a theater of war, in which any chances for success will depend upon how Britain's adversaries, be they inner or outer, will use physical conditions of environment, how they will adapt to them and disable the Englishmen to defend a vast but alien and even inimical country without possible transportation of numerous reinforcements from the metropolis.[103]

According to Veniukov and other military scholars, a paucity of logistical infrastructure and the vulnerability of communication routes definitely prevented British military commanders from undertaking counteroffensive operations against Tsarist troops at the initial stage of a future campaign. The multiethnic and multireligious composition of the Indian army was regarded as an additional obstacle to the British counterstroke. Some British military writers grumbled in their essays that the Anglo-Indian army "possessed neither the devoted attachment to our rule nor the ability to be more than a neutral factor in the question to make us desire such a reform."[104] Besides, native soldiers were not expected by Russian strategists to demonstrate their high fighting spirit in case of a Russian attack.[105]

It might be an oversimplification, however, to ignore some Russian contemporary journalists, who drew public attention to the threat of a Muslim uprising in the rear of the Russian armies, similar to that in the Caucasus region during the Russo-Turkish War of 1877–78. For example, Vasiliev submitted a note to Miliutin warning him of British endeavors to furnish some bellicose nomadic tribes on the southern frontier of Turkestan with war matériel. Curiously enough, Vasiliev even attributed to the British a design to employ agents provocateurs to "preach socialism [*sic*] to the Moslem subjects of the tsar in the empire."[106]

On February 13, 1878, a British navy squadron sailed into the Marmara Sea and dropped anchor in view of the Prince Islands. Immediately, the Tory Cabinet interpellated and Parliament voted for a credit of £6 million; military reservists were called out in the British Isles, and seven regiments of the Indian army were transported from India to Malta. Mindful of these war preparations, coupled with the unprecedented diplomatic pressure upon Saint Petersburg by Whitehall, the Tsarist generals stopped their troops at the gates of Constantinople. When chauvinistic campaigns in the press reached their culmination, and the military parties in both countries urged their governments to commence a military campaign, a new Russo–British armed conflict seemed imminent to everybody in Europe.

Under such circumstances, Colonel Leonid Sobolev, a former active officer in Turkestan and the chief of the Main Staff's Asian Division, suggested that Miliutin send to Kabul a special Russian envoy, who would coordinate a march of Cossacks toward the Upper Oxus and further to India via Afghanistan. This planned action was considered by Sobolev to constitute retaliation upon the British for their anti–Russian intrigues both in the Balkans and the Near East and, in this way, to divert the attention of Whitehall from the Turkish Straits.[107] Sobolev predicted that

> the movement of Russian troops will not only shake but destroy the British Empire in India, while the aftermath of such destruction will be of so immense significance that the whole world is convulsed. England then will be deleted from the register of the great powers and Russia will represent herself as an absolute master of Asia.[108]

Supported by Miliutin, Sobolev addressed his plan to Governor-General Kaufman, whose staff proceeded to draft it in full detail. The situation became even more dangerous after Mikhail Skobelev, the victorious "white general" in the Russo–Turkish War, proposed to the tsar to form an alliance with Sher Ali Khan for the purpose of ensuring a safe transition of invaders through his domains on their route to the Indus River.[109] In his turn, Kaufman suggested taking Afghanistan under the protection of Russia after the example of Bokhara, and to convert Persia into a similar vassal state. The implementation of these plans, to Kaufman's mind, would frustrate British policy in the Balkans and diminish the prestige of Great Britain as a great power in Asia. On April 4, 1878, he sent a ciphered telegram to Count Feodor Heiden, the head of the Main Staff:

> The interests of England may be in jeopardy if Turkestan detachments are removed closer to the Amu [Daria], to Sherabad, while the corps of 10,000–15,000 to be transported from the Caucasus region and Petro-Alexandrovsk on the Caspian coast in order to march toward Merv. The success depends on the position of Afghanistan. It is possible to get in contact with the ruler.[110]

Two weeks later, Miliutin reported to the tsar that, though the march to India appeared to him immensely risky, given the lack of appropriate expeditionary forces and the deficit in the military budget, the Russians would be able to reconnoiter accessible routes to Hindustan and pacify warlike nomads in Afghanistan.[111]

After a preliminary armistice between Russia and Turkey was signed in Santo Stephano, Alexander II conferred with his ministers and experts on perspectives for Russian policy in Central Asia. A memo from the privy counselor, Nikolai Tornau, called for a direct invasion of India through Astrabad in Persian Khorasan, and Herat in North Afghanistan.[112] Although Alexander Bariatinsky and Tornau, supported by Kaufman, all advocated this plan, Nikolai Giers, Nikolai Kryzhanovsky, and the grand dukes seemed rather skeptical about its realization. Miliutin, for his part, pointed out the prematureness of such an advance toward India, though he did not discard the general scheme. He proposed instead to invade the territory of North Afghanistan with sixty companies of infantry (12,000 combatants) and twenty-six Cossack squadrons (3,328 horsemen).[113]

Significantly, Ronald Thomson, the British minister to Tehran, inter-cepted a copy of the statement exposing Russia's strategic goals. As he commented on the hazards of Russian intervention of the Raj,

> Its general tenor bore on the necessity of restraining the greed and rapacity of the "Despot of the seas"; it said that the English exche-quer was enriched by 20,000,000 pounds a year from the rev-enues of India, and that the entire gain to Great Britain from the whole of India was 6.5 million pounds a day; that if the English were expelled from India, tumults would subvert the government and extinguish the political influence possessed by England with other nations; it was not intended, however, that Russia should seize India herself, but that the English should be dispossessed of it, and the country restored to its former possessors, inasmuch as the people of India would be in revolt and rebellion when they hear that Russian troops are marching towards their country to restore to them their freedom. Another factor in the successful accomplishment of this plan would be an understanding with the Afghans, who eagerly await the opportunity which the approach of an ally would give them to avenge the past of England. The movement of Russian troops towards India would compel the English to detach a large portion of her military force to defend her territory and thus her power would be weakened in Europe.[114]

Typically, Miliutin envisaged secret contacts with a number of Indian maharajas and the Armenian priests employed by Russian intelligence agents in Afghanistan and India.[115]

In the course of military preparations, the Tsarist strategists also debated the role of Persia and the situation in Turkmenia. Although the Turkmenian problem is thoroughly studied in the next section, the Persian question needs to be narrated here.

Despite Persia's typical state of decay in the second half of the nine-teenth century, some contemporaries regarded it as a regional state of paramount strategic significance. According to Lieutenant Colonel Arthur Cory, this country occupied a flanking position, which would enable any willing power to inflict a blow upon Russian Turkestan and the Caucasus.[116] In Eugene Schuyler's view, "the only danger to India from Russia lies through Persia."[117] Ludvig Iessen, an official on the staff of the Russian Foreign Ministry, likewise dwelt upon Persia's essential role as a continental bridge between the Mediterranean and South Asia.[118]

However, other military writers pointed to the fact that a defensive alliance with Tehran would only expand the theater of operations and annoy the emir of Afghanistan, Sher Ali Khan, to the benefit of Britain. That is why Persia's benevolent neutrality, in their judgment, would suit Russia's interests more than a Russo-Persian alliance of any kind.[119] At the same time, the shah's government avoided taking the side of Britain or Russia in bargaining with the great powers. For instance, Malcolm Khan, the Persian minister to London, made it clear to Lord Salisbury that

> the policy pursued by Russia was bringing about the annexation of Merv, a measure which Persia could prevent with the assistance of England; the most obvious mode of rendering such assistance was by placing Herat in her hands, though there were other means at hand, notably more effective armaments. In short, this was the critical moment, the point from which the policy of Persia must definitely turn towards Russia or England.[120]

Meanwhile, Miliutin's instructions to Kaufman of April 25, 1878, spurred the preparations for the Indian march. They proclaimed a temporary reinforcement of Turkestan District troops of up to 12,000 men in the initial period, plus 8,000 supplementary recruits to be delivered to the theater of operations by July 1878. The main column of invaders, commanded by Major General Mikhail Trotsky, was designated to proceed via Bokhara and Samarkand to Kabul and the Khyber Pass; the second detachment, headed by Colonel Alexander Grotenhelm, was directed to advance from the Russian Trans-Caspian stronghold Petro-Alexandrovsk to Chardjui; and the third contingent, under the command of Major General Abramov, was bound to set off from Samarkand across the Alai Mountains to invade Chitral and move further into the Valley of Kashmir. Adjutant General Kaufman took responsibility for the general supervision of the campaign. He was committed by the tsar to delegate a plenipotentiary ambassador to Sher Ali Khan.[121]

Pursuant to this general scheme, the marching units consisted of 12,000 infantry men and 4,292 Cossacks armed with 50 artillery cannons and 12 rocket batteries. Yet, by July 17, 1878, the troops, which were concentrated at Djam, a settlement 45 kilometers south of Samarkand, amounted to merely 9,600 infantry and 3,560 mounted combatants suffering from severe sandstorms and extreme heat.[122] According to a final report on the operation, only one column reached the assembly point, while the supplementary detachments had not left the places of their permanent deployment in a final count.[123]

On August 1, 1878, even the assembled battalions were disbanded after the Russian and Ottoman Empires had signed the peace treaty at the Berlin Congress. It may be regarded as an unsuccessful demonstration of military power, though the firsthand accounts testified to the gravity of intentions on the Russian side. According to Ivan Yavorsky, who was an eyewitness of the "military fever" in Tashkent in May 1878, both military chiefs and privates were immensely enthusiastic about the future offensive, though its ultimate goal seemed to them rather vague; nobody among rank-and-file soldiers or subalterns knew for sure what kind of adversary they would have to fight in a week or so.[124]

The march toward India failed for several reasons. An overall exhaustion of the Russian half-feudal economy because of the Russo-Turkish War was apparent to everybody in the Romanovs' Empire, while inadequate logistics, especially the railroads between European Russia and Central Asia, contributed to unfavorable conditions. The deficit of troops, war matériel, and provisions in quantity and quality in order to wage war on a massive scale revealed the obvious uselessness of the original scheme of the military campaign. Finally, the concerns of the Muslim nations not to welcome a promulgated Russian invasion of Afghanistan, Persia, or India were evidently not far from the truth. The allegations of other kinds, for example, that of the contagious diseases which prevented Tsarist generals from their march to India, lay beyond any critics.[125]

On the other side, it appears absolutely incorrect to depict this project and all the steps taken by Kaufman and his subordinates as a mere nonaggressive stroll, or rattling the saber on the Turkestan frontier in order to teach a lesson to the snobbish British.[126] This chapter has already demonstrated that the whole operation was meticulously elaborated by military planners who embarked on bringing it to life, though they stopped at the initial stage. Suffice it to pay heed to the fact that Kaufman set up his headquarters in the field on June 7, 1878. Typically, the tsar directed the war minister to equalize the deployment of the assembled detachments at Djam for a real military campaign.[127]

This inference is vindicated by the attention attributed to the "Indian march" in London and Calcutta. Lord Salisbury, the newly appointed foreign secretary, got the first, though slightly distorted, information about the matter from the ambassador to Constantinople as early as May 12, 1878. The ambassador miscalculated the overall quantity of active Russian troops at 50,000 combatants.[128] Later, the acting foreign minister, Nikolai Giers, categorically insisted in a conversation with Ambassador Loftus that

> there had been a moment when war appeared to be almost imminent, and that, under those circumstances, no doubt the military commanders conceived it to be their duty to make such arrangements as might be essential and serviceable to their country.[129]

According to the British diplomat, Giers denied that any Russian intrigues in Kabul were in progress at that time, though the ambassadorial mission headed by Major General Nikolai Stolietov had already started off from Tashkent to Kabul. Although the Tsarist government regarded this mission as another shrewd diplomatic move to induce the emir of Afghanistan to side with Russia, it seems absolutely wrong to suppose that Stolietov had left Tashkent for Kabul with instructions received from Miliutin alone.[130] It was Giers who informed Kaufman about the objectives of Stolietov's mission on May 11, 1878. The acting foreign minister considered Stolietov capable of provoking the emir's distrust and opposition to any British diplomatic overture, in exchange for Russian subsidies and obligation to ally with Afghanistan in case of an eventual armed encroachment by Britain.[131]

The inspection of Kaufman's correspondence with Sher Ali Khan in the Persian language for nearly a decade, from March 1870 to February 1879—which was captured by the British after they occupied Kabul in the course of the Second Anglo-Afghan War—also revealed the hidden agenda of Stolietov's ambassadorial mission: It aimed to encourage Sher Ali to allow Russian expeditionary corps to pass through his emirate to India and return safely. The Tsarist government, in the name of Stolietov, proposed making the ruler a presumptive heir of the Turkish sultan—"a puppet in the hands of the British," the very idea for which Stolietov had to inculcate in the mind of the Kabul ruler. In addition, the Russian envoy was instructed to take over the command of a joint Russo-Afghan army, if the potentate of Afghanistan agreed on a military alliance with Russia.[132]

On August 22, 1878, the staff of the Russian Embassy, escorted by more than three hundred Cossacks and Bokharian horsemen, entered Kabul. Stolietov and his military suite were accorded a hearty welcome in an atmosphere of magnificent Oriental ceremonies. During his two-week stay in Kabul, the Russian envoy met with the emir almost every day. The draft Russo-Persian Boundary Convention, which the envoy rendered to the emir, contained eleven articles. Pursuant to this document, the Afghan ruler would have to acknowledge that his country was Russia's protectorate, while the governor-general of Turkestan would take responsibility for any military aid that might be granted to Kabul by the Russian Empire. British secret agents also reported to London that the Russians offered Rs 30 million to the emir to allow the Tsarist armies to pass freely through Afghanistan to India.[133]

Significantly, it was Kaufman who strongly insisted on taking Afghanistan under Russian protection, according to his both private and official correspondence to Miliutin and Alexander II. Yet after consultations, which the tsar and the war minister held with diplomatic and military experts, the notion of a protectorate was turned down by the emperor himself. Alexander II ordered the willful Turkestan governor-general to pursue a more cautious policy with regard to the intricate situation in Europe and the Near East.[134] Besides, the tough negative reaction by the British, who were annoyed by Kaufman's secret projects exposed in a series of panicky telegrams from Calcutta, also devalued Stolietov's mission. According to the intelligence from Kabul, on which the viceroy predicated his alarmist messages to the home Cabinet, the Russians planned to build a railroad from Samarkand to Kabul via Herat along with a telegraph line from Samarkand to Kandahar, and they also planned to install depots for food and forage in the most important logistical hubs of Afghanistan.[135] A memorandum to the War Office on recent Russian military preparations in Central Asia contained the following observations by Colonel F. Clarke:

> The Russians are extending their influence daily over the Kyrgyz of the Alai and Pamir. They have been surveying recently at Sarikol on the Pamir, only nine or ten marches from Gilgit in Kashmir. They are within ear-shot of those principalities of the Upper Oxus, which, while glorying in their independence and tracing their descent from Alexander of Macedon, have been lately annexed, much against their will, to Afghanistan, from the people of which country they differ in religion.[136]

Even such an antagonist to "forward" policy as the duke of Argyll manifested his annoyance with Russian intrigues in Afghanistan:

> I must at once express my opinion that under whatever circumstances or from whatever motives, the Russian mission was sent and was received, it was impossible for the British government to acquiesce in that reception as the close of our transactions with the Emir upon the subject of missions to his court. We cannot allow Russia to acquire predominant, or even co-equal, influence with ourselves in Afghanistan. The Cabinet was, therefore, not only justified in taking, but it was imperatively call upon to take measures to ascertain the real object of that mission, and if it had any political character, to secure that no similar mission should be sent again.[137]

Symptomatically, Miliutin recorded in his personal diary on September 22, 1878:

> The Afghan developments presented a new ground for England to be nervous. In London they are unable to bear the reality that Sher Ali welcomed the Russian ambassadorial mission most heartily while at the same time rebuffing the British one. But what a noise they will make on learning that the Afghan ruler had dispatched his own ambassador to Tashkent with a plea to take Afghanistan under the aegis of Russia and with the promise that he would not receive any Englishman in Kabul without the "permission" of General von Kaufman.[138]

What seems even more important, Stolietov promised to the emir to come back to Kabul with 30,000 Russian troops to protect the Afghan ruler from the British intervention or, in any case, to accommodate roughness in relations between Kabul and Calcutta. On leaving the Afghan capital for Tashkent, he directed a group of diplomats and military officers to stay in the city in anticipation of the Russian expeditionary forces, which were due to arrive in Kabul as guarantors of Sher Ali's security. At the same time, the emir handed a special message to Stolietov designated for Alexander II, whereby the emir paid full homage to the Russian emperor.[139]

It would appear probable to presume that the British military-diplomatic mission headed by Major General Neville Chamberlain with an escort of 250 Indian horsemen set off for Kabul in its turn only after Lytton had prevailed on Disraeli and Salisbury that Britain was confronted with a challenge to lose its domination of Afghanistan in favor of Russia.[140] As Major General Gorlov reported from London on October 6, 1878, Britain would launch a war against the regime of Sher Ali even at the risk of a confrontation with Russia, though the majority of politicians as well as the press were convinced that the latter would not interfere with the Anglo-Afghan dispute at all.[141]

In fact, the disinclination of the Russian Foreign Ministry to acknowledge and clarify the objectives and results of Stolietov's ambassadorial mission irritated Salisbury and Lytton. It was only on September 27, after this major general had already returned to Russia and informed the tsar about the situation in Afghanistan, when Gorchakov told the British chargé d'affaires, G. T. Plunkett, that Stolietov's mission should be looked upon merely as a polite, goodwill visit to the emir and that the Russian emperor would not give up his right to dispatch such missions to anyone else in future.[142]

Soviet historians misinterpreted the march toward India planned by the Tsarist strategists in the summer of 1878 and presented Stolietov's escapade as purely peaceful, devoid of any intention to establish a military alliance with Sher Ali.[143] Although the staff of the embassy was awarded decorations and promoted in rank by the tsar,[144] the secret Russo-Afghan alliance proved abortive because the Russian government preferred to abstain from giving any assistance to the ill-fated emir in his hour of need.

Despite the fact that Stolietov's diplomatic fiasco was recognized by the Tsarist ministers, the Russian ambassador to Britain, Prince Alexander Lobanov-Rostovsky, shifted the blame for this failure to the general himself in an interview with Lord Granville.[145]

The story of the British invasion of Afghanistan and the calamities of the Second Anglo-Afghan War, which continued from November 1878 to May 1879, falls outside the scope of this book.[146] What does, however, pertain to the subject was the desire of some British military thinkers to rely upon the assistance of local residents in the struggle against the bellicose Pashtuns.[147] According to reports by native scouts who penetrated inaccessible valleys of Kafiristan from time to time, the indigenous people who inhabited the hill area sandwiched between Afghanistan and British India were of fair skin, had light hair, and worshiped gods but not Allah, as did neighboring Muslim tribes. Hence, a special secret mission commanded by William Lockhart was sent to the principalities in the Hindu Kush to spy on the land in the aftermath of the Anglo-Afghan War. Significantly, the First Scout Corps was also recruited in 1878 from local tribesmen, mainly the Afridis, to protect the current traffic of trade caravans through the Khyber Pass from mounted and armed bandits.[148]

Meanwhile, the Tsarist government declined all requests by Sher Ali Khan to send a Russian expeditionary corps to repulse the British invasion of the country. The Afghan emissaries dispatched by the Kabul ruler to Kaufman proved likewise abortive. When repeatedly asked by the emir about any means of military assistance from the Russians, Major General Nikolai Razgonov, who had been left by Stolietov in Afghanistan as chief representative of the tsar, could merely recommend that Sher Ali wage a guerrilla war against the advancing Anglo-Indian troops.[149] At midnight on December 13, 1878, the last few members of the Russian military-diplomatic mission escaped from Kabul to the northern Afghan town of Mazari-Sharif. Consequently, Sher Ali had nothing to do but to follow his insolvent patrons to the territory of Russian Turkestan, where he died on February 20, 1879. As Miliutin wrote in his diary, "Now we are inclined to make an attempt to resume all our previous agreements with England on Central Asia in order to preserve the independence of Afghanistan, which is necessary to maintain a political balance of power in Russo-British relations."[150]

This meant that Saint Petersburg had actually betrayed its potential ally, along with undertaking a fruitless project to convert Afghanistan into a new Russian vassal state, similar to Bokhara and Khiva. Yet Gorchakov attempted to mollify Kaufman and to explain this retreat from Kabul as a compromise with the British side to avoid interference with the affairs of Afghanistan in exchange for the noninvolvement of Calcutta in the political situation within the borders of Russian Turkestan. Trying to find additional arguments for such a decision, Gorchakov contended that "any sympathies of Asian rulers are extremely insecure, shaky and may involve us in complications which will lead to an imminent breach in the relations with England."[151]

Interestingly, on entering Kabul, the British troops found many things that reminded them of the Russians' short-term sojourn in the capital of Afghanistan. As the commander in chief, General Frederick Roberts, recalled later,

The Afghan *sirdars* [dignitaries] and officers were arrayed in Russian pattern uniforms, Russian money was found in the treasury, Russian wares were sold in the bazaars, and although the roads leading to Central Asia were certainly no better than those leading to India, Russia had taken more advantage of them than we had to carry on commercial dealings with Afghanistan.[152]

The author of the present volume concurs with Brian Robson, a modern historian of the Second Anglo-Afghan War, that the failure of the Russian march to India and the fiasco of Stolietov's ambassadorial mission to the court of the emir predetermined in no small measure the context of the Treaty of Gandamak in 1879, which granted significant concessions to Britain in Afghanistan, including control over the country's foreign policy. The conclusion of the treaty actually led to the establishment of the "buffer zone" amid Russian and British colonial possessions in the Middle East and Inner Asia, which Clarendon and Gorchakov had debated as early as in the 1860s.[153] It should, however, be borne in mind that on losing the Afghan set of the Great Game, Russia was anxious to make a retaliatory move in Turkmenia to revive its prestige and influence throughout Central and East Asia.

THE TURKMEN PROBLEM IN THE GREAT GAME

By the end of the 1870s, Turkmenia remained the only independent area in Central Asia that lay beyond Russian or British spheres of influence, though the rulers of Persia, Afghanistan, Khiva, and Bokhara competed for domination over the Turkmen people. Although the Turkmen consisted of four main tribes—the Yomuds (150,000 men and women), the Teke Turkmen (300,000), the Ersaris (150,000), and the Alimis (250,000)—and countless minor ethnic groups, rambling about spatial arid steppes and deserts from one pasture to another in search of forage for their livestock, a sedentary population also remained in a few oases. Apart from the Turkmen, other nations, such as the Kurds and the Pashtuns, also inhabited Trans-Caspia, concentrated in the districts bordering the territories of Persia and Afghanistan.

The climatic conditions of Trans-Caspia, as described by European travelers, appeared even more severe than those in the Bokharian or Khokandian khanates. Extremely hot weather in the period from April to November; gusty winds imbued with microscopic grains of sand; little fresh drinking water; unexpected attacks by insects like termites and midges, along with poisonous spiders and snakes; the danger of contagious diseases, including pestilence, cholera, and dysentery—all these hindrances prevented various invaders from any attempt to penetrate to the region.

In the course of the Khivian expedition mentioned in the previous chapter, Tsarist military administrators, and above all Governor-General Kaufman, required the Yomuds to pay 300,000 rubles of indemnity for the association with the khan of Khiva against the Russians. According to Burnaby and Schuyler, the indemnity debt was only a pretext for a sudden attack by Tsarist troops on this Turkmen tribe at the end of July 1873. This resulted in the massacre of the Yomuds, the devastation of their *kishlaks* (villages), and the capture of their livestock.[154] Significantly, the ruler of Khiva benefited greatly from this merciless destruction of the northern Turkmen tribes, inasmuch as his domains were saved from frequent forays.[155] After the subjugation of the Youmud Turkmen, just two Turkmen districts—the Akhal and Merv oases—remained independent.

Meanwhile, on March 21 1874, Tsar Alexander II adopted the Regulations for the Establishment of the Trans-Caspian Province and appointed Major General Nikolai Lomakin to the post of military governor. This decision symbolized a new step toward the complete conquest of Turkmenia. A note by Sobolev agreed that

a regular organization of our Central Asian theater of military operations appears urgent especially at present time, when the government of Great Britain spares no efforts to consolidate its position in South Asia, from the western part of Asia Minor to the boundaries of India.[156]

The reconnaissance trips undertaken by Lomakin throughout Trans-Caspia in the years 1875–76 testified to the gravity of Russian preparations for a new military campaign.[157] Such military planners as Skobelev, Cherniaev, Grodekov, and Kuropatkin urged Saint Petersburg to launch a war as soon as possible in the light of the recurring trips being undertaken by the British emissaries Colonel Baker and Colonel Charles Macgregor, Major Napier, and Captain Butler to the area under consideration. According to the reports from the Russian consuls staying in the towns on the Persian border, the British agents instigated an immediate unification of the most numerous Turkmen tribes in a sort of confederation under the patronage of Persia in order to oppose the coming Russian advance. The British were mentioned as having supplied the Turkmen with money and war matériel, encouraging them to resist the Russians by all means.[158] However, these plans were doomed to failure, because other local ethnic communities—for example, the Kurds and Armenians—drastically repulsed any overtures by the emissaries from Calcutta in the course of enduring internecine feuds between different Turkmen clans. At the same time, the shah of Persia disliked any possible resistance by the Turkmen, fearing that it would diminish his power in the northern provinces.[159]

Typically, Nikolai Grodekov, the acting chief of the headquarters in the field during the abortive "Russian march to India" in 1878, drafted a proposal for the conquest of North Afghanistan, also called Afghan Turkestan by contemporary European explorers. His idea was to establish another buffer state at the approaches to British India. In Grodekov's opinion, the conquest aimed to bring anti-Russian propaganda in Persia to a standstill. He wrote that

> the English military thinkers manifested that in case of war with Russia, they should capture Tehran and the southern Caspian coastline. Then the British army would occupy positions on the flank of the routes leading from the eastern Caspian coast to Herat. After the seizure of Tehran and the establishment of a coalition with the Turks, the British army would move to Tiflis, instigate Caucasian nations, and rise up with all the "murky forces" of Asia against Russia in the name of Islam.[160]

According to Grodekov, the Russian occupation of the Teke oasis in proximity to Persian Khorasan would counterbalance the British influence in the region. Simultaneously, Major General Arzas Ter-Gukasov, then the military governor of Trans-Caspia, and Colonel Nikolai Petrusevich, a military expert and explorer of the Amu Daria region, propounded a scheme to subjugate independent Turkmen tribes in four years, and calculated total spending for this campaign at 40 million rubles. Moreover, they put forward a key march route for the Russian assault upon the Turkmen—from the Caspian Sea along the mountain range of Koppet Dagh to Akhal Teke, Merv, and further to the southern oases of Penjdeh and Herat.[161]

In a note to Kaufman, Petrusevich maintained that

if we launch a war against England and have to move toward British India, we ought to pass through the oasis of Akhal Teke, and the Teke Turkmen would never let us go freely without combat; hence, we should cope with them in order to advance forward.... We need to acquaint the tribes living in these lands with the name of Russia and get in touch with them, or otherwise, if we have to operate in the area interposing between Herat, Kabul, and the Indian borders, there we shall not be able to find even guides![162]

If the analysts from the Turkestan Military District were more inclined to identify the Turkmen problem with the situation in Afghanistan, their colleagues in the Caucasus Viceroyalty tackled it through the lens of Russian interests in Persia and Asia Minor. The concept of Lieutenant General P. P. Pavlov, the head of the staff of the Caucasus Military District, exposed the motives of the Russian movement to Merv from the west. Commenting on a series of urgent procedures to be executed in order to stabilize the situation on the frontier, Pavlov contended that "the occupation of the Teke oasis will be an initial, and one may say, principal step in a final settlement of the Merv problem—the boundary delimitation between the possessions of Persia, Afghanistan, and Bokhara." He further devoted attention to inner tribal links and anticipated involvement of the Turkmen of Merv in the battle for Akhal Teke.[163]

Referring to Pavlov's opinion, General Adjutant Prince Dimitry Sviatopolk-Mirsky, the assistant to the commander in chief of the Caucasus army, sent a lengthy memorandum to his patron, Grand Duke Mikhail Nikolaevich, on February 19, 1879. Sviatopolk-Mirsky agreed with the Russian ambassador in London, Count Peter Shuvalov, on the policy to be pursued in Trans-Caspia in order to offset the British intrigues in the region. The former proposed setting up a direct operative line stretching from the Caspian mouth of the Atrek River through the oasis of Akhal Teke to Herat. Moreover, Sviatopolk-Mirsky regarded the conquest of Akhal Teke as one of the principal objectives of the subsequent military campaign. He believed that its occupation by the Russians would prevent local inhabitants from falling under the British protectorate in the aftermath of the Second Anglo-Afghan War. "The verity would seem to hold that the defense of India against Russia's encroachments would be a more complicated issue on the agenda of the Englishmen if they have Afghanistan in their rear, than if they have it in front of themselves," opined Sviatopolk-Mirsky. He further asserted that

> it won't be in the British power to command such a vast country as Afghanistan, maintain social order inside it and provide obedience of its population; besides, should a war with Russia break out, it seems difficult to secure military communications to supply a large quantity of troops with necessary war matériel, when Russian detachments intrude into Afghanistan as saviors.... I surmise that the Persian government will not permit our troops to pass though Persia, and it will be better to us to avoid such a route.[164]

Correspondence between high-ranking Russian military officers and diplomats reveals their concern about resolute British opposition to any Russian attempt to capture Merv. As the Foreign Office stated in copious memos that were regularly handed to Russian diplomatic representatives in London, the most probable route for which the Russians

might opt for their conquest of southern Turkmenia would be a movement to Merv.[165] Responding to a note from Gorchakov, Lord Derby
notified the Russian chancellor that

> whenever may be the ultimate destiny of Russia in the course of
> its civilizing mission in Central Asia, it is impossible not to see
> that, in view of the present conditions of the Turkmen tribes, of
> the relations in which they stand to the ruler of Afghanistan on
> the one hand, and those between that ruler and the government
> of India on the other, that each successive advance of the Russian
> frontier towards Afghanistan may involve complications, which it
> is equally the interest of both England and Russia to avoid, and
> may raise up the most serious obstacles to the continued pursu-
> ance of the policy which has hitherto guided both powers alike to
> maintain intact the integrity of Afghan territory.[166]

An anti-British revolt, which broke out in Kabul at the end of the
Second Anglo-Afghan War, diverted the attention of Calcutta from
Turkmenia. Under such favorable circumstances, Russian military planners were anxious to inflict an immediate offensive blow upon the
strongholds of the Teke Turkmen.[167] Commenting on the conditions of
the Treaty of Gandamak, Major General Alexander Gorlov reported to
Miliutin on June 4, 1879, that the British had occupied fifteen mountain passes, separated Baluchistan from Afghanistan, and shortened the
direct route from India to Persia by moving the frontier of the Raj far
to the west.[168] Characteristically, on July 15, 1879, Baron Alexander
Jomini, Russia's deputy foreign minister, declared to Lord Dufferin, the
British ambassador to Saint Petersburg, that

> although we do not intend to go to Merv, or to do anything
> which may be interpreted as a menace to England, you must not
> deceive yourself, for we shall create a base of operations against
> England, once the British government threatens our position in
> Central Asia by the occupation of Herat.[169]

The massacre of the British diplomatic mission headed by Major Louis Cavagnari, the political resident in Kabul, precipitated Lomakin's attack against Geok Tepe, a Turkmen stronghold on the way to Merv, in September 1879. According to the British press, the expeditionary forces cleared the caravan roads between Krasnovodsk and Khiva from numerous mounted bandit gangs and liberated more than 40,000 slaves.[170] Yet the expedition under the command of Lomakin ended in a defeat at the approaches to Geok Tepe, which caused the expedient retreat of the military contingents back to the starting point, Krasnovodsk, on September 27, 1879. This defeat was evidently attributed not to a shortage of troops but to inappropriate military guidance. Mikhail Terentiev's account contains horrible details of the debacle: The Turkmen hacked all the captured Russian prisoners of war to pieces and carved sebum off the cadavers to heal the wounds of their own combatants.[171]

In the meantime, the Disraeli government drafted a program to further the British advance in the region. Apart from the suppression of local guerrillas, it even envisaged initially the devastation of Kabul and the subsequent removal of the administrative center to Kandahar. Besides, the implementation of the program would lead to setting up a line of military outposts in the distance, from Peshawar via Gazni to Kandahar; the secession of Herat to Persia in exchange for its loyalty, once the Anglo-Russian confrontation had occurred; and, what was even more important, the institution of control over Merv spearheaded against Russian Turkestan.[172]

The electoral victory of the Liberal Party, which was chaired by the indefatigable Gladstone, relaxed the tension in Russo-British relations. On June 20, 1880, Queen Victoria notified the new prime minister that "Russia is our real enemy and rival—the only one, perhaps, we have."[173] As Reginald Esher, the private secretary of Lord Hartington, prophesied in a letter to Lord Rosebery, "In the course of the next five years you may have the Russians at Merv, the Persians avowed friendly to Russia and hostile to us, and Abdur Rahman [the new Afghan emir] playing into the hands of Skobelev."[174]

Meanwhile, the high-ranking Russian military officers were obsessed with the idea of restoring their prestige after Lomakin's fiasco. Provided Trans-Caspia submitted to the Caucasus Viceroyalty, the staff officers in Tiflis summarized the strategic goals in a memorandum on February 3, 1880:

> Even if England refrains from the occupation of Herat and cedes it to Persia, her agents will come to this town and the Persian government will not be able to prevent their contacts with the local Turkmen. Our task in Central Asia, therefore, is to make the Englishmen defend themselves. To achieve the goal, we need to set up a frontier along the Hindu Kush, Parapamirs and the crest of Koppet Dagh; to put it differently, all the rivers and flows running from the aforesaid mountains to the north and west, and entering the Amu Daria or its tributaries, should be brought under our control. In this way, the southern frontier will assume both scientific and strategic meaning; and we shall be separated from British possessions geographically, having a chance to threaten them in Afghanistan, and, consequently, in India.[175]

In anticipation of the second assault upon Geok Tepe and because of the Anglo-Afghan war accompanied with internal feuds of the claimants to the Kabul throne, the two rival powers actively reconnoitered Turkmenia and northern Persia. As Sobolev informed Skobelev, who took charge of the expeditionary forces committed to fight the Teke Turkmen, the British intensified their subversive activity in Trans-Caspia, especially after they suffered defeat from the Afghans in the battle at Maiwand near Kandahar in July 1880. Some "newswriters" recruited by the Russians from the native people reported to their spymasters that British emissaries were rumored by the Tsarist authorities to have imposed higher poll taxes on the locals, made them betray Islam and adopt Christian Orthodoxy, and taken away with them the Turkmens' young girls.[176]

Most characteristically, one such emissary, whose activity in northern Persia and southern Turkmenia attracted the close interest of the Tsarist administration during the years 1879–82, was a certain Edmund O'Donovan, a special correspondent for *The Daily News*. According to Hopkirk, O'Donovan's original intention was to follow the troops commanded by Skobelev in their march to Geok Tepe, yet the general disapproved of O'Donovan's attendance because of his Russophobic views.[177] When O'Donovan reached Merv, in spite of Persian obstructiveness and Russian prohibition, he addressed the assembled Turkmen chieftains on the urgency of a pan-Turkish alliance backed by Britain to counteract the Russian offensive. Having charted Merv, adjacent districts, and the routes to the Persian frontier town of Mashhad, O'Donovan was an eyewitness to the storm of Geok Tepe by the battalions under the command of Skobelev on January 23–24, 1881. Shortly afterward, this "envoy of the free-living Turkmen to European states," as he called himself, left Turkmenia for Constantinople through Persia. Significantly, anonymous Russian informants in Mashhad intercepted and copied all the confidential reports that O'Donovan used to mail to London, including rough sketches and maps of the strongholds.[178]

A secret mission carried out by another emissary—Lieutenant Colonel Charles Stewart, of the Fifth Punjab Infantry Regiment—likewise contributed to the British survey of the northern provinces of Persia and Trans-Caspia. Disguised as an Armenian horse trader, Stewart established a network of native scouts and "newswriters" who collected information about Russian contingents in Turkmenia. Oddly enough, according to Hopkirk, Stewart saw his compatriot O'Donovan several times but decided not to expose himself to the latter.[179]

Ivan Zinoviev, the minister to Tehran, later to become the head of the Foreign Ministry's Asian Department, reported to Giers about the ambiguity of English strategy:

On the one hand, they [the British] are trying to intimidate the Merv Turkmen by the rumors of the Afghan Emir intending to launch a military expedition against Merv to revenge himself upon the nomads for their forays into the province of Herat last autumn. But on the other hand, they [the British] seek to inculcate upon the inhabitants of Merv the urgency of coming to an agreement with the Emir in order to throw away Russian claims and obtain the right to urge England's moral as well as material collaboration.[180]

It needs to be noted that the capture of Geok Tepe was followed by the horrible massacre of more than 6,500 defenders inside the stronghold along with 8,000 Turkmen fugitives, mostly unarmed women and children. The news of this "victory" impressed other Turkmen tribes and shocked the European public. Although historians have differed in their comments upon its moral aspect, the accounts of eyewitnesses disproved the picture of the Cossacks' "benevolent" attitude toward their foes, as one may conclude after reading some publications by Soviet and current Russian authors.[181] In fact, Skobelev allowed his soldiers to sack Geok Tepe for three days, because he held it as a principle that "in Asia the duration of peace is in direct proportion to the slaughter you inflict upon the enemy. The harder you hit them, the longer they will be quiet afterwards."[182] To distinguish this bloody conqueror of the Turkmen, Alexander III raised him to the rank of infantry general and awarded him the Saint George Military Cross.

The subsequent conquest of Akhal Teke and Ashgabat brought the Turkmen tribes' resistance to an end. Although the Tsarist diplomats sought to mollify the Foreign Office with declarations that nothing could compel the Russians to advance to Merv, the London Cabinet fully realized that the last independent fortified oasis would become easy prey for the Tsarist generals in the near future, especially after the emperor's edict was issued on March 24, 1881, mandating the annexation of the lands of the Teke Turkmen.[183]

To survey current developments in the region, the above-mentioned Colonel Nikolai Grodekov and Pavel Lessar, a former military engineer who later went into diplomatic service, set out on two independent reconnaissance missions to Khorasan in the second half of 1881.[184] Along with the fact that the Tsarist government received valuable nuggets of information on the situation in Persia, the trips seemed to accelerate the conclusion of the secret Russo-Persian Boundary Convention on December 21, 1881. Interestingly, the British remained unaware of this document until 1884.[185] It fixed a boundary line along the flow of the Atrek River, or for the strip of territory from the eastern spurs of the Koppet Dagh to the Upper Oxus—the last no-man's land lying between Russian Turkestan and the domains of the shah. Apart from the clauses mentioned above, the convention proclaimed Persia's non-interference in the affairs of the Turkmen tribes. It also allowed Russian troops to pass through Persian territory on their way to the lands of the Turkmen. In Article VII of the convention, the Tsarist government reserved the right to station political agents in the Persian provinces adjacent to Russian Turkestan.[186]

The Russo-Persian Boundary Convention laid the foundations for the future preponderance of entrepreneurs, traders, and financial dealers from the Romanovs' Empire in the north of Persia. They hurried to make capital investments in industrial concessions, establish banks, and construct highways along with telegraph lines. At the same time, Russian physicians assisted local authorities in arresting epidemics of cholera and pestilence, while a separate Cossack brigade of about 2,000 horsemen was deployed in Tehran to serve as personal guardians of the shah.

After the subjugation of the Teke Turkmen, some military commanders and dignitaries at the Court of Saint Petersburg began to think that it was time for the army to stop on the frontiers that it had attained in the course of its conquest of Turkestan. For example, Lev Kostenko, a military statistician, called for a dialogue with Britain:

It will be particularly advantageous to us to have England— a strong and mighty power, as our neighbour-state. The fear of our approach to the frontiers of India will gradually vanish after the Englishmen become convinced that no ambitious designs and no self-interested calculations guide Russia in her progressive movement in Central Asia, but the sole desire to pacify the country, to give impulse to its productive forces, and to open out the shortest route by which she can transport the products of her Turkestan possessions to the European part of the empire.[187]

Simultaneously, Charles Marvin, the British traveler and journalist, noted in a résumé of his private interviews with a few distinguished Russian generals and statesmen in 1882:

It is a great disadvantage to England and Russia that the political writers of each country know so little of one another. Occasional intercourse would dissipate many of those erroneous impressions that mar the friendly relations of the peoples. Most of the English writers on Central Asia are personally unacquainted with Russia, and have no knowledge of the Russian language. The majority of them are good judges of the Central Asian question from Indian standpoint, having served in India; but they know nothing of the Russian aspect of the problem, except what they derive from the exaggerated and distorted intelligence appearing in the newspapers.[188]

Lord Ripon, the viceroy of India, corresponded with Hartington, offering a similar, albeit slightly modified, opinion on the latest developments in Asia. The viceroy poured ridicule upon Russophobia in Britain:

I believe that the fear of an invasion of India by the Russians, at all events in our days is purely chimerical, and I dismiss it at once for all practical purposes; but there is more plausibility in the notion that as the Russians approach our frontiers more nearly, they may when they are on bad terms with us try to stir up discontent and trouble by intrigues carried on within our dominions, and the real question, therefore, is how can such intrigues be best met and defeated?[189]

However, the "forwardists" among the high-ranking Tsarist officials still nourished plans of further expansion. Thus, on returning from India, where he had been collecting intelligence on Anglo-Afghan relations during the war, the well-known Major General Nikolai Stolietov reported to Miliutin on March 3, 1880:

In order to provoke a total revolt in India, we need a formidable trigger, either our conflict with England, or decisive misfortunes of the Englishmen in Afghanistan, or England's war against the Ottomans or Persians.[190]

A new governor-general of Turkestan, Mikhail Cherniaev, also shared this opinion. According to Marvin, Cherniaev claimed that "Russia has no intention or desire to attack India, but if you [Marvin] ask if an invasion is possible or not, I must answer in the affirmative, although I admit the task would not be an easy one."[191] Similarly, Prince Alexander Dondukov-Korsakov, the viceroy of the Caucasus, sent to Saint Petersburg one memo after another in attempts to persuade the tsar that "Russia should deliberately play the role of a formidable power in the East, pressing England to be more compliant in other regions of the world, and above all, in Europe."[192]

Yet, to create a smoke screen for the annexation of Merv, which was called by local natives "the Queen of the World" because of its ancient history and strategic significance, the Tsarist government agreed to start a new round of negotiations with London in 1882. Simultaneously, Lieutenant Maksud Alikhanov, accompanied by another officer (both disguised as Muslim merchants), arrived in Merv to prepare for the peaceful surrender of the oasis to the Russians. It appears probable to consider that the invitation of some Turkmen dignitaries and elders, sympathetic with Russia, to attend the pompous ceremony of the coronation of Tsar Alexander III in May 1883, affected the intention of the Merv Turkmen to come with the Russians on friendly terms, once their representatives became convinced of how mighty and rich was the Russian Empire.[193] One should, however, take into consideration the British military involvement in Egypt and Sudan in the period of the Russians' creeping annexation of the Merv oasis, though, as many historians argue, this undertaking actually canceled all the promises and guarantees given to the Foreign Office by Gorchakov and Giersin in the years 1879–82.[194] Besides, the initiative of some British military administrators, who were unaware of the Russo-Persian Convention of 1881, to suggest that the shah take the Merviles under his suzerainty was given the cold shoulder in Tehran.[195]

On February 13, 1884, Lieutenant General Alexander Komarov, the governor of Trans-Caspian Province, reported to the tsar by telegraph that

> I [Komarov] have the pleasure to inform Your Imperial Majesty
> that today in Ashgabat the Khans of four tribes of Merv Turkmen
> and twenty-four chosen delegates, one for every 2,000 *kibitkas*
> [pavilions], accepted unconditional allegiance to Your Majesty;
> confirming the same by solemn oath for themselves and the
> whole people of Merv.[196]

After Major General Komarov, who commanded the expeditionary
corps deployed about 150 kilometers from Merv, gave its inhabitants
a parole of honor of noninterference with their domestic affairs, the
senior men decided to accept Russian rule.

Although Whitehall and the media were not astonished at the annexation of Merv, the British diplomatic representatives in Saint Petersburg
and the experts of the Intelligence Branch of the Quartermaster-
General's Department in London rushed into a discussion on the current Russian progress in South Trans-Caspia.[197] Some ardent "forwardists," like Vambery, even took the news as a false rumor. He commented
in *The Times* on February 23, 1884:

> Strange indeed! The most unruly adventures of the Central Asian
> steppes, who boasted twenty years ago before the writer of these
> lines that royalty is not according to their taste, and that with them
> everybody is a king.... Well, these adventurers and thieves have
> now suddenly become anxious to get a chief—nay, an Emperor;
> and, to our great amazement, they show willingness to be gov-
> erned, taxed, and led on the path of modern civilization by the
> mighty tutor on the Neva.[198]

This episode contributed to the criticism of the Liberal Cabinet
by the political opposition for "inactivity" and the decline of Britain's
prestige, especially in light of the social disorder that this new territorial acquisition by the Russians might instigate in India.[199] As
Salisbury, the leader of the Conservative Party in the House of Lords,
expressed it on March 10, 1884, the great challenges with which the
British administration might be confronted were "the production

of intrigues and rebellions among the natives of India, the gradual weakening of respect, for the English arms, dissatisfaction toward the English Raj, and the crumbling away of our resources before Russia has struck a blow against our frontier."[200] However, the official *Journal de Saint Petersburg* and the tabloids, like *Novoe Vremya* and *Nedelia*, speculated in February and March 1884 on "the placid tenor of debates in the British Parliament" with regard to the problem of Turkmenia.[201]

In response to the seizure of Roshan, Shugnan, and Wahan, once the vassal Pamir principalities of Bokhara, by the army of Abdur Rahman backed by the viceroy of India, the Tsarist generals took under their authority the Sarakh Turkmen, who had originally paid tribute to the emir of Kabul. In July 1884, both the Russian and British sides agreed to establish a Joint Boundary Commission on the delimitation of the Russian and Afghan territories.[202]

Now the British public regarded the Penjdeh oasis, lying 110 kilometers south of Herat and occupied by Afghan troops, as the last section of the Turkmen territory free from Tsarist rule. As W. Baxter, a member of Parliament, juxtaposed the conquest of Khokand with the annexation of the Turkmen even before the seizure of Merv,

At present there is a similar uneasiness about Merv, and the Russophobes party are using all their efforts to show either that the Russians must not be allowed to take Merv, or if they do take it that Herat must be occupied.[203]

In Baxter's opinion, international arbitration might be used by the great powers as an effective political instrument to settle the Turkmen problem once and for all. The politician also recommended to the government to "allow the Russians plainly to understand what limits they could not pass in their onward movement,"[204] though such military thinkers as Macgregor, Cardwell, and Beaufort—together with renowned experts and explorers like Rawlinson, Vambery, Marvin, and Michel—differed on the best means of protection for the British interests in the Middle East and Inner Asia.[205]

Charles Macgregor, for instance, insisted in his book *The Defence of India* that Britain should set up an anti-Russian continental coalition in coordination with Germany, Austria-Hungary, and the Ottoman Empire, in order to have enough manpower at hand and gain easy access to all vulnerable strategic points in Russian territory. Next, Macgregor thought that it was appropriate for London to ally with Persia in order to establish an Anglo-Persian condominium over Herat and Turkmenia. Moreover, he also regarded an alliance with China as worthy of consideration. Finally, he believed that the organization of a Muslim rebellion in the khanates of Central Asia also deserved the government's attention. In his vision, it would facilitate a blockade by the Royal Navy of the Turkish Straits and other strategic Russian seaports. Macgregor's book was published in Russian soon after the first British edition, and so it was also known in Russia.[206]

Meanwhile, Tsar Alexander III adopted a project of a branch railway to the south of Merv. With its implementation, Russia would acquire absolute domination of the approaches to Afghanistan and, ipso facto, India.[207] A special conference in Saint Petersburg on Christmas Eve of 1884 adopted a scheme for a new Russian frontier line, to be moved from Merv to the oasis of Penjdeh.[208]

Although the Russo-British Joint Boundary Commission bogged down in a maze of futile technicalities, being unable to reach a compromise agreement, and the Tsarist diplomats proceeded to assure their British counterparts that "*une bonne entente*" (*sic*) with Russia was a sine qua non for the prolongation of British rule in India,[209] Saint Petersburg launched a propaganda campaign in the European press. The Russophile media alleged that the Turkmen of Penjdeh were strongly in favor of coming under the Russian protectorate, following the other Turkmen tribes. As if responding to their plea, the Cossack detachments and infantry battalions commanded by General Komarov approached Penjdeh to meet the avant-garde of the emir's troops on the fortified positions.

In the spring of 1885, statesmen and diplomats did not spare efforts to settle the Penjdeh problem. What annoyed the Foreign Office most of all was a threat of eventual seizure by Tsarist troops of the Zulficar

Pass leading directly to Herat.[210] In his concluding commentaries on the military significance of Penjdeh, Colonel A. Cameron, a staff member of the India Office's Political and Statistical Department, emphasized that

> every demand of Russia, in respect of a change of this frontier, is in direct connection with an intended advance on Herat, and that her sole desire is to gain every possible advantage beforehand for the inevitable campaign against India.[211]

The risk of a further Russo-British armed confrontation seemed so evident that Queen Victoria begged Alexander III to take the problem under his own command.[212] Yet on March 30, 1885, a column of troops headed by Lieutenant Alikhanov attacked the Afghan military detachments and forced them to retreat. Interestingly, the day of the skirmish strangely coincided with the emir's visit to Viceroy Lord Dufferin. According to statistics on this armed clash, the Afghans lost more than 500 men killed or wounded, while the Russian casualties were estimated at 42 Cossacks. In his report to higher military commanders, Major General Komarov attributed this assault to the menace of the Afghan breakthrough to Merv and further to Bokhara. He also mentioned the British military instructors, headed by Major General P. Lumsden, who ostensibly had recommended to the emir not to avoid a full-scale war against Russia.[213]

Although Dufferin acknowledged the presence of British officers in Penjdeh,[214] the British envoy to Tehran, Peter Thompson, cited somewhat different intelligence on the armed incident, maintaining that the Russians had provoked it with unexpected cannon fire on the Afghans' positions. Accordingly, the casualties of the Russian and Afghan sides ran, by Thompson's estimate, to respectively 250 and 255 combatants. The diplomat cabled to Granville on April 21, 1885, that

> the Afghans did all they could to avoid conflict, and it was solely owing to their patience and forbearance during two months of incessant irritation that peace has been preserved so long.[215]

Although Britain's involvement in the "holy war" waged by the Sudan rebellions under the banner of the Mahdi, or the new Muslim prophet, drew the attention of the United Kingdom's statesmen and the public away from the Penjdeh incident, the Foreign Office vehemently protested against the acts of violence committed by Tsarist expeditionary forces in South Trans-Caspia, especially in view of the Russo-British negotiations on the Afghan boundary's delimitation, which were in full swing.[216] It was just at that time when the British press labeled the state of mind of some British policymakers as "mervosity," while military analysts again feverishly calculated the volume of Russian troops in Turkestan.[217]

"The panic on the stock market, the vote of extraordinary credits, the occupation of Port Hamilton (off Korea) and other precautionary measures (including the printing of posters announcing the beginning of hostilities) [sic] were all signs that a great power conflict was closer than at any time since 1878," writes Paul Kennedy in his study of British foreign policy.[218] One prominent statesman later recalled that "under these conditions there was nothing for Gladstone to do but to adopt a determined attitude in the face of such a menace, and he promptly came down to the House [of Commons] and demanded a vote of credit of 11 mln pounds, and directed both the Admiralty and the War Office to take preparatory steps for the mobilization of the forces of the Empire."[219] According to Prince Vladimir Metschersky (see chapter 2), the tsar, inspired by the congratulations of the German emperor on the "brilliant victory at Penjdeh," promised to spend all his personal savings on a war against Britain if the state budget could not stand it. Metschersky recorded in his diary that

the first half of 1885 was a nervous period, for we lived in the atmosphere of a war threat by England because of the Afghan question.... In spite of the negotiations between England and Russia, the British government demonstratively intimidated us with their aggressive arrangements: troops were being prepared to set off to India; the Parliament unanimously voted for the credit of 11 million pounds; there were rumors of the English occupation of the Hamilton Island in the Japanese Sea and the diplomatic talks with Turkey regarding the intrusion of the British Navy to the Black Sea, etc.[220]

As had frequently happened before, a new wave of jingoism arose in both empires. According to Prince Kropotkin, a Russian political refugee in London, a phantom of the continental coalition, which the British government was about to establish in order to wage hostilities against the Tsardom in Asia, was again rumored in the emigrant coteries.[221] "The whole world, European and Asiatic," commented a Russian political observer, "has been waiting for this war for a long time and considers it to be inevitable. Today, or tomorrow, or later; because of Penjdeh, or Korea, or Bosporus, or because of diplomatic correctness, but it will definitely break out—everybody knows and anticipates it, but not everybody confesses it to himself."[222]

The "hawks" at the Court of Saint Petersburg and the military on the frontiers in Asia urged the government to take a tough stance in relations with London. For example, the governor-general of Turkestan, Nikolai Rosenbach, frightened the emperor with panicked reports on the secret trips of British military officers to the territory of Bokhara in the spring of 1885.[223] In spite of the fact that the foreign secretary, Lord Granville, refuted these insinuations, Giers informed Yegor Staal, the Russian ambassador to London, of the designs on the side of the Russian Main Naval Staff to lay mines in the bay of Vladivostok as a useful means to reciprocate the British war preparations in Hong Kong.[224] On April 27, 1885, the war minister general adjutant, Peter Vannovsky, authorized the Naval Ministry with respect to the transportation of additional manpower to the Central Asian theater of operations on board the steamers of the Caspian Sea Flotilla.[225] The Russian Pacific Squadron was also instructed to be ready for the beginning of a cruising war in order to break the major ocean lines of communications between Britain and its overseas dominions—Canada and Australia—as well as those with China and India.[226] On May 30, 1885, Zinoviev, the former ambassador to Constantinople, told Madam Novikoff, an eminent Russian public figure in Britain, that

England cannot give up her unfair tricks. Instead of being honestly united with us, instead of representing a compact power of Russia and England in the eyes of Asiatic tribes, England is now arming Herat against us.[227]

On the British side, the numerous secret notes and articles in the press suggested the measures of defense to be taken against the Russian advance in Trans-Caspia, such as the recall of the ambassador for consultations, coercion of the Persian shah to protest against the Russian acts of aggression, sending a squadron of battleships into the Persian Gulf, the construction of a railroad from the Gulf to Tehran, and even the inspiration of an appeal by the emir of Kabul to all the Muslims to launch a "holy war" against the infidels throughout Central Asia.[228] A memorandum by the experts in the Admiralty to the Cabinet in May 1885 envisaged the installation of a naval base in the Korean Straits as well as the protection of trade by patrolling commercial sea routes with squadrons of light cruisers.[229] Yet even at the apogee of military hysteria, a well-informed British statesman expressed skepticism about the effect of jingoistic propaganda:

Public attention is wholly engrossed in the prospects of war with Russia. For my part, I do not believe that Russia's objective is India. Consequently I see no reason why, if war is staved off now, peace should not be maintained until war breaks out in Eastern Europe, when we should, in any case, have allies who are not now procurable.[230]

In this context, *The Times* considered the only way to prevent further escalation of confrontation was the resumption of the delimitation negotiations by the Joint Boundary Commission.[231] As a Russian diplomat later evaluated the state of Russo-British relations in the summer of 1885, "one sometimes wonders how peace could have been maintained."[232]

The fall of the Liberal Cabinet in June 1885 caused a relaxation of tension between Russia and Britain, though some Tsarist strategists still foresaw a resumption of the armed confrontation.[233] The instability in

Europe because of German intrigues and the impending regrouping of the great powers compelled London and Saint Petersburg to resolve the Penjdeh conflict as soon as possible. On the other side, according to British sources, some military thinkers regarded the French peril in Africa as far more imminent and formidable than the Russian bogey.[234]

Hence, the Afghan boundary commission resumed activities to work out a final agreement on September 22, 1885, though the process of demarcation continued for another three years.[235] If the Penjdeh District went under the command of Russia, the emir of Afghanistan managed to keep the strategic Zulficar Pass in his possession. During the subsequent two years, other segments of the disputed frontier were compromised by peaceful negotiations, but the British government, annoyed by the Russo-Persian Treaty of 1881, concluded the Anglo-Persian Convention on September 30, 1885, which counterbalanced the Russian influence upon Tehran by prohibiting free passage of foreign military contingents through Persian territory.[236]

Thus, a kind of fragile equilibrium between Russia and Britain had been established by the mid-1880s. Its foundations included both static and dynamic components, the former based upon the frontiers, and mutually recognized in the Middle East and Inner Asia, while the latter depended, as one American historian denoted it, on "each party's ability to exert leverage over the other."[237] Both empires arrived at a strategic stalemate at the culmination point of the Great Game. They managed to keep their strategic position in Central Asia safe, while Russia's threat to India as well as Britain's menace to Turkestan lost its pressing urgency. Not coincidentally, therefore, pragmatism and realism gradually took over the uncompromising enmity toward the Romanovs' Empire in U.K. ruling circles, a stance that was defined by a prominent British diplomat as "a policy of despair" in 1880. "I am no apologist for Russia and I do not doubt that corruption and oppression are too often the characteristics of her rule," he admitted in a lengthy note to Lord Hartington, the state secretary for India, "and that it may often happen that her designs are of a kind which we may justly condemn and oppose; but she is, at all events, a great fact, and it should be remembered that, from a Russian point of view, England may naturally be considered as the chief obstacle to the attainment of some of the most cherished objects of her national ambition."[238]

Symbolically, in October 1885, the Tory Cabinet headed by Salisbury invited two Russian colonels, Temler and Odoevsky-Maslov, to be present at the military maneuvers of the Anglo-Indian troops that took place in the North-West Province of India. The tsar, for his part, sent special gifts to the six British officers who accompanied the Russian visitors.[239]

Yet a transition period from confrontation to collaboration occupied the next two decades of bilateral relations, while the focus of the Great Game gradually shifted to other parts of Asia—the Pamirs, Tibet, and Manchuria.

CHAPTER 5

STRATEGIC STALEMATE, 1886–1903

From the shores of the Pacific and the heights of the Himalayas, Russia could dominate not only the affairs of Asia but those of Europe as well.

—Sergei Witte, Russian finance minister

Listen in the North, my boys, there's trouble in the wind.
Tramp, O Cossacks, troop in front, grey great coats behind.
Trouble on the frontier of a most amazing kind,
Trouble on the waters of the Oxus.

—Rudyard Kipling, "The Sacred War Song of the Mavericks"

This chapter first describes the scramble for the Pamirs between Britain, Russia, and China throughout the 1880s and 1890s. The Pamirs—a remote area of Central Asia with an arid continental climate, tiny population, and treacherous mountain passes—remained one of the least-surveyed parts of the world at the turn of the twentieth century. Next, the chapter reconsiders the final round of the Great Game at the western approaches to India, which shaped not only the situation in Afghanistan but also developments in other parts of East Asia. This round was epitomized by such events as a diplomatic struggle for the concession of the Baghdad railway and a journey across the Persian Gulf by the British viceroy in India, Lord Curzon. Finally, the chapter visits quite a new "playfield" in the Great Game, the enigmatic land of Tibet, where the Cabinet of Saint Petersburg sought to neutralize London's desires to control the Tibetan Buddhists. In this complex round of the Game, Britain sought to link India to China via Tibet, but the Tsarist government tried to create a springboard for encircling China and opening a second front against British rule in India. Though far-flung Tibet might be regarded as merely a secondary playfield in the general Russo-British "tournament of shadows," in fact it had no less significance for the rival powers than did Persia, Afghanistan, or the khanates of Central Asia.

THE RUSSO-BRITISH SCRAMBLE FOR THE PAMIRS

As it ensued from the events recounted in earlier chapters, the Great Game culminated in a strategic deadlock, which shifted the Anglo-Russian competition to new areas, such as the Pamirs, Tibet, and Manchuria. The advanced positions occupied by Tsarist Russia in the 1870s and 1880s provided it with both advantage and motivation for the continuation of the forward policy in East Asia, similar to how its victorious war against the Ottoman Empire in 1877–88 spurred on the activation of its Balkans policy.[1]

By the mid-1880s, few territories in Asia might be called no-man's lands lying outside the sphere of influence of any great power. According to Captain Andrei Snesarev, who traversed this region several times and commanded a garrison of Russian frontier guards in a fortified military stronghold of Murghab,[2] the Pamirs were situated within the confines of the Zaalai Mountains to the north, the Hindu Kush to the south, the Upper Amu Daria River to the west, and the Sarikol Hills to the east. Although its total area was 70,415 square miles, it only had a population of about 16,000 males and females, of Turk origin in its eastern section and of the Tajik nationality in its western segment. Owing to the tiny population and treacherous mountain passes, this remote area with its arid continental climate remained one of the least-surveyed parts of the world at the turn of the twentieth century.[3]

However, owing to the intensive explorations in the last quarter of the nineteenth century, some European travelers and native scouts, either in the British or the Russian service, chartered this less accessible area, where three empires—Russian, British, and Chinese—met.[4] In Tashkent and Osh, Simla and Calcutta, Peking and Kashgar, civil and military officers contributed as the frontier lines of the three empires came closer to each other. In the 1890s, the distance between Russian, British, and Chinese avant-garde cordon outposts scarcely exceeded 200 miles in some sectors of the Game's "playfield," for example, in North Karakorum.

It also needs to be kept in mind that after the British subjugation of Punjab and the Russian conquest of Central Asia, the rival Russian and British empires had attained their natural, or "scientific," frontiers there. Pursuant to the Russo-British agreement of 1872–73, the Russian sphere of influence was limited to the right bank of the Upper Amu Daria, whereas the British sphere was limited to its left side. For the fact that the Khanate of Khokand commanded the Pamirs principalities— Shignan, Roshan, and Wakhan in the early nineteenth century but then yielded them—first, to the Bokharian emir, and shortly afterward, to the Tsarist colonial administration—Saint Petersburg proceeded to look upon these possessions as lying within the Russian sphere of influence.[5] Yet the later military expansion by Yakub Beg of Kashgaria into the Pamirs dramatically modified the status of these hill states. Moreover, the conclusion of the Treaty of Saint Petersburg in 1881 enabled the Qing government to reestablish its suzerainty over the district of Kuldja and to claim that the Pamirs should be incorporated in the Manchu Empire. It took nearly a year for the Russian and Chinese commissioners to demarcate the disputable sector of the no-man's-land up to the Lake of Kara-Kul. But the arduous task of demarcating the whole frontier line was still not done.[6]

Meanwhile, the ruler of Badakshan, a vassal of Abdur Rahman, the emir of Afghanistan, unexpectedly occupied Shignan, Roshan, and Wakhan in the summer of 1883. Bronislav Grombchevsky and other Russian explorers reported to Tashkent and Saint Petersburg about the mass atrocities committed by the Afghan military contingents in Shignan, from which local residents escaped to the territory controlled by the Tsarist authorities.[7] Yet London turned a deaf ear to the protests of the Russian Foreign Ministry, though Lord Ripon addressed a letter of inquiry on the situation in the Pamirs to Abdur Rahman.[8] While supporting the idea of a three-party boundary commission to settle the conflict, the British government granted an extra subsidy of Rs 1.2 million to the emir, in order to use his troops as covering armed forces against, they believed, the imminent Russian advance to Chitral and Gilgit—the "buffer states" like Shignan located between the Raj and Russian Turkestan. Although the Pamirs and the principalities lying to the south of it—such as Hunza (Kanjut), Nagar, and Yasin—had no agricultural or economic value for any conqueror, with the exception of ruby mines in the Chitral Valley, the logic of the Great Game predetermined the British and Russian leadership circles to secure their preponderance at the approaches to India and Tibet.[9]

Russian and British functionaries in the "far pavilions," who sought to win the favor of the local chieftains who commanded trade routes and strategic mountain passes in "the broad belt of independent barbarism,"[10] were major participants in the scramble for the Pamirs, which Britain, Russia, and China, along with the emir of Afghanistan, conducted throughout the 1880s and 1890s. As one prominent "gamer" wrote to Lord Lansdowne, then the Indian viceroy, in July 1890,

> We [the British] have here in the centre of Central Asia four nations grouped around some desert mountains: the Afghans afraid of the Chinese, and the Chinese afraid of the Afghans; the English suspicious of the Russians advancing south, and the Russians suspicious of the English advancing north.[11]

For the London Cabinet, it would be more appropriate if the pusillanimous, decadent Celestial Empire took the whole Pamirs under the aegis, interposing itself in this way between the Russian and British possessions.[12] Conversely, the Peking government was interested in the prolongation of Russia's competition with Britain in Inner Asia. As Younghusband—then a young subaltern of the King's Dragoon Guards, and later to be commissioned to the Indian Intelligence Branch of the Quartermaster-General's Office—summarized the regional policies pursued by the Manchu Dynasty,

> The Chinese officials, too, are favourably disposed to us, though when Russian and English interests clash, to prevent annoyance from the Russians, who have a consul at Kashgar, while we are unrepresented, they are inclined to side with the Russians rather than with us; and though they look upon ourselves and the Russians as barbarians, I think they look upon us as the less barbaric of the two, and respect us as the conquerors of India.[13]

In the years 1885–86, prompted by the Penjdeh incident, Colonel William Lockhart, a highly experienced and qualified deputy quarter-master-general of the Indian Intelligence Branch, thoroughly explored the Valley of Chitral abutting the Raj. The members of this mission conjectured that no Russian invasion force of substantial quantity could use the passes in the Pamirs for a breakthrough to India, either in winter or summer, because their march route might be quite easily blocked, both by snow avalanches and relentless surges of flowing water. Nevertheless, infiltration by minor armed groups of saboteurs through these gaps would endanger social stability in India.[14]

Almost simultaneously, another respected explorer, Ney Elias, a brilliant geographer, experienced traveler, and intelligence agent, surveyed the roads leading from Eastern Turkestan through the Pamirs and the Hindu Kush to India. As directed by Sir Henry Mortimer Durand, the foreign secretary of the government of India, Elias diligently pursued inspection of the terrain and collected valuable intelligence about local residents. More important, he mapped the Upper Oxus River Basin, where, in his opinion, a frontier line between the Qing Empire and Afghanistan ought to be drawn, separating in this way the territory of Russian Turkestan from that of British India.[15]

Apart from the British, other European travelers—for example, a group of French explorers—also surveyed the Pamirs intensively in the 1880s and 1890s.[16] However, it was Captain Grombchevsky, the officer in the service of the Russian Main Staff, who caught the attention of the Indian government.[17] Just at that time, Ishak Khan, the ruler of Badakhshan and a cousin of Abdur Rahman, mutinied against the suzerain in the fall of 1888, making the emir withdraw his military contingents from North Afghanistan. Moreover, the rebel chieftain snatched at a chance to assure the Russian authorities in Turkestan of his loyalty and appealed to the governor-general, Nikolai Rosenbach, for military aid.[18] That is why Grombchevsky, escorted by a few Cossacks, found himself in the epicenter of events; but he was late to assist Ishak Han because the revolt was ruthlessly suppressed by Abdur Rahman's punitive military contingent shortly before the arrival of the Russian emissary, in the spring of 1889. Symptomatically, Durand commented on the intelligence about Grombchevsky's expedition with the phrase "The game had begun," signaling the start of combat for the Pamirs.[19]

Under these circumstances, Grombchevsky had to search for another claimant to the vassalage of Russia. He was instructed by the Main Staff to pay a visit to Safdar Ali Khan, the sovereign of Hunza, who had previously informed Nikolai Petrovsky, the consul to Kashgar, of his desire to become a Russian subject. A study of diplomatic correspondence reveals that although Grombchevsky was directed only to reconnoiter the state of affairs in Hunza, he exceeded his instructions when he admonished Safdar Ali about military and financial backing from Russia on the condition that Safdar Ali submit to imperial protection. The Russian emissary went so far as to assure the khan that military instructors would arrive in the hill principality to drill a small army of the khan, and war munitions would be supplied to his state in due course. These messages from Consul Petrovsky to Safdar Ali—which were later confiscated by the British expeditionary forces in Baltit, a key fortress on the way to Hunza—exemplified the Russian intrigues at the court of the emir, who in turn sent his representatives to the town of Osh to obtain weaponry from the Russians for the anti-British resistance.[20]

The travel impressions penned by Grombchevsky in his diary on October 23–25, 1889, vindicated an unexpected rendezvous with Captain Younghusband at Khaian Aksai, when the Russian officer, at his own initiative, handed in to his British counterpart a correct chart of the Upper Oxus with all its surveyed tributaries. Shortly afterward, the government of India utilized this chart as a basic map for delimiting the Pamirs' frontier. "We bade a farewell to each other, promising to continue cooperation and keeping on correspondence. The British expedition, particularly its courageous chief, impressed me greatly," wrote Grombchevsky in his diary.[21] Despite these welcoming contacts, Younghusband directed his Russian colleague to "a route of absolutely no importance, leading from nowhere to nowhere," with a vague perspective on safe travel.[22] The motive for this "dirty trick" seemed to be not fears of an impending Russian invasion of the northern hill states adjacent to the Raj but the deposits of gold and nephrite in the South Pamirs, which had attracted the attention of British entrepreneurs.[23] Interestingly, a new encounter of Younghusband with Grombchevsky, which occurred in Yarkand a year later, on October 9 and 10, 1890, seemed at first glance friendly enough, but the British explorer veiled the real objective of his mission to Xinjiang with the necessity to intercede between the Afghans and the Chinese on the boundary issue.[24]

The reports by other Russian explorers tramping around the Pamirs at that time—such as Potanin, Pokotilo, Notovich, and the brothers Grumm-Grzhymailo, to mention but a few—as well as the messages by Petrovsky from Kashgaria led the Tsarist government to conclude that the time had come to annex the Pamirs and expel the British and the Chinese from minor hill states, like Hunza and Nagar. Both memoranda by military experts and editorials in the press referred to the vassal dependence of the countries under consideration upon the Khanate of Khokand—now an integral part of Russian Turkestan.[25] The military on the spot supported the occupation of the Pamirs for purely strategic considerations. One of them, a certain Staff Captain Skersky, recommended that the government annex the province for two main reasons—first, to threaten Badakhshan to such an extent that an armed conflict there would inevitably take up the majority of the Afghan troops, at the expense of the main theater of operations at Herat; and second, to cut off the territory of Afghanistan from the military bases in British India once a new Russo–British war began.[26]

For their part, official staff members and political commentators in Britain and India concentrated upon the closure of the last remaining gap on the northern frontier of the Raj. To furnish this narrative with a striking instance, one should mention, above all, George Nathaniel Curzon—the renowned traveler, statesman, and public figure—who examined the problem of the "scientific frontier" in Anglo-Russian relations. Referring to the Russian advance against India, still antici-pated by the general public, Curzon maintained that

> in its particular application to the northwestern borders of India, the phrase "a scientific frontier" practically means a border line drawn on the far side of the passes through the mountains that command the Indus Valley, instead of a line excluding them from British territory.[27]

To Curzon's thinking, the existing Russian frontier in Central Asia could in no small measure be regarded as a "scientific" one. Therefore, the Tsarist government aspired to attain a frontier line marked by a combination of physical, ethnographical, and political factors. According to Curzon, the most likely areas of new conquests by Tsarist generals would be Kashgaria, "a portion of the Chinese Empire most subject to Russian influence," and the Upper Oxus in the Pamirs, where the arti-ficial character of the Russian frontier seemed most apparent. Although Curzon denied a wish "to impute any sinister or Machiavellian motive to Russia's policy," its advance to Asia should be arrested by Britain; but, even more significant, the British government ought to cooperate with its rival as much as possible "in the great work of subduing the East to the West."[28]

At the risk of uttering commonplaces, one must admit that Curzon's concept, so well narrated in his voluminous book on contemporary developments in Central Asia, *Russia in Central Asia and the Anglo-Russian Question*, to a certain extent shaped subsequent British policy in Asia, owing to its scrupulous analysis of all potential routes for the Russian invasion of India, not excluding those through high mountain passes in the Pamirs.[29] Typically, in a review of the history of British relations with Hunza and Nagar, Lieutenant Colonel Edward Elles, the assistant to the quartermaster-general on the staff of the Intelligence Branch in Calcutta, pointed out that

> the government of India in 1888, in their dispatch to the Secretary of State, considered that the importance of Hunza lay in the fact that from it Chinese Turkestan could be reached by passes then unexplored and that immediately to the north, across the Kilik Pass, laid the gap between Afghanistan and China. By pushing through this gap, or by becoming the successor of the Chinese in Kashgar, the Russians might at any time acquire very inconvenient rights or claims over Kanjut [the other cognomen of Hunza], unless the suzerainty of Kashmir were previously established.[30]

To monitor Russian and Chinese intrigues in the Pamirs, the government of India had reinstalled the British political officer in Gilgit by 1889 (a post that was initially established as early as in 1878 during the Russo-Turkish War). Moreover, the Kashmir Imperial Service Troops, a newly established paramilitary contingent of the Anglo-Indian army, was put in charge of the Pamirs frontier garrisons in the early 1890s. Thus new strategic approaches to the defense of India suggested by both Charles Macgregor and Curzon were brought to life at the initial stage of reorganization.[31]

The pleas for help from the rulers of Punjab and Kashmir to the Russian emperor, mentioned earlier in the book, intensified just at the apogee of Russo-British rivalry. One of them, Dulep Singh, a younger son of Maharaja Ranjit Singh, who had consolidated Punjab in the course of the First Anglo-Afghan War, arrived in Russian Turkestan in 1887 on a covert mission that was quite unexpected by the local Tsarist authorities. In his appeal to Tsar Alexander III, this Indian prince claimed that he represented the majority of big landowners and, on their behalf, requested the Russian emperor to become a new suzerain of Hindustan. According to Dulep Singh, the Indian maharajas were mostly ill disposed toward British rule and therefore would be happy to join the invading forces, bringing with them an army of 300,000 volunteers, in order to force the withdrawal of all the British from India. At the very end of his message, the heir to the Punjabi throne invited two or three English-speaking military officers from Russia to investigate the state of affairs in British India.[32] As Richard Popplewell correctly pointed out,

> The Government of India's anxiety that Russia might exploit the grievances of Indian princes reached its height during the Viceroyalty of Lord Dufferin (1884–88). For a brief time, it seemed possible that opportunities might be open for Russian subversion in the key strategic province of the Punjab.[33]

After Dufferin's tenure in office came to an end "amidst a storm of regret from all classes of Her Majesty's subjects" in November 1888, no signs of improvement were seen in the country.[34] In spite of the tsar's circumspect reaction to the appeals from some Indian princes, the British intelligence service suspected that the Russians continued their espionage activity inside the Raj. On November 12, 1891, Lord Cross, the secretary of state for India, supported Lansdowne's negative opinion of a trip taken by Count de Kreutz and Baron de Nolde, both on the Russian military service: "You are quite right in keeping them out of Kashmir, but I dislike any Russian in India. Whatever their professed object, there is always an ulterior object behind, and the less we see of them the better."[35]

Even the round-the-world voyage carried out by the heir to the Russian throne, Nikolai Romanov, in 1890–91 caused annoyance in London and Calcutta. "I do not at all like this tour of the tsesarevitch," wrote Cross to Lansdowne on November 7, 1890, "Of course, I am not speaking of the man, but of his attendants. I think it is quite right that we should have two such Russian-speaking Britons as Wallace and Harding attached to the visitors, so as to prevent any mischief, and at all events to be able to keep watch and ward of them."[36]

To neutralize the influence of Russia upon Indian native elites and neutralize their hatred of the British, Lansdowne assembled all the Indian princes at a durbar (congress) of all the native princes in 1892. The omnipresent Russian menace to India, intensified by the signing of the Russo-French military alliance, was again on the political agenda.[37] Even before this event, Lord Kimberley, then the state secretary for India, remarked that the hostility of France toward Britain played everywhere to Russia's hand, while the director of military intelligence, Major General Henry Brackenbury, admitted that the worst combination the British had any reason to dread was a Franco-Russian alliance against the United Kingdom. A private trip made by Lord Randolph Churchill to Russia in October 1887 with the objective of sounding out Russian designs in Europe and Asia corroborated concerns of this kind.[38]

In a memorandum sent to the war secretary, Edward Stanhope, on August 7, 1887, the indefinite stance of the home Cabinet regarding delimitation of the northwest frontier of India and Afghanistan suffered harsh criticism from Major General Brackenbury.[39] Meanwhile, the British "forwardists" urged division of the Pamirs by the great powers, excluding Russia, in order to "do away with the robbery, violence, and oppression chronic in the states lying between the British, Russian, and Chinese frontiers."[40]

Conversely, the defensive projects drafted by the commander in chief of the Anglo-Indian army, General Frederick Roberts, to oppose a joint Franco-Russian assault upon the Raj intensified the flow of official correspondence between the state secretary and the viceroy in the early 1890s.[41] For example, Kimberley informed Lansdowne in July 1893 that

> there cannot, I think, be the smallest doubt that this nation would not go to war with Russia for Shignan and Roshan, and what is now happening about Siam emphasizes the importance of not getting into quarrel with Russia. A combination between Russia and France is perhaps the most formidable of all possible combinations against us. I fear that our very strained relations with France will, in any event, make Russia more difficult to deal with.[42]

Similarly, George Curzon cautioned the Cabinet of Saint James against Russo-French collaboration in Asia. His commentary in the journal *The Nineteenth Century* in August 1893 drew a special attention from the Russian Legation in London.[43]

However, as early as the summer of 1891, Colonel Mikhail Ionov, the commander of the Second Turkestan Line Battalion, led an expedition to reconnoiter those gaps in the Indian defenses that Calcutta had belatedly sought to fill before the anticipated Russian advance. According to the instructions from the Turkestan governor-general, Alexander Vrevsky, another objective of Ionov was to demonstrate military strength in the Pamirs in order to frustrate the division of the whole region between the British and the Chinese. While Ionov and his Cossacks erected a number of boundary pillars in the high mountains to demark a frontier line, they coerced a small contingent of the Qing frontier guards to retreat back to Chinese territory. In addition, Ionov deported the British explorers, Younghusband and Davison, whom he had met in the hills, on the pretext of their unrestrained activities in the Russian section of the Pamirs. The Tory Cabinet was infuriated by this provocative action and was terrified by information, albeit inaccurate, that Russian troops were entering the Pamirs and moving toward the Indian frontier with the obvious intention "to seize a number of forts, which protected the passes penetrating the mountains into India," so it energetically remonstrated against the policy of the "accomplished facts" threatening to bring two empires to an open breach of their relations.[44] As General Roberts later reminisced, he and his staff were ready "to go for the Russians" in the autumn of 1891. To retaliate for the consolidation of Russian power in the minor Pamirs states, the independent British expeditionary corps had captured Hunza by the end of 1891 and incorporated its territory into the British Empire.[45] Although Consul Petrovsky intimidated the Qing authorities in Xinjiang with the seizure by Tsarist troops of Sarikol and other boundary strongholds in the Pamirs, provided the Chinese ignored the British occupation of Hunza, he failed to egg the former on to open armed conflict with the latter.[46]

The breadth of this study merely permits a skeleton outline of Ionov's saga, inasmuch as Russian and British historians described this episode of the Great Game in full detail.[47] Yet it needs to be mentioned that regular expeditions to the Pamirs by the Cossacks under the command of Colonel Ionov spurred the Foreign Office to offer to the Tsarist Foreign Ministry to specify the principles of boundary delimitation in the region. Although the Russians insisted on strict adherence to the Granville-Gorchakov agreement of 1873, the Foreign Office pointed to a number of strategic, commercial, and ethnoreligious developments that had destabilized the state of affairs. The diplomatic contacts throughout the winter and spring of 1892 were, however, interrupted by a new Russian advance to the Upper Oxus.[48]

Thus it is small wonder that the Cabinet of Saint James, and especially the government of India, sought to combine both diplomatic and military methods in the scramble for the Pamirs, though Yegor Staal, the ambassador to London, recurrently assured Whitehall of the tsar's sincerest intention to settle the frontier problem in the distant areas as soon as possible.[49] "If the intelligence which I sent you from Berlin is well-founded," communicated Kimberley to Lansdowne on September 1, 1892, "the Russians are playing a bold game on the Pamirs.... I hope, however, they may be more reasonable than we expect. The worst of it is that it is impossible to believe a word they say."[50]

The defeat inflicted upon the Afghans by Ionov's military unit in the skirmish at Yeshil Gol in the summer of 1892 and his new attacks against the Chinese boundary posts compelled both London and Calcutta to ally with the emir of Afghanistan—though, as Lansdowne admitted, "it would be at best a risky proceeding."[51] The British press claimed the fulfillment of obligations to uphold Abdur Rahman in order to arrest Russian progress and coerce Saint Petersburg to accomplish the delimitation of the Pamirs.[52] In January 1893, Kimberley expressed his dissatisfaction with Russia's policies in a private letter to Lansdowne:

The answer of the Russian Government to Morier [the British ambassador in Saint Petersburg] as to the Pamirs is a most characteristic document. They evidently mean to postpone agreeing to any delimitation until they have established themselves on the line they have determined to occupy. I expect that, as soon as the weather permits, Colonel Ionov will resume his operations, and that we shall hear that Russian posts have been established at Bozai Gumbaz [a strategic pass in the Hindu Kush] and as far east as may be necessary to remove all obstacles to the free passage of Russian troops. I have no anticipation that the Chinese will offer any real opposition, and I should not be surprised to hear that the Emir has come to a secret understanding with Russia.[53]

The special conferences convened by Tsar Alexander III from April 1892 to March 1893 adopted the strategy of consecutive parleys on the Pamirs problem, first with the Chinese and then with the British. Meanwhile, the Turkestan governor-general formed the Pamirs Task Force in mid-1893. It consisted of one infantry battalion, three hundred Cossacks, and a battery of mountain artillery under the command of the same Mikhail Ionov who was later promoted to the position of military governor of Semipalatinsk Province.[54]

In his study of the Pamirs delimitation, Captain Zaichenko, a military expert on the Main Staff, correctly noted that this spatial region represented a field of conflicts between Russia and Britain for decades in the nineteenth century.[55] Not coincidentally, therefore, Russian preparations for hostilities at the approaches to the Raj caused a new tidal wave of Russophobia in the British public and governing elites, when the Foreign, War, and India offices concurred in the decision to expel the Russians from the northern slopes of the Hindu Kush by every means, not excluding military force.[56]

Summing up the evidence introduced here, it is not difficult to acknowledge that the struggle between "inactivists" and "forwardists" continued among the British ruling elites. The fall of the Tory government and the formation of the fourth Cabinet of William Gladstone in 1892 again changed the political landscape in the direction of coming to friendly terms with Russia. As this Liberal leader told one journalist, "The accordance between England and Russia makes a deposit of successful settlement of all great political problems of the universe."[57] That is why the Foreign Office made a proposal to Saint Petersburg in February 1893 to set up a Joint Boundary Commission in the Pamirs following the pattern of the bilateral committee dealing with the Afghan frontier.

Significantly, a similar dynamic was evident in Russian leadership circles. On May 31, 1893, Staal informed Lord Rosebery, the foreign secretary in the Liberal Cabinet, that with the domains of two empires perpetually approaching each other in High Asia, it was time to secure stability in a new boundary agreement predicated on the principles of mutual benefit. Symptomatically, the Russian diplomat used the phrase "*entente commune*," which, to his mind, ought to be included in the articles of a future pact.[58]

To exclude a secret Russo-Afghan or Russo-Chinese bargain on the Pamirs behind the backs of the British, Durand signed a special agreement with the emir of Afghanistan on November 12, 1893. Pursuant to it, the so-called Corridor of Wakhan was established, referring to a strip of the mountainous terrain, only a dozen miles wide at its narrowest part, that effectively separated Russian and British possessions. Henceforward, this corridor became incorporated into the Emirate of Afghanistan.[59] Furthermore, a frontier line called the "Durand Line" after the head of the British delegation to the boundary commission demarked the territories of British India and Afghanistan.[60]

In light of the Anglo-Afghan agreement of 1893, London urged Saint Petersburg to renounce all claims for the occupation of the high mountain corridors in the Pamirs. The diplomatic experts recommended to Whitehall "to enter into a bilateral military arrangement, according to which the Russian government would engage that her troops should not pass the line of the Murghab and that Great Britain should engage that hers should not advance beyond Gilgit, Jasin, Mastudj, and Chitral." In fact, the Russians were obliged not to cross the 38th meridian of latitude, while Hunza and Nagar, similarly to Kashmir, came under British protection. The British also proposed that their Russian counterparts give due notice to the opposite party in case any military action was needed in the frontier zone.[61] As Count Vladimir Lamsdorf, the foreign minister's chief counselor, wrote in his diary on May 3, 1894, "The Sovereign [Alexander III] believes that we shall reach a final agreement with the Englishmen regarding the Pamirs, without making any substantial concessions to them."[62]

In the spring of 1895, the British occupied Chitral, a nominal vassal state of the Kashmiri ruler, as a punitive military action to release the political officer and his escort, who had been besieged by rebels in the fortress. This action frustrated the plans of some Russian military officers to march through the Hindu Kush and seize this hill principality.[63] In spite of mutual collaboration on the Armenian problem and the Sino-Japanese conflict, the Russian Foreign Ministry demanded detailed explanations from the Foreign Office after it received the news of the British advance to Chitral.[64] Also, Russia's nervousness increased just at this time because of German intrigues against Saint Petersburg and friendly intercourse between Paris and London, which, in the view of the Tsarist government, might even lead to the revival of the Crimean coalition of the 1850s.[65]

In spite of all these unfavorable factors, both sides agreed on the delimitation of the Pamirs via an exchange of diplomatic notes between Kimberley and Staal on March 11, 1895, which symbolized the end of the Great Game in the Hindu Kush—though the demarcation of the frontier was only completed half a year later.[66] With this agreement, the last section of no-man's land in Asia was divided between the contracting parties, which meant that they had reached their "scientific" frontiers. Although Russia gained the larger part of the Pamirs, Britain secured its occupancies in India, and China actually restored order in Xinjiang, making any further advance impossible, except at the risk of war.

The majority of the general public and British statesmen, like Rosebery, were content to see this long-fought rivalry coming to an end.[67] But the "military party" in Saint Petersburg, as well as generals in the "far pavilions" of Asia—Major General Aleksei Kuropatkin, the military governor of Trans-Caspia, being a typical case—did not cease provoking the government to conduct an adventurous policy during the period when the attention of the great powers was diverted to the Sino-Japanese War of 1894–95.[68]

An account by Ralph Cobbold, an American traveler mentioned earlier in the book, who visited the Pamirs in 1897–98, testified to the ambitions for Inner Asia that were still cherished by the Tsarist officer corps,

> It appears that the plans for the invasion of Badakshan and Chitral from the Upper Oxus are a matter of common discussion at the dinner table of the Governor of Ferghana, and the officers at Charog [a boundary post in the Pamirs at the Upper Oxus] told me that at Marghilan the present Russo-Afghan frontier of the Oxus is considered as a purely temporary arrangement, and likewise the boundary fixed by the Pamirs Commission as by no means permanent. They affirm that in due course they will advance their frontier to the Hindu Kush on the south and cross the Oxus and occupy Badakshan. They anticipate that our government will give way, and not dare to risk a war with them on behalf of the Emir.[69]

This situation would become even worse, wrote some British political experts, if a scramble for the Kabul throne began after the death of the aged Abdur Rahman Khan. In this very case, the Russo-French alliance might be used by Saint Petersburg as insurance for the more reserved British stance with regard to Afghanistan.[70] George Curzon, who took a scheduled trip to the Afghan capital as the private, honorable guest of the emir himself, also shared this opinion, though Abdur Rahman had sworn eternal fidelity to Britain on behalf of his heirs.[71]

In a broader sense, despite the fact that the Russo-British delimitation of the Pamirs may be considered an important new step toward ending the frontier disputes between the two states, it was too early to surmise that the seeds of concord would inevitably grow into a pragmatic plant of a long-term collaboration. The Russian and British cabinets kept on watching each other's activities in different frontier zones with suspicion, dispatching agents provocateurs to instigate local nationalists or religious fanatics to rise up against colonial authorities, as happened in 1897–98 in Waziristan, which belonged to the British sphere of influence, and in the province of Ferghana, in the territory of Russian Turkestan.[72]

In this context, the situation at the western approaches to India was worth taking into consideration, for it shaped not only the situation in Afghanistan but also developments in other parts of East Asia.

THE FINAL ROUND OF THE GREAT GAME AT THE APPROACHES TO INDIA

As was stated earlier in the book, Tsarist strategists continued to brood over the projects of a march to India, notwithstanding the diplomatic compromises described above. Conversely, British military experts, whether sincerely or strategically, kept on regarding the Raj as in jeopardy from Russia, though the pattern of their thinking underwent certain modifications in the course of the Great Game. If at the initial stage they devoted more attention to Russian desires to uphold the native princes inside Hindustan in order to restore the former Mogul Empire,[73] and then they took heed of clandestine Russian activity among the bellicose mountain tribes in the northwest frontier zone, at the final stage of the Game their consideration was given to the highland passes in the Pamirs and the Hindu Kush, most of which were available to the Cossacks in their avalanche assault upon the flatlands of India. Such military writers as Roberts and Malleson speculated about this attack in numerous secret memos and open publications.[74] Typically, Younghusband, then the political agent in Chitral, reported to his superiors in February 1895 that

> these wild tribes are capable of being used as a weapon against us, and it would be impossible for us to remain in the plains and simply await attack whenever that might be made, because, if that were done, the Russians would be able to quietly establish themselves among the numerous tribes who inhabit the mountain belt and roll them off in one great avalanche on the plains of India whenever they chose to do so.[75]

As if to confirm these apprehensions, Kuropatkin drafted a detailed scheme for a Russian assault upon India through Afghanistan and the Pamirs as early as the mid-1880s. As Captain Grierson of the War Office's Intelligence Branch, who thoroughly analyzed it, pointed out,

> The author of this scheme realizes the fact that an invasion of India from the present Russian possessions could not be carried out in one campaign, and therefore, proposes in a first campaign to occupy Herat, Meimana, Balkh, and Badakshan; and in a second, undertaken some two or three years later, to take Kashmir, Kashgar, Kabul, and Kandahar. He thinks that after the latter successes the British Empire in India would be in such a "pitiable state" that little more exertion would be required on that part of the Russians to make short work of it.[76]

But what really struck the British expert was the close coincidence of Kuropatkin's plan with Macgregor's scenarios for a Russian advance to India from Trans-Caspia and Turkestan. Later, Charles Marvin (see chapter 4), reviewed all the Russian projects of an offensive nature against the Raj,[77] while V. T. Lebedev, the General Staff officer, digested them in a brochure that exposed three top objectives for an invasion: first, to oust Britain from the Middle East; second, to command the lines of transportation communications from Europe to Asia; and third, to open the way for an ice-free seaport. "Our victories over the Englishmen may result in the constitution of either the Russo-Indian monarchy or a number of independent states, or a federation of states under the patronage of Russia," argued Lebedev in 1898, "or, finally, in the conservation of British rule on conditions of the close cooperation between Russia and Great Britain."[78] Lebedev's essay was translated into English and became a topic of the lively discussions among British officers in the Anglo-Indian army. Interestingly, twenty-five years later, Feodor Raskol'nikov, a highly placed Soviet official, mocked the objectives and chances of a march to India as absolutely utopian:"One can hardly imagine Tsarist generals acting as apostles of the Indian revolution!" he stated ironically in one of his essays on the problem.[79]

To obtain intelligence on the situation in the states adjacent to Russian Turkestan, the Tsarist authorities meticulously monitored the activity of the government of India to consolidate the frontier and prepare it for a hypothetical attack by British expeditionary military forces.[80] For example, Lieutenant General Nikolai Protsenko, the head of the headquarters of Trans-Caspia, reported to the Main Staff in the fall of 1892 about the construction of fortifications, telegraph lines, and high roads. The recruitment of natives to join auxiliary paramilitary formations and reforms in the regular Anglo-Indian army also seemed to be on the agenda of war preparations. "All these arrangements are made by the Englishmen in conformity with the general project of hostilities against Russia, and more rapidly than before, as if in the foresight of an impending armed crisis in Anglo-Russian relations," observed Protsenko.[81]

On the eve of the twentieth century, the attention of Saint Petersburg was drawn to Lord Curzon's plans for the reorganization of military task formations according to three key principles. First, the viceroy intended to avoid the concentration of troops in remote military camps located far from the bases of supply. Second, he was eager to encourage the residents of the frontier areas to police the tribal lands by themselves. And third, he proposed constructing railways and high roads in order to substantially improve military logistics in the northwest section of Hindustan. As initiated by Curzon, the renovation of the British intelligence service in India would also contribute to strengthening the empire's defenses. In November 1901, the administrative reform carried out by the viceroy led to the unification of the districts on the frontier in Punjab with the contiguous tribal areas along the Durand Line. "As long as we rule India, we are the greatest power in the world," explained Curzon in a 1901 letter to Arthur Balfour, the leader of the Conservatives in the House of Commons; "if we lose it, we shall drop straight away to a third-rate power."[82] According to a modern historian, Curzon's policy in India was to make the country "a homogeneous compound instead of a heterogeneous mixture," and this, he believed, could only be attained by a strong central government that commanded both princes and provinces of India. That is why the viceroy "abolished internal differences of rule and promoted uniformity in education and fiscal systems."[83]

As is well known, consular staffers often spied on the countries and cities of their accreditation in the course of their legal duties. For example, the annual budget of the Russian Consulate in Bombay came to 22,500 rubles, including 5,250 rubles spent on espionage operations against the British authorities.[84] In September 1900, Lamsdorf, then the acting Russian foreign minister, instructed Pavel Klemm, the consul general in Bombay, to collect, collate, and analyze intelligence about the political situation and naval activity in this seaport. "India is of top significance to us [the Russians], because it remains the most vulnerable part of the British Empire, a sensible nerve, whereon a single touch, in case of emergency, may force the government of the Queen to convert Britain's hostile attitude into tolerance in all questions of mutual interest," maintained Lamsdorf in his instructions to Klemm. "According to the information we have at hand," he continued, "the self-seeking policy of Great Britain in India and the snobbish attitude of Englishmen to native residents still arouse the deep hatred of the population of multimillions."[85] In turn, the consul-general reported to Saint Petersburg that "the Anglo-Indian officials regarded the foundations of British rule in India laying not in the imaginary gratitude of the people but just in numerous caste superstitions and multiethnic diversities."[86]

The Russian Main Staff continued to collect intelligence both from the trips of officially sent military officers and the covert missions of secret agents dispatched to India. Between just 1897 and 1904, Lieutenant Colonel Serebrennikov, Lieutenant Colonel Kornilov, Captain Novitsky, Staff Captain Snesarev, and Lieutenant Colonel Polosov, to mention only a few officers, carried on their reconnaissance travels to Kashmir and the North-West Frontier Province of India with the permission of the British authorities. On returning to Russia, they reviewed the geographical features, customs, and traditions of the lands they had successfully traversed, while focusing on the state of political affairs.[87]

With respect to the secret emissaries who were sent to the Asian countries, Esaul (equivalent of captain in the Cossack troops) David Livkin, a specialist in Oriental languages, may be called a typical case.

Disguised as Mahomed Hasanov, a Persian dealer in the trade of precious stones, Livkin managed to surreptitiously penetrate the Raj through the seaport of Madras in the late 1898. He set up a spy network of local nationals with the help of a few Muslim merchants in Hyderabad. Along with gathering information about the epidemiological situation in the northern Indian states, where pestilence ran rampant at the moment, Livkin succeeded in collecting political intelligence. His secret reports to Saint Petersburg led to a reassessment by the Tsarist government of the actual state of domestic affairs in India. As he wrote in a conclusive report,

> The English dominance remains extremely consolidated, because their rule is a paragon of organization. Conceding for a moment that a revolt or a local mutiny occurs somewhere, immediately a sufficient amount of troops will be assembled to suppress it, due to the appropriate routes of transportation and railways in existence. Although the English presence in India is scarcely visible, their command of the situation is exercised efficiently everywhere in the country.[88]

Despite the stalemate in the Great Game, many Turkestan staff officers aspired "to wash up their high-boots in the Indian Ocean," after Afghanistan would yield to Russian power and a hypothetical uprising of Indian nations would facilitate invasion of the peninsula. Not surprisingly, one of the poems by Prince Esper Ukhtomsky, an eminent expert on Oriental studies and a close confidant of Tsar Nicholas II, was titled "We Shall Be in India Tomorrow."[89] Another illustration of the disposition to reach the "warm ocean" was a diary entry which a certain Russian volunteer officer in the Boers' service recorded during the war in South Africa. Being aware that the Tsarist Empire was still assuming glory and dignity, this person favored the spontaneous, fatal, and unstoppable progress of Russia in Asia, guided by Providence itself.[90]

Russian maritime activity in the last decades of the nineteenth century also irritated Britain. Although some key problems of the Great Game in the Far East, including those regarding the Pacific Squadron, are discussed in the next chapter, the situation at the other potential theaters of operations deserves analysis here. According to the official correspondence of the officers staffing the Admiralty, there is strong evidence to believe that the British naval attachés accredited in Russia thoroughly studied the personnel, ammunition, and dockyards of the Russian fleets in the Baltic, Black, and Caspian seas. Much attention was paid to the survey of the Russian sea fortresses as well as to the plans of a landing operation on the British Isles. Some British naval experts pointed to the boost in the buildup of the fast cruisers and vessels of the so-called Russian Volunteer Fleet.[91]

Characteristically, in 1887 the rumors of an impending sea war with Britain circulated in Saint Petersburg. Russian military writers speculated on the possible operations of the fast cruisers equipped with the newest torpedo apparatus, which was able to sink British merchantmen and avoid counterattacks of battleships. A popular slogan for the new naval program, which the Tsarist government set in motion in the late 1880s, was "Britannia no longer rules the waves!"

In response, the Admiralty proposed introducing a two-power standard, which was to become the famous core of British naval policy for the next forty years. The new Naval Defence Bill passed Parliament in 1889 while British strategists began to envisage a maritime war against a coalition of Russia and France. Symptomatically, William Langer, a prominent American specialist in diplomatic history, alluded to a novel by W. Le Queux, *The Great War in England in 1897*, which came out at that time. According to Langer, the author depicted a Franco-Russian invasion of Britain that resulted in the surrender of major industrial centers, such as Manchester and Birmingham, to the alliance, along with a fatal assault by the Russians and French upon London.[92]

Those Russian admirals and generals who attended a special conference on the development of the Russian fleet at the beginning of December 1895 presented to the tsar a more balanced vision of the naval competition. They concurred in the plan to prevent British battleships from entering the Black Sea via the Turkish Straits, while simultaneously preparing a strong squadron to fight the Germans in the Baltic and seeking an ice-free port somewhere in the Far East.[93] Three years later, an incident at Fashoda, an African settlement where British and French expeditionary forces collided in 1898, and a scramble for concessions in China spurred the Tsarist government to make improvements to sea fortresses in the Black Sea and Baltic Sea, in case Russia, allied with France, needed to get involved in an armed clash between London and Paris.[94] The Russian ambassador reported to Count Mikhail Muraviev, the foreign minister, on a new wave of jingoistic hysteria in U.K. military and naval circles. Characteristically, Nicholas II penned a rhetorical question in the margin of the document: "Why does England have a right to arm herself so audaciously among the universal peace?"[95]

The Boer War of 1899–1902 and the defeats suffered by British troops at its initial stage spawned illusions of geostrategic compensations that Russia would demand from Great Britain in return for its neutrality during the conflict. Lamsdorf specified these "compensations" as naval bases in the Mediterranean and Black Seas, or in the Persian Gulf and the Far East. In his view, London should make concessions to Saint Petersburg in Persia and Afghanistan. He recommended that Nicholas II establish direct diplomatic contacts with Kabul. On February 6, 1900, the Russian Legation in London delivered a memorandum to the Foreign Office arguing for the tsar's intention to implement this recommendation. Although the Russians reassured Whitehall that they continued to look upon Afghanistan as a state lying outside their sphere of influence, Mikhail Ignatiev, the political resident in Bokhara, proposed that the emir open direct trade relations between Tashkent and Kabul.[96]

Significantly, the scenarios for Russian foreign policy in different regions, including Central and East Asia, which Muraviev put forward in his humble report to the tsar early in 1900, in essence followed from Lamsdorf's general vision of foreign affairs. The latter, in turn, continued to regard Britain as Russia's foremost foe, particularly outside Europe. Moreover, the defeats of active British troops in South Africa induced the tsar to take a more aggressive stance in relations with the United Kingdom.[97]

On the other side, a majority of British military experts, with Brackenbury and Roberts as typical, still concurred in the opinion that geostrategic competition would inevitably lead to Russo-British confrontation in the mountain areas of the Pamirs or Hindu Kush. To avoid the Cossacks surreptitiously crossing the Indus River, a July 18, 1898, memorandum from Major General John Ardagh, who replaced Brackenbury as head of military intelligence, advocated that

> we should endeavour to secure a frontier which will keep her [Russia] as far away as possible, lest, when the time for actual demarcation arrives, we may find the Russians as inconveniently near to us as they now are on the north of Chitral. This same reasoning applies to Tibet as a buffer region. Unless we secure the reversion of Lhasa, we may find the Russians there before us.[98]

Apart from the Tibet problem, which is considered below, British military analysts recommended that the home Cabinet inflict a three-pronged preventive strike on Russia's communications with its Trans-Caspian dominions—first, from Batum or another seaport of a similar strategic importance on the Black Sea; second, from a base in the Mediterranean through Asia Minor; and, third, from a naval stronghold in the Persian Gulf through continental Persia.[99] Although the most authoritative members of both the Tory and Liberal cabinets, including prime ministers, demonstrated a skeptical stance with regard to these projects, almost all of them agreed with the conclusion, as Lord Salisbury wrote in a missive to Lansdowne at the end of the 1880s, that even "a single defeat at the hands of Russia could have catastrophic repercussions in India."[100] The fact that Salisbury's scenario for the "forward" policy had always been pragmatic and moderate should also be taken into consideration, because he really sought to advance frontiers to the points from which the buffer states—like Afghanistan, Kashmir, and even Persia—could be supported by the British authorities and at the same time command volatile tribes in the hill areas along the Russian and Chinese frontiers.[101]

Yet this political course depended heavily upon the attitude of Asian rulers toward Europeans. Countless summaries of intelligence and memoranda by political residents and military officers testified to the fact that the Foreign Office and the government of India persistently suspected Oriental potentates of having played a double game with Britain by trying to drive the wedge between London and Saint Petersburg. A typical instance was Abdur Rahman Khan of Afghanistan, who corresponded secretly with Tashkent via Herat throughout the 1890s while assuring Calcutta of his loyalty to Britain. Not coincidentally, therefore, the tsar's decision to begin a direct diplomatic dialogue with the emir as well as the construction of a branch line from the Trans-Caspian Railway to the Afghan border at Kushka in 1899 and 1900 infuriated Viceroy Curzon and the members of the Unionist Cabinet.[102]

Consequently, the Boer War encouraged Tsar Nicholas II to revive previous aggressive designs regarding Herat and Badakshan. The death of Abdur Rahman in 1901 only escalated the tension, inasmuch as any agreement between Afghanistan and European powers was regarded by the Afghan ruling elites as a personal deal by the emir. That is why the British were compelled to rebuild their relationship with each new ruler in that country while Habibulla, who ascended the throne after the demise of his father, intended initially to get rid of British protection as soon as possible. "It was reported," ran the summary for British intelligence dated July 1902, "that correspondence was going on between the emir [Habibulla] and the Russians, the result of which was that the Emir had bound himself to keep his country free from English influence, while Russia guaranteed to him in return her assistance, should Afghanistan fall under the English attack."[103]

This information verified perpetual blackmail of the government of India by Habibulla, who disseminated information on a Russian envoy's alleged arrival in Kabul across all of Central Asia. The alarmist messages from Calcutta compelled Arthur Balfour, Salisbury's political successor, to propose a withdrawal from any serious pledge to the emir, at the same time maintaining the status quo by suggesting direct arrangement with Russia.[104] Alternatively, Curzon dispatched a special mission to Kabul headed by Louis Dane, the foreign secretary of India's government. This mission aimed to coerce Habibulla to sign a new treaty with the British that would supersede the earlier agreements concluded in 1880 and 1893 by the late Abdur Rahman.[105] While bullying the emir with the inevitable Russian offensive against Herat and, simultaneously, granting him new subsidies, Dane succeeded in persuading Habibulla to reach a new arrangement with Britain on March 21, 1905. To all appearances, the Russian defeat in the war with Japan deprived the emir of resolution to continue even a semblance of an independent policy.[106]

Persia proved to be another state at the approaches to India for which the Great Game had entered a less hectic phase after the Penjdeh incident was settled peacefully in 1885 and, in the aftermath, the Joint Boundary Commission delimited the Russo-Persian frontier by 1887. Tension increased again, however, when the shah invited Berlin to stipulate its political and commercial advent to Persia. This initiative led to the sending of the first German ambassador to Tehran in the spring of 1885. Yet Otto von Bismarck rejected the shah's proposal to delegate a group of military instructors to his country as well as his request to invest German capital in railway construction.[107]

This activity impelled Russian and British representatives to consolidate their positions in Persia, because any kind of unexpected German infiltration of Middle East and Inner Asia jeopardized those rights and privileges that London and Saint Petersburg had gained there long before.[108] With the conclusion of a special agreement with the shah in 1883, the Tsarist government denied free access for transiting products from Europe to Persian markets through the Caucasus. Russo-Persian and Anglo-Persian banks were opened in Tehran with governmental participation, and private insurance companies began to operate in the country in the 1890s. Both Russian and British entrepreneurs competed for telegraph and tobacco concessions in Persia. Late in the nineteenth century and early in the twentieth century, Saint Petersburg and London granted several loans to the shah's government in order to control the country's financial assets.[109]

Although the British fleet displayed the Union Jack in the Persian Gulf and at the mouth of the Karun River, a tributary of the Shatt-al-Arab that served as a significant inner transportation artery, the Russians actually came to command the central provinces by means of a special Cossack Brigade (see chapter 4).[110] By the mid-1890s, this brigade submitted to the sovereign alone as his personal Horse Guards. In a private letter to Valentine Chirol, a respected political observer at *The Times*, the British envoy to Tehran, Sir Cecil Spring-Rice, expressed his appreciation for the role of the brigade as a formidable means of influence upon Persian elites:

> The only disciplined force here is 1,000 Cossacks, armed and officered by the Russians. They can take Tabrez in one day, Mashhad in two, Teheran in six. Should the Persians do anything the Russians dislike, the Russians can move their troops forward. We can only operate in the Gulf ports, threatening them far less than the capital.[111]

Analogously, Chirol himself devoted much attention to "the men of the Cossack Brigade" in his analyses of the Middle Eastern and Asian question in connection with the defense of India. In his view, all retired horsemen were usually sent off to the provinces, where they could act "as guards to the governors, agents of Russian influence and for the collection of information required by their Russian employers."[112] There is every reason to believe, therefore, that the brigade became an integral part of the Persian political scene, according to the reminiscences recorded by Major General Vladimir Kosogovsky, who was charged with this cavalry detachment in the 1890s.[113] Conversely, the military unit confined British pressure upon the Persian government, in spite of perpetual friction between the Russian envoys to Tehran and the chiefs of the brigade. "It is commanded by a Russian general in the service of the shah," wrote a French scholar at the turn of the twentieth century, "and this general corresponds directly to the war minister, similar to how the director of the Russo-Persian Bank communicates with the tsar's finance minister."[114]

For their part, the British sought to transform Persia into a stable buffer state and restore their diminished prestige in the remote provinces, especially Khorasan, where a new, effective center of espionage was established, for Mashhad continued to be the great sacred town of the Shiite Muslims.[115] To attain these objectives, Salisbury appointed Sir Henry Drummond Wolff to the new position of minister to Tehran in October 1887. Wolff was obliged to pay particular attention to the northeastern Persian borders and to persuade the government of the shah to consolidate administrative power on the spot. As a British scholar emphasized, Britain was scared not of the power of Russia but, above all, of the weakness of Persia.[116] In fact, however, Wolff's main task was to counteract the Russian influence upon Persia by the proliferation of free trade regulations and the encouragement of political reforms. On arriving in Tehran, Wolff proposed to the Russian envoy, Prince Nikolai Dolgorukov, to civilize the ancient kingdom through mutual effort. "It seems to me," wrote the British diplomat, "that while promoting prosperity of this country and assisting her to develop resources, two neighbours may have neutral territory between their boundaries, which would benefit from their support and wholesome influence."[117]

Consequently, Russo-British diplomatic correspondence verified the Russians' cautious attitude toward negotiations with their British counterparts on the problems of Persia, especially regarding railway construction. This issue was thoroughly discussed by the Russian ambassador to London, Baron Yegor Staal, in his conversation with Wolff as well as in the latter's memorandum on impediments in Anglo-Russian relations dated September 2, 1889.[118] To go no deeper into the matter, it is only necessary to point out that Wolff failed to invite the Russian diplomats at the shah's court to side with Britain in the promotion of urgent political reforms. Regrettably, however, the shah's official visits to Saint Petersburg and London following Wolff's private rendezvous with Alexander III in Berlin in October 1889 proved to be abortive. In an interview with Wolff, the British ambassador to Russia, Sir Robert Morier, explained to his colleague that Wolff's expectation of Russia joining hands with Britain to pursue a civilizing mission in the Middle East and Inner Asia seemed far from reality. To Morier's mind, the Tsarist government was convinced that Russia would become a guiding star in the ascendant for its Asian possessions, and their poverty and decline would only induce local nations to strive for its patronage.[119] As if to vindicate this statement, on November 12, 1890, Shah Nasir-u-Din pledged himself to Russia not to construct railroads on its territory and not to grant concessions to any foreign company or individual for the next ten years.[120]

However, the London Cabinet's understanding of current Persian affairs frequently thwarted that exposed by Calcutta. This essential disagreement stemmed from the distribution of responsibility for Persia between the Foreign Office, which monitored the situation in the empire's northern provinces, including Tehran, and the government of India, which was in charge of affairs in the southern provinces, including those adjacent to the Persian Gulf.[121] This differentiation of opinions may be illustrated by Curzon's classic book on the problems of Persia, *Persia and the Persian Question*, which was published in 1892, soon after the author's return from his famous trip to the Middle East. Simultaneously, this book shattered the illusions of those statesmen who had been cherishing hopes for Russo-British collaboration on regional problems:

> Russia regards Persia as a power that may temporarily be tolerated, that may even require sometimes to be humored or caressed, but that in the long run is irretrievably doomed. She regards the future partition of Persia as a prospect scarcely less certain of fulfillment than the achieved partition of Poland; and she has already clearly made up her own mind as to the share which she will require in the division of the spoils.[122]

Indeed, various Tsarist military and diplomatic thinkers did not forsake their criticism of the British political course in the Middle East and Inner Asia, scarcely distinguishing between those nuances in approaches to concrete problems for which London or Calcutta attempted to find appropriate solution in the course of the Great Game. For example, the adjutant general, Dondukov-Korsakov, the viceroy of the Caucasus (see chapter 4), foresaw further political expansion by Britain to Trans-Caspia following its commercial penetration of the region.[123] Another Russian military expert, Aleksei Kuropatkin, then the governor of Trans-Caspia, shared Korsakov's deep concerns about Britain's economic preponderance in Persia. On visiting Tehran in 1895 with a special message for Nasir-u-Din, he reported to Tsar Nicholas II that, notwithstanding Russia being a neighbor state of the Persian market, "the greater part of it still remains in the sphere of the British commercial influence, let alone Azerbaijan, wherein German trade has been recently rooted."[124]

Apart from Britain's advance to the northern provinces of Persia, the Russians were annoyed by British undertakings in Seistan, the southern province, through which, as the Indian government was perfectly convinced, Tsarist troops might also invade India, unless they failed to break through Herat to the Indus.[125] In the opinion of Lieutenant General Feodor Palitsyn, the chief of the General Staff, the British occupation of Seistan would seriously confine Russian ambitions to reach the Indian Ocean by a march across Persian territory.[126] Similarly, a German expert compared Bandar-Abbas, a seaport of strategic significance on the Persian Gulf, with Vladivostok, the "naval gates" of Russia on the Pacific Ocean. He even foretold the eventual establishment of a direct pan-Asiatic railway connection between the Far East and the Turkish Straits through Siberia, Turkestan, and Persia.[127]

To survey all possible routes for a Russian invasion of India through Persia, the Foreign Department at Simla dispatched Percy Sykes, an Orientalist and explorer, on a mission of reconnaissance to Baluchistan. As Curzon and General Horatio Kitchener, the commander in chief of the Anglo-Indian army in 1902–7, later estimated the strategic significance of this region,

The danger of complete Russian ascendancy in Seistan (apart from the greater facilities that it would provide for an attack upon Kandahar) appears to us to lie not in any opening that it might afford for an invasion of India through Baluchistan in the direction of Sind, but in the opportunities that it would provide for unsetting and embroiling the Beluch border from Seistan through Mehran to the sea. Already Russia, through her agents in Seistan, is perpetually intriguing with discontented or restless spirits on that border, and a situation might easily be developed which would cause us the same sort of trouble as we are so familiar with on the Pathan frontier of India.[128]

According to intelligence collected by Sykes in 1893–94, Russian spymasters installed a network of informants and scouts in the southern section of Persia to agitate for the Romanovs' Empire. The principal function of Sykes, who was raised to the rank of the consul in Mashhad, was daily monitoring of the Russians' activities in Persia, especially among local nations.[129]

In the meantime, the Russian Main Staff persisted in reporting to the tsar on British designs to engineer a circular railway from the sacred town of Qum via Esfahan that would enable the British to put the central and eastern provinces of Persia under their direct command. Besides, the government of India intended to erect a cluster of fortified outposts on the pattern of the strongholds that had been built earlier on the northwest frontier of the Raj.[130] Finally, the Russian Consulate in Baghdad obtained information on the British preponderance in the trade and commercial transactions between the minor Arabic states in the Persian Gulf.[131]

The demise of Nasir-u-Din in 1896 provoked a sudden, albeit quite expected, destabilization of the domestic situation in Persia. British diplomats—for example, Durand—feared an imminent Russian occupation of Tehran and the provinces bordering the Caspian Sea.[132] In fact, however, neither Saint Petersburg nor London was in a position to take responsibility for the maintenance of the territorial integrity of Persia. "It would seem to be much better," recommended George Curzon, "where rival interests are frankly divergent—for either party to play its own game, instead of affecting a community of interest which does not exist, and which would only be assumed by one party at any rate as a blind."[133]

The ascendancy of Muzzafar-u-Din to the throne did not improve the state of affairs. To all appearances, the threat of disintegration of both Persia and the Ottoman Empire prompted Salisbury to propose to Nicholas II an agreement on the Turkish Straits during the tsar's visit to London in the fall of 1896.[134] Two years later, the British prime minister modified his proposal by including partition of the Ottoman and Qing empires. In February 1899, Durand revealed an idea for Russian and British spheres of interest, which were to be established in Persia. Even Curzon, who doggedly opposed any concord with Saint Petersburg, admitted that "if Russia could be made to agree to spheres of interest in Persia all would be well, if not, the Cabinet would have to take action to thwart Russian activities in Persia."[135]

These arguments notwithstanding, there still remained skeptical opinions among high-ranking military and diplomats. Most typically, Spring-Rice commented on the stalemate in Persia, addressing his message from Tehran to a Foreign Office official on August 23, 1899:

> There seems to be a general belief in England that England and Russia might come to an agreement for the establishment of spheres of interest in Persia. The residents here and the natives laugh at the idea. It is quite true that Russia does not appear to wish to take any part of Persia; she has enough to do elsewhere and quite enough territory at present. But if she wants anything she wants the whole. Persia is the route by which she intends to reach the sea, and one end of a road is not much use without the other.... Her best policy is gradually to prepare the ground, to disintegrate Persia, and to prevent Persia from improving—to wait for an opportunity when England is engaged somewhere and to pounce.[136]

The treatment of the Persian question by the Tsarist government seemed to corroborate this skepticism. "We [the Russians] face another problem in the Middle East [and Asia]," stated an editorial in *Novoe Vremya*' on November 13, 1899: "We must reach a coast of the ocean [Indian] in order to come out to a wider space of world transport logistics at the point which locates not too far from the European part of the empire. That is why the shortest and straightest way to the ocean lies through Persia."[137] Similarly, on December 13, 1902, Foreign Minister Lamsdorf instructed Count Alexander Benkendorf (who succeeded Staal as ambassador to London): "Should delimitation of spheres of influence in Persia be adopted by both powers according to the English ambitions, Russia would not benefit any advantages, while, at the same time, Great Britain would gain far more rights than she possesses at present. The Imperial Government persistently eschewed, therefore, any bargains of this kind with England on the ground of Persian affairs." However, in a concluding paragraph, Lamsdorf did not exclude Russo-British rapprochement, which, however, "ought not to infringe upon their historic rights."[138]

The penetration of Russian men-of-war into the Persian Gulf on the eve of the twentieth century could not but lead to aggravation of tension in the region. Certainly, this naval action was another means of retaliation at a time when Britain's hands remained tied in South Africa. It is common knowledge that first the Portuguese and then the British had prevailed in the Gulf's political life and commerce since medieval times. Both Liberal and Tory cabinets signed treaties with some local rulers—the sultan of Oman, and the sheikhs of Bahrain and Kuwait in the last quarter of the nineteenth century. But shortly afterward, the new naval powers set about sending missions to the Arabic states located on the Gulf. A visit of a Japanese warship to the Gulf ports in 1880 was followed by a visit of the American frigate *Brooklyn*, which arrived in Bushire six years later. An Austrian-Hungarian training vessel and an Italian gunboat sailed to the Gulf the next year. A German warship also reached it in 1895. Finally, France began to dispatch its merchant vessels to the Arabian Sea.

According to archival records, a chance visit of the Russian auxiliary cruiser *Nizhny Novgorod* to the emirates of Muscat and Yask in September 1893 opened a new front for Russo-British competition in Asian countries.[139] Interestingly, Lord Northbrook had prophetically written to the India Office two decades earlier that "an attempt to extend Russian territory or a Russian protectorate to the shores of the Persian Gulf would be so direct a menace to India that it would justify a resort to arms for the purpose of securing our present supremacy in it." He suggested, therefore, proclaiming the Gulf a sphere of British interests as early as May 1873.[140]

George Curzon, a member of the Directorate of the Anglo-Persian Banking Corporation and an informal leader of the so-called old

Persian hands in the British establishment, headed a "crusade" for the maintenance of the Persian Gulf in Britain's orbit after his nomination to the post of the viceroy of India.[141] Curzon and the champions of the "forward" policy conjectured that any rival power, including Russia, would undermine the British position, once it occupied even a narrow coastal strip with a naval base or a coal station on the Gulf. Such an occupation, they believed, would definitely impress indigenous Arab residents and assist Britain's efforts to consolidate its rule in India, which in turn would lead to massive casualties among the British officers in the region and useless costs in the long run. As Curzon sarcastically remarked in his book on the situation in Persia,

> A Russian port in the Persian Gulf, that dear dream of so many a patriot from the Neva or the Volga, would even in times of peace, import an element of unrest into the life of the Gulf that would shake the delicate equilibrium so laboriously established, would wreck a commerce that is valued at many million pounds and would let loose again the passions of jarring nationalities only too ready to fly at each others' throats.[142]

Characteristically, as viceroy, Curzon intensified a routine correspondence with the British consuls, political residents, and agents in the Gulf area, such as Percy Cox and Colonel Robert Mid They kept informing him about all the important developments there during his tenure. Mindful of the real state of affairs, he drew the attention of the Cabinet and Salisbury himself to the anti-Turkish uprising in Yemen, to Russian designs to set up a coal station in Kuwait, to the activity of Russian epidemiologists in the south of Persia, and to French ambitions to occupy Muscat. His plan, dated September 1899, to counteract the great powers' advance upon Persia and the Gulf by active means, not excluding military force, was thwarted by the balanced political course pursued by Salisbury, not to mention Durand's opinion noted above.[143]

A visit by a German cruiser to Bushire in late March 1899 worried the British representatives and the government of India. It was especially alarming in the period of war preparations to invade the

Boer republics, which later compelled Calcutta to arrange for the trans-portation of more than 8,000 British troops and 3,000 native soldiers to the South African theater of operations.[144] The rumors of Russia's acquiring rights over the Persian port of Bandar-Abbas from the shah's government intensified apprehensions of its sinister desires in East Asia. "The presence of Russians and other foreigners in various parts of the Gulf has been frequently reported; in many cases they appear to be connected with the illicit trade in arms," commented political analysts in the summary submitted to the attention of Curzon.[145] The situation became tenser after the European press published information about a group of French battleships, destined to sail to Madagascar, that had just passed through the English Channel. "George Curzon telegraphs from India that he thinks they mean an intrigue on the Persian Gulf and wants them shadowed," wrote one high-ranking British administrator to his son on November 2, 1899.[146] This occurred just at the time when the Russian Naval Ministry sent a shallow-draft gunboat to the Gulf at the initiative of the Russian envoy to Tehran, in order "to indicate to the British and the local authorities alike that we [the Russians] con-sider access to the Gulf open to the ships of all nations, despite the wish of the British government to turn it into a closed sea within the sphere of her exclusive interests."[147]

The Russian gunboat made a tour of the Persian Gulf ports during March and April 1900. This visit was followed by naval missions by three other Russian warships—*Varyag, Askold,* and *Boyarin* (in the latter case, the Russian cruiser was accompanied by the French battleship *Infernet*) in 1901–3—and the first merchantman *Kornilov* shipped Russian manufactures and commodities to the Arab sheikhs in February 1901. Sergei Witte, the influential finance minister, submitted memoranda to the emperor on the establishment of direct shipping links between the Russian ports on the Black Sea and the Persian Gulf.[148]

This and other undertakings by the government to consolidate Russia's position in the Middle East testified to the seriousness of the situation—whether Saint Petersburg's conclusion of a trade convention with Tehran in February 1903, the construction of railroads in Turkestan, the protection of Muscat by the Russian fleet, the establishment of coal stations, or the acquisition of harbors in the Gulf. As a British military officer noted in a report to the War Office:

> The general consensus of optimism seems to be that when the Tashkent–Orenburg railroad is finished, or nearly so, a forward move may be expected, which will probably be a railway advance through Persia with a seaport as its ultimate objective.[149]

Curzon was likewise pessimistic about the security of British interests in the region. "Should a Russian naval port be constructed in the Gulf, and should a Russian Fleet (most likely in connection with the French) be called into existence in the Indian Ocean," he wrote to the India Office, "it is impossible, either for the protection of our trade, or for the safety of our own shores, that we could remain content with the existing strength of the East India squadron. We should have to place the ports on the eastern coasts of India in a state of more finished defence."[150] Conversely, the Cabinet of Saint Petersburg regularly gave the cold shoulder to nearly all diplomatic overtures made by the Unionist government to Russia. Typically, Nicholas II penned on the margins of a report from Staal in November 1901: "I will not stir a finger to come to any agreement with England."[151]

To counteract Russia's activities in the region, and in particular to dilute the impression made by the tours of its men-of-war to the Persian Gulf, the Indian government sent the *Renown*, a new battleship of the East India Squadron, to the Gulf. Yet the provincial Persian authorities and Arab sheikhs were reported to ignore the arrival of the battleship.[152] "Shall we give away Bandar-Abbas to Russia?" inquired political observers and military writers in their condemnation of the policy pursued by the Cabinet.[153]

That was why Lansdowne announced a special political declaration in the House of Lords on May 5, 1903. Predicated on the Curzonian argument that India should be defended at the distant approaches to the peninsula, including Arabia and the Gulf,[154] the foreign secretary warned the great powers that any attempt to set up a naval base or a fortified port in the south of Persia or on the minor sea islands would be regarded "as a very grave menace to British interests" and would be resisted with all means at Britain's disposal.[155] To soften his intimidating language, unusual in a diplomatic protocol, Lansdowne announced that His Majesty's Government would guarantee free trade and open enterprise activity to the all non-British private companies in the region.[156] This statement was warmly applauded to by all "true imperialists." "You may judge how satisfied I was," Curzon remarked triumphantly to Salisbury soon after Lansdowne's speech in Parliament. "This is what I contended for in a language which has since become famous in my book eleven years ago; it is what I have argued and pleased for in scores of letters to you during the last four years;...and therefore,...I cannot help feeling some personal sense of congratulations."[157]

Along with the diplomatic struggle for the concession of the Baghdad railway at the beginning of the 1900s, Lord Curzon's journey across the Persian Gulf appeared to be the last song of the Great Game in the Middle East before the outbreak of the Russo-Japanese War. The viceroy had proposed a tour of the Gulf for the first time in May 1901. But Britain's general involvement in the Boer War was the main argument for Salisbury and Lansdowne to veto this undertaking. Two years later, after Lansdowne proclaimed British special rights in May 1903, Curzon became fully convinced that the time had come to make an inspection of the imperial outposts in the Gulf. This time the Cabinet found no persuasive excuse to impede this trip.[158]

On November 16, 1903, Curzon, accompanied by his wife, Mary, set off from the port of Karachi toward the Sultanate of Muscat on board the flagship *Hardinge* with an escort of four warships. His journey across the Persian Gulf lasted nearly three weeks. Beside Muscat, the viceroy paid official visits to other Arab sheikhs, including the rulers of Sharja and Kuwait. He also attended the harbors of Bandar-Abbas and Bushire on the Persian coast, though he refused to land in the terminal port of his journey because of the anti-British intrigues being pursued by the Russian consul general, Nikolai Passek.[159]

Historians have differed on whether there was a hidden agenda for Curzon's trip to the Persian Gulf. David Gilmour, for example, considered it to be of purely ceremonial importance, although he acknowledged that "the tour also provided an opportunity for the navy to examine the strategic conditions of the Gulf in case it had to defend parts of it from a Russian attack."[160] Other authors, like Curzon's biographer, Lord Ronaldshay, insisted that there was great merit in the viceroy's abating Russia's sinister plans to subjugate Persia and seize a naval base in the Gulf.[161] The Soviet scholar Grigory Bondarevsky accused Curzon of frustrating Russo-British diplomatic contacts in the fall of 1903 that might have precipitated official negotiations on the peaceful settlement of their disputes in Asia.[162]

This negative reasoning notwithstanding, the journey should be regarded as one of the last turns of the Great Game in the Middle East, though this assessment should not bring the reader to the inference that henceforward it fell outside the scope of Russian and British policies.

THE TIBETAN "PLAYFIELD" IN THE GREAT GAME

"The Land of Snows," or "the Heart of Asia," as many Europeans usually called Tibet, had always attracted their thinking, while remaining an enigmatic land, with inaccessible mountain terrain controlled by the Qing Dynasty since the second half of the eighteenth century. The rumors of enormous mineral resources concentrated in Tibet together with ancient legends of the mysterious people who inhabited it under the supreme authority of the Dalai Lama, an earthly embodiment of Bodhisattva, inspired numerous explorers from Europe to make their way to this "lost world."[163]

Politically, the Cabinet of Saint Petersburg sought to neutralize London's desires to control Tibetan Buddhists and thus frustrate London's goal of manipulating the adepts of Lamaism in Southern Siberia, Altai, and Kalmykia.[164] In a secret memo to the Main Staff, Nikolai Golovin, an officer with a special commission at the headquarters of the Turkestan Military District, portrayed Tibet as the next cockpit in the Great Game because of the vacuum of Qing power there and the advance of the Kashmiri rulers, whose armies regularly penetrated into southern areas of Tibet, plundering both the sedentary population and caravans of transit traders. Golovin further maintained that

> the Englishmen were not likewise lenient toward Buddhism, destroying even those Buddhist monuments, which have existed ever since ancient times; and they did not hesitate to burden the Buddhists with high taxes, especially in the aftermath of Yakub Beg's coming to Kashmir that coupled with intensive contacts between him and the British political agents, like Forsyth and Shaw, on the shipping of war matériel and dispatch of military instructors to Kashgaria.[165]

Golovin proposed to his superiors to send a qualified intelligence agent on a confidential mission to Lhasa to reconnoiter the state of matters there, initiate contacts with local officials, and collect information on British designs in the province. A group of ten Buddhist monks who were familiar with all the details of the route to the Tibetan capital should accompany the agent, disguised as a pilgrim. Moreover, Golovin meticulously outlined four possible scenarios for the expedition, the spending on which, according to his report, would amount to 12,000 rubles.[166] Dimitry Miliutin inquired with the Foreign Ministry on the practical expediency of this suggested expedition to Tibet. In reply, Nikolai Giers, the acting minister, contended that though the proposal seemed of interest, it might be implemented by Colonel Mikhail Przhevalsky, who was about to set off for his third trip to Inner Asia. In this case, admitted Giers, Golovin might be attached to the staff of the mission.[167]

Simultaneously, Przhevalsky himself sent a note to the head of the War Ministry's Asian Division. From his point of view, "the scientific research will camouflage the real political objectives of the expedition and ward off the inference of our adversaries."[168] He also specified that there was an urgent necessity to place the Dalai Lama, the most influential Buddhist spiritual leader, under Russian protection in order to prevent him from coming into the orbit of British policy.[169]

As is well known, the third and fourth expeditions to Lhasa undertaken by Przhevalsky failed to reach the sacred city. Yet no authentic archival records have been found that might shed light on a confidential mission to Lhasa made by a person in the guise of a pilgrim or a lama in compliance with Golovin's proposal. To all appearances, by the mid-1880s, the Tsarist government for the moment had given up the idea of any further invasion of Tibet and had shifted its attention toward more significant "playfields"—Afghanistan and Turkmenia, though the Russian consulates continued to monitor the situation in Burma, Nepal, and other minor states abutting British India.[170]

Tibet's isolated position and its strategic meaning as a natural, unsurpassable obstacle on the northeast frontier of the Raj encouraged the government of India to institute a special training center at the Dehra Dun hill station in the suburbs of Simla as early as in 1863 to school a few selected local nationals on how to survey Tibet. As was mentioned in the earlier chapters, these native scouts, known as pundits, contributed greatly to exploring and mapping the most faraway places in High Asia. Significantly, they managed to discover gold and silver mines in the upper flows of the three great Asian rivers—the Indus, Sutlej, and Brahmaputra—at a height of 16,300 feet.[171] Characteristically, Ekai Kawaguchi, a Japanese Buddhist monk, who was consulted by the most experienced pundit, Sarat Chandra Das, before visiting Lhasa disguised as a Chinese physician, recorded in his diary in 1901 that the natives were aware of a desire on the part of the British to take possession of the gold mines from the Qing authorities.[172]

This situation changed by the end of the 1880s. Apart from the Russian threat, two more aspects assumed crucial meaning—the impending collapse of the Qing Empire, and the armed confrontation between Nepal and Tibet in 1884–85, when the Indian government preferred to uphold the Nepalese, who offered military assistance to Calcutta in the event of war with Russia. The strategic position of Nepal, bordering the Raj in the northeast, somehow matched the location of Afghanistan on its northwest frontier. As Ney Elias reported to the Foreign Office in March 1887, "undoubtedly, the Russians were attracted to Tibet as the back door to intrigue with Nepal." This brilliant explorer felt concern for Russia being able to make British relations with Katmandu as unpredictable as they seemed to be with Kabul.[173]

Thus, while Britain sought to link India to China via Tibet, the Tsarist government endeavored to create a springboard in the Land of Snows for the encirclement of the Qing Empire in the south along with opening a second front against British rule in India in the northeast direction.[174]

To stave off the implementation of such a scenario, London had to rely on both military and economic means. In the fall of 1888, more than 2,000 Anglo-Indian troops invaded the Chumbi Valley—a gateway to Lhasa. The aggression occurred after the convention of 1886 between Britain and China had ceased to regulate the state of affairs. In 1890 the government of India and the Chinese *amban* (again, the provincial Qing chief administrator) signed another agreement on the delimitation of the boundaries in the triangle of Burma, Sikkim, and Tibet. Three years later, Calcutta and Peking endorsed the new trade regulations between British India and Tibet. All these documents laid the foundations for further British policies to open the Land of Snows for commerce, on the one hand, and to frustrate any designs of geostrategic adversaries to link Russian Turkestan to French Indochina, on the other.[175] Typically, a British businessman engaged in overseas commerce wrote to *The Englishman*, a daily newspaper that came out in China,

> If the valley of that great river Yangtze is to be preserved from encroachment, it is important that neither France nor Russia should be allowed to thrust an arm between it and India. We must be dominant in Tibet both on account of present advantages and future possibilities.[176]

In March 1893, Peter (Zhamtsaran) Badmaev—a baptized Buriat Mongol who had graduated from Saint Petersburg University, then served in the Foreign Ministry's Asian Department, and called himself a Tibetan doctor of medicine—submitted to Sergei Witte an ambitious project aimed at bringing Mongolia, Manchuria, and Tibet under the Romanovs' scepter. This objective might be achieved, according to Badmaev, at minimal risk of military conflict and at little cost by the instigation of an uprising against Manchu rule along with the construction of a branch railway line from Lake Baikal to the city of Lanchow and further to Xinjiang in the territory of the Qing Empire. The project also envisaged a propaganda campaign to be launched among the national minorities of China in order to position the Russian tsar as the real protector of Asian peoples from Westernization.[177] Interestingly, the British ambassador to Saint Petersburg, Sir Nicholas O'Connor, reported to London on his interview with Witte on January 1, 1898. The Russian finance minister allegedly drew his hand over a few provinces of China depicted on a map of the Celestial Empire and solemnly announced that Russia would probably absorb all these territories sooner or later, provided the great Trans-Siberian Railway and the hinterland of China were linked together by a cluster of branch lines.[178]

Although Tsar Alexander III initially turned down Badmaev's scheme as a fantastic dream, Witte solicited the emperor for a budget of 2 million golden rubles to be allocated to the newly established trading tea company run by the dexterous Tibetan doctor. In November 1893, the tsar subsidized Badmaev with a loan for ten years at a 4 percent rate of interest. The Russian consuls in Urga, Kuldja, and Kashgar were required by the Foreign Ministry to keep a close eye on his activities in Mongolia, Xinjiang, and Tibet.[179] Copious memoranda delivered by this adventurer to the attention of Nicholas II in the late 1890s and early 1900s constituted testimony that Britain's preponderance in Tibet would severely impinge upon Russia's prestige in East Asia and undermine its overwhelming influence upon China. The Tsarist government hence ought to establish secret diplomatic contacts with the Dalai Lama in order to take Tibet under the Russian protectorate. Thus, the reconnaissance missions under the cover of Badmaev's trading company left Saint Petersburg for Lhasa to spy in Mongolia and Tibet. At the same time, encouraged by Tsarist officials, tens of youngsters from the Buriat and Kalmuck nations made pilgrimages to the most prominent Tibetan monasteries to become Buddhist monks and, simultaneously, part-time agents for Russian influence in the Land of Snows.[180]

It was small surprise, then, that Badmaev's machinations caused a great deal of anxiety in Calcutta and London, where Lhasa was looked upon as a bridgehead for further Russian penetration of High Asia, a screen against Russian encroachment on India from the northeast, and a religious center of Buddhism. As Younghusband illustrated, Britain's genuine fear of the Russian invasion of Tibet was that it would lead to a concentration of British armed forces on the Tibetan frontier, which, at the same time, would weaken the defense of India in the northwest sector.[181] Austin Waddel, a physician who had accompanied Younghusband in his famous march to Lhasa in 1903–4, likewise admonished British public opinion against the disastrous effect that Russia's eventual preponderance in Tibet would have had upon Britain's position in Central and East Asia. According to Waddel, under the worst circumstances, many Himalayan minor states would set up hostile alliances, which would require of the government enormous military spending to prevent their breaking through the defense line of the Raj.[182]

A lecture delivered by a certain Gombozhab Tsybikov—one of the Buriat pilgrims to Central Tibet in the 1890s and early 1900s, and later to become a professor of Buddhology at the University of Vladivostok—at the annual meeting of the Imperial Russian Geographical Society verified apprehensions of this kind. The speaker reasoned why the Tsarist government should take the status of Tibet into consideration:

> Russia could hardly regard Tibet as a profitable consumer market for her goods, but it is important to her as a pivotal area of Lamaism, so popular among the modern Mongols, Buriats, and Kalmucks living under subordination of the Russian Empire.[183]

The Sino-Japanese War of 1894–95 exposed the impending breakup of Imperial China to the outer world. The great powers then commenced an uncompromising scramble for concessions and spheres of interest in the Far East. Under these circumstances, Russian strategists determined upon a good sendoff in the conduct of the clandestine political contacts with Tibetan lamas. On June 4, 1895, O'Connor worriedly wrote to the viceroy, Lord Elgin, that

> some time ago some Russian officers [Vsevolod Roborovsky and Petr Kozlov] had been in communication with the Tibetan authorities…and impressed upon them the importance of main-

taining friendly relations with the Russians who were alone able to protect them against the ambitious designs of the English who evidently coveted possession of Tibet.[184]

Consequently, the lease of the Chinese naval bases by Germany and Russia in 1897–98 caused an escalation of international tension in the Far East. The British occupation of Weihaiwei, a retaliatory arrangement aimed to arrest the advance of its rivals to the Pacific, also stimulated Russian secret missions and expeditions to arrive in Tibet on the eve of the twentieth century. For example, a mission by Captain Baranov, a former adjutant of Przhevalsky, visited Tibet in 1898–99. Baranov passed envelopes with emergency messages to the thirteenth Dalai Lama, Tubten Gyatso, who had been inaugurated as the supreme ruler in 1894. The latter was asked to send the envelopes to the nearest Russian post of frontier guards if Anglo-Indian troops risked invading Tibet. However, the Dalai Lama passed these envelopes to the Chinese *amban* in order to be backed up by the Peking government in the event of an armed conflict with the British.[185]

In the late 1890s, Agvan Dorzhiev and Petr Kozlov, two outstanding pathfinders, greatly contributed to the setting up of political contacts between Russia and Tibet. According to Dorzhiev's autobiography, written in 1921–22, he came from a family of Khalkha Mongols living in a village to the south of Ulan-Ude, the administrative center of Russian Buriatia. At the age of twenty-one, Dorzhiev made a pilgrimage to Tibet as a Buddhist monk. There, he was educated in the monasteries for a few years and went on to become a professor of metaphysical philosophy at Drebung Monastery, where he rose to the rank of *lozang dorpe*, the equivalent of a bishop in Christianity. His deep knowledge of the Buddhist canon and initial noninvolvement in internecine quarrels at the Court of the Dalai Lama XIII motivated his promotion to the post of private tutor and counselor to Tubten Gyatso in 1889.[186]

Three decades later, Dorzhiev recalled that Anglo-Tibetan relations were impaired because of the British occupation of Sikkim, a traditional vassal state of Tibet. "To the extent of my understanding," he wrote in his autobiography, "I surmised that as far as the Russians are opposing the British, the Russians are able to aid the Tibetans to avoid the seizure of their country by the Englishmen. And that it is necessary to elucidate the state of things in Tibet to the Russian side."[187]

Dorzhiev persistently enforced his plan to assure the Dalai Lama and other high-ranking Buddhist priests, who were ignorant of the realities in world politics, that Russia and Britain were waging a competition with each other in Asia. Although the Manchu Dynasty was declining, argued Dorzhiev, Russia might become the only possible ally of Tibet against Britain. "If Russia takes Tibet under her protection," he contended, "the Tsarist government will be benevolent to the Buriats and their religion. And Tibet will escape the maw of aliens."[188] Dorzhiev's concept corresponded with the personal intention of the young Dalai Lama to gain independence from China, taking into account Peking's actual noninterference with the British encroachments upon the hill principalities of Sikkim and Ladakh in 1890–92.[189]

It was Dorzhiev who initiated the first Tibetan unofficial mission to be delegated to Saint Petersburg, ostensibly with the objective of collecting financial donations for the construction of a Buddhist temple in the Russian capital. In December 1898, the tsar received Dorzhiev in a private audience, with Prince Ukhtomsky and Doctor Badmaev also attending. Imbued with the perspective to obtain extensive political and commercial rights in Tibet, Nicholas II promised to uphold the Tibetans in their struggle for autonomy, if not independence, against either the Qing or British empires. The tsar also recommended that the war minister, Kuropatkin, dispatch to Lhasa a group of military instructors furnished with various types of war matériel to supply the Tibetans.[190]

Reciprocally, three months later, the British political representative in Sikkim arrived at Yatung, a small settlement on the Tibetan border, to meet the Chinese *amban*. During their interview, the latter warned the British officer that if the government of India insisted on the signing of a boundary convention without Lhasa, the Tibetan government might apply for support to Russia. Other high-profile lamas confirmed this information to the British delegate, which actually meant that Dorzhiev's mission to Saint Petersburg had assumed political meaning.[191]

The fact that Dorzhiev labored hard against Britain's interests in High Asia should not be interpreted, however, as irrefutable evidence that he was being paid by the Russian War Ministry, though he was rumored to have been attached as an interpreter to the staff of the last expedition conducted by Przhevalsky as early as in 1884.[192] "I do not think he was or is more of an intriguer than any Asiatic would be when confronted with, to him, such a new and intricate question as Tibet's policy in Central Asian politics and in relation to the great empires it neighbours," reported William Rockhill, the American envoy to China, to Washington after his first talk with Dorzhiev on November 10, 1908.[193] Conversely, Dorzhiev's trip around France, Britain, and Italy in 1899 and 1900 as well as his discourse with Georges Clemenceau, the French politician of a chauvinist tenor, led to the conclusion that he had persevered in searching for an ally among the European great powers, either in alliance with or even apart from Russia.

According to the entries in his diaries, Dorzhiev met Nicholas II for the second time in mid-October 1900. During his stay in Yalta, the astute monk convinced the autocrat that the Tibetans had anticipated an earthly protector who would act as the sword of God to defend them from numerous foes. Dorzhiev called Nicholas the Stepson of Heaven and the 169th incarnation of Buddha, an allusion perfectly corresponding with the latter's ambition to become the "Lord of the Pacific."[194] Not coincidentally, Dorzhiev made this trip at the apogee of the British misfortunes in the Boer War and the so-called Boxer Uprising in China. Directed by the tsar, Lamsdorf also met Dorzhiev as a diplomatic representative of the Grand Lama. Characteristically, *Journal de Saint Petersburg* published an official communiqué of the audience in the luxurious palace of Livadia on October 19, 1900.[195]

Meanwhile, the reconnaissance expeditions commanded by Tsybikov, Zerempil, and Narzounof—the Buriat and Kalmuck subjects in the tsar's service who were disguised as Buddhist pilgrims—surveyed the routes and gold mines at the approaches to Lhasa. As early as April 18, 1899, George Hamilton, the India Office secretary, admonished Curzon in a ciphered secret memorandum against the private company of a certain influential pro-British entrepreneur (Baron Rothschild?), whose activity might be preempted by the advance of the Russians if the gold fields located between Trokjalang and Shigatze fell under their control.[196]

According to intelligence obtained by Sarat Chandra Das and other pundits on returning from Russia, Dorzhiev handed to the Dalai Lama a paper roll recording the Russian emperor's good acts. This roll specified many benefits that all Buddhists would obtain by the maintenance of friendly relations with such a great monarch and proposed to arrange a trip by the Dalai Lama to Saint Petersburg so he could convert the emperor to the Buddhist faith. Dorzhiev told his patron of the legend of the mysterious Shangri-La and a mighty Buddhist prince, who was bound to emerge in a country lying "somewhere to the north of Kashmir" and bring the whole world under his rule. The young and gentle tsar, Dorzhiev added, could be the incarnation of this prince, who was temporarily pretending to be a Christian merely on the grounds of expedience.[197]

This legend, coupled with the dismaying British encroachments upon Tibet, led the assembly of the highest lamas and chieftains to vote to send a third political mission to the Russian capital under the command of the omnipresent Dorzhiev, whose influence upon the ruler of Tibet definitely overshadowed that of the pro-British or pro-Chinese groups in the Dalai Lama's administration.

Thus, the staff of the third mission delegated to Russia by the Tibetan potentate was furnished with exclusive diplomatic credentials. It needs to be noted that Nicholas II welcomed the extraordinary Tibetan ambassador at the Grand Palace of Peterhof on July 6, 1901. As Cecil Spring-Rice confessed in a letter to one of his correspondents five years later: "The real reason is the idea, which he [the tsar] has fixed in his mind that, if he assumes or is given the right to act as temporal protector of the chief center of the Buddhist faith, he will become the moral chief of the continent of Asia."[198] To encourage these aspirations, Dorzhiev presented to Nicholas II a draft Russo-Tibetan treaty of alliance, engraved on a golden plate. A special conference was held in Saint Petersburg to discuss the proposed agreement, but it was rejected by the majority of the government. In spite of the aspirations of Saint Petersburg to undermine the British position in High Asia with the help of the Tibetans guided by their spiritual leader, the skeptical attitude to the projected secret alliance by such leading political statesmen as Witte and Lamsdorf led the negotiations to nothing.[199] Yet the tsar assured Dorzhiev of his personal strong desire to act in support of Tibet at any time and despite any British remonstrations. The Tibetan envoy was granted a lavish present from Nicholas II—a bishop's vestments for the Russian Orthodox Church. Before the departure, Dorzhiev was required to convey special messages from Nicholas II and Lamsdorf to the Dalai Lama to assure friendly relations between Russia and Tibet. While the press enthusiastically commented on this visit, two caravans of 200 and 300 camels each—loaded with silver bars, other luxurious gifts, and, certainly, war matériel—set off to Lhasa from the Russo-Mongolian border.[200]

In parallel with the diplomatic activities by Dorzhiev, Lieutenant Petr Kozlov, an explorer who was one of Przhevalsky's intimate assistants and friends, conducted a special reconnaissance mission to Eastern Tibet. As early as in the winter of 1899–1900, Kozlov, escorted by three officers and fourteen Cossacks, traveled from Urga to Lhasa. As Colonel Macswiney of the Indian Intelligence Branch reported to his commanders, "Not satisfied with scheming for a port in the Persian Gulf, Russia is bent on being before us in Tibet. Lieutenant Kozlov's objective is Lhasa, by the Emperor's special command."[201]

Although Kozlov failed to reach the Tibetan capital, owing to the categorical prohibition by the administration of Chamdo, a boundary Tibetan outpost 300 miles from the capital,[202] he collected valuable nuggets of intelligence about the latest political developments, geographical features, and ethnoreligious composition of Tibet. According to Kozlov, it might be divided into three relatively separate regions: Central, Eastern, and Northern. If the first part was governed by the Dalai Lama himself, the Eastern and Northern sections were controlled by the Qing authorities. In Kozlov's view, the Tibetans ceased to place confidence in the Manchu Dynasty after the Chinese defeat in 1895 and the occupation of Peking by the allied European troops in August 1900. Yet they did not hold enough war potential to shake the yoke of the Qings by themselves and therefore sought a mighty sponsor to help them achieve the independence of Tibet, the Russian sovereign being number one on the list.[203]

The information gathered by Lieutenant Kozlov, who was promoted to the rank of captain after his return from the Tibetan expedition in 1901, underlay the dossier on the situation in Tibet, which the General Staff officers regularly delivered to the attention of Kuropatkin, Lamsdorf, Witte, and the emperor himself during the period 1901–3. Their memoranda envisaged secret military support to be provided to Lhasa in compliance with the semiofficial intercourse established between the Russian and Tibetan courts.[204]

Reciprocally, British leadership circles and the general public disliked the prospect of Cossacks patrolling the streets of Lhasa, as Dorzhiev told some Tibetan dignitaries in 1902. It would appear probable that most British statesmen, and Curzon above all, were convinced that as long as the Qing Empire maintained territorial integrity, at least in the regions bordering Russia, the latter would pose no direct menace to India's northeast frontier, but if the Manchu rulers collapsed as they had done in the war against Japan, followed by the great powers' ruthless scramble for concessions and spheres of interest in the Far East, Tibet could fall under Russian influence, which would lead to the emergence of another zone of Anglo-Russian confrontation in High Asia.[205] Besides, some politicians, including the viceroy of India, suspected that the tsar was anxious to channel traditional Chinese xenophobia into the anti-Western policies of the Peking government, to the benefit of Russia.[206]

On June 11, 1901, Curzon forwarded to Hamilton a memorandum on the Russian ambitions in Tibet. To Curzon's mind, Britain was unable to hamper Russia from conquering Mongolia or Chinese Turkestan, but the Cabinet was bound to prevent the establishment of a Russian protectorate in Tibet, which would definitely constitute "a distinct menace" and "a positive source of danger" to the Indian Empire. "If Russia reaches the borders of Nepal," argued the viceroy, "that country will be converted into a new Afghanistan instead of becoming a buffer state between us and Russia."[207] While focused on galvanizing an active British policy toward Asian states, Curzon grumbled in a report to the India Office at the end of 1901,

Acquiescence in the aims of Russia at Teheran or Mashhad will not save Seistan. Acquiescence in Seistan will not turn her eyes from the Gulf. Acquiescence in the Gulf will not prevent intrigue and trouble in Baluchistan. Acquiescence at Herat and in Afghan Turkestan will not save Kashgar. Acquiescence at Kashgar will not divert Russian eyes from Tibet. Each morsel but whets her appetite for a pan-Asiatic dominion. If Russia is entitled to these ambitions, still more is Britain entitled, nay compelled, to defend that which she has won, and to resist the minor encroachments which are only a part of the larger plan.[208]

The viceroy actually proposed a refreshed concept of an active Indian defense, which needed to be reinforced in every possible direction of invasion. "Tibet is, I think, much more likely in reality to look to us for protection than to look to Russia," wrote Curzon in a private letter to Hamilton, "and I cherish a secret hope that the communication which I am trying to open with the Dalai Lama may inaugurate some sort of relations between us."[209] As an Indian historian remarked, "Curzon not only moved the pieces in the Great Game on the traditional squares of Persia and Afghanistan, but also, for the first time, brought Tibet within its scope."[210]

However, all the attempts of the viceroy to address the Dalai Lama, first through the *amban* and then directly by sending couriers with messages to the Potala Palace, the residence of the Tibetan ruler, ended in a fiasco. As early as March 1899, the viceroy let Hamilton know about the stalemate in Tibetan policy:

We seem to be moving in a vicious circle. If we apply to Tibet, we either receive no reply, or are referred to the Chinese Resident. If we apply to the latter, he excuses his failure by his inability to put any pressure on Tibet.[211]

The "almost royal honours"—which Dorzhiev, as the representative of "the Tibetan priestly junta," in Curzon's own words, had received from the tsar in Saint Petersburg—shocked the viceroy, who could not be aware of the real state of relations between Russia and Tibet because of the lack of agents "as efficient…as are employed by Russia" on the northern borders of Sikkim, the British vassal state. Meanwhile, the news of the Russians' aspirations to sign a separate convention on Tibet with China as a condition sine qua non for the evacuation of Tsarist troops from Manchuria after the suppression of the Boxer Uprising, reached Calcutta and London. In February 1902, Maharaja Chandra Shamsher Jang, the prime minister of Nepal, informed Colonel Pears, the British political resident in Katmandu, about a proposal made to him by the Dalai Lama himself for joint armed resistance to a probable invasion of Tibet. According to the maharaja, he received intelligence about the intentions of the Chinese governor-general of Sichuan and the rulers of Bhutan and Ladakh to enter the anti-British "coalition" allegedly propped up by Russia. Pursuant to this crafty plan, British expeditionary forces would be enticed into the high Himalayan passes and annihilated there by Tibetan combatants with the help of explosive charges, which Russian military engineers would install in the mountains to provoke snow avalanches down to the battalions on the march.[212]

Various panicked rumors of sinister Russian designs in Tibet circulated in the Indian and Chinese press. For example, three Tsarist military instructors were reported to have arrived in Lhasa to supply the Tibetan troops with modern machine guns, while some local Chinese governors were said to have been bribed by the Tsarist military authorities not to impede the transportation of Russian war matériel to Tibet.[213] In April 1902, the Reuters news agency announced that Pavel Lessar, the Russian minister to Peking, had suggested to the Qing government that Peking should grant Tibet independence, a request that the government of India interpreted as the first step toward the conversion of the former Qing Province into a protectorate of Russia.[214] The report by Sir Ernest Satow, the envoy to Peking, which was submitted to the Foreign Office on August 2, 1902, shattered the initial ignorance of Balfour and Lansdowne with regard to the media scandal. In fact, Satow supplemented his memorandum with a copy of the Russo-Chinese Convention on Tibet, which *The China Times*, *The Tientsin Daily News*, and the Japanese dailies published in July 1902. Presumably, it consisted of twelve articles that allegedly ceded China's rights on Tibet to Saint Petersburg in exchange for its support to Peking in dealing with Britain, Germany, and Japan. In conformity with the document, Russian political and military representatives would be positioned in Lhasa, in order to supervise the foreign policy of Tibet and, what seemed even more significant, to have a hand in the exploitation of Tibetan mineral wealth, notably the gold mines.[215]

As mentioned above, Russian activities in Tibet, whether real or fantastic, became a decisive argument for Curzon to resuscitate an active defense of India. "Russia has concluded some sort of agreement with the Tibetan government which will presently result in a Russian envoy to Lhasa and a little later in a Russian protectorate," he wrote indignantly to the Foreign Office in mid-1902. "This is a challenge to our power and position wholly unprovoked, entirely unwarrantable, fraught in my opinion with the most prompt and strenuous resistance. If we do nothing now—while all the cards are still in our hands—we shall deserve the worst that could befall us."[216]

Reluctant to embark on any international ventures in the aftermath of the Boer War, and mindful of enormous expenditures, the home Cabinet deliberated between "hard" and "soft" power. In the first instance, many London politicians were concerned about a coercive solution of the problem, which might be interpreted as a pattern to be emulated by the Russians in Afghanistan or Persia. The interests of the "old China hands" were also threatened by the impending breakup of China.[217] Hence, the Foreign Office recurrently sounded out an agreement with Russia on the affairs of Tibet in the spring and summer of 1903. One could be led to believe that the Cabinet—and especially the Committee of Imperial Defence, which had been established as an influential interdepartmental coordinative agency (see chapter 4)—discussed a bargain whereby the Russians might have receded from close relations with Tibet in return for a more collaborative approach by the British to Russian desires vis-à-vis Afghanistan.[218] Some historians have argued for an even broader convention regarding Russian and British spheres of interest in Persia, Afghanistan, Kashgaria, Mongolia, and Tibet, which the governments might have concluded in 1904, except that the Russo-Japanese War broke out in February of that same year.[219]

Although the Tsarist diplomats sought to dissipate British fears about Russian intentions to take Tibet under the scepter of the Romanovs,[220] the Unionist Cabinet tended to share Curzon's conception of Russian agents as being able to upset the tranquillity of minor Himalayan states bordering the Raj. "The story of the Russo-Chinese agreement as to Tibet," Lansdowne told the Cabinet members on October 1, 1902, "is supported by a good deal of evidence."[221] The memorandum on the Russian occupation of Manchuria signed by Admiral Evgeny Alekseev, the governor-general of Kwantung, and General Tsen Tsi, the governor of Mukden Province, on October 27, 1900, also exacerbated British consternation that a similar scenario might be brought to life by the Russians in Tibet.[222]

To frustrate any chance for Russo-Tibetan rapprochement, Curzon proposed sending a "diplomatic mission" to the Court of the Dalai Lama, escorted by "a sufficient force to ensure its safety." Officially, it aimed to pursue negotiations on "a treaty of friendship and trade with the Tibetan government"; however, Curzon's genuine purpose was to counterbalance Russian influence upon the Land of Snows.[223] His memorandum of January 18, 1903, on the necessity of a resolute British response to the Russian challenge in High Asia and a ritual Russophobe campaign in the British press compelled the London Cabinet to endorse the sending of a special ambassadorial mission to Tibet. According to some British newspapers, the Russians had already secured Peking's permission to carry out the geological exploration of Tibet; they were reported to have dispatched a few Cossack squadrons to reinforce native troops defending Lhasa and delivered war matériel to equip the Tibetan army; the tsar's secret emissaries were seen by occasional witnesses at the Court of the Dalai Lama, whom they allegedly subsidized with colossal sums of money. Some journalists argued that Russia was going to construct a new strategic railway through Tibet, and that the Russian General Staff was working on military plans of attack against India through Tibet, Sikkim, and Bhutan.[224]

On February 19, 1903, the Cabinet directed Lansdowne and Hamilton "to see whether some modus vivendi could be arrived at which would diminish the perpetual friction" between the British and the Russians in Asia.[225] In his response to a memorandum sent to him by the Russian ambassador, Alexander Benkendorf, Lansdowne maintained that

> as we [the British] are much more closely interested in Tibet than Russia, if Russia displays activity, we must reply by a greater display. We are simply trying to get the Tibetans to fulfill the Treaty of 1890, and it is no use trying through China.[226]

In his lecture on the budget of India, Curzon no doubt drew upon the plan to coerce the Dalai Lama to accept British "friendship" on the terms suggested by the viceroy. As some contemporaries metaphorically remarked, Lord Curzon was about to abandon the previous policy of "patient waiting" in favor of a new offensive course of "impatient hurry." "India is like a fortress with the vast moat of the sea on two of her faces, and with mountains for her walls on the remainder," wrote Curzon in a letter to Hamilton. "But beyond those walls extends a glacis of varying breadth and dimensions. We do not want to occupy it, but we cannot afford to see it occupied by our foes."[227]

The energetic viceroy was lucky to find an ardent supporter—Colonel Francis Younghusband, who "was enchanted with the prospect of leading a mission to Tibet." "This is a really magnificent business I have dropped in for," the colonel confided to his father on May 21, 1903. "What has brought matters to this head," he added, "is that the Russians have concluded, or tried to conclude, a secret treaty with Tibet—though their Ambassador in London has sworn to Lord Lansdowne that such a thing is the very last thing in the world that his government would dream of doing. However, from India, Peking, Paris, and Saint Petersburg identical reports arrive, so evidently an attempt at least has been made by the Russians to get hold of Tibet; and so I am being sent to forestall them and to put our relations with Tibet on such footing that we will be able to prevent any other power gaining a predominant influence there."[228] In his memorandum, dated October 26, 1903, Younghusband again sought to motivate the British march to Lhasa, citing the snobbishness of Tibetan lamas, aggressiveness of Tsarist generals, and weakness of the local Qing authorities—a set of arguments so typical to all the "players" of the Great Game in the Land of Snows:

> With Russian influence growing as it has done; with the Dalai Lama sending autograph letters to the tsar and his officials while he refuses to receive letters from the Viceroy and his representatives, we can not afford to allow our own influence to decline, and we are compelled by the natural necessities of the situation to take measures to insure, indeed, that it not only equals, but predominates over that of the Russians.[229]

The first attempt by Younghusband as chief frontier commissioner to hold negotiations with the Dalai Lama's plenipotentiary representatives at Khamba Jong, a medieval monastery in the territory of Tibet, ended in failure in April 1903. But his second mission—accompanied by a 1,200-strong military escort, mostly of Gurkhas and Sikhs under the command of Brigadier General James Macdonald—fought their way to Lhasa, in spite of the weather's whims and the armed resistance of irregular Tibetan combatants, from November 1903 to August 1904.[230] The story of this expedition, which was perfectly described by eyewitnesses and studied by academic scholars, falls outside the scope of this study.[231] To go no deeper into the matter here, it is necessary to specify that Younghusband and his fellow officers were disappointed to find in the Tibetan arsenals of arms merely thirty rifles delivered from Russia to Lhasa. A "rifle factory" in the capital, which British spies mentioned in their reports to Simla long before the expedition, was in reality a small workshop run by two Muslim renegades from the Raj. Likewise, the members of the British mission failed to find any mountain cannons or machine guns either in Lhasa or other Tibetan fortresses.[232]

Although Younghusband was shown a draft Russo-Chinese treaty on the mutual protection of Tibet, this document appeared to have been drawn up as early as the beginning of the 1890s. Besides, it had never been officially adopted by Saint Petersburg or Peking. Hence, the chief frontier commissioner acknowledged his fiasco—his failure to find any artifacts of the Russian presence in Tibet on a larger scale. Moreover, both the Grand Lama and nearly all Tibetan dignitaries, including Dorzhiev, had fled Lhasa before the British arrival in the city. "No trace was discovered of the 'skilled mechanicals' or the military advisers from Asiatic Russia who had been so often postulated in the mission's reports," stressed Fleming in his study.[233]

At first glance, this expedition might be regarded as a triumph of the "forwardist" concept in Asia, especially when juxtaposed with a series of military defeats on land and at sea that the Russians suffered in the course of war with Japan (see chapter 6). In fact, however, the Younghusband mission had achieved two main objectives, as Curzon articulated them in a memorandum of June 25, 1904: first, to constitute official diplomatic relations between the British Empire and Tibet; and second, to prevent the establishment of a Russian protectorate on the northeast frontier of the Raj. "We want to make sure that Tibet will keep the new treaty, when signed; that she will not intrigue with Russia; and that, as soon as our backs are turned, the situation which we have made such sacrifices to prevent is not at once resumed," maintained Curzon in a note summing up Britain's achievements in High Asia.[234]

Indeed, the Anglo-Tibetan Convention, which was enforced by the British upon the Tibetan government in the absence of the Dalai Lama, symbolized the British preponderance in Tibet. Pursuant to Article IX, no portion of Tibetan territory should be ceded to any state, sold, leased, mortgaged, or otherwise given for occupation to any foreign power. In addition, the eventual attendance of a British political agent at Lhasa and a huge sum of indemnity ($£500,000$) imposed on Tibet were to ensure British rights in the Heart of Eurasia. Conversely, this was the first diplomatic act of international law that Tibet, as a sovereign state, had signed with a European great power.[235]

Yet this convention was a Pyrrhic victory for Curzon, Younghusband, and other "forwardists." First of all, the general public's attitude toward the conquest of Tibet ranged from outright condemnation to a slightly apprehensive curiosity.[236] The Liberals sharply criticized the Cabinet, and especially Curzon, for this military operation, which was wasteful in spending at the time of the Russo-Japanese War and had been undertaken in the face of the German menace in Europe. Some respected, high-ranking officials in the government of India, mostly opponents of Curzonian imperialist policy, grumbled at Younghusband for exceeding his commission. For example, Kitchener anticipated the undesirable effect that this undertaking would have upon the reformation of the Indian army for the lack of subsidies spent on the march to Lhasa.[237] At the same time, nearly all concerned powers, including the United States, were disquieted by the British victory. William Rockhill, a respected American specialist on Tibet and a counselor to John Hay, the secretary of state, informed British ambassador Satow that

> the mission to Tibet was a most unfortunate step which will inevitably result in impairing Chinese prestige, control and sovereignty over what we all hold to be an integral part of the Chinese Empire, and may be later on used by some other Power as a valid precedent for territorial acquisition in China. Then again we think the reasons given for this "War with Tibet" quite insufficient, the interests of trade unimportant and the danger from Russia, in that quarter at least, too small to justify the means adopted by the Indian government.[238]

As a matter of fact, the Younghusband expedition and the Anglo-Tibetan Convention of 1904 reflected a new political reality. The fact was that Peking had ceded to London to overrule Tibet. Furthermore, Younghusband's failure to capture the Dalai Lama and the latter's escape from Lhasa to Urga indicated a vacuum of administrative power in the territory of Tibet. This might unleash a new rivalry, not only in the Land of Snows but also in Eastern Turkestan and Mongolia. Respectively, Curzon's far-reaching designs to replace the pro-Russian Dalai Lama with the more pragmatic Panchen Lama, who occupied the second position in the lamas' hierarchy, were considered by contemporaries, including the members of the London Cabinet, as inappropriate and utopian.

For example, John Brodrick, then the head of the War Office, communicated to Lord Ampthill, the acting governor-general of India in the absence of the viceroy: "The difference between us and Curzon is that we think the battle can be better fought out in London than in Lhasa."[239]

So it was small wonder that Younghusband's mission generated a most unfavorable impression among the Russian public. The mass media in Saint Petersburg and Moscow scrutinized the route of the expedition and described all the hardships with which it was confronted in the Himalayas. *Novoe Vremya*, for instance, critically summarized Russia's attitude to Britain's presence in Tibet:

> All in all, the Englishmen have decided to subjugate Tibet, for India is not enough for them, and they would like to extend her frontier to the north. In anticipation of the occupation of the Yangtze Valley, the Englishmen secure to guarantee in advance their rights upon the country, where the sources of this Chinese Nile are situated.[240]

The expedition organized by Curzon in 1903–4 definitely contributed to Anglophobia in Russia. It was reinforced, moreover, with the signing of the Anglo-Japanese Alliance in 1902 and London's sympathies vis-à-vis Tokyo, which London did not hide during the armed confrontation between Russia and Japan in the Far East, in spite of Britain's officially proclaimed neutrality. Referring to the intelligence obtained by Consul-General Klemm in Bombay about Kitchener's feverish war preparations on the northwest frontier of India, Lamsdorf informed Kuropatkin about Britain's secret support of Japan in the anti-Russian military coalition.[241] The majority of Russian military analysts believed that the Cabinet of Saint James sought to restore its political prestige in Asia by the initiation of a "small victorious military campaign" against Tibet.[242]

Although on November 7, 1903, Benkendorf told Lansdowne of the tsar's desire "to remove all source of misunderstanding between two governments" and spoke in favor of "a change for the better" in Russo-British relations,[243] the intelligence concerning the Anglo-Indian troops marching to Lhasa infuriated Nicholas II and his ministers. The Tsarist government reacted negatively to King Edward's intention to settle all existing disputes regarding Afghanistan and Tibet. On November 17, 1903, Benkendorf presented a note of protest to the Foreign Office concerning the Younghusband expedition. Thus, a good chance for the commencement of Russo-British negotiations was lost (see chapter 6).

Klemm would send to the chief of the Foreign Ministry's Asian Department one panicked report after another, accusing the government of India, and Curzon in particular, of having the ambition to set up a political agency in Lhasa on a permanent basis. Conversely, he informed Saint Petersburg of the British attempts to cause discord in Russo-Chinese relations by fabricating pieces of news about secret Russian emissaries landing in Tibet and instructing local residents on how to erect fortifications and use modern weapons against the British.[244] To verify these data, including those intercepted by Russian intelligence agents, Captain Kozlov was directed to evaluate the results of the Younghusband expedition. However, the explorer came to the following conclusion:

> Russia should join Britain in the opening of Tibet, but, at the same time, it is necessary to insist on her equal participation in the establishment of her political representatives there to remove all barriers for Lamaist pilgrims and goods on caravan routes from Russia to Tibet.

At the end of his note, Kozlov urged a special expeditionary corps to be delegated to Lhasa for a military demonstration similar to that made by Younghusband.[245] It is also noticeable that Kozlov, following the example of other Russian military experts, was convinced of the British desire to take the Chinese naval base in Weihaiwei under their control as a kind of "fee" from China for the withdrawal of British troops from Tibet.[246]

It needs to be mentioned in this connection that as early as 1902, the Tsarist government was determined to send a secret reconnaissance mission to Tibet commanded by two Kalmycks—Pod'esaul (a title meaning "staff captain" for Cossack troops) Naran Ulanov and the Lama Dambe Ulianov. Yet the preparations for this trip took another two years. The significance of this mission could be illustrated by noting the audience that Nicholas II had granted to the staff members of the mission before their departure in January 1904. The emissaries were instructed to observe the activities of Younghusband and his expeditionary brigade. According to the archival records, the autocrat also encouraged Ulanov and Ulianov "to incite the Tibetans against the English." To attain this objective, Kuropatkin charged the War Ministry to allocate more than 14,000 rubles to the expedition. Besides, another Russian agent, Buda Rabdanov, who was disguised as a Lamaist pilgrim, set off to the Chinese town of Dazinlu to act as a liaison officer.[247] In April 1904, for example, Rabdanov informed the above-mentioned Dorzhiev that Russia's preparations for a full-scale military campaign on the northwest frontier of India were in full swing. On receiving this news, the Grand Lama was expected to agree with a plan to remove his residence to the territory of Russia.[248]

It took the expedition more than a year to make its way to Lhasa through Russian Turkestan and Kuldja. The premature demise of Ulanov because of an unknown contagious disease compelled Dambe Ulianov to take command of the mission. The Russian emissaries were accorded a hearty welcome in Tibet as brilliant experts on Lamaism. They stayed in the capital from the end of May to mid-August 1905 collecting information on British activities in the region. Ulianov was received in audiences by the Lama Goldan Tiva-Rambuche, who acted as the ruler of Tibet in the absence of the Dalai Lama. The latter assured Ulianov that both the Buddhist clergy and general public hated British occupation troops deployed in the Chumbi Valley, and anticipated the return of the superior Lamaist priest to Lhasa. Inspired by Dorzhiev and other secret emissaries, Lamsdorf and Kuropatkin began to elaborate a scheme for the Dalai Lama's coming back to Lhasa in the company of a special Russian political officer.[249]

At nearly the same time, Lieutenant Colonel Lavr Kornilov, a highly qualified General Staff officer, became the commander in chief of the Russian army, and much later, in July 1917, he was commissioned to collect intelligence on Kitchener's military reforms in India shortly before the end of the Japanese War.[250] According to Consul Klemm's reports, the Russian emissary failed to arrive in the city incognito and was introduced to Sir Archibald Genter, lieutenant general of the Bombay army, in February 1904. Strange as it may seem, Kitchener did not frustrate Kornilov's intention to tour all the main strategic strongholds in the north of India, where he was welcomed by the British military commanders on the spot. Yet Kornilov's baggage—including his personal diary, photo camera, and binoculars—were stolen by unknown thieves in Peshawar, just on the day of his departure back to Bombay.[251]

The Dogger Bank incident in October 1904, which followed the signing of the Anglo-Tibetan Convention, marked the lowest ebb of Russo-British relations since the Penjdeh crisis in 1884–85 (see chapter 6). On October 31, 1904, the vice consul in Bombay, Alexei Nekrasov, informed Saint Petersburg of the instruction that Curzon had allegedly given to Kitchener as to moving active troops to Kabul and Kandahar, should a Russo-British war begin.[252] In these circumstances, the Tsarist government decided to forward another covert mission, this time to Urga, to sound out the Dalai Lama's plans regarding his return to Tibet. Kuropatkin directed the same Captain Kozlov to accompany the grand priest on his route from Urga to Lhasa. His commission should be also a routine collection of intelligence on the state of affairs in Mongolia after the Russo-Japanese War.[253]

On arriving in Urga and receiving an audience with the Dalai Lama in April 1905, Kozlov reported to the Main Staff that the Tibetan ruler expected the European powers to acknowledge the independence of Tibet. Besides, the Dalai Lama told Kozlov that the Tibetan government in exile had managed to preserve tranquillity among the Mongolian Lamaists, owing to the good relations between Tibet and Russia, for the Tsarist armies, fighting the Japanese in Manchuria, needed peace and tranquillity in their rear.[254] As a result, the Russians arranged for the surreptitious departure of the Dalai Lama from Urga in December 1906, first to the Monastery of Gumbut on Chinese territory and then to Lhasa. Yet the Tsarist government, especially Alexander Izvolsky, who acceded to the post of foreign minister in May 1906, regarded the attendance of any Russian political agent in Tibet as an act of provocation, in light of the Russo-British diplomatic consultations that were in full swing at that moment.[255]

On the other side, supported by other continental European powers, Russian diplomacy strongly remonstrated against the occupation of Lhasa and the provisions of the Anglo-Tibetan Convention of 1904. These reprimands were coupled with the home Cabinet's disinclination to rush into a full-scale military conflict with Russia. It needs to be mentioned that London was not always prompt in reporting to Calcutta the intelligence it received from Saint Petersburg. Yet when information of this kind was received, it was often dismissed by the Russophobes in the civil and military establishments of the Raj.[256]

By the turn of the new century, the Unionist government faced the real danger of a new European armed conflict because of the negative effect that the military expedition against Tibet had on the international image of Britain. "We must make it clear"—wrote John Brodrick, the state secretary for India, to Lord Ampthill, the governor of Madras and the acting viceroy of India, early in October 1904—"that Younghusband had 'sold' us. It had become too much like the usual Russian device as it was. Things got really bad at the Foreign Office as Lansdowne felt his honour involved."[257] To reduce criticism and the ill disposition of the European and British general public vis-à-vis the military venture in the Himalayas, the home Cabinet directed Younghusband and Macdonald to withdraw troops from Lhasa only after the British representatives revised the Anglo-Tibetan Convention with the government of Tibet.[258] Nevertheless, on October 6, 1904, the British military contingent set off from the Tibetan capital on their return march to the Indian border. According to Russian intelligence sources, their going away was accompanied by "damnations of those Tibetans whose relatives had been killed or wounded in the confrontation with the British," but Younghusband wrote in his diary that the residents of Lhasa bade a friendly farewell to the members of his mission.[259]

In fact, Balfour and Lansdowne shifted all responsibility for the outcome of the expedition to Younghusband and Curzon. The prime minister indignantly wrote that the former had disobeyed explicit orders from London, making it impossible "to clear ourselves from the very unjust imputation of copying the least creditable methods of Russian diplomacy." Moreover, the Cabinet regarded Younghusband as guilty of insubordination for leaving Lhasa without amending the Anglo-Tibetan Convention as instructed.[260] It is not difficult to acknowledge, therefore, that Younghusband became a victim of the contradictions in the external political course pursued by the Unionist Cabinet.[261] Soon afterward, Curzon retired from the position of the Indian viceroy, to which he had been appointed for a second tenure in 1903. His successor—Lord Minto—embarked on a more cautious political course, resembling "masterly inactivity," though General Kitchener continued to reform the Anglo-Indian army up to 1909.

A new Anglo-Chinese Convention, signed on April 27, 1906, symbolized the compromise that London and Peking had finally achieved on the Tibetan problem. The document endorsed China's political suzerainty over the Land of Snows, while Britain managed to secure its commercial rights in the country. The home Cabinet substantially reduced an incredibly huge indemnity imposed upon Tibet by Younghusband.[262] All these diplomatic achievements notwithstanding, the position of Tibet between three empires still seemed far from stable and secure.

In the nature of any surface impressions, Tibet might be regarded as merely a secondary "playfield" in the general Russo-British "tournament of shadows," a myth that absolutely contradicted its role in the Great Game.[263] In fact, it had no less significance to the rival powers than Persia, Afghanistan, or the khanates of Central Asia.[264] Yet it seems an exaggeration to confine the scope of the Great Game to the Anglo-Russian competition in the Land of Snows, because the struggle in the Far East seemed to have contributed to the end of the Game in no small measure.[265]

CHAPTER 6

THE END OF THE GAME

Turkestan, Afghanistan, Trans-Caspia, Persia—to many these words breathe only a sense of utter remoteness, or a memory of strange vicissitudes, and of moribund romance. To me, I confess, they are the pieces on a chess board upon which is being played out a game for the domination of the world.

—George Nathaniel Curzon

This final chapter concentrates on the Far East, to which the focus of the Great Game slowly but surely shifted at the start of the twentieth century. From the Trans-Siberian Railway to Port Lazarev on the Korean Peninsula and Port Hamilton on the Korean Gulf, both the Russians and the British found many places to play the Game. In the end, most ruling elites in the Russian Empire began to understand that any serious clash with Britain could provoke the downfall of the autocratic regime and the empire's collapse. So even diehard Anglophobes at the Court of Saint Petersburg and in the "far pavilions" of Asia had to acknowledge the urgency of bringing the Great Game to its inevitable end.

The chapter further dwells upon the diplomatic revolution of 1902–7, which took place in the context of two very different societies. On one hand, Britain had attained a climax of power, with its unprecedented material supremacy through industrialization, 80 percent urban residents, and annual foreign trade of £800 million. On the other hand, the Russian Empire remained mostly agricultural and rural, with barely 10 to 15 percent of the population living in cities and £119 million in foreign trade. In this context, there was perpetual quarreling between Britain and Russia at all strategic points, which in turn caused heavy spending. So there were economic motivations to end this conflict. Eventually, Russo-British rapprochement flowered in the years 1905–6, and the Great Game could be considered to have ended by mid-1907, when the Anglo-Russian Convention was signed.

Finally, the chapter argues that, although the crucial turning point in world politics at the onset of the twentieth century—the establishment of ententes between leading states—was the result of momentary necessity and never erased underlying problems, it meant a real breakthrough not only in Russo-British relations but also in the great powers' general conduct of foreign policy. Thus, the Great Game's final impact on Asian countries is worthy of separate, careful consideration. For instance, with respect to the conventional wisdom on the lasting effects of the very different Russian and British models of colonial rule, though the latter phase of Russian economic policy in Asia progressed toward a more European model, ironically the British champions of protectionism came to dominate colonial policy by the beginning of the twentieth century.

THE FAR EAST ON THE CHESSBOARD OF THE GREAT GAME

For a short period after the Second Opium War and the suppression of the Taiping Rebellion, British and Russian statesmen still recognized the significance of the Far East for world politics. Yet in the 1870s and 1880s, this part of Asia ceased to attract the attention of the great powers. Although, at first, a new apprehension of "inveterate commercialism" came over the Foreign Office in the Gladstonian era, and then the Middle East assumed the attention of the London Cabinet in the Disraeli period, the Tsarist government focused upon the subjugation of Central

Asia along with the colonization of Eastern Siberia. A desire to reach "natural frontiers which rationalized the Russian imperial expansion eastwards was supplemented with an irrational motivation of securing the borders of the 'Orthodox Tsardom.'"[1]

The standstill that characterized the posture of affairs in Chinese Turkestan after a turbulent period made it possible for the Russian government to concentrate upon other zones of strategic importance in East Asia—above all, Priamur Province. A special conference held in Saint Petersburg on July 29, 1883, adopted a twofold plan for the administrative reorganization that aimed to motivate the political and economic development of the Amur River Basin in order to promote Russia's political and economic influence upon its neighboring states—including China, Japan, and the United States—as well as to safeguard the empire's Pacific provinces from any foreign invasion. That is why the governor-generalship of the Priamur region was established in the late 1880s, including three districts of Zabaikal, Amur, and Ussuri, plus two autonomous subdistricts—Sakhalin Island and the Kamchatka Peninsula.[2] This approach seemed the prompter, the more insistently Peking aspired to restore its former possessions in the Pacific. The claims to the Amur and Ussuri basins, as well as to some frontier territories in Russian Turkestan, made by the Peking government in 1885–86, when Russia and Britain were balancing on the brink of war in Afghanistan and Turkmenia, intensified international tension in Asia.[3]

Meanwhile, long before the Sino-Japanese War of 1894–95, merely sporadic threats emanated from the Tsarist government to the British political position and commercial preponderance in the Far East; for instance, in 1885 Alexander III decided to set up a naval base at Port Lazarev on the Korean Peninsula to make Russia's military protection available to the Korean king. Reciprocally, the British Cabinet approved the occupation by the Marine Corps of Port Hamilton at the sea entrance to the Korean Gulf.[4]

The paucity of military means sufficient for a synchronized attack against the Afghan troops in Penjdeh and the British naval squadron in the Pacific compelled the Tsarist government to evacuate from Port Lazarev. Conversely, however, the Russians embarked on the realization of the tremendous Trans-Siberian Railway project in the early 1890s. Although some British authors regarded it as "a shabby bureaucratic affair" and "the most expensive peaceful undertaking in modern history up to that time,"[5] the railway's strategic consequences could hardly be overestimated. When finished, the railroad linked the Tsarist Empire's Pacific provinces to its European region. Besides, it enabled the transportation of manpower and war ammunition to the hinterland of Eurasia, where the British navy could launch no adequate counterattack against Tsarist troops.

Mindful of the railway construction in Turkestan and the Far East on a larger scale, some British politicians devoted much time to speculations on the results.[6] "I have felt for a very long time past," admonished the secretary of state for India, George Hamilton, in a private message to the Indian viceroy, Lord Curzon, on November 2, 1899, "that we must, so far as Russia is concerned, acknowledge the changed condition that the extension of railroads has made in the relative fighting powers of Great Britain and Russia." Significantly, Hamilton was rather pessimistic at the end of his letter: "I do not believe that we can fight Russia on land successfully except in the neighborhood of our frontiers in India."[7]

At the same time, the situation in Europe, especially the latest developments in the Balkans and the Near East, made Salisbury and his Cabinet encourage the tsar's ambitions in the Far East. "With Russia involved in Manchuria," emphasized Major General John Ardagh, "our anxiety over her activity in Afghanistan, Persia and Turkey will be relieved, and also lessen any chance France may have felt for Russian support."[8] Thus, the focus of the Great Game slowly but surely shifted to the Far East at the turn of the new century.

Similarly, as followed from a report on the Russian Pacific provinces by Major General Henry Brackenbury dated May 1, 1886, British strategists realized perfectly that they could hardly wage war against Russia to the west of the Caspian Sea without the support of the Ottoman Empire, together with the Muslim population in the Middle East. So they were barely able to launch a military campaign in East Asia without such an ally as China. In the early 1890s, some officers at the War

Office and Admiralty strongly advocated a joint assault by British naval forces, backed by Chinese land troops, upon Vladivostok, Nikolaevsk, Possiet, and Khabarovka—the principal Russian footholds in the Far East. Otherwise, Britain would need to side with China in restoring the territories that Russia had filched from the Qing Empire when the latter was in trouble because of the Taiping Rebellion and the Second Opium War. According to Brackenbury, London would kill two birds with one stone by removing this constant menace to British trade in the North Pacific and simultaneously taking Chinese foreign policy under its control.[9] Curzon, who shared this concept, also argued that Britain's task in the Far East was twofold: It ought to reshape the Qing Empire as well as create a trilateral alliance with China and Japan in order to counteract any aggression of "the perfidious Muscovites."[10]

A close study of the Russian General Staff's records reveals that the Tsarist government was incapable of efficiently defending its possessions in East Asia, once such an alliance was reached. It is common knowledge that the British fleet surpassed the combined French and Russian naval forces in all aspects, and the Russian Bear actually had no chance of defeating the British Whale at sea.[11] Besides, by 1890 China had built up the North Pacific's largest navy, which was stationed at Port Arthur. Vladivostok's position as the "dominator of the East" was all the more threatened from Kirin and Port Arthur, because Priamur Province largely depended on imports of food and war matériel by sea before the Trans-Siberian Railway was put into operation on the eve of the Russo-Japanese War.[12] Regardless of an ability of Russian troops to occupy a defensive position on Chinese territory immediately after the outbreak of hostilities, they found themselves needing reinforcements from the Irkutsk and Omsk military districts, which could arrive at the scene of military operations after a few weeks. This would give the Chinese a favorable opportunity to restore Priamur and Ussuri provinces under the aegis of the Peking government by the time the new "cannon fodder" would begin fighting.[13]

A way out of this strategic deadlock might be found in the destruction of the British naval stations in the Pacific. The archival records testify to a plan to land Russian troops in Hong Kong and

Singapore in order to occupy these sea fortresses. If they succeeded, Britain's shipping lines between China and India would be broken, and any transportation communication with its overseas colonies would be disrupted. Symptomatically, a special commission was set up in Vladivostok on May 10, 1888, to consider all the pros and cons of such a scenario for a naval war that Russian cruisers could wage against the British and Chinese fleets. Half a year later, the commission—which was chaired by First Rank Captain Stepan Makarov, who was later to become commander in chief of the Russian Pacific Squadron—drafted a detailed plan for the cruising war in the ocean space between Canada and Australia. In spite of the enormous hardships that the Russian cruisers might be face if a maritime campaign began, the officers of the Main Naval Staff discussed it in the period before the Sino-Japanese War. Characteristically, many Tsarist military experts pointed to the "negative effect" that an eventual Anglo-Sino-Japanese alliance would have upon Russian designs on Hong Kong and Singapore.[14]

The big powers' struggle for preponderance in Korea seemed to become another major factor in the affairs of the Far East. Korea's position as a "bridge" between China and Japan, coupled with rich mineral resources and a voluminous stock of timber on the peninsula, made it a bone of discord between Russia, Britain, China, and Japan. The "opening" of Korea by the Japanese in 1876 and the encroachments of Russia and Britain upon some of its seaports in the mid-1880s, mentioned earlier in this chapter, marked a new era in Korean history. Moreover, the Treaty of Shimonoseki, which ended the Sino-Japanese War, abrogated the nominal Chinese suzerainty of Korea in 1895.[15]

After the British evacuated their marine detachments from the Komundo Islands in February 1887, a special conference convened by the tsar on May 8, 1888, adopted a resolution that put forth a preventive policy aimed at not allowing other great powers "to turn Korea into a tool of the anti-Russian policy."[16] With the beginning of armed conflict between Japan and China in July 1894, a newly convened special conference in Saint Petersburg recognized the neutrality of Korea and confirmed the prewar status quo on the Korean Peninsula.[17]

The Japanese victory in the war against the Qing Empire totally reshaped the geopolitical landscape of the Far East. It was Japan, not China, that since 1894–95 had become one of the major competing powers in the scramble for East Asia. If the Country of the Rising Sun was looked upon in Europe as a "military dwarf" in the period before the Sino-Japanese War—according, for example, to impressions that Nicholas as the heir to the throne gained during his unofficial visit to Japan in 1891[18]—its emergence as another warlike empire threatened to interfere with a diplomatic duel between Russia and Britain.

This problem underlay the disagreement of generals, public leaders, and intellectuals on a strategy for Far Eastern policies. Although before the Sino-Japanese War most Tsarist statesmen, in particular diplomats, claimed that a balance of power between Russia, Britain, China, and Japan should be maintained in order to contest London's influence upon Peking,[19] the strengthening of Japan's position in the aftermath of hostilities opened up three alternatives for the Tsarist government in the Pacific: first, to come to an agreement with Japan on spheres of interest in Manchuria and Korea; second, to pursue a concord with Britain and other European powers to reduce Tokyo's ambitions; or third, to impose a treaty of alliance on China in order to bring it into the Russian orbit.[20]

Adjutant General Nikolai Obruchev was partial to the first scenario, which envisaged Russian occupation of North Manchuria. In his view, Russia should not mind Korea coming under the suzerainty of Japan. He was impressed by the rapid victory that the Japanese had won over the Chinese army and navy, and he pointed to the enormous logistical difficulties that Russian troops would face in an armed clash with Japan.[21]

Grand Duke Aleksei Alexandrovich, a general-admiral and uncle of Nicholas II, supported the second scenario. He argued that Russia's counteractions against the Country of the Rising Sun would only drive it into the arms of the British. To stave off such an outcome and isolate Tokyo by peaceful means, he advocated, Saint Petersburg ought to initiate a joint diplomatic demarche of the European powers against the Japanese encroachments on China.[22]

Prince Alexander Lobanov-Rostovsky, the Russian foreign minister in 1895–96, supported this concept. According to a humble note that he submitted to the tsar on April 6, 1895, provided that Britain continued to rely upon China in its anti-Russian policy, London would regard Japan as a major potential rival in the Pacific, especially after the collapse of the Celestial Empire. At the same time, as an emerging naval power, Japan could hardly abstain from a future contest with Britain, at least in the seas washing the Chinese coast. Thus, the foreign minister anticipated the continuation of a political dialogue with Britain in the Far East following the pattern of Russo-British collaboration that solved the Pamirs problem.[23]

However, when Saint Petersburg failed to implicate London in a joint diplomatic intervention against Japan in April 1895, Sergei Witte, the finance minister, backed by Peter Vannovsky, the war minister, persuaded Nicholas II adopt a third type of action. Infatuated with an ambitious project to create a sort of "Russian India" in East Asia, the tsar and some of his closest advisers finally determined on a collaboration with the decrepit Qing monarchy, even at the expense of friendly, or at least neutral, relations with Japan.[24]

According to reconnaissance reports, notes, and plans elaborated by the General Staff officers, most of them were convinced that China was to become Russia's natural strategic partner; otherwise, it might jeopardize Russian interests on the Pacific if pro-Western lobbying groups gained the upper hand at the Peking Court.[25] Thus, the very dynamics of the Great Game in Xinjiang, Tibet, and Mongolia, referred to in earlier chapters, incited Tsarist strategists to enter an international scramble for Korea and Manchuria. Typically, Alfred Mahan, a U.S. Navy captain and a respected naval strategist, juxtaposed Russia's advance to the Pacific with its endeavors to obtain a stronghold in the Persian Gulf.[26] Conversely, Japan's territorial gains in Korea threatened to violate the balance of power in favor of so-called neomercantilist railway imperialism, as some authors labeled the policy being pursued on the outskirts of the Russian Empire.[27]

In a note on the situation in the Far East, a General Staff colonel, Vladimir Altfan, claimed that only Korea could provide Russia with a desired naval base in the Pacific. "Our roadway to Korea is going through Manchuria," wrote the expert. "Korea is an objective, whereas

Manchuria remains merely a means to achieve the goal."[28] Another military observer, Prince Volkonsky, thought Korea should be converted into a Russian protectorate, following the example of Bokhara.[29] Furthermore, Major General Nikolai Chichagov, the acting chief of staff of the Priamur Military District, investigated modernization and rearmament of the Japanese army and navy in the course of its preparations for open conflict with Russia, which, as he believed, would break out in 1903–4. Significantly, this strategist openly recommended Japan as the most likely ally for Britain in a future Pacific war.[30]

Summing up the opinions of Russian political observers on Far Eastern policy in the 1890s, several other diverse views also need to be taken into consideration. Some contemporaries severely criticized Qing statecraft and urged the Tsarist government to come to friendly terms with Japan, especially before the war of 1894–95.[31] Other writers created an image of the Pan-Asiatic Empire, with Manchuria as its industrial heart, that would emerge in the Pacific under the aegis of Russia.[32] Also heard were voices of Russian journalists who bullied the general public about the so-called yellow peril, a slur invented by Ivan Levitov, who published a series of pamphlets about the ominous designs of the yellow race in Asia (see below).[33] Finally, a group of commentators in the mass media admonished readers against the establishment of a Japanese marionette kingdom embracing the Russian Pacific provinces, Manchuria, and Korea and resembling Manchukuo, a monstrous puppet state created by Tokyo much later, in the early 1930s.[34]

On June 9, 1896, the Russo-Chinese Protocol was signed in Moscow, granting to the Russians the right to construct a railroad in Manchuria. In compliance with its provisions, China was bound to consult with Russia on foreign policy. Saint Petersburg set up the Russo-Chinese Bank and promised Peking to delegate military officers to drill not only Chinese but also Korean troops in anticipation of a new Japanese assault.[35] It is common knowledge, however, that Russian policies in Korea fluctuated between a compromise with Japan pursuant to the Nishi-Rosen agreement of April 25, 1898, and encouragement of the Korean emperor against the Chinese and Japanese in the late 1890s.[36]

If many Russian intellectuals regarded the advance to Northeast Asia as a preemptive attack on China in view of the strategic designs cherished by other great powers, London saw it as new evidence of the encirclement of the Raj by buffer states hostile to Britain. In this way, both a static and dynamic equilibrium in the Far East, based upon British economic preponderance, might have come to an end.[37]

Yet there were other nuances in the stances of British statesmen, public figures, and journalists. Lord Curzon, for example, mostly specified the negative geostrategic effect of the Russians' deep penetration into the Celestial Empire. Commenting on the Great Game in this section of Asia, he argued in 1896 that

> it is Russia who threatens her [the Qing Empire's] frontiers in Chinese Turkestan and on the Pamirs; Russia who is always nibbling, in scientific disguise, at Tibet; Russia who has designs on Manchuria; Russia whose shadow overhangs Korea; Russia who is building a great Trans-Continental railway that will enable her to pour troops into China at any point along 3,500 miles of contiguous border.[38]

Curzon drew the attention of the home Cabinet to the difficulties that commercial and naval shipping in the Yellow Sea and the Yangtze Basin would face, provided that Russia was able to station permanent squadrons at Port Lazarev or Fusan. Characteristically, the "old China hands," who ran big commercial enterprises in the Far East, strongly supported this notion.[39] As Charles Beresford, a retired rear admiral and a high-profile public figure, described his visits to Hong Kong, Shanghai, and other major Chinese cities in 1898–89,

> The British merchants further pointed out that if Russia openly annexes Manchuria, Korea is cut off and entirely at her mercy; Mongolia would easily be absorbed and the great horse-breeding ground for the whole of China with it. This would give Russia control over the hordes of irregular cavalry that have before now overrun the whole of China, and also give them control of a

hardy and stalwart population of many millions, that only need to be drilled and disciplined to make as fine soldiers as any in the world. They also pointed out that if Russia were once in this possession there would be nothing to prevent her sweeping down from the north of China to the centre and from the centre to India, thus paralyzing British trade and commerce.[40]

Sir Valentine Chirol, a leading editor of *The Times*, also shared the apprehensions of the Russian "avalanche" threatening to nullify British special interests in the Pacific. He was fully aware that if Saint Petersburg were determined to assume guardianship of the Chinese Empire, this "sick man of the Far East" would "pass away and his inheritance be formally appropriated."[41]

A broader interpretation of the subject in question may be found in an essay by Albert Beveridge, an American journalist, who dwelt upon Russian Far Eastern policy in a 1903 pamphlet. His metaphorical description of the Russian advance ran as follows:

So the Russian advance is a commercial and financial move-ment, from Gibraltar-like Vladivostok, on the north, all along the shores of the Pacific, into the very citadel of English power on China's extreme south. It is a diplomatic advance, too, throughout every province of the Flowery Kingdom [Korea] as well as on the Chinese extreme south. It is an advance by merchant vessels and war-ships from Odessa to Port Arthur; by Russian peasantry, cultivated farms, and permanent homes over the rich grain-fields of the Ussuri littoral, and even within the borders of Manchuria; by towns and cities and all activities of peace into the very centre of Manchuria, which until this very moment the world's wisest statesmen have insisted and believed, though with the faith of fear, was permanently Chinese territory.[42]

Along with drawing parallels between Russian and German advanc-es, Beveridge accentuated a dangerous situation caused by Berlin's intrusion into the Pacific region. He urged London's Cabinet to pay more attention to the German menace to Britain, for it appeared to him much graver than the notorious Russian bogey.[43] Furthermore, British worries about this new global competitor were exacerbated by Germany's occupation of Kiaochow, a strategic Chinese naval fortress on the Shandong Peninsula, along with its diplomatic intrigues against Britain all over the world and the growing British–German commercial rivalry in Asian markets.[44]

If Curzon and other "forwardists" in the British ruling elites insisted on the establishment of an anti-Russian alliance—first, with the Qing Empire in the period before the Sino-Japanese War; and later, with Japan, especially after the signing by London and Tokyo of the Treaty of Commerce and Navigation in 1894 and Japan's victory in the armed conflict with China[45]—some other groups in British leadership circles were more inclined to come to an agreement with Russia in view of three interrelated developments: the strengthening of its position in the region; the existence of the Russo-French Alliance; and, more important, the aggrandizement of the Second Reich in Europe.

With regard to the role played by Russia as a Pacific power, Demetrius Boulger, the political observer mentioned in the earlier chapters, wrote in the *Fortnightly Review*: "The process has been precisely the same as has led this country [Britain] to predominance in all the waters of the world, and to penetrate in every continent wherever a profitable territory could be acquired without disproportionate difficulty."[46] Referring to the Russo-French collaboration in the making of an anti-Japanese diplomatic demarche, also propped up by Germany in April 1895, Robert Hart, the inspector-general in the service of the Peking government, asserted that things looked worse and worse as far as Britain was more and more out of the running, because "Russia and France were hauling in the line hand over hand," while the British "would soon be feeling the grip tightening."[47] One should also bear in mind that a coalition of continental great powers including Germany aimed to pacify the Far East in a manner threatening not only Japanese commercial and political interests but also British aspirations there. "Above all, it is important to us to safeguard the independence and integrity of Korea," penned Lamsdorf in his diary on February 16, 1895, "because even such occasional cooperation will restrain British ambitions on Asia, setting the European problems in a quite different perspective."[48]

Not coincidentally, the policy of "splendid isolation" was gradually going out of fashion in Britain due mainly to challenges that London had to rebuff in the late 1890s. "Peking shows signs of a new scrimmage," wrote Hart in a private letter to his friend on the eve of the twentieth century; "it looks as if England in the Chinese question would have Russia, France, Germany, and China, all four against her."[49] Hence, more and more politicians advocated a defensive policy of alliances that London ought to pursue in Asia. A book about travels to the overseas colonies by Henry Norman, a British journalist, was a typical case of such views. Norman raised a rhetorical question—"Why not to enter an agreement with Russia in the Far East in order to delimit spheres of influence there in spite of controversies over European affairs?"—in the epilogue of his volume, which was published right after the end of the Sino-Japanese War.[50] Mindful of the latest developments in the Far East, Hart wrote to his correspondent in London on June 7, 1896: "As regards policy—facts should be looked in the face: we cannot stop, we cannot snuff out Russia, and the best thing for England would be a friendly understanding with that big power."[51]

The author of the present volume has already had occasion to comment on the policies that Salisbury adopted in keeping with his attitude toward Russia. Although an overall evaluation of his diplomacy falls outside the scope of this book, its Far Eastern direction is undoubtedly worth more thorough consideration.[52] A general key to understanding Salisbury's approach may be found in his saying dated December 1885: "The power able to strengthen her position in China, shall take the upper hand in the world trade."[53] This explained his attempts to maintain British arbitrage in the affairs of the Far East in order to secure the frontiers of India. At the same time, his pragmatic attitude toward Russia proved to be far from open Russophobia. "The Russians are rather vindicating my view that they are not such terrible fellows after all," he claimed in a letter to Lord Lytton at the climax of the Russo-Turkish War of 1877–78. The experienced British statesman was convinced that "Russia does not differ widely from many other civilized states."[54] Although Salisbury dismissed the immediate danger of any Russian intrusion into India, he preferred to take a tough stance in relations with the traditional rival empire. "If Russia satisfies us that there is not room in Asia for herself and us also, our policy to her must be of a very internecine and probably also, of effective character," he stated, manifesting the principles of his diplomacy in September 1885, and instructing Robert Morier, the chargé d'affaires in Saint Petersburg, who was later to become the ambassador to Russia.[55]

Thus it was small wonder that the Conservative prime minister did not lose a favorable chance to sound the possibility of coming to a compromise with Nicholas II during his first visit to Britain. Instead of making alluring though ungrounded declarations, Salisbury proposed to the autocrat to negotiate the burning issues of the long-term Anglo-Russian competition in the Turkish Straits, Persia, India, and the Far East, given that all the other big powers would not oppose such reconsideration. Notes of his meetings with the tsar at Balmoral on September 27–29, 1896, revealed the intentions of the prime minister to reconceive bilateral relations in order to put an end to the Great Game. Yet Nicholas suspiciously regarded such advances of the British side as a diplomatic trap bound to drive a wedge into Russia's cooperation with the European continental states—France and Germany—and also into the Russo-Chinese defensive alliance.[56]

The scramble for concessions and naval bases in the Far East incited Salisbury to repeat his overtures to the emperor in January 1898. This time, however, he focused upon the situation in China. The gravity of the Far Eastern crisis even compelled the prime minister to move Envoy Sir Nicholas O'Connor from Peking to Saint Petersburg. At the same time, the latter was instructed by the Foreign Office to risk another discussion with the Russians on their policy in Asia. According to O'Connor's report, "Muraviev was ready to consider at once any proposal which would bring about a closer understanding (entente) [sic] between the two countries."[57] Despite the tsar's spontaneous wish, the Russian government suspended even tentative negotiations on the pretext that Britain's loan to China and its occupation of Weihaiwei violated the fragile balance of interests in the northeastern provinces of the Celestial Empire.[58] Reciprocally, the Tsarist diplomats gave the cold shoulder to the Foreign Office's proposal to convene an international conference on the problems of the Far East, following the tested model of the Berlin Congress that had partitioned Central Africa in 1884–85.[59]

As Salisbury proclaimed in an annual lecture at the conference of the Primrose League, Russia had made a great mistake in getting hold of Port Arthur, because it would definitely be of no use to it whatsoever.[60] Expectedly, the proponents of imperialist policy, including the members of the China Association, advocated the occupation of Weihaiwei. According to Staal's report on March 2, 1898, Sir William Harcourt, then the leader of the Liberal opposition in the House of Commons, and Curzon had defined a policy pursued by the Cabinet in the Far East as guided by a three-pronged principle: preservation of the integrity and independence of China, protection of treaty rights, and security of free trade.[61] Although Salisbury and the senior ministers of his government regarded this action as a "consolation prize" to satisfy parliamentary criticism, Curzon described the decision as "a declaration on our [British] part that we have not abandoned the field in North China to our rivals, but that equally with them we demand a voice in the protection of our interests in that quarter, and in the regulation of China's future."[62]

Some scholars have correctly argued that the Russophobia in the United Kingdom had an effect on Salisbury's inclination to agree with the Tsarist government on the problems of the Far East.[63] A negative stereotype of Russia in the mentality of the British political leaders married with the aspiration to maintain the Ottoman Empire and protect India. Doubtlessly, whatever kind of Russophobe polemic was prevalent in the British media, its tenor remained the same: Great Britain had to check Russian ambitions on China, Korea, and the whole of East Asia by diplomatic or military means in order to save from destruction both its formal and informal empires.[64] To illustrate British antipathy toward the Tsardom, it is sufficient to allude to the opinion avowed by Colonel Nikolai Yermolov, the Russian military attaché to London. In a kaleidoscopic panorama of Victorian Britain, he specified a paradoxical apprehension of the notorious Russian peril by the ruling circles and general public. "They all consider a war with Russia as a naval operation somewhere in the Pacific, and nothing else," he reported to the Main Staff on March 21, 1898. "The understanding that England is confronted with troubles in India (inroads of warlike mountain tribes, pestilence, financial deficit, poverty, inadequate logistical infrastructure of the theater of military operations), encourages Saint Petersburg to bridle her aggressive ambitions in the Far East."[65]

So it was small wonder that Russian bureaucrats and intellectuals paid the British back in their own coin. Typically, Lieutenant Colonel Waters, the British military attaché to Saint Petersburg, characterized these emotions in the following way:

Russian feeling towards Great Britain is fervent almost beyond all powers of comprehension. Indeed, I have been assured, the animosity towards us [the British] is stronger now than it was at the time of the Crimean War, while it is by no means confined to grown-up individuals of any particular class. On the contrary, it is general, and is taught to, felt, and expressed by schoolboys and schoolgirls, the rising generation.... As a nation we are respected, but the distrust, of which mention has been made, and which existed before the Sino-Japanese War, shows no signs of abatement, and is intensely strong in the breasts of both Anglophile and Anglophobe. How often we are told, "I like the English, but hate their policy." It is much to be regretted that suspiciousness of English designs has been a flourishing plant, ever bearing new fruit, and more firmly rooted than ever in the ground of the national mind.[66]

Fortunately, sound pragmatism and goodwill usually took over in Russo-British relations, at least when Saint Petersburg and London would deal with particular issues on the international agenda. Such was the case with the construction of the Chinese railways. The signing of a compromise agreement on April 28, 1899, symbolized another step on the long path to ending the Great Game in Asia, though it merely included the delimitation of British and Russian spheres of railway concessions. Nevertheless, the accord eliminated the danger of Russian interference with British commercial interests in the basin of the Yangtze River, while London agreed to avoid any confrontation with Saint Petersburg in the so-called Chinese northeastern crescent, or Manchuria.[67]

Yet in spite of this pragmatic approach, the Anglophobes at the Court of Saint Petersburg suspected that the British Cabinet had plans to draw the Russians away from Manchuria, impose their own schemes for army reorganization on the Peking government, and offer it a new loan for the construction of the strategic railway from Shanghai to Niuzhuan. As Staal reported to Muraviev, Whitehall was going "to stab Russia's back" in the Far East. Simultaneously, Russian military representatives in China weighted all pros and cons with regard to the strategic position of Weihaiwei—a naval base leased by Britain to monitor Russian activity in the Zhili Gulf in 1898.[68]

These challenges were coupled with the war preparations that the government of India was allegedly intensifying on the northwest frontier. Reciprocally, Nicholas II directed Kuropatkin to reinforce the troops in Turkestan with infantry detachments and Cossack squadrons, while the celebrated military expert Veniukov was sent off by the Main Staff for a two-year reconnaissance tour to the Far Eastern states in order to investigate the state of affairs in light of the overtures made by London to Peking.[69]

At the same time, there were prudent and farsighted British politicians who, like Rosebery, anticipated "a cordial accord with Russia, which would make it possible to settle all disputable matters in Asia."[70] Another renowned public figure, Robert Spence Watson, the president of the National Liberal Federation from 1890 to 1902, founded the Society of the Friends of Russian Freedom. This organization edited *Free Russia*, a magazine that differentiated the autocratic regime from the Russian intellectual elites and ordinary people.[71] Furthermore, General Edward Cazelet, a distinguished military strategist, set up the Anglo-Russian Literary Society in the early 1890s and chaired it for thirty years, until his death in 1923. On the Russian side, two grand dukes, Georgii and Konstantin, patronized this organization, while Nicholas II even granted an audience to its members a couple of times in 1896–97.[72]

Owing to the positive tendency in Russo-British relations, even though they were violated by occasional Russophobic and Anglophobic propagandistic campaigns in the press, Muraviev assured O'Connor that the Russian government desired to cultivate very friendly relations with Great Britain, especially in the Far East. Their talk took place on June 15, 1898. Having rejected any aspirations for economic concessions in the Yangtze Basin, Muraviev saw no reason "why a spirit of latent and still less of militant antagonism should exist between the two countries."[73]

At the risk of being too reductionist, one may come to the conclusion that the ambivalence of Russian policy in Asia should be looked upon as a compromise between chauvinistic, Pan-Slavic, and less aggressive pro-European elite groups at the Court of Nicholas II. The German intrigues in Europe and Asia, accompanied by the alarmist media, contributed to an increase in Anglophobia in Russia and also to Russophobia in Great Britain. One typical anti-Russian pamphlet was by Joseph Popowski, an Austrian journalist, who argued in 1890 that "the plans of campaign against India in the archives of the Russian Chief Staff may be counted by the hundreds, and every year fresh ones are sent in." He further impeached the London Cabinet of political inactivity, military incompetence, and absolute complacency concerning Russia's advance in Asia. Consequently, he recommended that the British side join in the coalition of the Central Powers—Germany and Austria-Hungary—in order to arrest a forthcoming march of the Cossacks to India. The English translation of his pamphlet came out in the United Kingdom three years later.[74]

Confidence and security have always been the major problems of international relations in modern times. Thus, on November 21, 1895, Lobanov-Rostovsky wrote to Staal with regard to Britain's involvement in the Armenian crisis: "Doubtlessly, the tactics of Lord Salisbury appeared far to be looked upon as worthy of trust. Moreover, his actions and statements could often arouse concerns which seemed quite justified." Accordingly, Salisbury admitted in a letter to one diplomat that "it was something to do with Manchuria; I found I could not trust them [the Russians and Germans]."[75]

The mistrust that was deeply rooted in the fabric of Russo-British relations during the Great Game, along with new challenges in world politics, revealed to the United Kingdom the urgent necessity of searching for a potential ally—first at the regional and then at the global levels, which in turn meant the end of Britain's "splendid isolation." More and more statesmen and public leaders began to acknowledge, especially in the course of the Boer War, the importance of a defensive alliance with another power that could ensure the long-term stability of Britain's imperial frontiers and, above all, its possessions in Asia.[76]

Given the fact that London and Calcutta were disappointed with China's defeat in the armed conflict with Japan, the British government and general public turned their eyes to the latter as a possible political partner in the Far East after 1895. While criticizing the obvious military impotence of the Qing army and navy, *The Times* highly appreciated the military potential of Japan: "The one side is well armed, well disciplined, and well led; the other is none of these things."[77]

Reciprocally, Japanese sympathy for Britain gained more and more supporters amid both leadership circles and the general public. In fact, many Britons were impressed by a certain similarity in the two nations' geographical positions as island states combined with the Japanese people's aspirations to rapidly modernize their country.[78] The unprecedented economic activity of Russia and Germany on the shores of the Pacific likewise spurred Anglo-Japanese rapprochement. "The general feeling in Japan is that England is her natural ally; not for love of us, but for hatred of Russia," averred a British diplomat in a letter to a friend in Tokyo as early as in May 1893.[79] Suffice it to quote editorials in *Jiji Shimpo*, a leading Tokyo newspaper, maintaining that it was "England, and England alone, that could be safely relied upon for continued friendship." The author further adduced the following arguments in favor of arriving at a good understanding between the two states:

England keeps herself aloof from European politics and maintains undisputed supremacy of the seas. England and Japan are natural allies; they have immense common interests to safeguard against a common foe. Russia's schemes in these regions are a direct menace to the interests of both Japan and England. For her own part, Japan is prepared to sacrifice everything in order prevent Russia from obtaining a naval station in Korea or Manchuria, and England must be equally interested in averting this. This community of interests inevitably draws the two countries into a natural alliance, an alliance far stronger than such as are usually concluded by treaty.[80]

At the same time, as Robert Maccordock, a respected American diplomat, correctly stated, Britain favored a policy of coercing the Peking government to open domestic markets to imports. The concept of "open doors" in the Far East—which was articulated by the American secretary of state, John Hay, in a circular note to all powers concerned on September 6, 1899—thwarted the Russian policy of a trade monopoly in the markets of northern and western China by retaining high duties on imported articles.[81] But even earlier, Ernest Satow, the British ambassador to Tokyo, reported to Salisbury of his talk with Count Okuma, the Japanese prime minister, on October 22, 1896, when the latter "responded that he did not know what the aims of Russia might be, but, in his view, doubtlessly, it seemed to the general advantage that China should remain independent and discharge the function for which she was so well fitted, that of a market for the commerce of the whole world."[82]

With the breakup of China becoming more and more actual, even such "true imperialists" as Curzon and Younghusband became more inclined to conclude an agreement with the Country of the Rising Sun. "When required upon the alliance of Japan," commented Curzon on the British lease of Weihaiwei, "if we abdicate in the north she will have no alternative but to come to terms with her adversaries."[83] Similarly, Younghusband wrote to Curzon on August 9, 1898:

If the Russians bully the Chinese into giving away some interest of ours in Manchuria for instance, I would not support the Chinese to resist the Russian demand, for I believe in the last resort the Chinese would practically leave us to fight the Russians over it, when as a matter of fact it is not our business to do this, but the business of the Chinese to do it.[84]

The restraint that the Tsarist government imposed upon its collaboration with Britain in the Far East and Germany's ambivalent stance with regard to the integrity of the Qing Empire annoyed London. The Unionist Cabinet, with the possible exception of Salisbury, considered Japan a military partner, both for curbing the expansion of other great powers, in particular Russia and Germany, and for opening the Chinese market to British exports.[85]

Tension in the Far East escalated with the Boxer Uprising and the punitive expedition launched by the international contingent of troops against the rebels besieging diplomatic missions in Peking for several weeks. The Russians' occupation of Manchuria, coupled with their provocations on the frontiers of Persia and Afghanistan and intrigues in Tibet, mentioned in an earlier chapter, pushed the British government into a defensive alliance with Japan in January 1902. As many scholars have contended, this event symbolized the first practical step in the reconsideration of Britain's "splendid isolation" in the post-Victorian epoch.[86]

The Anglo-Japanese Alliance shocked bureaucratic elites and the public in Europe and Russia. Even some leading British statesmen, like Salisbury, believed that big "white" powers of the modern age were increasingly endangered by the hostile yellow race, above all by the Chinese and Japanese.[87] Yet the Unionist Cabinet, chaired by Prime Minister Arthur Balfour after the retirement of Salisbury, prepared to develop the Anglo-Japanese military collaboration. According to the correspondence between the War Office and the India Office, British and Japanese military representatives conferred on the situation in the Pacific on July 7, 1902. This meeting resulted in an accord as to a mutual exchange of secret data about Manchuria and Korea. The allies decided to establish a joint Intelligence Bureau in Shanghai or Tientsin—the two biggest Chinese cities. Interestingly, Major General Fukushima, the head of the Japanese military secret service, paid a visit to Curzon late in the same year.[88] Besides, British bankers lavishly credited large sums of money to their Japanese collaborators, while European manufacturers fulfilled delivery orders for armaments from Tokyo in the course of its large-scale war preparations. Furthermore, British naval officers were reported to drill the crews of some Japanese men-of-war and allegedly commanded them during the Battle of Tsushima in May 1905.[89]

The institution of the Russian Viceroyalty in the Far East and the inauguration by the tsar of the Special Committee on the Affairs of the Far East in August–October 1903 impelled a flood of reports, notes, and memoranda by British experts to the Unionist Cabinet. The authors regarded an impending Russo-Japanese conflict through the lens of a possible emergence of the anti-British coalition of continental states. The Admiralty, for instance, carried out a strategic war game at the Royal Naval College in Greenwich in 1903. The scenario envisaged cooperation with the friendly Japanese in the Pacific in order to protect Britain's naval bases against Russian attacks, while the British Mediterranean Fleet was bound to fight a joint Russo-French Flotilla,[90] though Balfour argued for a neutral stance in the war—but being benevolently disposed, however, to Japan:

We [Great Britain], of course, are little for Korea, except as it affects Japan. From every other point of view (except trade), there could be nothing better for us than that Russia should involve herself in the expense and trouble of Korean adventure, with the result that at the best she would become possessed of a useless province, which would cost more than it brought in, which could only be retained so long as she kept a great fleet in the Far East, and a large army thousands of miles from her home base, and which would be a perpetual guarantee that whenever Russia went to war with another power, no matter where or about what, Japan would be upon her back.[91]

London actually washed its hands in the conflict, leaving Russia "to engage herself so deeply in Manchuria that she would have neither the time nor money to spend on Constantinople or the Persian Gulf."[92]

Balfour and the majority of the Committee of Imperial Defence (CID) considered, moreover, that once Russia won the war, it would consolidate its alliance with France, then launch open aggression against India, and finally win total domination in the Middle East.[93]

To prevent the implementation of such a scenario, the members of the CID discussed the necessary arrangements to be taken in order to obstruct free passage by the Russian Black Sea Fleet through the Turkish Straits. Their conference was held on January 27, 1904, two weeks before the outbreak of the Russo-Japanese War, which ended in a decision to frustrate attempts by the Russian squadron of battleships to sail off to the Pacific from the Black Sea theater of naval operations. Prime Minister Balfour warned the Russian ambassador that any such endeavor would be regarded by the Cabinet of Saint James as open aggression against the United Kingdom. Thus, a new alignment of forces in the Far East, in spite of Britain's official neutrality, became a reality.[94]

As war operations intensified in the Far East, the Russophobes in Great Britain urged that more attention be devoted to the imperial defenses. Typically, as early as February 18, 1904, Lieutenant Colonel Napier, the military attaché in Russia, reported to Charles Scott, the ambassador in Saint Petersburg, that

> if matters go badly with Russia in the Far East on land as well as by sea, it is possible she will look southwards to retrieve some of her lost prestige in what is regarded by many Russians as an easier and more profitable campaign towards India, or endeavour by a large concentration of troops to intimidate England into a policy opposed to Japan.[95]

Being deeply concerned about Russia's hostile reaction to the pro-Japanese tenor of British foreign policy, the CID considered that "the Russian frontier in all parts of the world should be studied with a view to ascertain any points of weakness which might be utilized for attack in the event of war."[96] Furthermore, the experts of this coordinative body elaborated an ambitious program of the naval defense of

Australia aimed to safeguard British interests in the South Pacific—the sea gates to India.[97]

Although the Tsarist government was annoyed by the closure of the Turkish Straits to Black Sea Fleet battleships, it realized the negative effect that Britain's direct involvement in the war would have had upon the Russian position in Europe. "To tell the truth," acknowledged one high-ranking Russian official in mid-1904, "Japan is supported by the whole of Europe in a moral sense, partly officially and partly secretly, with minor exceptions, for there are no resolute protests against her violation of international maritime law and those atrocities against the civil population she commits in Korea." Interestingly, he cautioned the Tsarist government against British intentions to provoke a Russo-Chinese War with the purpose of drawing the Russians completely out of the Northeast Pacific.[98]

With the pursuit of war, the tension in bilateral relations escalated to the utmost, because the tsar decided to send a squadron of light cruisers on long-distance raids to stop war supplies bound for Japan. Apart from the interception of smugglers on the open sea, they were directed to patrol the Mediterranean and Red Sea, operating on the main sea routes from Europe to India.[99] Thus it was small wonder that initial British dislike of these operations developed into strong official remonstrations and an anti-Russian campaign in the press, filled with accusations of cynical violations of maritime law by the men-of-war.[100]

The Dogger Bank incident, which occurred on this large sandbank in the coastal North Sea waters off Hull, marked the lowest point in the bilateral relationship since the mid-1880s. On October 22, 1904, a panicky Russian flotilla, destined for Port Arthur and Vladivostok, mistook British fishing trawlers for Japanese torpedo boats and fired on them in the deep nighttime mist, sinking one and damaging their own cruiser, *Aurora*. In response, the furious British media called the Russians "this fleet of lunatics."[101] However, according to Alexander Izvolsky, who served as Russian foreign minister from 1906 to 1910, this final tottering on the brink of war led to a perception that the two empires should agree on a compromise in the near future.[102]

Although a comprehensive account of the Russo-Japanese conflict falls outside the scope of the study, it is important to emphasize that more and more pragmatically thinking bureaucrats in the Russian governing elites became aware that London and Saint Petersburg ought to stay away from any hostilities, especially stemming from incidents similar to the one at Dogger Bank. For example, Andrei Kalmykov, a young Russian diplomat trained in Oriental studies, recalled an interview with Pavel Lessar, the highly qualified diplomatic staff member mentioned above. When asked by Kalmykov in October 1904: "Will England attack Russia?" Lessar looked at his interlocutor, smiled, and said: "Let her try, she'll be the worse for it." "And we? Are we not to attack first?" "No reason to," he answered.[103]

Sergei Kolokolov, a graduate of the Institute of Oriental Studies in Vladivostok, who had succeeded Petrovsky in the post of consul-general in Kashgar in 1904, was another official, albeit from a younger generation, who shared this opinion. To his mind, both Russian and British officials on the spot should beware of any misunderstandings that their activity might spawn in Asiatic countries. Kolokolov even came in close contact with George Macartney, the British consul in Chinese Turkestan, to settle the question of Sarikol, a strategic stronghold and trade center in the Eastern Pamirs.[104]

Despite their long-term rivalry and misrepresentations of one another, the new challenges that Russia and Great Britain confronted in Europe and Asia began to afflict not only the mentality of bureaucrats but also of ordinary people in both countries. One of them seemed to be apprehension about the "yellow race" winning victory over the "white race." As Lord Esher, a high-profile figure in British political life, expressed it in a letter to his son on July 22, 1904,

The Japs do not seem to have found Kuropatkin an easy nut to crack. Still, they have turned him with his back to the sea—so that his line of communication is badly threatened. Should they have enough troops, and fresh troops, they may destroy part of his army. I am glad that he has made a good fight and that the West is not hopelessly beaten by the East. It would not be a good thing for us, in the long run, if that were so.[105]

And Robert Hart in his regular correspondence to a friend made this suspicion more clear.

The Chinese idea is still divided: Some are sure the Russians must win eventually and trim accordingly; others are believers in Japan, but among them an ugly feature is developing for they begin to gloat over and express the conviction that the next step will be for Japan to rid China of every foreigner![106]

Significantly, after the Tsarist armies and fleet suffered defeats, some British statesmen began to believe that once Japan won the war, it would be considered Australia's most imminent threat. As *The Pall Mall Gazette* wrote in May 1904, "We acknowledge their [Japanese] splendid qualities,...but we feel assured that their ideas cannot blend with our own, and that their influence would have a disintegrating effect on our future development."[107] And Pavel Klemm, the Russian consul in Bombay, reported to the Foreign Ministry that the Japanese military success in the battle of Mukden in February 1905 gave a real fright to the government of British India.[108]

These concerns notwithstanding, the Foreign Office renewed the Anglo-Japanese Alliance in August 1905. The discussion at the regular CID meeting on April 12, 1905, revealed Whitehall's ambivalent stance with regard to its Far Eastern ally:

In any extension, it is essential that the defensive character of the treaty should be strictly maintained, and that the provisions should be so framed as neither to constitute a menace, in reality, or in appearance to the position and interests of friendly powers, such as France and the U.S., nor to be regarded as an Anglo-Japanese Alliance against Europe.

Significantly, some Cabinet members proposed adjusting the Anglo-Japanese Alliance to the situation in the Middle East, which meant eventual incorporation of the Ottoman Empire into it. A leakage of confidential information even led the Russian ambassador to Constantinople to inquire of his British counterpart about a projected tripartite Anglo-Japanese-Turkish coalition in January 1906.[109]

A study of the CID's papers, along with British diplomatic correspondence, exposes the objectives that the London Cabinet was going to attain in Asia with the prolongation of the agreement with Tokyo. First, the aggressive ambitions of the "war party" in Russia should be restrained by extending the agreement's scope to India and making it operative in the event of the signatory being at war with one foe, instead of two or more. Then, the German kaiser's aspirations in the Pacific ought to be restrained by Anglo-Japanese naval collaboration. Finally, the activities of the proponents of the Pan-Asiatic doctrine in Japan should be taken under British control. Not coincidentally, the Admiralty submitted a special memorandum to the Cabinet in December 1905 urging that Anglo-Japanese signaling and cipher codes be reciprocally put into operation. Similarly, they recommended that the Cabinet allow exchanges of intelligence along with providing various kinds of facilities on the sea to each other, also according to a principle of reciprocity, pursuant to the treaty's secret supplements.[110]

References to the multifaceted impact of the Russo-Japanese armed confrontation on the Great Game should be made in the context of the Far Eastern crisis. Above all, as a modern Japanese historian has pointed out, the war brought changes to the connections between local regions and international relations in the northeastern crescent zone of the Pacific, promoting the reformation of the Qing Empire.[111] In the second instance, the collapse of the Tsarist armies encouraged nationalists of all sorts, including those in the Indian Empire. Characteristically, George Clark, the secretary of the CID, argued in 1908 that "Russia's defeat had raised questions about Europe's right and ability to rule the rest of the world and so, ironically, had done more to weaken the British Empire than all its blustering threats to invade Afghanistan."[112] To him and such statesmen as Curzon and public figures as Chirol, the emergence of Japan had contributed to the aspirations of those Indian nationalists who sought the "guidance and assistance" of Japan in the liberation of their mother state.[113]

Thus, paradoxical as it may seem, the downfall of Russia's prestige in Asia proved to be a setback for Whitehall similar to its hypothetical victory in the war against Japan, because many British officials regarded, however mistakenly, the stability of their rule in India as being put in jeopardy because of the Russians' desire for revenge. Apart from psychological motives, some military thinkers in London and Calcutta— General Kitchener being typical—pointed to the extension of the Russian railway network, which, they strongly believed, brought a march to the Raj within the bounds of practicability. According to the plan adopted by the tsar, one strategic railroad started at the ports on the Caspian Sea and continued via Merv to the fortified railhead at Kushk, which was situated merely 500 miles from Kandahar. Another railway went from Orenburg to Charjui on the Amu Daria (Oxus) via Tashkent and Samarkand, with a branch line to the Afghan border at Termez. Not coincidentally, Lord Minto, who succeeded Curzon in the post of viceroy, reported with alarm to London about the arrival of Russian military boats at the Oxus early in 1906.[114] Along with the above-mentioned directions of a Russian advance, there was a Persian route through Seistan via the future extension of the railway from Djulfa to Mashed. There is every reason to believe, therefore, that as the Russo-Japanese War continued, Whitehall revised its estimates of the Russian threat due to the improvement of the logistical, mainly railway, system that linked the European provinces of the Romanovs' Empire to Central Asia, Eastern Siberia, and Manchuria. As a modern researcher correctly wrote, many British politicians referred to it as "a sword of Damocles" hanging over Britain's head.[115]

Not coincidentally, therefore, the CID outlined three scenarios for the war against Russia in 1904–5—marked with the letters A for Europe, B for Central Asia, and C for the Caucasus and the Black Sea Basin— while Colonel Yermolov reported to his superiors on Kitchener's design to inflict a preventive blow upon Russian Turkestan with the seizure of Herat and occupation of Seistan, followed by the invasion of Trans-Caspia.[116] To justify this information, one should bear in mind that in the period under consideration, Russian troops in Turkestan amounted to 42,000, plus 30,000 in the army of the emir of Bokhara, along with

75,486 British and 155,240 native soldiers, plus irregular detachments of allied troops, reaching a total of 333,000 officers and soldiers. This is why the calculations verified Clark's opinion, who called it "sheer lunacy" to imagine that Russia could sustain large forces in Afghanistan.[117]

Finally, the experience with Russo-Japanese hostilities, as David Macdonald correctly remarked, brought about the necessity of eliminating foreign "complications," so as to restore the domestic order violated by the Russian Revolution in 1905.[118] The majority of ruling elites in the Russian Empire began to understand that any such complication—for example, a clash with Britain—could provoke the downfall of the autocratic regime and the collapse of the Romanovs' dynasty. Hence, even diehard Anglophobes at the Court and in the "far pavilions" of Asia had to acknowledge the urgency of bringing the Great Game to its inevitable end.

THE DIPLOMATIC REVOLUTION OF 1902–7

By the beginning of the twentieth century, the British Empire seemed to have attained a climax of power. Free trade, industrialization, and the huge Royal Navy had provided the British with unprecedented material supremacy. Suffice it to compare the foreign trade of the United Kingdom, amounting annually to £800 million, with the analogous indicator of Russian trade turnover, not exceeding £119 million a year. Although the total proportion of urban residents in the British Isles came to almost 80 percent, the Russian Empire remained mostly rural, with thin swaths of townsfolk and the middle class making up barely 10 to 15 percent of the population.[119]

The celebration of Queen Victoria's Diamond Jubilee in 1897 aimed to demonstrate that the British Empire—though "a congeries of different parts moving at different speeds," as the famous American historian Paul Kennedy sarcastically called it—still possessed enormous potentials for war, not merely to maintain its leading position in world politics but also to spread its influence to other regions of strategic or economic importance.[120] Although British foreign policy before 1914 was concentrated in the hands of a small, relatively homogenous ruling elite, which was aristocratic at its core,[121] more and more statesmen and public figures now aspired to reshape this motley congregation of dominions, settlements, and colonies into a coherent world power, capable of safeguarding its own "place under the sun." After the end of the Boer War, the empire became a panacea for all domestic troubles in the eyes of the British public, for whom industrial modernization was progressing to the general benefit of people who were interested in "markets, civilization, security and future greatness."[122]

However, most thoughtful observers fully realized that the British empire was faced with strategic overextension, given that it was charged with various commitments to a motley conglomerate of dominions and minor colonial possessions all over the world. In fact, the necessity for the empire to honor these obligations, along with a desire for it to keep on playing its traditional role of international arbiter, put an end to the policy of "splendid isolation" in the decade before World War I. To all appearances, British leadership circles faced a difficult dilemma: either to preserve an "open door empire" predicated on the principles of free trade and laissez-faire, or to convert its domains into an autocratic "empire fortress" protected by a system of military alliances and high interdictory custom duties.[123]

In any case, some historians opine that the reorientation of British foreign policy began with the decision of Salisbury's second Cabinet to remain in Egypt in 1889. Hence, Turkish territorial integrity, along with any kind of cooperation with Germany or Austria-Hungary, had lost their significance to the prime minister and his colleagues.[124] Salisbury described this process in a private message in August 1896—"I do not know that I can sum up the present trend of English policy better than by saying we are engaged in slowly escaping from the dangerous errors of 1846–56"—implying, above all, a confrontation with Russia and the preservation of the Ottoman Empire by any means.[125]

On the other side, Russian diplomatic correspondence vindicated the advocates of aggression in the Far East who sought to accommodate any remonstrations by Whitehall against the Russian encroachment upon Korea. That is why the majority of Tsarist strategists renounced the idea of a trilateral Anglo-Japanese-Russian alliance that some British diplomats offered to Saint Petersburg on the eve of the twentieth century. Characteristically, Staal reported to Nicholas II in November 1901:

A trilateral alliance with Great Britain and Japan would facilitate the settlement of the most complicated problems in the Far East, but, it seems to me, that to find a formula for such an alliance is as difficult as to discover the quadrature of circle. Besides, this alliance, perhaps, meets the interests of Britain more than ours.

The tsar concurred with his representative in this evaluation and, consequently, rejected Salisbury's proposal to commence diplomatic consultations with Russia on the problems of the Turkish Straits, Central Asia, and the Far East.[126] Furthermore, the conclusion of the Anglo-Japanese Alliance in 1902, mentioned earlier in this chapter, demonstrated the prematureness of Russo-British rapprochement at that time.[127]

Meanwhile, the rise of Kaiserreich as an industrial and commercial superpower stimulated ambitious naval programs pursued by Kaiser Wilhelm II and his naval minister, Grand Admiral Alfred von Tirpitz, in the 1900s. Mindful of this growing German peril, Curzon foresaw in a letter to Hamilton that

the most marked feature in the international development of the next quarter of a century will be, not the advance of Russia— that is in any case inevitable—or the animosity of France—that is hereditary—but the aggrandizement of the German Empire at the expense of Great Britain; and I think that any English Foreign Minister, who desires to serve his country well, should never lose sight of that consideration.[128]

While British intelligence agents and strategists concentrated upon Russia's potential for war during the late 1880s and early 1900s, the military resources of Germany drew the attention of Whitehall no sooner than February 1903.[129] As a result, Britain's long-term opposition to the

Russian command of the Turkish Straits also came to an end: "It [control over the Straits] would carry with it, as has been pointed out above, some naval advantages to Russia," ran the proceedings of the Cabinet meeting on February 11, "but these are not of the decisive character which has sometimes been supposed."[130]

Many Russian statesmen, diplomats, and intellectuals likewise reconsidered a new role for Germany in international affairs. As early as May 1891, Lamsdorf prophetically remarked in his personal diary:

Zinoviev [the head of the Foreign Ministry's Asian Department] argues that the whole policy of Russia should be aimed at the conclusion of an agreement with the London Cabinet; certainly, the time has not yet come, in his view, but he thinks that we must get railway lines and material resources in Central Asia prepared to achieve this objective. Central Asia represents a cockpit where we shall struggle or agree with England in the near future. If we arrive at a final understanding, it will become a masterpiece of the art of diplomacy![131]

In spite of a strong pro-German party at the Court of Saint Petersburg, including the empress and grand dukes themselves, who regularly counteracted any step in Russian foreign policy that they regarded as a threat to the traditional collaboration between two dynasties—the Romanovs and Hohenzollerns[132]—the Russian general public soon became aware that the kaiser's government was pursuing a policy that was detrimental to the interests of Pan-Slavism. Paradoxically, the defeat in the Far East intensified the Germanophobia in Russia. Interestingly, Andrei Kalmykov, whose reminiscences are alluded to earlier in this chapter, recalled that when he interrogated Colonel Alexander Mikhelson, the military attaché to Berlin, about how the Germans treated the Russians after the Japanese War, the latter answered: "With contempt, like impoverished relatives."[133]

An interview that William Stead, a renowned editor of *The Times*, held with the Russian diplomat Pavel Lessar in 1899 may be given as another typical indication of the moods that prevailed among Russian governing elites. During their talk, Lessar admitted that now, Russia is economically and politically a hundred years behind England. In a century's time she may have caught you up, but the notion of an Anglo-Russian war now is a mere bêtise. The nations whom you will fight in the near future are Germany and the USA. They are the neck-and-neck rivals of England. Sooner or later they will strike at your supremacy on the sea, and how absurd you will look if you have broken your teeth and wasted your resources on Russia.

A metaphor that Lessar used in this discourse to compare Russia's attitudes toward Britain and Germany impressed Stead most of all:

England is our [Russian] bad-tempered cat, Germany is our good-tempered tiger. You may scratch and swear as you please, you can never be anything but a nuisance to Russia. With Germany, it is different. Germany's conduct to Russia in all matters is perfect.... But Germany, if she should ever quarrel with Russia, can strike at our head. Therefore, as nations have to adjust their calculations according to their vital needs, not according to the sentimental moods of their peoples, Russia, while rejoicing in all the good turns Germany does her, and resenting all the bad turns England tries to do to her, can never forget that she is never in real danger from England, while Germany always can strike at the heart.[134]

Meanwhile, the escalation of international tension in the second half of 1903, caused by the Russo-Japanese scramble for Korea and the great powers' race for the Baghdad Railway in the Middle East, spurred Whitehall to renew diplomatic advances to Saint Petersburg about a cluster of problems in Asia almost simultaneously with the Anglo-French negotiations that led to the establishment of the Entente Cordiale in April 1904.[135]

However, Saint Petersburg again turned a deaf ear to the draft agreement on the delimitation of spheres of influence that the Foreign Office had circulated to Russia in January 1904, when Nicholas II had determined to start "a short victorious war" against Japan that would augment the world prestige and power of the "invincible empire."[136]

The present volume seeks to expose the misunderstanding of the Russo-Japanese War as an event that delayed the start of official Russo-British diplomatic negotiations. Quite the contrary, to this author's mind, the hostilities in the Far East accelerated Russo-British rapprochement, because the Tsarist government was worried less by the German penetration of North Persia than by Britain's alliance with Japan. Characteristically, Lamsdorf informed Kuropatkin immediately after the Japanese launched their first naval attack against Port Arthur that

> with regard to Britain's eventual policy in the future, one should certainly bear in mind that on declaring officially that she had assumed allied obligations to Japan, she is capable, under certain circumstances, of siding with our adversary. Consequently, some preparatory arrangements may not be unnecessary in the event of the rupture of Russo-British relations. On the other hand, however, it seems to me that open war preparations against England, which [preparations] still find no excuse in her policy toward Russia, would impel the government of Great Britain to resort to actions unfriendly to us, and, in this way, to impinge on our position in other countries where Russian and British interests collide.[137]

The significance of the Far Eastern problem for the Russo-British relationship may be illustrated by the proceedings of the special conference that was held in the Russian capital on April 4, 1904. The empire's leading military and civil officials were assembled to debate a new naval program for the next ten years. As Count Geiden, the assistant of the chief of the Main Naval Staff, wrote to Lamsdorf,

> England fears Russia's influence on Persia and Afghanistan, but the time will come when she realizes that it is not Russia, needing merely Persian cotton and exporting to Persia mineral raw materials and sugar, in other words, the products which England is unable to export to that country, rivals Britain there, but Germany

that aspires to draw her away from the Middle East [and Inner Asia] by exporting metal and chemical products. The sooner the borders of England and Russia come closer to each other in Afghanistan, the easier and stronger an agreement with England on the problems of Asian policy will be to mutual benefit.

In addition, Geiden argued in favor of "a comprehensive political and economic rapprochement with England to pacify the Near East by the maintenance of a trilateral Anglo-Franco-Russian alliance in the Mediterranean."[138]

A study of British diplomatic correspondence in the early twentieth century leads one to conclude that this particular period saw a real beginning for a new approach by British leadership circles to Russia. The London Cabinet devoted much attention to Saint Petersburg's aspiration to abstain from any steps in 1904–5 that might be interpreted by the British government and public opinion as directed against their national interests. "The war with Japan," wrote Lansdowne to Sir Cecil Spring-Rice, then the chargé d'affaires in Russia, "rendered the present moment unfavorable for entering upon any negotiations, but the Russian government had never shown themselves to sincere understanding provided that His Majesty's Government would formulate clearly the equitable conditions upon which they [the Russians] desired that it should be established."[139]

The threat of the "yellow peril" to European civilization had assumed particular popularity in various swaths of Russian society by the onset of the twentieth century. Suffice it to say that many political observers began to allude to *Apologia for Russia*, an 1895 pamphlet by W. Probyn-Nevins, who advocated an alliance of the two major Christian empires of modern times—Britain and Russia—in their crusade against decadent and cruel Oriental potentates.[140] That was why the war minister, Kuropatkin, averred in a memo to Nicholas II that "as far as China is concerned, the future danger for Russia from this empire of 400,000,000 people is beyond all doubt. The most vulnerable part of the Russian frontier, as it was eight hundred years ago, remains that great gateway of peoples through which the hordes of Genghis Khan had poured into Europe."[141] Implicitly, Lamsdorf concurred with Kuropatkin in this argument when he informed Benkendorf that nobody could evaluate the disasters that the national liberation movements of Asian nations would bring to both empires.[142] As Dimitry Yanchevetsky, a political analyst and secret agent specializing in the problems of the Far East, commented on the rapprochement between London and Tokyo: "The Anglo-Japanese friendship is a historical fallacy of the British government, similar to Britain's enduring hostility to every foreign action that Russia had taken since the Crimean War."[143]

Both sides used new trial balloons for their intentions in mid-1905, after the Tsarist armies and naval squadrons had sustained defeats in the Far East. Although the debacles at Mukden and Tsushima encouraged Wilhelm II to try again to instigate a continental coalition of Germany, Russia, and France in July 1905, the renewal of the Anglo-Japanese Alliance and the negative reaction of Paris to even a hint of Russo-German collaboration compelled the Tsarist government, first, to apply to the City of London for a loan to cover the deficit in the state budget and, second, to agree to preliminary diplomatic consultations on the cases of Persia, Afghanistan, and Tibet.

Taking into account the contingency of a political bargain with the London Cabinet, the tsar, at the same time, bluffed his cousin Willy with the aspirations of the British side to settle all disputes in Asia with Russia as soon as possible. "England is trying energetically to come to an agreement with us on the problems of the frontiers in Asia," Nicholas II informed Wilhelm II in September 1905. "But I don't wish to commence any talks with her at all," continued the Russian sovereign, seeking to delude his crowned relation.[144] Meanwhile, *Novoe Vremya* published one editorial after another inspired by those coteries in Saint Petersburg who championed the relaxation of international tension as a necessary objective for Russian policy after the fiasco in the Far East.[145] "These [editorials] have been the subject of a favourable comment in the English press," wrote Charles Hardinge, the ambassador to Saint Petersburg, to Lansdowne on October 8, 1905, "and have certainly been the means of affecting a détente in the relations of the press of the two countries."[146]

Typically, Mikhail Fedorov, who was proficient in Oriental and economic studies, held that contemporary Russian interests, if interpreted impartially, meant "the conclusion of peace or even alliance with Britain rather than the promotion of absolutely a bizarre hatred to her."[147] Yet the liberal media in the United Kingdom, not to mention India, continued to publish critical commentaries on Russian policy in Asia until October 1905, when the democratic revolution compelled Nicholas II to initiate domestic political reforms. Following *The Times*, many British periodicals began to argue that Russia and Britain were natural allies challenged by the other continental powers in Europe, meaning Germany and Austria-Hungary. Such respected journalists as Donald Wallace, later to be promoted to the rank of equerry to the king, and Edward Dillon, a political observer, together with Bernard Pares, an expert on the medieval history of Russia, contributed greatly to the British media's assuming more tolerance with respect to domestic affairs in Tsarist Russia.[148]

Although historians have meticulously studied the origins of this diplomatic rapprochement,[149] it seems imperative to stipulate the decisive motivations of both governments to convert even tentative advances, no matter how important they were in reality, into the routine practice of negotiations. Apart from notorious German intrigues in Europe and the Near East, which were fully recognized by Whitehall in 1906, a combination of other long-standing factors, mentioned above, had its apparent effect upon the state of things. And above all, it was an obvious stalemate in the Great Game that moved Russo-British dialogue forward from the neutral point in the aftermath of the war in the Far East.[150]

A deadlock that characterized Russo-British relations at that time was well perceived by both the Committee of Imperial Defence and the Russian General Staff. According to the calculations made by British experts, the home Cabinet would have to send a military contingent of 500,000 as reinforcements to the Anglo-Indian army in the event of a sudden Russian assault upon the Raj. Mindful of the unprecedented budget allocations to the Boer War, the Treasury would hardly be able to sustain such an extra burden of spending during the feverish international naval arms race.[151] Conversely, Russian financial resources were totally exhausted because of the war with Japan and social disorder in the provinces of the empire. As is well known, the Russian government was granted a joint Anglo-French loan in April 1906 owing either to pressure by Paris upon London or to some high-ranking Foreign Office officials who lobbied for it among members of Parliament, though the new Liberal Cabinet applied to Saint Petersburg for the reimbursement of the private property lost by British subjects in the Far East in the hostilities of 1904–5.[152]

The democratization of the autocratic regime in Russia and the coming of the Liberals to power in Britain also contributed to the beginning of diplomatic parleys. In fact, a new generation of states-men, like Alexander Izvolsky and Edward Grey, manifested themselves in the world diplomacy. Their belief system differed considerably from the mentality of those politicians who had taken their official positions early in the climax of the Great Game. What is even more important, their conception of international relations was not confined to merely European problems.[153]

In comparison with Lamsdorf, who was regarded as Witte's protégé, Izvolsky was descended from an aristocratic family that had served the Romanovs since the onset of their reign. This talented statesman's abil-ity to establish intimate contacts with all European sovereigns, includ-ing Edward VII, enabled him to enjoy the confidence of Nicholas II, to the extent that even Empress Alexandra preferred not to interfere with his policies. According to his memoirs, it was during several consequent interviews with the British monarch, whom he met in Copenhagen early in 1904, when the idea of the Russo-British entente struck him for the first time.[154]

Touching upon Grey's conception of British foreign policy, one should bear in mind his recurrent appeals to the previous Cabinet to abandon "splendid isolation" in favor of more permanent alliances, not excluding those with France or Russia in Asia. Significantly, he mani-fested these claims long before he entered the Foreign Office as the state secretary in December 1905 and advocated, therefore, the conclu-sion of the Anglo-French Entente as an embryo for a wider coalition of states determined to stop Germany's aggressiveness.[155] Soon afterward, Grey informed Spring-Rice about his conversation with Benkendorf on the urgency of reaching an Anglo-Russian understanding. The foreign secretary was convinced that Russia was supported by Britain in its aspiration to regain prestige and influence after the debacle of 1905, and thus Russia should be grateful to Britain and sympathize with the British concept of a renewed balance of power in the world.[156]

Apart from such prominent figures as Izvolsky and Grey, many other politicians, senior military officials, and high-profile public figures contributed to the immediate start and successful finish of the Russo-British negotiations. The role of informal contacts between Edward VII and Nicholas II is also worthy of note. Suffice it to mention a British proposal to arrange for the informal visit of the king to Russia in January and February 1906.[157] At the same time, while the British were distressed by the unremitting attempts of influential pro-German dignitaries at the tsar's court—for example, the chair of the State Council of Defense, Grand Duke Nikolai Nikolaevich the junior; and the chief of the General Staff, Lieutenant General Feodor Palizin—to thwart mutual rapprochement, the Russians were no less worried by a Russophobic campaign that the military thinkers like Kitchener, the statesmen like Curzon, and the journalists like Vambery waged in Parliament, government ministries, and the media. Many senior officials and military commanders of various ranks also disbelieved "on the spot" any kind of Russo-British cooperation.[158] As Premen Addy argued in his study of British policy in Tibet, "so keen was the home government to reach a settlement with Russia that the Foreign Office during the talks consulted only the India Office, the prime minister and Lord Ripon [the former viceroy], almost totally ignoring the Indian authorities."[159] That is why Grey arranged for regular meetings of the CID, while Izvolsky assembled high-ranking bureaucrats at a few special conferences in order to bridge over any misunderstanding of the continuing Russo-British diplomatic dialogue. It is also worthy of note that interdepartmental quarrels, frequently coupled with personal ambitions, also distorted the process. One may recall that a conflict between Curzon, Kitchener, and Brodrick resulted in the viceroy leaving, or the antipathy of Izvolsky to the above-mentioned Grand Duke Nikolai Nikolaevich the junior.[160] Typically, Izvolsky described the Russian General Staff in a letter to Benkendorf as "having learnt and forgotten nothing." "They speculate on Seistan, the Persian Gulf, the Indian Ocean, etc., like they used to debate on the problems of Manchuria, Korea, and the Pacific Ocean prior to the Japanese War," complained the foreign minister of being misunderstood by the high-ranking military.[161]

It was the First Moroccan Crisis in 1905–6 that triggered an official Russo-British discussion—which, however, did not prevent the heads of the Russian and French general staffs from proceeding with forming a coalition for war against Britain in the aftermath of the Algeciras conference.[162] Meanwhile, encouraged by the cooperation in the course of the crisis, the Liberal Cabinet bogged down in debates on the urgency of embarking on direct negotiations with Russia without French mediation. These became even more intensive when Clarke and Kitchener submitted a joint memorandum to the CID, which proposed to reinforce the Anglo-Indian army in the light of the latest events, causing a substantial increase in overall defense spending.[163] Besides, the London Cabinet did not exclude eventual disorder or even chaos on the empire's Asian frontiers, if a total collapse of the Tsarist Empire were to occur due to a new wave of revolution. As a secret agent reported to the Indian Intelligence Branch on July 7, 1905, after his trip to Central Asia, "the popular belief is that the Russian Empire is on its last legs; Russian influence and prestige have sunk to the vanishing point."[164]

According to British diplomatic records, the leading members of the Cabinet—Grey, Asquith, Haldane, and Morley—made a final decision on the start of negotiations with Russia at an informal dinner on April 24, 1906. In the four-hour debates on the subject, they all concurred on the necessity to respond positively to the Russian overtures and to delegate Arthur Nicolson, an experienced staff member of the Foreign Office who was renowned for his work at the Algeciras conference, to make an official visit to Saint Petersburg to present the British position.[165]

A careful study of diplomatic correspondence and accounts of eyewitnesses reveals that, though the Russians were the first who considered the Foreign Office's position as to possible negotiations before the general elections of 1905,[166] it was the Liberal Cabinet (and person-ally Edward Grey), that initiated Russo-British rapprochement from December 1905 to April 1906. Accordingly, one could be led to believe that the Great Game came to an end in the interval between December 1905 and August 1907, when the Anglo-Russian Convention was signed. In these years, the foreign secretary did his utmost to assure the British ruling elites and general public that there could be no alterna-tive to a compromise with Russia, provided the Cabinet wished to stop perpetual quarrelling with it at all strategic points, which in turn caused heavy budgeted spending. Grey was convinced that not only Asian nations but also Germany would benefit from a continuation of hatred toward Russia in British public opinion.[167] Moreover, the state secretary pointed to a unique chance for the Liberal Cabinet to reduce tension on the perimeter of the imperial frontiers by coming to friend-ly terms with Saint Petersburg.[168] Addressing Theodore Roosevelt, the American president, Grey defined the objectives for Anglo-Russian diplomatic contacts in December 1906:

> We wish to preserve and strengthen Entente with France; oth-erwise she will sign her own treaty with Germany because of fear of our betrayal.... In order to complete this basis, we wish to conclude agreement with Russia.... If we do not become friends, at least, we will not remain foes.[169]

For his part, Izvolsky did his best to organize a propaganda campaign in the press to persuade the Russian public to become more receptive to collaboration with the United Kingdom. A series of special conferences that he convened at the behest of the tsar on September 20, 1906, and February 14, April 27, and August 24, 1907, aimed to revoke interdepart-mental disagreements and elaborate a unified approach for the Russian leadership vis-à-vis the projected understanding with Britain.[170]

Delimitation of spheres of influence in Persia, construction of the Baghdad Railway, and the situation in Afghanistan proved to be the initial burning issues that attracted the attention of the Russian and British governments. Significantly, Izvolsly managed to remove the most formidable objections to the agreement in question, as avowed by some high-ranking military thinkers, especially Lieutenant General Feodor Palizin, only after the Russo-Japanese Convention was signed on July 30, 1907. As a British historian correctly remarked, for Russia the concord with Britain was, in a sense, a supplement to the secret treaty with Japan.[171] Reciprocally, the Russo-Japanese accord also had a special meaning for London, because the pacification of the Far East enabled the Tsarist government to concentrate on European problems. That is why Grey welcomed and closely watched the official Russo-Japanese consultations. "It is important that our negotiations should be included practically pari passu with the Japanese negotiations," wired Grey to Nicolson in April 1907. "I have impressed upon Komura [the Japanese foreign minister] that the two ought now to proceed simultaneously, though there should be nothing tripartite about them."[172]

In addition, Izvolsky believed that it was very important to get approval of the final draft by the governors-general, especially Nikolai Grodekov, the Turkestan "viceroy," who even convened a seminar of his staff officers on May 27, 1907, to elaborate a positive evaluation of the Russo-British détente.[173]

The official talks between Alexander Izvolsky and Arthur Nicolson actually began in Saint Petersburg on June 7, 1906, after Nicolson, the newly appointed British ambassador, was received by the emperor in an audience. It was the problem of Tibet that both contracting parties had chosen as a "touchstone" for the negotiations, which proceeded for the next fourteen months, including two main stages—the initial, from June to November 1906; and the decisive, from March to August 1907.[174] It needs to be mentioned that the diplomatic consultations were held against the backdrop of several notable international political events: the Second Hague Conference on disarmament in Europe, the scramble for the Baghdad Railway by the great powers, the conclusion of the Anglo-Chinese Convention on Tibet, and the signing of the Franco-Japanese Treaty.

The breadth of the author's purpose for the present volume permits only a skeleton outline of the Russo-British negotiations. Although the discussion of the Tibetan question took a relatively short period for the parties to concur on main principles, in spite of intrigues by the Dalai Lama in attempts to drive a wedge between the great powers,[175] the Afghan problem became a real barrier for the elaboration of the agreement because of the parties' conflicting political, military, and economic ambitions in the region. In the Afghan case, one should bear in mind the Anglo-Afghan Treaty of March 21, 1905. Pursuant to this document, Habibulla Khan renewed all Afghan commitments to the British Empire, at the same time disavowing any idea of an immediate attack against Russian Turkestan, which some of his counselors had recommended launching.[176]

With regard to the delimitation of Russian and British spheres of influence in Persia, both empires were annoyed with the antimonarchical revolutionary movement that extended to the central and northern provinces in 1906–7, and the race for economic supremacy with Germany.[177] The British anticipated the strengthening of Germany's position on the flank of the Suez Canal, whereas the Russians did their best in order, as Spring-Rice observed in a report to the Foreign Office, "to put a stopper on a German scheme for a railway into Persia from the East."[178] To prevent the German advance, Saint Petersburg decided to turn Northern Persia into "a veiled protectorate of Russia," in Hardingee's words.[179] Paradoxically, however, this objective would be unattainable without a closer collaboration with Britain on both political and economic aspects. That is why the agreement on Russian and British spheres of influence in this state, with a neutral buffer zone between them, laid the foundation for a general détente in bilateral relations.[180]

The negotiations on the Afghan and Persian questions were given new momentum in November 1906, when Charles Hardinge, then the British under–foreign secretary, acknowledged Russia's general right to aspire to the Turkish Straits in an interview with S. Poklevsky-Kozel, the Russian chargé d'affaires in London. The contingency of this issue was illustrated by Zinoviev in a letter to Izvolsky:

It has become extremely desirable that our Black Sea Fleet be cured of its impotency and that access to the Mediterranean be secured for it. It appears possible to raise this question only on condition that we are able to establish sincere cooperation with England. All plans for attack upon India are untenable and must be relegated to the field of fantasy. Concessions could be made by our side regarding the Central Asian question in case England is prepared to assist in solving the problem of the Straits.[181]

As Nicolson recalled later, after the telegram from Poklevsky-Kozel about the recognition of Russian interests in the Turkish Straits by the Foreign Office had reached Saint Petersburg, Izvolsky "blossomed into a happy man." In a discourse with the ambassador, the foreign minister regarded this statement as a "real breakthrough," an epochal event in the history of bilateral relations. Thus, starting at the end of 1906, a more friendly perception of the British stance regarding Persia prevailed among those in Russian leadership circles. To stipulate an exclusive right of Russian battleships to free passage through the Straits, Izvolsky handed a confidential memorandum to Nicolson on April 14, 1907.[182] In this way, the Russian foreign minister overruled stubborn opposition to the British draft by the Court, the State Council of Defence, and the Main Staff. He managed, moreover, to gain the support of Arkady Stolypin, the last productive Tsarist prime minister, who was in charge of the government in the years 1906–10.[183] It was at that time when the editorial board of *The Times* confidentially asked Izvolsky to promote tolerance and a benevolent attitude toward Britain among the Russian general public.[184]

The primary archival sources do not vindicate the finding shared by some historians of Izvolsky's surrender to Grey's claims in the course of negotiations, especially on the Afghan question.[185] In fact, the diplomats agreed on a final compromise on nearly all points, save the situation in three regions—the Turkish Straits, the Persian Gulf, and Mongolia. With regard to the Bosporus and Dardanelles, the Foreign Office relegated debates to the back burner on the pretext of considering the great powers' positions, above all those of Germany and Austria-Hungary, and avoiding the Ottoman Empire's eventual hatred for Britain.[186] Reciprocally, Izvolsky assured Grey of Russia's noninterference in the affairs of the Arabian sheikhs around the Persian Gulf.[187] As for the so-called Mongolian formula—which meant British reconciliation with the Russian encroachments upon Mongolia, which remained an integral province of the Qing Empire—Grey recommended that Izvolsky, together with Japan, solve this problem in a separate treaty.[188]

On August 31, 1907, in Saint Petersburg, Izvolsky and Nicolson signed the Arrangement on Tibet and the Arrangement on Persia along with the Convention on Afghanistan, with each document comprising five articles. A special supplement was attached to the Arrangement on Tibet concerning the withdrawal of British expeditionary forces from the Chumbi Valley. The subsequent exchange of ratification notes took place on September 25 that same year.[189] Significantly, the Russian side insisted that the documents relating to Persia and Tibet were called not *conventions* but *arrangements*, taking into account the probable negative reaction by Tehran and Peking to their provisions. Although Grey favored more obligatory clauses, he failed to convince Izvolsky. Later, the European public, following the commentaries by political observers and journalists, referred to the three documents as one Anglo-Russian Convention of 1907.[190]

The news of the accord attained by the formerly irreconcilable geostrategic contenders impressed and even shocked many—especially those statesmen and public figures who could not believe that Saint Petersburg and London had been able to come to any compulsory arrangement at all. Different pro-and-contra opinions were rumored in European capitals and at the courts of Oriental autocrats. Although senior French officials, quite predictably, welcomed the rapprochement, most politicians and military experts in Germany evaluated it in a skeptical manner. "No one will reproach England for such a policy," observed the German ambassador to Saint Petersburg, Wilhelm von Shoen; "one can only admire the skill with which she has carried out her plans. These plans need not necessarily be ascribed to any anti-German tendency, yet Germany is most affected by the agreement." Significantly, Kaiser Wilhelm penned in the margins of this dispatch: "Yes, when taken all around, it is aimed against us."[191]

The Qing authorities, which sustained a merely nominal suzerainty over Tibet, abstained from open remonstrations about the accord, because their interests had been secured by a series of previous agreements with Britain, Russia, and Japan, but Habibulla, the emir of Afghanistan, did not recognize the articles of the Anglo-Russian Convention with regard to his country. Moreover, he rejected all British attempts to persuade him to make an official visit to London in order to agree on a compromise with Whitehall.[192] According to Hopkirk, the signature of the Anglo-Russian Convention humiliated the peoples of Afghanistan and Persia, because they were "shared out" between two empires without even being consulted.[193] Yet the Persians seemed to have resented the Russo-British bargain most of all. Both the champions of monarchy and the democratic leaders, who had looked upon England as a guarantor of the sovereignty and territorial integrity of their country against the encroachments of Tsarist Russia, called the convention "an alliance with the devil." As one nationalistic newspaper claimed, Russia had benefited from the agreement while Britain "had deceived Persia" when it sided with "the foes of civilization and justice."[194] Spring-Rice, then the British minister in Tehran, grumbled to Grey that the natives called all the British renegades who had "betrayed the Persian people."[195]

The reception of this "masterful piece of statesmanship," as a Tsarist diplomatic officer labeled the Anglo-Russian Convention,[196] by the British and Russian general publics needs a more profound consideration in order to justify its role in the end of the Great Game. Typically, a chorus of Grey's partisans in Britain balanced the voices of his implacable opponents, especially in India and other overseas territories of the empire. *The Times'* editorial dated September 2, 1907, for example, praised the conclusion of the convention by saying that "the peace of Asia and the prospect of some eventual reduction of the heavy military burden of India are worth some sacrifice." The author was convinced that "it will rank among the most important instruments for securing the peace of the whole world."[197] According to *The Spectator*, the convention secured the Persian Gulf from Russian penetration, ending "the crisis of this long disease of anxiety about Russian intentions."[198] "Above all, the newspapers stressed its great historical significance, because a certain modus vivendi in Central Asia has been established," reported Poklevsky-Kozel from London to the foreign minister on October 2; "they also express their hope that this diplomatic act puts an end to the policy of mutual competition and distrust, when both sides constantly suspected each other of ambitious designs and did their utmost to counteract each other's arrangements."[199]

The City of London also supported the "bargain." Early in 1908, the Imperial Bank of Persia informed the Foreign Office about the great satisfaction with which they appreciated the understanding with Russia relating to Persia.[200] As Grey wrote to Nicolson of the British public's reception of the entente a month later: "People here do not think that the Convention, as an isolated bargain, is a good one; but they will be pleased if it leads to a general friendly attitude of Russia towards us. Hoping and expecting this, they have cordially approved of the Convention, and Russia must be careful not to disappoint them."[201]

This opinion was shared by some leading political observers. Edward Dillon, for example, specified in the *Contemporary Review* that

> Sir Arthur Nicolson's achievement, far-reaching and beneficent in its results, deserves greater recognition than the successful conduct of a military campaign. Summing up the advantages it confers upon us, one may fairly say that it has laid the specter of an Anglo-Russian conflict solved in the Middle East, insured the maintenance of all British concessions situated within Russia's sphere of influence in Persia, and deprived other states of the power of causing a sudden panic among ourselves, or precipitating a sanguinary war between the British and Russian peoples.[202]

In a broader sense, as Paul Kennedy correctly stated, most Liberals were tempted by the argument that an Asian agreement would eliminate the prospect of an enormously costly war for the defense of India, just as the profits—financial, political, and other—that might flow from the creation of an Anglo-French-Russian bloc fascinated the Russians.[203]

Responding to those analysts who supposed that the isolation of Germany was a major objective for both London and Saint Petersburg in removing barriers for collaboration, another political observer hidden under the pseudonym "Calchas" argued in the *Fortnightly Review* that there was not a shadow of truth in the suggestion that the British had tried to engineer a countercoalition, because the Anglo-Russian Convention simply equalized diplomatic conditions in Eurasia.[204] As Benkendorf reported to Saint Petersburg, Grey and the Liberal Cabinet feared either the collapse of the Tsarist regime or its unexpected conversion into a pro-German military dictatorship. In the latter case, any chance for Britain to attain any comprehensive understanding with Russia would have been frustrated.[205]

Among the most relentless critics of the Anglo-Russian entente were several distinguished experts on Oriental studies and practice—Curzon, Spring-Rice, Vambery, Chirol, Morrison, and the like. Oddly enough, their views concurred with the negative reception of the agreement by some liberals and also leftist journalists, such as L. Wolf and H. Brailsford, who strongly believed that "a predatory Tsarist bureaucracy, as hostile to the liberty of other people as to her own," using the phrase of Spring-Rice, would be simply unable to be transformed into a partner of democratic Britain within a few months.[206] And the information from Saint Petersburg appeared to correspond perfectly with such a low evaluation of the Tsarist administration. As Chirol wrote to his colleague Morrison on September 2, 1907, "Only ten days ago Stolypin and Izvolsky were outvoted at the Council of State to which the Agreement was finally submitted, and everything depended upon the Emperor's last word, which was decided and decisive."[207] The *Daily News* supposed that until a parliamentary order of state had been established in Russia, the British government should ignore it.[208] Not coincidentally, in April, June, and July 1907, mass protest meetings against the Russo-British rapprochement took place in London, Manchester, and other industrial cities of Britain at the initiative of Labour Party activists, whereas their Administrative Council adopted a resolution that condemned Whitehall for plotting an alliance with the autocratic Tsardom.[209] Bernard Pares, the above-mentioned expert on Russian and Slavonic studies, expressed these emotions in a metaphor: "The establishment of a frankly constitutional regime in Russia will be like the establishment of a common language, in which England and Russia can converse freely."[210]

Arminius Vambery, for his part, also flung invectives at the Russo-British accord. The famous Orientalist called the agreement "a humiliating Convention" in the eyes of the peoples of Persia, Afghanistan, and China, because it violated their sovereign rights and territorial integrity while making possible both Russian and German aggressive designs. According to Vambery, "the Convention, instead of being useful to British interests in Asia, does a good deal of harm by strengthening the deeply rooted optimism prevailing in England with regard to Asiatic affairs."[211] Characteristically, the members of the Indian government, including Minto and Kitchener, severely criticized the agreement. Impressed by their criticism, the American consul-general in Calcutta told his government that the convention was regarded by them as "all that it ought not to be."[212]

But it was Lord Curzon who definitely crusaded against the ratification of this diplomatic act. Speaking in the House of Lords on February 6, 1908, for one and a quarter hours, he avowed disbelief in any sincere wish by the Russians to settle all disputable questions with Britain. "I have been reluctantly driven to the conclusion," declared the former viceroy, "that, whatever may be the ultimate effects produced, we have thrown away to a large extent the efforts of our diplomacy and of our trade for more than a century; and I do not feel at all sure that this treaty in its Persian aspect, will conduce either to the security of India, to the independence of Persia, or to the peace of Asia." The "bargain," Curzon told the audience, was "doubtful in respect of Afghanistan, bad in respect of Tibet, and worse in respect of Persia." His general verdict called it a humiliation of British prestige in Asia.[213] As one historian expressed it, "to Curzon's mind the agreement with Russia surrendered all that the British government had been fighting for over the past century and it gained nothing in return."[214]

However, the parliamentary debates demonstrated support for the Russo-British détente by the majority of the ruling elites and general public in the British Isles. Lansdowne, Sanderson, and Grey himself consistently advocated the Anglo-Russian Convention and disclaimed any proposed amendments to its provisions. They assured both members of Parliament and the public that the document would safeguard

Britain's position in Central and East Asia. Thomas Sanderson, the permanent undersecretary for foreign affairs, argued in his speech to the House of Commons that "positive and permanent engagements had been given concerning Persia and Afghanistan in place of the rather fluid assurances which were all that Russia had previously been willing to offer."[215] According to Grey, "it will be much nearer the truth to say that under this Agreement we [the British] have given up nothing that was not gone before"; and "what we have gained strategically is real, while the apparent sacrifices, we have made commercially, are not real." Grey's conclusive argument sounded in the same manner:"Had we taken up the attitude of refusing to negotiate with Russia, the events which have since taken place on the Indian Frontier and in Persia must have brought the two countries [Britain and Russia] measurably nearer conflict."[216] According to the foreign secretary, Russia "has undergone a spectacular humiliation in the Far East and she could only regain her position as a great power by adding British friendship to the French alliance."[217]

Following these arguments, one could be led to believe that the Anglo-Russian Convention promised to stabilize the empire and save substantial spending on imperial defense through its reduction of the Russian threat to India. To put it differently, the conclusion of the convention signified "strategic foreign policy at its best, using foreign policy to maximize Britain's ability to defend her interests."[218]

For his part, Izvolsky declared to the Russian government:"We must put our interests in Asia on a reasonable footing; otherwise we shall simply become an Asiatic state, which would be the greatest disaster for Russia."[219] Judging from the evaluations typical in the ruling circles and mass media, their assessments of the Anglo-Russian Convention also differed, though a positive reflection prevailed. "A glance at the Russian press of all shades and opinions showed conclusively how it was welcomed as the visible sign of a new era in Anglo-Russian relations," wrote Hardinge in a memorandum about King Edward VII's visit to Reval in June 1908, "On expressing my surprise that such papers as the *Novoe Vremya*, which I had always regarded when in Russia as the bitterest foe of England, had now become the ardent supporters of an

Anglo-Russian understanding, His Majesty [Nicholas II] admitted that he also was astonished at the rapidity with which the feeling had spread, and that he had never been so surprised as when he had read recently in a chauvinistic 'rag' called the *Sviet* a warm article in praise of England, and urging closer relations between the two countries."[220] This evaluation given by one of the leading British diplomats refuted a statement by some modern scholars that the Russians in their mass neglected the entente with Britain.[221]

It is doubtless that many Russian analysts and public figures contended with such an outcome of the long race for supremacy in Asia. One of them, Nikolai Notovich—himself a direct participant in the Great Game, who had repeatedly made secret trips to the Middle East and India—published a pamphlet that advocated a historic compromise with Britain.[222] Another famous figure of a higher public caliber, Maksim Kovalevsky, estimated the wholesome effect of the Anglo-Russian Convention on Russian foreign and domestic policies in the following way:

> The further rapprochement of our mother state with the country, which has the greatest interests as well as the largest influence on Asia of all other European states, will be conducive to the maintenance of peace in the Far East, similar to how a closer acquaintance with English political life will contribute to the organic development of our state establishments.[223]

According to the military commander Alexei Kuropatkin, "Russia and England, as Asian powers, should work in conjunction, so as to uphold order in Central Asia and counteract a common menace from the Far East in the future."[224] As another respected military thinker, Nikolai Grodekov, wrote to Izvolsky on March 17, 1908, the Anglo-Russian accord would surely pacify the peoples of Central Asia, whereas the continuation of struggles between the two empires would bring their rule in the Middle East and India to a collapse. Analogously, the governor-general stressed in an annual humble report of 1907 to the tsar that the entente with Britain had put an end to the period of disturbances and conflicts in bilateral relations and opened a new era of "mutual support of the Europeans in Asia."[225] Roman Rosen, the ambassador to Tokyo and later to Washington, was likewise enthusiastic about the prospects for Russo-British political dialogue, viewing it through the lens of a future Anglo-American-Russian alliance in East Asia.[226]

Their opponents disapproved of the agreement in a way that was similar to how it was fought in the United Kingdom. Obviously, some of them shared Bismarck's low assessment of Britain as one of "those dexterous powers, with whom it is not only impossible to form any lasting alliance but who cannot be relied upon with any certainty, because in England the basis of all political relations is more changeable than in any other state."[227] Besides, the pro-German dignitaries, like some members of the imperial Romanov family, dreaded Russia's eventual rupture with Germany and sought economic and political privileges to be granted to German industrial companies and banks in the Middle East and Far East. To Witte, for example, it appeared a triumph of British diplomacy, making it impossible for Russia to annex Persia. He believed that Saint Petersburg had lost free access to Kabul and Afghan Turkestan. Under such circumstances, he was convinced, Afghanistan as a buffer state would be converted into somewhat a "loaded gun" directed against Russia.[228]

The military experts, such as Andrei Snesarev and Mikhail Grulev, doubted that the Anglo-Russian Convention would have any positive effect on Asia's Russian client states, such as Persia, while appreciating a general "spirit" of cooperation with Britain.[229] According to Alexander Rediger, a respected Russian military thinker who headed the War Ministry in the years 1906–8, the stabilization of the situation in Central Asia would not prevent Britain from further strengthening the Indian army.[230]

It should be stressed that evaluations of the 1907 Anglo-Russian Convention varied throughout the twentieth century. For example, Georgy Chicherin, the head of the People's Commissariat for Foreign Affairs in Bolshevik Russia, opined that "it was sponsored by the Russian metallurgical imperialism."[231] Andrei Zaionchkovsky, a celebrated Russian military historian, maintained that Russia did not benefit at all from the Anglo-Russian Convention, because Britain was unable to support Tsarist armies in war operations against Germany or Austria-Hungary on the continent.[232] Anatoly Ignatiev, a Soviet specialist in the history of international relations, observed that it was the national liberation movement that molded a certain basis for Russo-British collaboration in 1907.[233] The Uzbek historian Goga Khidoiatov claimed that the delimitation of Russian and British spheres of preponderance in Asia had served merely as a smokescreen for Britain to prepare new aggression against the peoples of the Middle East and Inner Asia.[234] Conversely, Pio-Carlo Terenzio, a Swiss expert on the history of international law, held that the Anglo-Russian Convention merely signified the emergence of an anti-German coalition.[235] According to American scholars, "the fundamental importance of the Anglo-Russian Entente of 1907 was potential rather than substantive," because it "hindered rather than furthered the British quest for security," or it even became "a stepping-stone to the First World War."[236]

However, the author of the present volume fully adheres to the views of those historians who have argued that the Anglo-Russian Convention meant the most radical reformation of British external policy since the days of Ellenborough, Wellington, and Palmerston.[237] As this study reveals, it was modeled on the pattern of the Russo-Austrian Agreement of 1897 respecting the situation in the Balkans, and the Anglo-French Entente of 1904 regarding colonial possessions in Africa and Asia.[238]

The Anglo-Russian Convention settled or at least accommodated the seemingly irreconcilable disputes between Russia and Britain in the region from Persia to the Far East. For London, as Thomas Otte correctly wrote, it "reduced Russia's perennial threat to Britain's Indian possession and its other Central Asian interests and so reduced the dangers of imperial overstretch."[239] One may also believe that it was not the Russian defeat in the war of 1904–5 but the Anglo-Russian agreement that diminished fears of Tsarist Russia in British leadership circles and among ordinary people.[240] The author of the present volume agrees with John Gooch's objective assessment of the convention, given in his preface to a collection of the British documents on the origins of World War I:

"India ceased to bulk large, indeed to bulk at all in the cycles of strategic debate in England. The fear of a Russian advance in Persia continued, but the burden of preserving stability in Central Asia fell on the diplomats rather than on the soldiers."[241]

Indeed, the events in the interval 1902–7 symbolized a diplomatic revolution in the history of international affairs and of Britain's relations with foreign powers—in particular, because a new system of ententes was instituted in Eurasia, respectively between Britain and Japan, Britain and France, France and Japan, Russia and Japan, and, last, Britain and Russia, not to mention the Russo-French alliance that had come into existence much earlier. Although each of them did not prove to be an alliance based on mutual sympathies, it had to be carefully nurtured, as David French correctly remarked,[242] because, in practice, entente provided for signatories freedom of action within the fixed territorial zones along with cooperation within other zones and good comradeship everywhere. Thus, long-standing political alliances began to replace the fragile ad hoc coalitions of states in international affairs that had been typical of the so-called Vienna world order throughout the nineteenth century. As is well known, the Entente as a general counterbalance to the Triple Alliance developed for nearly thirty years from 1891–93 to 1922–23. With regard to Russo-British relations, the 1907 convention completely transformed their atmosphere and laid the foundation for their military collaboration during World War I.

In conformity with these arguments, the Anglo-Russian Convention may be truly regarded as the end of the Great Game, whereas the contributors to the architecture of the Russo-British rapprochement—such as Grey, Nicolson, Izvolsky, and Benkendorf, to mention but a few— that led to this epochal transformation should be considered crucial.[243] Although Russian and British "hawks" amid ruling elites repeatedly claimed that the Anglo-Russian accord would not survive in the decade before World War I, the Great Game ceased to remain the mainstream in the Russo-British relationship. As *The Times'* editorial said,

Taken as a whole, the Anglo-Russian Convention will, we hope and truly believe, fulfill the purpose set forth in its preamble. It settles by mutual consent the different questions affecting the interests of the two powers in Asia, and, if loyally carried out, it should remove an antagonism which, whether real or imaginary, has for the last half century and more continually threatened the peace of the world.[244]

Edward Grey seemed to be absolutely right when he announced in a lecture delivered to a British audience on October 20, 1905, shortly before he took up the post of foreign secretary, that "the spirit of the agreement is more important than the letter of the agreement."[245] Symptomatically, *The Times* reproduced the tenor of this uttering in 1912 as a commentary on the visit of the British parliamentary delegation to Russia in return for the similar visit of the State Duma's representatives to London three years earlier: "The Anglo-Russian understanding is much more than an understanding between two governments: It is rooted in a genuine mutual sympathy between two nations; and has thus an element of stability and permanence such as no paper agreement between diplomats could hope to possess."[246]

THE GAME'S FINAL IMPACT ON ASIAN COUNTRIES

It should be stressed that although the crucial turning point in world politics at the onset of the twentieth century—the establishment of ententes between leading states—was the result of momentary necessity and never erased underlying problems, it meant a real breakthrough not only in Russo-British relations but also in the great powers' general conduct of foreign policy. And even though "diplomatic revolutions have not worked smoothly," as an American historian rightly remarked,[247] the Great Game's impact on Asian countries is worthy of separate, careful consideration.

At the beginning of the Great Game, Central and East Asia were characterized by more or less medieval political, social, economic, and cultural features. Then the competition between British and Russian civilizing patterns led to modern changes in all spheres of daily routine. Instead of the social apathy, economic backwardness, and political anarchy in which they had been stuck for centuries, local nations gradually began to awake under the influence of innovations that were brought to them by many the Great Game's "players" of different caliber: politicians, military staff, civil administrators, even merchants and journalists, both British and Russian.

It is striking how many analysts drew comparisons between the Russian and British models of colonial rule, for example, in Central Asia, India, Tibet, and even Manchuria.[248] In a sense, the media of both countries waged propaganda wars against the adversary to cover up their own weaknesses and to eulogize imperial policies in remote areas. Yet despite specific elements, an inference can be drawn from historical sources that no matter how intensive the Great Game was in different periods, some common qualities distinguished the Russian and British styles of dealing with Oriental peoples.[249]

In contrast to the Russian pattern of colonial rule—which was predicated on territorial acquisition followed by rigid political control over the indigenous population, along with an imposition of settlements by military colonists who combined their military service and agricultural labor on fertile lands—British trade colonialism emerged from the empire's long-standing exploitation of the natural resources of Asian countries, though Britain's industrial development likewise required capital investments in setting up modern infrastructure, such as telegraph lines, railways, high roads, and depots in India and other sections of its colonial periphery. In accordance with the available statistical data, by the 1880s Hindustan had absorbed £270 million in British capital, or about one-fifth of total British overseas investment.[250] Although Russian Turkestan remained a financial "black hole" of the empire in the long run, a fact that puzzled British statesmen and public figures,[251] India provided economic growth for the United Kingdom and the well-being of the British. It is problematic, therefore, to agree with those historians who maintain that Britain abstained from "putting anything back into the soil" of its dominions.[252] Yet it needs to be noted that there were Oriental potentates who were looking forward to their minor states becoming protectorates of Russia in order to preserve their prerogatives as traditional feudal rulers backed by the powerful white tsar of the Romanovs' Empire.

Thus, if a group of respected statesmen, colonial officers, journalists, and public activists apologetically praised British rule in India as the "Golden Age" of the empire,[253] other eyewitnesses—for example, Alexander Gardner, a colonel of artillery in the service of Maharaja Ranjit Singh of Kashmir—compared India's position as one of the richest countries in ancient times with its demoralizing mode of existence under the aegis of Great Britain throughout the nineteenth century, when the Indian population became poorer and social conditions deteriorated.[254] To corroborate this opinion, many Russian observers stigmatized the "rapacious rule" of the British in India, especially their treatment of natives as "a lower race in mentality, morality, and healthiness." The Russian press frequently alluded to such vernacular periodicals as *The Indian Express*, which regularly commented on the antipathy or distrust between the British and natives.[255]

Apart from journalists, Russian military officers and diplomatic officials unanimously agreed on British rule's negative impact on Asian countries, India in particular. For example, David Livkin, who had sojourned in the Raj for several months, reported to the Main Staff:

> The Englishmen used every occasion to point out to natives and the whole world that they had made great progress in the spheres of people's education, transport communication and a system of sewerage. In fact, however, these achievements are nothing in comparison with benefits which England derives from India. Should the government of Britain not regard this country as a profitable enterprise, she [India] could enjoy more prosperity and not suffer such calamities as famine, epidemic diseases, etc., as she does now.[256]

The officer claimed that whereas barely 1 percent of the Indians were literate, even they were deprived of any chance to make an administrative career, unlike loyal subjects of the tsar of Turkish origin in Russian Central Asia.

Analogously, Consul-General Pavel Klemm delivered to the Foreign Ministry his highly critical assessments of the British government of

India in the period of Curzon's Viceroyalty—1899–1905. According to the consul-general to Bombay, the viceroy "curtailed any independence of action of local princelings"; "turned them completely into pawns in the hands of British Political Agents"; "reduced the autonomy of the vernacular press" by the prohibition against revolutionary propaganda and the introduction of a regime of state secrecy; canceled free elections in the Indian universities; and annihilated a traditional, competitive system of career promotion for civil officers.[257]

At the same time, though the majority of Tsarist subjects genuinely saw the Russian conquest of Asian countries as a result of God-ordained destiny, believing in their progressive and beneficial rule over the natives, Western politicians and intellectuals severely criticized Russian administrative practices toward Oriental races. This biased approach, rooted in decades of Russo-British opposition in Asia, was predicated on a number of stereotypes rather than on any objective concept.[258] This study reveals, however, that it would not be fair to ignore the achievements under Russian rule, such as the stabilization of frontiers, strengthening of internal security, reduction of petty feuds between neighboring tribes and social groups, improvement in logistics, and establishment of secular schools, libraries, and hospitals. Indeed, even natives agreed that the incorporation of the Central Asian peoples into the Russian Empire was more progressive than living under the Persian, Afghan, or Manchu rulers. Symptomatically, many Europeans were convinced that Russian military occupation, repressions against Pan-Islamic dissidents, and despotism in the treatment of local rulers notwithstanding, its pattern of colonial government proved to be not less progressive and sometimes more efficient than that of the British. As the renowned British scholar Charles Trevelyan wrote in *The Times*, referring to the Russian conquest of Turkmenia,

> Peace and security of life and property, which are the foundations of every other improvement, have been substituted for rapine and personal outrage. These darkest of all the dark places of the Earth were full of the habitations of cruelty. Their pacification and settlement were beyond our reach, and we ought not to obstruct

Russia in her costly and difficult task by habitual misconstruction and depreciation.[259]

Doubtless, in the political sphere, the subjugation of nomadic tribes and medieval khanates anchored the frontiers of the Romanovs' Empire and integrated natives into the modern social order, though the Tsarist authorities exempted their Muslim subjects from conscription. According to Aleksei Kuropatkin, the military governor of Trans-Caspia in the 1890s, addressing a group of British tourists in Ashgabat,

> We [the Russians] may boast with perfect truth that thirty-five years during which Central Asia has enjoyed the blessings of a firm and civilized rule, have been years of sustained progress, of daily-increasing strength in the bonds of attachment and good-will which unite these subject peoples to the inhabitants of other Russian provinces.[260]

Conversely, Russian tolerance for local traditions revived the aspirations of dissidents to stir up anti-Russian uprisings, for example, the Andizhan revolt in 1897–98. It is disputable whether Russian rule was less progressive than British rule in the fields of education, industry, and social standards, but Russian rule was definitely more understandable for natives who were not ready to fully accept Western civilization. Not coincidentally, many diplomatic and military analysts stated that whereas the British caused the local people to feel inferior, the Russians wished them to behave somewhat as if they were at home. That is why Durand quite correctly held that whereas the Russian position in Asia was natural, the British one proved to be artificial.[261]

Significantly, both Russian and European travelers juxtaposed the ambivalent attitude of Oriental merchants—for example, Bokharian or Kashgarian—toward Britain with that toward Russia; though upholding the efforts of the British to impose fair trade rules on Asian markets, they appreciated the military power and political prestige of the white tsar, who was mighty enough to send off countless armies to conquer new territories in Asia.[262]

Compared with the British Empire, which embraced a cluster of overseas domains "resembling an interim commercial office set up to gain certain profits," as one Russian political observer critically argued in 1897,[263] Russia's principal idiosyncrasy was its territorial continuity in Eurasia. Similar to the boom in railway construction for the British in India, Tsarist engineers and administrators managed to create a web of railroads linking the empire's European part to its outskirts, including Central Asia and Manchuria. Although their key role, unlike the railways operated by the British, was more strategic than commercial,[264] the opinion of a German observer regarding the Central Asian Railroad seems very true:

> It has cut through the desert belt which England regarded as a protection for India,...it has made possible the simultaneous reinforcement of large masses of troops from Turkestan, the Caucasus and Volga regions to Ashgabat and Merv, and has firmly connected the province of Trans-Caspia with its true natural center, Turkestan; Russia's prestige in Central Asia has been consolidated;...[the] Russification...of its Asiatic possessions has been forwarded by an entire generation.[265]

Yet this and other railroads, which linked together different Russian provinces, gradually assumed economic significance. Despite the growing cargo traffic along the Central Asian Railroad at the beginning of the twentieth century, the Orenburg-Tashkent Railway still provided transportation for manufactures from Turkestan to Russia; for example, in 1908 the overall turnover amounted to 14.5 million rubles, and, in the reverse direction, to 11.8 million rubles.[266]

By the 1890s, Tsarist bureaucrats at all levels had awakened to Turkestan's economic potential. After Ivan Vyshnegradsky, the finance minister, visited the Tashkent Exhibition in 1890, he called Turkestan "a jewel in the crown of the Russian tsar," for the region had definitely become the empire's principal source of raw cotton and silk.[267] It was, claimed a Russian journalist, "a colony indissolubly linked to the Empire," a natural market for Russian products, and a potential area for peasant colonization.[268]

Yet this study reveals that though the latter phase of Russian economic policy in Asia progressed toward a more European model, along with a gradual reduction of protectionist measures and the introduction of conventional trade tariffs in the relations with principal partner states,[269] the champions of neomercantilism and protectionism among the British ruling elites were about to take the upper hand in colonial policy by the beginning of the twentieth century. The suppression of domestic industries and monopolization of markets in Asian countries ceased to be a special feature of Russian colonial rule. The jingoistic tenor in Parliament and the press reflected the ambivalent challenge with which Whitehall was confronted at the last stage of the Great Game: the necessity to consolidate overseas possessions, and simultaneously the urgency to bridle German ambitions in Europe to preserve the general balance of power.[270]

In the Russian case, the concept of Siberia and Central Asia as a cradle for a new, growing nation was formulated by statesmen and intellectuals at the end of the nineteenth century. Thus, a pattern of colonial rule suffered modification from the purely military-to-economic model at that time.[271] Characteristically, by 1881 about 30,000 Russians had settled in Semirechie, a province of Turkestan, though the Russian prohibition on purchasing farmland in the Emirate of Bokhara or the Khanate of Khokand had remained in force until the beginning of World War I.[272] The regulations of the Turkestan governor-generalship, introduced in 1886, accelerated the Cossack colonization of southern Turkestan. A similar dynamic was evident in Priamur Province and Manchuria before the Russo-Japanese War. New, extended areas for peasant colonization in the Asian part of the Russian Empire emerged in the years 1906–10, in compliance with the agrarian reform initiated by Prime Minister Arkady Stolypin.[273] At the same time, according to annual financial reports, the Tsarist government began to encourage foreign capital investments in Central Asia.[274] Symptomatically, after the Anglo-Russian Convention was concluded, a Russian observer held that "our immediate policy in the Orient should be a policy of economic arrangements based on peaceful cultural collaboration and friendship with certain states."[275]

Thus, the role of the Great Game in transformations of fundamental importance could be underestimated by later generations.

REVERBERATIONS OF THE GREAT GAME

The free trade foundations are brilliant as they may be, but England herself got into the habit of utilizing them only on achieving "industrial adolescence"; while we [Russia] are still very far from this age; and our concessions to England in trade should not obscure current demands of our commerce and industry.

—Peter Stremoukhov, head of the Foreign Ministry's Asian Department, 1869, quoted by Naftula Khalfin in his dissertation

The Russians have subjugated people who were easy to conquer, and the general result of all this, and of the rumors of untold legions of soldiers stationed in Russia proper, is to impress the Oriental mind with the idea that the Russians have a greater strength in comparison with the British than they perhaps actually have.

—Francis Younghusband, *The Heart of a Continent*, 1896

After the two powers settled their disputes in Persia, Afghanistan, and Tibet in 1907, the Anglo-Russian Friendship Committee was set up, along with the Anglo-Russian Chamber of Commerce in 1909, which nearly coincided with the visit of the Duma's delegation to Parliament.

Bernard Pares, the leading British expert on Slavonic studies, founded the School of Russian Studies at the University of Liverpool in 1907 and began printing *The Russian Review* five years later.[1] Austen Chamberlain, one of the Conservative Party's ruling elite, attended a ceremony marking the establishment of the Russo-English Bank in Saint Petersburg on April 8 the same year.[2] As Bruce Lockhart, the British vice consul in Moscow, later recalled, half a dozen British military officers began to arrive in Moscow to study the Russian language, while the Muscovites were eager to accord them a hearty welcome.[3]

Although some journalists still aimed their arrows of criticism at the autocratic regime in Russia,[4] the British leadership circles and general public ceased to look upon the great continental empire as a half-barbaric country, especially after the ambitious Arkadii Stolypin initiated social reforms to accelerate Russia's industrial modernization in the years 1907–10. Symptomatically, Edward Grey expressed a feeling of sympathy with the Russian people in the House of Commons during the visit of Edward VII to the tsar in June 1908:

> I see in Russia a great race, much of its power undeveloped still, its character still growing not yet come to its full strength but with new thoughts and new energies beginning to stir the race. I am convinced it will have a great part in the world. Much of the peace of the world may depend, and much of the welfare both of Russia and ourselves, must depend upon the relations between us.[5]

Therefore, it was small wonder that the end of the uncompromising rivalry between the two empires modified their external policies in various aspects. On March 20, 1908, the India Office secretary, John Morley, sent a memorandum to Lord Minto concerning the influence of the Anglo-Russian Convention on the reduction of military spending, especially those expenditures dedicated to the defense of India.[6] In August, Ellis Barker, a correspondent for the journal *The Nineteenth Century and After*, observed that "during the last two years there has not been a single complaint about Russian emissaries in Asia. It must be acknowledged that Russia has behaved with the greatest correctness and loyalty towards this country [Great Britain]."[7]

A close interrelation of Asian and European problems, especially in connection with the emerging German peril, led Grey to wire the following instructions to the British Embassy in Saint Petersburg on August 30, 1909:

> You should declare to the Imperial Government in strictest confidence that we have received a suggestion from German Government not only for a discussion of naval expenses but for a general assurance of friendly political relations.... It is very essential that this be kept secret as I am very hopeful it would result in something of general pacific character to which France and Russia would become parties, and any chance may be lost by premature diffusion.[8]

Grey's opinion, which would have been incredible during the period of the age-old Russo-British rivalry, testified to the fact that the spirit of collaboration and support was gradually replacing traditional deterrence and animosity. As the permanent undersecretary of the Foreign Office, Charles Hardinge, argued in January 1909, "Our whole future in Asia is bound up with the necessity of maintaining the best and most friendly relations with Russia." Three months later—in a memorandum that was endorsed by Grey, Asquith, and Edward VII himself—Hardinge maintained that even a pro-German orientation by Russia vis-à-vis Europe should not lead to the collapse of Anglo-Russian understanding vis-à-vis Asia.[9] The Committee of Imperial Defence, the Ministry for War, the Admiralty, and the General Staff began to reconsider their strategic plans, shifting focus from the defense of the Hindu Kush, Hong Kong, and Singapore to the protective measures to be immediately taken in the northwestern sector of Europe against a sudden assault upon the British Isles by the Germans.[10]

A similar dynamic was evident among many statesmen, intellectuals, and even ordinary people in Russia. For example, Andrei Semenov

Tien-Shansky, the president of the Imperial Russian Geographic Society, stated in March 1908 that

> it is time for us to realize that our tense relations with England through nearly all the last century were mostly inspired by misunderstanding, unawareness, and permanent mutual irritation.... After we have delimited the spheres of our influence in Asia, and after England has understood that Russia intended to threat her neither in India nor on her trade sea routes, she began to trust us, and the agreement was signed, which may be converted into an alliance. We shall benefit tremendously by mitigating hostility toward us in either the Far or Near East with its help.[11]

The withdrawal of British troops from the Chumbi Valley in February 1908, pursuant to the clauses of the Anglo-Russian Convention, encouraged even such an Anglophobe as Agvan Dorzhiev to propose to the Tsarist Foreign Ministry to take Tibet under a joint condominium of the two empires. For his part, Aleksei Kuropatkin, the former war minister, also argued for the eventual division of Chinese Turkestan between Russia and Britain.[12]

Meanwhile, Saint Petersburg and London cooperated effectively at the Afghan-Persian border, where a joint Russo-British contingent of frontier guards controlled the situation in order to repulse any penetration by German agents through Persia into Afghanistan. Mindful of the chaos and disintegration that the Pan-Islamic or nationalistic movements might bring to the Middle East and Inner Asia, Whitehall made no remonstrations against the suppression of the revolution in Persia by the Cossack Brigade in the service of the shah. Reciprocally, Russia's noninterference in the Kuwait crisis in 1912 enabled Britain to protect its position in the Persian Gulf against German encroachments. As the military attaché to London, Lieutenant General Yermolov, reported to the Main Staff after his trip to the Raj in 1911, the administration of India sought "closer military rapprochement with us on the foundations of the Anglo-Russian Convention of 1907."[13] It also needs to be noted that, following the prolongation of the Anglo-Japanese Alliance in 1905 and 1911, a series of Russo-Japanese arrangements on the status quo of Manchuria and Inner Mongolia were signed in 1910–12.[14]

With the benefit of hindsight, one could be led to believe that the Anglo-Russian Convention of 1907 became a precedent for an international partnership between Russia and Britain as well as other foreign states in the aftermath of the Great Game. Certainly, the Game's end did not spawn harmony in these relationships; the former adversaries continued to defend their interests in Persia, Afghanistan, India, Xinjiang, Tibet, and Mongolia, though by far less aggressive means than in the nineteenth century and in accordance with the designs of the partner state. Yet the foundations of the Russo-British understanding seemed fragile to many politicians and public leaders, whereas the frictions caused by different approaches to European problems might bring détente in Asia to an end. That is why Russian and British intelligence structures continued secret operations in the zones of potential conflict.[15] However, as Hardinge commented in his discourse with Nicholas II, then in Reval, in a letter to Grey,

> There might be occasional divergence of views in small matters, but the identity of the national interests of England and Russia in Europe and Asia would far outweigh any possible results from such trivial differences of opinion.[16]

Moreover, traditional stereotypes in the mentality of high-ranking officials and also in public opinion still impeded the transformation of the accord into an alliance.[17] Not coincidentally, some historians have argued that the Russians sympathized with the British merely, so to say, at a chancery level, whereas a chauvinistic trend overruled the aspirations of the Tsarist regime to cooperate with Britain on friendly terms, after the public order and international prestige of the Russian Empire had been restored before the outbreak of World War I. They thought that it was unrealistic to believe that the interests of the partner states could be molded in such a way as to march together in Asia, when the London Cabinet disliked the Pan-Slavic moods that took the upper hand in Russia from 1910 to 1913.[18] In fact, the opponents of the rapprochement on both sides drew the attention of their governments to violations of the spirit of the Anglo-Russian Convention: the recruitment of native spies by the British intelligence service to secretly penetrate Russian Central Asia in 1908–10, the distribution of "tickets for citizenship" to local residents by the British Consulate in Kashgar in 1911, the Russian consulates' activity in Persian boundary settlements through 1912–14, and a plan for the occupation of Mesopotamia and railway construction from Basra to Mosul concocted by the British General Staff in 1912.[19]

By the summer of 1914, most bureaucrats and military thinkers in both Russia and Britain had realized that the time had already come to reconsider the Anglo-Russian Convention of 1907 in the light of current developments in world politics. For example, the India Office proposed to give Russia a free hand in Chinese Turkestan and Outer Mongolia in return for the adequate compensation that Britain would get in Tibet.[20] The pressure of Saint Petersburg on the shah's government, especially in the neutral zone, also annoyed Whitehall. The consolidation of Saint Petersburg's military potential and its rapid industrial progress induced London to seek a compromise with Berlin in Africa and Asia, in order to prevent Russia's eventual abandonment of the 1907 convention.[21] As Nicolson wrote on the eve of the Great War, this uncertainty in the Anglo-Russian relationship "increases my fear lest Russia in giving us up in despair will take steps towards bringing herself into closer relations with Germany, and of course such a new course of policy on her part would seriously react upon our relations with her in the Mid and Far East."[22]

Contrary to such apprehensions, in January 1914, Tsar Nicholas II endorsed the strengthening of the ties binding the two empires, despite the opposition of pro-German elements in the Russian and British ruling circles.[23] Nevertheless, this "dancing on a tightrope"—as Nicolson called the new round of Russo-British negotiations that started on the eve of World War I and continued until the Russian Revolution of 1917—could hardly stop collaboration. Apart from a naval convention and the situation in the Balkans, the governments discussed the issues to be settled in the face of the challenges resulting from the new state of affairs in the atmosphere of intensive war preparations.[24] For example, the copious memoranda from the Foreign Office and the India Office's Political Department submitted to the Cabinet focused upon those concessions in Xinjiang and even in Afghan Turkestan that Britain was ready to make to Russia in return for the absorption by the British of Tibet and the neutral zone in Persia.[25] Reciprocally, Tsarist strategists, Kuropatkin being an example, projected "corrections" of Russia's borders in the Middle East and China, let alone occupation of the Turkish Straits and partition of the Ottoman Empire.[26]

Due to Russo-British collaboration in the course of World War I, secret German expeditions failed to penetrate Persia, Afghanistan, Tibet, and Mongolia. Thus, London and Saint Petersburg prevented these countries from falling into the orbit of the Central Powers.[27] Furthermore, since the Napoleonic Wars, Cossack and Sepoy had contended side by side against their common foe—the Turks—in Mesopotamia, "instead of glowering at one another across the mountains and deserts of innermost Asia."[28]

It seems useless to surmise what particular format the Anglo-Russian relationship would have assumed in Eurasia if Russia had not given up its obligations as a member state of the Entente in March 1918. However, one thing is doubtless—the Great Game had come to an appropriate end and could be never revived by the former rivals in a new guise.

For half a century, the Great Game reflected a variety of conflicting trends, ranging from diplomatic dialogue and exchanges of valuable nuggets of topographic data between London and Saint Petersburg to their feverish race for territories, resources, and markets, which recurrently brought the empires to the brink of war. This study has revealed the interchange of "light and darkness" in Russo-British relations, though competition and collaboration seemed to have always accompanied their policies in Central and East Asia. When the spirit of "forwardism" took over in the mentality of policymakers, as happened in the years 1877–88 and 1884–85, the Game led to the revival of national phobias and jingoism among ruling elites and the general public. Conversely, along with delimitations of borders and spheres of influence, the spirit of "peaceful coexistence" began to overrule both the leadership and ordinary people, as occurred in the early 1870s and in the mid-1890s.

Webster's Dictionary gives a dozen nuances of meaning for the word "game." Yet the one that seems the most appropriate for the subject of this study is "any test of skill and endurance."[29] The author of the present volume is convinced that the mainstream of the Great Game cannot be reduced to expeditions of explorers or intelligence operations, though they doubtless affected Anglo-Russian relations. Not coincidentally, those intelligence agencies that emerged in the course of the Game originated modern special task forces—such as the British Special Air Service, the U.S. Army's Green Berets and Delta Force, and the Russian Special Military Contingents—that excel "both in the aims they hope to achieve and, indeed, in the way that they seek to achieve them."[30]

As this study has also demonstrated, the economic, cultural, and ethnosocial aspects of Russo-British dualism in competition/collaboration also need to be given careful consideration. To the mind of the author of the present volume, though the British ruling elites were initially obsessed with mostly economic objectives in reforming Asiatic nations, Russia embarked on the Great Game in order to augment the prestige of its empire and to extend its frontiers as far to the east and south as possible. It seems, therefore, that in both cases the civilizing mission proved to be equally important and essential. The end of the Russo-British rivalry in the early 1900s saw, however, an inverse correlation between the economic and strategic components in the Asian policies of the two empires. For Russia, an aspiration for industrial modernization came to the forefront, particularly after its defeat in the Far East; for Great Britain, political ambitions became the most significant determinants, also taking into account the claims expressed by miscellaneous associations of "Indian, Persian, or China hands."[31]

The research distilled in this volume proves that it would be superficial to charge Russia alone with aggressiveness on its Asian frontiers. In this respect, a really important point, though one neglected by many scholars, is that the Great Game included a struggle between two very different cultural paradigms—one based upon the values of the Protestantism, competitiveness, free trade, and civil liberties; the other resting on the dogmas of Christian Orthodoxy, state patronage, mercantilism, and political autocracy.[32] As a modern Russian historian has described the image of Russia in the Western mentality during the Victorian period, "a closer geographic neighborhood of the autocratic power, which had subjugated vast territories in Eurasia, provoked a feeling of depression and potential threat to them in the minds of contemporary European observers."[33]

Certainly, there was a gap in industrial and social development between Britain and Russia; if the former had already completed its industrial modernization, the latter had merely commenced it in the course of the reforms that Tsar Alexander II had imposed upon the empire during the 1860s and 1870s. This incongruity underlay the principles to which the British and Russian leadership circles adhered in the conduct of their Asian policies, though the general public and mass media tended to compare their administration of imperial outskirts, whether in Central Asia, India, or the Far East. Thus, many Europeans shared a stereotypical misconception of the Russians as deplorably bad businessmen, and of the British as divinely gifted entrepreneurs.[34]

This study of the Great Game has shown that it was a competition of adequate opponents.[35] And they sometimes played it blindfolded, because at the initial stage both London and Saint Petersburg knew the "chessboard" of the Game too little, while unexpected inference from outside might distort its course, though ostensibly well calculated in advance. Besides, the members of the Victorian wealthy upper class used a mirror image of the Tsarist Empire to represent their own expansion as a cluster of reciprocal moves to counteract Russia's doomed progress in Asia. In a broader sense, the majority of British statesmen realized perfectly well that thanks to its geostrategic position, military potential, and ethnocultural proximity, Russia could suggest to Asian potentates, traditional elites, and ordinary people a model of modernization that they regarded as more adaptable and well calibrated for implementation than that of the accelerated progress offered by Britain. As Lord Napier correctly asserted in 1875,

The Russians, being Asiatic themselves, and constantly absorbing the people of the countries which they conquer, take a firmer root in the ground they occupy than we seem ever likely to do in India.[36]

The author of the present volume also shares a concept with David Gillard, who wrote in his book about how political ascendancy in Asia was the real prize in this competition, accompanied by recurring tension in Anglo-Russian relations.[37] Not coincidentally, for example, the Tsarist colonial authorities did their utmost to convert Tashkent, the capital of Turkestan, into a symbol of the Russians' superiority over the British in their invasion of Asia.[38]

At the same time, the debates that historians still continue to have about whether the priority in Russian or British colonial rule was political motives or economic motives seems counterproductive.[39] As this study has established, the roles of these motivations varied in importance at different stages of the two empires' competition in Asia. It is also quite wrong to assume that the Great Game resulted from the courageous and pioneering spirit of successful individuals. In fact, nearly all the celebrated "players" did not act entirely at their own risk but were commissioned to fulfill a concrete task by central governments or officials in the "far pavilions." Furthermore, an equally narrow approach to the Game would be to interpret it as merely a military-political confrontation of the two empires as they aspired to defend or, conversely, to conquer Asian territories.[40] Above all, as the author of the present volume has explained, the modernization of backward, traditional, preindustrial societies underlay the Game's agenda. Although the Russian pattern differed from the British model, as has been shown in this book, and though the majority of British statesmen and members of the public paradoxically viewed Russia as both a rival empire and an underdeveloped area that needed British expertise to nurture it,[41] a generalization can also be made regarding the Eurocentrism, Christianity, and racial superiority that both London and Saint Petersburg exhibited in the course of pursuing their civilizing missions in the Oriental countries.

Finally, this comprehensive survey of the Great Game leads one to believe that it became an inseparable element of the Russo-British relationship in the Victorian and Edwardian epochs. In fact, the Game spawned such defining geopolitical terms as "buffer state," "scientific frontier," and "sphere of influence" (or "interests"), which laid the foundations for understanding modern world politics. For Britain, where Liberal Cabinets regularly changed places with ones headed by Conservatives, it really created a continuity of foreign policy, to which Lord Rosebery once drew attention in an oration.[42] Furthermore, the Game brought into diplomatic practice the concepts of détente and entente, which are widely used by current political leaders.

If one considers the origins, stages, and results of the Great Game, it is easy to arrive at the conclusion that nobody lost or won this competition.[43] Similarly, in the view of the author of the present volume, the Game can neither be called a "Victorian cold war" with the benefit of hindsight, nor prolonged to continue into any period of the twentieth century after the Anglo-Russian Convention on Persia, Afghanistan, and Tibet was signed in 1907, signifying the end of Britain's "splendid isolation." London and Saint Petersburg started to play the Game right after the Crimean War, when, as a Russian strategist metaphorically wrote, Britain "threw down the gauntlet under the walls of Sebastopol" and Russia "accepted the challenge."[44] The two empires continued their rivalry until they realized that the mastery of Asia by a single power was a geostrategic utopia. Yet their perpetual competition in Asia had a multifaceted impact upon the Asian nations, the most formidable one being their eventual incorporation into the process of globalization. That is why the Great Game deserves to be remembered as making a highly significant contribution not only to the development of Russo-British relations but also to the general contour of world politics in the twentieth century.

A NOMINAL ROLL OF THE RULERS, STATESMEN, DIPLOMATS, AND MILITARY OFFICERS ENGAGED IN THE GREAT GAME, 1856–1907

RUSSIAN EMPERORS (TSARS)

Name	Period of Reign
Alexander II	1855–81
Alexander III	1881–94
Nicholas II	1894–1917

BRITISH MONARCHS

Name	Period of Reign
Queen Victoria	1837–1901
King Edward VII	1901–10

RULERS OF PERSIA, AFGHANISTAN, AND THE KHANATES OF CENTRAL ASIA

Name   *Period of Reign*

PERSIA

Shah Nasir-u-Din............................ 1848–96

Shah Muzaffar-u-Din.................... 1896–1907

AFGHANISTAN

Dost Mohamed Khan.................... 1842–63

Sher Ali Khan.............................. 1863–65; 1869–79

Mohamed Afzal Khan................... 1865–67

Mohamed Azim Khan.................. 1867–69

Yakub Khan 1879

Abdur Rahman Khan................... 1880–1901

Habibulla Khan 1901–19

BOKHARA

Nasrulla Khan 1826–60

Said Muzaffar-u-Din Khan........... 1860–85

Said Abdul al-Ahad Khan 1885–1910

KHIVA

Said Mohamed Khan.................... 1856–64

Mehmet Rahim Khan.................. 1864–1910

KHOKAND

Mohamed Khudayar Khan 1845–58; 1865–75

Malle Khan 1858–62

Said Mohamed Khan.................... 1862–65

Said Nasir-u-Din Khan 1875–76

RUSSIAN FOREIGN MINISTERS

Name	*Term in Office*
Alexander Gorchakov	1856–82
Nikolai Giers	1882–95
Alexander Lobanov-Rostovsky	1895–96
Mikhail Muraviev	1896–1900
Vladimir Lamsdorf	1900–1906
Alexander Izvolsky	1906–10

BRITISH SECRETARIES OF STATE FOR FOREIGN AFFAIRS

Name	*Term in Office*
Earl of Clarendon	1853–58; 1865–66; 1868–70
Earl of Malmesbury	1858–59
Lord John Russell	1859–65
Earl of Derby	1866–68; 1874–78
Earl Granville	1870–74; 1880–85
Marquis of Salisbury	1878–80; 1885–86; 1887–92; 1895–1900
Earl of Rosebery	1886; 1892–94
Earl of Kimberley	1894–95
Marquis of Lansdowne	1900–1905
Sir (Viscount) Edward Grey	1905–15

RUSSIAN GOVERNORS-GENERAL OF TURKESTAN

Name	*Term in Office*
Konstantin Kaufman	1867–82
Mikhail Cherniaev	1882–84
Nikolai Rosenbach	1884–89

Alexander Vrevsky 1889–98

Sergei Dukhovskoi 1898–1901

Nikolai Ivanov 1901–4

Nikolai Teviashov 1904–5

Dimitry Subbotich 1905–6

Nikolai Grodekov 1906–8

BRITISH VICEROYS OF INDIA

Name	*Term in Office*
Viscount Canning (governor-general, 1856–58)	1858–62
Earl of Elgin	1862–63
Sir John Lawrence	1864–69
Earl of Mayo	1869–72
Lord Northbrook	1872–76
Lord Lytton	1876–80
Marquis of Ripon	1880–84
Earl of Dufferin	1884–88
Marquis of Lansdowne	1888–94
Earl of Elgin	1894–99
Lord Curzon	1899–1905
Earl of Minto	1905–10

RUSSIAN AMBASSADORS TO THE UNITED KINGDOM

Name	*Term in Office*
Phillip Brunnov	1855–74
Peter Shuvalov	1874–79
Alexander Lobanov-Rostovsky	1880–82

Yegor Staal 1884–1903

Alexander Benkendorf 1903–17

BRITISH AMBASSADORS TO THE RUSSIAN EMPIRE

Name	*Term in Office*
Lord Wodehouse	1856–59
Sir John Crampton	1859–61
Lord Napier	1861–65
Sir Andrew Buchanan...................	1865–72
Lord Loftus	1872–79
Earl of Dufferin...........................	1879–82
Sir Edward Thornton	1882–86
Sir Robert Morier........................	1886–94
Sir Frank Lascelles	1894–99
Sir Charles Scott	1899–1904
Sir Charles Hardinge	1904–6
Sir Arthur Nicolson......................	1906–10

Sources: National Archives of the United Kingdom–Public Record Office, FO/181; Indian Office Library and Records, Mss Eur F 111-112; H. Mackinder, *India. Eight Lectures* (London: G. Philip & Son, 1910); A. Ward and G. Gooch, eds., *The Cambridge History of British Foreign Policy, 1783–1919* (Cambridge: Cambridge University Press, 1923), vol. 3; Viscount Mersey, *The Viceroys and Governors-General of India, 1757–1947* (London: John Murray, 1949); P. Woodruff, *The Men Who Ruled India* (London: Jonathan Cape, 1953), vol. 2; E. Benians et al., eds., *The Cambridge History of the British Empire* (Cambridge: Cambridge University Press, 1959), vol. 3; M. Holdsworth, *Turkestan in the Nineteenth Century: A Brief History of Bokhara, Khokand and Khiva* (Oxford: Central Asian Research Centre, 1959); R. Pierce, *Russian Central Asia, 1867–1917: A Study in Colonial*

Rule (Berkeley: University of California Press, 1960); B. Robson, *The Road to Kabul: The Second Afghan War 1878–1881* (London: Arms and Armour Press, 1986), 283; Memet Yetisgin, "How the *Times* of London Covered and Interpreted Russian Expansion into Central Asia in the Second Half of the 19th Century," Ph.D. diss., Texas Technological University, 2000.

NOTES

INTRODUCTION

1. The political situation in Central Asia immediately after the collapse of the Soviet Union in the early 1990s is studied, e.g., by Stephen Page, "The Creation of a Sphere of Influence: Russia and Central Asia," *International Journal* 49, no. 4 (1994): 788–813. For contemporary "takes" on the Great Game, see, e.g., Ian Cuthbertson, "The New 'Great Game' (Central Asia and the Transcaucasus)," *World Policy Journal* 11, no. 4 (1994): 31ff.; M. E. Ahrari, *The New Great Game in Muslim Central Asia*, McNair Paper 47 (Washington, D.C.: Institute for National Strategic Studies, National Defense University, 1996); Anatol Lieven, "The (Not So) Great Game," *National Interest*, Winter 1999–2000, 69ff., http://www.nationalinterest.org/article/the-not-so-great-game-411; Alec Rasizade, "The Specter of a New 'Great Game' in Central Asia," *Foreign Service Journal*, no. 11 (2002): 48–52, http://www.afsa.org/fsj/nov02/greatgame.pdf; Lutz Kleveman, "The New 'Great Game,'" *The Nation*, February 16, 2004; and Ivan Sukhov, "Soldat 'Bol'shoi Igry,'" *Vremia Novostei*, February 26, 2009.

2. Peter Hopkirk, *The Great Game: On Secret Service in High Asia* (Oxford: Oxford University Press, 1990), 123.

3. Gerald Morgan, "Myth and Reality in the Great Game," *Asian Affairs* 60 (new ser. 4), pt. I (1973): 55–65, at 55; Karl Meyer and Shareen Brysac, *Tournament of Shadows: The Great Game and the Race for Empire in Asia* (London: Abacus, 1999), 126–27; Robert Johnson, *Spying for Empire: The Great Game in Central and South Asia, 1757–1947* (London: Green Hill Books, 2006), 53.

4. Peter Hopkirk, *The Quest for Kim: In Search of Kipling's Great Game* (Oxford: Oxford University Press, 1996), 6–7.

5. Meyer and Brysac, *Tournament of Shadows*, 127.

6. Peter Fleming, *Bayonets to Lhasa: The First Full Account of the British Invasion of Tibet in 1904* (London: Rupert Hart-Davis, 1961), 30; Milan Hauner, "The Last Great Game," *Middle East Journal* 38, no. 1 (1984): 72–84, at 72.

7. Meyer and Brysac, *Tournament of Shadows*, 126.

8. *The Hansard Parliamentary Debates* (London: C. Buck, 1908), ser. 3, vol. 71, cols. 1011–12.

9. Edward Said, *Orientalism* (London: Routledge & Kegan Paul, 1978), 121.

10. Max Beloff, *Imperial Sunset, Volume 1: Britain's Liberal Empire, 1897–1921* (London: Methuen, 1969), 1, 5.

11. A British Subject, *The Great Game: A Plea for a British Imperial Policy* (London: Simpkin, Marshall, 1875), 174–75.

12. David Fromkin, "The Great Game in Asia," *Foreign Affairs* 58, no. 4 (1980): 936–51, at 936.

13. Alastair Lamb, *Britain and Chinese Central Asia: The Road to Lhasa, 1767 to 1905* (London: Routledge & Kegan Paul, 1960), x; John Macgregor, *Tibet: A Chronicle of Exploration* (London: Routledge & Kegan Paul, 1970), 256.

14. Rudyard Kipling, *Kim* (London: Macmillan, 1966; orig. pub. 1901), 285–86. For a detailed analysis of Kipling's novel, see especially the depiction of the Great Game given by Hopkirk, *Quest for Kim*, 202–22.

15. Francis Younghusband, *The Heart of a Continent: A Narrative of Travels in Manchuria across the Gobi Desert, through the Himalayas, the Pamirs, and Hunza 1884–1894* (London: John Murray, 1904), 238.

16. Henry Whigham, *The Persian Problem: An Examination of the Rival Positions of Russia and Great Britain in Persia with some Account of the Persian Gulf and the Baghdad Railway* (London: Isbister, 1903), 1–2.

17. See especially George Curzon, *Russia in Central Asia in 1889* (London: Frank Cass, 1889); George Curzon, *Persia and the Persian Question*, 2 vols. (London: Longmans, Green, 1892); and George Curzon, *Problems of the Far East: Japan-Korea-China* (London: Archibald Constable, 1896).

18. E.g., see Halford Mackinder, *India* (London: G. Philip and Son, 1910); and Karl Haushofer, *Geopolotik des Pazifischen ozeans* (Berlin: K. Vowinckel Verlag, 1924).

19. See Morton Kaplan, *System and Process in International Relations* (New York: John Wiley & Sons, 1957).

20. Henry Davis, *The Great Game in Asia, 1800–1844* (London and Oxford: H. Milford and Oxford University Press, 1927).

21. Guy Wint, *The British in Asia* (London: Faber & Faber, 1947), 142.

22. Michael Edwardes, *Playing the Great Game* (London: Hamish Hamilton, 1975), vii–viii. On the origins of this term, also see Narendra Singh Sarila, *The Shadow of the Great Game: The Untold Story of India's Partition* (London: Archibald Constable, 2006).

23. David Gillard, *The Struggle for Asia, 1828–1914: A Study in British and Russian Imperialism* (London: Methuen, 1977), 9, 95.

24. Morgan, "Myth and Reality," 64–65; Gerald Morgan, *Anglo-Russian Rivalry in Central Asia: 1810–1895* (London: Frank Cass, 1981), 133–58.

25. Edward Ingram, *The Beginning of the Great Game in Asia, 1828–1834* (London: Clarendon Press, 1979), 13, 339.

26. Edward Ingram, *Commitment to Empire: Prophesies of the Great Game in Asia, 1797–1800* (Oxford: Clarendon Press, 1981), 17.

27. Ibid., 399–401.

28. Edward Ingram, *In Defence of British India: Great Britain in the Middle East, 1775–1842* (London: Frank Cass, 1984), 7.

29. Ibid., 152.

30. Fromkin, "Great Game in Asia," 936–51.

31. Gordon Whitteridge, *Charles Masson of Afghanistan: Explorer, Archaeologist, Numismatist and Intelligence Agent* (London: Aris and Phillips, 1986), 114.

32. Hopkirk, *Great Game*, 2. Also see Peter Hopkirk, *Trespassers on the Roof of the World: The Race for Lhasa* (London: John Murray, 1982); and Peter Hopkirk, *On Secret Service East of Constantinople: The Plot to Bring Down the British Empire* (London: John Murray, 1994).

33. Meyer and Brysac, *Tournament of Shadows*, xxv. For the genesis of this concept, see Gillard, *Struggle for Asia*, 181–85.

34. Lawrence James, *The Rise and Fall of the British Empire* (London: Little, Brown, 1994), 180.

35. Peter Brobst, *The Future of the Great Game: Sir Olaf Caroe, India's Independence and the Defence of Asia* (Akron: University of Akron Press, 2005), 75.

36. Charles Allen, *Duel in the Snows: The True Story of the Younghusband Mission to Lhasa* (London: John Murray, 2004), 18.

37. Johnson, *Spying for Empire*; Jules Stewart, *Spying for the Raj: The Pundits and the Mapping of the Himalaya* (Phoenix Mill, U.K.: Sutton Publishing, 2006).

38. Frederick Hitz, *The Great Game: The Myth and Reality of Espionage* (New York: Vintage Books, 2005), 6, 61.

39. Patrick French, *Younghusband: The Last Great Imperial Adventurer* (London: HarperCollins, 1994), 122.

40. See current scholarship on this subject: Mikhail Ryzhenkov, "'Rol' voennogo vedomstva Rossii v razvitii otechestvennogo vostokovedeniia v XIX–nachale XX vv.," Kand. diss., Institut vostokovedeniia AN SSSR, 1991; K. Suteeva, "Russkie voennye istoriki XIX v. o prichinakh i motivakh dvizheniia Rossii na Vostok (v Sredniuyu Asiyu i Yuzhnyi Kazakhstan)," http://www.kungrad.com/history/st/rushis/.

41. Mikhail Grulev, *Sopernichestvo Rossii i Anglii v Srednei Asii* (Saint Petersburg: V. Berezovsky, 1909), 1–3.

42. For a modern view of Soviet historians, see N.V. Terentieva, "Sovetskaia istoriografiia anglo-russkogo sopernichestva v Srednei Asii v pervoi polovine XIX v.," Kand. diss., Barnaul'skii gosudarstvennyi universitet, 2003; and A. G. Dankov, "Otechestvennaia i britanskaia istoriografiia o sopernichestve Rossii i Velikobritanii v Tsentral'noi Asii (XIX–nachalo XXI vv.)," Kand. diss., Tomskii gosudarstvennyi universitet, 2009.

43. Alexander Popov, "Bor'ba za sredneasiatskii platzdarm," *Istoricheskie zapiski* 7

(1940): 182–235; Evgeny Steinberg, *Istoriia britanskoi agressii na Srednem Vostoke* (Moscow: Voennoe izdatelstvo, 1951); Goga Khidoiatov, *Iz istorii anlo-russkikh otnoshenii v Srednei Asii (60-ye–70-ye gg. XIX v.)* (Tashkent: Fan, 1969); Nina Kiniapina, "Sredniaia Asiia vo vneshnepoliticheskikh planakh tsarisma (50-e–80-e gg. XIX v.)," *Voprosy istorii*, no. 2 (1974): 36–51; Olga Zhigalina, *Velikobritaniia na Srednem Vostoke (XIX–nachalo XX v.): Analiz vneshnepoliticheskikh kontseptsii* (Moscow: Nauka, 1990).

44. Naftula Khalfin, *Angliiskaia kolonial'naia politika na Srednem Vostoke (70-t gg. XIX v.)* (Tashkent: Sredneaziatskii gosudarstvennyi universitet, 1957); Naftula Khalfin, *Politika Rossii v Zentralnoi Asii* (Moscow: Nauka, 1960); Naftula Khalfin, *Prisoedinenie Srednei Asii k Rossii (60-e–90-e gg. XIX v.)* (Moscow: Nauka, 1965); Naftula Khalfin, *Rossiia i khanstva Srednei Asii (pervaia polovina XIX v.)* (Moscow: Nauka, 1974).

45. Sergei Porokhov, *Bitva imperii: Angliia protiv Rossii* (Moscow: AST-Astrel', 2008), 6.

46. Alexander Shirokorad, *Russia-England, neizvestnaia voina, 1857–1907* (Moscow: AST, 2003); Mikhail Leontiev, *Bolshaia Igra* (Moscow: AST-Astrel', 2008).

47. Leontiev, *Bolshaia Igra*, 9.

48. For the most interesting studies. see Firuz Kazemzadeh, *Russia and Britain in Persia, 1864–1914* (New Haven, Conn.: Yale University Press, 1968); Parshotam Mehra, *The Younghusband Expedition: An Interpretation* (London: Asia Public House, 1968); Fida Mohammad Hassnain, *British Policy towards Kashmir (1846–1921): Kashmir in Anglo-Russian Politics* (New Delhi: Sterling, 1974); Hossein Nazem, *Russia and Great Britain in Iran (1900–1914)* (Teheran: Sherkat Iran Chap, 1975); Premen Addy, *Tibet on the Imperial Chessboard: The Making of British Policy towards Lhasa, 1899–1905* (Calcutta: Academic Publishers, 1984); Furen Wang and Wenting Suo, *Highlights of Tibetan Policy* (Peking: New World Press, 1984); Myung Hyun Cho, *Korea and the Major Powers: An Analysis of Power Structure in East Asia* (Seoul: Research Center for Peace and Unification of Korea, 1989); Kulbhushan Warikoo, *Central Asia and Kashmir: A Study in the Context of Anglo-Russian Rivalry* (New Delhi: Gian, 1989); Nayana Goradia, *Lord Curzon: The Last of the British Moguls* (Delhi: Oxford University Press, 1993); Chakravarty Sukash, *Afghanistan and the Great Game* (Delhi: New Century, 2002); and Pirouz Mojtahed-Zadeh, *The Small Players of the Great Game: The Settlement of Iran's Eastern Borderlands and the Creation of Afghanistan* (London: Routledge, 2004).

49. Memet Yetisgin, "How the *Times* of London Covered and Interpreted Russian Expansion into Central Asia in the Second Half of the Nineteenth Century," Ph.D. diss., Texas Technical University, 2000, 168–69.

50. For current monographs on the Persian question, see Anthony Wynn, *Persia in the Great Game: Sir Percy Sykes—Explorer, Consul, Soldier, Spy* (London: John Murray, 2003); John Tchalenko, *Images from the Endgame: Persia through a Russian Lens, 1901–1914* (London: Al-Saqi Press, 2006); Laura Akhmedova, *Politika Anglii v zone Persidskogo zaliva v poslednei treti XIX–nachale XX v. (1870–1914)*

(Saint Petersburg: Sankt-Peterburgskii gosudarstvennyi universitet, 2006); Elena Andreeva, *Russia and Iran in the Great Game: Travelogues and Orientalism* (London: Routledge, 2007); and Nugsar K. Ter-Oganov, "Persidskaia kazachya brigada: Period transformatsii (1894–1903)," *Vostok*, no. 3 (2010): 69–79.

On the situation in the khanates of Bokhara, Khiva, and Khokand, see Page, "Creation"; N. A. Abdurakhimova and G. K. Rustamova, *Kolonial'naia sistema vlasti v Turkestane vo vtoroi polovine XIX–pervoi chetverti XX vv.* (Tashkent: Tashkentskii gosudarstvennyi universitet, 1999); Zh. B. Alymbaeva, "Istoriografiia zavoevaniia Turkestana Rossiei v XIX–nachale XX v.," Kand. diss., Tashkentskii gosudarstvennyi universitet, 2002; Daniel Brower, *Turkestan and the Fate of the Russian Empire* (London: Routledge, 2003); Natalia N. Lisitsyna, "Zakaspiiskii krai v anglo-russkikh otnosheniiakh (1880–1917)," Kand. diss., Moskovskii otkrytyi pedagogicheskii universitet, Moscow, 2006; Jeff Sahadeo, *Russian Colonial Society in Tashkent, 1865–1923* (Bloomington: Indiana University Press, 2007); Olga A. Yegorenko, "Bukharskii Emirat v period ptotektorata Rossii (1868–1920): Istoriographiia problemy," Kand. diss., Rossiiskii gosudarstvennyi universitet turizma i servisa, Moscow, 2008; and S. N. Abashin, D. Yu. Arapov, and N. Ye. Bekmakhanova, eds., *Tsentral'naia Asiia v sostave Rossiiskoi imperii* (Moscow: Novoe literaturnoe obozrenie, 2008).

On the Afghan problem, see D. S. Richards, *The Savage Frontier: A History of the Anglo-Afghan Wars* (London: Macmillan, 1990); Pirouz Mojtahed-Zadeh, *The Amirs of the Borderlands and Eastern Iranian Borders* (London: Urosevic Foundation, 1995); and Christine Noelle, *State and Tribe in Nineteenth-Century Afghanistan: The Reign of Amir Dost Muhammad Khan (1826–1863)* (Richmond, U.K.: Curzon Press, 1997).

On the struggle for the control over the Pamirs, see O. B. Bokiev, *Zavoevanie i prisoedinenie Severnogo Tadzhikistana, Pamira i Gornogo Badakhshana k Rossii* (Dushanbe: Tadzhikskii gosudarstvennyi universitet, 1994); Andrei Smirnov, "U sten Indii: Pamirskie pokhody pri Alexandere III," *Rodina*, no. 8 (2001): 67–70; Aleksei Postnikov, *Skhvatka na "kryshe mira": Politiki, razvedchiki, generally v bor'be za Pamir v XIX v.* (Moscow: Ripol-Klassik, 2005); and Arutiun Ulunian, "Britanskii konzept 'etnopoliticheskogo prostranstva' v 'Bol'shoi Igre' i ego krushenie (70-e–80-e gg. XIX v.)," *Istoricheskoe prostranstvo: Problemy istorii stran SNG*, no. 1 (2009): 175–90.

On the modern and contemporary history of Chinese Turkestan (Xinjiang), see Paul Henze, "The Great Game in Kashgaria: British and Russian Missions to Yakub Bek," *Central Asia Survey*, no. 2 (1989): 61–95; Dinara Dubrovskaia, *Sud'ba Sintsiana: Obretenie Kitaem novoi granitsy v kontse XIX v.* (Moscow: Russian Academy of Sciences Institute of Oriental Studies, 1998); Hodong Kim, *Holy War in China: The Muslim Rebellion and State in Chinese Central Asia, 1864–1877* (Stanford, Calif.: Hoover Institution Press, 2004); Alexander Kolesnikov, *Russians in Kashgaria (vtoraia polovina XIX–nachalo XX v.): Missii, ekspeditsii, puteshestviia*

(Bishkek: Raritet, 2006); and Vadim Obukhov, *Skhvatka shesti imperii za Sinkiang* (Moscow: Veche, 2007).

On the Great Game in Tibet, see Helen Hundley, "Tibet's Part in the 'Great Game,'" *History Today* 43 (1993): 45–50; John Snelling, *Buddhism in Russia: The Story of Agvan Dorzhiev, Lhasa's Emissary to the Tsar* (Shaftsbury, U.K.: Element, 1993); David Schimmelpenninck van der Oye, "'Tournament of Shadows: Russia's Great Game in Tibet," *Tibetan Review* 29, no. 1 (1994): 13–20; Alex MacKay, *Tibet and the British Raj: The Frontier Staff, 1904–1907* (Richmond, U.K.: Curzon Press, 1997; Tatiana Shaumian, *Tibet: The Great Game and Tsarist Russia* (New Delhi: Oxford University Press, 2000); Nikolai Kuleshov, "Agvan Dorjiev, the Dalai Lama's Ambassador," in *The History of Tibet*, vol. 3, edited by A. Mackay (London: RoutledgeCurzon, 2003), 57–68; Michael MacRae, *In Search of Shangri-La: The Extraordinary True Story of the Quest for the Lost Horizon* (London: M. Joseph, 2003); P. L. Madan, *Tibet: Saga of Indian Explorers (1864–1894)* (New Delhi: Manohar, 2004); Wendy Palace, *The British Empire and Tibet 1900–1922* (London: Routledge, 2005); and Alexander Andreev, *Tibet v politike tsarskoi, sovetskoi i postsovetskoi* (Saint Petersburg: Saint Petersburg State University–Nartang, 2006).

On the British countermeasures to lay off the alleged Russian invasion of India, see Derek Waller, *The Pundits: British Exploration of Tibet and Central Asia* (Lexington: University Press of Kentucky, 1990); Christopher Alan Bayly, *Empire and Information: Intelligence Gathering and Social Communication in India, 1780–1870* (Cambridge: Cambridge University Press, 1996); Charles Allen, *Soldier Sahibs: The Men Who Made the North-West Frontier* (London: John Murray, 2000); Charles Allen, *Duel in the Snows: The True Story of the Younghusband Mission to Lhasa* (London: John Murray, 2004); Pavel Litvinov, "Britanskaia Indiia i russkii Turkestan vo vtoroi polovine XIX–nachale XX v.," in *Rossiia–Indiia: perspektivy regional'nogo sotrudnichestva*, edited by G. I. Kuznetsov (Moscow: Institut vostokovedeniia RAN, 2001), 60–68; S. Mahajan, *British Foreign Policy, 1874–1914: The Role of India* (London: Routledge, 2002); Ian Barrow, *Making History, Drawing Territory: British Mapping in India, c. 1756–1905* (New Delhi: Oxford University Press, 2003); Robert Johnson, "Russians at the Gates of India? Planning the Defense of India, 1884–1899," *Journal of Military History* 67, no. 3 (2003): 697–743; Ben Hopkins, *The Myth of the "Great Game": The Anglo-Sikh Alliance and Rivalry*, Occasional Paper 5 (Cambridge: Centre of South Asian Studies, University of Cambridge, 2004), 1–36; Konstantin Kubanov, "Pokhody v Indiiu v proektakh rossiiskikh voennykh i politicheskikh deiatelei XVIII–nachala XX v.," Kand. diss., Nizhnevartovskii gosudarstvennyi gumanitarnyi universitet, Nizhnevartovsk, 2007; Kublushan Warikoo, ed., *Himalayan Frontiers of India: Historical, Geo-Political and Strategic Perspectives* (London: Routledge, 2009); and S. A. Bogomolov, "Strategicheskie osnovy politiki Britanskoi Indii na severo-zapadnom frontier (poslednyaia tret' XIX v.)," *Vostok*, no. 4 (2010): 34–44.

On the Russo-British rivalry in the Far East region, see S. Paine, *Imperial Rivals: Russia, China and Their Disputed Frontier, 1858–1924* (Armonk, N.Y.: M. E. Sharpe, 1996); John Evans, *Russian Expansion on the Amur, 1848–1860: The Push to the Pacific,* 2 vols. (New York: Edwin Mellen Press, 1999); David Schimmelpenninck van der Oye, *Toward the Rising Sun: Russian Ideologies of Empire and the Path to War with Japan* (DeKalb: Northern Illinois University Press, 2001); Vladimir Moiseev, *Rossiia i Kitai v Tsentralnoi Asii (vtoraia polovina XIX v.–1917 g.)* (Barnaul: Az Buka, 2003); Aleksei Voskresensky, *Kitai i Rossiia v Evrazii* (Moscow: Muravei, 2004); Dimitry Pavlov, *Russko-iaponskaia voina 1904–1905 gg.: Sekretnye operatsii na sushe i na more* (Moscow: Materik, 2004); and Thomas Otte, *The China Question: Great Power Rivalry and British Isolation, 1894–1905* (Oxford: Oxford University Press, 2007).

51. Edwardes, *Playing,* 3; also see V. K. Chavda, *India, Britain, Russia: A Study in British Opinion (1838–1878)* (Delhi: Sterling, 1967), 23.

52. Ingram, *In Defence,* 2; Ingram, *Commitment,* 17; Ingram, *Beginning,* x, 13.

53. Ingram, *In Defence,* 7, 11.

54. Leontiev, *Bolshaia Igra,* 16.

55. The author of the present volume agrees with Edmund Clubb, the American diplomat who served as consul in Urumchi, Mukden, Vladivostok, and Chanchun for more then twenty-five years; see Edmund Clubb, *China and Russia: The Great Game* (New York: Columbia University Press, 1971), 91–103.

56. Alexander Orlov, *Soiuz Peterburga i Londona: Rossiisko-Britanskie otnosheniia v epokhy napoleonovskikh voin* (Moscow: Progress-Traditsiia, 2005), 325. For further information on the history of Russo-British relations in the period of Alexander I (1801–25) and Nicholas I (1825–55), see Alexander Orlov, *"Teper" vizhu anglichan vblizi': Britaniia i britantsy v predstavleniiakh rossiian o mire i o sebe (vtoraia polovina XVIII–pervaia polovina XIX vv.)—Ocherki* (Moscow: Giperboreia, Kuchkovo Pole, 2008).

57. Phillip Darby, *Three Faces of Imperialism: British and American Approaches to Asia and Africa. 1870–1970* (New Haven, Conn.: Yale University Press, 1987), 56. For deeper insight into economic tendencies, see A. J. H. Latham, *The International Economy and the Underdeveloped World* (London: Croom Helm, 1978).

58. For more information on the so-called Eastern question in Russo-British relations, see, e.g., Matthew Anderson, *The Eastern Question, 1774–1923: A Study in International Relations* (London and New York: Macmillan and St. Martin's Press, 1966); Nina Kiniapina, ed., *Vostochnyi vopros vo vneshnei politike Rossii, konets XVIII–nachalo XX v.* (Moscow: Nauka, 1978); A. L. Macfie, *The Eastern Question, 1774–1923* (London: Longman, 1989); and Vladilen Vinogradov, "Russko-tutetskaia voina 1877–1878 gg. i evropeiskie derzhavy," *Novaia i Noveishaia istoriia,* no. 1 (2009): 127–43.

59. Quoted by Georgii Chicherin, *Stat'i i rechi po voprosam mezhdunarodnoi politiki* (Moscow: Izdatel'stvo sotsial'no-economicheskoi literatury, 1961), 86.

60. Jennifer Siegel, *Endgame: Britain, Russia and the Final Struggle for Central Asia* (London: I. B. Tauris, 2002), 197. This concept is supported by other British scholars; e.g., see Alex Marshall, *The Russian General Staff and Asia, 1800–1917* (London: Routledge, 2006), 161–62.

61. Alastair Lamb, *British India and Tibet, 1766–1910* (London: Routledge & Kegan Paul, 1986), 283.

62. Johnson, *Spying for Empire*, 24.

63. Morgan, *Anglo-Russian Rivalry*, 200–214.

64. Brobst, *Future of the Great Game*, xiii; for a similar opinion, see Hauner, " Last Great Game," 73–74, 200.

65. Francis Younghusband, *The Light of Experience: A Review of Some Men and Events of My Time* (London: Archibald Constable, 1927), 107. On the "diplomatic revolution" in the early twentieth century, e.g., see Evgeny Sergeev, "Diplomaticheskaia revoliuysiia' 1907 g. v otnosheniiakh Rossii i Velikobritanii," *Vostok*, no. 2 (2008): 80–93; William Mulligan, *The Origins of the First World War* (Cambridge: Cambridge University Press, 2010), 49–62.

66. Hopkirk, *Great Game*, 2.

67. Quoted by Keith Jeffrey, "The Eastern Arc of Empire: A Strategic View, 1850–1950," *Journal of Strategic Studies* 5, no. 4 (1982): 531–45, at 534.

68. On the conception of "three fronts" in Asia, see I. Strebelsky, "The Frontier in Central Asia," in *Studies in Russian Historical Geography*, vol. 1, edited by J. Bates and R. French (London: Academic Press, 1983), 143–73.

69. Quoted by Arutiun Ulunian, *Novaia politicheskaia geographiia* (Moscow: Institute of World History, 2009), 127.

70. It is interesting to compare the travel diaries by prominent Russian and European explorers, e.g., those penned by Nikolai Przhevalsky and Arminius Vambery—see Nikolai Przhevalsky, "Sovremennoe polozhenie Tsentral'noi Asii," *Russkii vestnik* 186 (1886): 473–524; and Arminius Vambery, *His Life and Adventures* (London: T. Fisher Unwin, 1914). Also see descriptions of relief, flora, and fauna in Central and Inner Asia by Dimitry Logofet and Vladimir Obruchev, *Na granitsakh Srednei Asii: Putevye ocherki* (Saint Petersburg: V. Berezovsky, 1909), 1–3; and Vladimir Obruchev, *Ot Kiakhty do Kul'dgi: Puteshestvie v Zentralnuiu Asiiu i Kitai* (Moscow: Izdatel'stvo Akademii Nauk, 1950).

71. Milan Hauner, *What Is Asia to Us? Russia's Asian Heartland Yesterday and Today* (Boston: Unwin Hyman, 1990), 41.

72. For the most valuable published documents, see C. U. Aitchinson, comp., *A Collection of Treaties, Engagements, and Sanads Relating to India and Neighboring Countries*, 14 vols. (Calcutta: Government of India Central Publication Branch, 1932); G. Gooch and H. Temperley, eds., *British Documents on the Origins of the War 1898–1914* (London: His Majesty's Stationery Office, 1929), vols. 1–5, 7, 10; and Dominic Lieven, ed., *British Documents on Foreign Affairs: Reports and Papers*

from the Foreign Office Confidential Print—Russia, 1859–1914 (Washington, D.C.: University Press of America, 1983–89), pt. I, ser. A, vols. 1–6.

73. *Sbornik geograficheskikh, topograficheskikh i statisticheskikh materialov po Asii*, 83 vols. (Saint Petersburg: Tipografiia Glavnogo Shtaba, 1883–1910). For a short review of this collection, see Warren Walsh, "The Imperial Russian General Staff and India: A Footnote to Diplomatic History," *Russian Review* 16, no. 2 (1957): 53–58, at 54–55; and Edwin Bilof, "China in Imperial Russian Military Planning, 1881–1887," *Military Affairs* 46 (1982): no. 2, 69–75, at 70.

74. For an evaluation of Lieutenant Colonel Serebrennikov's contribution to the historiography of Central Asia, see L. R. Mirzaeva, "Sbornik 'Turkestanskii krai' A. G. Serebrennikova i ego znachenie dlia sredneasiatskoi istoriografii," Kand. diss., Institut istorii i arkheologii AN Uzbekskoi SSR, 1963. The most informative contemporary publications of archival documents are by V. N. Trotsky, ed., *Materialy dlia opisaniia Khivinskogo pokhoda 1873 g.* (Tashkent: Shtab Turkestanskogo voennogo okruga, 1881–82), pts. 1–2; Russia, Foreign Ministry, *Afghanskoe razgranichenie: Peregovory mezhdu Rossiei i Velikobritaniei 1872–1885* (Saint Petersburg: Foreign Ministry, 1886); Russia, War Ministry, *Russia and Great Britain in Central Asia* (Tashkent: Shtab Turkestanskogo voennogo okruga, 1908); and A. G. Serebrennikov, ed., *Turkestanskii krai: Sbornik materialov dlia istorii yego zavoevaniia* (Tashkent: Shtab Turkestanskogo voennogo okruga, 1914–15), vols. 17, 19, 20–22. For similar publications from the Soviet period, see E. D. Grimm, ed., *Sbornik dogovorov i drugikh dokumentov po istorii mezhdunarodnykh otnoshenii na Dal'nem Vostoke (1842–1925)* (Moscow: Institut vostokovedeniia, 1927); V. V. Struve et al., eds., *Materialy po istorii Turkmen i Turkmenii: Iranskie, bukharskiei i khivinskie istochniki XVI–XIX vv.* (Moscow: Akademia Nauk SSSR, 1938), vol. 2; A. Ilyasov, ed., *Prisoedinenie Turkmenii k Rossii. Sbornik dokumentov* (Ashkhabad: Akademiia Nauk Turkmenskoi SSR, 1960); Efim Rezvan, comp., *Russian Ships in the Gulf, 1899–1903* (Reading, U.K.: Ithaca Press, 1993); P. M. Shastitko, ed., *Russko-indiiskie otnosheniia v XIX v. Sbornik arkhivnykh dokumentov i materialov* (Moscow: Vostochnaia literatura, 1997); and T. N. Zagorodnikova, comp., *"Bol'shaia" igra' v Tsentral'noi Asii: "Indiiskii pokhod" russkoi armii—Sbornik arkhibnykh dokumentov* (Moscow: Institut vostokovedeniia RAN, 2005).

75. On the activity of native spies, see especially Charlotte Macgregor, ed., *The Life and Opinions of Major-General Sir Charles Metcalfe Macgregor* (Edinburgh: W. Blackwood and Sons, 1888), vol. 2; Sarat Chandra Das, *Indian Pundits in the Land of Snow* (Calcutta: Baptist Mission Press, 1893); and Henry Brackenbury, *Some Memories of My Spare Time* (Edinburgh: W. Blackwood and Sons, 1909). Apart from the works cited above, see, e.g., an impressive book by Charles Allen, *Soldier Sahibs*.

CHAPTER 1

1. See Samuel Huntington, *The Clash of Civilizations and the Remaking of the World Order* (New York: Simon & Schuster, 1996).

2. See Alfred Rieber, "Sravnivaia kontinental'nye imperii," in *Rossiiskaia imperiia v sravnitel'noi perspective*, edited by Aleksei Miller (Moscow: Novoe izdate'stvo, 2004), 33–70.

3. Political journalists and academic scholars in European countries have been debating the credibility of Peter's will since the first half of the nineteenth century; see L. Locart, "The Political Testament of Peter the Great," *Slavonic Review*, no. 37 (1937): 38–53; I. I. Pavlenko, "Tri zavetschaniia Petra I," *Voprosy istorii*, no. 2 (1979): 129–44; and Ye. Danilova, "Zavetschanie Petra Velikogo," in *Problemy metodologii i istochnikovedeniia istorii vneshnei politiki Rossii*, edited by Aleksei Narochnitsky (Moscow: Nauka, 1985), 213–79. According to current scholarship, a certain Polish emigrant in Paris fabricated the "will" in order to split the anti-French coalition of Austria, Prussia, Russia, and Britain; see Sergei Mezin, "'Zavetschanie Petra Velikogo': Evropeiskie mify i rossiiskaia real'nost," *Rossiiskaia Istoriia*, no. 5 (2010): 18–27. Despite the apocryphal nature of the document, European journalists did not hesitate to cite it; e.g., see Francis Skrine and Edward Ross, *The Heart of Asia: A History of Russian Turkestan and the Central Asian Khanates from the Earliest Times* (London: Methuen, 1999), 409. Also see Archibald Colquhoun, *Russia against India: The Struggle for Asia* (London: Harper & Brothers, 1900), 199. Strange as it may seem, even some modern authors study it as an authentic source; see Pirouz Mojtahed-Zadeh, *Small Players of the Great Game: The Settlement of Iran's Eastern Borderlands and the Creation of Afghanistan* (London: RoutledgeCurzon, 2004), 18–19; and Mikhail Leontiev, *Bol'shaia Igra* (Moscow: AST-Astrel, 2008), 10–13.

4. Quoted by Memet Yetisgin, "How the *Times* of London Covered and Interpreted Russian Expansion into Central Asia in the Second Half of the 19th Century," Ph.D. diss., Texas Technological University, 2000, 77–78.

5. There are many studies on Russia's aggrandizement under the autocrat regime; especially see Ivo Lederer, ed., *Russian Foreign Policy: Essays in Historical Perspective* (New Haven, Conn.: Yale University Press, 1962); Barbara Jelavich, *St Petersburg and Moscow: Tsarist and Soviet Foreign Policy, 1814–1974* (Bloomington: Indiana University Press, 1974); Taras Hunczak, ed., *Russian Imperialism from Ivan the Great to the Revolution* (New Brunswick, N.J.: Rutgers University Press, 1974); John Le Donne, *The Russian Empire and the World, 1700–1917: The Geopolitics of Expansion and Containment* (New York: Oxford University Press, 1997).

6. Alfred Mahan, *The Problem of Asia and Its Effect upon International Policies* (London: S. Low, Marston, 1900), 44; for the juxtaposition of Russian aggressive ambitions with those of the British, also see 25, 56.

7. For a scrupulous study of ethnic groups in Asia by Russian scholars, e.g., see

Vasilii Grigoriev, *Rossiia i Asiia: Sbornik issledovanii i statei po istorii, ethnographii i geographii* (Saint Petersburg: Tipographiia Panteleevykh, 1876).

8. Lance Davis and Robert Huttenback, *Mammon and the Pursuit of Empire* (Cambridge: Cambridge University Press, 1986), 71.

9. Ronald Hyam, "The Primacy of Geopolitics: The Dynamics of British Imperial Policy, 1763–1963," in *The Statecraft of British Imperialism*, edited by Robert King and Robin Kilson (London: Frank Cass, 1999), 29.

10. Robert Huttenback, "The 'Great Game' in the Pamirs and Hindu Kush: The British Conquest of Hunza and Nagar," *Modern Asian Studies* 9, no. 1 (1975): 1–29, at 2.

11. On the culmination of British power in the reign of Queen Victoria, especially see James Morris, *Pax Britannica: The Climax of an Empire* (London: Faber & Faber, 1968); Kenneth Bourne, *The Foreign Policy of Victorian England, 1830–1902* (Oxford: Clarendon Press, 1970); Dennis Judd, *The Victorian Empire* (London: Weidenfeld & Nicolson, 1970); Bernhard Porter, *The Lion's Share: A Short History of British Imperialism, 1850–1970* (London: Longmans, 1975); and Ronald Hyam, *Britain's Imperial Century, 1815–914: A Study of Empire and Expansion* (London: Batsford, 1976).

12. David Armitage, *The Ideological Origins of the British Empire* (Cambridge: Cambridge University Press, 2002), 198; C. C. Eldridge, *Victorian Imperialism* (London: Hodder & Stoughton, 1978), 123.

13. A. J. H. Latham, *The International Economy and the Underdeveloped World, 1865–1914* (London: Croom Helm, 1978), 175; Leonid Semenov, *Rossiia i Angliia: Economicheskie otnosheniia v seredine XIX v.* (Leningrad: Leningradskii gosudarstvennyi universitet, 1975), 4, 153.

14. Dominic Lieven, ed., *British Documents on Foreign Affairs: Reports and Papers from the Foreign Office Confidential Print—Russia, 1859–1914* (Washington, D.C.: University Press of America, 1983–89), vol. 1, 117.

15. George Curzon, *Russia in Central Asia in 1889 and the Anglo-Russian Question* (London: Frank Cass, 1967; orig. pub. 1889), 376; Mikhail P. Fedorov, *Sopernichestvo torgovykh interesov na Vostoke: Doklad na zasedanii Soveta obtschestva vostokovedov* (Saint Petersburg: Elektro-tipographiia Stoikovoi, 1903), 14. In 1876, another analyst proudly remarked that "Russian calicoes are delivered all over Central Asia to successfully compete with equivalent British fabrics"; see Mikhail Terentiev, *Rossiia i Angliia v bor'be za rynki* (Saint Petersburg: V. Merkuriev, 1876), 34. For a survey of the economic penetration of the Middle East and Inner Asia by Russia, see A. Lunger, "The Economic Background of the Russian Conquest of Central Asia in the Second Half of the Nineteenth Century," Ph.D. diss., University of London, 1952.

16. Quoted by Maria Rozhkova, *Ekonomicheskie sviasi Rossii so Srednei Asiei, 40-e–60-e gg. XIX v.* (Moscow: Izdatelstvo Akademii nauk, 1963), 97.

17. See Kirill Ivanov, "Tamozhennaia politika Rossiiskoi imperii v kontse XIX–

nachale XX v.: Perekhod k sisteme konventsional'nykh torgovykh soglashenii,"
Kand. diss., Saint Petersburg State University, 2006, 29–31.

18. Jules Stewart, *Spying for the Raj: The Pundits and the Mapping of the Himalaya*
(Phoenix Mill, U.K.: Sutton, 2006), 32. On Russo-Persian commercial relations
in the first half of the nineteenth century, see Sergei Sukhorukov, *Iran mezhdu
Britaniei i Rossiei: Ot politiki do ekonomiki* (Saint Petersburg: Aleteia, 2009), 53–108.

19. Rozhkova, *Ekonomicheskie sviasi Rossii*, 59–60.

20. Naftula Khalfin, "Politika Rossii v Srednei Asii i anglo-russkoe sopernichestvo
(1857–1876)," doct. diss., Moskovskii gosudarstvennyi pedagogicheskii institut,
1962, 26.

21. On the Russian economic policy in Turkestan, especially see Yetisgin, "How the
Times of London Covered and Interpreted Russian Expansion," 240–99; N. A.
Abdurakhimova, "Stanovlenie i osobennosti ekonomicheskoi politiki Rossii v
Turkestane vo vtoroi polovine XIX–nachale XX vv.," *Istoricheskoe prostranstvo:
Problemy istorii stran SNG*, nos. 1–4 (2008): 62–88.

22. Zinaida Kastel'skaia, *Iz istorii Turkestanskogo kraia (1865–1917)* (Moscow:
Vostochnaia literatura, 1980), 60; Abdurakhimova, "Stanovlenie i osobennosti
ekonomicheskoi politiki," 74–76.

23. Galina Romanova, *Ekonomicheskie otnosheniia Rossii i Kitaia na Dal'nem Vostoke
XIX—nachalo XX v.* (Moscow: Nauka, 1987), 45.

24. *New York Times*, March 21, 1869, quoted by Yetisgin, "How the *Times* of London
Covered and Interpreted Russian Expansion," 71.

25. Ibid.

26. *Obsor vneshnei torgovli Rossii po evropeiskim i asiatskim granitsam* (St. Petersburg:
Departament tamozhennykh sborov, 1883), 11, 17.

27. Karl Marx, "The Future Results of the British Rule in India," *New York Daily
Tribune*, August 8, 1853.

28. A. Subbotin, *Rossiia i Angliia na sredneaziatskikh rynkakh: Istoriko-ekonomicheskii
etiud* (Saint Petersburg: Ekonomicheskii zhurnal, 1885), 27.

29. Quoted by John Michell and Robert Michell, eds., *The Russians in Central Asia*
(London: E. Stanford, 1865), 47–48.

30. Russian State Library Manuscript Division, fond (f.; collection) 169, opis' (op.;
inventory) 36, delo (d.; file) 36, listy (ll.; folios) 1–2.

31. Augustus Loftus, *The Diplomatic Reminiscences, 1837–1862*, 2 vols. (London:
Cassell, 1892), vol. 1, 271.

32. Arkhiv vneshnei politiki Rossiiskoi Imperii (hereafter, AVPRI), f. 133, op. 469, d.
79, ll. 585–86; Lieven, *British Documents*, pt. 1, ser. A, vol. 1, 287.

33. Edward Said, *Orientalism: Western Conceptions of the Orient* (New York: Vintage
Books, 1979), 121.

34. George Curzon, "The True Imperialism," *The Nineteenth Century and After* 63,
no. 371 (1908): 151–65, at 155. This is a printed record of Lord Curzon's speech
on December 11, 1907. Characteristically, a farewell appeal by the speaker to

the audience at the Birmingham City Hall sounded like this: "Cling humbly but feverently to the belief that so long as we are worthy, we may still remain one of the instruments through whom He chooses to speak to mankind"; ibid., 165.

35. Subbotin, *Rossiia i Angliia*, 73.

36. E.g., see Yetisgin, "How the *Times* of London Covered and Interpreted Russian Expansion," 45–46.

37. Ibid., 48. On the "Peter Pan" theory, see Phillip Darby, *Three Faces of Imperialism: British and American Approaches to Asia and Africa, 1870–1970* (New Haven, Conn.: Yale University Press, 1987), 48.

38. Seymour Becker, *Russia's Protectorates in Central Asia: Bokhara and Khiva, 1865–1924* (Cambridge, Mass.: Harvard University Press, 1968), 23.

39. Queen Victoria's dealing with foreign policy is illustrated by the duke of Argyll's correspondence with Lord Northbrook. Typically, on July 15, 1873, the former reproached the latter for not having mailed an epistle to Her Majesty during a prolonged space of time, "as the Queen has a real interest in letters, and attaches value to being kept *au fait* of all important affairs and even of smaller details"; see India Office Library and Records (hereafter, IOLR), Mss Eur C 144/9, Argyll to Northbrook, London, July 15, 1873. For an evaluation of Queen Victoria's role in British foreign policy, see Andrew Sinclair, *The Other Victoria: The Princess Royal and the Great Game of Europe* (London: Weidenfeld & Nicolson, 1981).

40. David Fromkin, "The Great Game in Asia," *Foreign Affairs* 58, no. 4 (1980): 936–51, at 951.

41. Alexander Rediger, *Istoriia moei zhizni: Vospominaniia voennogo ministra* (Moscow: Kanon-Press–Kuchkovo Pole, 1999), vol. 2, 157.

42. Larisa Zakharova, "Alexander II i mesto Rossii v mire," *Novaia i noveishaia istoriia*, no. 2 (2005): 164–93, at 178–79.

43. Quoted by George Lensen, ed., *Russia's Eastward Expansion* (Englewood Cliffs, N.J.: Prentice Hall, 1964), 91.

44. Gwendolen Cecil, *Life of Robert, Marquis of Salisbury*, 4 vols. (London: Hodder & Stoughton, 1921–32), vol. 3, 231, Salisbury to Morier, London, September 15, 1885.

45. David Mackenzie, "Expansion in Central Asia: St Petersburg vs. the Turkistan Generals (1863–1866)," *Canadian Slavic Studies* 3, no. 2 (1969): 286–311, at 286; David Mackenzie, *Imperial Dreams, Harsh Realities: Tsarist Russian Foreign Policy, 1815–1917* (Fort Worth: Harcourt Brace College Publishers, 1994), 91.

46. Quoted by Philip Guedalla, *Palmerston* (London: Hodder & Stoughton, 1926), 193–94.

47. On Palmerston's activity as foreign secretary, also see Algernon Cecil, *British Foreign Secretaries, 1807–1916: Studies in Personality and Policy* (London: G. Bell and Sons, 1927), 131–226.

48. Robert Blake, *Disraeli* (London: Eyre and Spottiswoode, 1966), 577.

49. A. L. Kennedy, *Salisbury, 1830–1903: Portrait of a Statesman* (London: John Murray, 1971), 92; G. Cecil, *Life of Robert*, vol. 3, 231; Robert Taylor, *Lord*

Salisbury (London: Allen Lane, 1975), 45; David Steele, *Lord Salisbury. A Political Biography* (London: University College London Press, 1999), 105.

50. Colin Matthew, *Gladstone, 1809–1874* (Oxford: Clarendon Press, 1986), 188; Roy Jenkins, *Gladstone: A Biography* (New York: Random House, 1995), esp. 500–516.

51. David Steele, "Salisbury at the India Office," in *Salisbury: The Man and His Policies*, edited by Robert Blake and Hugh Cecil (New York: St. Martin's Press, 1987), 117–18. For a comparison of Salisbury and Disraeli's views upon the threat of Russian invasion of Afghanistan in the 1870s, see John Charmley, *Splendid Isolation? Britain, the Balance of Power and the Origins of the First World War* (London: Hodder & Stoughton, 1999), 18–19.

52. Blake, *Disraeli*, 574–75; Agatha Ramm, "Lord Salisbury and the Foreign Office," in *The Foreign Office, 1782–1982*, edited by Roger Bullen (Frederick, Md.: University Publications of America, 1984), 47.

53. According to Richard Temple, who occupied the posts of foreign secretary and financial secretary in the Indian government and was the governor of Bengalia and Bombay from the 1850s to the 1870s, John Wyllie, a colonial officer, used the expression "masterly inactivity" for the first time in his comment on British policy in *The Edinburgh Review* in January 1867; see Richard Temple, *Men and Events: My Time in India* (London: John Murray, 1882), 342.

54. William Dawson, "Forward Policy and Reaction," in *The Cambridge History of British Foreign Policy, 1783–1919*, edited by A. Ward and G. Gooch (Cambridge: Cambridge University Press, 1923), vol. 3, 72.

55. Richard Bruce, *The Forward Policy and Its Results* (London: Longmans, Green, 1900), 325.

56. Dawson, "Forward Policy," 72.

57. V. K. Chavda, *India, Britain, Russia: A Study in British Opinion, 1838–1878* (Delhi: Sterling, 1967), 225.

58. Lawrence James, *The Rise and Fall of the British Empire* (London: Little, Brown, 1994), 180.

59. Nikolai Yerofeev, *Tumannyi Al'bion: Angliia i anglichane glazami russkikh, 1825–1853* (Moscow: Nauka, 1982), 271–72.

60. Anthony Cross, "Britanskii vzgliad na Rossiiu: Proiskhozhdenie, zhivuchest' i izmenenie natsional'nykh stereotipov myshleniia v period s XVI v. do Krymskoi voiny," in *Ot Elizabeth I do Elizabeth II: Problemy Britanskoi istorii v novoe i noveishee vremia*, edited by Andrei Sokolov (Yaroslavl: Yaroslavskii gosudarstvennyi pedagogicheskii universitet, 2008), 21–32.

61. John Gleason, *The Genesis of Russophobia in Great Britain: A Study of the Interaction of Policy and Opinion* (Cambridge, Mass.: Harvard University Press, 1950), 3, 16, 279.

62. Charles Allen, *Soldier Sahibs: The Men Who Made the North-West Frontier* (London: John Murray, 2000), ix–x.

63. Viscount Mersey, *The Viceroys and Governor-Generals of India, 1757–1947*

(London: John Murray, 1949), 3.

64. George Woodcock, *The British in the Far East* (New York: Atheneum, 1969), 35.

65. Morris, *Pax Britannica*, 267.

66. Mark Bence-Jones, *The Viceroys of India* (London: Archibald Constable, 1982), 1.

67. For a brilliant narration of the British colonial rule in India, also see John Kaye, *Lives of Indian Officers: Illustrative of the History of the Civil and Military Services of India* (London: A. Strahan, 1867), vols. 1–2; Philip Woodraft, *The Men Who Ruled India* (London: Jonathan Cape, 1953–54), vols. 1–2; and Bence-Jones, *Viceroys*.

68. Lucien Wolf, ed., *Life of the First Marquis of Ripon* (London: John Murray, 1921), vol. 1, 80.

69. Allen, *Soldier Sahibs*, 6.

70. National Archives of the United Kingdom–Public Record Office, FO 539/9, Rumbold to Clarendon, Saint Petersburg, May 19, 1864.

71. Robert Johnson, *Spying for Empire: The Great Game in Central and South Asia, 1757–1947* (London: Greenhill Books, 2006), 61.

72. Richard Robbins, *The Tsar's Viceroys: Russian Provincial Governors in the Last Years of the Empire* (Ithaca, N.Y.: Cornell University Press, 1987), 244–45.

73. Michael Edwardes, *Playing the Great Game* (London: Hamish Hamilton, 1975), 15.

74. Quoted by Alexander Popov, "Iz istorii zavoevaniia Srednei Asii," *Istoricheskie zapiski* 9 (1940): 198–242, at 202; Helene Carrère d'Encause, "Systematic Conquest," in *Central Asia, 130 Years of Russian Dominance: A Historical Overview*, edited by Edward Allworth (Durham, N.C.: Duke University Press, 1994), 149–50.

75. See O. A. Gopov, "Rol' ofitserov General'nogo shtaba v osutschestvlenii vneshnei politiki Rossiiskoi imperii na musul'manskom Vostoke vo vtoroi polovine XIX v.," Kand. diss., Institut vostokovedeniia RAN, Moscow, 2004.

76. Dimitry Miliutin, *Dnevnik*, 4 vols. (Moscow: Gosudarstvennaia biblioteka Lenina, 1950), vol. 4, 143.

77. Frederick Burnaby, *A Ride to Khiva: Travels and Adventures in Central Asia* (London, 1877), 86.

78. Mikhail Terentiev, *Istoriia zavoevaniia Srednei Asii*, 3 vols. (Saint Petersburg: V. Komarov, 1906), vol. 2, 66.

79. See Oleg Airapetov, *Zabytaia kariera "Russkogo Mol'tke": Nikolai Nikolaevich Obruchev (1830–1904)* (Saint Petersburg: Aleteia, 1998), 270.

80. Karl Meyer and Shareen Brysac, *Tournament of Shadows: The Great Game and the Race for Empire in Central Asia* (London: Abacus, 1999), 186.

81. Mackenzie, "Expansion," 286–311.

82. Yetisgin, "How the *Times* of London Covered and Interpreted Russian Expansion," 27.

83. Great Britain, Parliament, *Papers Relating to Tibet* (London: His Majesty's Stationery Office, 1904); Great Britain, Parliament, *Further Papers Relating to Tibet* (London: His Majesty's Stationery Office, 1904).

84. Dimitry Miliutin, *Vospominaniia, 1863–1864* (Moscow: Rosspen, 2003), vol. 5, 520.

85. Tsentralnyi Gosudarstvennyi Arkhiv Respubliki Uzbekistan, f. I-1, op. 1, d. 34, l. 256.

86. Quoted by David Schimmelpenninck van der Oye, "Ex Orient Lux: Ideologies of Empire and Russia's Far East, 1895–1904," Ph.D. diss., Yale University, 1997, 36.

87. For further details, especially see Derek Waller, *The Pundits: British Exploration of Tibet and Central Asia* (Lexington: University Press of Kentucky, 1990); Ian Barrow, *Making History, Drawing Territory: British Mapping in India, c. 1756–1905* (New Delhi: Oxford University Press, 2003); and P. L. Madan, *Tibet: Saga of Indian Explorers* (New Delhi: Manohar, 2004); Stewart, *Spying for the Raj*.

88. Madan, *Tibet*, 137.

89. Dimitry Miliutin, *Vospominaniia, 1856–1860* (Moscow: Rosspen, 2004), vol. 3, 168.

90. John Morell, *Russia and England: Their Strength and Weakness* (New York: Riker, Thorne, 1854), 11.

91. David Urquhart, *Progress of Russia in the West, North, and South by Opening the Sources of Opinion and Appropriating the Channels of Wealth and Power* (London: Truebner, 1853), 438.

92. Ibid., 291 ff. For the current interpretation of the impact of the Caucasus problem upon the Russo-British competition, see Vladimir Degoev, *Bol'shaia igra na Kavkaze: Istoriia i sovremennost'* (Moscow: Russkaia mysl', 2003), 117–55.

93. George de Lacy Evans, *On the Designs of Russia* (London, 1828); George de Lacy Evans, *On the Practicability of an Invasion of India, and on the Commercial and Financial Prospects and Resources of the Empire* (London, 1829).

94. Gosudarstvennyi arkhiv Rossiiskoi Federatsii (hereafter, GARF), f. 730, op. 1, d. 519, ll. 1–3 rev.

95. J. B. Kelly, *Britain and the Persian Gulf, 1795–1880* (Oxford: Clarendon Press, 1968), 456. On the Anglo-Persian War of 1856–57, see P. P. Bushev, *Herat i anglo-persidskaia voina 1856–57 gg.* (Moscow: Vostochnaia literatura, 1959).

96. GARF, f. 730, op. 1, d. 241, ll. 1–32.

97. C. U. Aitchinson, comp., *A Collection of Treaties, Engagements, and Sanads Relating to India and Neighboring Countries*, 14 vols. (Calcutta: Government of India Central Publication Branch, 1932), vol. 13, 85–86; Arkhiv vneshnei politiki Rossiiskoi Imperii (hereafter, AVPRI), f. 133, op. 469, d. 76, 1857, ll. 42–50 rev.

98. IOLR / L/P&S /18 /A3, 1–8. As a highly placed official claimed in the memo on the agreement between Emir Dost Mohamed and East India Company on February 9, 1857, "the best policy [of Britain] would be to consent to the independence of Herat" (p. 8).

99. AVPRI, f. 133, op. 469, d. 205, 1857, ll. 1–135. This is correspondence between the Russian diplomatic mission in Tehran and the Foreign Ministry concerning the repercussions of the Anglo-Persian War.

100. Kelly, *Britain and the Persian Gulf*, 287. On Russo-Persian relations in the first

half of the nineteenth century, also see Peter Avery, *Modern Iran* (London: Ernest Benn, 1965), 37–40.

101. John McNeill, "The Progress and Present Position of Russia in the East," in *The Great Game: Britain and Russia in Central Asia*, edited by Martin Evans (London: RoutledgeCurzon, 2004), 104. The first edition of this pamphlet came out in London as early as 1836.

102. Quoted by F. P. Verney, "Six Generations of Czars," *The Nineteenth Century*, no. 148 (1889): 827–37, at 829.

103. Archibald Thornton, "The Reopening of the 'Central Asian Question,' 1864– 1869," *History*, 41, nos. 141–43 (1956): 122–36, at 123.

104. For a contemporary assessment of Dost Mohamed's life and political activity, see Victor Langlois, *Herat: Dost Mohammed et les influences politiques de la Russie et de l'Angleterre dans l'Asie centrale* (Paris, 1864). A modern reappraisal is given by Christine Noelle, *State and Tribe in Nineteenth-Century Afghanistan: The Reign of Amir Dost Muhammad Khan (1826–1863)* (Richmond, U.K.: Curzon Press, 1997).

105. Malcom Yapp, *Strategies of British India: Britain, Iran and Afghanistan, 1798–1850* (Oxford: Clarendon Press, 1980), 307.

106. On the activity of Vitkevich in Afghanistan, see Ivan Blaramberg, *Vospominaniia* (Moscow: Nauka, 1978). Comparative analyses of the missions by Vitkevich and Burnes are given by Naftula Khalfin, *Rossiia i khanstva Srednei Asii (pervaia polovina XIX v.)* (Moscow: Nauka, 1974), 243–55; and Meyer and Brysac, *Tournament of Shadows*, 77–110. The Soviet historian Naftula Khalfin investigated the mysterious suicide of Lieutenant-Captain Vitkevich in early May 1839; see Naftula Khalfin, "'Drama v spal'ne otelia," *Voprosy istorii*, no. 10 (1966): 216–20.

107. On the history of the First Anglo-Afghan War and Second Anglo-Afghan War, especially see Archibald Forbes, *The Afghan Wars 1839–42 and 1878–80* (London: Seeley, 1892); James Eliott, *The Frontier: The Story of the North-West Frontier of India* (London: Cassell, 1968), 13–44; and D. S. Richards, *The Savage Frontier: A History of the Anglo-Afghan Wars* (London: Macmillan, 1990), 17–57.

108. Geoffrey Wheeler, "Russian Conquest and Colonization of Central Asia," in *Russian Imperialism from Ivan the Great to the Revolution*, ed. Hunczak, 22.

109. Mastura Kalandarova, "Geopolitika Anglii v Tsentral'noi Asii v 20–30-e gg. XIX v.," Kand. diss., Institut vostokovedeniia, Moscow, 1995, 12–13.

110. Terentiev, *Istoriia zavoevaniia Srednei Asii*, vol. 1, 20.

111. A. I. Maksheev, *Istoricheskii obzor Turkestana i nastupatel'nogo dvizheniia v nego russkikh* (Saint Petersburg: Voennaia tipografiia, 1890), 99.

112. Further details are given by Khalfin, *Rossia i khanstva Srednei Asii*, 199–221; also see Begaamaly Dzhamgerchinov, *Prisoedinenie Kirgizii k Rossii* (Moscow: Sotsial'no-ekonomicheskoe izdatel'stvo, 1959), 83–124.

113. On the details of the campaign against Khiva by General Vasily Perovsky in 1839, see Maksheev, *Istoricheskii obzor Turkestana*, 143–214; and Alexander Popov, "Bor'ba za sredneasiatskii platzdarm," *Istoricheskie zapiski* 7 (1940): 182–235.

114. S. Zykov, "'Ocherk utverzhdeniia russkogo vladychestva na Aral'skom more i reke Syr Daria s 1847 po 1862 g." *Morskoi sbornik* 59, no. 6 (1862): 298–348, at 311–12.

115. On the fates of both Stoddart and Conolly, see Joseph Wolff, *Narrative of a Mission to Bokhara in the Years 1843–1845, to Ascertain the Fate of Colonel Stoddart and Captain Conolly*, 2 vols. (London: J. Parker, 1845).

116. Alexander Shepelev, *Ocherk voennykh i diplomaticheskikh snoshenii Rossii so Srednei Aziei* (Tashkent: Tipografiia Voenno-narodnogo upravleniia, 1879), pt. 1, 67–70; Meyer and Brysac, *Tournament of Shadows*, 128–30; Yetisgin, "How the *Times* of London Covered and Interpreted Russian Expansion," 82; Aleksei Postnikov, *Skhvatka na "Kryshe mira": Politiki, razvedchiki, geography v bor'be za Pamir v XIX veke* (Moscow: Ripol-Classik, 2005), 84–85; Johnson, *Spying for Empire*, 86–87. According to Terentiev, "there was no doubt, that if they [Charles Stoddart and Arthur Conolly] had moved from the town [of Bokhara] to the lodgings of the Russian mission, they would have been saved by Russian diplomats who would have taken them to Orenburg"; see Terentiev, *Istoriia zavoevaniia Srednei Asii*, vol. 1, 197–98.

117. Thornton, "Reopening," 122. On the efforts of Nicolas I to come to Britain on friendly terms, especially see Harold Ingle, *Nesselrode and the Russian Rapprochement with Britain, 1836–1844* (Berkeley: University of California Press, 1976).

118. See "Buffer State," http://www.statemaster.com/encyclopedia/Buffer-state.

119. Manuel Sarkisianz, "Russian Conquest in Central Asia: Transformation and Acculturation," in *Russia and Asia: Essays on the Influence of Russia on the Asian Peoples*, edited by Wayne Vucinich (Stanford, Calif.: Hoover Institution Press, 1972), 284. For a compendium of documents, including unique records by Persian, Bokharian, and Khivian news writers, on the history of Turkmenistan from the sixteenth century to the period of its subjugation to Russia, see V. V. Struve, ed., *Materialy po istorii Turkmen i Turkmenii* (Moscow: Izdatel'stvo Akademii nauk SSSR, 1938), vol. 2, esp. 205–322, 355–638.

120. Struve, *Materialy po istorii*, vol. 2, 304.

121. *The Times*, December 29, 1854; quoted by Yetisgin, "How *The Times* of London Covered and Interpreted Russian Expansion," 88.

122. Kalandarova, "Geopolitika Anglii," 17.

123. Alim Aminov and Abdusamad Babakhodzhaev, *Ekonomicheskie i politicheskie posledstviia prisoedineniia Srednei Asii k Rossii* (Tashkent: Izdatelstvo Uzbekistan, 1966), 41.

124. A. G. Serebrennikov, ed., *Turkestanskii krai* (Tashkent: Tipographiia Turkestanskogo voennogo okruga, 1915), vol. 20, 130.

125. AVPRI, f. 701, op. 1, 1854, f. 4, ll. 35–36, 108; quoted by Postnikov, *Skhvatka na "Kryshe mira,"* 106–8, who maintains that Muslim instructors had finally refused to leave for Khiva. Conversely, Memet Yetisgin argues for the arrival of three native officers to the Court of Mohamed Khudayar Khan; see Yetisgin, "How the

Times of London Covered and Interpreted Russian Expansion," 87.

126. AVPRI, f. 701, op. 1, 1854, f. 4, ll. 29–30.

127. Friedrich von Hellwald, *Die Russen in Zentralasien; Eine geographisch-historische Studie* (Vienna:Verlag des Verfassers, 1869), 191–92.

128. Jack Dabbs, *History of the Discovery and Exploration of Chinese Turkestan* (The Hague: Mouton, 1963), 5; Boris Gurevich, *Mezhdunarodnye otnosheniia v Tsentral'noi Asii v XVII–pervoi polovine XIX v.* (Moscow: Nauka, 1983), 161.

129. Dabbs, *History*, 11 ff.;Vadim Obukhov, *Skhvatka shesti imperii: Bitva za Sinkiang* (Moscow:Veche, 2007), 7–18. For a contemporary geostrategic analysis, see Justin Huggler and Clifford Coonan, "China Reopens a Passage to India," *The Independent*, June 20, 2006.

130. Gurevich, *Mezhdunarodnye otnosheniia*, 259–72.

131. Nikolai Klimenko, *Kolonial'naia politika Anglii na Dal'nem Vostoke v seredine XIX veka* (Moscow: Nauka, 1976), 12–13, 32–33.

132. John Evans, *Russian Expansion on the Amur, 1848–1860:The Push to the Pacific*, 2 vols. (NewYork: Edwin Mellen Press, 1999), vol. 1, 20.

133. M. I. Romanova, "Anglo-russkoe morskoe sopernichestvo na Dal'nem Vostoke v seredine XIX v. i otnoshenie k nemu liberal'nykh krugov Velikobritanii," *Rossiiskii flot na Tikhom okeane: Istoriia i sovremennost'*, no. 2 (1996): 11–15.

134. R. Quested, *The Expansion of Russia in East Asia, 1857–1860* (Kuala Lumpur: University of Malaysia Press, 1968), 282.

135. Quoted by Roman Bogdanov, "Vospominaniia amurskogo kazaka o proshlom, s 1849 po 1880 g.," *Priamurskie vedomosti*, nos. 340–44 (1900): 348–49.

136. Klimenko, *Kolonial'naia politika Anglii*, 32–33; Evans, *Russian Expansion*, vol. 1, 88.

137. Thomas Otte, "'It's What Made Britain Great': Reflections on British Foreign Policy from Malplaquet to Maastricht," in *The Makers of British Foreign Policy*, edited by Thomas Otte (Basingstoke, U.K.: Palgrave, 2002), 11.

138. Leonid Bogdanovich, "Angliia i Rossiia v Srednei Asii," *Russkaia mysl'* 2 (1900): 139–61; 3: 19–29 (at 139).

CHAPTER 2

1. George Clarke, *Russia's Sea Power: Past and Present, or the Rise of the Russian Navy* (London: John Murray, 1898), 33–36.

2. Alexander Popov, comp., "Angliiskaia politika v Indii i russko-indiiskie otnosheniia v 1897–1905 gg.," *Krasnyi Arkhiv* 6, no. 19 (1926): 53–63.

3. Ronald Robinson and John Gallagher, *Africa and the Victorians:The Climax of Imperialism* (NewYork:Anchor Books, 1968), 13. For a general assessment of Britain's colonial rule, see Bernhard Porter, *The Lion's Share: A Short History of British Imperialism, 1850–1970* (London: Longman, 1975). A current evaluation

of the situation in the Raj in the 1850s is given by Charles Allen, *Soldier Sahibs: The Men Who Made the North-West Frontier* (London: John Murray, 2000).

4. See Warren Walsh, "The Imperial Russian General Staff and India: A Footnote to Diplomatic History," *Russian Review* 16, no. 2 (1957): 53–58, at 57.

5. Mikhail Terentiev, *Istoriia zavoevaniia Srednei Asii*, 3 vols. (Saint Petersburg: V. Komarov, 1906), vol. 1, 43; Sergei Idarov, "Znachenie Indii v politike Rossii s Turtsiei i Angliei," *Russkii vestnik* 171, no. 6 (1884): 487–553, at 487.

6. Quoted by Petr Shastitko, ed., *Russko-indiiskie otnosheniia v XIX v.* (Moscow: Vostochnaia literatura, 1997), 28. For a documentary survey of these plans, see "Proekt ekspeditsii v Indiu, predlozhennykh Napoleonom Bonapartom imperatoram Pavlu I i Alexandru I v 1800 i 1807–1808 gg.," *Sbornik geographicheskikh, topographicheskikh i statisticheskikh materialov po Asii* 23 (1886): 1–93; and Feodor Lobysevich, *Postupatel'noe dvizhenie v Sredniuiu Asiiu v torgovom i diplomatichesko-voennom otnosheniiakh* (Saint Peterburg: Obtschestvennaia pol'za, 1900), 60–61. Also see Idarov, "Znachenie Indii," 519–49.

7. Cited by V. P. Metscherskii, *Moi vospominaniia (1850–1894)* (Saint Petersburg: V. Metscherskii, 1897), vol. 3, 195.

8. George de Lacy Evans, *On the Designs of Russia* (London, 1828), 120–24, 240–42.

9. John McNeill, "The Progress and Present Position of Russia in the East," in *The Great Game: Britain and Russia in Central Asia*, edited by Martin Evans (London: RoutledgeCurzon, 2004), 104–5.

10. Nikolai Yerofeev, *Tumannyi Al'bion: Angliia i anglichane glazami russkikh, 1825–1853* (Moscow: Nauka, 1982), 273.

11. Anonymous, *India, Great Britain, and Russia* (London, 1838), 2–3, 11, 33–35.

12. Ivan Vernadskii, *Politicheskoe ravnovesie i Angliia* (Moscow: Moscow State University, 1855), 70, 85.

13. Arkhiv Vneshnei Politiki Rossiiskoi Imperii (hereafter, AVPRI), fond (f.; collection) 133, opis' (op.; inventory) 470, delo (d.; file) 62 (1882), listy (ll.; folios) 169, Giers to Morenheim, Saint Petersburg, 1882.

14. Tsentral'nyi Gosudarstvennyi Arkhiv Respubliki Uzbekistan, f. 715, d. 25; Rossiskii gosudarstvennyi voenno-istoricheskii arkhiv (hereafter, RGVIA), f. 800, op. 1, d. 18291, ll. 3–15; Platon Chikhachev, "Zapiska o vozmozhnosti osutschestvleniia Rossiei ekspeditsii v Indiu," *Sbornik geographicheskikh, topographicheskikh i statisticheskikh materialov po Asii* 23 (1886): 105–29; Archibald Colquhoun, *Russia Against India: The Struggle for Asia* (London: Harper & Brothers, 1900), 18; Alexander Lobanov-Rostovsky, *Russia and Asia* (Ann Arbor: G. Wahr, 1951), 119–25.

15. Konstantin Kubanov, "Pokhody v Indiiu v proektakh rossiiskikh voennykh i politicheskikh deiatelei XVIII–nachala XX vv.," Kand. diss., Nizhnevartovsk: Nizhnevartovskii gosudarstvennyi gumanitarnyi universitet, 2007, 18.

16. Gosudarstvennyi Arkhiv Rossiiskoi Federatsii (hereafter, GARF), f. 730, op. 1, d. 271, ll. 1–14 rev.; also see Ivan Blaramberg, *Vospominaniia* (Moscow: Nauka,

1978); Evgeny Steinberg, *Istoriia britanskoi agressii na Srednem Vostoke* (Moscow: Voennoe izdatel'stvo, 1951), 54–55.

17. Otdel rukopisei Rossiskoi gosudarstvennoi biblioteki, f. 169, op. 50, d. 55, l. 119; Shastitko, *Russko-indiiskie otnosheniia*, 87–89; . P. Bushev, *Herat i anglo-persidskaia voina 1856–57 gg.* (Moscow: Vostochnaia literatura, 1959), 26–27.

18. Shastitko, *Russko-indiiskie otnosheniia*, 88, 93–94; Naftula Khalfin, "Politika Rossii v Srednei Asii i anglo-russkoe sopernichestvo (1857–1876)," doct. diss., Moskovskii gosudarstvennyi pedagogicheskii institut, 1962, 74–75.

19. Shastitko, *Russko-indiiskie otnosheniia*, 96.

20. V. K. Chavda, *India, Britain, Russia: A Study in British Opinion, 1838–1878* (Delhi: Sterling, 1967), 212–13.

21. AVPRI, f. 137, op. 475, d. 41, 1857, ll. 172–172 rev., annual report of the foreign minister to the tsar, December 1857.

22. Shastitko, *Russko-indiiskie otnosheniia*, 121–26, 139–41, 142; Naftula Khalfin, *Missii iz Indiiu v Rossiiu vo vtoroi polovine XIX veka* (Moscow: Vostochnaia literatura, 1963); Kubanov, "Pokhody v Indiiu," 23.

23. Sidney Cotton, *Nine Years on the North-West Frontier of India, from 1854 to 1863* (London: R. Bentley, 1868), 284–85. Valuable assessments of the British policy during the Sepoy Mutiny are given by William Muir, ed., *Records of the Intelligence Department of the Government of the North-West Provinces of India during the Mutiny of 1857* (Edinburgh: Clark, 1902), vols. 1–2; and Frederick Roberts, *Forty-One Years in India from Subaltern to Commander-in-Chief* (London: Macmillan, 1902), vol. 1, 414–37. Soviet historians used to argue that the Tsarist authorities allegedly abstained from sending secret agents to India throughout the latter half of the nineteenth century; e.g., see Khalfin, "Politika Rossii v Srednei Asii," 39–40.

24. Keith Jeffrey, "The Eastern Arc of Empire: A Strategic View, 1850–1950," *Journal of Strategic Studies* 5, no. 4 (1982): 531–45, at 537.

25. Karl Meyer and Shareen Brysac, *Tournament of Shadows: The Great Game and the Race for Empire in Central Asia* (London: Abacus, 1999), 151.

26. James Morris, *Pax Britannica: The Climax of an Empire* (London: Faber & Faber, 1968), 137. On reverberations of the Sepoy Mutiny in Central Asia, also see Anwar Khan Mohammad, *England, Russia and Central Asia (A Study in Diplomacy), 1857–1878* (Peshawar: University Book Agency, 1963); and Pavel Litvinov, "Britanskaia Indiia i russkii Turkestan vo vtoroi polovine XIX–nachale XX v.," in *Rossiia–Indiia: perspektivy regional'nogo sotrudnichestva*, edited by G. I. Kuznetsov (Moscow: Institut vostokovedeniia RAN, 2001), 60–68.

27. AVPRI, f. 133, op. 470, d. 62 (1882), l. 173, Giers to Morenheim, Saint Petersburg, 1882.

28. Cited by Phillip Darby, *Three Faces of Imperialism: British and American Approaches to Asia and Africa, 1870–1970* (New Haven, Conn.: Yale University Press, 1987), 26.

29. AVPRI, f. 137, op. 475, d. 41, 1857, ll. 172–172 rev.

30. Shastitko, *Russko-indiiskie otnosheniia*, 91.

31. GARF, f. 730, op. 1, d. 121, ll. 1–40, Ignatiev's personal diary of his sojourn in London, 1857.

32. H. Edwards, *Russian Projects against India: From the Tsar Peter to General Skobelev* (London: Remington, 1885), 158–9.

33. GARF, f. 730, op. 1, d. 511, ll. 1–2 rev., draft report by Ignatiev to the Main Staff, London, 1857. Also see Dimitry Romanovsky, *Zametki po sreneaziatskomu voprosu* (Saint Petersburg: Vtoroe otdelenie Kantseliarii Ego Imperatorskogo Velichestva, 1868), x; on the two competing lines of the Russian Asian policy, see 25–27.

34. GARF, f. 730, op. 1, d. 511, ll. 1–30, draft note by Ignatiev, 1859.

35. N. N. Dlusskaia, comp., "Zapiski N. G. Zalesova," *Russkaia starina* 115 (1903): 21–37, 321–40.

36. Dimitry Miliutin, *Dnevnik*, 4 vols. (Moscow: Gosudarstvennaia biblioteka Lenina, 1950), vol. 4, 208.

37. GARF, f. 730, op. 1, d. 507, ll. 1–12, note by Ignatiev on the position of Russia and Britain in case of a war, Saint Petersburg, July 17, 1863.

38. Rossiiskii Gosudarstvennyi Arkhiv Voenno-Morskogo Flota, f. 410, op. 2, d. 2621, ll. 1–4 rev., instruction by Rear Admiral Popov, the commander of the Pacific Squadron, to the captain of the corvette *Novik*, April 27, 1863. On the challenges with which the Russian navy was confronted after the Crimean War, see Alexander Nidermiller, *Ot Sevastopolia do Tsusimy: Vospominaniia—Russkii flot za vremia s 1866 po 1906 gg.* (Riga: M. Didkovsky, 1930).

39. GARF, f. 730, op. 1, d. 507, ll. 4 rev.–5.

40. Dlusskaia, "Zapiski," 324.

41. RGVIA, f. 400, op. 1, d, 4913, ll. 2–9 rev.; Stepan Khrulev, 'Zapiska o pokhode v Indiiu', *Russkii Arkhiv,* 1882, vol. 3, no. 5, pp. 42–66.

42. Mikhail Veniukov, "Trans-Ili and Chu Districts," in *The Russians in Central Asia*, edited by John Michell and Robert Michell (London: E. Stanford, 1865), 404.

43. Steinberg, *Istoriia britanskoi*, 52–54; E. A. Orlov, "Vopros ob 'oborone Indii' ot 'russkoi ugrozy' v istoriografii," in *Protiv kolonialisma i neokolonialisma*, edited by V. I. Danilov (Moscow: Nauka, 1975), 38–59; B. S. Mannanov, "Sovremennaia burzhuaznaia istoriografiia o nekotorykh aspektakh istoriografii anglo-russkikh otnoshenii na Srednem Vostoke (iz istorii 'Bol'shoi igry')," in *Fal'sifikatory istorii (kritika burzhuaznoi istoriografii Srednei Asii i stran zarubezhnogo Vostoka)*, edited by M. M. Khairullaev and N. A. Khalfin (Tashkent: Fan, 1985), 51–75. For a modern interpretation of this discussion by Western scholars, especially see Alex Marshall, *The Russian General Staff and Asia, 1800–1917* (London: Routledge, 2006), 131–62.

44. Petr Shastitko, "K voprosu o mificheskoi 'russkoi ugroze' Indii," in *Protiv falk'sifikatsii istorii kolonialisma*, edited by K. Popov (Moscow: Vostochnaia literatura, 1962), 182–96.

45. Friedrich Engels, "Russia's Advance in Central Asia," *New York Daily Tribune*, November 3, 1858.

46. For a British evaluation of Russian political missions, see Gerald Morgan, *Anglo-Russian Rivalry in Central Asia: 1810–1895* (London: Frank Cass, 1981), 86–99; R. Quested, *The Expansion of Russia in East Asia, 1857–1860* (Kuala Lumpur: University of Malaysia Press, 1968), 64–275. A Soviet interpretation of the expeditions is presented by Nina Kiniapina, "Tri rossiiskie missii v Sredniuiu Asiiu," in *Kavkaz i Sredniaia Asiia vo vneshnei politike Rossii. Vtoraia polovina XVIII v.–80-e gg. XIX v.*, edited by N. S. Kiniapina, M. M. Bliev, and V. V. Degoev (Moscow: Moscow State University, 1984), 256–69.

47. AVPRI, f. 137, op. 475, d. 42, 1858, ll. 171 rev.– 172.

48. RGVIA, f. 483, op. 1, d. 53, l. 12 rev.

49. National Archives of the United Kingdom–Public Record Office (hereafter, PRO), FO 65/867, 1860.

50. GARF, f. 730, op. 1, d. 292, ll. 1–3 rev.

51. RGVIA, f. 483, op. 1, d. 53, ll. 1–6 rev.

52. PRO/FO 181/338; PRO/FO 65/867, 1858; GARF, f. 730, op. 1, d. 272, ll. 1–11 rev.; d. 315, ll. 1–6; Khalfin, "Politika Rossii v Srednei Asii," 30; Viktoria Khevrolina, *Rossiiskii diplomat graf Nikolai Pavlovich Ignatiev* (Moscow: Institut rossiiskoi istorii, 2004), 32–62.

53. Peter Hopkirk, *The Great Game: On Secret Service in High Asia* (London: John Murray, 1990), 296.

54. Otdel pis'mennykh istochnikov Gosudarstvennogo istoricheskogo muzeia, f. 208, op. 1, d. 1, ll. 50–59 rev. For a rather informative diary about this trip penned by Iganiev's private secretary in 1858, see G. Kuelman, *A Journey to Khiva*, in PRO/FO 65/867, 1859 (trans. by A. Michell).

55. On the anti-Russian coalition of the Turkic khanates backed by the Ottoman Empire, see L. R. Mirzaeva, "Sbornik 'Turkestanskii krai' A. G. Serebrennikova i ego znachenie dlia sredneasiatskoi istoriografii," Kand. diss., Institut istorii i arkheologii AN Uzbekskoi SSR, 1963, 17. A British view of such a project is given by John Strong, "'The Ignatiev Mission to Khiva and Bokhara in 1858," *Canadian Slavonic Papers* 17, nos. 2–3 (1975): 236–69.

56. See S. V. Zhukovsky, *Snosheniia Rossii s Bokharoi i Khivoi za poslednee trkhsotletie* (Petrograd: Trudy Obschestva russkikh orientalistov, 1915), 146–55, esp. 155.

57. GARF, f. 730, op. 1, d. 300, ll. 1–26, report by Ignatiev to Alexander II about his trip to Khiva and Bokhara, Saint Petersburg, January 1859.

58. Nikolai Ignatiev, *Missiia v Khivu i Bokharu v 1858 g. fligel'-adjiutanta polkovnika N. Ignatieva* (Saint Petersburg: Gosudarstvennaia tipografiia, 1897), 274–75.

59. Khevrolina, *Rossiiskii diplomat*, 35.

60. Friedrich von Hellwald, *Die Russen in Zentralasien: Eine geographisch-historische Studie* (Vienna: Verlag des Verfassers, 1869), 9–10; Nina Kiniapina, "Sredniaia Asiia vo vneshnepoliticheskikh planakh tsarisma (50-e–80-e gg. XIX v.)," *Voprosy istorii*, no. 2 (1974): 36–51. For a study of Khanykov's career as an explorer in Oriental countries, especially see Naftula Khalfin and Ekaterina Rassadina, *N. V.*

Khanykovz: Vostokoved i diplomat (Moscow: Nauka, 1977).

61. AVPRI, f. 137, op. 475, d. 42, 1858, ll. 144 rev.–45.

62. Ibid., f. 133, op. 469, d. 165, 1858, ll. 2–6.

63. Mary Holdsworth, *Turkistan in the Nineteenth Century: A Brief History of the Khanates of Bokhara, Khokand and Khiva* (Oxford: Central Asian Research Institute, 1959), 51; Hopkirk, *Great Game*, 290; Memet Yetisgin, "How the *Times* of London Covered and Interpreted Russian Expansion into Central Asia in the Second Half of the 19th Century," Ph.D. diss., Texas Technological University, 2000, 89.

64. Dimitry Miliutin, *Vospominaniia: 1856–1860* (Moscow: Rosspen, 2004), vol. 3, 197.

65. India Office Library and Records (hereafter, IOLR), L&PS/5/18, 72–72 rev., 74.

66. Hopkirk, *Great Game*, 290. On the results of Khanykov's mission to Khorasan and Afghanistan, also see Khalfin and Rassadina, *N. V. Khanykovz*, 119–42.

67. For a contemporary evaluation of the missions of Ignatiev and Khanykov, see A. I. Kalinin, "O nekotorykh aspektakh sredneaziatskoi politiki Rossii v 40–80-kh XIX v.," *Vostochnyi arkhiv*, nos. 4–5 (2000): 49–54.

68. RGVIA, f. 447, op. 1, d. 4, ll. 16–19, memorandum by Zakharov, Kuldja, August 1857.

69. AVPRI, f. 137, op. 475, d. 41, ll. 206 rev.–207.

70. Chokan Valikhanov, *O sostoianii Altyshara, ili shesti vostochnykh gorodov kitaiskoi provintsii Nan-Lu v 1858–1859 gg.* (Alma-Ata: Akademia nauk Kazakhskoi SSR, 1962), vol. 2. For the details of this covert activity, see Alexander Popov, "Iz istorii zavoevaniia Srednei Asii," *Istoricheskie zapiski* 9 (1940): 198–242, at 199–204; Khalfin, "Politika Rossii v Srednei Asii," 106–13; and Kiniapina, "Sredniaia Asiia vo vneshnepoliticheskikh planakh tsarisma," 36–51.

71. Chokan Valikhanov, *Chinese Turkestan and Dzungaria* (London: E. Stanford, 1865).

72. Dimitry Miliutin, *Vospominaniia: 1863–1864* (Moscow: Rosspen, 2003), vol. 5, 512–13; Popov, "Iz istorii zavoevaniia Srednei Asii," 205–10.

73. AVPRI, f. 138, op. 467, d. 3, l. 11 rev.

74. E.g., see PRO/FO 181/336, Wodehouse to the Foreign Office, Saint Petersburg, January 24, 1857; and Friedrich Engels, "Persia and China," *New York Daily Tribune*, June 5, 1857. On the origins of the Second Opium War, see W. Soothill, *China and the West: A Sketch of Their Intercourse* (London: Oxford University Press, 1925), 137–53.

75. Quoted by John Evans, *Russian Expansion on the Amur, 1848–1860: The Push to the Pacific*, 2 vols. (New York: Edwin Mellen Press, 1999), vol. 1, 110.

76. Quoted by Vladimir Miasnikov, *Dogovornymi statýami utverzhdeny: Diplomaticheskaia istoriia russko-kitaiskoi granitsy XVII-XX vv.* (Moscow: Institut Dal'nego Vostoka RAN, 1996), 274.

77. PRO/FO 181/354, Crampton to Russell, Saint Petersburg, September 14 and October 7, 1859.

78. Quoted by Alexandra Zakharova, "Alexander II i mesto Rossii v mire." *Novaia i noveishaia istoriia*, no. 2 (2005): 164–93, at 179.

79. Augustus Loftus, *The Diplomatic Reminiscences, 1837–1862*, 2 vols. (London: Cassell, 1892), vol. 1, 292–316. For one of the best studies of the Russo-Chinese delimitation of the territories on the Amur and Ussuri in the late 1850s, see S. Paine, *Imperial Rivals: China, Russia and Their Disputed Frontiers* (Armonk, N.Y.: M. E. Sharpe, 1996), 49–106.

80. Quoted by A. N. Khokhlov, "Voennaia pomotsch Kitaiu v kontse 50-kh–nachale 60-kh gg. XIX v.," in *Strany Dal'nego Vostoka i Yugo-Vostochnoi Asii (istoriia i ekonomika)*, edited by I. S. Kazakevich (Moscow:Vostochnaia literatura, 1967), 123–24.

81. Under these circumstances, Russia dispatched to China 10,000 rifles and a battery of six field guns with 300 shells and spare parts while a few Russian military instructors were drilling six Chinese subalterns and sixty rank-and-file soldiers from November 1861 to January 1862; see Khokhlov, "Voennaia pomotsch Kitaiu," 127–29.

82. Cited by Nikolai Klimenko, *Kolonial'naia politika Anglii na Dal'nem Vostoke v seredine XIX v.* (Moscow: Nauka, 1976), 65, 71.

83. A. Buksgevden, *Russkii Kitai: Ocherki diplomaticheskikh otnoshenii Rossii s Kitaem* (Port Arthur: Novyi Krai, 1902), 23, 57; Evans, *Russian Expansion*, vol. 1, 103. On Ignatiev's mission to China in 1859–60, see Vladimir Miasnikov, *Dogovornymi statýami utverzhdeny*, 264–94; and Vladimir Moiseev, *Rossiia i Kitai v Tsantral'noi Asii (vtoraia polovina XIX v.–1917 g.)* (Barnaul: Az Buka, 2003), 21–41.

84. See Khevrolina, *Rossiiskii diplomat*, 63–96.

85. AVPRI, f. 730, op. 1, d. 149, ll. 28 rev.–29.

86. Ibid, ll. 34, 50–50 rev.; Buksgevden, *Russkii Kitai*, 112–18.

87. Cited by Hopkirk, *Great Game*, 300.

88. On the mapping of Central and East Asia, including Priamur Province and Mongolia, by Russian explorers and scouts, see Mikhail Veniukov, *Iz vospominanii* (Amsterdam, 1895), vol. 1, 201–78.

89. Popov, "Iz istorii zavoevaniia Srednei Asii," 208.

90. Quoted by Khalfin, "Politika Rossii v Srednei Asii," 137.

91. A. G. Serebrennikov, comp., *Sbornik materialov po zavoevaniiu Turkestanskogo kraia* (Tashkent:Tipografiia Shtaba Turkestanskogo voennogo okruga, 1914–15), vol. 17, pt. 1, 68–75.

92. RGVIA, f. 483, op. 1, d. 66, ll. 1–24.

93. Zakharova, "Alexander II," 175.

94. AVPRI, f. 137, op. 475, d. 44, 1860, ll. 269–75.

95. GARF, f. 730, op. 1, d. 2170, l. 2, cited by Khevrolina, *Rossiiskii diplomat*, 116.

96. GARF, f. 730, op. 1, d. 507, ll. 4–5.

97. RGVIA, f. 447, op. 1, d. 5, l. 1 rev.

98. *The Times*, January 9, 1857.

99. Barbara Jelavich, *St Petersburg and Moscow: Tsarist and Soviet Foreign Policy, 1814–1974* (Bloomington: Indiana University Press, 1974), 171.

100. Arkhiv Instituta vostochnykh rukopisei Rossiskoi Akademii nauk (hereafter, AIVR RAN), f. 115, op. 1, d. 6, ll. 6–7, extract from the manuscript by Andrei Snesarev, *Rossiia i Angliia v Srednei Asiii i Indiia (Russia and England in Central Asia and India)* (Saint Petersburg, 1906); Roman Rosen, *Forty Years of Diplomacy*, 2 vols. (New York: Alfred A. Knopf, 1922), vol. 1, 37.

101. Quoted by E.V. Bunakov, "K voprosu o politicheskikh sviasiakh Rossii s Vostochnym Turkestanom v pravlenie Yakub-Bega (1865–1877)." *Akademiia nauk Uzbekskoi SSR. Bulletin*, no. 5 (1945): 21–24, at 22. On Obruchev's strategic views, see Oleg Airapetov, *Zabytaia kar'era 'Russkogo Moltke': Nikolai Nikolaevich Obruchev (1830–1904)* (Saint Petersburg: Aleteia, 1998), esp. 270.

102. For Gorchakov's memoranda on the Russian policies in Central Asia, see Serebrennikov, *Sbornik materialov*, vol. 19, pt. 1.

103. Quoted by Michael Edwardes, *Playing the Great Game* (London: Hamish Hamilton, 1975), 86.

104. Firuz Kazemzadeh, "Russia and the Middle East," in *Russian Foreign Policy. Essays in Historical Perspective*, edited by Ivo Lederer (New Haven, Conn.: Yale University Press, 1962), 495–96; David Mackenzie, "Expansion in Central Asia: St Petersburg vs. the Turkistan Generals (1863–1866)," *Canadian Slavic Studies* 3, no. 2 (1969): 286–311, at 289–90.

105. AIVR RAN, f. 115, op. 1, d. 6, l. 19.

106. Serebrennikov, *Sbornik materialov*, vol. 17, pt. 2, 196–201.

107. I. Strebelsky, "The Frontier in Central Asia," in *Studies in Russian Historical Geography*, vol. 1, edited by J. Bates and R. French (London: Academic Press, 1983), 169.

108. AVPRI, f. 133, op. 469, d. 78, 1864, ll. 470–74. For an English translation of this diplomatic circular, see IOLR/F132/37, 1–4. It is incorporated in the India Office Lyall Collection of documents, in a file titled "England and Russia in Asia, 1864–1907." One of the earliest publications of Gorchakov's circular letter was in a leaflet by Hubert Jerningham, *Russia's Warnings* (London: Chapman and Hall, 1885). For its modern interpretation, see Archibald Thornton, *Doctrines of Imperialism* (New York: J. Wiley and Sons, 1965), 65. Thornton arrived at a surprising conclusion: that the ideas articulated by Gorchakov laid down the foundations of the famous British "double mandate" concept in the League of Nations.

109. G. R. Aberigh-Mackay, [*Some*] *Notes on* [*the Situation in*] *Western Turkistan* (Calcutta: Thacker, Spink, 1875), 22.

110. For a detailed account and professional commentaries by eyewitnesses, see Romanovsky, *Zametki po sreneaziatskomu voprosu*, 123–91; and Konstantin Abaza, *Zavoevanie Turkestana: Rasskazy iz voennoi istorii, byta i nravov tuzemtsev v obtschedostupnom izlozhenii* (Saint Petersburg: M. Stasiulevich, 1902).

111. Dominic Lieven, ed., *British Documents on Foreign Affairs: Reports and Papers from*

the Foreign Office Confidential Print—Russia, 1859–1914 (Washington, D.C.: University Press of America, 1983–89), ser. A, pt 1, vol. 1, 93, memorandum by T. Michell, attaché to the British Embassy in Saint Petersburg, December 4, 1865.

112. AVPRI, f. 133, op. 469. d. 78, 1858, ll. 370–370 rev., Clarendon to Gorchakov, London, January 16, 1858.

113. IOLR/L&PS/5/256/3 rev., minutes by Lieutenant General Outram, Calcutta, January 4, 1860. According to John Le Donne, the duke of Wellington claimed as early as in 1829 that "the worst combination" Britain had any reason to dread might be "an alliance of France and Russia against her"; see John Le Donne, *The Russian Empire and the World, 1700–1917* (New York: Oxford University Press, 1997), 329.

114. PRO/ FO 65/ 867, no. 66.

115. Ben Hopkins, *The Myth of the "Great Game": The Anglo-Sikh Alliance and Rivalry,* Occasional Paper 5 (Cambridge: Centre of South Asian Studies, University of Cambridge, 2004), 17–18, 34.

116. Arminius Vambery, *His Life and Adventures* (London: T. Fisher Unwin, 1914), 308.

117. On the reorganization of the Anglo-Indian army, see Cotton, *Nine Years*, 311–52; Charlotte Macgregor, ed., *The Life and Opinions of Major General Sir Charles Metcalfe Macgregor.* 2 vols. (Edinburgh: W. Blackwood and Sons, 1888), 119–211. A more critical assessment is prevalent in a book by T. Moreman, *The Army in India and the Development of Frontier Warfare, 1849–1947* (London and New York: Macmillan and St. Martin's Press, 1998), 42–53.

118. Robert Johnson, *Spying for Empire: The Great Game in Central and South Asia, 1757–1947* (London: Greenhill Books, 2006), p. 28.

119. Gerald Morgan, "Myth and Reality in the Great Game," *Asian Affairs* 60 (new ser. 4), pt. I (1973): 55–65, at 58.

120. Ibid., 55.

121. Hopkins, *Myth*, 15. For a meticulous analysis of the intelligence process, especially see Christopher Bayly, *Empire and Information: Intelligence Gathering and Social Communication in India, 1780–1870* (Cambridge: Cambridge University Press, 1996), 10–55.

122. T. Escott, *The Story of British Diplomacy: Its Makers and Movements* (London: T. Fisher Unwin, 1908), 369; Richard Deacon, *A History of the British Secret Service* (New York: Taplinger, 1970), 123.

123. Bayly, *Empire and Information*, 365.

124. William Beaver, "The Development of the Intelligence Division and Its Role in Aspects of Imperial Policy Making, 1857–1901: The Military Mind of Imperialism," Ph.D. diss., Oxford University, 1976, 10.

125. Meyer and Brysac, *Tournament of Shadows*, 208; Jules Stewart, *Spying for the Raj: The Pundits and the Mapping of the Himalaya* (Phoenix Mill, U.K.: Sutton, 2006), 48–49.

126. Stewart, *Spying for the Raj*, 56; Derek Waller, *The Pundits: British Exploration of Tibet and Central Asia* (Lexington: University Press of Kentucky, 1990), 32.

127. To the modern perception of the pundits' activities, cited earlier in this book, may be added a concept developed by Richard Popplewell, *Intelligence and Imperial Defence: British Intelligence and the Defence of the Indian Empire, 1904–1924* (London: Frank Cass, 1995), 21–22.

128. Johnson, *Spying for Empire*, 116.

129. RGVIA, f. 400, op. 1, d. 4806, ll. 1–3 rev., memorandum by Veniukov, 1872. Some secret missions under discussion are also analyzed by Johnson, *Spying for Empire*, 98–117; and by Aleksei Postnikov, *Skhvatka na "Kryshe mira": Politiki, razvedchiki, geography v bor'be za Pamir v XIX veke* (Moscow: Ripol-Classik, 2005), 108–9.

CHAPTER 3

1. See D. I. Romanovsky, *Zametki po sredneaziatskomu voprosu* (Saint Petersburg: Tipografiia Vtorogo otdeleniia sobstvennoi kantseliiarii Ego Imperatorskogo Velichestva, 1868), x.

2. India Office Library and Records (hereafter, IOLR), L/P&S/5/19/413B–413B rev.

3. Ibid.

4. Arkhiv Vneshnei Politiki Rossiiskoi Imperii (hereafter, AVPRI), fond (f.; collection) 184, opis' (op.; inventory) 520, delo (d.; file) 269, listy (ll.; folios) 2–4.

5. Rossiskii gosudarstvennyi voenno-istoricheskii arkhiv (hereafter, RGVIA), f. 431, op. 1, d. 31, ll. 62–64 rev., Novitsky to the Main Staff, London, November 11, 1864.

6. Keith Jeffrey, "The Eastern Arc of Empire: A Strategic View, 1850–1950," *Journal of Strategic Studies* 5, no. 4 (1982): 531–45, at 543.

7. *The Times*, June 16, 1865.

8. For further information on Russian military campaigns against Khokand and Bokhara, see Sidney Cotton, *A Prophecy Fulfilled, 1869: The Central Asian Question* (Dublin and London: W. MacGee and Simpkin, Marshall, 1878); Lev Kostenko, "Istoricheskii ocherk rasprostraneniia russkogo vladychestva v Srednei Asii," *Voennyi sbornik*, no. 8 (1887): 145–78; no. 9: 5–37; no. 10: 139–60; no. 11: 5–35; A. I. Maksheev, *Istoricheskii obzor Turkestana i nastupatel'nogo dvizheniia v nego russkikh* (Saint Petersburg: Voennaiia tipografiia, 1890), 219–88; Giliary Siarkovsky, "O Turkestanskikh pokhodakh 1864–1865," *Voennyi sbornik* 197, no. 2 (1891): 357–81; 198, no. 3: 157–64; Mikhail Terentiev, *Istoriia zavoevaniia Srednei Asii*, 3 vols. (Saint Petersburg: V. Komarov, 1906), vol. 1, 336–425; A. G. Serebrennikov, comp., *Sbornik materialov po zavoevaniiu Turkestanskogo kraia* (Tashkent: Tipografiia Shtaba Turkestanskogo voennogo okruga, 1914–15), vols. 20 and 22; Alexander Popov, "Iz istorii zavoevaniia Srednei Asii," *Istoricheskie zapiski* 9 (1940): 198–242; and Naftula Khalfin, *Prisoedinenie Srednei Asii k Rossii (60–90-e gg. XIX v.)* (Moscow: Nauka, 1965). Valuable studies are presented by David Mackenzie, "Expansion

in Central Asia: St Petersburg vs. the Turkistan Generals (1863–1866)," *Canadian Slavic Studies* 3, no. 2 (1969): 286–311; and David Mackenzie, "Turkistan's Significance to Russia (1850–1917)," *Russian Review* 33, no. 2 (1974): 167–88.

9. Petr Pashino, *Turkestanskii krai v 1866 g. Putevye zametki* (Saint Petersburg: Tiblen, 1868), 82.

10. Terentiev, *Istoriuia zavoevaniia Srednei Asii*, vol. 1, 269–70.

11. Mikhail Veniukov, *Rossiia i Vostok: Sobranie geograficheskikh i politicheskikh statei* (Saint Petersburg: V. Bezobrazov, 1877), 173.

12. AVPRI, f. 138, op. 467, d. 5, ll. 1–41. This is a memorandum by Brunnov on the current alignment of political forces in Great Britain that was submitted for the consideration of Grand Duke Alexander, the heir to the Russian throne, London, April 29, 1864.

13. IOLR / Mss Eur F 90/3/16, Lawrence to Wood, Calcutta, May 27, 1865; Lawrence to Ripon, Calcutta, April 20, 1866. These letters are referred to in Sarvapalli-Gopal, *British Policy in India, 1858–1905* (Cambridge: Cambridge University Press, 1965), 46.

14. National Archives of the United Kingdom–Public Record Office (hereafter, PRO), FO 65/1212, Lawrence to Northcote, Simla, September 3, 1867. Interestingly, the annual report of 1864 by the Russian Foreign Ministry's Asian Department to the emperor indirectly testified to this assertion; see Veniukov, *Rossiia i Vostok*, 197; Popov, "Iz istorii zavoevaniia Srednei Asii," 226; and AVPRI, f. 137, op. 475, d. 53, ll. 217 rev.–221 rev.

15. Terentiev, *Istoriuia zavoevanoia Srednei Asii*, vol. 1, 425.

16. Seymour Becker, *Russia's Protectorates in Central Asia: Bokhara and Khiva, 1865–1924* (Cambridge, Mass.: Harvard University Press, 1968), 164. On the role of Bokharian Jews in the trade with Russia, see Vladimir N. Shkunov, "Bukharskie evrei i torgovye sviazi Rossii s khanstvami Srednei Asii vo vtoroi povine XVIII–XIX v.," *Vostok*, no. 4 (2010): 129–33.

17. Helene Carrère d'Encause, "Systematic Conquest," in *Central Asia, 130 Years of Russian Dominance: A Historical Overview*, edited by Edward Allworth (Durham, N.C.: Duke University Press, 1994), 132–33; Memet Yetisgin, "How the *Times of London* Covered and Interpreted Russian Expansion into Central Asia in the Second Half of the 19th Century," Ph.D. diss., Texas Technological University, 2000, 96–97.

18. PRO/FO 65/868, extract from the secret report, Saint Petersburg, May 14, 1865.

19. Dimitry Logofet, *Strana bespraviia: Bukharskoe khanstvo i ego sovremennoe sostoianie* (Saint Petersburg: V. Berezovskii, 1909), 18–19.

20. Mikhail Veniukov, *Opyt voennogo obozreniia russkikh granits v Asii* (Saint Petersburg: V. Berezovskii, 1873), 141.

21. Arminius Vambery, *Ocherki Srednei Asii* (Moscow: A. Mamontov, 1868), 172–88.

22. PRO/ FO 65/868, Buchanan to Russell, Saint Petersburg, September 12, 1865.

23. See Mackenzie, "Conquest," 208–34.

24. Mary Holdsworth, *Turkistan in the Nineteenth Century: A Brief History of the Khanates of Bukhara, Kokand and Khiva* (Oxford: Central Asian Research Institute, 1959), 55.

25. Serebrennikov, *Sbornik materialov*, vol. 20, pt. II, 127. Kryzhanovsky to Gorchakov, Orenburg, October 23, 1865.

26. A group of conservative politicians, headed by Prince Bariatinsky and Count Shuvalov, opposed the military reforms promoted by Dimitry Miliutin, whereas, for example, Mikhail Cherniaev, a very ambitious military commander, frequently came up against other "Turkestan generals"—Verevkin, Romanovsky, and Kryzhanovsky; see Otdel Pis'mennykh Istochnikov Gosudarstvennogo Istoricheskogo Muzeia (hereafter, OPI GIM), f. 208, op. 1, d. 6, ll. 15–16, 40–51; and Dimitry Miliutin, *Vospominaniia, 1865–1867* (Moscow: Rosspen, 2005), vol. 6, 343–44.

27. PRO/ FO 85/869.

28. Mackenzie, "Turkistan's Significance," 170–71.

29. Serebrennikov, *Sbornik materialov*, vol. 20, pt. II, 187–88, Kryzhanovsky to Cherniaev, Orenburg, November 14, 1865. On Cherniaev's military career in Central Asia, see David Mackenzie, *The Lion of Tashkent: The Career of General M. G. Cherniaev* (Athens: University of Georgia Press, 1974), 34–66.

30. Becker, *Russia's Protectorates*, 25–43.

31. AVPRI, f. 137, op. 475, d. 56, 1867, ll. 334–35; Anonymous, *Russian Advance in Asia, 1873* (London: War Office, 1873), 55–56; Popov, "Iz istorii zavoevaniia Srednei Asii," 215.

32. Miliutin, *Vospominaniia*, vol. 7, 58.

33. Alexander Lobanov-Rostovsky, *Russia and Asia* (Ann Arbor: George Wahr, 1951), 152.

34. Mikhail Veniukov, *Iz vospominanii*, 3 vols. (Amsterdam, 1895–1901), vol. 2, 162; Logofet, *Strana bespraviia*, 168.

35. OPI GIM, f. 307, op. 1, d. 15, ll. 31–32, 41, 71–72, memorandum by Major General Swistunov, August 27, 1870.

36. Veniukov, *Iz vospominanii*, vol. 2, 154–55.

37. OPI GIM, f. 307, op. 1, d. 24, l.5.

38. Khalfin, *Prisoedinenie Srednei Asii k Rossii*, 225–41; Alexander Vasiliev, "Vzaimootnosheniia Osmanskoi imperii i gosudarstv Tsentral'noi Asii v seredine XIX–nachale XX vv.," Kand. diss., Rossiiskaia akademiia gosudarstvennoi sluzhby, Moscow, 2007, 19–22; Yetisgin, "How the *Times* of London Covered and Interpreted Russian Expansion," 109–10.

39. Yetisgin, "How the *Times* of London Covered and Interpreted Russian Expansion," 112.

40. Serebrennikov, *Sbornik materialov*, vol. 17, pt. II, 211–21, memorandum by Stremoukhov, Saint Petersburg, December 1864.

41. Miliutin, *Vospominaniia*, vol. 7, 219–22; Popov, "Iz istorii zavoevaniia Srednei

Asii," 228. It should be noted that the fortress of Novo-Petrovsk was the first Russian stronghold on the Caspian eastern coast built up by Russian military engineers, as early as in 1854; see Romanovsky, *Zametki po sredneaziatskomu voprosu*, 5. Yet it was Krasnovodsk that assumed the status of the principal base for the advance to Trans-Caspia. A few years afterward, the fort of Chikishlar was erected on the delta of the Atrek River, an episode to which the British military observers also devoted attention for its strategic value in the course of the conquest of Central Asia; see *The Daily News*, April 24, 1873.

42. Veniukov, *Iz vospominanii*, vol. 2, 155; Mackenzie, "Turkistan's Significance," 173. The Russian statistics for 1868–75 revealed the following financial results of the Tsarist policy in Turkestan: receipts, 10,588,459 rubles; expenditures, 29,497,415 rubles; see PRO/FO 539/14, correspondence respecting Russian proceedings in Central Asia, 1874–77.

43. Rossiiskii gosudarstvennyi istoricheskii arkhiv (hereafter, RGIA), f. 954, op. 1, d. 112, l. 18 rev., memorandum by Kaufman, Tashkent, December 16, 1868. The same archival collection contains Kaufman's appeal to the townsfolk of Samarkand and the rural population in its suburbs in the Russian and Persian languages on May 4, 1868. By this proclamation, the Tsarist viceroy mandated the movement of tax payments from the emir's treasury to the budget of the Turkestan governor-generalship; see RGIA, f. 954, op. 1, d. 113, ll. 1–1 rev.

44. RGVIA, f. 483, op. 1, d. 91, ll. 1–11 rev., Kryzhanovsky to Reitern, Orenburg, October 1865. Arguably, in the opinion of another champion of Kaufman's policy—Mikhail Terentiev—the authentic sum of receipts amounted to 3,123,329 rubles while expenditures hardly came to 2,509,157 rubles, with a balance surplus of nearly 614,000 rubles in 1873, if the indemnity payments by Bokhara, Khokand, and Khiva to Russia were taken into account; see Mikhail Terentiev, *Rossiia i Angliia v Srednei Asii* (Saint Petersburg: P. Merkuriev, 1875), 312–13. For an analysis of these calculations, also see Mackenzie, "Turkistan's Significance," 174.

45. Becker, *Russia's Protectorates*, 58.

46. Otdel Rukopisei Rossiiskoi Gosudarstvennoi Biblioteki (hereafter, OR RGB), f. 169, op. 36, d. 36, ll. 1–2, Russell to Brunnov, London, September 16, 1865.

47. OPI GIM, f. 208, op. 1, d. 6, ll. 43–44, Cherniaev to Poltoratsky, Tashkent, December 20, 1865.

48. AVPRI, f. 184, op. 520, d. 296, ll. 8–9 rev., Brunnov to Gorchakov, London, November 9, 1866.

49. PRO/ FO 65/869/62-4, Buchanan to Clarendon, Saint Petersburg, November 28, 1866. As, e.g., Gorchakov admitted to Buchanan, the ambassador to Russia, in 1869, "Doubtless, there is a desire among Russian military men, who wish to gain decorations, that we should make further conquests in Central Asia." Interestingly, the British diplomat, in his turn, acknowledged that "if any circumstances should occur to disturb the present good understanding of two

governments, it could only come from the unauthorized action of officers on the frontiers"; see Anonymous, *Russia and England in Central Asia: A Problem* (New York: American Church Press, 1873), 5.

50. Quoted by Agatha Ramm, ed., *The Political Correspondence of Mr. Gladstone and Lord Granville, 1868–1876*, 2 vols. (London: Royal Historical Society, 1952), vol. 2, p. 433.

51. IOLR / Mss Eur C 144/9, Northbrook to Argyll, Calcutta, March 28, 1873.

52. Adrian Preston, "Sir Charles Macgregor and the Defense of India, 1857–1887," *Historical Journal* 12, no. 1 (1969): 58–77, at 65; also see W. Hunter, *A Life of the Earl of Mayo, Fourth Viceroy of India*, 2 vols. (London: Smith, Elder, 1875), vol. 2, 122–26.

53. Hunter, *Life of the Earl of Mayo*, vol. 1, 154–56, memorandum by Gladstone, London, November 10, 1870. On Russia's initiative to revise the Paris Peace Treaty of 1856, see V. P. Metschersky, *Moi vospominaniia*, 3 vols. (Saint Petersburg: V. Metschersky, 1897–1912), vol. 2, 135–36; P. Knaplund, *Gladstone's Foreign Policy* (London: Frank Cass, 1970), 63–64.

54. Anonymous, *Russia and England*, 13.

55. See Paul Kennedy, *Strategy and Diplomacy* (London: George Allen & Unwin, 1983), 13–39.

56. Hunter, *Life of the Earl of Mayo*, vol. 1, 272.

57. Cotton, *Prophecy Fulfilled*, 5.

58. Cited by Karl Meyer and Shareen Brysac, *Tournament of Shadows: The Great Game and the Race for Empire in Central Asia* (London: Abacus, 1999), 154.

59. IOLR/L&PS/18/C 4/1-20, memorandum by Rawlinson on the Central Asian question, London, July 20, 1868. For Russian commentaries on this document, see Leonid Bogdanovich, "Angliia i Rossiia v Srednei Asii," *Russkaia mysl'* 2 (1900): 139–61; 3: 19–29.

60. IOLR/L&PS/18/C 4/1-20, memorandum by Rawlinson.

61. Quoted by Michael Edwardes, *Playing the Great Game* (London: Hamish Hamilton, 1975), 95.

62. OR RGB, f. 169, op. 65, d. 25, ll. 13–14, Kaufman to Miliutin, Tashkent, March 7, 1872.

63. IOLR / Mss Eur F 111/115, *Correspondence Respecting the Relations between the British Government and That of Afghanistan since the Accession of the Emir Sher Ali Khan (1863–1878)* (London: Her Majesty's Stationery Office, 1878), 51.

64. Quoted by A. Ward and G. Gooch, eds., *The Cambridge History of British Foreign Policy, 1783–1919* (Cambridge: Cambridge University Press, 1923), vol. 3, 75.

65. Quoted by Hunter, *Life of the Earl of Mayo*, vol. 1, 279, 281.

66. IOLR/B 380/2. Mayo to Argyll, Simla, July 1, 1869.

67. IOLR/L&PS/18/C 5/3-7, note by Macleod, lieutenant governor of Punjab, Lahore, October 10, 1869.

68. Analysis by Tenderden of the papers presented to Parliament respecting Central Asia, London, November 30, 1879. A general course of negotiations was also

considered by O.T.B. [Bailey?] in the memorandum submitted to the attention of the India Office on November 31, 1881; see IOLR/L/P&S/18/c 31/1b.

69. IOLR/P&PS/18/A 147/1–8, correspondence on Russian assurances with regard to Afghanistan, 1869–85, Gorchakov to Brunnov, Saint Petersburg, March 7, 1869.

70. IOLR/L&PS/18/A 91/1–9, memorandum by the India Office Political and Secret Department on the Russo-Afghan boundary delimitation, London, May 2, 1893.

71. AVPRI, f. 184, op. 520, d. 328, ll. 14–15 rev., Gorchakov to Kaufman, Saint Petersburg, March 30, 1870.

72. PRO/FO 65/870, extracts from Russian and British periodicals, 1869.

73. Firuz Kazemzadeh, *Russia and Britain in Persia, 1864–1914* (New Haven, Conn.: Yale University Press, 1968), 25. A modern version of the Russo-British cooperation in Persia is given by Elena Andreeva, *Russia and Iran in the Great Game: Travelogues and Orientalism* (London: Routledge, 2007), chap. 4.

74. AVPRI, f. 137, op. 475, d. 61, 1870, ll. 288–89, annual report of the foreign minister to Alexander II, Saint Petersburg, December 1870.

75. Ibid., ll. 297–97 rev.; also see W. K. Fraser-Tytler, *Afghanistan: A Study of Political Developments in Central and Southern Asia* (London: Oxford University Press, 1967), 120–36.

76. Quoted by Terentiev, *Rossiia i Angliia v Srednei Asii*, 257, humble report by Gorchakov to Alexander II, Heidelberg, September 3, 1869. For current interpretations of the Afghan problem in the course of the Great Game, also see Sukash Chakravarty, *Afghanistan and the Great Game* (Delhi: New Century, 2002), 56.

77. Edwardes, *Playing*, 96; George Alder, *British India's Northern Frontier, 1865–95: A Study in Imperial Policy* (London: Longmans, 1963), 287–99.

78. PRO/FO 65/869, no. 311, Buchanan to Gorchakov, Saint Petersburg, July 2, 1869.

79. GARF, f. 677, op. 1, d. 454, l. 32, minutes by Kutaisov, London, October 1871.

80. John Le Donne, *The Russian Empire and the World, 1700–1917* (New York: Oxford University Press, 1997), 184.

81. Adrian Preston, "British Military Policy and the Defense of India, 1876–1880," Ph.D. diss., University of London, 1966, p. 32; Preston, "Sir Charles Macgregor," 62.

82. PRO/FO 65/870/112-117, government of India's memorandum on northern boundaries of Afghanistan, Simla, July 7, 1869. On Forsyth's negotiations with Gorchakov and Stremoukhov, see Douglas Forsyth, *Autobiography and Reminiscences* (London: Bentley, 1887), 43-53.

83. AVPRI, f. 147, op. 485, d. 1699, l. 4, review of the Russo-British negotiations on the affairs of Central Asia; ibid., f. 184, op, 520, d. 346, ll. 7 rev.–8, 37–40, Gorchakov to Kaufman, Saint Petersburg, November 4, 1871; ibid., f. 184, op. 520, d. 363, ll. 6–9, Granville to Loftus, London, January 24, 1873 (intercepted by Russian secret agents).

84. Popov, "Iz istorii zavoevaniia Srednei Asii," 226–27.

85. Frederick Roberts, *Forty-One Years in India from Subaltern to Commander-in-Chief*, 2 vols. (London: Macmillan, 1897), vol. 2, 46–47.

86. Quoted by J. Dutchie, "Some Further Insights into the Working of Mid-Victorian Imperialism: Lord Salisbury, the 'Forward' Group and Anglo-Afghan Relations, 1874-1878," *Journal of Imperial and Commonwealth History* 8, no. 3 (1980): 182–83; Kazemzadeh, *Russia and Britain*, 26–28.

87. AVPRI, f. 184, op. 520, d. 297, ll. 8–17, memorandum by Mackenzie, the former consul in Persia, to Brunnov, London, November 1, 1866; also see Alexander Popov, "Anglo-russkoe sopernichestvo na putiakh Irana," *Novyi Vostok* 12 (1926): 127–48.

88. See Aleksei Kuropatkin, *Kashgaria: Historical and Geographical Sketch of the Country—Its Military Strength, Industries and Trade* (Calcutta: Thacker, Spink, 1882), 21; and Jack Dabbs, *History of the Discovery and Exploration of Chinese Turkistan* (The Hague: Mouton, 1963).

89. The staff members of the Intelligence Branch in Simla could not identify the origins of the Dungans. According to their report, the latter "adopted the Chinese language, dress, customs and outward appearance, though taller, stronger, and better made. In religion the Dungans belong to the Sunni sect of Mohammedans"; see IOLR/L/Mil/17/14/74., W. Malleson, ed., *Military Report on Kashgaria prepared in the Division of the Chief of the Staff, Intelligence Branch* (Simla: Government Monotype Press, 1907), 94.

90. Demetrius Boulger, *The Life of Yakoob Beg, Athalik Ghazi and Badaulet, Emir of Kashgar* (London: W. Allen, 1878), 1–13, 14–21. For a contemporary analysis, see Le Donne, *Russian Empire*, 187; Vasily Petrov, *Miatezhnoe "serdtse" Asii: Sinkiang—kratkaia istoriia narodnykh dvizhenii i vospominaniia* (Moscow: Kraft+, 2003), 163–64; Alexander Kolesnikov, *Russkie v Kashgarii: Vtoraia polovina XIX—nachalo XX v. Missii, ekspeditsii, puteshestviia* (Pishkek: Raritet, 2006), 6.

91. Significantly, in 1866 the Anglo-Indian trade with Chinese Turkestan amounted to Rs 100,000, whereas by 1868 it had increased to Rs 1,038,000; see M. Baskhanov, "Politika Anglii v otnoshenii gosudarstva Yakub-Bega," in *Iz istorii mezhdunarodnykh otnoshenii v Tsentral'noi Asii (srednie veka i novoe vremya)*, edited by G. Iskhakov (Alma-Ata: Gylym, 1990), 110–11.

92. For a detailed analysis of these uprisings, see Owen Lattimore, *Inner Asian Frontiers of China* (London: Oxford University Press, 1940), 181–87. The origins of the Dungans rebellion were studied by A. K. Geins, "O vosstanii musul'manskogo naseleniia, ili dunganei, v Zapadnom Kitae," *Voennyi sbornik*, no. 8 (1866): 185–208, at 193. Also see Chu Wen-Djang, *The Moslem Rebellion in Northern China, 1862–1878: A Study of Government Minority Policy* (The Hague–Paris: Mouton, 1966), 18–23, 24–55; Chu Wen-Djang presents another version of how the insurrection broke out as a result of the armed clash between the Chinese and Uighur volunteers, who were committed by the local Qing authorities to counterattack a large gang of Taiping rebels at the approaches to the city of Kashgar.

93. S. Paine, *Imperial Rivals: Russia, China and Their Disputed Frontier, 1858–1924* (Armonk, N.Y.: M. E. Sharpe, 1996), 107–73.

94. RGVIA, f. 400, op. 1, d. 48, ll. 183–83 rev., Miliutin to Gorchakov, Saint Petersburg, September 28, 1866.

95. OPI GIM, f. 307, op. 1, d. 56, ll. 103–55, Povestvovanie Bega Kuli-bega o kashgarskom khane Yakub Bege. According to this record, Yakub Beg was born approximately in 1822–23. This narration was later translated and published by I. Pervyshev, comp., "Resale-i-Yakubi: Vospominaniia o Yakub-beke kashgarskom Kamil'-Khana-Ishana," *Istorik-Marxist*, no. 3 (1940): 127–35. The Uigur authentic sources on the uprising of 1864 and the later activity of Yakub Beg were reconsidered by K. Usmanov, "'Uigurskie istochniki o vosstanii v Sinkiange 1864 g." *Voprosy istorii*, no. 2 (1947): 87–89. Further information on this question is given by Daut Isiev, *The Uighur State of Yettishar (1864–1877)* (Moscow: Nauka, 1981), 53–54.

96. RGVIA, f. 400, op. 1, d. 48, ll. 189–222, note by Colonels Geins and Gutkovskii on the origins of the Dungans rebellion in Eastern Turkestan, Saint Petersburg, March 26, 1866. Apart from this work, information about Yakub Beg is given by Robert Michell, *Eastern Turkistan and Dzungaria and the Rebellion of the Dungans and Taranchis, 1862–1866* (London: E. Stanford, 1871); Nikolai Pantusov, *Voina musul'man protiv kitaitsev* (Kazan: Kazanskii universitet, 1881), vols. 1–2; Pavel Fesenko, *Istoriia Sinqianga* (Moscow: Institut vostokovedeniia, 1935), 79–120; Dimitry Tikhonov, "Vosstanie 1864 g. v Vostochnom Turkestane," *Sovetskoe vostokovedenie* 5 (1948): 155–72; M. Sushanlo, "Dunganskoe vosstanie vtoroi poviny XIX v. i rol' v nem Bai Yanhu," Kand. diss., Institut vostokovedeniia AN SSSR, 1953; V. A. Moiseev, *Rossiiai i Kitai v Tsentral'noi Asii (vroraia polovina XIX v.–1917 g.)* (Barnaul: Az Buka, 2003), 42–66; and Hodong Kim, *Holy War in China: The Muslim Rebellion and State in Chinese Central Asia, 1864–1877* (Stanford, Calif.: Hoover Institution Press, 2004).

97. Louis Frechtling, "Anglo-Russian Rivalry in Eastern Turkistan, 1863–1881," *Journal of the Royal Central Asian Society* 26, pt. 3 (1939): 471–89, at 473.

98. Moiseev, *Rossiiai i Kitai*, 42–66.

99. Arminius Vambery, *Central Asia and the Anglo-Russian Frontier Question: A Series of Political Papers* (London: E. Smith, 1874), 156.

100. On the claims of British commercial associations to the home Cabinet, see Alastair Lamb, *Britain and Chinese Central Asia: The Road to Lhasa, 1767–1905* (London: Routledge & Kegan Paul, 1960), 125. Diplomatic maneuvers by Russia, Britain, and China are thoroughly investigated by Richard Pierce, *Russian Central Asia, 1867–1917: A Study in Colonial Rule* (Berkeley: University of California Press, 1960), 27–28.

101. RGVIA, f. 400, op. 1, d. 48, l. 21, Khrutschov to Miliutin, Omsk, January 6, 1866.

102. Ibid., ll. 347–51 rev., Pavlinov to Stremoukhov, Kuldja, February 1, 1867.

103. Ibid., d. 4774, ll. 1–10 rev., memorandum by Vorontsov-Dashkov on the Russian

position in Central Asia, 1867.

104. Robert Johnson, *Spying for Empire: The Great Game in Central and South Asia, 1757–1947* (London: Greenhill Books, 2006), 110.

105. Quoted by A. Akhmetzhanov, "Agressivnye ustremleniia angliiskogo kapitalizma v Zapadnom Kitae v 60-e–70-e gg. XIX v.," *Alma-Atinskii pedagogicheskii institut im. Abaia: Uchenye zapiski* 11, no. 1 (1956): 141–54, 144.

106. For further detailed information on Hayward's mission, see John Keay, *Where Men and Mountains Meet: The Explorers of the Western Himalayas, 1820–1875* (London: John Murray, 1977), 224.

107. PRO/FO 65/871, memorandum by Robert Michell, March 25, 1870.

108. A modern reassessment of this and other missions is given by Peter Hopkirk, *The Great Game: On Secret Service in High Asia* (London: John Murray, 1990), 324–29; and Johnson, *Spying for Empire*, 110–23.

109. RGVIA, f. 400, op. 1, d. 126, ll. 31–39, Gorchakov to Miliutin, Saint Petersburg, December 9, 1868.

110. George Henderson and Allan Hume, *Lahore to Yarkand: Incidents of the Route and Natural History of the Countries Traversed by the Expedition of 1870 under T. D. Forsyth* (Lahore: Niaz Akhmad, 1981), 7.

111. Forsyth, *Autobiography*, 54–89; Popov, "Iz istorii zavoevaniia Srednei Asii," 235. For further fragmental nuggets of information on this trip, see Great Britain, Parliament, *Forsyth's Mission: Extracts of Correspondence Relating to the Mission of Mr. Douglas Forsyth to Yarkand* (London: Her Majesty's Stationery Office, 1871).

112. Terentiev, *Rossiia i Angliia v Srednei Asii*, 137–38; Isiev, *Uighur State*, 41–42.

113. Donald Rayfield, *The Dream of Lhasa: The Life of Nikolai Przhevalsky (1839–88), Explorer of Central Asia* (London: P. Elek, 1976), 93. Rayfield points out that Yakub Beg's chief minister, Zaman Beg, camouflaged his pro-Russian position with the pro-Turkish declarations; see Vasiliev, "Vzaimootnosheniia Osmanskoi imperii," 23–24.

114. Miliutin, *Vospominaniia*, vol. 7, 332.

115. Le Donne, *Russian Empire*, 188–89.

116. RGVIA, f. 400, op. 1, d. 292, ll. 1–5 rev., Gorchakov to Miliutin, Saint Petersburg, November 3, 1871.

117. Ibid., d. 128, ll. 315–16, Khrutschov, the governor-general of Western Siberia, to Miliutin, Omsk, October 22, 1870; RGIA, f. 954, op. 1, d. 116, ll. 1–11, note by Kaufman on the plan of military operations in China, Tashkent, June 20, 1871. On the Ili crisis, see Pierce, *Russian Central Asia*, 28–29; Dinara Dubrovskaia, *Sud'ba Sinkianga: Obretenie Kitaem "novoi granitsy" v kontse XIX v.* (Moscow: Institut vostokovedeniia, 1998), 131–64; Le Donne, *Russian Empire*, 188–89; and Moiseev, *Rossiiai i Kitai*, 116–33.

118. RGVIA, f. 165, op. 1, d. 195, ll. 9–12 rev., draft amendments by Lieutenant General Kolpakovsky to the agreement signed by Captain Kaulbars with Yakub Beg, June 20, 1872. Also see Alexander Kaul'bars, "Zametki o Kul'dzhinskom

krae," in *Materialy dlia statistiki Turkestanskogo kraia*, vol. 3 (Saint Petersburg: K. Trubnikov, 1874), 115–49; Boulger, *Life of Yakoob Beg*, 192–94; Miliutin, *Vospominaniia*, vol. 7, 541; and Fesenko, *Istoriia Sinkianga*, 118–19.

119. RGVIA, f. 165, op. 1, d. 195, l. 6 rev.

120. Kostenko, "Istoricheskii ocherk rasprostraneniia russkogo vladychestva," 147.

121. Quoted by Chu Wen-Djang, *Moslem Rebellion*, 175.

122. Derek Waller, *The Pundits: British Exploration of Tibet and Central Asia* (Lexington: University Press of Kentucky, 1990), 144–68. On Forsyth's second mission to Kashgaria, especially see Douglas Forsyth, *Report of a Mission to Yarkand in 1873* (Calcutta: Foreign Department Press, 1875); Forsyth, *Autobiography*, 90–126; Henry Bellew, *Kashmir and Kashgar: A Narrative of the Journey of the Embassy to Kashgar in 1873–7* (London: Truebner, 1875); Frechtling, "Anglo-Russian Rivalry," 481–83; Isiev, *Uighur State*, 43–46; Baskhanov, "Politika Anglii," 120–21; S. Kliashtornyi, A. Kolesnikov, and M. Baskhanov, *Vostochnyi Turkestan glazami evropeiskikh puteshestvennikov* (Alma-Ata: Gylym, 1991), 44–76; and Aleksei Postnikov, *Skhvatka na "kryshe mira": Politiki, razvedchiki, generally v bor'be za Pamir v XIX v.* (Moscow: Ripol-Klassik, 2005), 138–57.

123. AVPRI, f. 137, op. 475, d. 69, 1874, ll. 209–10.

124. IOLR/L&PS/18/72, memorandum by Hertslet on the Russian advance in Eastern Turkestan, London, January 21, 1873, 1–10.

125. Preston, "Sir Charles Macgregor," 67.

126. Cited by W. Habberton, *Anglo-Russian Relations Concerning Afghanistan, 1837–1907* (Urbana: University of Illinois Press, 1937), 88.

127. RGVIA, f. 165, op. 1, d. 4807, ll. 1–12; Bogdanovich, "Angliia i Rossiia," 142.

128. *The Hansard Parliamentary Debates* (London: C. Buck, 1908), 1873, series 3, vol. 215, cols. 873–74; *The Times*, April 23, 1873.

129. PRO/FO 65/875, memorandum by Michell, Saint Petersburg, January 20, 1873. On the reaction of British leadership circles, see Alder, *British India's Northern Frontier*, 165–89; L. Morris, "Anglo-Russian Relations in Central Asia, 1873–1887," Ph.D. diss., University of London, 1968, 35; and Marina Aisenshtat and Tamara Gella, *Angliiskie partii i kolonial'naia imperiia Velikobritanii v XIX v. (1815–seredina 1870-h gg.)* (Moscow: Institut vseobtschei istorii RAN, 1999), 194.

130. Augustus Loftus, *The Diplomatic Reminiscences, 1837–1862*, 2 vols. (London: Cassell, 1892), vol. 2, 55; also see Habberton, *Anglo-Russian Relations*, 35; and Nina Kiniapina, "Sredniaia Asiia vo vneshnepoliticheskikh planakh tsarisma (50-e–80-e gg. XIX v.)," *Voprosy istorii*, no. 2 (1974): 36–51, at 46–47.

131. Quoted by Yetisgin, "How the *Times* of London Covered and Interpreted Russian Expansion," 114.

132. OPI GIM, f. 307, op. 1, d. 10, ll. 52–53, letter by a Russian slave from Khiva, 1872.

133. G. R. Aberigh-Mackay, [*Some*] *Notes on* [*the Situation in*] *Western Turkistan* (Calcutta: Thacker, Spink, 1875), 41.

134. OPI GIM, f. 307, op. 1, d. 10, ll. 78–94, 96–117 rev., 124–50. On the draft of

a military campaign against Khiva submitted to the War Ministry, see Mikhail Skobelev, "Posmertnye bumagi," *Istoricheskii vestnik* 10, no. 10 (1882): 109–38; no. 11: 275–94, at 131–38. For further information on Kaufman's contribution to the expedition, see Evgeny Glutschenko, *Geroi Imperii: Portrety rossiiskikh kolonial'nykh deiatelei* (Moscow: XXI v.–Soglasie, 2001), 78 ff.

135. The futility of these attempts may be seen in *The Times*, November 19, 1872. Interestingly, the shah of Persia even interceded with the tsar for his troops as auxiliary forces being able to join the Russians in the campaign against Khiva; see AVPRI, f. 137, op. 475, d. 66, 1873, ll. 196–97 rev., annual humble report by the foreign minister to the tsar, Saint Petersburg, 1873; OPI GIM, f. 307, op. 1, d. 10, ll. 58–58 rev., Kaufman to Said Mohamed Khan, Tashkent, June 11, 1873.

136. Miliutin, *Vospominaniia*, vol. 7, 543.

137. For a description of the military campaign against Khiva, see Kostenko, "Istoricheskii ocherk rasprostraneniia russkogo vladychestva," 20–37, 139–60; Maksheev, *Istoricheskii obzor Turkestana*, 313–26; Terentiev, *Istoriia zavoevaniia Srednei Asii*, vol. 2; and Becker, *Russia's Protectorates*, 65–78.

138. Gerald Morgan, *Anglo-Russian Rivalry in Central Asia: 1810–1895* (London: Frank Cass, 1981), 132.

139. PRO/FO 539/11, correspondence respecting Central Asia, 1873–74; OPI GIM, f. 307, op. 1, d. 14, ll. 1–286, collection of diaries and memories penned by the officers who participated in the military campaign against Khiva, 1873; Yetisgin, "How the *Times* of London Covered and Interpreted Russian Expansion," 120–23.

140. *The Times*, June 26, 1873.

141. Francis Trench, *The Russo-Indian Question, Historically, Strategically, and Politically Considered* (London: Macmillan, 1869), 151.

142. See Veniukov, *Iz vospominanii*, vol. 2, 228.

143. Arminius Vambery, *Sketches of Central Asia* (London: W. Allen, 1868), 33.

144. F. Wellesley, *With the Russians in Peace and War: Recollections of a Military Attaché in Russia* (London: E. Nash, 1905), 299–300.

145. RGVIA, f. 483, op. 1, d. 95, ll. 4–5, Cherniaev to Kryzhanovsky, Tashkent, December 7, 1865; Serebrennikov, *Sbornik materialov*, vol. 21, pt. 1, 310–11, Romanovsky to Kryzhanovsky, Tashkent, July 5, 1866. On the missions of Indian Maharajas to Russia, see Naftula A. Khalfin, *Missii iz Indii v Rossiiu vo vtoroi polovine XIX v.* (Moscow: Vostochnaia literatura, 1963); Petr Shastitko, ed., *Russko-indiiskie otnosheniia v XIX v. Sbornik arkhivnykh dokumentov i materialov* (Moscow: Vostochnaia literatura, 1997), 88.

146. Quoted by Aberigh-Mackay, [*Some*] *Notes*, 91.

147. Trench, *Russo-Indian Question*, 150.

148. See, e.g., Alexander Halliday, *The Retention of India* (London: Tinsley Brothers, 1872), 143–44; Aberigh-Mackay, [*Some*] *Notes*, 58; Anonymous, *Russian Advance*, 49–54; and Richard Temple, *Men and Events of My Time in India* (London: John Murray, 1882), 93.

149. Vambery, *Sketches*, 58–59. The same view was reflected in a brochure by Colonel Henry Green, the superintendent and later commander of the northwest frontier of Sind; see Henry Green, *The Defence of the North-West Frontier of India with Reference to the Advance of Russia in Central Asia* (London: Harrison, 1873), 1–36.

150. Richard Deacon, *A History of the British Secret Service* (New York: Taplinger, 1970), 123–24; B. Parritt, *The Intelligencers: The History of the British Military Intelligence up to 1914* (Ashford, U.K.: Intelligence Corps Association, 1971), 97–99; Thomas Fergusson, *British Military Intelligence, 1870–1914: The Development of a Modern Intelligence Organization* (Frederick, Md.: University Publications of America, 1984), 15–34; Christopher Andrew, *Secret Service: The Making of the British Intelligence Community* (London: Heinemann, 1985), 11.

151. William Beaver, "The Development of the Intelligence Division, and Its Role in Aspects of Imperial Policy Making, 1854–1901: The Military Mind of Imperialism," Ph.D. diss., University of Oxford, 1976, iii–iv, 26–27.

152. Especially see Mohammad Anwar Khan, *England, Russia and Central Asia (A Study in Diplomacy), 1857–1878* (Peshawar: University Book Agency, 1963), 54; Preston, "British Military Policy," 72, 76–77; Preston, "Sir Charles Macgregor," 64–69; Edwardes, *Playing*, 125–27; Peter Burroughs, "Imperial Defense and the Victorian Army," *Journal of Imperial and Commonwealth History* 15, no. 1 (1986): 55–72; Christopher Bayly, *Empire and Information: Intelligence Gathering and Social Communication in India, 1780–1870* (Cambridge: Cambridge University Press, 1996), 365–69; Waller, *Pundits*, 193–208; Ian Barrow, *Making History, Drawing Territory: British Mapping in India, c. 1756–1905* (New Delhi: Oxford University Press, 2003), 18–50; Johnson, *Spying for Empire*, 118–50; and Jules Stewart, *Spying for the Raj: The Pundits and the Mapping of the Himalaya* (Phoenix Mill, U.K.: Sutton, 2006), 50–71.

153. Ch. V. Gal'kov, "Turkestanskii voenno-topographicheskii otdel i ego raboty po kartographirovaniiu Srednei Asii (1867-1914)," Kand. diss., Sredneasiatskii gosudarstvennyi universitet, 1958, 54; Mikhail Ryzhenkov, "Rol' voennogo vedomstava Rossii v razvitii otechestvennogo vostokovedeniia (XIX–nachalo XX v.), Kand. diss.‚ Indtitut vostokovedeniia, 1991, 11; A. A. Vigasin, ed., *Istoriia otechestvennogo vostokovedeniia s serediny XIX v. do 1917 g.* (Moscow: Vostochnaia literatura, 1997), 141–42.

CHAPTER 4

1. Demetrius Boulger, *England and Russia in Central Asia* (London: Allen, 1879), vol. 1, 90.

2. Alexander Mediakov, *Istoriia mezhdunarodnykh otnoshenii v novoe vremya* (Moscow: Prosvetschenie, 2007), 394.

3. Christopher Howard, *Splendid Isolation: A Study of Ideas Concerning Britain's International Position and Foreign Policy during the Latter Years of the Third Marquis of Salisbury* (London: Macmillan, 1967), 76.

4. Quoted by Robert Blake, *Disraeli* (London: Eyre and Spottiswoode, 1966), 577.

5. Henry Pirbright, *England's Policy in the East* (London: Chapman and Hall, 1877), 91.

6. Sergei Korff, *Russia's Foreign Relations during the Last Half Century* (London: Macmillan, 1922), 29–30.

7. Roundell Palmer, ed., *Earl of Selborne, Lord High Chancellor: Memorials Personal and Political, 1865–1895* (London: Macmillan, 1898), pt. 2, vol. 1, 444–58. On a comparative analysis of Disraeli's political course by British and Russian historians, see Blake, *Disraeli*; C. Eldridge, *England's Mission: The Imperial Idea in the Age of Gladstone and Disraeli* (Chapel Hill: University of North Carolina Press, 1974); Igor' Parfenov, *Kolonial'naia ekspansiia Velikobritanii v poslednei treti XIX v. (dvizhutschie sily, formy i metody)* (Moscow: Nauka, 1991); and Vladimir Trukhanovsky, *Benjamin Disraeli, ili istoriia odnoi neveroiatnoi kar'ery* (Moscow: Nauka, 1993).

8. See, N. S. Kiniapina, M. M. Bliev, and V. V. Degoev, eds., *Kavkaz i Sredniaia Asiia vo vneshnei politike Rossii: Vtoraia polovina XVIII v.–80-e gg. XIX v.* (Moscow: Moscow State University, 1984), 304.

9. Nikolai Tcharykov, *Glimpses of High Politics* (London: George Allen & Unwin, 1931), 159.

10. Henry Rawlinson, *England and Russia in the East: A Series of Papers on the Political and Geographical Condition of Central Asia* (London: John Murray, 1875), 134.

11. Rossiiskii Gosudarstvennyi Voenno-Istoricheskii Arkhiv (hereafter, RGVIA), fond (f.; collection) 431, opis' (op.; inventory) 1, delo (d.; file) 44, listy (ll.; folios) 10–15, Kutaisov to Miliutin, London, March 4, 1873. The reaction of various sections of the leadership circles to how Russia and Britain rivaled each other in the Middle East is analyzed by Tamara Gella, "Politicheskie krugi Velikobritanii o russko-angliiskom sopernichestve na Srednem Vostoke (60-e–nachalo 70-kh gg. XIX v.)," in *Rossiia i Evropa: Diplomatiia i kul'tura*, edited by A. Chubarian (Moscow: Nauka, 1995), 117–28.

12. Edward Cazalet, *England's Policy in the East: Our Relations with Russia and the Future of Syria* (London: E. Stanford, 1879), iii–iv.

13. Ibid., 18. Charles Marvin, a correspondent to *The Newcastle Weekly Chronicle* and *The Army and Navy Magazine*, argued that the reconstruction of the old riverbed of the Oxus would greatly contribute to the aggrandizement of Russian power in the Middle East; see Charles Marvin, *Reconnoitering Central Asia: Pioneering Adventures in the Region Lying between Russia and India* (London: Sonnenschein, 1884), 215.

14. D. A. Miliutin, *Dnevnik*, 4 vols. (Moscow: OR RGB, 1947–50), vol. 1, 181. For further information on Russian railway projects, see Petr Shastitko, ed., *Russko-indiiskie otnosheniia v XIX v. Sbornik arkhivnykh dokumentov i materialov* (Moscow: Vostochnaia literatura, 1997), 155–63.

15. Boulger, *England and Russia*, vol. 2, 124–25.

16. Richard Popplewell, *Intelligence and Imperial Defense: British Intelligence and the Defense of the Indian Empire, 1904–1924* (London: Frank Cass, 1995), 36.

17. Owen Lattimore, *Inner Asian Frontiers of China* (London: Oxford University Press, 1940), 235.

18. Ibid., 236. See also Arutiun A. Ulunian, "Britanskii konzept 'etnopoliticheskogo prostranstva' v 'Bol'shoi Igre' i ego krushenie (70-e–80-e gg. XIX v.)," *Istoricheskoe prostranstvo: Problemy istorii stran SNG*, no. 1 (2009): 175–90.

19. Gosudarstvennyi Arkhiv Rossiiskoi Federatsii (hereafter, GARF), f. 678, op. 1, d. 453, l. 99, note by Veniukov, 1874; Mikhail Veniukov, *Rossiia i Vostok* (Saint Petersburg: V. Bezobrazov, 1877), 259; Mikhail Annenkov, *Akhal-Tekinskii oazis i puti v Indiiu* (Saint Petersburg: Tipographiia Peterburgskogo voennogo okruga, 1881), 6.

20. F. Hellwald, *Die Russen in Centralasien: Eine geographisch-historische Studie* (Vienna: Verlag des Verfassers, 1869), 99–100. Petr Pashino, who combined his activity as a journalist with commitments as an intelligence agent, and Ivan Minaev, a professor at Saint Petersburg University, who repeatedly visited India in 1873–79 and 1880–86, summarized impressions of the trips in their essays; see Petr Pashino, *Vokrug sveta. Po Indii: Putevye vpechatleniia* (Saint Petersburg: A. Suvorin, 1885), vol. 1; and Ivan Minaev, *Dnevniki puteshestvii v Indiiu i Birmu, 1880 i 1885-6 gg.* (Moscow: Izdatel'stvo AN SSSR, 1955). The hidden agenda of these travels is exposed by Charles Marvin, *Reconnoitering Central Asia: Pioneering Adventures in the Region Lying between Russia and India* (London: W. Sonnesheim, 1884), 252–63; Shastitko, *Russko-indiiskie otnosheniia*, 165–77, 181–98. Also see RGVIA, f. 431, op. 1, d. 54, ll. 13–15, the war minister's instructions to Professor Minaev, Saint Petersburg, December 1879.

21. Some Russian historians still share the traditional Soviet concept of the catastrophic results of the British colonial rule in India in comparison with the "progressive mission" carried on by the Tsarist administration in Central Asia; e.g.,, see L. N. Khariukov, *Anglo-russkoe sopernichestvo v Tsentral'noi Asii i ismailism* (Moscow: Moscow State University, 1995), 15–16.

22. Mark Mancall, "The Ch'ing Tribute System: An Interpretive Essay," in *The Chinese World Order: Traditional China's Foreign Relations*, edited by J. Fairbank (Cambridge, Mass.: Harvard University Press, 1968), 82.

23. Feodor Martens, *Rossiia i Angliia v Srednei Asii* (Saint Petersburg: E. Gartier, 1880), 8.

24. A British Subject, *The Great Game: A Plea for a British Imperial Policy* (London: Simpkin, Marshall, 1875), 174–75.

25. India Office Library and Records (hereafter, IOLR), Mss Eur C 144/11, Salisbury to Northbrook, London, July 17, 1874.

26. Ibid., Salisbury to Northbrook, London, May 22, 1874.

27. Quoted by V. G. Trukhanovsky, *Bendjamin Disraeli, ili istoriia odnoi neveroiatnoi kariery* (Moscow: Nauka, 1993), 314–15; also see James Morris, *Pax Britannica: The Climax of an Empire* (London: Faber & Faber, 1968), 75.

28. IOLR / Mss Eur C 144/11, Salisbury to Northbrook, London, November 12, 1874.

29. Boulger, *England and Russia*, vol. 2, 368.

30. IOLR/L&PS/18/C 13, memorandum by Bellew, London, June 24, 1875; *The Times*, February 17 and March 1, 1876; Richard Temple, *Men and Events of My Time in India* (London: John Murray, 1882), 93–94; Memet Yetisgin, "How the *Times* of London Covered and Interpreted Russian Expansion into Central Asia in the Second Half of the 19th Century," Ph.D. diss., Texas Technological University, 2000, 139.

31. Helene Carrère d'Encause, "Systematic Conquest," in *Central Asia, 130 Years of Russian Dominance: A Historical Overview*, edited by Edward Allworth (Durham, N.C.: Duke University Press, 1994), 146.

32. Demetrius Boulger, *Central Asian Portraits: The Celebrities of the Khanates and the Neighbouring States* (London: W. Allen, 1880), 184.

33. Aleksei Kuropatkin, *Kashgaria: Historical and Geographical Sketch of the Country— Its Military Strength, Industries and Trade* (Calcutta: Thacker, Spink, 1882), 5.

34. For the most comprehensive firsthand account of the Khokandian war, see A. I. Maksheev, *Istoricheskii obzor Turkestana i nastupatel'nogo dvizheniia v nego russkikh* (Saint Petersburg: Voennaia tipografiia, 1890), 329–50.

35. Arkhiv Vneshnei Politiki Rossiiskoi Imperii (hereafter, AVPRI), f. 137, op. 475, d. 73, 1875, ll. 247 rev.–262; *The Times*, May 8, 1876.

36. RGVIA, f. 400, op. 1, d. 488, l. 1, Vasiliev to Miliutin, Saint Petersburg, November 20, 1876.

37. Ibid., ll. 2–2 rev.

38. Mikhail Veniukov, "Mezhdunarodnye voprosy v Asii," *Russkii vestnik*, no. 6 (1877): 499.

39. Mikhail Veniukov, *Opyt voennogo obozreniia russkikh granits v Asii*, 2 vols. (Saint Petersburg: V. Bezobrazov, 1873–76), vol. 1, 381. A detailed telling of Veniukov's geopolitical studies is presented by Anatoly V. Remnev, "U istokov rossiiskoi imperskoi geopolitiki: Aziatskoe 'pogranichnoe prostranstvo' v issledovaniiakh M. I. Veniukova," *Istoricheskie zapiski*, 4, no. 122 (2001): 344–69.

40. Aleksei Kuropatkin, *Russko-kitaiskii vopros* (Saint Petersburg: Novoe Vremya, 1913), 87.

41. Otdel Pis'mennykh Istochnikov Gosudarstvennogo Istoricheskogo Muzeia (hereafter, OPI GIM), f. 307, op. 1, d. 44, ll. 1–2, Kaufman to Yakub Beg, Tashkent, July 12, 1875; V. S. Kadnikov, "Iz istorii Kul'dzhinskogo voprosa," *Istoricheskii vestnik* 124, no. 6 (1911): 893–909, at 896; RGVIA, f. 846, op. 1, d. 6823, l. 261, minutes by Stremoukhov to Geiden, Saint Petersburg, June 7, 1870.

42. Kuropatkin, *Kashgaria*, 4–5.

43. E.g., see Bronislav Grombchevsky, *Otchet o poezdke v Kashgar i iuzhnuiu Kashgariiu v 1885* (Novyi Margellan: Shtab Turkestanskogo voennogo okruga, 1886), 112; Richard Pierce, *Russian Central Asia, 1867–1917: A Study in Colonial Rule* (Berkeley: University of California Press, 1960), 28–29.

44. RGVIA, f. 165, op. 1, d. 222, ll. 1–10 rev., draft report by Kuropatkin to Kaufman

and the Main Staff, Tashkent, October 1876.

45. D. A. Isiev, *Uigurskoe gosudarstvo Yettishar (1864–1877)* (Moscow: Nauka, 1981), 45–46; M. Baskhanov, "Politika Anglii v otnoshenii gosudarstva Yakub-Bega," in *Iz istorii mezhdunarodnykh otnoshenii v Tsentral'noi Asii (srednie veka i novoe vremya),* edited by G. Iskhakov (Alma-Ata: Gylym, 1990), 126–27.

46. Demetrius Boulger, *The Life of Yakoob Beg, Athalik Ghazi and Badaulet, Amir of Kashgar* (London: W. Allen, 1878), 211–35; Edmund Clubb, *China and Russia: The "Great Game"* (New York: Columbia University Press, 1971), 115; A. A. Kolesnikov, *Russkie v Kashgarii (vtoraia polovina XIX–nachalo XX v.): Missii, ekspeditsii, puteshestviia* (Pishpek: Raritet, 2006), 133–41.

47. Quoted by Anonymous, *Russia and England in Central Asia: A Problem* (New York: American Church Press, 1873), 14.

48. GARF, f. 730, op. 1, d. 433, l. 2 rev., minutes by Ignatiev, June 1881; see also Louis Frechtling, "Anglo-Russian Rivalry in Eastern Turkistan, 1863–1881," *Journal of the Royal Central Asian Society* 26, pt. 3 (1939): 471–89, at 485.

49. The British intelligence officers investigated the sudden death of Yakub Beg in a memorandum to the India Office dated January 1907. According to the reliable accounts of eyewitnesses, on May 28, 1877, Yakub Beg became greatly exasperated with his secretary, Hamal, whom he killed with the butt end of his gun. He then set upon his treasurer, Sabir Akhem, whom he also began to beat. In the conflict, the emir received a blow that rendered him senseless and from which he died on May 29. The stories that Yakub Beg was poisoned by his son or that he himself took poison after he was defeated by the Qing army seem groundless; see IOLR/L/MIL/17/14/74, 173.

50. Quoted by Kadnikov, "Iz istorii Kul'dzhinskogo voprosa," 899.

51. National Archives of the United Kingdom–Public Record Office (hereafter, PRO), FO 418/10/1, correspondence respecting the Russo-Chinese Treaty, 1878–80, pt. 1; see also Lattimore, *Inner Asian Frontiers,* 27; Immanuel Hsue, *The Ili Crisis: A Study of Sino-Russian Diplomacy, 1871–1881* (Oxford: Clarendon Press, 1965), 11–12.

52. Hsue, *Ili Crisis,* 123.

53. On the negotiations about the restitution of the Ili District, see Hsue, *Ili Crisis,* 153–70; Aleksei Voskresensky, *Diplomaticheskaia istoriia russko-kitaiskogo Sankt-Peterburgskogo dogovora 1881 g.* (Moscow: Pamiatniki istoricheskoi mysli, 1995); and V. A. Moiseev, *Rossiia i Kitai v Tsentral'noi Asii (vroraia polovina XIX v.–1917 g.)* (Barnaul: Az Buka, 2003), 171–210.

54. Voskresensky, *Diplomaticheskaia istoriia,* 112. For a slightly reconsidered version, see Aleksei Voskresensky, *Kitai i Rossiia v Evrasii: Istoricheskaia dinamika politicheskikh vzaimovliianii* (Moscow: Muravei, 2004), 9–202.

55. J. Bland, *Li Hung-Chang* (London: Archibald Constable, 1917), 189–90.

56. For further details of the Ili crisis, see Edwin Bilof, "China in Imperial Russian Military Planning, 1881–1887," *Military Affairs* 46 (1982): no. 2, 69–75.

57. Rossiiskii Gosudarstvennyi Arkhiv Voenno-Morskogo Flota (hereafter, RGA VMF), f. 410, op. 2, d. 4040, ll. 18–18 rev., Gorlov to Miliutin, London, November 13, 1877. On November 1, 1876, twelve Irish high-ranking nationalists offered their assistance to the Tsarist government in the coming war with Britain; see RGA VMF, f. 410, op. 2, d. 4048, ll. 34–35.

58. Ibid., ll. 1–15, Semechkin to the Main Naval Staff, Saint Petersburg, March 1878.

59. Ibid., d. 4040, ll. 40–40 rev. Admiral Petschurov, the acting naval minister, to Lesovsky, Saint Petersburg, January 12, 1878.

60. PRO/Adm/231/6, memorandum by Hall and Eastman, London, March 14, 1885, 1–30.

61. Ibid., 31–33.

62. Pierre Renouvin, *La question d'Extrême-Orient, 1840–1940* (Paris: Libraire Hachette, 1946), 105.

63. John Fairbank, ed., *The I. G. in Peking: Letters of Robert Hart—Chinese Maritime Customs 1868–1907* (Cambridge, Mass.: Harvard University Press, 1975), vol. 2, 327, Hart to Campbell, Peking, June 22, 1880.

64. RGVIA, f. 400, op. 1, d. 646, ll. 2–4.

65. Ibid., d. 653, ll. 2–4 rev., Lesovsky to the Naval Ministry, Alexandria, July 30, 1880.

66. Ibid., d. 581, ll. 23–24, Russian plenipotentiary envoy to Japan Struve to Giers, Tokyo, February 3, 1881.

67. H. Lansdell, *Russian Central Asia*, 2 vols. (Boston: Houghton Mifflin, 1885), 256; G. Lacost, *Rossia i Velikobritaniia v Tsentral'noi Asii* (Tashkent: Shtab Turkestanskogo voennogo okruga, 1908), 15; V. I. Petrov, *Miateznoe "serdtse" Asii: Sinkiang—kratkaia istoriia narodnykh dvizhenii i vospominanii* (Moscow: Kraft Plius, 2003), 203–7.

68. See, e.g., E. Kiernan, *British Diplomacy in China: 1880 to 1885* (Cambridge: Cambridge University Press, 1939), 58–72; Hsue, *Ili Crisis*, vii; and A. Akhmetzhanov, "Vozvratschenie Rossiei Kul'dzhinskogo raiona Kitaiu," *Alma-Atinskii pedagogicheskii institut im. Abaia: Uchenye zapiski* 14, no. 2 (1957): 69–90.

69. PRO/F 539/15, minutes by Lytton on the affairs of Central Asia and the position of Russia and Britain, Simla, September 4, 1878.

70. Frechtling, "Anglo-Russian Rivalry," 488; GARF, f. 730, op. 1, d. 433, ll. 1–11 rev., memorandum by Ignatiev to Gorckakov, June 1878.

71. Grombchevsky, *Otchet o poezdke v Kashgar*, 90.

72. Clarmont Skrine and Pamela Nightingale, *Macartney at Kashgar: New Light on British, Chinese, and Russian Activities in Sinkiang, 1890–1918* (London: Methuen, 1973), 24–25.

73. AVPRI, f. 143, op. 491, d. 444, ll. 1–152, Petrovsky's reports to Kapnist, the head of the Foreign Ministry's Asian Department, Kashgar, 1886–90.

74. Ibid., d. 475, ll. 296–97, Petrovsky to Kapnist, Kashgar, September 12, 1887. For an evaluation of Petrovsky's personal features by British travelers, see Francis

Younghusband, *The Heart of a Continent* (London, John Murray, 1904), 276–77; Ralph Cobbold, *Innermost Asia: Travel and Sport in the Pamirs* (London: William Heinemann, 1900), 66–67. On how Petrovsky treated European explorers, see Kolesnikov, *Russkie v Kashgarii*, 18–19.

75. Skrine and Nightingale, *Macartney at Kashgar*, 25.

76. Quoted by Robert Johnson, *Spying for Empire: The Great Game in Central and South Asia, 1757–1947* (London: Greenhill Books, 2006), 167–68.

77. AVPRI, f. 143, op. 491, d. 493, ll. 2–23, note by Petrovsky on the methods of reconnaissance conducted by colonial scouts, Kashgar, February 16, 1887.

78. See, e.g., AVPRI, f. 143, op. 491, d. 493, ll. 37–40, Petrovsky to Kapnist, Kashgar, May 31, 1891.

79. Cobbold, *Innermost Asia*, 199, 279–80.

80. RGVIA, f. 483, op.1, d. 120, l. 171, survey by Colonel Beliavsky, Saint Petersburg, December 5, 1884.

81. E.g., see N. Zeland, *Kashgaria i perevaly Tian-Shania: Putevye zapiski* (Omsk: Tipographiia okruzhnogo shtaba, 1887); and Lev Kostenko, "Dzhungariya: Voenno-statisticheskii ocherk," *Sbornik geographicheskikh, topographicheskikh i statisticheskikh materialov po Asii* 28 (1887): 1–341.

82. *Pioneer Mail*, Calcutta, July 26, 1885.

83. For a typical firsthand travel account, see Alexander Hosie, *Three Years in Western China* (London: Philip and Son, 1897). There are many books and magazine articles covering these travels. For current assertions, see Johnson, *Spying for Empire*, 165–80; Aleksei Postnikov, *Skhvatka na "kryshe mira": Politiki, razvedchiki, generally v bor'be za Pamir v XIX v.* (Moscow: Ripol-Klassik, 2005), 224–379; V. G. Obukhov, *Skhvatka shesti imperii: Bitva za Sinkiang* (Moscow: Veche, 2007), 25–31; Ye. Boikova, "Rossiiskie voennye ekspeditsii v Mongolii v kontse XIX v.," in *Altaica*, edited by V. M. Alpatov (Moscow: Institut vostokovedeniia, 1997), 23–33; and Mariia Bugrova, "Britanskie ekspedirsii v Kitai i sosednie raiony (70-e-90-e gg. XIX v.)," *Oriens*, no. 1 (2008): 116–27. Besides, the works by John Keay are worthy of note; see John Keay, *Where Men and Mountains Meet: The Explorers of the Western Himalayas, 1820–1875* (London: John Murray, 1977); and John Keay, *The Gilgit Game: The Explorers of the Western Himalayas, 1865–1895* (Hamden, Conn.: Archon Books, 1979).

84. RGVIA, f. 165, op. 1, d. 242, ll. 1–18.

85. Quoted by Peter Hopkirk, *The Great Game: On Secret Service in High Asia* (London: John Murray, 1990), 379.

86. IOLR/L&PS/C 23/1/12–13, Loftus to Derby, Saint Petersburg, April 27, 1875.

87. Quoted by Leslie Harris, "British Policy on the North-West Frontier of India, 1889–1901," Ph.D. diss., University of London, 1960, 24–25.

88. See Alexander Popov, "Iz istorii zavoevaniia Srednei Asii," *Istoricheskie zapiski* 9 (1940): 198–242, at 241. In interviews with some high-ranking Tsarist statesmen and generals, Marvin mentioned Lytton's proposal to invade Russian Turkestan in 1876.

In the latter's view, a Muslim revolt that British agents might instigate in the rear of Tsarist armies would facilitate a counteroffensive by the Anglo-Indian troops; see Charles Marvin, *The Russian Advance towards India: Conversation with Skobeleff, Ignatiev, and Other Distinguished Russian Generals and Statesmen on the Central Asian Question* (London: Sampson Low, Marston, Searle, and Rivington, 1882), 160.

89. RGVIA, f. 400, op. 1, d. 470, l. 13, Miliutin to Fredericks, Moscow, November 10, 1876.

90. Quoted by Adrian Preston, "British Military Policy and the Defense of India, 1876–1880," Ph.D. diss., University of London, 1966, 307. For a current, revised perspective on how Lord Salisbury tackled international problems, see Thomas Otte, "'Floating Downstream?' Lord Salisbury and British Foreign Policy, 1878–1902," in *The Makers of British Foreign Policy*, edited by T. Otte (Basingstoke, U.K.: Palgrave, 2002), 98–127.

91. IOLR / Mss Eur E 218/518/2, Lytton to Salisbury, Calcutta, May 28, 1877.

92. For a detailed description of reconnaissance missions and their contribution to the Great Game, see Marvin, *Reconnoitering Central Asia*; A. G. Isachenko, *Russkoe geographicheskoe obtschestvo: 150 let* (Moscow: Progress-Pangeia, 1995); and Johnson, *Spying for Empire*, 110–50. A telegram from the Russian Consulate in Tehran to the Foreign Ministry on the expedition of Captain Charles Napier, who visited Persian Khorasan and South Turkmenia in 1874–76 at the recommendation of the Persian foreign minister, was a testimony of this boom; see RGVIA, f. 400, op. 1, d. 531, ll. 2–3, Shimanovsky, Russian chargé d'affaires in Persia, to the Foreign Ministry, Tehran, December 18, 1876. Further information on Napier's secret mission is given by Hopkirk, *Great Game*, 366–67.

93. See, e.g., IOLR/L&PS/18/A 9, memorandum by O.T.B. [Bailey?], Simla, July 20, 1875, 1–11.

94. RGVIA, f. 400, op. 1, d. 420, ll. 17–17 rev., Miliutin to Kaufman, Saint Petersburg, December 10, 1875. It should be noted that Miliutin insisted on the intelligence officer Lieutenant Colonel Shneur's back route to Russia via India seven years later. The war minister directed his subordinate to gather all available nuggets of intelligence on current developments in the Raj; see RGVIA, f. 400, op. 1, d. 646, ll. 178–178 rev., Giers to Miliutin, Saint Petersburg, March 12, 1881. For a lively telling of Burnaby's ride to Khiva, also see Hopkirk, *Great Game*, 365–79.

95. For more comprehensive analyses, see Victor Winstone, *The Illicit Adventure: The Story of Political and Military Intelligence in the Middle East from 1898 to 1926* (London: Jonathan Cape, 1982); Thomas Fergusson, *British Military Intelligence, 1870–1914: The Development of a Modern Intelligence Organization* (Frederick, Md.: University Publications of America, 1984); Christopher Andrew, *Secret Service: The Making of the British Intelligence Community* (London: Heinemann, 1985); and Evgeny Sergeev, *Russian Military Intelligence in the War with Japan, 1904–05: Secret Operations on Land and at Sea* (London: Routledge, 2007), 11–30.

96. PRO/CAB/17/93. On the establishment of the Colonial Defence Committee, see J. P. Mackintosh, "The Role of the Committee of Imperial Defense before 1914," *English Historical Review* 77, no. 304 (1962): 490–503, at 490–91; and Denis Judd, *Balfour and the British Empire* (London: Macmillan, 1968), 24.

97. Gwendolen Cecil, *Life of Robert, Marquis of Salisbury*, 4 vols. (London: Hodder & Stoughton, 1921–32), vol. 2, 168.

98. See George Hamilton, *Parliamentary Reminiscences and Reflections, 1886–1906* (New York: Dutton, 1917), 307.

99. J. A. S. Colquhoun, "Essay on the Formation of an Intelligence Department for India," *Proceedings of the United Service Institution of India* 4, no. 18 (1875): 1–73; G. T. Plunkett, "On the Organization of an Intelligence Department," *Proceedings of the United Service Institution of India* 4, no. 19 (1875): 123–28. For a firsthand account of the eyewitness, see Henry Brackenbury, *Some Memories of My Spare Time* (Edinburgh: W. Blackwood & Sons, 1909).

100. Johnson, *Spying for Empire*, 145.

101. J. A. S. Grenville, *Lord Salisbury and Foreign Policy: The Close of the Nineteenth Century* (London: Athlone Press, 1964), 302.

102. IOLR / Mss Eur F 111/115; *Further Papers Relating to the Affairs of Afghanistan (Afghanistan No. 2)* (London: Her Majesty's Stationery Office, 1878), Lytton to Carnarvon, Calcutta, January 21, 1877; Lytton to Salisbury, Calcutta, April 25 and May 21, 1877. Also see Preston, "British Military Policy," 312–14; and Farida Yuldasheva, *Iz istorii angliiskoi kolonial'noi politiki v Afghanistane i Srednei Asii (70-e—80-e gg. XIX v.)* (Tashkent: Fan, 1963), 86–90.

103. Mikhail Veniukov, *Kratkii ocherk angliiskikh vladenii v Asii* (Saint Petersburg: V. Bezobrazov, 1875), 2–3.

104. Boulger, *England and Russia*, vol. 2, 50.

105. Annenkov, *Akhal-Tekinskii oazis*, 33. It should be also noted that Pashino proposed to the foreign minister to contact Nana Sahib, a hero of the Sepoy Mutiny, who was living in exile in the town of Munipur on the Burmese frontier. Pashin projected to persuade Nana Sahib to become a leader of the new anti-British uprising provoked by the Russians in India; see Mikhail Ryzhenkov, ed., *"Bol'shaia igra" v Tsentral'noi Asii: "Indiiskii pokhod" russkoi armii* (Moscow: Institut vostokovedeniia RAN, 2005), 53–55, Pashino to Giers, April 9, 1878.

106. F. Wellesley, *With the Russians in Peace and War: Recollections of a Military Attaché* (London: Eveleigh Nash, 1905), 301–2.

107. E.g., see Johnson, *Spying for Empire*, 146.

108. AVPRI, f. 138, op. 467, d. 734, l. 3 rev. For a thorough analysis of the structure of the Anglo-Indian army, also see RGVIA, f. 1396, op. 2, d. 2195, ll. 23–54 rev., note by Major General Alexander Geins, the governor of Turgai Province, April 15, 1878.

109. Mikhail Skobelev, "Posmertnye bumagi," *Istoricheskii vestnik* 10, no. 10 (1882): 109–38; no. 11: 275–94 (at 122 and 279); Mikhail Skobelev, "Proekt M. D.

Skobeleva o pokhode na Indiiu," *Istoricheskii vestnik* 14, no. 12 (1883): 543–55. Skobelev was convinced that Central Asia should be transformed into a base for future military campaigns against the British in Asia; see Skobelev, "Posmertnye bumagi," 293. For the evaluation of Skobelev's projects by contemporaries, see Marvin, *Russian Advance*, 105; and H. Edwards, *Russian Projects against India from the Czar Peter to General Skobeleff* (London: Remington, 1885), 260–93. The official Soviet concept is presented by Evgeny-Steinberg, "'Angliiskaia versiia o 'russkoi ugroze' Indii v XIX–XX vv.," *Istoricheskie zapiski* 33 (1950): 47–66, at 59–60. Oddly enough, some Russian journalists continue to eulogize Skobelev's schemes of the march to British India; see, e.g., Valentin Masal'sky, *Skobelev: Istoricheskii portret* (Moscow: Andreevskii flag, 1998), 214.

110. RGVIA, f. 846, op. 1, d. 17, ll. 3–4, reproduced by Ryzhenkov, *"Bol'shaia igra,"* 44.
111. A. Ilyasov, ed., *Prisoedinenie Turkmenii k Rossii: Sbornik dokumentov* (Ashgabad: Izdatel'stvo AN Turkmenskoi SSR, 1960), 332–36, Miliutin to Alexander II, Saint Petersburg, April 20, 1878.
112. RGVIA, f. 846, op. 1, d. 17, ll. 8–13, note by Tornau, March 3, 1878.
113. OR RGB, f. 169, op. 3, d. 2, l. 54, entry in Miliutin's diary, April 16, 1878; Ryzhenkov, *"Bol'shaia igra,"* 80–84; V.V. Korneev, "Tsentral'noaziatskii region v voennoi politike Rossii (XVIII–nachalo XX v.)," *Oriens*, no. 4 (2004): 5–16, at 12–13.
114. IOLR/L&PS/18/ C 23/1/31.
115. Ibid., C 20/5.
116. Arthur Cory, *Shadows of Coming Events, or the Eastern Menace* (London: Henry S. King, 1876), 10.
117. Eugene Schuyler, *Turkestan* (London: S. Low, M. Searle, and Rivington, 1876), vol. 2, 264–65.
118. AVPRI, f.138, op. 467, d. 757a, ll. 11–13 rev., note by Iessen, December 1, 1876.
119. Ryzhenkov, *"Bol'shaia igra,"* 45–46, 49–50.
120. IOLR/L&PS/18/C 23/2/19.
121. RGVIA, f. 1396, op. 2, d. 2195, ll. 2–6 rev., Miliutin to Kaufman, Saint Petersburg, April 25, 1878.
122. RGVIA, f. 846, op. 16, d. 6919, ll. 69–93, Kaufman to Miliutin, Tashkent, February 10, 1879.
123. See, e.g., Alexander Lobanov-Rostovsky, *Russia and Asia* (Ann Arbor: George Wahr, 1951), 164; and Hopkirk, *Great Game*, 380. Kazemzadeh and Johnson miscalculate the number of the military contingents prepared to march toward India; see Johnson, *Spying for Empire*, 146.
124. Ivan Yavorsky, *Puteshestvie russkogo posol'stva po Afghanistanu i Bukharskomu khanstvu v 1878–1879 gg.* (Saint Petersburg: Tipographiia M. Khana, 1882), vol. 1, 2.
125. E.g., see Korneev, "Tsentral'noaziatskii region," 13.
126. Ryzhenkov, *"Bol'shaia igra,"* 30–31. For the grounds of such apprehensions, see K. G. Kubanov, "Pokhody v Indiiu v proektakh rossiiskikh voennykh i politicheskikh deiatelei XVIII–nachala XX v.," Kand. diss., Nizhnevartovskii

gosudarstvennyi gumanitarnyi universitet, 2007, 22.

127. Ryzhenkov, *"Bol'shaia igra,"* 102, directions by Kaufman for the activity of the troops in the Turkestan Military District, Tashkent, June 7, 1878; RGVIA, f. 400, op. 1, d. 588, ll. 5–5 rev.

128. National Archives of India, Foreign Department (hereafter, NAI FD), August 1878, no. 4; reproduced by Ryzhenkov, *"Bol'shaia igra,"* 92.

129. PRO/FO 539/15; *Further Correspondence Respecting Russian Proceedings in Central Asia* (London: Her Majesty's Stationery Office, 1878), Loftus to Salisbury, Saint Petersburg, July 3, 1878.

130. Morris, *Pax Britannica*, 117–47.

131. RGVIA, f. 1396, op. 2, d. 2195, ll. 75–76 rev., Giers to Kaufman, Saint Petersburg, May 11, 1878.

132. IOLR/L&PS/18/A 38/1–45, Russian correspondence with Kabul, March 1870–February 1879, especially see 25–27; NAI FD, July 1878, no. 95-104; reproduced by Ryzhenkov, *"Bol'shaia igra,"* 94–95, British secret agent to the deputy commissioner of Peshawar Major Louis Cavagnari, Peshawar, May 13, 1878. RGVIA, f. 1396, op. 2, d. 2195, ll. 87–95 rev., Kaufman's instructions to Major General Stolietov, Tashkent, June 7, 1878.

133. RGVIA, f. 846, op. 2, d. 16, ll. 10–17, supplement to Kaufman's report, Tashkent, September 21, 1878; reproduced by Ryzhenkov, *"Bol'shaia igra,"* 156–59; also see Frederick Roberts, *Forty-One Years in India from Subaltern to Commander-in-Chief*, 2 vols. (London: Macmillan, 1897), vol. 2, appendix V, 477; NAI FD, December 1878, no. 668, British secret agent to Salisbury, Quetta, October 8, 1878. And see Ryzhenkov, *"Bol'shaia igra,"* 171.

134. Ibid., ll. 2–9 rev., Kaufman to Miliutin, Tashkent, September 21, 1878; ibid., op. 1, d. 24, ll. 25–25 rev., Miliutin to Kaufman, Saint Petersburg, October 2, 1878. Also see Mikhail Terentiev, *Istoriia zavoevaniia Srednei Asii*, 3 vols. (Saint Petersburg: V. Komarov, 1906), vol. 2, 458–61; and Feodor Raskol'nikov, "Rossiia i Afghanistan: Istoricheskii ocherk," *Novyi Vostok* 4 (1923): 12–48, at 34–35.

135. Dominic Lieven, ed., *British Documents on Foreign Affairs: Reports and Papers from the Foreign Office Confidential Print—Russia, 1859–1914* (Washington, D.C.: University Press of America, 1983–89), vol. 1, 318, Cavagnari to the India Office, Peshawar, June 18, 1878.

136. PRO/FO 539/15/108, memorandum by Clarke, August 10, 1878.

137. Duchess of Argyll, *George Douglas the Eighth Duke of Argyll: Autobiography and Memoirs* (London: John Murray, 1906), vol. 1, 330.

138. D. A. Miliutin, *Dnevnik*, 4 vols. (Moscow: OR RGB, 1947–50), vol. 3, 93.

139. Yavorsky, *Puteshestvie russkogo*, vol. 2, 83–85; Terentiev, *Istoriia zavoevaniia Srednei Asii*, vol. 2, 450, 457.

140. RGVIA, f. 846, op. 2, d. 16, ll. 62–64, Lytton to Sher Ali Khan, Calcutta, November 6, 1878 (intercepted by the Russian intelligence service).

141. RGVIA, f. 401, op. 3, d. 15, 1878, ll. 75–76 rev., Gorlov to Miliutin, London,

October 6, 1878.

142. NAI FD, January 1879, no. 3, Plunkett to Salisbury, Saint Petersburg, September 27, 1878; reproduced by Ryzhenkov, *"Bol'shaia igra,"* 167.

143. See Naftula Khalfin, *Proval britanskoi agressii v Afghanistane (XIX–nachalo XX v.)* (Moscow: Sotsial'no-economicheskoe izdatel'stvo, 1959), 95; Petr Shastitko, "'K voprosu o mificheskoi 'russkoi ugroze' Indii," in *Protiv falk'sifikatsii istorii kolonialisma,* edited by K. Popov (Moscow: Vostochnaia literatura, 1962), 194–95; Goga Khidoiatov, *Iz istorii anglo-russkikh otnoshenii v Srednei Asii v kontse XIX v. (60–70-e gg.)* (Tashkent: Fan, 1969), 258–93; and Alexandr Shirokorad, *Russia–England, neizvestnaia voina, 1857–1907* (Moscow: AST, 2003), 119–24. Also see a short review of the problem in the preface to Ryzhenkov, *"Bol'shaia igra,"* 31–39.

144. PRO/FO 539/19/43-5, Granville to Dufferin, London, January 28, 1881.

145. E.g., see RGVIA, f. 846, op. 2, d. 16, ll. 68–70 rev., Miliutin to Kaufman, Saint Petersburg, December 18, 1878.

146. For the firsthand accounts of eyewitnesses see Roberts, *Forty-One Years,* vol. 2, 118–242; Palmer, *Earl of Selborne,* vol. 1, 456 ff.; and Archibald Forbes, *The Afghan Wars 1839–42 and 1878–80* (London: Seeley, 1892), 161–327. For contemporary analyses, see Preston, "British Military Policy," 460–511; Brian Robson, *The Road to Kabul: The Second Afghan War, 1878–1881* (London: Arms and Armour Press, 1986); and D. S. Richards, *The Savage Frontier: A History of the Anglo-Afghan Wars* (London: Macmillan, 1990), 74–101.

147. On the origins and history of the Pathans, especially see Olaf Caroe, *The Pathans: 500 B.C.–A.D. 1957* (Oxford: Oxford University Press, 1984).

148. Johnson, *Spying for Empire,* 112; C. Trench, *The Frontier Scouts* (London: Jonathan Cape, 1985), 8. On the ethnic origins of the modern Kalasha tribesmen living in the frontier area amid Afghanistan and Pakistan, see Ulunian, "Britanskii konzept," 182. For the role of ethnic groups, especially that of the Afridis, in the Great Game, see Johnson, *Spying for Empire,* 200; and Ulunian, "Britanskii konzept," 182–84. On Lokhart's mission to the northern hill states of Hindustan, see Keay, *Gilgit Game,* 75–83; Johnson, *Spying for Empire,* 162–64; and Postnikov, *Skhvatka na "kryshe mira,"* 254–55.

149. Yavorsky, *Puteshestvie russkogo,* vol. 2, 81; NAI, Foreign Department, 1878, no. 874, Major Macoley to Colonel Monro, November 14, 1878, reproduced by Ryzhenkov, *"Bol'shaia igra,"* 197.

150. Miliutin, *Dnevnik,* vol. 3, 98.

151. RGVIA, f. 165, op. 1, d. 238, ll. 1–3 rev., Gorchakov to Kaufman, Saint Petersburg, January 23, 1879.

152. Roberts, *Forty-One Years,* vol. 2, 247.

153. Robson, *Road to Kabul,* 280.

154. F. Burnaby, *A Ride to Khiva: Travels and Adventures in Central Asia* (London, 1877), 217; *The Times,* November 16, 1876. Schuyler, vol. 2, 264–65. On Kaufman's directions concerning the massacre of the Yomuds, see E. A. Glutschenko, *Geroi*

Imperii: Portrety rossiiskikh kolonial'nykh deiatelei (Moscow: XXI v.–Soglasie, 2001), 108–15.

155. Yetisgin, "How the *Times* of London Covered and Interpreted Russian Expansion," 131–32.

156. OPI GIM, f. 307, op. 1, d. 24, ll. 7–8 rev., note by Sobolev, Saint Petersburg, late 1878–early 1879; also see Kostenko, "Dzhungariya," 152; Sergei Martirosov, "Anglo-russkoe sopernichestvo v period prisoedineniia Turkmenii k Rossii," Kand. diss., Moskovskii gosudarstvennyi pedagogicheskii institut, 1966, 17.

157. On Lomakin's expeditions, see Grodekov, *Voina v Turkmenii*, vol. 1; and Aleksei Kuropatkin, *Zavoevanie Turkmenii* (Saint Petersburg: V. Berezovskii, 1899), 77–220. For a fresh interpretation, see Yetisgin, "How the *Times* of London Covered and Interpreted Russian Expansion," 142–43.

158. E.g., see *The Times*, July 14, 1879.

159. Tsentral'nyi Gosudarstvennyi Arkhiv Respubliki Uzbekistan (hereafter, TGA RUZ), f. 1, op. 34, d. 437, ll. 1–2, Colonel Grotenhelm to Kaufman, February 5, 1879; RGVIA, f. 846, op. 1, d. 6907, l. 69; TGA RUZ, f. 545, op. 1, d. 1552, ll. 147–52; also see D. Davletov and A. Ilyasov, *Prisoedinenie Turkmenii k Rossii* (Ashkhabad: Ylym, 1972), 123.

160. OPI GIM, f. 307, op. 1, d. 23, ll. 28 rev.–29, Draft project of the march to Afghanistan by Grodekov, March 30, 1879; also see Grodekov, *Voina v Turkmenii*, vol. 1, 134.

161. Grodekov, *Voina v Turkmenii*, vol. 1, 170–74.

162. Ilyasov, *Prisoedinenie Turkmenii k Rossii*, 371, 373, note by Petrusevich, 1879.

163. Ibid., 373–74, minutes by Pavlov, January 1879.

164. RGVIA, f. 846, op. 1, d. 28, ll. 50–58, Sviatopolk-Mirsky to Grand Duke Mikhail Nikolaevich, Tiflis, February 19, 1879.

165. Lieven, *British Documents*, vol. 2, 67, Foreign Office memorandum on the correspondence with the Russian Government in regard to Merv, 1874–84, London, February 25, 1884.

166. PRO/FO 539/14, correspondence respecting Russian proceedings in Central Asia, 1874–77, memorandum by Her Majesty's Government on Russian policy in Central Asia, London, October 25, 1875.

167. IOLR/F111/115. Great Britain, Parliamentary Papers, *Correspondence relating to the Affairs of Afghanistan (Afghanistan Nos. 1, 2, 3)* (London: Her Majesty's Stationery Office, 1880); Great Britain, Parliamentary Papers, *Correspondence Relating to the Affairs of Afghanistan (Afghanistan Nos. 1, 2, 3, 4, 5)* (London: Her Majesty's Stationery Office, 1881).

168. RGVIA, f. 401, op. 3, d. 1, 1879, ll. 185–86, Gorlov to Miliutin, London, June 4, 1879.

169. Lieven, *British Documents*, vol. 2, 71, Foreign Office memorandum on the correspondence with the Russian government in regard to Merv.

170. *The Times*, October 9, 1879. The Turkmens' forays, which aimed to capture

slaves, or the so-called *alamans*, were analyzed by British and Russian military explorers; see Pavel Ogorodnikov, *Na puti v Persiiu i eyo Prikaspiiskie provintsii* (Saint Petersburg: M. Popov, 1878). Interestingly, Ogorodnikov pointed out that the price for a slave on Central Asian markets varied from 30 to 60 Persian tomans, equivalent to 100–200 rubles or £10 to £20.

171. Terentiev, *Istoriia zavoevaniia Srednei Asii*, vol. 3, 22.

172. RGVIA, f. 401, op. 3, d. 1, 1879, ll. 191–92, Gorlov to Miliutin, London, September 23, 1879; Grodekov, *Voina v Turkmenii*, vol. 2, 22–25.

173. Quoted by Cedric Lowe, *The Reluctant Imperialists: British Foreign Policy, 1878–1902* (London: Routledge & Kegan Paul, 1967), vol. 1, 93.

174. Maurice Brett, ed., *Journals and Letters of Reginald Viscount Esher* (London: I. Nicholson & Watson, 1934), vol. 1, 72.

175. Ilyasov, *Prisoedinenie Turkmenii k Rossii*, 466–67, memorandum by the staff officers at the headquarters of the Caucasus Viceroyalty, Tiflis, February 3, 1880.

176. OPI GIM, f. 307, op. 1, d. 38, correspondence between Sobolev and Skobelev, especially see ll. 6–7 rev., Sobolev to Skobelev, Saint Petersburg, April 14, 1880; ll. 112–19 rev., Sobolev to Skobelev, Saint Petersburg, August 22, 1880; ll. 144–46, Skobelev to Sobolev, Shirvan, March 12, 1881.

177. Hopkirk, *Great Game*, 404–5.

178. On the activity of Edmund O'Donovan, see TGA RUZ, f. 1, op. 34, d. 540, ll. 10–12, Zinoviev to the Foreign Ministry's Asian Department, Tehran, November 1881; RGVIA, f. 846, op. 1, d. 6935, Gorlov to Miliutin, London, November 1881; RGVIA, f. 400, op. 1, d. 704, ll. 9–10, Rerberg, the military governor of Trans-Caspian Province, to the Main Staff, Ashgabat, June 24, 1881; Ibid., f. 400, op. 1, d. 704, ll. 19–25 rev., Colonel Aminov, the acting head of the staff of Trans-Caspian Province, to the Main Staff Military-Scientific Committee, Ashgabat, January 31, 1882; Terentiev, *Istoriia zavoevaniia Srednei Asii*, vol. 3, 141; Grodekov, *Voina v Turkmenii*, vol. 3, 140–42, and vol. 4, 96; and Pavel Lessar, "O'Donovan: The Khan of Merv," *Novoe Vremya*, no. 2765 (1883). The mails sent by O'Donovan to *The Daily News* in the interval between 1879 and 1881 may be found in OPI GIM, f. 307, op. 1, d. 41, especially, ll. 188–90. Oddly enough, Soviet historians, on the one hand, accused O'Donovan of espionage to the detriment of Russians, but on the other, described O'Donovan's meeting with Vlasov, the Russian consul in Resht (Persia), with whom O'Donovan shared intelligence on the situation in Turkmenia; see Steinberg, "'Angliiskaia versiia,'" 61; Mikhail Tikhomirov, *Prisoedinenie Merva k Rossii* (Moscow: Vostochania literature, 1960), 210–14; and Davletov and Ilyasov, *Prisoedinenie Turkmenii k Rossii*, 215–27. For a complementary recounting, see Edmund O'Donovan, *The Merv Oasis: Travels and Adventures East of the Caspian during the Years 1879–80–81, Including Five Months' Residence among the Teke of Merv* (London, 1882).

179. Hopkirk, *Great Game*, 402, 404–5, 407.

180. RGVIA, f. 846, op. 1, d. 70, ll. 30–33, Zinoviev to Giers, Tehran, March 22, 1882.

181. For a detailed firsthand description of the Geok Tepe operation, see Grodekov, *Voina v Turkmenii*, vol. 3, 296; and A. Prioux, *Les Russes dans l'Asie Centrale: La dernière Campagne de Skobelev (1880–1881)* (Paris: Librairie Militaire de L. Baudoin, 1886); On Skobelev's activity in Trans-Caspia, see Nikolai Knorring, *General Mikhail Dimitrievich Skobelev: Istoricheskii etiud* (Paris: Illustrirovannaia Rossiia, 1939), vol. 1, 155–80; Tikhomirov, *Prisoedinenie Merva k Rossii*, 52–54; Khidoiatov, *Iz istorii anglo-russkikh*, 403–5; Glutschenko, *Geroi Imperii*, 315–16; V. M. Mukhanov, "Mikhail Dmitrievich Skobelev," *Voprosy istorii*, no. 10 (2004): 57–81, at 73; Masal'sky, *Skobelev*, 143–234; Andrei Sholokhov, *Polkovodets, Suvorovu ravnyi, ili minskii korsikanets Mikhail Skobelev* (Moscow: Yunivestmedia, 2008), 229–54; and Oleg Airapetov, *Vneshniaia politika Rossiiskoi imperii 1801–1914* (Moscow: Evropa, 2006), 355–59.

182. Marvin, *Russian Advance*, 98–99.

183. Lieven, *British Documents*, vol. 2, 74–75, Dufferin to Granville, Saint Petersburg, March 8, 1881. Addressing the House of Commons, a Liberal member of Parliament argued that due to the recent conquest of Turkmenia, Russia had not only seized enormous space of fertile lands but had also incorporated more than 60,000 light cavalry horsemen in her army; see *The Hansard Parliamentary Debates* (London: C. Buck, 1908) series 3, vol. 262, col. 2302-231, June 10, 1881.

184. The state of affairs in Afghanistan, Persia, and Turkmenia was meticulously analyzed by Nikolai Grodekov, *Cherez Afganistan: Putevye zametki* (Saint Petersburg: Novoe vremya, 1880); and Pavel Lessar, *Zametki o Zakaspiiskom krae i sopredel'nykh stranakh* (Saint Petersburg: A. Suvorin, 1884). On the British apprehension of these trips, see Prioux, *Les Russes*, 160–61; and Charles Marvin, *The Russians at Merv and Herat, and Their Power of Invading India* (London: W. Allen, 1883), 258–71.

185. See Maksud Alikhanov-Avarsky, *V gostiakh u Shaha. Ocherki Persii* (Tiflis: Ya. Liberman, 1898), 7–8; Mary Macarthy, "Anglo-Russian Rivalry in Persia," *University of Buffalo Studies* 4, no. 2 (1925): 27–67, at 27–35.

186. GARF, f. 568, op. 1, d. 146, ll. 1–5 rev., Russo-Persian Convention, Tehran, December 21, 1881; IOLR/L&PS/18/C 46/1–3, memorandum by A.W.M. on the Russian advance in Central Asia, 1872–85, Simla, May 5, 1885; *Afganskoe razgranichenie: Peregovory mezhdu Rossiei i Velikobritaniei, 1872–1885* (Saint Petersburg: Ministerstvo inosrannykh del, 1886), 14; and Grodekov, *Voina v Turkmenii*, vol. 4, 107–11. On the consequences of the Russo-Persian agreement, see Lieven, *British Documents*, pt. 1, ser. A, vol. 2, 141–46, memorandum by Colonel Karavayev, November 27, 1886. For a view of Soviet historians, see, e.g., Goga Khidoiatov, *Britanskaia ekspansiia v Srednei Asii (Penjdeh, March 1885)* (Tashkent: Fan, 1981), 65.

187. Lev Kostenko, *The Turkestan Region, Being a Military Statistical Review of the Turkestan Military District of Russia, or Russian-Turkestan Gazetteer* (Calcutta: Office of the Superintendent of Government Printing, 1882–84), vol. 3, 209.

188. Marvin, *Russian Advance*, 43.

189. Quoted by Lucien Wolf, ed., *Life of the First Marquis of Ripon*, 2 vols. (London: John Murray, 1921), vol. 1, 58–59. See also a memorandum by Lord Ripon to the Cabinet on Central Asian policy, September 2, 1881, PRO/CAB/37/5/17; Lowe, *Reluctant Imperialists*, vol. 2, 37.

190. Shastitko, *Russko-indiiskie otnosheniia*, 245–46, Stolietov to Miliutin, March 3, 1880.

191. Marvin, *Russian Advance*, 132–33; OPI GIM, f. 203, op. 1, d. 56, ll. 49–71 rev., note by Sergei Bronsky, adjutant of Lieutenant General Cherniaev, Tashkent, 1880.

192. AVPRI, f. 147, op. 485, d. 1696, ll. 1–42; TGA RUZ, f. 1, op. 2, d. 710, ll. 3–30, memorandum by Dondukov-Korsakov, viceroy of the Caucasus, to Vannovsky, Tiflis, June 26, 1884; RGIA, f. 932, op. 1, d. 463, ll. 1–54, correspondence by Dondukov-Korsakov to Vannovsky on the incorporation of Turkmen lands in the Russian Empire, Tiflis, June 29–November 17, 1884.

193. Tcharykov, *Glimpses*, 161.

194. E.g., see J. Marriott, *Anglo-Russian Relations 1689–1943* (London: Methuen, 1944), 138.

195. IOLR/L&PS/18/A 48/1-8, memorandum by Napier, January 10, 1882.

196. *The Times*, February 16, 1884; quoted by Yetisgin, "How the *Times* of London Covered and Interpreted Russian Expansion," 158.

197. IOLR/L&PS/18/A 50, note by Burne, February 20, 1882; Mss Eur F 111/699/1-34, note by Beaufort, 1884.

198. *The Times*, February 23, 1884.

199. Johnson, *Spying for Empire*, 158.

200. Rose Greaves, *Persia and the Defense of India, 1884–1892: A Study of the Foreign Policy of the Third Marquis of Salisbury* (London: Athlone Press, 1959), 67; Cedric Lowe, *The Reluctant Imperialists: British Foreign Policy, 1878–1902*, 2 vols. (London: Routledge & Kegan Paul, 1967), vol. 1, 76.

201. Martirosov, "Anglo-russkoe sopernichestvo," 29.

202. AVPRI, f. 147, op. 485, d. 1699, ll. 17–77, review of the Russo-British negotiations on the occupation of Merv and the Penjdeh crisis, 1884–85; Terentiev, *Istoriia zavoevaniia Srednei Asii*, vol. 3, 395; Greaves, *Persia*, 53–69.

203. W. Baxter, *England and Russia* (London: S. Sonneschein, 1885), 32–33.

204. Ibid., 33, 72–73.

205. For typical examples, see Charles Macgregor, *The Defence of India: A Strategical Study* (Simla: Government Central Branch Press, 1884); F. Beaufort, *Russian Advances in Asia* (London: Ministry of Defence, 1884); Marvin, *Russians at Merv and Herat*, 61–123; *The Times*, February 23, 1884; and IOLR/L&PS/18/A 133/1-4, memorandum by Michell, December 1, 1884. The concept of Uzbeck historians for a propaganda campaign in the British press is given by Khidoiatov, *Britanskaia ekspansiia*, 141–44.

206. Macgregor, *Defence of India*, 105–44. Also see a Russian translation of his book in *Sbornik geographicheskikh, topographicheskikh i statisticheskikh materialov po Asii*

43 (1891): 1–264; 44:1–212. For a profound study of Macgregor's contribution to the elaboration of strategy and tactics of imperial defense, see Adrian Preston, "Sir Charles Macgregor and the Defense of India, 1857–1887," *Historical Journal* 12, no. 1 (1969): 58–77, esp. 75–77. For an assessment of his work by a Russian military writer, see Andrei Snesarev, *Afghanistan* (Moscow: Gosudarstvennoe izdatel'stvo, 1921), 227–28.

207. GARF, f. 568, op. 1, d. 90, ll. 1–12, journal of the special conference in the Foreign Ministry on the Russo-Afghan boundary problem, Saint Petersburg, January 12, 1885; Marvin, *Russians at Merv and Herat*, 352–82.

208. Lobanov-Rostovsky, *Russia and Asia*, 178–79; Alexandre Meyendorff, ed., *Correspondence diplomatique du Baron de Staal (1884–1900)* (Paris: Libraire des Sciences Politiques et Sociales, 1929), vol. 1, 177, Giers to Staal, Saint Petersburg, March 27, 1885. As a British expert stated, if the Russians approached Penjdeh not from the Upper Oxus but from the Caspian coast via Merv, they would avoid many difficulties in their march to India; see Lansdell, *Russian Central Asia*, vol. 2, 489.

209. Symptomatically, Giers mentioned in the telegram to Yegor Staal, the ambassador to London, that the Russian objective was "to establish a good frontier between the zones of influence of both powers—Britain and Russia"; see Meyendorff, *Correspondence diplomatique*, vol. 1, 41–42, Giers to Staal, Saint Petersburg, July 17, 1884; ibid., 42–50, Giers to Staal, Saint Petersburg, July 18, 1884.

210. GARF, f. 568, op. 1, d. 92, ll. 23–32, Lord Granville to Staal, London, March 13, 1885. On Dufferin's perception of the "buffer state" policy, see *The Cambridge History of British Foreign Policy, 1783–1919*, edited by A. W. Ward and G. P. Gooch (Cambridge: Cambridge University Press, 1923), vol. 3, 188–89.

211. IOLR/L&PS/18/A 60/1–6, memorandum by Cameron, April 19, 1885.

212. Ward and Gooch, *Cambridge History*, vol. 3, 189.

213. Terentiev, *Istoriia zavoevaniia Srednei Asii*, vol. 3, 250; A. N. Maslov, "Rossiia v Srednei Asii (Ocherk noveishikh priobretenii)," *Istoricheskii vestnik* 20 (1885): 372–423, at 422; Dimitry Logofet, *Na granitsakh Srednei Asii: Putevye ocherki*, 3 vols. (Saint Petersburg: V. Berezovsky, 1909), vol. 2, 24–38. Also see Z. R. Nuriddinov, "Angliia i afghano-russkoe razgranichenie v 80-3 gg. XIX v.," *Tashkentskii gosudarstvennyi pedagogicheskii institute: Uchenye zapiski—Istoriia* 33, no. 2 (1962): 250–329, at 314–15; Khidoiatov, *Britanskaia ekspansiia*, 116–61; Greaves, *Persia*, 70–84. A current interpretation of the Penjdeh incident is presented by Natalia N. Lisitsyna, "Pendinskoe srazhenie 1885 goda: Novye dokumenty," *Vostochnyi arkhiv*, nos. 11–12 (2004): 66–72.

214. PRO/FO65/1242/3140, Dufferin to Granville, Simla, May 3, 1885; also see Barbara Jelavich, "British Means of Offence against Russia in the Nineteenth Century," *Russian History* 1, pt. 2 (1974): 119–35, at 130.

215. AVPRI, f. 184, op. 520, d. 542, ll. 25–32, Thomson to Granville, Tehran, April 21, 1885 (intercepted by the Russian intelligence service).

216. A. Yate, *England and Russia Face to Face in Asia: Travels with the Afghan Boundary*

Commission (Edinburgh and London: W. Blackwood and Sons, 1887), 311–60.

217. PRO/FO 65/1233; PRO/FO 65/1237, memoranda by Murray on the distribution of Russian troops in the Turkestan Military District and Trans-Caspia, January 2 and March 4, 1885.

218. Paul Kennedy, *The Realities behind Diplomacy: Background Influences on British External Policy, 1865–1900* (London: George Allen & Unwin, 1981), 93–94. Characteristically, some personal messages of ordinary British people to Alexander III illustrated the state of public opinion. E.g., one correspondent wrote to the tsar: "You are about to go to war with England, and I for one hope you will get beaten and I think my countrymen think the same. You are a regular tyrant and you have my curses. I hope you may get beaten and killed. This is all I have to say. Your Enemy." see GARF, f. 677, op. 1, d. 473, l. 5, May 1885.

219. Hamilton, *Parliamentary Reminiscences*, 267.

220. V. P. Metschersky, *Moi vospominaniia*, 3 vols. (Saint Petersburg: V. Metschersky, 1897–1912), vol. 2, 189–90; also see Airapetov, *Vneshniaia politika*, 375.

221. Korff, *Russia's Foreign Relations*, 34.

222. Sergei Yuzhakov, *Anglo-russkaia raspria: Nebol'shoe predislovie k bol'shim sobytiiam—Politicheskii etud* (Saint Petersburg: Tovaritschestvo 'Obtschaia pol'sa', 1885), 3.

223. Meyendorff, *Correspondence diplomatique*, vol. 1, 68, Giers to Staal, Saint Petersburg, March 8, 1885.

224. Ibid., 174–75; 186–87, Granville to Giers, London, March 25, 1885; Giers to Staal, Saint Petersburg, April 18, 1885. On the plan of the Admiralty to wage a war in the Pacific against Russia, see RGA VMF, f. 417, op. 1, d. 70. ll. 1–1rev., Giers to Shestakov, the deputy naval minister, Saint Petersburg, March 30, 1885.

225. RGA VMF, f. 417, op. 1, d. 83, ll. 1–1 rev., Vannovsky to Admiral Chikhachev, the naval minister, April 15, 1885.

226. Ibid., f. 410, op. 2, d. 4048, ll. 65–77 rev., May 1885; OR RNB, f. 856, op. 637a, d. 12, ll. 31 rev., 34–34 rev., 43. Entries in the diary by Admiral Shestakov, the deputy naval minister, March 21 and 26 and April 23, 1885.

227. W. Stead, ed., *The M.P. for Russia: Reminiscences and Correspondence of Madam Olga Novikoff* (London: A. Melrose, 1909), vol. 2, 221.

228. PRO/WO/110/9, memorandum by Alison, April 18, 1885; IOLR/L&PS/18/A 64/1–2, Captain Barrow to Lieutenant General Lumsden, July 3, 1885; ibid., L&PS/18/A 66/1–2, memorandum by R.H.S.C., July 7, 1885; PRO/WO/110/9, memorandum by Beaufort, 1885; Richard Russel, *India's Danger and England's Duty* (London: Ward, Lock, 1885), 23–37; Charles Showers, *The Cossack at the Gate of India* (London: Simpkin, Marshall, 1885), 16–18; George Towle, *England and Russia in Asia* (Boston: J. Osgood, 1885), 42–44, 92–108; John Adye, *Russia in Central Asia* (Gibraltar, 1885), 5–10; Captain Heumann, *Les Russes et les Anglais dans l'Asie Centrale* (Paris: Libraire Militaire, 1885), 7.

229. PRO/ADM/231/6/1–17, memorandum on the protection of commerce by patrolling the ocean routes by convoys, May 1885; also see Kiernan, *British*

Diplomacy, 188–207.

230. Brett, *Journals*, vol. 1, 113–14, Esher to Wolseley, Orchard Lea, April 17, 1885.

231. *The Times*, 11 April 1885.

232. Korff, *Russia's Foreign Relations*, 33.

233. RGAVMF, f. 417, op. 1, d. 93, ll. 1–5, Vannovsky to Chikhachev, July 26, 1885; also see Yate, *England and Russia*, 442–44; W. Habberton, *Anglo-Russian Relations Concerning Afghanistan, 1837–1907* (Urbana: University of Illinois Press, 1937), 56; W. Langer, *The Diplomacy of Imperialism, 1890–1902*, 2 vols. (New York: Alfred A. Knopf, 1935), vol. 1, 309–14.

234. William Beaver, "The Development of the Intelligence Division, and Its Role in Aspects of Imperial Policy Making, 1854–1901: The Military Mind of Imperialism," Ph.D. diss., University of Oxford, 1976, 337.

235. PRO/FO/65/1358, Afghan Boundary Delimitation, 1887–88, protocols signed by Major General Komarov and Lieutenant Colonel Iate; Lobanov-Rostovsky, *Russia and Asia*, 180.

236. Yuzhakov, *Anglo-russkaia raspria*, 86; David Mackenzie, *Imperial Dreams, Harsh Realities: Tsarist Russian Foreign Policy, 1815–1917* (Fort Worth: Harcourt Brace College Publishers, 1994), 130. For the study of the Afghan Boundary Commission at work, see Morris, *Pax Britannica*, 356–428.

237. George Liska, *Cycles of East-West Conflict in War and Peace* (Baltimore: Johns Hopkins University Press, 1982), 47.

238. IOLR/L/P&S/18/C 84/1–6, note by Mallet to Hartington, London, September 25, 1880.

239. AVPRI, f. 147, op. 485, d. 904, ll. 4–4 rev., 6, 29–30 rev.; Shastitko, *Russko-indiiskie otnosheniia*, 256–57.

CHAPTER 5

1. See Mikhail Pokrovsky, *Diplomatiia i voiny tsarskoi Rossii v XIX stoletii* (Moscow: Krasnaia nov', 1923), 322–23.

2. S. N. Rostovsky, "Tsarskaia Rossiia i Sinkiang v XIX–XX vv.," *Istorik-Marxist* 3, no. 155 (1936): 36–53, at 38; A. A. Kolesnikov, *Russkie v Kashgarii (vtoraia polovina XIX–nachalo XX v.): Missii, ekspeditsii, puteshestviia* (Pishpek: Raritet, 2006), 20.

3. Andrei Snesarev, *Pamiry (Voenno-geografichcheskoe opisanie)* (Tashkent: Shtab Turkestanskogo voennogo okruga, 1903), 1–2, 50, 107–19. For further information on the expeditions undertaken by Russian travelers in the Pamirs, see Viktor Dubovitsky, "Nikolay Leopol'dovich Korzhenevsky: Imia na karte Pamira," 2007, available at www.ferghana.ru.

4. See Edward Knight, *Where Three Empires Meet: A Narrative of Recent Travel in Kashmir, Western Tibet, Gilgit, and the Adjoining Countries* (London: Longmans, 1897).

5. See Bronislav Grombchevsky, *Nashi interesy na Pamire: Voenno-politicheskii ocherk* (Saint Petersburg: Tipographiia Peterburgskogo voennogo okruga, 1891), 1; Mikhail Terentiev, *Istoriia zavoevaniia Srednei Asii*, 3-vols. (Saint Petersburg: V. Komarov, 1906), vol. 3, 394; and Lavr Kornilov, *Kashgaria ili Voctochnyi Turkestan: Opyt voenno-statisticheskogo opisaniia* (Tashkent: Tipographiia shtaba Turkestanskogo voennogo okruga, 1903). In addition, see the study of the problem of the Pamirs by O. B. Bokiev, *Zavoevanie i prisoedinenie Severnogo Tadzhikistana, Pamira i Gornogo Badakhshana k Rossii* (Dushanbe: Tadzhikskii gosudarstvennyi universitet, 1994).

6. Aleksei Postnikov, *Skhvatka na "kryshe mira": Politiki, razvedchiki, generally v bor'be za Pamir v XIX v.* (Moscow: Ripol-Klassik, 2005), 216–18.

7. Arkhiv Rossiiskogo Geographicheskogo Obtschestva (hereafter, ARGO), fond (f.; collection) 45, opis' (op.; inventory) 1, delo (d.; file) 6, listy (ll.; folios) 218–20, a travel diary by Grombchevsky, August 29, 1889.

8. India Office Library and Records (hereafter, IOLR), Mss Eur F 111/144/317-8, 463, 466; Great Britain, Parliamentary Papers, *Correspondence respecting Affairs of Asia (Central Asia No. 1)* (London: Her Majesty's Stationery Office, 1884); also see Postnikov, *Skhvatka na "kryshe mira,"* 251–54.

9. Arkhiv Vneshnei Politiki Rossiiskoi Imperii (hererafter, AVPRI), f. 147, op. 485, d. 688, ll. 5–11, Staal to Giers, London, April 3, 1895; Grombchevsky, *Nashi interesy na Pamire*, 2; Nina Luzhetskaia, *Ocherki istorii Vostochnogo Gindukusha vo vtoroi polovine XIX v.* (Moscow: Nauka, 1986), 3–4. For current interpretations of the Great Game in the Pamirs, see John Keay, *The Gilgit Game: The Explorers of the Western Himalayas, 1865–1895* (Hamden, Conn.: Archon Books, 1979).

10. Quoted by D. Woodman, *Himalayan Frontiers: A Political Review of British, Chinese, and Russian Rivalries* (London: Barrie and Rockliff, Cresset Press, 1969), 85.

11. Ibid., 93.

12. IOLR / Mss Eur F 111/113, correspondence in regard to the Pamirs frontier, 1890–91, Godley, the permanent undersecretary of state for India, to Salisbury, London, August 14, 1890.

13. Quoted by Woodman, *Himalayan Frontiers*, 88. On Younghusband's activities in the region, see George Seaver, *Francis Younghusband: Explorer and Mystic* (London: John Murray, 1952); Anthony Verrier, *Francis Younghusband and the Great Game* (London: Jonathan Cape, 1991); Patrick French, *Younghusband: The Last Great Imperial Adventurer* (London: HarperCollins, 1994).

14. Keay, *Gilgit Game*, 75–83; Robert Johnson, *Spying for Empire: The Great Game in Central and South Asia, 1757–1947* (London: Greenhill Books, 2006), 163; Luzhetskaia, *Ocherki istorii*, 54–55; Postnikov, *Skhvatka na "kryshe mira,"* 220–21.

15. Interestingly, British and Russian scholars differed in their assessment of the missions undertaken by Ney Elias in 1885–86. If Robert Johnson highly appreciates the explorer's contribution to the defense of India with regard to Gilgit, Chitral and Hunza, Mikhail Postnikov specifies that he failed to induce

local Chinese authorities to ally with the British against the Russians; see Johnson, *Spying for Empire*, 167; and Postnikov, *Skhvatka na "kryshe mira,"* 258. On the activity of Elias in Kashgaria, the Pamirs, and the Hindu Kush, especially see Gerald Morgan, *Ney Elias: Explorer and Envoy Extraordinary in High Asia* (London: George Allen & Unwin, 1971).

16. Knight, *Where Three Empires Meet*, 353; Johnson, *Spying for Empire*, 184; Postnikov, *Skhvatka na "kryshe mira,"* 275.

17. Regretfully, there is merely a single essay on Grombchevsky's life and activity translated from Polish into Russian: Jadwiga Chudzikowska and Jan Jaster, *Ludzie Wielkiej Przygody* (Warsaw, 1955); in the Russian translation, *Ludi velikoi otvagi* (Moscow: Gosudarstvennoe izdatel'stvo geografiicheskoi literatury, 1957), 247–52.

18. Bronislav Grombchevsky, *Doklad v Nikolaevskoi Akademii General'nogo Shtaba, March 26, 1891* (Tashkent: Shtab Turkestanskogo voennogo okruga, 1891), 2.

19. Woodman, *Himalayan Frontiers*, 72.

20. Arkhiv Vneshnei Politiki Rossiiskoi Imperii (hereafter, VPRI), f. 147, op. 485, d. 1296, ll. 7–8 rev., 20–23 rev., 47–52 rev., Zinoviev to Vannovsky, Tehran, April 28, 1888; Petrovsky to Zinoviev, Kashgar, August 26, 1888; and Grombchevsky to Petrovsky, October 5, 1888. On Grombchevsky's mission to Hunza and British concerns, also see ARGO, f. 45, op. 1, d. 2, ll. 1–260, Grombchevsky's diary of travel to Kanjut [Hunza] and Raskem in 1888; Robert Huttenback, "The 'Great Game' in the Pamirs and Hindu Kush: The British Conquest of Hunza and Nagar," *Modern Asian Studies* 9, no. 1 (1975): 1–29, at 26; Luzhetskaia, *Ocherki istorii*, 57–58; Johnson, *Spying for Empire*, 184–85, 279.

21. ARGO, f. 45, op. 1, d. 6, ll. 409–18, entry in the diary, October 23–25, 1889.

22. IOLR/L&PS/8/3, Younghusband to Parry Nisbet, the British Political Resident in Kashgaria, October 26, 1889. This episode is mentioned by all modern authors, e.g., see Peter Hopkirk, *The Great Game: On Secret Service in High Asia* (London: John Murray, 1990), 455–57; Verrier, *Francis Younghusband*, 111–12; French, *Younghusband*, 77; Postnikov, *Skhvatka na "kryshe mira,"* 236–38; Johnson, *Spying for Empire*, 187.

23. ARGO, f. 45, op. 1, d. 6, ll. 598–604, Grombchevsky's diary, October 28, 1889; AVPRI, f. 188, op. 761, d. 431, ll. 1–6, Grombchevsky to Petrovsky, September 15, 1889; ibid., ll. 7–17, Grombchevsky to the Imperial Russian Geographical Society, Saint Petersburg, January 22, 1891.

24. ARGO, f. 45, op. 1, d. 6, ll. 897–98, Grombchevsky's diary, October 10, 1890; also see Francis Younghusband, *The Light of Experience* (London: Archibald Constable, 1927), 54–55; Postnikov, *Skhvatka na "kryshe mira,"* 238–39.

25. For example, see ARGO, f. 45, op. 1, d. 10, ll. 1–12 rev., minutes by Grombchevsky on the modern political situation in the Pamirs khanates, February 4, 1890; *Novoe Vremya*, January 28 (February 9), 1891.

26. Quoted by Warren Walsh, "The Imperial Russian General Staff and India: A Footnote to Diplomatic History," *Russian Review* 16, no. 2 (1957): 53–58, at 56.

27. George Curzon, "The Fluctuating Frontier of Russia in Asia," *The Nineteenth Century* 144 (1889): 267–83, at 267.

28. Ibid., 283. Also see George Curzon, "The 'Scientific Frontier' an Accomplished Fact," *The Nineteenth Century* 136 (1888): 901–17; George Curzon, "The Unscientific Frontier of Russia in Asia," *The Nineteenth Century*, no. 143 (1889): 1–17. Significantly, the British high-ranking military shared Curzon's vision of the frontier problem. E.g., Major General C. Brownlow wrote to him on April 23, 1889: "Your article on our true policy in India is the best exposition of the subject that I have yet read. Since I saw you I have met Brackenbury, and I told him that I thought you knew more about the whole question than any man alive, soldier or civilian"; see Earl Ronaldshay, *The Life of Lord Curzon*, 3 vols. (London: Ernest Benn, 1928), vol. 1, 148.

29. See George Curzon, *Russia in Central Asia and the Anglo-Russian Question* (London: Frank Cass, 1967, orig. pub. 1889).

30. IOLR / Mss Eur F 111/113, minutes by Elles, Simla, 1892.

31. In the final count, the British annexed Gilgit to establish a military base there to counteract "the Bolshevik menace" in 1918–20. For further information on the role of Kashmir in Anglo-Russian relations, see Fida Mohammad Hassnain, *British Policy towards Kashmir (1846–1921): Kashmir in Anglo-Russian Politics* (New Delhi: Sterling, 1974), esp. 60, 115.

32. Gosudarstvennyi Arkhiv Rossiiskoi Federatsii (hereafter, GARF), f. 568, op. 1, d. 80, ll. 1–2, Dulep Singh to Alexander III, May 22, 1887. Also see the correspondence on Dulep Singh's arrival in Russia given by Petr Shastitko, ed., *Russko-indiiskie otnosheniia v XIX v. Sbornik arkhivnykh dokumentov i materialov* (Moscow: Vostochnaia literatura, 1997), 265–81. Significantly, Lamsdorf incorporated a telegram by the Austrian-Hungarian consul in Bombay to Vienna intercepted by the Russian secret service. The consul anticipated the British being coerced to come to agreement with any invader in order to avoid a general uprising in India, see V. N. Lamsdorf, *Dnevnik, 1886–1890* (Moscow: Gosudarstvennoe izdatel'stvo, 1926), 212.

33. Richard Popplewell, *Intelligence and Imperial Defense: British Intelligence and the Defense of the Indian Empire, 1904–1924* (London: Frank Cass, 1995), 24.

34. Frederick Roberts, *Forty-One Years in India from Subaltern to Commander-in-Chief*, 2 vols. (London: Macmillan, 1897), vol. 2, 428. Roberts sharply criticized the policy pursued by Lord Dufferin in India in the following way: "This [Lansdowne's appointment to the post of viceroy] augured well for the abandonment of the traditional, selfish, and, to my mind, shortsighted policy of keeping aloof, and I hoped that endeavours would at last be made to turn the tribesmen into friendly neighbors, to their advantage and ours instead of being obliged to have recourse to useless blockade or constant and expensive expeditions for their punishment, or else to induce them to refrain from troubling us by the payment of a heavy blackmail" (p. 429).

35. H. Lansdowne, *The Marquess of Lansdowne Correspondence with the Secretary of State for India, 1888–1894*, 5 vols. (Calcutta: Indian Government Office, 1894), vol. 1, 52, Lansdowne to Cross, Calcutta, March 20, 1889; vol. 3, 83, Cross to Lansdowne, London, November 12, 1891. Also see [An] Indian Officer [Frederick Roberts], *Russia's March towards India*, 2 vols. (London: Sampson Low, Marston, 1894), vol. 2, 78.

36. Lansdowne, *Marquess of Lansdowne Correspondence*, vol. 2, 95, Cross to Lansdowne, London, November 7, 1890.

37. AVPRI, f. 188, op. 761, d. 431, l. 54. Petrovsky to the Foreign Ministry's Asian Department, Kashgar, April 9, 1892. On the gradual modification of the Russian appreciation of the great powers in the 1880s, see Irene Gruening, *Die Russische oeffentliche Meinung und ihre Stellung zu den Grossmaechte vom Berliner Kongress bis zum Abschluss des franko-russischen Buendnis* (Berlin: F.W. Universitaet zu Berlin, 1927).

38. National Archives of the United Kingdom–Public Record Office (hereafter, PRO), WO/33/47, Official reports by the director of military intelligence, 1887. Also see John Le Donne, *The Russian Empire and the World, 1700–1917* (New York: Oxford University Press, 1997), 329, 331. For the evaluation of Churchill's trip to Russia, see K.V. Kasparian, "Rossiisko-britanskie otnosheniia v 80-e gg. XIX v. Konets politiki 'blestiatschei isoliatsii' Velikobritanii," in *Problemy otechestvennoi i zarubezhnoi istorii: Mneniia, oysenki, razmyshleniia—Uchenye zapiski kafedry otechestvennoi i zarubezhnoi istorii Piatigorskogo gosudarstvennogo lingvisticheskogo universiteta'*, edited by V. P. Yermakov (Piatigorsk: Piatigorskii gosudarstvennyi lingvisticheskii universitet, 2008), vol. 10, 212–40.

39. IOLR/L&PS/18/C 57/1–6, memorandum by Brackenbury, London, August 7, 1887.

40. W. Barnes, "Colonel Grombchevsky's Expeditions in Central Asia, and the Recent Events on the Pamirs," *Imperial and Asiatic Quarterly Review* 3, no. 5 (1892): 17–52, at 48.

41. E.g., see IOLR/L/MIL/17/14/80, memorandum by Roberts, Simla, October 14, 1890.

42. Ibid., Kimberley to Lansdowne, London, July 27, 1893.

43. A. Meyendorff, ed., *Correspondence diplomatique du Baron de Staal (1884–1900)*, 2 vols. (Paris: Libraire des Sciences Politiques et Sociales, 1929), vol. 2, 218–19.

44. On the preparations for this expedition and Ionov's subsequent encounter with British surveyors, see Rossiiskii Gosudarstvennyi Voenno-Istoricheskii Arkhiv (hereafter, RGVIA), f. 165, op. 1, d. 337, ll. 1–2, Petrovsky to the Foreign Ministry's Asian Department, Kashgar, September 20, 1891; AVPRI, f. 188, op. 761, d. 431, ll. 34–41, Vrevsky to Vannovsky, Tashkent, October 17, 1891; Lansdowne, *Marquess of Lansdowne Correspondence*, vol. 3, 69, 81, Cross to Lansdowne, London, September 24 and November 5, 1891. Also see IOLR / Mss Eur F 111/113, correspondence with regard to the Pamirs frontier, 1890–91, 156–86; Seaver, *Francis Younghusband*, 145. On British remonstrations, see Verrier, *Francis Younghusband*, 134; and

Johnson, *Spying for Empire*, 190. For the account of the eyewitness, see Francis Younghusband, *The Heart of a Continent* (London: John Murray, 1904), 289–94. A current interpretation of the episode by a distant descendant of Francis Younghusband is given by Tom Broadbent, *On Younghusband's Path: Peking to Pindi* (Aldwick, U.K.: Head-Hunter Books, 2005).

45. IOLR/L&PS/18/A 83/1–12, note by C.S.B[ailey], The Complication with Hunza, January 25, 1892; Algernon Durand, *The Making of a Frontier: Five Years Experience and Adventures in Gilgit, Hunza, Nagar, Chitral, and the Eastern Hindu Kush* (London: Murray, 1899), 254–70; Terentiev, *Istoriia zavoevaniia Srednei Asii*, vol. 3, 399. Interestingly, the troops under the command of Durand put the machine guns to use against the Hunza defenders for the first time in military history; see U. Rustamov, "Iz istorii angliiskoi agressii na granitsakh Pamira v kontse 80-kh gg. i v nachale 90-kh gg. XIX v.," *Institut vostokovedeniia An Uzbekskoi SSR: Trudy* 2 (1954): 70–79, at 77–78.

46. Huttenback, "'Great Game,'" 25–26.

47. Meyendorff, *Correspondence diplomatique*, vol. 2, 157–61, Morier to Giers, Saint Petersburg, January 25, 1892; Giers to Morier, Saint Petersburg, January 29, 1892. On Ionov's expeditions to the Pamirs, also see Boris Tageev, *Pamirskie pokhody 1892–1895: Desiatiletie prisoedineniia Pamira k Rossii* (Warsaw: Tipografiia Gubernskogo pravleniia, 1902), 44–47; Captain Zaichenko, *Pamiry i Sarikol (ocherk vozniknoveniia, posledovatel'nogo razvitiia i sovremennogo polozheniia Pamirskogo voprosa)* (Tashkent: Shtab Turkestanskogo voennogo okruga, 1903), 41–42; Terentiev, *Istoriia zavoevaniia Srednei Asii*, vol. 3, 401–2; Seaver, *Francis Younghusband*, 144–45; Verrier, *Francis Younghusband*, 115–41; French, *Younghusband*, 93–95; Hopkirk, *Great Game*, 467–69; Postnikov, *Skhvatka na "kryshe mira,"* 324–25; and Johnson, *Spying for Empire*, 190–94. For further information on the mapping of the Pamirs by Ionov and his escort during the expedition in 1891, see Postnikov, *Skhvatka na "kryshe mira,"* 317. A British chronicle of Ionov's marches may be found in IOLR / Mss Eur F 111/700/1– 23; and see W. Maclean and J. Ardagh, *Russian Advances in Asia* (London: Intelligence Branch of the Quartermaster-General's Department, 1895).

48. AVPRI, f. 138, op. 467, d. 126/131, ll. 2–3, 6–7, Morier to Giers, Saint Petersburg, January 2, 1892; Giers to Morier, Saint Petersburg, January 22, 1892; ibid., f. 147, op. 485, d. 826, ll. 6–7, Sakharov, the head of the Main Staff, to Lamsdorf, Saint Petersburg, May 3, 1903. The British military officers captured this letter in Hunza in the spring of 1903. On London's reaction to a new expedition conducted by Ionov to the Pamirs in July and August 1892, see IOLR/L&PS/18/A 86 a/1–5, note by S. C. B[ailey], the Russian Expedition to the Pamirs of 1892, August 12, 1892. For the Russian reappraisal of the Pamirs delimitation, see Kornilov, *Kashgaria ili Voctochnyi Turkestan*, 44–48.

49. Meyendorff, *Correspondence diplomatique*, vol. 2, 183, 186–88, Staal to Giers, London, August 23, 1892; Staal to Shishkin, the deputy foreign minister, London,

October 1892.

50. Lansdowne, *Marquess of Lansdowne Correspondence*, vol. 4, 56, Kimberley to Lansdowne, London, September 1, 1892.

51. Ibid., 83, 105, 141, Kimberley to Lansdowne, London, November 24, 1892; Lansdowne to Kimberley, Simla, September 6 and November 3, 1892. On the Russo-Afghan armed clash in the Pamirs, see Tageev, *Pamirskie pokhody*, 86–91.

52. *The Times,* August 25, 1892.

53. Lansdowne, *Marquess of Lansdowne Correspondence*, vol. 5, 7, Kimberley to Lansdowne, London, January 19, 1893.

54. AVPRI, f. 188, op. 761, d. 431, ll. 85–96, journals of the special conferences on the Pamirs, Saint Petersburg, April 27 and May 11, 1892; ibid., f. 138, op. 467, d. 126/131, ll. 40–45 rev., journal of the Special Conference on the Pamirs, Saint Petersburg, March 15, 1893.

55. Zaichenko, *Pamiry i Sarikol*, 114.

56. Le Donne, *Russian Empire*, 331. On Ionov's military expeditions to the Pamirs in 1891–94, also see Mikhail Gertsulin, "Dvizhenie letuchego otriada polkovnika Ionova v Rushan v 1893 g.," *Voennyi sbornik*, no. 4 (1900): 272–89; O. B. Bokiev, "Anglo-russkoe sopernichestvo v Srednei Asii v sviasi s prisoedineniem territorii Tadzhikistana k Rossii," in *Aktual'nye problemy istorii i istoriografii Srednei Asii (vtoraia polovina XIX–nachalo XX v.)*, edited by M. B. Babakhanov (Dushanbe: Tadzhikskii gosudarstvennyi universistet, 1990), 3–29; Andrei Smirnov, "U sten Indii: Pamirskie pokhody pri Alexandere III," *Rodina*, no. 8 (2001): 67–70.

57. Quoted by Leonid Bogdanovich, "Angliia i Rossiia v Srednei Asii," *Russkaia mysl'* 2 (1900): 139–61; 3: 19–29 (at 20).

58. Cited by W. Habberton, *Anglo-Russian Relations Concerning Afghanistan, 1837–1907* (Urbana: University of Illinois Press, 1937), 63.

59. Great Britain, Foreign Office, *Correspondence relating to the Occupation of Chitral* (London: Her Majesty's Stationery Office, 1896), 30–31. On the exchange of opinions between London and Calcutta on the subject, see Lansdowne, *Marquess of Lansdowne Correspondence*, vol. 5, 95–97, 98–99, 114–16, Lansdowne to Kimberley, Simla, July 4 and 11 and August 1, 1893. The negotiations between Durand and Abdur Rahman were analyzed by some contemporaries, e.g., Richard Bruce, the political agent in Baluchistan and commissioner in Punjab; see Richard Bruce, *The Forward Policy and Its Results* (London: Longmans, Green, 1900), 243–85. For a comprehensive review, see J. Harris, "British Policy on the North-West Frontier, 1889–1901," Ph.D. diss., University of London, 1960, 2, 108–36, 416–29; and Postnikov, *Skhvatka na "kryshe mira,"* 385.

60. RGVIA, f. 400, op. 1, d. 1832, ll. 2–18, short review of the British war preparations in the northwest frontier zone of India by Lieutenant General Protsenko, head of the headquarters of Trans-Caspia, 1895.

61. IOLR/L&PS/18/A 93/1–7, minutes by Bayley on the proposals of the Russian government on the Pamirs delimitation, April 7, 1894. Also see IOLR / Mss Eur

F 111/113; and G. Cockerill, *A Few Notes on the Possible Lines of Advance from the Russian Base upon Chitral and Gilgit* (Simla: Government Central Printing Office, 1894).

62. V. N. Lamsdorf, *Dnevnik, 1894–1896* (Moscow: Mezhdunarodnye otnosheniia, 1991), 61.

63. AVPRI, f. 147, op. 485, d. 688, ll. 1–2, Kimberley to Lascelles, the ambassador to Russia, London, March 15, 1895 (communicated to Lobanov-Rostovsky, the Russian foreign minister, on March 19, 1895). The detailed account of the British expedition to Chitral may be found in IOLR / Mss Eur F 111/115; *Correspondence Relating to Chitral* (London: Her Majesty's Stationery Office, 1895); and *Correspondence Relating to the Occupation of Chitral* (London: Her Majesty's Stationery Office, 1896).

64. Lamsdorf, *Dnevnik, 1894–1896*, 204.

65. As early as in March 1887, Admiral Ivan Shestakov, the acting naval minister, recorded in his diary: "The Germans appear to conquer us peacefully more rapidly and on a larger scale than we thought before!" (see OR RNB, f. 856, op. 637a, d. 14, l. 33). On the Franco-British diplomatic contacts in 1893–94, see Lamsdorf, *Dnevnik, 1894–1896*, 378.

66. More information about the negotiations on the Pamirs delimitation is given by Bogdanovich, "Angliia i Rossiia," 3:148; Tageev, *Pamirskie pokhody*, 142–44; Harris, "British Policy," 422–24; Woodman, *Himalayan Frontiers*, 97–98; Cedric Lowe, *The Reluctant Imperialists: British Foreign Policy, 1878–1902*, 2 vols. (London: Routledge & Kegan Paul, 1967), vol. 1, 187–90; and Peter Brown, *Die Verteidigung Indiens, 1800–1907: Das Problem der Vorwaertsstrategie* (Cologne: Boehlau Verlag, 1968), 148–51. The routine work of the Pamirs Boundary Commission is thoroughly described by Postnikov, *Skhvatka na "kryshe mira,"* 387–411.

67. *Pall Mall Gazette*, January 3, 1895; *The Times*, April 23, 1895; also see Memet Yetisgin, "How the *Times* of London Covered and Interpreted Russian Expansion into Central Asia in the Second Half of the 19th Century," Ph.D. diss., Texas Technological University, 2000, 235. According to the editorial in *The Contemporary Review* for May 1895, Rosebery spoke in favor of the rapprochement between Russia and Britain at the London Guild Hall. He maintained that the two empires were more allies than rivals, because both powers had common interests in Asia that should lead to a consolidation of their influence upon hundreds of millions nonwhite natives; the British statesman emphasized that "if England associates with Russia to harmonize Asiatic policy, their supremacy will be accepted as natural and fair by all European powers"; see RGVIA, f. 165, op. 1, d. 4807, ll. 13–18, clippings from the British periodicals, 1895.

68. RGVIA, f. 400, op. 1, d. 1832, ll. 19–39 rev., report of Kuropatkin to Obruchev, the head of the Main Staff, Ashgabat, November 14, 1895.

69. Ralph Cobbold, *Innermost Asia: Travel and Sport in the Pamirs* (London: William Heinemann, 1900), 269.

70. IOLR/L&PS/18/A 110/1–12, note on the Afghan succession and Russia's advance by Sir William Lee-Warner, Simla, August 26, 1896.

71. IOLR / Mss Eur F 111/53/143–49, Curzon's speech at the Royal Institution of Great Britain, London, May 10, 1895; IOLR / Mss Eur F 111/56/1–22, memorandum by Curzon on his visit to the Emir of Afghanistan, November 12–December 2, 1894.

72. IOLR / Mss Eur F 111/688/1–6, summary by Captain Douglas and Colonel Murray, Simla, March 1, 1899; ibid. F 111/695. Memorandum by Captain Douglas on Russia's capability to operate against North Afghanistan, 1899, Simla, 1899; AVPRI, f. 147, op. 485, d. 695, ll. 170–71, Petrovsky to the Foreign Ministry's Asian Department, Kashgar, June 16, 1899; Arkhiv Instituta Vostochnykh Rukopisei (hereafter, AIVR)-RAN, f. 115, op. 1, d. 122, ll. 2–8, instructions for the commander of the Pamirs task force, Tashkent, July 4, 1902. On the activity of British secret agents in the vassal Pamirs states in 1900–5, see Naftula Khalfin, *Rossiia i Bukharskii Emirat na Zapadnom Pamire (konets XIX–nachalo XX v.)* (Moscow: Vostochnaia literatura, 1975), 12–47. On the suppression of the Pathans' uprising in 1897–98, see IOLR / Mss Eur F111/115, *Papers Regarding British Relations with the Neighboring Tribes on the North-West Frontier of India and the Military Operations Undertaken against Them during the Years 1897–1898*, 2 vols. (London: Her Majesty's Stationery Office, 1898); Harris, "British Policy," 270–311; D. S. Richards, *The Savage Frontier: A History of the Anglo-Afghan Wars* (London: Macmillan, 1990), 129–41.

73. E.g., see Alexander Halliday, *The Retention of India* (London: Tinsley Brothers, 1872), 142. For a digest of articles on the subject, especially in the Anglo-Indian press, supplemented with critical remarks by the author, see G. R. Aberigh-Mackay, [*Some*] *Notes on* [*the Situation in*] *Western Turkistan* (Calcutta: Thacker, Spink, 1875).

74. IOLR/L/MIL/17/14/80/14–30, 36–45, 163–69, memoranda by Roberts to the government of India, Simla, December 31, 1883; Madras, May 22, 1885; Fort William, February 6, 1889, etc.; George Malleson, *Herat: The Granary and Garden of Central Asia* (London: W. Allen, 1880); George Malleson, *The Russo-Afghan Question and the Invasion of India* (London: G. Routledge & Sons, 1885).

75. IOLR/L&PS/18/A 95/1–11, note by Younghusband on the northern frontier of India, February 1895.

76. PRO/WO/106/6208/1–2, analysis by Grierson of General Kuropatkin's scheme for the invasion of India, August 1886. The top secret plans elaborated by Kuropatkin, who anticipated a two-pronged Russian attack upon the Turkish Straits and India, are thoroughly examined by William Beaver, "The Development of the Intelligence Division, and Its Role in Aspects of Imperial Policy Making, 1854–1901: The Military Mind of Imperialism," Ph.D. diss., University of Oxford, 1976, 158–90.

77. R. Pethybridge, "British Imperialists in the Russian Empire," *Russian Review* 30, no. 4 (1971): 346–55, at 351.

78. V. Lebedev, *V Indiiu! Voenno-statisticheskii i strategicheskii ocherk—Proekt budutschego pokhoda* (Saint Petersburg: A. Porokhovtschikov, 1898), 150.

79. F. Raskol'nikov, "Rossiia i Afghanistan: Istoricheskii ocherk," *Novyi Vostok* 4 (1923): 12–48, at 26.

80. On the role of native soldiers as the vanguard forces in the march to India, see IOLR/L&PS/18/C 62/1–13, secret memorandum addressed to General Komarov by a Muslim agent, who had been traveling for fourteen months in India, Afghanistan, and Turkestan, March 15, 1890.

81. RGVIA, f. 400, op. 1, d. 1626, ll. 1–6 rev., note by Protsenko to the Main Staff, September–October 1892.

82. Cited by Aaron Friedberg, *The Weary Titan: Britain and the Experience of Relative Decline 1895–1905* (Princeton, N.J.: Princeton University Press, 1988), 220. For an evaluation of Curzon's administrative reforms, see Collin Davies, "Lord Curzon's Frontier Policy and the Formation of the North-West Frontier Province, 1901," *Army Quarterly* 13 (1927): 261–73; Harris, "British Policy," 312–83; P. Braun, *Die Verteidigung Indiens, 1800–1907: Das Problem der Vorwaertsstrategie* (Cologne: Boehlau Verlag, 1968), 152–72; and David Gilmour, *Curzon* (London: Papermac, 1994), 191–203. On Russian concerns about Curzon's policy in India, see Popplewell, *Intelligence and Imperial Defense*, 42–56. For the current Russian evaluation of British strategies on the frontiers of India, see Sergei Bogomolov, "Strategicheskie osnovy politiki Britanskoi Indii na severo-zapadnom frontier (poslednyaia tret' XIX v.)," *Vostok*, no. 4 (2010): 34–44.

83. Viscount Mersey, *The Viceroys and Governors-General of India, 1757–1947* (London: John Murray, 1949).

84. Rossiiskii Gosudarstvennyi Arkhiv Voenno-Morskogo Flota (hereafter, RGA VMF), f. 417, op. 1, d. 1707, l. 12 rev. Also see PRO/FO/65/1725/66-67, note on the British consulates in Central Asia and the Russian Consulate in India, 1875–99.

85. Quoted by Alexander Popov, comp., "Angliiskaia politika v Indii i russko-indiiskie otnosheniia v 1897–1905 gg.," *Krasnyi Arkhiv* 6, no. 19 (1926): 53–63, at 59–60, Lamsdorf to Klemm, Saint Petersburg, September 19, 1900.

86. Ibid., 63, Klemm to the Foreign Ministry's Asian Department, Bombay, June 10, 1902. On the history of the Russian Consulate in Bombay, which began to function on November 22, 1900, see M. T. Kozhekina, "Forpost Rossii na Indostane: K 100-letiyu rossiskogo konsul'stva v Indii," *Vostochnyi arkhiv*, nos. 6–7 (2001): 35–46.

87. E.g., see A. Polosov, *Severo-zapadnaia granitsa Indii* (Saint Petersburg: Berezovsky, 1902). The commentaries on this book are given by Naftula Khalfin, *Angliiskaia kolonial'naia politika na Srednem Vostoke (70-e gg. XIX v.)* (Tashkent: Sredneasiatskii gosudarstvennyi universitet, 1957), 194.

88. RGVIA, f. 970, op. 3, d. 1594, l. 74, report of Esaul David Livkin to the Main Staff, 1899. On the missions to India undertaken by the Russian military, also

see Petr Shastitko, ed., *Rossiiskie puteshestvenniki v Indii XIX–nachala XX veka: Dokumenty i materially* (Moscow: Nauka, 1990), 159–234; and Evgeny Primakov, ed., *Ocherki istorii rossiiskoi vneshnei razvedki* (Moscow: Mezhdunarodnye otnosheniia, 1997), vol. 1, 172–80.

89. Esper Ukhtomsky, *Iz proshlogo* (Saint Petersburg:Vostok, 1902), 7. On the Russian strategic views upon frontiers in Asia, see RGVIA, f. 165, op. 1, d. 4777, ll. 1–12, summary of Asian frontiers compiled by Staff Captain Levitsky according to a lecture delivered by Major General Zolotarev at the Academy of the General Staff, Saint Petersburg, 1902. An overall evaluation of the Russian projects on the eve of the twentieth century is given by Alexis Krause, *Russia in Asia: A Record and Study, 1558–1899* (London and New York: G. Richards and H. Holt, 1900), 148–71.

90. Evgeny Augustus, "Vospominaniia uchastnika anglo-burskoi voiny 1899-1902 gg.," *Varshavskii voennyi zhurnal* 3 (1902): 219–28.

91. PRO/ADM/231/7/9, précis of official and other reports, London, August 1885. Also see numerous reports and memoranda by naval officers to the Admiralty Intelligence Department through 1887–94 in PRO/ADM/231/10/9; PRO/ADM/231/14/179, 182, 184, 187; PRO/ADM/231/18/62b, 69c, 254; etc.

92. William Langer, *The Diplomacy of Imperialism. 1890-1902,* New York: A. Knopf, 1935, p. 469.

93. RGAVMF, f. 410, op. 2, d. 2621, ll. 24–26 rev., journal of the special conference on the development of the Russian fleet, Saint Petersburg, December 1, 1895.

94. Ibid., f. 417, op. 1, d. 1896, ll. 2–7 rev., November 28, 1898–April 26, 1899. On the evaluation of the Russo-French military conventions signed in 1892–94, see V. N. Lamsdorf, *Dnevnik, 1891–1892* (Moscow: Akademiia, 1934), 336–40, minutes by Obruchev, Saint Petersburg, June 12, 1892.

95. RGAVMF, f. 417, op. 1, d. 1896, ll. 6–7 rev., Staal to Muraviev, London, November 23, 1898.

96. PRO/CAB/1/4/283/2/1–21, memorandum by Tilley respecting the relations between Russia and Great Britain, London, January 15, 1905; IOLR/L/PS/18/A 165, memorandum by J.E.S. of India Office Political Department on the direct relations between Russia and Afghanistan, London, June 10, 1907.

97. GARF, f. 568, op. 1, d. 84, ll. 1–30, memorandum by Lamsdorf on the Russian foreign affairs in connection with the Anglo-Boer War, Saint Petersburg, February 12, 1900; Alexander Popov, comp., "Tsarskaia diplomatiia o zadachakh Rossii na Dal'nem Vostoke," *Krasnyi Arkhiv* 5, no. 16 (1926): 3–29.

98. PRO/FO/17/1361, memorandum by Ardagh to the Foreign Office, London, July 18, 1898.

99. Apart from Macgregor's classic study of the Indian defense, these views were discussed in numerous reports, memoranda, and essays; e.g., see PRO/CAB/37/13, memorandum by Rothwell to the Cabinet, London, July 7, 1884; and PRO/CAB/37/19/8, memorandum by Brackenbury to the War Office, London,

January 25, 1887. Those commentaries by strategists and military experts that are worthy of being taken into account are reproduced by Charles Dilke and Spenser Wilkinson, *Imperial Defence* (London: Macmillan, 1892), 95–173; [An] Indian Officer [Frederick Roberts], *Russia's March*, vol. 2, 273–97; H. B. Hanna, *Can Russia Invade India?* (London: Archibald Constable, 1895), 37–52; and George Clarke, *Imperial Defence* (London: Imperial Press, 1897), 205–6. More British plans of how to counteract the Russian threat are interpreted by R. Greaves, *Persia and the Defense of India, 1884–1892: A Study in the Foreign Policy of the Third Marquis of Salisbury* (London: Athlone Press, 1959), 36–41; Lowe, *Reluctant Imperialists*, vol. 2, 45–46; B. Jelavich, "British Means of Offence against Russia in the Nineteenth Century," *Russian History* 1, pt. 2 (1974): 119–35, at 129; Friedberg, *Weary Titan*, 216–17; Robert Johnson, "Russians at the Gates of India? Planning the Defense of India, 1884–1899," *Journal of Military History* 67, no. 3 (2003): 697–743. A general review of the problem is presented by S. Mahajan, *British Foreign Policy, 1874–1914: The Role of India* (London: Routledge, 2002).

100. Quoted by D. Gillard, "Salisbury and the Indian Defense Problem, 1885–1902," in *Studies in International History*, edited by K. Bourne and D. Watt (London: Longman, 1967), 242.

101. J. B. Kelly, "Salisbury, Curzon and the Kuwait Agreement of 1899," in *Studies in International History*, edited by K. Bourne and D. Watt (London: Longmans, 1967).

102. PRO/FO/106/1, summaries of military intelligence, 1898–99; PRO/FO/106/2, Abdur Rahman to Curzon, Kabul, 1899; PRO/FO/106/3, Hamilton to Curzon, London, February 23, 1900, and Curzon to Hamilton, Simla, May 17, 1900.

103. IOLR / Mss Eur F 111/696/1902.

104. Ibid., Mss Eur F 132/37, memorandum by Balfour on the relations with Afghanistan, London, December 16, 1902.

105. E.g., see PRO/FO/106/10, correspondence between Dane and Curzon on Dane's mission to Habibulla Khan, December 1904–January 1905.

106. PRO/FO/106/11; IOLR / Mss Eur F 132/37.

107. Firuz Kazemzadeh, *Russia and Britain in Persia, 1864–1914* (New Haven, Conn.: Yale University Press, 1968), 143–44.

108. On the British evaluation of the German role in Asia, see Valentine Chirol, *The Middle Eastern Question or Some Political Problems of Indian Defence* (London: John Murray, 1903), 185–99.

109. Mary Macarthy, "Anglo-Russian Rivalry in Persia," *University of Buffalo Studies* 4, no. 2 (1925): 27–67; Boris Anan'ich, "Angliia i Rossiia v Persii nakanune soglasheniia 1907 g.," Kand. diss., Leningrad State University, 1980, 9–12. According to Russian statistics, the debt of Persia to Russia amounted to 72.2 million rubles (£7.2 million) in 1906, while her financial obligation to Britain did not exceed 2 million rubles (£200,000); see Alexander Popov, comp., "Anglo-russkoe sopernichestvo v Persii v 1890–1906 gg.," *Krasnyi Arkhiv* 1, no. 56 (1933): 33–64, at 61. A contemporary British evaluation of the Russian

influence upon Persia is given by Valentine Chirol, *Fifty Years in a Changing World* (London: Jonathan Cape, 1927), 159–60.

110. Nugsar Ter-Oganov, "Persidskaia kazachya brigada: Period transformatsii (1894–1903)," *Vostok*, no. 3 (2010): 69–79.

111. S. Gwynn, ed., *The Letters and Friendships of Sir Cecil Spring Rice*, 2 vols. (London: Archibald Constable, 1929), vol. 1, 289, Spring-Rice to Chirol, Tehran, September 15, 1899.

112. Chirol, *The Middle Eastern Question, or Some Political Problems of Indian Defense* (London: John Murray, 1903), 256.

113. Vladimir Kosogovsky, "Persiia v kontse XIX v. (dnevnik generala Kosogovskogo)," *Novyi Vostok* 3 (1923): 446–69; Vladimir Kosogovsky, "Ocherk razvitiia persidskoi kazachiei brigady," *Novyi Vostok* 4 (1923): 390–402.

114. A. Rouire, *La rivalité Anglo-Russe au XIXe siècle en Asie: Golfe Persique—Frontière de l'Inde* (Paris: Librairie A. Colin, 1908), 78.

115. The role of this province, which had assumed new significance in the period of the Great Game, is perfectly studied by L. Morris, "British Secret Service Activity in Khorassan, 1887–1908," *Historical Journal* 27, no. 3 (1984): 657–75. On the deterioration of the British position in Persia in the last quarter of the nineteenth century, as viewed by an Asiatic observer, see Selim Faris, *The Decline of British Prestige in the East* (London: T. Fisher Unwin, 1887), esp. 90–-30.

116. Greaves, *Persia*, 20.

117. Cited by Kazemzadeh, *Russia and Britain*, 157.

118. Meyendorff, *Correspondence diplomatique*, vol. 2, 44, 49–51, Staal to Giers, London, August 8 and 27, 1889; PRO/FO/539/45, memorandum by Wolff, London, September 2, 1889.

119. Kazemzadeh, *Russia and Britain*, 184.

120. Greaves, *Persia*, 120–36.

121. Chirol, *Fifty Years*, 151. It should be noted that Curzon as the Viceroy of India criticized Salisbury's foreign policy. E.g., he complained to Hamilton in a private message on September 6, 1899: "We live in that institution [the Foreign Office], as a three years' experience enabled me to judge, from hand to mouth. There are no settled principles of policy in relation to any part of the world; and everyone from the exalted head down to the humbled clerk sits there anxiously waiting to see what will turn up next"; quoted by J. A. S. Grenville, *Lord Salisbury and Foreign Policy: The Close of the Nineteenth Century* (London: Athlone Press, 1964), 296–97.

122. Curzon, *Persia and the Persian Question* (London: Longmans, Green, 1892), 593–94. Interestingly, one of Curzon's three daughters, Lady Alexandra Metcalfe, recalled that in the 1950s "a tattered copy was treasured in the British Embassy in Teheran, read by all the diplomatic staff as the guide that rivaled all others," whereas "another copy was highly valued by the BBC staff at Bush House"; see Peter King, ed., *Curzon's Persia* (London: Sidgwick and Jackson, 1986), 9.

123. AVPRI, f. 147, op. 485, d. 1696, ll. 1–41, note by Dondukov-Korsakov on the situation in Trans-Caspia, January 26, 1887. For a recent study of the role of Trans-Caspia in Russo-British relations, see Nataliya N. Lisitsyna, "Zakaspiiskii krai v anglo-russkikh otnosheniiakh (1880–1917)," Kand. diss., Moskovskii otkrytyi pedagogicheskii universitet, Moscow, 2006.

124. Aleksei Kuropatkin, *Vsepoddaneishii otchet o poezdke v Teheran v 1895 g.* (1895), 42.

125. See David Maclean, *Britain and Her Buffer State: The Collapse of the Persian Empire, 1890–1914* (London: Royal Historical Society, 1979), 24.

126. Popov, "Anglo-russkoe sopernichestvo v Persii," 63.

127. Hermann Brunnhofer, *Russlands Hand ueber Asien: Historisch-geographische Essays zur Entwicklungsgeschichte des russischen Reichsgedankens* (Saint Petersburg: Typographie der Aktien Gesellschaft, 1897), 45.

128. PRO/CAB/1/4/371, memorandum by Curzon and Kitchener on the provisional report of the Defence Committee on the Indian defense, Simla, August 7, 1903.

129. Anthony Wynn, *Persia in the Great Game: Sir Percy Sykes—Explorer, Consul, Soldier, Spy* (London: John Murray, 2003), 24–37, 137.

130. V. A. Kosogovsky, *Iz tegeranskogo dnevnika polkovnika V.A. Kosogovskogo*, edited by G. M. Petrob and G. L. Bondarevskii (Moscow: Vostochnaia literatura, 1960), 135.

131. RGIA, f. 560, op. 45, d. 77, ll. 11–13 rev., Consul Mashkov to the Russian chargé d'affaires in Tehran, Baghdad, January 22, 1896.

132. PRO/FO/539/72/1–16, memorandum by Durand, Tehran, September 27, 1895.

133. Ibid., FO/539/73/2 rev., memorandum by Curzon, London, April 12, 1896.

134. Robert Taylor, *Lord Salisbury* (London: Allen Lane, 1975), 170.

135. Quoted by Grenville, *Lord Salisbury*, 298.

136. Gwynn, *Letters and Friendships*, vol. 1, 285–86, Spring-Rice to Villiers, Tehran, August 23, 1899.

137. *Novoe Vremya*, November 13, 1899; the editorial was titled "Russia's Great Task in the Middle Asiatic East."

138. Irina Rybachenok, comp., *Korennye interesy Rossii glazami eyo gosudarstvennykh deiatelei, diplomatov, voennykh i publitsistov* (Moscow: Institut rossiskoi istorii RAN, 2004), 343, Lamsdorf to Benkendorf, Saint Petersburg, December 13, 1902.

139. Efim Rezvan, *Russian Ships in the Gulf, 1899–1903* (Reading, U.K.: Ithaca Press, 1993), 2–3.

140. IOLR/L&PS/18/C 94/1–5, note by Lee-Warner on the British interests in Persia and the Gulf, May 5, 1899.

141. Grigory Bondarevsky, *Angliiskaia politika i mezhdunarodnye otnosheniia v basseine Persidskogo zaliva (konets XIX—nachalo XX v.)* (Moscow: Nauka, 1968), 32–33.

142. Curzon, *Persia*, vol. 2, 465. On the views of Curzon's proponents, see W. K. Fraser-Tytler, *Afghanistan: A Study of Political Developments in Central and Southern Asia* (London: Oxford University Press, 1967), 113.

143. Bondarevsky, *Angliiskaia politika*, 104–6, 122.

144. RGA VMF, f. 417, op. 1, d. 2032, ll. 5–6 rev., Kruglov, the consul in Baghdad, to the Russian Embassy in Constantinople, April 13, 1899. The estimation of Anglo-Indian troops sent to South Africa in the course of the Boer War is given by Ronaldshay, *Life of Lord Curzon*, vol. 2, 69.

145. IOLR / Mss Eur 111/689/1–9, summary by Douglas and Barrow on the principal events during 1899, Simla, March 2, 1900.

146. M. Brett, ed., *Journals and Letters of Reginald Viscount Esher*, 2 vols. (London: Ivor Nicholson and Watson, 1934), vol. 1, 241.

147. Quoted by Rezvan, *Russian Ships*, 4. For the correspondence on the dispatch of a Russian gunboat to the Gulf, see RGA VMF, f. 417, op. 1, d. 2032, ll. 7–7 rev., Tyrtov to Muraviev, Saint Petersburg, May 29, 1899.

148. AVPRI, f. 144, op. 488, d. 4067, ll. 1–215, collection of documents on the Russian warships' visits to the Persian Gulf, 1901–3. Further details are given by Rezvan, *Russian Ships*, 5–22; Petr Ostrikov, "K istorii imperialisticheskoi ekspansii Anglii v Irane v nachale XX v.," in *Protiv falk'sifikatsii istorii kolonialisma*, edited by K. Popov (Moscow: Vostochnaia literatura, 1962), 77–103; Laura Akhmedova, *Politika Anglii v zone Persidskogo zaliva v poslednei treti XIX–nachale XX v.* (Saint Petersburg: Sankt-Peterburgskii universitet, 2006), 45–77.

149. PRO/CAB/6/1/24 D, report by Captain Smyth, London, June 6, 1903.

150. IOLR/L&PS/18/C 105/1-6, minutes by Curzon, October 28, 1901.

151. Quoted by Bondarevsky, *Angliiskaia politika*, 451.

152. Rezvan, *Russian Ships*, 18.

153. E.g., see H. Whigham, *The Persian Problem* (London: Isbister, 1903), 57–76.

154. PRO/CAB/6/1/100/1–10, memoranda by the War Office Intelligence Department, London, March 10, 1903.

155. Quoted by Beryl Williams, "The Strategic Background to the Anglo-Russian Entente of August 1907," *Historical Journal* 9, no. 3 (1966): 360–73, at 362.

156. *The Hansard Parliamentary Debates* (London: C. Buck, 1908), Lords, series 4, vol. 121, col. 1348, May 5, 1903. Also see Lord Newton, *Lord Lansdowne. A Biography* (London: Macmillan, 1929), 242–43; Hossein Nazem, *Russia and Great Britain in Iran (1900–1914)* (Tehran: Sherkat Iran Chap, 1975), 14.

157. Quoted by Parshotam Mehra, *The Younghusband Expedition: An Interpretation* (London: Asia Publishing House, 1968), 98.

158. Gilmor, *Curzon*, 268.

159. Chirol, *Fifty Years*, 168–70; Ronaldshay, *Life of Lord Curzon*, vol. 2, 305–19; Bondarevsky, *Angliiskaia politika*, 495–98. On the failure of Curzon's landing in Bushire in November 1903, see Sergei V. Chirkin, *Dvadtsat' let sluzhby na Vostoke: Zapiski tsarskogo diplomata* (Moscow: Russkii put', 2006), 105–7.

160. Gilmor, *Curzon*, 269–70.

161. Ronaldshay, *Life of Lord Curzon*, vol. 2, 101–2.

162. Bondarevsky, *Angliiskaia politika*, 495–98.

163. On the interpretation of Tibet as the "Land of Snows" or the "Roof of the

World," especially see Thomas Gordon, *The Roof of the World: Being the Narrative of a Journey over the High Plateau of Tibet to the Russian Frontier and the Oxus Sources on the Pamirs* (Edinburgh: Edmonton and Douglas, 1876); Sven Hedin, *Central Asia and Tibet: Towards the Holy City of Lhasa*, 2 vols. (London: Hurst and Blackett, 1903). For further information about the explorers of Tibet, see John Macgregor, *Tibet: A Chronicle of Exploration* (London: Routledge & Kegan Paul, 1970).

164. Nikolai Kaznakov, the governor-general of Western Siberia, rather pessimistically evaluated the development of this part of the Russian Empire; see RGIA, f. 948, op. 1, d. 64, ll. 1–17, a humble report by Kaznakov to the tsar, 1875.

165. RGVIA, f. 400, op. 1, d. 554, ll. 1–2, minutes by Golovin, April 1878.

166. Ibid., ll. 3–5 rev.

167. Ibid., ll. 10–10 rev., Giers to Miliutin, Saint Petersburg, July 18, 1878.

168. Ibid., d. 553, ll. 3–4, memorandum by Przhevalsky, Saint Petersburg, September 6, 1878.

169. David Schimmelpenninck van der Oye, "Ex Oriente Lux: Ideologies of Empire and Russia's Far East, 1895–1904," Ph.D. diss., Yale University, 1997, 31–32.

170. For further analysis of the situation in Burma, especially after the mission by Forsyth to Mandalay in May 1875, see RGVIA, f. 431, op. 1, d. 54, ll. 1–12 rev., note by an anonymous military expert to Miliutin, Saint Petersburg, January 26, 1877; AVPRI, f. 147, op. 485, d. 988, ll. 10–11 rev., Mendeleev to the Naval Ministry, Nice, December 6, 1878.

171. IOLR / Mss Eur F 111/842, anonymous, notes on the Gold Mines of Tibet, March 28, 1899. Also see Alexander Andreev, *Tibet v politike tsarskoi, sovetskoi i postsovetskoi* (Saint Petersburg: Saint Petersburg State University–Nartang, 2006), 59.

172. Ekai Kawaguchi, *Three Years in Tibet* (Madras: Theosophical Publishing Society, 1909), 405. For a brief review of Kawaguchi's clandestine activity in Lhasa and his contacts with Sarat Chandra Das, see Peter Hopkirk, *Trespassers on the Roof of the World: The Race for Lhasa* (London: John Murray, 1982), 148–58.

173. PRO/FO 17/1055, report by Elias to the Foreign Office on Tibet, March 5, 1887.

174. Wang Furen and Suo Wenting, *Highlights of Tibetan Policy* (Beijing: New World Press, 1984), 120.

175. AVPRI, f. 147, op. 485, d. 907, ll. 45–45 rev., extracts from *The Chinese Times*, 1890. Also see Alastair Lamb, *Britain and Chinese Central Asia: The Road to Lhasa, 1767–1905* (London: Routledge & Kegan Paul, 1960), 241; and Mehra, *Younghusband Expedition*, 73.

176. Quoted by Mehra, *Younghusband Expedition*, 149.

177. Sergei Witte, *Vospominaniia* (Berlin: Slovo, 1922), vol. 1, 39. For a comprehensive study of Badmaev's note, see Andrew Malozemoff, *Russian Far Eastern Policy 1881–1904* (Berkeley: University of California Press, 1958), 48–49.

178. See Peter Fleming, *Bayonets to Lhasa: The First Full Account of the British Invasion of Tibet in 1904* (London: Rupert Hart-Davis, 1961), 29. On Badmaev's political career, see John Snelling, *Buddhism in Russia: The Story of Agvan Dorzhiev, Lhasa's*

Emissary to the Tsar (Shaftsbury, U.K.: Element, 1993), 85–86.

179. AVPRI, f. 188, op. 761, d. 362, ll. 15–16 rev., 17–19 rev., Vladimir Luba, the consul in Urga, to Pavlov, chargé d'affaires in Peking, Urga, January 9 and December 6, 1897. On the loan to Badmaev, see Vladimir Semennikov, ed., *Za kulisami Tsarisma: Arkhiv tibetskogo vracha P.A. Badmaeva* (Leningrad: Gosudarstvennoe izdatel'stvo, 1925), 83–85; Malozemoff, *Russian Far Eastern Policy*, 49.

180. Semennikov, *Za kulisami Tsarisma*, 49–75; Kawaguchi, *Three Years*, 495–96.

181. Francis Younghusband, *India and Tibet* (London: John Murray, 1910), 75.

182. Austin Waddel, *Lhasa and Its Mysteries* (London: John Murray, 1905), 39.

183. Gombozhab Tsybikov, *O tsentral'nom Tibete* (Saint Petersburg: Imperatorskoe russkoe geographicheskoe obtschestvo, 1903), 32. It is worthy of note that approximately 160,000 Buriats and 200,000 Kalmucks inhabited the Russian Empire in the late 1890s and early 1900s; see Tatiana Shaumian, *Tibet: The Great Game and Tsarist Russia* (New Delhi: Oxford University Press, 2000), 16. On Tsybikov's activity as an expert in the Buddhist faith, see Snelling, *Buddhism*, 74–75.

184. Quoted by Lamb, *Britain and Chinese Central Asia*, 236.

185. Macgregor, *Tibet*, 287. A careful study of the Dalai Lama's life and political activity is made by Tokan Tada, *The Thirteenth Dalai Lama* (Tokyo: Centre for East Asian Cultural Studies, 1965). A more recent evaluation is presented by Nikita Voul', "Politicheskaia istoriia Tibeta vo vremia pravleniia Dalai-Lamy XIII," Kand. diss., Sankt-Peterburgskii gosudarstvennyi universitet, Saint Petersburg, 2007.

186. Dorzhiev's enigmatic personality attracted the attention of contemporaries and academic scholars throughout the twentieth century; e.g., see Lamb, *Britain and Chinese Central Asia*, 253–56. His activity as a diplomatic mediator between Tibet and Russia and later as a public and religious activist is analyzed by Macgregor, *Tibet*, 281–96; Snelling, *Buddhism*, 77–89; Aldar Damdinov, "Agvan Dorzhiev: Diplomat, politicheskii, obstchestvennyi i religioznyi deiatel,'" Kand. diss., Irkutskii gosudarstvennyi universitet, 1996, 1–23; Shaumian, *Tibet*, 21–34; Nikolai Kuleshov, "Agvan Dorjiev, the Dalai Lama's Ambassador," in *The History of Tibet*, vol. 3, edited by A. Mackay (London: RoutledgeCurzon, 2003), 57–68; and Andreev, *Tibet v politike*, 77–103.

187. Agvan Dorzhiev, *Predanie o krugosvatnom puteshestvii ili povestvonaie o zhizni Agvana Dorzhieva* (Ulan-Ude: Buriatsky institute obtschestvennykh nauk SO RAN, 1994), 51.

188. Agvan Dorzhiev, *Zanimatel'nye zametki: Opisanie puteshestviia vokrug sveta* (Moscow: Vostochnaia literatura, 2003), 47–48.

189. Alexandre Ular, *A Russo-Chinese Empire* (London: Archibald Constable, 1904), 169–70.

190. Dorzhiev, *Predanie*, 53; Andreev, *Tibet v politike*, 81.

191. Shaumian, *Tibet*, 14. Contrary to the accounts of eyewitnesses and those of Dorzhiev himself, modern Russian authors still negate both the political aspect of Dorzhiev's mission and the Tsarist government's promises of support to Tibet;

e.g., see Kuleshov, "Agvan Dorjiev," 61–64.

192. This intelligence is given by W. Filchner, *Sturm ueber Asien: Erlebnisse eines diplomatischen Geheimagenten* (Berlin: Verlag Neufeld and Henius, 1924), 4–5. Some Indian scholars reanimated this concept; see Mehra, *Younghusband Expedition*, 136–37. Yet the majority of British authors, like their Russian colleagues, criticized this opinion; see Snelling, *Buddhism*, 39.

193. Quoted by Macgregor, *Tibet*, 353.

194. PRO/FO/65/1601, Hardinge to Lansdowne, Saint Petersburg, October 17 and 31, 1900; Gwynn, *Letters and Friendships*, vol. 2, Spring-Rice to Hardinge, March 15, 1906. On the tsar's ambitions in Asia, see Premen Addy, *Tibet on the Imperial Chessboard: The Making of British Policy towards Lhasa, 1899–1905* (Calcutta: Academic Publishers, 1984), 186. The distinguished Swedish traveler Sven Hedin likewise alluded to the ancient prophesy that said that "the Tsagan Khan, or White Emperor, would some day rule over the whole world, conquer Tibet and destroy Lhasa"; Hedin, *Central Asia and Tibet*, vol. 2, 35.

195. Frederick O'Connor, *On the Frontier and Beyond* (London: John Murray, 1931), 28.

196. IOLR / Mss Eur F 111/342, Hamilton to Curzon, London, April 18, 1899; Snelling, *Buddhism*, 287.

197. IOLR / Mss Eur F 111/342, memorandum by B.M.G. on the alleged missions between Russia and Tibet, April 26, 1902; Kawaguchi, *Three Years*, 497–99. It is noticeable that Lev Berlin, the first Soviet researcher of Dorzhiev's missions to Russia, studied his activities in the context of the Tibetan struggle for independence, see Lev Berlin, "Khambo Agvan Dorzhiev (k bor'be Tibeta za vezavisimost')," *Novyi Vostok* 3 (1923): 139–56. Interestingly, Georgy Chicherin, the renowned Soviet people's commissar for foreign affairs, published a special article on the history of the national liberation movement in Tibet; see Georgy Chichern, " Novyi uspekh Vostoka," *Izvestiia*, August 12, 1925. On the political interpretation of the legend of Shangri-La and a Buddhist prince—the "savior of Tibet"— especially see David Schimmelpenninck van der Oye, "'Tournament of Shadows: Russia's Great Game in Tibet," *Tibetan Review* 29, no. 1 (1994): 13–20, at 18.

198. Quoted by Fleming, *Bayonets to Lhasa*, 43–44.

199. Snelling, *Buddhism*, 85. For the text of the Russo-Tibetan draft treaty, see Ular, *Russo-Chinese Empire*, 306; Angus Hamilton, *Problems of the Middle East* (London: Eveleigh Nash, 1909), 216–17.

200. PRO/FO 535/3, correspondence respecting the affairs of Tibet, 1903, pt. 3; Dorzhiev, *Predanie*, 57, 90; Dorzhiev, *Zanimatel'nye zametki*, 52–54; Kawaguchi, *Three Years*, 505–6; Braun, *Die Verteidigung Indiens*, 190; Shaumian, *Tibet*, 29; Andreev, *Tibet v politike*, 94, 102–3.

201. Quoted by Verrier, *Francis Younghusband*, 174.

202. RGIA, f. 948, op. 1, d. 132, ll. 12–17 rev., Kozlov to the Imperial Russian Geographical Society, Chamdo, December 1900.

203. RGIVIA, f. 2000, op. 1, d. 1086, ll. 1–3, note by Kozlov on Tibet, June 1900.

204. Ibid., f. 447, op. 1, d. 60, ll. 7–30 rev., note by Staff Captain Rossov on the significance of Tibet in the Russian interpretation, March 1903.

205. See Addy, *Tibet*, 52–53. On Lord Curzon's Tibetan policy from 1899 to 1902, also see Lamb, *Britain and Chinese Central Asia*, 239–74.

206. See Ular, *Russo-Chinese Empire*, 168.

207. Quoted by Andreev, *Tibet v politike*, 107.

208. Quoted by Lamb, *Britain and Chinese Central Asia*, 239–40.

209. Quoted by Mehra, *Younghusband Expedition*, 116.

210. S. Gopal, *British Policy in India, 1858–1905* (Cambridge: Cambridge University Press, 1965), 235.

211. Quoted by G. Gooch, "Continental Agreements, 1902–1907," in *The Cambridge History of British Foreign Policy, 1783–1919*, edited by A. W. Ward and G. P. Gooch (Cambridge: Cambridge University Press, 1923), vol. 3, 322.

212. Kawaguchi, *Three Years*, 697–98; Filchner, *Sturm ueber Asien*, 64; Lamb, *Britain and Chinese Central Asia*, 267; Mehra, *Younghusband Expedition*, 149.

213. IOLR / Mss Eur F 111/342, reports from the Intelligence Branch to the government of India, 1902.

214. Lamb, *Britain and Chinese Central Asia*, 268; Shaumian, *Tibet*, 34, 50.

215. AVPRI, f. 188, op. 761, d. 402, ll. 3–4; Earl of Ronaldshay, *On the Outskirts of Empire in Asia* (Edinburgh: W. Blackwood and Sons, 1904), 353; Fleming, *Bayonets to Lhasa*, 45–46; Macgregor, *Tibet*, 303–6.

216. Quoted by Michael Edwardes, *Playing the Great Game* (London: Hamish Hamilton, 1975), 147–48.

217. PRO/FO 539/88, further correspondence respecting Central Asia, 1904; e.g., see the editorial in *The Transcaspian Review*, December 16, 1903.

218. See Younghusband, *India and Tibet*, 79–83; Alastair Lamb, *British India and Tibet, 1766–1910* (London: Routledge & Kegan Paul, 1986), 254.

219. Lamb, *British India and Tibet*, 283–84.

220. E.g., see AVPRI, f. 188, op. 761, d. 402, ll. 6–6 rev., Lamsdorf to Lessar, Saint Petersburg, September 17, 1902. For further information on the Russo-British diplomatic consultations, see V. A. Teplov, *Angliiskaia ekspeditsiia v Tibet* (Saint Petersburg: V. Komarov, 1904), 39, 43–44; Younghusband, *India and Tibet*, 82; Gwynn, *Letters and Friendships*, vol. 1, 362–87.

221. PRO/FO 17/1554; FO 17/1745, minutes by Lansdowne, London, October 1, 1902; Lamb, *Britain and Chinese Central Asia*, 275; Fleming, *Bayonets to Lhasa*, 48.

222. The details of the so-called Alekseev-Tsen agreement were analyzed by Ivan Korostovets, *Rossiia na Dal'nem Vostoke* (Peking: Vostochnoe Prosvetschenie, 1922), 128–29.

223. PRO/FO 17/1745, Curzon to Hamilton, Calcutta, November 13, 1902. For a thorough analysis of Curzon's initiative, especially see Lamb, *Britain and Chinese Central Asia*, 279 ff.; Fleming, *Bayonets to Lhasa*, 48, 55–56; Macgregor, *Tibet*, 306; and Snelling, *Buddhism*, 106.

224. PRO/FO 535/1, correspondence respecting the affairs of Tibet. 1903, pt. 1, Hosie to Townly, Chengtu, August 1, 1903; Teplov, *Angliiskaia ekspeditsiia*, 65; Snelling, *Buddhism*, 109; Fleming, *Bayonets to Lhasa*, 155; Shaumian, *Tibet*, 37.

225. Mehra, *Younghusband Expedition*, 170, Balfour to King Edward VII, London, February 19, 1903.

226. Quoted by William Dawson, "Forward Policy and Reaction" in *Cambridge History*, ed. Ward and Gooch, vol. 3, 324.

227. Ibid., 326.

228. Quoted by Fleming, *Bayonets to Lhasa*, 71. Also see Charles Allen, *Duel in the Snows: The True Story of the Younghusband Mission to Lhasa* (London: John Murray, 2004), 20.

229. PRO/FO 535/1, 1903, pt. 1, memorandum by Younghusband, Simla, October 26, 1903.

230. Younghusband, *India and Tibet*, 150–295; Filchner, *Sturm ueber Asien*, 72–73; Hopkirk, *Great Game*, 508–12.

231. The most informative accounts of the Younghusband expedition were published by Edmund Candler, *The Unveiling of Lhasa* (London: E. Arnold, 1905); Perceval Landon, *The Opening of Tibet* (New York: Doubleday, Page, 1905); Laurence Waddell, *Lhasa and Its Mysteries: With a Record of the British Tibetan Expedition of 1903–1904* (London: John Murray, 1905); William Ottley, *With Mounted Infantry in Tibet* (London: Smith, Elder, 1906); Younghusband, *India and Tibet*; and O'Connor, *On the Frontier*, 24–73. Various academic interpretations are given by Seaver, *Francis Younghusband*, 201–50; V. P. Leontiev, *Inostrannaia ekspansiia v Tibete v 1888–1919 gg.* (Moscow: Izdatel'stvo AN SSSR, 1956); Lamb, *Britain and Chinese Central Asia*, 275–317; Fleming, *Bayonets to Lhasa*; Mehra, *Younghusband Expedition*; Macgregor, *Tibet*, 307–47; Verrier, *Francis Younghusband*, 179–91; French, *Younghusband*, 202–52; Allen, *Duel in the Snows*; Wendy Palace, *The British Empire and Tibet 1900–1922* (London: RoutledgeCurzon, 2005), 1–14; and Andreev, *Tibet v politike*, 105–32.

232. Waddell, *Lhasa*, 122; Allen, *Duel in the Snows*, 287.

233. Fleming, *Bayonets to Lhasa*, 268.

234. IOLR / Mss Eur F 111/342, memorandum by Curzon, London, June 25, 1904.

235. Great Britain, Parliamentary Papers, *Further Papers Relating to Tibet (Tibet No. 2)* (London: His Majesty's Stationery Office, 1904), 4–7; Mehra, *Younghusband Expedition*, 385–86. The Anglo-Tibetan negotiations in September 1904 were depicted by Waddell, *Lhasa*, 308–14, and Younghusband, *Light of Experience*, 99–100. For Russian commentaries on the Anglo-Tibetan Convention, see Leontiev, *Inostrannaia ekspansiia*, 217–18.

236. Fleming, *Bayonets to Lhasa*, 137.

237. Younghusband, *Light of Experience*, 86. For further information on Kitchener's army reforms in India, especially see George Arthur, *Life of Lord Kitchener*, 2 vols. (London: Macmillan, 1920), vol. 2, 140–41; and Evgeny Steinberg, "Angliiskaia

versiia o 'russkoi ugroze' Indii v XIX–XX vv.," *Istoricheskie zapiski* 33 (1950): 47–66, at 63.

238. Quoted by Addy, *Tibet*, 128.

239. Cited by Mehra, *Younghusband Expedition*, 279, Brodrick to Ampthill, May 20, 1904. On the Cabinet's attitude toward Younghusband's expedition to Tibet, also see Ronaldshay, *On the Outskirts*, 361–62; and Owen Lattimore, *Inner Asian Frontiers of China* (London: Oxford University Press, 1940), 237.

240. *Novoe Vremya*, July 15, 1903. The apprehension of the Tibetan problem in the Russian press is studied by G. Telepina, "Russkaia pechat' o politike Anglii v Tibete v nachale XX v.," *Institut Dal'nego Vostoka: Informatsionnyi bulletin*, no. 120, pt. 2 (1983): 62–71.

241. Steinberg, "Angliiskaia versiia," 64.

242. Teplov, *Angliiskaia ekspeditsiia*, 69.

243. Quoted by Mehra, *Younghusband Expedition*, 216.

244. AVPRI, f. 188, op. 761, d. 402, ll. 37a–37b, 43, and f. 147, op. 485, d. 927, ll. 7–11, Klemm to Hartvig, Bombay, November 14 and 29, 1903, and January 7, 1904.

245. ARGO, f. 18, op. 1, d. 40, ll. 3 rev.–4, Kozlov to the Main Staff, 1904.

246. RGVIA, f. 2000, op. 1, d. 1086, ll. 6–7, Lasarev to Tselebrovsky, the chief of the Main Staff Military Statistical Department, Paris, October 19, 1904.

247. AVPRI, f. 188, op. 761, d. 402, l. 68, Lamsdorf to Lessar, Saint Petersburg, February 1, 1904; GARF, f. 568, op. 1, d. 82, l. 31 rev., note by Alexander Izvolsky on the Tibetan question, June 12, 1906. For a thorough description of the Ulanov-Ulianov mission, see Primakov, *Ocherki istorii*, vol. 1, 183–90. Regrettably, Patrick French mistakenly wrote of Lamsdorf's ignorance of this expedition; see French *Younghusband*, 187. On Dorzhiev's role at the Court of the Dalai Lama while staying in Mongolia, see Filchner, *Sturm ueber Asien*, 85–107.

248. AVPRI, f. 188, op. 761, d. 402, ll. 107–8, Rabdanov to Dorzhiev, Dazinlu, July 27, 1904.

249. Primakov, *Ocherki istorii*, 188–89.

250. AVPRI, f. 147, op. 485, d. 927, ll. 33–34 rev., Klemm to Hartvig, Bombay, February 23, 1904.

251. Ibid., d. 1094, ll. 3–3 rev., Klemm to the Foreign Ministry's Asian Department, Bombay, February 23, 1904.

252. Ibid., f. 147, op. 485, d. 927, ll. 177–78, Nekrasov to Hartvig, Bombay, October 31, 1904.

253. ARGO, f. 18, op. 1, d. 42, ll. 1–2, draft note on the trip to Urga by Kozlov, March 8, 1905.

254. RGVIA, f. 2000, op. 1, d. 1086, ll. 9–10, final report by Kozlov on the mission to Urga, Saint Petersburg, September 4, 1905. For the reminiscences by Kozlov of his meetings with the Dalai Lama, see ARGO, f. 18, op. 1, d. 134, ll. 10–17. For a printed version of this report, see Petr Kozlov, "Tibetskii Dalai Lama," *Izvestiia Russkogo geographicheskogo obtschestva* 2 (2003): 77–92.

255. AVPRI, f. 188, op. 761, d. 402, ll. 96–96 rev., Lamsdorf to Lessar, Saint Petersburg, July 18, 1904. On the question of the Dalai Lama's stay in Mongolia and return to Lhasa, see Shaumian, *Tibet*, 94–116; and Andreev, *Tibet v politike*, 132–53. On the British attitude toward the Dalai Lama, see Palace, *British Empire and Tibet*, 53–72.
256. Verrier, *Francis Younghusband*, 14.
257. Quoted by Mehra, *Younghusband Expedition*, 335.
258. Allen, *Duel in the Snows*, 290.
259. An inquisitive reader can compare the interpretations of Lhasa residents' attitude toward the British as described by Leontiev, *Inostrannaia ekspansiia*, 102; and by Younghusband, *India and Tibet*, 144–48.
260. Mehra, *Younghusband Expedition*, 352; Allen, *Duel in the Snows*, 293.
261. Younghusband, *India and Tibet*, 295–97, 335–40. Characteristically, Younghusband was awarded the double order of knighthood, KCIE, in 1905 by King Edward VII for his contribution to the Tibetan expedition, in spite of all the accusations of insubordination by his opponents; see Seaver, *Francis Younghusband*, 251.
262. AVPRI, f. 188, op. 761, d. 402, ll. 217–18, Anglo-Chinese Convention on Tibet, Peking, April 27, 1906.
263. Schimmelpenninck van der Oye, "Tournament of Shadows," 19.
264. Lamb, *British India and Tibet*, 245–46.
265. For example, see Voul', "Politicheskaia istoriia Tibeta," 11.

CHAPTER 6

1. On the Russian territorial expansion in Eastern Siberia, especially see Anatoly Remnev, *Rossiia Dal'nego Vostoka: Imperskaia geografiia vlasti XIX—nachalo XX vv* (Omsk: Omskii gosudarstvennyi universitet, 2004).
2. Rossiiskii Gosudarstvennyi Voenno-Istoricheskii Arkhiv (hereafter, RGVIA), fond (f.; collection) 400, opis' (op.; inventory) 1, delo (d.; file) 856, listy (ll.; folios) 94–109; also see Rossiiskii Gosudarstvennyi Arkhiv Voenno-Morskogo Flota (hereafter, RGAVMF), f. 410, op. 2, d. 2621, ll. 5–13. Note by an anonymous Russian naval expert on the significance of the Far East to Russia, 1883.
3. India Office Library and Records (hereafter, IOLR), Mss Eur C 144/5. Northbrook to Dufferin, London, January 9, 1885; Kuropatkin, *Russko-kitaiskii vopros* (Saint Petersburg: Novoe Vremya, 1913), 90.
4. Henry Norman, *The Peoples and Politics of the Far East* (New York: Charles Scribner's Sons, 1895), 369–71; Mary Wilgus, *Sir Claude Macdonald, the Open Doors, and British Informal Empire in China, 1895–1900* (New York: Garland, 1987), 26–27; Bella Pak, "Rossiiskaia diplomatiia i Koreia (1876–1898)," Kand. diss., Institut Vostokovedeniia RAN, Moscow, 2007, 27. Robert Hart, the inspector general of Chinese Customs, wrote to his private correspondent four years before the

conflict of interests on the Korean Peninsula: "Some people think it is Korea that is coveted; others that preparations are made to meet England or other powers in the waters; others that Korea will be annexed and China pay the expenses, etc."; see John Fairbank, ed., *The I. G. in Peking: Letters of Robert Hart—Chinese Maritime Customs 1868–1907* (Cambridge, Mass.: Harvard University Press, 1975), vol. 1, 339. Hart to Campbell, Peking, September 26, 1880.

5. Steven Marks, *Road to Power: The Trans-Siberian Railroad and the Colonization of Asian Russia, 1850–1917* (London: I. B. Tauris, 1991), xii, 217.

6. National Archives of the United Kingdom–Public Record Office (hereafter, PRO), WO/106/6279, memorandum by Grierson, London, 1893.

7. Quoted by Leonard Young, *British Policy in China, 1895–1902* (Oxford: Clarendon Press, 1970), 39–40. Hamilton to Curzon, London, November 2, 1899.

8. PRO/WO/30/40/14, memorandum by Ardagh, London, July 19, 1900; also see Young, *British Policy*, 41.

9. PRO/WO/106/6217, report by Brackenbury, London, May 1, 1886.

10. *The History of the Times* (London: Office of the Times, 1947), vol. 3, 186–87; e.g.,, see Curzon's commentary on the Far Eastern question in *The Times*, June 16, 1894.

11. RGA VMF, f. 417, op. 1, d. 1273, reports by Lieutenant Ukhtomsky, the Russian naval attaché in Great Britain, to the Main Naval Staff, London, 1894–96.

12. John Le Donne, *The Russian Empire and the World, 1700–1917* (New York: Oxford University Press, 1997), 184.

13. Konstantin Vogak, "Extracts from Reports, 1893–1894," *Sbornik geograficheskikh, topograficheskikh i statisticheskikh materialov po Asii* 60 (1895): 1–204. On the Tsarist army's preparations for a war against China, see Andrew Malozemoff, *Russian Far Eastern Policy 1881–1904* (Berkeley: University of California Press, 1958), 24; and E. Bilof, "China in Imperial Russian Military Planning, 1881–1887," *Military Affairs* 46 (1982): no. 2, 69–75, at 73–74.

14. RGA VMF, f. 417, op. 1, d. 332, ll. 15–16 rev., Admiral Shestakov, the naval minister, to Vannovsky, Saint Petersburg, June 22, 1887; ibid., d. 296, ll. 2–14, note by Lieutenant Colonel Tisengausen, Saint Petersburg, October 20, 1887; ibid., d. 429, ll. 1–4, 5–12, note by Captain Second Rank Rodionov, Saint Petersburg, June 12, 1888; ibid., l. 20, "Proceedings of the Commission on the Cruising War in the Pacific Ocean, Vladivostok, November 7, 1888"; ibid., ll. 84–90, note by Vice-Admiral Kaznakov, Saint Petersburg, February 7, 1892; ibid., ll. 102–8, note on possibility of a cruising war by Lieutenant Sergeev, Saint Petersburg, February 4, 1893. Also see V. Stetcenko, *Kreisery i Tikhii Okean* (Saint Petersburg: Tipografiia Morskogo Ministerstva, 1893).

15. On the place of Korea in the world politics, see Eugene Kim and Hankyo Kim, *Korea and the Politics of Imperialism, 1876–1910* (Berkeley: University of California Press, 1967); Myung Hyun Cho, "Korea and the Major Powers: An Analysis of Power Structures in East Asia," Ph.D. diss., Research Center for Peace

and Unification of Korea, Seoul, 1989.

16. Alexander Popov, comp., "Pervye shagi russkogo imperialisma na Dal'nem Vostoke," *Krasnyi Arkhiv* 3, no. 52 (1932): 54–61; *Proceedings of the Special Conference on the Acquisition of Korea, Saint Petersburg*, May 8, 1888, quoted by Pak, "Rossiiskaia diplomatiia i Koreia," 29.

17. Alexander Popov, "Pervye shagi russkogo imperialisma," *Proceedings of the Special Conference on the Sino-Japanese War, Saint Petersburg, August 21, 1894*, 65–66.

18. A standard account of the Grand Tour is given by Esper Ukhtomsky, *Travels in the East of Nicholas II When Cesarewitch* (London: Archibald Constable, 1900), vols. 1–2. For contemporary British commentaries on the visit of Tsarevich Nicholas to Japan, see Alexander Michie, *The Englishman in China during the Victorian Era* (Edinburgh: W. Blackwood and Sons, 1900), vol. 2, 321–23. For a thorough analysis of the visit, see David Schimmelpenninck van der Oye, "Ex Oriente Lux: Ideologies of Empire and Russia's Far East, 1895–1904," Ph.D. diss., Yale University, 1997, 115–28.

19. Aleksei Narochnitsky, *Kolonial'naia politika kapitalisticheskikh derzhav na Dal'nem Vostoke* (Moscow: Gospolitizdat, 1956), 569; Vladimir Miasnikov, *Dogovornymi stat'iami utverdili: Diplomaticheskaia istoriia russko-kitaiskoi granitsy XVII–XIX vv.* (Moscow: Institut Dal'nego Vostoka RAN, 1996), 296.

20. Alexander Popov, "Pervye shagi russkogo imperialisma," *Proceedings of the Special Conference on the Policy towards Japan, Saint Petersburg, February 1, 1895*, 67–74. On the Manchurian problem in the Russian Far Eastern policy, see R. Quested, *"Matey" Imperialists? The Tsarist Russians in Manchuria 1895–1917* (Hong Kong: Centre of Asian Studies, University of Hong Kong, 1982); and David Wolff, *To the Harbin Station: The Liberal Alternative in Russian Manchuria* (Stanford, Calif.: Stanford University Press, 1999).

21. Alexander Popov, "Pervye shagi russkogo imperialisma," *Proceedings of the Special Conference on the Policy towards Japan, Saint Petersburg, April 11, 1895*, 102.

22. Ibid., 80–82.

23. Ibid., 74–76, Humble Note by Lobanov-Rostovsky to Nicholas II, Saint Petersburg, April 6, 1895.

24. David Schimmelpenninck van der Oye, *Toward the Rising Sun: Russian Ideologies of Empire and the Path to War with Japan* (DeKalb: Northern Illinois University Press, 2001).

25. Dimitry Putyata, *Kitai: Ocherki geographii, ekonomicheskogo sostoianiia, administrativnogo i voennogo ustroistva Sredinnoi imperii* (Saint Petersburg: Voennaia tipografiia, 1893), 5–6.

26. Alfred Mahan, *The Problem of Asia and Its Effect upon International Policies* (London: S. Low, Marston, 1900), 56, 119.

27. Ronald Robinson, "Railways and Informal Empire," in *Railway Imperialism*, edited by C. Davis and Kenneth Wilburn (New York: Greenwood Press, 1991), 192.

28. RGVIA, f. 400, op. 1, d. 2119, ll. 5–54, note by Colonel Altfan, Saint Petersburg,

October 1896.

29. Ibid., f. 165, op. 1, d. 449, ll. 1–26, note by Lieutenant Volkonsky, Saint Petersburg, December 15, 1897.

30. Ibid., f. 400, op. 1, d. 4972, ll. 1–32, report by Major General Chichagov, Khabarovsk, 1898.

31. E.g., see A. Maksimov, *Nashi zadachi na Tikhom okeane: Politicheskie etudy* (Saint Petersburg: Tipografiia P. I. Babkina, 1894).

32. Remnev, *Rossiia Dal'nego Vostoka*, 345.

33. E.g., see Ivan Levitov, *Zheltaia Rossiia* (Saint Petersburg: Tipografiia G. A. Bernsteina, 1901), 37–50.

34. F. A. Tarapygin, *Kitai* (Saint Petersburg, 1904).

35. Gosudarstvennyi Arkhiv Rossiiskoi Federatsii (hereafter, GARF), f. 568, op. 1, d. 126, draft of the Russo-Chinese defensive alliance against Japan, May 9, 1896; IOLR / Mss Eur F 111/76, Captain of the RMS *Narcissus* to Jordan, the Consul General, Seoul, June 11, 1897; Admiral Buller of the RMS *Centurion* to the Admiralty, Hong Kong, December 15, 1897. On the Russian policy in Korea, including the activities of her military instructors, see Aleksei Narochnitsky, "Angliia, Rossiia i koreiskii vopros nakanune napadeniia Yaponii na Kitai let m 1894 g.," *Istoricheskie zapiski*, no. 24 (1947): 160–83; Boris Pak, *Rossiia i Koreia* (Moscow: Vostochnaia literatura, 1979), 134–38, 160–79, 189–96, 272–76. The Korean emperor was staying at the Russian diplomatic mission from February 11, 1896, to February 20, 1897; see Yury Soloviev, *Vospominaniia diplomata* (Moscow: Izdatel'stvo sozial'no-ekonomicheskoi literatury, 1959), 56–100. On the reconnaissance activity by the Russian consul general in Korea, see Dimitry Pavlov, *Russko-Yaponskaia voina 1904–1905: Sekretnye operatsii na sushe i na more* (Moscow: Materik, 2004), 267–85.

36. GARF, f. 568, op. 1, d. 211, ll. 1–20, *Obsor snoshenii s Yaponiei po Koreiskim delam s 1895 g.* (Saint Petersburg: Tipografiia V. F. Kirshbauma, 1906); GARF, f. 568, op. 1, d. 145, ll. 3-47 rev., *Diplomaticheskaia perepiska po Koree*, October 3, 1895–June 22, 1898. The struggle inside the high-ranking Tsarist bureaucracy over Far Eastern policy is examined by Boris Romanov, *Rossiia v Man'chzhurii* (Leningrad: Gospolitizdat, 1928); Malozemoff, *Russian Far Eastern Policy*; and Richard Storry, *Japan and the Decline of the West in Asia, 1894–1943* (London: Macmillan, 1979), esp. 37.

37. On major trends in the West attitude toward Russia, see George Liska, *Russia and the Road to Appeasement: Cycles of East-West Conflict in War and Peace* (Baltimore: Johns Hopkins University Press, 1982), 47–48.

38. George Curzon, *Problems of the Far East: Japan–Korea–China* (London: Archibald Constable, 1896), 277.

39. In December 1897, one respected associate appealed to the War Office on the Russian threat to the British trade in the Far East: "It appears to me, we may consider that Russia has practically the control of Manchuria and will sooner or later command Korea, unless Japan prevents her." This observer saw another

danger for British interests in the forthcoming resignation of Robert Hart, who held the position of the inspector general at the Imperial Maritime Customs; see IOLR / Mss Eur F 112/1/1b, Faukes to Goshen, Spye Park, December 26, 1897.

40. Charles Beresford, *The Break-Up of China* (London: Harper & Brothers, 1899), 63.

41. Valentine Chirol, *The Far Eastern Question* (London: Macmillan, 1896), 66.

42. Albert Beveridge, *The Russian Advance* (New York: Harper & Brothers, 1903), 4–5.

43. Ibid., 152–72.

44. PRO/WO/106/17, correspondence on the Occupation of Kiaochow by Germany, 1897–98. Also see B. L. Putnam Weale, *The Reshaping of the Far East* (London: Macmillan, 1905), vol. 2, 463. On how Germany intimidated Britain with the Russian threat to British interests in the Far East, see Hermann Brunnhofer, *Ruslands Hand ueber Asien: Historisch-geographische Essays zur Entwicklungsgeschichte des russischen Reichsgedankens* (Saint Petersburg: Typographie der Aktien Gesellschaft, 1897), esp. 31–32.

45. Chirol, *Far Eastern Question*, 153. As he believed, "a conservative alliance" between Britain and Japan "can alone find favour with British public opinion." Also see *History of the Times*, vol. 3, 188. It should be mentioned that *The Times* had reduced its criticism of Russian foreign policy shortly after the end of the Russo-Japanese War; see ibid., 427.

46. Demetrius Boulger, "Why Not a Treaty with Russia?" *Fortnightly Review* 68, no. 406 (1900): 677–86, at 680.

47. Fairbank, *I. G. in Peking*, vol. 2, 1037, Hart to Campbell, Peking, October 20, 1895.

48. V. N. Lamsdorf, *Dnevnik, 1894–1896* (Moscow: Mezhdunarodnye otnosheniia, 1991), 140.

49. Fairbank, *I. G. in Peking*, vol. 2, 1183, Hart to Campbell, Peking, January 15, 1899.

50. Henry Norman, *The Peoples and Politics of the Far East* (New York: Charles Scribner's Sons, 1895), 590.

51. Fairbank, *I. G. in Peking*, vol. 2, 1067, Hart to Campbell, Peking, June 7, 1896.

52. For a comprehensive study of Salisbury's political course in the period under discussion, especially see J. A. S. Grenville, *Lord Salisbury and Foreign Policy: The Close of the Nineteenth Century* (London: Athlone Press, 1964).

53. Quoted by Evgeny Sergeev, *Politika Velikobritanii i Germanii na Dal'nem Vostoke, 1897–1903 gg.* (Moscow: Institute of World History RAN, 1998), 22. On the Far Eastern policy of Salisbury and his Cabinet, see A. Kennedy, *Salisbury, 1830–1903: Portrait of a Statesman* (London: John Murray, 1971), 269–76, 308, 321–22.

54. G. Cecil, *Life of Robert, Marquis of Salisbury*, 4 vols. (London: Hodder & Stoughton, 1921–32), vol. 2, 154–55, Salisbury to Lytton, London, July 6, 1877.

55. Ibid., vol. 3, 231, Salisbury to Morier, London, September 15, 1885.

56. IOLR / Mss Eur F 112/9/1–3, notes on Salisbury's memo of his conversations with the emperor of Russia at Balmoral, September 27–29, 1896; Robert Taylor, *Lord Salisbury* (London: Allen Lane, 1975), 170.

57. Dominic Lieven, ed., *British Documents on Foreign Affairs: Reports and Papers from*

the Foreign Office Confidential Print—Russia, 1859–1914 (Washington, D.C.: University Press of America, 1983–89), vol. I, 6, O'Connor to Salisbury, Saint Petersburg, January 20, 1898. Interestingly, Muraviev uttered this declaration in the manner almost similar to that used by Sergei Witte in his interview with O'Connor half a year earlier, in August 1897; see A. Palmer, "Lord Salisbury's Approach to Russia, 1898," *Oxford Slavonic Papers* 6 (1955): 102–14, at 104; Young, *British Policy*, 57.

58. Arkhiv Vneshnei Politiki Rossiiskoi Imperii (hereafter, AVPRI), f. 138, op. 467, d. 163/165, ll. 3–5 rev., 6–7, memorandum by Lamsdorf, Saint Petersburg, February 9, 1898; note by O'Connor to the Russian Foreign Ministry, Saint Petersburg, February 12, 1898.

59. Sergeev, *Politika Velikobritanii i Germanii na Dal'nem Vostoke*, 43.

60. Quoted by Beveridge, *Russian Advance*, 96.

61. A. Meyendorff, ed., *Correspondence diplomatique du Baron de Staal (1884–1900)*, 2 vols. (Paris: Libraire des Sciences Politiques et Sociales, 1929), vol. 2, 373, Staal to Muraviev, London, March 2, 1898.

62. IOLR / Mss Eur F 111/76, memorandum by Curzon, London, March 13, 1898.

63. E.g., see Palmer, "Lord Salisbury's Approach," 114.

64. Wilgus, *Sir Claude Macdonald*, 40.

65. RGVIA, f. 431, op. 1, d. 61, ll. 74–74 rev., Yermolov to the Main Staff, London, March 21, 1898.

66. Lieven, ed., *British Documents*, pt. 1, ser. A, vol. 2, 310–11, Waters to Goshen, Saint Petersburg, October 13, 1896.

67. Young, *British Policy*, 267–94; Nakami Tatsuo, "Qing China Northeast Crescent: The Great Game Revisited," in *The Russo-Japanese War in Global Perspective: World War Zero*, vol. 2, edited by David Wolff et al. (Leiden: Brill, 2007), 513–29, esp. 518.

68. GARF, f. 568, op. 1, d. 82, ll. 10–12, Staal to Muraviev, London, November 23, 1898; RGVIA, f. 447, op. 1, d. 41, ll. 17–17 rev., Grodekov to Sakharov, the head of the Main Staff, Nikol'skoe, August 13, 1898; AVPRI, f. 138, op. 467, d. 160/162, ll. 5–6 rev., Kuropatkin to Muraviev, Saint Petersburg, November 29, 1898; RGVIA, f. 147, op. 1, d. 57, ll. 23–28, Vogak to the Main Staff, Tientsin, October 3, 1910.

69. Alexander Popov, comp., "Anglo-russkoe soglashenie o razdele Kitaia 1899 g.," *Krasnyi Arkhiv* 6, no. 25 (1927): 111–34, at 131, Lessar to Muraviev (privately), London, December 6, 1898; RGVIA, f. 400, op. 1, d. 646, ll. 9–11, Obruchev to Veniukov, Saint Petersburg, 1898.

70. Quoted by Tamara Gella, *Liberal'naia partiia Velikobritanii i imperiia v kontse XIX–nachale XX vv.* (Orel: Orlovskii gosudarstvennyi pedagogicheskii institut, 1992), 99–100.

71. Zara Steiner and Keith Neilson, *Britain and the Origins of the First World War* (Basingstoke, U.K.: Palgrave Macmillan, 2003), 85.

72. D. Galton, "The Anglo-Russian Literary Society," *Slavonic and East European*

Review 46, no. 107 (1968): 19–38; Apollon Davidson, "O roli kul'turnykh sviazei v mezhdunaridnykh otnosheniiakh: Anglo-Rossiiskoe literaturnoe obtschestvo (1892–1930 gg.)," *Novaia i noveishaia istoriia*, no. 4 (2009): 85–98. For the original views shared by the founder of the Society, see Edward Cazalet, *England's Policy in the East: Our Relations with Russia and the Future of Syria* (London: E. Stanford, 1879).

73. IOLR / Mss Eur F 111/93, O'Connor to Salisbury, Saint Petersburg, June 15, 1898.

74. Joseph Popowski, *Antagonismus der Englishen und Russischen Interessen in Asien: Eine Militaerpolitische Studie* (Vienna: Wilhelm Frick, 1890); for the British edition, see Joseph Popowski, *The Rival Powers in Central Asia or the Struggle between England and Russia in the East* (London: Archibald Constable, 1893), esp. 73, 102–3, 133–34, 202–3, 221.

75. Lamsdorf, *Dnevnik, 1894–1896*, 310, Lobanov-Rostovsky to Staal, Saint Petersburg, November 21, 1895; Kennedy, *Salisbury*, 393.

76. See Sneh Mahajan, "The Defence of India and the End of Isolation: A Study in the Foreign Policy of the Conservative Government, 1900–1905," *Journal of Imperial and Commonwealth History* 10, no. 2 (1982): 168–93.

77. *The Times,* January 24, 1895.

78. There were, however, those British political observers who doubted Japan's aggrandizement as a mighty industrial power; see IOLR / Mss Eur F 111/93, Satow to Curzon, Tokyo, January 11, 1898.

79. S. Gwynn, ed., *The Letters and Friendships of Sir Cecil Spring-Rice*, 2 vols. (London: Archibald Constable, 1929), vol. 1, 146.

80. IOLR / Mss Eur F 111/76/A, Lowther to Salisbury, Tokyo, July 9, 1895.

81. Robert Maccordock, *British Far Eastern Policy 1894–1900* (New York: Octagon Books, 1976), 358.

82. IOLR / Mss Eur F 111/75, Satow to Salisbury, Tokyo, October 22, 1896.

83. Ibid., F 111/76, memorandum by Curzon, London, March 13, 1898.

84. Ibid., F 111/93, Younghusband to Curzon, Rajputana, August 9, 1898.

85. Ian Nish, "British Foreign Secretaries and Japan, 1892–1905," in *Shadow and Substance in British Foreign Policy 1895–1939*, edited by B. Mackercher and D. Moss (Edmonton: University of Alberta Press, 1984), 60.

86. G. Gooch and H. Temperley, eds., *British Documents on the Origins of the War 1898–1914* (London: His Majesty's Stationery Office, 1929), vol. 2, 33, Jordan to Salisbury, Seoul, May 1, 1900; Grenville, *Lord Salisbury*, 401–2; Ian Nish, *The Anglo-Japanese Alliance: The Diplomacy of Two Island Empires, 1894–1907* (London: Athlone Press, 1966), 177–81; A. Rosenbaum, "The Manchurian Bridgehead: Anglo-Russian Rivalry and the Imperial Russian Railways of North China, 1897–1902," *Modern Asian Studies* 10, no. 1 (1976): 41–64, at 63; Peter Lowe, *Britain in the Far East: A Survey from 1819 to the Present* (London: Longman, 1981), 64–81.

87. On the perception of the "yellow peril" in Europe and Russia, especially see Schimmelpenninck van der Oye, *Toward the Rising Sun*, 82–103.

88. PRO/WO/106/48/G 3, Lieutenant General Wilson to Clarke, London, March 12, 1903.

89. Petr Ostrikov, "Angliiskaia pomotsch Yaponii vo vremia russko-iaponskoi voiny 1904–1905 gg.," *Kurskii gosudarstvennyi pedagogicheskii institute: Uchenye zapiski* 13 (1961): 91–116.

90. PRO/ADM/231/38/706, précis of the Strategic War Game carried out at the Royal Naval College, Greenwich, in the early part of 1903, October 1903, 1–19.

91. PRO/CAB/1/4/43, memorandum by Balfour, London, December 22, 1903.

92. Quoted by M. Hauner, *What Is Asia to Us? Russia's Asian Heartland Yesterday and Today* (Boston: Unwin Hyman, 1990), 137.

93. PRO/CAB/1/4/39, memorandum by Balfour, London, December 29, 1903.

94. Ibid., CAB/4/1/1/15b, memorandum by Balfour, London, January 28, 1904.

95. Ibid., FO/539/88, Napier to Scott, Saint Petersburg, February 18, 1904.

96. Ibid., CAB/2/1, minutes of the CID meeting, London, May 20, 1904.

97. V. Grudzinsky, *Na povorote sud'by: Velikaia Britaniia i imperskii federalism (posledniaia tret' XIX–pervaia chetvert' XX vv.)* (Cheliabinsk: Cheliabinskii gosudarstvennyi universitet, 1996), 158.

98. GARF, f. 568, op. 1, d. 205, ll. 1–3, note by Ilia Tolstoi, June 1904.

99. For further details on the cruiser war, see Evgeny Sergeev, *Russian Military Intelligence in the War with Japan, 1904–05: Secret Operations on Land and at Sea* (London: Routledge, 2007), 147–48.

100. PRO/FO/899/5/29, draft of a dispatch from Lansdowne to Hardinge, London, July 19, 1904.

101. Ibid., correspondence on the Hull incident, October 28–November 2, 1904; J. Marriott, *Anglo-Russian Relations, 1689–1943* (London: Methuen, 1944), 158. On the current interpretations of the Dogger Bank affair, see Sergeev, *Russian Military Intelligence*, 144–46.

102. Alexander Izvolsky, *Vospominaniia* (Moscow: Mezhdunarodnye otnosheniia, 1989), 31.

103. Andrei Kalmykov, *Memoirs of a Russian Diplomat: Outposts of the Empire, 1893–1917* (New Haven, Conn.: Yale University Press, 1971), 25–26.

104. Clarmont Skrine and Pamela Nightingale, *Macartney at Kashgar: New Light on British, Chinese and Russian Activities in Sinkiang, 1890–1918* (London: Methuen, 1979), 142, 157.

105. M. Brett, ed., *Journals and Letters of Reginald Viscount Esher*, 2 vols. (London: Ivor Nicholson and Watson, 1934), vol. 2, 61, Esher to Brett, London, July 22, 1904.

106. Fairbank, *I. G. in Peking*, vol. 2, 1415, Hart to Campbell, Peking, June 6, 1904.

107. IOLR / Mss Eur F 111/93, newspaper clippings, May 1904.

108. AVPRI, f. 147, op. 485, d. 932, ll. 45–48, Klemm to Gartvig, Bombay, March 15, 1905. For the British perception of the "yellow peril" in the period of the Russo-Japanese War, e.g., see Thomas Holdich, *England's Strength in Asia* (London: Central Asian Society, 1905).

109. PRO/FO/181/879, O'Connor to Grey, Constantinople, January 25, 1906.
110. Ibid., CAB/4/2/70b, memorandum by the Admiralty, London, December 7, 1905. On the discussion of the treaty, also see PRO/CAB/17/67, correspondence on the renewal of the Anglo-Japanese Alliance, 1905–6. For Britain's strategic objectives in the aftermath of the Russo-Japanese War, see PRO/FO/181/873, Hardinge to Grey, March 26, 1906. On regular attempts of Russian agents to bribe attendants in London in order to get access to confidential papers or intercept diplomatic correspondence, see PRO/FO/181/873, Hardinge to Spring-Rice (privately), March 20, 1906. On the aims of the renewed Anglo-Japanese Alliance, see Ian Nish, "Great Britain, Japan and North-East Asia, 1905–1911," in *British Foreign Policy under Sir Edward Grey*, edited by F. Hinsley (Cambridge: Cambridge University Press, 1977), 362–67. The German aspect in the British Far Eastern policy at the turn of the twentieth century is analyzed by Sergeev, *Politika Velikobritanii i Germanii na Dal'nem Vostoke.*
111. Tatsuo, "Qing China Northeast Crescent," 529.
112. Quoted by P. Towle, "The Russo-Japanese War and the Defense of India," *Military Affairs* 44, no. 3 (1980): 111–17, at 116.
113. T. Sareen, "India and the War," in *The Impact of the Russo-Japanese War,* edited by R. Kowner (London: RoutledgeCurzon, 2006), 245–46; Dominic Lieven, *Empire: The Russian Empire and Its Rivals* (London: John Murray, 2000), 109.
114. On the defense of India as a "hidden agenda" of the Russo-British diplomatic talks, see IOLR/L/P&S/10/54, report by Napier on the trip to Central Asia, Saint Petersburg, November 10, 1904; ibid., Mss Eur D 573/370/5, summary of Kitchener's minutes of July 19, 1905, on the military policy in India, Simla, August 1905; ibid., Mss Eur D 573/8, Minto to Morley, June 12, 1906; ibid., IOLR/L/P&S/A 166, note by Deane on the probable attitude of the frontier tribes of India to Russia in case of its invasion and on the frontier policy in this respect, Simla, July 13, 1906; PRO/CAB/17/60, memorandum by GSC on Anglo-Russian relations as affecting the situation in India, London, July 16, 1906; IOLR / Mss Eur D 573/37a/3, questions that require consideration by the subcommittee appointed by the prime minister to report upon the military requirements of India and the consequent demands on the military forces at home, London, January 10, 1907; Edwin Collen, *The Defence of India* (London: Harrison and Sons, 1906), 23–32.
115. Beryl Williams, "The Strategic Background to the Anglo-Russian Entente of August 1907," *Historical Journal* 9, no. 3 (1966): 360–73, at 363–64. For a comprehensive analysis of the Russian imperialistic railway policy in Central Asia, see Towle, "Russo-Japanese War," 114; Arutyun Ulunian, "Magistralisatsiia prostranstva: Tsentral'no-asiatskii vector v otsenkakh i prognosakh imperskikh voennykh i grazhdanskikh chinovnikov (konets XIX–nachalo XX v.)," *Irano-Slavika*, nos. 3–4 (2004): 16–23. For a comparison of the railway construction in Russian Turkestan with that in the Qing Empire, see Percy Kent, *Railway*

Enterprise in China: An Account of Its Origin and Development (London: E. Arnold, 1907), esp. 90–95.

116. RGVIA, f. 16532, op. 1, d. 6, ll. 7–8, report by Yermolov to the Main Staff, London, January 1905. On the role of military intelligence in the reorientation of Russian foreign policy in 1904–6, see A. V. Shalina, "Politika Velikobritanii v Srednei Asii i na Dal'nem Vostoke v 1904–1906 gg.: Ot protivostoiania s Rossiei k anglo-russkoi konvetsii (po doneseniiam rossiiskikh voennykh agentov)," in *Problemy vseobstchei istorii: sobytiia, liudi, fakty*, edited by I. Zhiriakov (Moscow: Moskovskii gosudarstvennyi oblastnoi pedagogicheskii universitet, 2000), 80–93.

117. G. Lakost, *Rossia i Velikobritaniia v Tsentral'noi Asii* (Tashkent: Shtab Turkestanskogo voennogo okruga, 1908), 70; Lieven, *Empire*, 109. The concentration of Russian troops in Turkestan in the beginning of the Russo-Japanese War aimed, apart from other objectives, to intimidate the Shah's government, which, as Lamsdorf pointed out to Benkendorf, "apparently yielded to perfidious inspirations of the British representative in Teheran"; see AVPRI, f. 184, op. 520, d. 1148, ll. 8–8 rev., Lamsdorf to Benkendorf, Saint Petersburg, June 9, 1904.

118. David Macdonald, "Tsushima's Echoes: Asian Defeat and Tsarist Foreign Policy," in *The Russo-Japanese War in Global Perspective: World War Zero*, vol. 1, edited by J. Steinberg et al. (Leiden: Brill, 2005), 562.

119. PRO/WO/106/48/E 3/1, memorandum by Robertson, London, January 17, 1902. A detailed commentary on the demographic statistics relating to Great Britain in the Edwardian period is given by Wilfried Mellers and Rupert Hildyard, "The Cultural and Social Setting," in *The Cambridge Cultural History of Britain, Volume 8: Early Twentieth-Century Century Britain*, edited by Boris Ford (Cambridge: Cambridge University Press, 1992), 3–44.

120. Paul Kennedy, *Strategy and Diplomacy 1870–1945* (London: George Allen & Unwin, 1983), 207.

121. Thomas Otte, "'Almost a Law of Nature?' Sir Edward Grey, the Foreign Office and the Balance of Power in Europe, 1905–1912," in *Power and Stability: British Foreign Policy, 1865–1965*, edited by Erik Goldstein and B. J. C. Mackercher (London: Frank Cass, 2003), 79.

122. C. C. Eldridge, *Victorian Imperialism* (London: Hodder & Stoughton, 1978), 190.

123. On different views on the British foreign policy in the late Victorian and Edwardian periods, see Kennedy, *Strategy and Diplomacy*, 13–39, 216–17.

124. E.g., see Eldridge, *Victorian Imperialism*, 239. Concise descriptions of this epoch are given by James Morris, *Pax Britannica: The Climax of an Empire* (London: Faber & Faber, 1968); Kenneth Bourne, *The Foreign Policy of Victorian England, 1830–1902* (Oxford: Clarendon Press, 1970); Dennis Judd, *The Victorian Empire* (London: Weidenfeld & Nicolson, 1970); Brian Porter, *The Lion's Share: A Short History of British Imperialism, 1850–1970* (London: Longman, 1975); and Robert Hyam, *Britain's Imperial Century 1815–1914: A Study of Empire and Expansion* (London: Batsford, 1976).

125. Cited by Lilian Penson, "The New Course in British Foreign Policy, 1892–1902," in *Essays in Modern History*, edited by Ian Christie (London and New York: Macmillan and St. Martin's Press, 1968), 321–22. On Salisbury's policy toward the partition of the Ottoman Empire in the period 1886–97, see Keith Wilson, *Empire and Continent: Studies in British Foreign Policy from the 1880s to the First World War* (London: Mansell, 1987), 1–30.

126. PRO/CAB/17/67, memorandum by C.L. Ottley, the Director of Naval Intelligence at the CID meeting, April 12, 1905. Grigory Bondarevsky, *Angliiskaia politika i mezhdunarodnye otnosheniia v basseine Persidskogo zaliva (konets XIX–nachalo XX v.)* (Moscow: Nauka, 1968), 451; Muriel Chamberlain, *"Pax Britannica"? 1789–1914* (London: Longman, 1988), 162, 170.

127. For a current alternative view on the end of "splendid isolation" as early as in the 1880s, see Konstantin Kasparian, "Rossiisko-britanskie vneshnepoliticheskie otnosheniia i dinasticheskie sviazi, 1837–1907 gg.," Kand. diss., Piatigorskii gosudarstvennyi lingvisticheskii universitet, 2006, 22.

128. Quoted by Earl Ronaldshay, *The Life of Lord Curzon*, 3 vols. (London: Ernest Benn, 1928), vol. 2, 117, Curzon to Hamilton, September 25, 1901.

129. E.g., see PRO/WO/106/6218, *The Strategic Aspect of the Western Frontiers of Russia* (London: War Office, 1888); ibid., WO/106/6221, *The Armed Strength of the Russian Empire* (London: Her Majesty's Stationery Office, 1893), vols. 1–2; ibid., CAB/3/1/1a, memorandum by Lieutenant Colonel Altham, London, August 12, 1901; ibid., WO/106/48/E 3/2, memorandum by Lieutenant Colonel Altham, London, August 15, 1901; ibid., WO/106/48/E 3/1, memorandum by Lieutenant General Robertson, London, January 17, 1902. On the emergence of the German peril, see ibid., CAB/1/6/20, memoranda by Lieutenant General Robertson, London, 7, February 10, 1903.

130. Ibid., CAB/4/1/1, report of the conclusion arrived at on February 11 in reference to Russia and Constantinople, London, February 23, 1903.

131. V. N. Lamsdorf, *Dnevnik, 1891–1892* (Moscow: Akademiia, 1934), 105–6, Saint Petersburg, May 6, 1891.

132. Sergei Korff, *Russia's Foreign Relations during the Last Half Century* (London: Macmillan, 1922), 39, 63; James Eliott, *The Frontier: The Story of the North-West Frontier of India* (London: Cassell, 1968), 48.

133. Kalmykov, *Memoirs*, 210–11.

134. William Stead, ed., *The M.P. for Russia: Reminiscences and Correspondence of Madame Olga Novikoff*, 2 vols. (London: A. Melrose, 1909), vol. 2, 230–31.

135. Lieven, ed., *British Documents*, vol. 2, 424, Spring-Rice to Sanderson, Saint Petersburg, November 25, 1903. To understand the vacillations of Nicholas II in his attitude toward Britain, one should also pay attention to an episode in the dynastic diplomacy, less known to the general public, notably, the fact that Alexander II carried on regular transactions of his annual income to the Bank of England from 1869 to 1881. The total sum reached £50 million and was

deposited in the private account of the Romanovs' family. Despite his pro-Boer stance, his grandson, Nicholas II, actually credited this sum to Queen Victoria in the beginning of the Boer War; see V.V.Vaal, "Zapiski: 1900—April–June," in *Anglo-burskaia voina 1899–1902 gg. Po arkhivnym materialam i vospominaniiam ochevidtsev*, compiled by N. G.Voropaev, et al. (Moscow:Vostochnaia literatura, 2001), 47.

136. PRO/FO/899/5/25A, Lansdowne to Benkendorf, London, January 1, 1904. For the details of the British overtures to Russia on delimitation of spheres of influence in Asia at that time, see John Charmley, *Splendid Isolation? Britain, the Balance of Power, and the Origins of the First World War* (London: Hodder & Stoughton, 1999), 331–95. As Hardinge reminisced later, it had taken four years to initiate the tentative diplomatic contacts in comparison with official negotiations that the two parties carried out for merely a year; see Charles Hardinge, *Old Diplomacy: The Reminiscences of Lord Hardinge of Penshurst* (London: John Murray, 1947), 146.

137. RGVIA, f. 2000, op. 1, d. 361, ll. 1–1 rev., Lamsdorf to Kuropatkin, Saint Petersburg, February 12, 1904.

138. GARF, f. 543, op. 1, d. 108, ll. 131–42 rev., Geiden to the Foreign Ministry, April 4, 1904.

139. Gooch and Temperley, *British Documents*, vol. 4, Lansdowne to Spring-Rice, London, May 4, 1904.

140. W. Probyn-Nevins, *Apologia for Russia* (London: Simpkin, 1895), 117–18.

141. Quoted by Richard Pierce, *Russian Central Asia, 1867–1917: A Study in Colonial Rule* (Berkeley: University of California Press, 1960), 298.

142. RGVIA, f. 2000, op. 1, d. 361, l. 105, Lamsdorf to Benkendorf, Saint Petersburg, August 30, 1904.

143. Dimitry Yanchevetsky, *Groza s Vostoka: Zadachi Rossii i zadachi Yaponii na Dal'nem Vostoke—Ocherki* (Reval: Reval'skie Izvestiia, 1907), 202.

144. Cited by Alevtina Ostal'tseva, *Anglo-russkoe soglashenie 1907 g.: Vliianie russko-iaponskoi voiny i revolutsii 1905–1907 gg.—Na vneshnyuyu politiku tsarisma i na peregruppirovku evropeiskikh derzhav* (Saratov: Saratovskii gosudarstvennyi universitet, 1977), 125.

145. E.g., see the editorials in *Novoe Vremya*, April 29, 1900, March 28, 1901, September 7, 1901, October 12, 1901, and November 22, 1901. For a study of Britain's image in Russian public opinion, see Lev Petukhov, "Obraz Velikobritanii v rossiiskom obstchestvennom mnenii v period anglo-burskoi voiny (1899–1902 gg.)." Kand. diss., Gosudarstvennyi akademicheskii universitet gumanitarnykh nauk, Moscow, 2008, esp. 14–16.

146. Gooch and Temperley, *British Documents*, vol. 4, 208–9, Hardinge to Lansdowne, Saint Petersburg, October 8, 1905.

147. Mikhail P. Fedorov, *Sopernichestvo torgovykh interesov na Vostoke* (Saint Petersburg: Elektro-tipographiia Stoikovoi, 1903), 325.

148. *History of the Times,* vol. 3, 427, 460–508. As Alexander Izvolsky recalled in his memoirs, in Britain Donald Wallace was considered the most eminent expert on Russian affairs. He lived in the country for a few years, spoke fluent Russian, and wrote a book about the Russian lifestyle. Moreover, he accompanied Nicholas as the heir to the throne when the young tsarevich visited India during his Grand Tour around the world in the early 1890s; see Izvolsky, *Vospominaniia,* 126. On the contribution to the improvement in Russo-British relations made by Wallace, Dillon, and Pares, see Bernard Pares, *My Russian Memoirs* (London: Jonathan Cape, 1931). For a modern revaluation of their activity before World War I, see Michael Hughes, "Bernard Pares, Russian Studies and the Promotion of Anglo-Russian Friendship, 1907–1914," *Slavonic and East European Review* 78, no. 3 (2000): 510–35. On the gradual alteration of appreciation of Russia in Britain, also see Lieven, *Empire,* 126–27.

149. S. Pashukanis, "K istorii anglo-russkogo soglasheniia 1907 g.," *Krasnyi Arkhiv,* nos. 2–3 (69–70) (1935): 3–39; L. Poltz, "Die Anglo-Russische Entente, 1903–1907," Ph.D. diss., Universitaet Winsen (Luhe), 1938; Rogers Churchill, *Anglo-Russian Convention of 1907* (Cedar Rapids, Iowa: Torch Press, 1939); Pio-Carlo Terenzio, *La Rivalité Anglo-Russe en Perse et en Afghanistan jusqu'aux Accords de 1907* (Paris: Rousseau, 1947), 115–65; V. M. Khvostov, *Istoriia diplomatii* (Moscow: Gospolitizdat, 1963), vol. 2, 606–12; Williams, "Strategic Background," 360–73; Beryl Williams, "Great Britain and Russia, 1905 to the 1907 Convention," in *British Foreign Policy under Sir Edward Grey,* edited by F. Hinsley (Cambridge: Cambridge University Press, 1977), 133–47; Beryl Williams, *The Politics of Entente: Essays on the Determinants of British Foreign Policy, 1904–1914* (Cambridge: Cambridge University Press, 1985); Ostal'tseva, *Anglo-russkoe soglashenie 1907 g.*; Keith Neilson, *Britain and the Last Tsar: British Policy and Russia 1894–1917* (Oxford: Oxford University Press, 1995); Otte, "'Almost a Law of Nature?'" 77–118; Evgeny Sergeev, "Anglo-rossiiskaia Antanta 1907 g. Novye aspekty," *Novaia i noveishaia istoriia,* no. 5 (2007): 50–65; Evgeny Sergeev, "Diplomaticheskaia revoliuysiia' 1907 g. v otnosheniiakh Rossii i Velikobritanii," *Oriens,* no. 2 (2008): 80–93.

150. Brett, *Journals and Letters of Reginald Viscount Esher,* vol. 2, 183; M. Beloff, *Imperial Sunset, Volume 1: Britain's Liberal Empire, 1897–1921* (London: Methuen, 1969), 106.

151. Williams, "Strategic Background," 367–68; George Searle, *A New England? Peace and War 1886–1918* (Oxford: Clarendon Press, 2004), 483.

152. Gooch and Temperley, *British Documents,* vol. 4, 214, Hardinge to Lansdowne, Saint Petersburg, October 21, 1905.

153. Neilson, *Britain and the Last Tsar,* 47–50; Evgeny Sergeev, "Imperskie voennye elity Rossii i Velikobritanii v kontse XIX–nachale XX vv.: Opyt sravnitel'nogo analiza," in *Rossiia i Britaniia: Sviazi i vzaimnye predstavleniia, XIX–XX vv.,* vol. 4, edited by A. Davidson (Moscow: Nauka, 2006), 228–47.

154. Izvolsky, *Vospominaniia,* 13, 177. Also see Terenzio, *Rivalité Anglo-Russe,* 123.

On the views and activity of the Russian foreign minister, see V. A. Yemets, "A. P. Izvolsky i perestroika vneshnei politiki Rossii (soglasheniia 1907 g.)," in *Rossiiskaia diplomatiia v portretakh*, edited by A. V. Ignatiev et al. (Moscow: Mezhdunarodnye otnosheniia, 1992), 336–55; Viktor Avdeev, "Alexander Petrovich Izvolsky," *Voprosy istorii*, no. 5 (2008): 65–79.

155. Edward Grey, *Twenty-Five Years 1892–1916*, 2 vols. (London: Hodder & Stoughton, 1926), vol. 2, 4; George Trevelyan, *Grey of Fallodon: The Life and Letters of Sir Edward Grey* (Boston: Houghton Mifflin, 1937), 94, 104; Keith Robbins, *Sir Edward Grey: A Biography of Lord Grey of Fallodon* (London: Cassell, 1971), 131.

156. Gooch and Temperley, *British Documents*, vol. 4, 218, Grey to Spring-Rice, London, December 13, 1905; Gwynn, *Letters and Friendships*, vol. 2, 53–54, Grey to Spring-Rice, London, December 22, 1905.

157. Gooch and Temperley, *British Documents*, vol. 4, 219–20, 221, Spring-Rice to Grey, Saint Petersburg, 3, January 16, 1906.

158. Williams, "Great Britain and Russia," 135.

159. Premen Addy, *Tibet on the Imperial Chessboard: The Making of British Policy towards Lhasa, 1899–1905* (Calcutta: Academic Publishers, 1984), 190.

160. On the quarrel between Curzon and his colleagues, especially see Philip Magnus, *Kitchener: Portrait of an Imperialist* (London: John Murray, 1958), 204–26; and David Gilmour, *Curzon* (London: Papermac, 1994), 318–46. On the opposition to Izvolsky's policy, see A. V. Ignatiev, ed., *Istoriia vneshnei politiki Rossii: Konets XIX–nachalo XX v.* (Moscow: Mezhdunarodnye otnosheniia, 1997), 206. For the views of opponents to agreement, see Lieven, ed., *British Documents*, vol. 4, 96–97, Nicolson to Grey, Saint Petersburg, June 16, 1906; and Gooch and Temperley, *British Documents*, vol. 4, 255–65, Nicolson to Hardinge, Saint Petersburg, January 2, 1907 (enclosure in the dispatch).

161. Quoted by B. H. Sumner, "Tsardom and Imperialism in the Far East and Middle East, 1880–1914," *Proceedings of the British Academy* 27 (1940): 37–38.

162. Khvostov, *Istoriia diplomatii*, vol. 2, 605–6. It should be mentioned, however, that the chief of the French Main Naval Staff still regarded it as useful to discuss a coalition war against Britain with his Russian colleagues; see RGA VMF, f. 417, op. 1, d. 2460, ll. 4–4 rev., Lieutenant Epanchin, the Russian naval attaché in France, to the Main Naval Staff, Paris, June 2, 1906.

163. Williams, "Strategic Background," 367–68.

164. IOLR / Mss Eur F 111/394, résumé of a report by the secret agent P.Q. on his journey in Russian Central Asia, July 7, 1905.

165. John Morley, *Recollections* (London: Macmillan, 1921), vol. 2, 137, Morley to Minto, April 25, 1906; Harold Nicolson, *Sir Arthur Nicolson, Bart., First Lord Carnock: A Study in the Old Diplomacy* (London: Archibald Constable, 1930), 206.

166. Gooch and Temperley, *British Documents*, vol. 4, 272, Nicolson to Grey, Saint Petersburg, January 27, 1907 (with commentaries by Hardinge in the margins of the report).

167. Grey, *Twenty-Five Years*, vol. 2, 153; Trevelyan, *Grey*, 94.

168. PRO/FO/371/371, Grey to Spring-Rice, London, July 16, 1907.

169. Quoted by Ostal'tseva, *Anglo-russkoe soglashenie 1907 g.*, 165.

170. For the records of these special conferences, see RGVIA, f. 2000, op. 1., d. 6643, ll. 80–85; d. 6926, ll. 85–99, 140–51. Some of proceedings were published by I. Reisner, "Anglo-russkaia konventsiia i razdel Afghanistana," *Krasnyi Arkhiv* 3, no. 10 (1925): 54–66; and by Pashukanis, "K istorii anglo-russkogo soglasheniia 1907 g.," 19–25. On the Russian chief military commanders' attitude to the convention, see Alex Marshall, *The Russian General Staff and Asia, 1800–1917* (London: Routledge, 2005).

171. Sumner, "Tsardom and Imperialism," 41.

172. Grey, *Twenty-Five Years*, vol. 1, 163–64, Grey to Nicolson, London, April 1, 1907. For the records of the Russo-Japanese negotiations, see Russian Foreign Ministry, *Dokumety, kasayutschiesia zakliucheniia mezhdu Rossiei i Yaponiei obtschepoliticheskogo soglasheniia, 17/30 July 1907* (Saint Petersburg: Tipogragiia V. F. Kirshbauma, 1907).

173. P. S. Kotliar, "Russko-afghanskie otnosheniia v seredine XIX–nachale XX v. i anglo-russkoe sopernichestvo na Srednem Vostoke," *Tashkentskii gosudarstvennyi pedagogicheskii institute: Uchenye zapiski. Istoriia* 33, no. 2 (1962): 57–249, at 221–23.

174. Gooch and Temperley, *British Documents*, vol. 4, 239–40, Nicolson to Grey, Saint Petersburg, June 7, 1906.

175. Interestingly, Badmaev was entirely responsible for bringing in Mongolian chiefs on the Russian side during the war with Japan; see Richard Deacon, *A History of the British Secret Service* (New York: Taplinger, 1970), 135–36. On the Tibetan issue in the Russo-British diplomatic dialogue, see PRO/FO/800/72, correspondence on Tibet, 1906–7; AVPRI, f. 188, op. 461, d. 402, ll. 222–26, a humble note by Izvolsky on Tibet to Nicholas II, Saint Petersburg, June 12, 1906; GARF, f. 559, op. 1, d. 7, ll. 1–2 rev., Benkendorf to Izvolsky, July 11, 1906; Alexander Popov, "Rossiia i Tibet," *Novyi Vostok* 20 (1928): 33–54. For the recent evaluations of this problem, see Nikolai Kuleshov, *Rossiia i Tibet* (Moscow: Vostochnaia literatura, 1992), 118–33; Tatiana Shaumian, *Tibet: The Great Game and Tsarist Russia* (New Delhi: Oxford University Press, 2000), 127–36; Alexander Andreev, *Tibet v politike tsarskoi, sovetskoi i postsovetskoi* (Saint Petersburg: Saint Peterburg State University–Nartang, 2006), 155–66. The revision of British policy in Tibet is described by Wendy Palace, *The British Empire and Tibet, 1900–1922* (London: RoutledgeCurzon, 2005).

176. IOLR/L/PS/18/A 169, Minto to Morley, Calcutta, June 12, 1906. See also W. Habberton, *Anglo-Russian Relations Concerning Afghanistan, 1837–1907* (Urbana: University of Illinois Press, 1937), 68–81. Also see ibid., L/PS/18/A 165, memo by J.E.S. of the India Office Political Department on the question of direct relations between Russia and Afghanistan, London, June 10, 1907. On the Dane's mission, see W. K. Fraser-Tytler, *Afghanistan: A Study of Political Developments in*

Central and Southern Asia (London: Oxford University Press, 1967), 178–79.

177. For summaries of the Russian and British economic interests in Persia, see I. Yagello, "Bagdadskaia zheleznaia doroga," *Svedeniia o stranakh, sopredel'nykh s Turkestanskim voennym okrugom* 85, no. 12 (1906): 9–10; and AVPRI, f. 144, op. 488, d. 4141, ll. 213–23, a record of the Special Conference on the Baghdad Railway and the Persian telegraph lines, Saint Petersburg, July 27, 1907. On the contour of political affairs in the country, see RGIA, f. 560, op. 45, d. 86, ll. 15–178, correspondence on the activity of the Cossack Brigade in Persia, 1906–11. On the German menace to Britain's position in the Middle East, see PRO/CAB/4/1/1/45b, 67b, 77b, a series of memoranda by the General Staff, 1904–6.

178. Gwynn, *Letters and Friendships*, vol. 1, 281, Spring-Rice to Villiers, Tehran, June 27, 1899.

179. Quoted by D. Maclean, *Britain and Her Buffer State: The Collapse of the Persian Empire, 1890–1914* (London: Royal Historical Society, 1979), 14.

180. See Marina Kalmykova, "Politika Velikobritanii v bor'be velikikh derzhav za neftianye istochniki Blizhnego i Srednego Vostoka v period s 1901 po 1920 gg.," Kand. diss., Vladimirskii gosudarstvennyi pedagogicheskii universitet, 2006; Ekaterina Romanova, *Put' k voine: Razvitie anglo-germanskogo konflikta, 1898–1914 gg.* (Moscow: Maks Press, 2008), 86–100; and Arutyun Ulunian, "Tsentral'no-Asiatskaia igra' rossiiskoi biurokratii (konets XIX–nachalo XX v.)," *Istoricheskoe prostranstvo: Problemy istorii stran SNG*, nos. 1–4 (2008): 89–107, at 97–98. For a general review of the Persian policy, see Firuz Kazemzadeh, *Russia and Britain in Persia, 1864–1914* (New Haven, Conn.: Yale University Press, 1968), chap. 7.

181. Quoted by Reisner, "Anglo-russkaia konventsiia," 65; see also W. Walsh, "The Imperial Russian General Staff and India: A Footnote to Diplomatic History," *Russian Review* 16, no. 2 (1957): 53–58, at 57–58.

182. Yuliia Luneva, "Chernomorskie prolivy v anglo-rossiiskikh otnosheniiakh (1907–1914 gg.), Kand. diss., Institut vseobtschei istorii RAN, Moscow, 2003, 20.

183. Yemets, "A. P. Izvolsky," 350. On the details of these negotiations, see Gooch and Temperley, *British Documents*, vol. 4, 232–305, esp. 254–55, Hardinge to Nicolson, London, November 28, 1906, and Grey to Nicolson, London, November 30, 1906. Also see Nicolson, *Sir Arthur Nicolson*, 238–43; Winston Churchill, *Great Contemporaries* (London: Fontana Books, 1937), 107–76.

184. AVPRI, f. 130, 1906, d. 97, l. 272, Kokovtsev, the finance minister, to Izvolsky, Saint Petersburg, November 15, 1906.

185. E.g., see Avdeev, "Alexander Petrovich Izvolsky," 73.

186. Gooch and Temperley, *British Documents*, vol. 4, 296, Nicolson to Grey, Saint Petersburg, May 8, 1907.

187. PRO/FO/800/241, private letters from Sanderson to Spring-Rice, 1907–8; Gooch and Temperley, *British Documents*, vol. 4, 475–80, 482–83, 491–93, correspondence between Grey and Spring-Rice on the affairs in Persia, 1907.

188. Ibid., 284–85, Nicolson to Grey, Saint Petersburg, March 26, 1907 (with the

enclosure of a note by Izvolsky to Nicolson), Saint Petersburg, January 5, 1907. Interestingly, Colonel Karl Mannerheim, later to become the founder of independent Finland, committed the last reconnaissance expedition from Tashkent via Xinjiang to Peking in the course of the Great Game; notably, from August 1906 to June 1908. It was aimed to collect intelligence on the state of affairs in those provinces of China, where Russia had special political as well economic interests. The information that Mannerheim procured during this trip enabled the Tsarist government to agree with Tokyo on the status of these territories; see Karl Mannerheim, "Otchet ob ekspeditsii v Kitai, 1906 –8," *Sbornik geographicheskikh, topographicheskikh i statisticheskikh materialov po Asii* 81 (1909); Karl Mannerheim, *Memuary* (Moscow: Vagrius, 1999), 30–44; S. G. Kliashtorny and A. A. Kolesnikov, comps., *Vostochnyi Turkestan glazami russkikh puteshestvennikov (vtoraia polovina XIX v.)* (Alma-Ata: Tipografiia AN Kazakhskoi SSR, 1988), 195–218; Aleksei Shkvarov, *General-Lieutenant Mannerheim* (Saint Petersburg: Russkaia voennaia enziklopediia, 2005), 206–40; Eleonora Ioffe, *Linii Mannerheima: Pis'ma i dokumenty: Tainy i otkrytiia* (Saint Petersburg: Zvezda, 2005), 68–89.

189. PRO/FO/899/6; C. U. Aitchinson, comp., *A Collection of Treaties, Engagements, and Sanads Relating to India and Neighboring Countries*, 14 vols. (Calcutta: Government of India Central Publication Branch, 1932), vol. 13; *Anglo-Russian Convention Signed on August 31, 1907, between Great Britain and Russia, Containing Arrangements on the Subject of Persia, Afghanistan, and Tibet (Russia No. 1)* (London: His Majesty's Stationery Office, 1908); Gooch and Temperley, *British Documents*, vol. 4. 618–20. For the Russian translation, see Andrei Zaionchkovsky, *Podgotovka Rossii k mirovoi voine v mezhdunarodnom otnoshenii* (Leningrad: Voennaia tipografiia, 1926), 350–54.

190. Gooch and Temperley, *British Documents*, vol. 4, 299–300, Nicolson to Grey, Saint Petersburg, August 20, 1907.

191. Quoted by Nicolson, *Sir Arthur Nicolson*, 257. For a French evaluation of the convention, e.g., see A. Rouire, *La rivalité Anglo-Russe au XIXe siècle en Asie: Golfe Persique—Frontière de l'Inde* (Paris: Libraire A. Colin, 1908), 239–98.

192. Kotliar, "Russko-afghanskie otnosheniia," 211–12.

193. Peter Hopkirk, *On Secret Service East of Constantinople: The Plot to Bring Down the British Empire* (London: John Murray, 1994), 93.

194. Kazemzadeh, *Russia and Britain*, 410; Hossein Nazem, *Russia and Great Britain in Iran (1900–1914)* (Tehran: Sherkat Iran Chap, 1975), 26.

195. Quoted by Dennis Wright, *The English amongst the Persians during the Qajar Period 1787–1921* (London: Heinemann, 1977), 30.

196. Kalmykov, *Memoirs*, 211.

197. *The Times*, September 2, 1907.

198. *The Spectator*, September 28, 1907.

199. RGVIA, f. 2000, op. 1, d. 6933, l. 143 rev., Poklevsky-Kozel to Izvolsky, London, October 2, 1907.

200. IOLR/L/P&S/18/C 140, memorandum by an anonymous author respecting the Anglo-Russian Convention, London, January 29, 1908.

201. Gooch and Temperley, *British Documents*, vol. 4, 616, Grey to Nicolson, London, February 24, 1908.

202. E. Dillon, "Foreign Affairs," *Contemporary Review* 92, no. 503 (1907): 699.

203. Paul Kennedy, *The Realities behind Diplomacy: Background Influences on British External Policy, 1865–1900* (London: George Allen & Unwin, 1981), 127.

204. Calchas, "The Anglo-Russian Agreement," *Fortnightly Review* 88, no. 490 (1907): 535–50, at 545. For the so-called Teutophobia in Britain, see Ellis Barker, "The Anti-British Policy of Germany," *The Nineteenth Century and After* 61, no. 367 (1907): 345–64.

205. Alexander Izvolsky, *Au service de la Russie: Correspondence diplomatique 1906–1911* (Paris: Les Editions Internationales, 1937), vol. 1, 325, Benkendorf to Izvolsky, London, July 7, 1906.

206. Gwynn, *Letters and Friendships*, vol. 2, 100, Spring-Rice to Hardinge, April 23, 1907. Also see Hughes, "Bernard Pares," 511–12; and Ian Packer, *Liberal Government and Politics, 1905–15* (London: Palgrave, 2006), 33.

207. Quoted in *History of the Times*, vol. 3, 503, Chirol to Morrison, London, September 2, 1907.

208. Quoted in RGVIA, f. 2000, op. 1, d. 977, l. 174, Benkendorf to Izvolsky, London, May 26, 1908.

209. See Lev Kertman, "O politicheskikh raznoglasiiakh v Anglii po voprosu o sblizhenii s tsarskoi Rossii v period i posle revolutsii 1905–1907 gg," *Nauchnye doklady vysshei shkoly: Istoricheskie nauki*, no. 1 (1961): 115–31, at 126.

210. Quoted by Hughes, "Bernard Pares," 516.

211. Arminius Vambery, "The Anglo-Russian Convention," *The Nineteenth Century and After* 62, no. 370 (1907): 895–904, at 903.

212. Quoted by R. Greaves, *Persia and the Defense of India, 1884–1892: A Study in the Foreign Policy of the Third Marquis of Salisbury* (London: Athlone Press, 1959), 193. On Kitchener's reception of the convention, see IOLR / Mss Eur D 573/37e, consideration by Lord Kitchener of the effect of the Anglo-Russian Convention on the strength of the army in India, Calcutta, October 21, 1907.

213. *The Hansard Parliamentary Debates* (London: C. Buck, 1908), series 4, vol. 183, cols. 1309–10. This extract of Curzon's discourse is also cited by Anthony Wynn, *Persia in the Great Game: Sir Percy Sykes—Explorer, Consul, Soldier, Spy* (London: John Murray, 2003), 163–64; and by Gilmour, *Curzon*, 377. Also see A. W. Ward and G. P. Gooch, eds., *The Cambridge History of British Foreign Policy, 1783–1919* (Cambridge: Cambridge University Press, 1923), vol. 3, 362.

214. Maclean, *Britain and Her Buffer State*, 76.

215. *Hansard Parliamentary Debates*, series 4, vol. 183, cols. 1327–28. Sanderson's oration in the House of Commons is quoted by Ward and Gooch, *Cambridge History*, vol. 3, 363. For Lansdowne's defense of the convention, see *Hansard*

Parliamentary Debates, series 4, vol. 184, cols. 1340–41. It is also quoted by Ward and Gooch, *Cambridge History*, vol. 3, 362.

216. *Hansard Parliamentary Debates*, series 4, vol. 184, cols. 476–97. For further arguments see ibid., vol. 190, cols. 234–46. Grey's oration in the House of Commons with regard to the visit of Edward VII to Russia, June 4, 1908. Also see Gooch and Temperley, *British Documents*, vol. 4, 616, Grey to Nicolson, London, February 24, 1908; Edward Grey, *Speeches on Foreign Affairs 1904–1914* (London: George Allen & Unwin, 1931), 55–76, 91–104. On the Russian analysis of the parliamentary debates, see RGVIA, f. 2000, op. 1, d. 977, ll. 64–65, Benkendorf to Izvolsky, London, February 18, 1908.

217. *Hansard Parliamentary Debates*, series 4, vol. 184, col. 496.

218. Keith Neilson, "'Control the Whirlwind': Sir Edward Grey as Foreign Secretary, 1906–16," in *The Makers of British Foreign Policy*, edited by T. Otte (Basingstoke, U.K.: Palgrave, 2002), 141.

219. Quoted by Sumner, "Tsardom and Imperialism," 42.

220. Gooch and Temperley, *British Documents*, vol. 5, 243–44, memorandum by Hardinge, Reval, June 1908.

221. For a typical example, see Jennifer Siegel, *Endgame: Britain, Russia and the Final Struggle for Central Asia, 1907–1914* (London: I. B. Tauris, 2002), 22.

222. Nikolai Notovich, *Rossiia i Angliia: Istoriko-politicheskii etyud* (Saint Petersburg: Gosudarstvennaia tipographiia, 1907), 16. A modern Russian historian even maintains that it was Notovich whom Rudyard Kipling depicted as a Tsarist spy and ruthless opponent of the British in his brilliant novel *Kim*; see Ulunian, "Tsentral'no-Asiatskaia igra'," 98.

223. Maksim Kovalevsky, "Nachalo russko-angliiskogo sblizheniia," *Vestnik Evropy*, no. 3 (1912): 241–64, at 264.

224. Lieven, ed., *British Documents*, vol. 5, 124, Colonel Wyndman, the British military attaché in Russia, to Nicolson, Saint Petersburg, March 21, 1908.

225. Quoted by R. M. Ter-Egiazarova, "Turkestanskoe general-gubernatorstvo i anglo-russkoe soglashenie 1907 g.," *Tashkentskii gosudarstvennui universitet: Nauchnye trudy* 343, pt. 1 (1969): 97–98.

226. R. Rosen, *Forty Years of Diplomacy*, 2 vols. (London: George Allen & Unwin, 1922), vol. 2, 48–49.

227. Quoted by Kennedy, *Salisbury*, 163.

228. S. Yu. Witte, *Vospominaniia*, 3 vols. (Berlin: Slovo, 1922), 434; Churchill, *Great Contemporaries*, 321.

229. See Andrei Snesarev, *Anglo-russkoe soglashenie 1907 g.* (Saint Petersburg: Obstchestvo revnitelei voennykh znanii, 1908), 23–25. Interestingly, his critical appreciation of the 1907 convention remained unchanged in the later decades; see Andrei Snesarev, *Afghanistan* (Moscow: Gosudarstvennoe izdatel'stvo, 1921), 242–44. On Grulev's more objective views, see Mikhail Grulev, *Sopernichestvo Rossii i Anglii v Srednei Asii* (Saint Petersburg: V. Berezovsky, 1909), 357–80.

230. Quoted by A. I. Zvavich, "Russko-angliiskie otnosheniia, 1909–1914," *Moskovskii oblastnoi pedagogicheskii institute: Uchenye zapiski* 105, no. 6 (1961): 73–103, at 78.

231. Georgy Chicherin, "Rossiia i asiatskie narody," *Vestnik NKID*, no. 2 (1919): 96.

232. Zaionchkovsky, *Podgotovka Rossii*, 147–49.

233. See Anatoly Ignatiev, *Russko-angliiskie otnosheniia nakanune Pervoi mirovoi voiny (1908–1914 gg.)* (Moscow: Izdatel'stvo sotsial'no-ekonomicheskoi literatury, 1962), 69.

234. G. A. Khidoiatov, *Iz istorii anglo-russkikh otnoshenii v Srednei Asii v kontse XIX v. (60–70-e gg.)* (Tashkent: Fan, 1969), 429.

235. Terenzio, *Rivalité Anglo-Russe*, 169.

236. Habberton, *Anglo-Russian Relations*, 81; Ira Klein, "The Anglo-Russian Convention and the Problem of Central Asia, 1907–1914," *Journal of British Studies* 11, no. 1 (1971): 126–47; Siegel, *Endgame*, vii–viii.

237. E.g., see Beloff, *Imperial Sunset*, 70; David Gillard, *The Struggle for Asia 1828–1914: A Study in British and Russian Imperialism* (London: Methuen, 1977), 177.

238. Gooch and Temperley, *British Documents*, vol. 4, 377, Hardingeee to Grey, London, December 23, 1905.

239. Otte, "'Almost a Law of Nature?'" 94.

240. Towle, "Russo-Japanese War," 115.

241. Gooch and Temperley, *British Documents*, vol. 4, 182.

242. David French, *British Strategy and War Aims 1914–1916* (London: George Allen & Unwin, 1986), 7.

243. For further evidence of this role, see Nicolas Basily, *Diplomat of Imperial Russia 1903–1917: Memoirs* (Stanford, Calif.: Hoover Institution Press, 1973). As another Russian diplomatic staffer positively profiled Benkendorf, the attitude of the British Foreign Office toward him was not only correct but also cordial throughout the Russo-Japanese War. This contributed to the prevention of British intervention in the Russo-Japanese War at the time of the Dogger Bank affair; see Dmitry Abrikosov, *Relevance of a Russian Diploma* (Seattle: University of Washington Press, 1964), 113.

244. *The Times,* September 25, 1907.

245. Trevelyan, *Grey*, 92; also quoted by Thomas Otte, "Old Diplomacy: Reflections on the Foreign Office Before 1914," in *The Foreign Office and British Diplomacy in the Twentieth Century*, edited by G. Johnson (London: Routledge, 2005), 41.

246. Cited by Hughes, "Bernard Pares," 532.

247. Klein, "Anglo-Russian Convention," 147.

248. For a comparison of the British administration of India with the Russian government of Manchuria, see Ivan Korostovets, *Rossiia na Dal'nem Vostoke* (Peking: Vostochnoe Prosvestchenie, 1922), 125–26.

249. This concept is also shared by Dietrich Geyer in his study of Russian imperialism; see Dietrich Geyer, *Der Russische Imperialismus: Studien ueber den Zusammenhang von innerer und auswaertiger Politik 1860–1914* (Goettingen:

Vandenhoeck und Ruprecht, 1977), 247–48.

250. Aaron Friedberg, *The Weary Titan: Britain and the Experience of Relative Decline 1895–1905* (Princeton, N.J.: Princeton University Press, 1988), 219.

251. As Salisbury informed Northbrook, Russian annual spending on Turkestan overran her profit by more than £800,000; see IOLR / Mss Eur C 144/11, Salisbury to Northbrook, London, February 26, 1875.

252. See, e.g., Hauner, *What Is Asia to Us?* 52. Oddly enough, some Russian revolutionary socialists believed that the Russian peasantry could act as renovators of Asia who would disseminate the principles of agrarian socialism amid rural residents in India and China, in order "to rally them against Western capitalist exploitation"; see Svetlana Lurie, "Rossiiskaia i Britanskaia imperii na Srednem Vostoke v XIX–nachale XX vv.: Ideologiia i praktika," Kand. diss., Institut vostokovedeniia RAN, 1996, 15.

253. Typically, a journalist of *The Times of India* wrote in the paper: "Day by day our grasp of India is becoming firmer, owing to improved communications, closer relations with the people, and the diffusion of European learning and western ideas. We are conferring countless blessings on the natives, we are to them a visible Providence, and they are daily becoming more conscious of the truth of this fact." See G. R. Aberigh-Mackay, *[Some] Notes on [the Situation in] Western Turkistan* (Calcutta: Thacker, Spink, 1875), 75. For a concept of the "Golden Age" of India under British rule, also see Alexander Halliday, *The Retention of India* (London: Tinsley Brothers, 1872), 36–37. For an analysis of the system of tribal levies and service allowances applied by the British in Asia, see Richard Bruce, *The Forward Policy and Its Results* (London: Longmans, Green, 1900), 145. Reference to Curzon's typical argumentation of the British conquest of India also deserves attention: "We came here [to India] in obedience to what I call the decree of Providence, for the lasting benefit of millions of the human race. We often make great mistakes here; but I do firmly believe that there is no government in the world that rests on so secure a moral basis, or is more fiercely animated by duty"; quoted by S. Gopal, *British Policy in India, 1858–1905* (Cambridge: Cambridge University Press, 1965), 225.

254. H. Pearse, ed., *Soldier and Traveler: Memoirs [Chiefly in His Own Words] of Alexander Gardner, Colonel of Artillery in the Service of Maharaja Ranjit Singh* (Edinburgh: W. Blackwood and Sons, 1898), 354. According to estimates based on archival records, the famine in the Raj was running rampant for eighteen years between 1876 and 1900, when more than 26 million people perished as a result of it; see G. A. Akhmedzhanov, *Sovetskaia istoriografiia prisoedinenie Srednei Asii k Rossii* (Tashkent: Fan, 1989), 27.

255. Andrei Snesarev, *Indiia kak glavnyi factor v sredneaziatskom voprose* (Saint Petersburg: Tipografiia A. Suvorina, 1906), 70, 132, 166–67; Arkhiv Rossiiskogo Geographicheskogo Obtschestva, f. 32, op. 1, d. 40, ll. 1–15, manuscript by Grigory Grumm-Grzhimailo, a famous Russian explorer, on the life of the

native population in British India, 1934.

256. Arkhiv InstitutaVostochnykh Rukopisei RAN, f. 115, op. 1, d. 120, ll. 15 rev.–16, report by Livkin, Saint Petersburg, September 26, 1899; quoted also by Petr Shastitko, ed., *Russko-indiiskie otnosheniia v XIX v. Sbornik arkhivnykh dokumentov i materialov* (Moscow:Vostochnaia literatura, 1997), 207–8.

257. Alexander Popov, comp., "Angliiskaia politika v Indii i russko-indiiskie otnosheniia v 1897–1905 gg," *Krasnyi Arkhiv* 6, no. 19 (1926): 53–63, Klemm to the Foreign Ministry's Asian Department, Bombay, September 14, 1905.

258. E.g., see Helene Carrère d'Encausse, "Organizing and Colonizing the Conquered Territories," in *Central Asia: 120Years of Russian Rule*, edited by Edward Allworth (Durham, N.C.: Duke University Press, 1989), 151–71; Alfred Rieber, "Persistent Factors in Russian Foreign Policy: An Interpretive Essay," in *Imperial Russian Foreign Policy*, edited by H. Ragsdale (Cambridge: Cambridge University Press, 1993), 315–59; and Seymour Becker, "The Russian Conquest of Central Asia and Kazakhstan: Motives, Methods, Consequences," in *Central Asia: Its Strategic Importance and Future Prospects*, edited by H. Malik (New York: St. Martin's Press, 1994), 21–38.

259. *The Times*, November 28, 1878, quoted by Memet Yetisgin, "How the *Times* of London Covered and Interpreted Russian Expansion into Central Asia in the Second Half of the 19th Century," Ph.D. diss., Texas Technological University, 2000, 295.

260. Quoted by Francis Skrine and Edward Ross, *The Heart of Asia: A History of Russian Turkestan and the Central Asian Khanates from the Earliest Times* (London: Methuen, 1999), 426.

261. IOLR/L/P&S/18/C 58, note by Durand, Simla, February 1, 1888.

262. E.g., see Vsevolod Krestovsky, "V gostiakh u Emira Bukharskogo. Putevoi dnevnik," *Russkii vestnik* 159, no. 2 (1884): 469–532; 170, no. 3: 113–54; 171, no. 5: 5–75; 171, no. 6: 608–59; 172, no. 7: 49–110; no. 8, 478–559. Also see George Curzon, "A Visit to Bokhara, the Noble," *Fortnightly Review* 51 (1889): 122–43.

263. K. Skalkovsky, *Vneshniaia politika Rossii i polozhenie inostrannykh derzhav* (Saint Petersburg: Tipografiia A. Suvorina, 1897), 407.

264. R. E. Glatfelter, "Russia, the Soviet Union, and the Chinese Eastern Railway," in *Railway Imperialism*, edited by C. Davis and K. Wilburn (New York: Greenwood Press, 1991), 142.

265. Quoted by David Mackenzie, "Turkistan's Significance to Russia (1850–1917)," *Russian Review* 33, no. 2 (1974): 167–88, at 179.

266. Ibid., 180.

267. Ibid., 178.

268. M. Brodovsky, *Kolonial'noe znachenie nashikh Sredne-Aziatskikh vladenii* (Moscow: Tipografiia D. Inozemtseva, 1891), 3–5. On the role of cotton production in Central Asia's economic links to Russia, see M. Holdsworth, *Turkistan in the Nineteenth Century: A Brief History of the Khanates of Bukhara,*

Kokand and Khiva (Oxford: Central Asian Research Institute, 1959), 18–19, 30; Seymour Becker, *Russia's Protectorates in Central Asia: Bokhara and Khiva, 1865–1924* (Cambridge, Mass.: Harvard University Press, 1968), 180–83; N. A. Abdurakhimova, "Stanovlenie i osobennosti ekonomicheskoi politiki Rossii v Turkestane vo vtoroi polovine XIX–nachale XX vv," *Istoricheskoe prostranstvo: Problemy istorii stran SNG*, nos. 1–4 (2008): 62–88, at 66–68. On the results of the Russian colonial administration in Turkestan before World War I, see N. A. Abdurakhimova and G. K. Rustamova, *Kolonial'naia sistema vlasti v Turkestane vo vtoroi polovine XIX–pervoi chetverti XX vv.* (Tashkent: Tashkentskii gosudarstvennyi universitet, 1999).

269. PRO/FO/405/45, 53, correspondence respecting trade with Chinese Turkestan, 1888–89, 1890–91; PRO/FO/405/67, further correspondence respecting trade with Chinese Turkestan, 1895–97; Lev Kleinbort, *Russkii imperialism v Asii* (Saint Petersburg: Znanie, 1906), 44–45.

270. E.g., see Graham Goodland, *British Foreign and Imperial Policy, 1865–1919* (London: Routledge, 2000).

271. Remnev, *Rossiia Dal'nego Vostoka*, 449.

272. Dimitry Logofet, *Strana bespraviia: Bokharskoe khanstvo i ego sovremennoe sostoianie* (Saint Petersburg: V. Beresovsky, 1909), 167–81.

273. David Mackenzie, "'The Conquest and Administration of Turkestan, 1860–1885," in *Russian Colonial Expansion to 1917*, edited by M. Rywkin (London: Manswell, 1988), 228; Daniel Brower, *Turkestan and the Fate of the Russian Empire* (London: RoutledgeCurzon, 2003), 26–56; Abdurakhimova, op. cit., pp. 65-6.

274. See Chiming Hou, *Foreign Investment and Economic Development in China, 1840-1937*, Cambridge, Mass.: Harvard University Press, 1965, p. 17; Nazem, op. cit., p. 173; Abdurakhimova, "Stanovlenie i osobennosti ekonomicheskoi politiki Rossii," 76–77.

275. Arkady Petrov, *Kak zastchistchayut svoi interesy v Asii Angliia i Rossiia* (Saint Petersburg: Alexander Popov, 1910), 43.

EPILOGUE

1. Michael Hughes, "Bernard Pares, Russian Studies and the Promotion of Anglo-Russian Friendship, 1907–1914," *Slavonic and East European Review* 78, no. 3 (2000): 510–35, at 520–21, 524–33; Zara Steiner and Keith Neilson, *Britain and the Origins of the First World War* (Basingstoke, U.K.: Palgrave Macmillan, 2003), 86.

2. Austen Chamberlain, *Politics from Inside: An Epistolary Chronicle 1906–1914* (London: Cassell, 1936), 471.

3. Bruce Lockhart, *British Agent* (New York: G. P. Putnam's Sons, 1933), 64.

4. On the British elite's criticism of Russia in the prewar years, see Keith Nelson, "Wishful Thinking: The Foreign Office and Russia 1907–1917," in *Shadow and Substance in British Foreign Policy 1895–1939*, edited by B. Mackercher and D. Moss (Edmonton: University of Alberta Press, 1984), 151–80. As the author correctly remarked, "The Foreign Office wished for Russian politics to become more liberal in order that Russia would be more acceptable as a British ally; at the same time they hoped that British politics would not become too liberal in order that Britain would be more acceptable as a Russian ally" (p. 156).

5. *The Hansard Parliamentary Debates* (London: C. Buck, 1908), series 4, vol. 190, cols. 234–46.

6. Indian Office Library and Records (hereafter, IOLR), Mss Eur D 573/37f. Morley to Minto, London, March 20, 1908.

7. Ellis Barker, "The Triple Entente and the Triple Alliance." *The Nineteenth Century and After* 63, no. 377 (1908): 1–17, at 9.

8. Arkhiv Vneshnei Politiki Rossiiskoi Imperii (hereafter, AVPRI), fond (f.; collection) 138, opis' (op.; inventory) 467, delo (d.; file) 284, (ll.; folios) 2–2rev., Grey to O'Beirne, London, August 30, 1909.

9. G. Gooch and H. Temperley, eds., *British Documents on the Origins of the War 1898–1914* (London: His Majesty's Stationery Office, 1929), vol. 5, app. 3; cited by D. Sweet and R. Langhorne, "Great Britain and Russia, 1907–1914," in *British Foreign Policy under Sir Edward Grey*, edited by F. Hinsley (Cambridge: Cambridge University Press, 1977), 242.

10. Paul Kennedy, *The Realities behind Diplomacy: Background Influences on British External Policy, 1865–1900* (London: G. Allen & Unwin, 1981), 131.

11. Andrei Semenov Tian-Shansky, *Nashi blizhaishie zadachi na Dal'nem Vostoke* (Saint Petersburg: Sankt-Peterburgskie Vedomosti, 1908), 66.

12. See Richard Pierce, *Russian Central Asia, 1867–1917: A Study in Colonial Rule* (Berkeley: University of California Press, 1960), 298.

13. Cited by M. T. Kozhekina, "Missiia generala N. S. Yermolova v Indiyu (1911 g.)," *Vostochnyi arkhiv*, nos. 2–3 (1999): 72–85, at 83.

14. *Novoe Vremya*, May 13, 1912; Andrei V. Piaskovsky, "Revolutsiia 1905–1907 gg. v Turkestane," Kand. diss., Institut istorii AN SSSR, 1956, 27; Sweet and Langhorne, "Great Britain and Russia," 237–42; A. Mackay, ed., *The History of Tibet* (London: RoutledgeCurzon, 2003), vol. 3, 66; Sergei V. Chirkin, *Dvadtsat' let sluzhby na Vostoke: Zapiski tsarskogo diplomata* (Moscow: Russkii put', 2006), 246. Significantly, Sergei Sazonov, who succeeded Izvolsky in the post of foreign minister, told a British Cabinet member in 1912 that Afghanistan remained a dangerous hotbed of Pan-Islamic propaganda, which destabilized the situation at the approaches both to Russian Turkestan and British India; see P. S. Kotliar, "Russko-afghanskie otnosheniia v seredine XIX–nachale XX v. i anglo-russkoe sopernichestvo na Srednem Vostoke," *Tashkentskii gosudarstvennyi pedagogicheskii institute: Uchenye zapiski. Istoriia* 33, no. 2 (1962): 57–249, at 235. The Russo-Japanese

rapprochement reached its culmination in the secret Convention signed on July 3, 1916, concerning the division of their spheres of interest in China, see P. Clyde, *International Rivalries in Manchuria, 1689–1922* (Columbus: Ohio State University Press, 1928), 147; and Victor Yakhontoff, *Russia and the Soviet Union in the Far East* (New York: Coward-Maccann, 1931), 65, 376–81.

15. See Rossiiskii Gosudarstvennyi Voenno-Istoricheskii Arkhiv (hereafter, RGVIA), f. 2000, op. 1, d. 980, ll. 20–22, report by the staffers of the Turkestan Military District on the organization of intelligence in British India, Tashkent, August 7, 1907; IOLR/L&PS/10/16, regulations issued by the Russian government on the British officers traveling in Central Asia, Saint Petersburg, September 8, 1908.

16. Edward Grey, *Twenty-Five Years: 1892–1916*, 2 vols. (London: Hodder & Stoughton, 1926), vol. 1., 215, Hardinge to Grey, London, July 12, 1908.

17. For these stereotypical opinions by conservative Russian statesmen, see Ivan Zinoviev, *Rossiia, Angliia i Persiia* (Saint Petersburg: Tipografiia A. Suvorina, 1912); and Skif, *Persidskii vopros: Anglo-russkoe soglashenie, ego osnovnye printsipy i tseli i piatilentie itogi* (Moscow: Tipografiia A. Strel'tsova, 1912).

18. E.g., see Ira Klein, "The Anglo-Russian Convention and the Problem of Central Asia, 1907–1914," *Journal of British Studies* 11, no. 1 (1971): 126–47, at 141; Lawrence James, *The Rise and Fall of the British Empire* (London: Little, Brown, 1994), 338; and Anthony Wynn, *Persia in the Great Game: Sir Percy Sykes— Explorer, Consul, Soldier, Spy* (London: John Murray, 2003), 164.

19. Dimitry Logofet, *Bukharskoe Khanstvo pod russkim protektoratom* (Saint Petersburg: V. Berezovsky, 1911), vol. 2, 225; I. G. Polinov, "Proiski angliiskikh i yaponskikh imperialistov v Sinkiange (konets XIX–nachalo XX vv.)," *Institut vostokovedeniia AN Uzbekskoi SSR, Trudy* 2 (1954): 80–90, at 83–84; Anton Vinokur, "Ot konfrontatsii k soglasovannomu kursu: Politika Velikobritanii i Rossii v Irane (1900–1914)," Kand. diss., Saint Petersburg: Sanktpeterburgskii gosudarstvennyi universitet, 2004, 19; James, *Rise and Fall of the British Empire*, 338.

20. National Archives of the United Kingdom–Public Record Office (hereafter, PRO), FO/535/15, memorandum by Crewe respecting the situation in the countries bordering on the northeastern frontier of India, London, July 12, 1912; quoted by D. Woodman, *Himalayan Frontiers: A Political Review of British, Chinese, and Russian Rivalries* (London: Barrie and Rockliff, Cresset Press, 1969), 106; also see Lev E. Berlin, "Angliia i Tibet," *Novyi Vostok* 2 (1922): 355–66, at 362–63.

21. Gooch and Temperley, *British Documents*, vol. 10, pt. 2, 775–76, Grey to Buchanan, London, March 18, 1914; PRO/FO 371/2073/22510, memorandum by Clarke on Anglo-Russian relations in Persia, London, July 23, 1914; quoted by Jennifer Siegel, *Endgame: Britain, Russia and the Final Struggle for Central Asia* (London: I. B. Tauris, 2002), 175–96; Thomas Otte, "Old Diplomacy: Reflections on the Foreign Office Before 1914," in *The Foreign Office and British Diplomacy in the Twentieth Century*, edited by G. Johnson (London: Routledge, 2005), 42.

22. PRO/FO 800/373, Nicolson to Buchanan, London, April 7, 1914; quoted by

Steiner and Neilson, *Britain and the Origins*, 98.

23. David Macdonald, "Tsushima's Echoes: Asian Defeat and Tsarist Foreign Policy," in *The Russo-Japanese War in Global Perspective: World War Zero*, vol. 1, edited by J. Steinberg et al. (Leiden: Brill, 2005), 559–60, 562.

24. Gooch and Temperley, *British Documents,*, vol. 10, pt. 2, 780–82, Buchanan to Grey, Saint Petersburg, April 3, 1914. For the current interpretations of Grey's policy on the eve and in the first period of World War I, see Yury Zhdanov, "Diplomatiia E. Greya i osnovnye napravleniia vneshnei politiki Velikobritanii v 1905–1916 gg.," Kand. diss., Leningradskii gosudarstvennyi universitet, 1986; and Andrei Plekhanov, "Anglo-russkie politicheskie otnosheniia v 1907–1914 gg.," Kand. diss., Gosudarstvennyi pedagogicheskii universitet, Vladimir, 2006.

25. E.g., see Gosudarstvennyi Arkhiv Rossiiskoi Federatsii, f. 601, op. 1, d.791, ll. 1–6, memorandum by the Foreign Office to the Russian Foreign Ministry, London, March 12, 1915; IOLR/L/L&S/18/A 172, memorandum by Macartney, London, August 23, 1915; IOLR/L/L&S/18/C 142, memorandum by the India Office Political Department on revision of the Anglo-Russian Convention of 1907, London, 1915; IOLR/L/L&S/18/C 163, extract from the secret note on revision of the Anglo-Russian Convention of 1907, New Delhi, September 29, 1916; Kotliar, "Russko-afghanskie otnosheniia," 235–37.

26. Alexander Lobanov-Rostovsky, *Russia and Asia* (Ann Arbor: G. Wahr, 1951), 255–56, quoted by Anatoly V. Remnev, "Kak obustroit' Rossiiu: Geopoliticheskie prognosy byvshego ministra Kuropatkina," *Rodina*, 2004, 32–34.

27. On the German activity in the Middle East and Inner Asia during World War I, see Peter Hopkirk, *On Secret Service East of Constantinople: The Plot to Bring Down the British Empire* (London: John Murray, 1994), 105–21; and Yurii N. Tikhonov, "Novyi istochnik po istorii 'Bol'shoi Igry' v Afghanistane v period dvukh mirovykh voin," *Vostochnyi arkhiv*, no. 13 (2005): 102–11.

28. Peter Hopkirk, *The Great Game: On Secret Service in High Asia* (London: John Murray, 1990), 522.

29. David B. Guralnik, ed., *Webster's New World Dictionary* (Oxford: Oxford and IBH, 1974), 397.

30. Adrian Weale, *Secret Warfare: Special Operations Forces from the Great Game to the SAS* (London: Hodder & Stoughton, 1997), xi.

31. See Lance Davis and Robert Huttenback, *Mammon and the Pursuit of Empire* (Cambridge: Cambridge University Press, 1986), 212–13.

32. On the specification of British imperialism in the nineteenth century, especially see John Mackenzie, *Propaganda and Empire: The Manipulation of British Public Opinion, 1880–1960* (Manchester: Manchester University Press, 1985); Robert Macdonald, *The Language of Empire: Myths and Metaphors of Popular Imperialism, 1880–1918* (Manchester: Manchester University Press, 1994); Judith Brown and William Louis, eds., *The Oxford History of the British Empire* (Oxford: Oxford University Press, 1999), vol. 3; Ronald Hyam, "The Primacy of Geopolitics:

The Dynamics of British Imperial Policy, 1763–1963," in *The Statecraft of British Imperialism,* edited by Robert King and Robin Kilson (London: Frank Cass, 1999), 27–52; Tamara Gella, "Liberalism i 'novyi imperialism' v Velikobritanii v 80–90-kh gg. XIX v.," *Novaia i noveishaia istoriia,* no. 2 (2001): 52–65; David Armitage, *The Ideological Origins of the British Empire* (Cambridge: Cambridge University Press, 2002); Robert Johnson, *British Imperialism* (Houndmills, U.K.: Palgrave Macmillan, 2003); Ivan Stepanov, "Ideologiia i politika britanskogo militarisma v kontse XIX–nachale XX v.," Kand. diss., Samarskii gosudarstvennyi universitet, Samara, 2006; and Philippa Levine, *The British Empire: Sunrise to Sunset* (London: Longman, 2007). A modern representation of Russian imperialism is given by Dietrich Geyer, *Der Russische Imperialismus: Studien ueber den Zusammenhang von innerer und auswaertiger Politik 1860–1914* (Goettingen: Vandenhoeck and Ruprecht, 1977); and Dominic Lieven, *Empire: The Russian Empire and Its Rivals* (London: John Murray, 2000).

33. Aleksei Zashihin, *"Gliadia iz Londona": Rossiia v obstchestvennoi mysli Britanii. Vtoraia polovina XIX–nachalo XX v. Ocherki* (Archangelsk: Pomorskii mezhdunarodnyi pedagogicheskii universitet, 1994), 97.

34. See R. Pethybridge, "British Imperialists in the Russian Empire," *Russian Review* 30, no. 4 (1971): 346–55, at 352–53.

35. This comparison was made as early as at the turn of the twentieth century; see Arminius Vambery, *Western Culture in Eastern Lands: A Comparison of the Methods Adopted by England and Russia in the Middle East* (London: Murray, 1906).

36. Quoted in IOLR/L/P&S/18/C 106, memorandum by Lee-Warner, Simla, November 6, 1902. For the influence of frontiers upon self-consciousness of ethnic groups, see Roman Ignatiev, "Vliianie politicheskikh granits na ethnicheskoe samosoznanie," Kand. diss., Institut ethnologii i antropologii RAN, Moscow, 2002.

37. David Gillard, *The Struggle for Asia, 1828–1914: A Study in British and Russian Imperialism* (London: Methuen, 1977), 2.

38. Jeff Sahadeo, *Russian Colonial Society in Tashkent, 1865–1923* (Bloomington: Indiana University Press, 2007), 69.

39. For further discussion by Russian historians, see Sergei Z. Martirosov, "Anglo-russkoe sopernichestvo v period prisoedineniia Turkmenii k Rossii," Kand. diss., Moskovskii gosudarstvennyi pedagogicheskii institut, 1966, 19; Maria K. Rozhkova, *Ekonomicheskie sviasi Rossii so Srednei Asiei, 40-e–60-e gg. XIX v.* (Moscow: Izdatelstvo Akademii nauk, 1963), 135; V. Ya. Basin and K. R. Nesimbaeva, "Vneshniaia torgovlia Rossii so stranami Vostoka na rubezhe XIX–XX vv.," in *Iz istorii mezhdunarodnykh otnoshenii v Tsentral'noi Asii (srednie veka i novoe vremya),* edited by G. Iskhakov (Alma-Ata: Gylym, 1990), 176–83; and Olga Yegorenko, "Bokharskii Emirat v period protektorata Rossii (1868–1920 gg.): Istoriia problemy," Kand. diss., Rossiiskii gosudarstvennyi universitet turizma, Moscow, 2008, 20.

40. E.g., see P. Waldron, *The End of Imperial Russia, 1855–1917* (Houndmills, U.K.: Macmillan, 1997), 107–8.

41. Pethybridge, "British Imperialists," 355.

42. Robert Rhodes James, *Rosebery: A Biography of Archibald Philip, Fifth Earl of Rosebery* (London: Weidenfeld and Nicolson, 1963), 192.

43. Khalfin, 'Politika Rossii v Srednei Asii," 40; Gillard, *Struggle for Asia*, 179.

44. It was Major General Leonid Sobolev who used this metaphor in a correspondence to the national daily *Rus'* in December 1884; see Firuz Kazemzadeh, "Russia and the Middle East," in *Russian Foreign Policy. Essays in Historical Perspective*, edited by Ivo Lederer (New Haven, Conn.: Yale University Press, 1962), 495–96.

SELECTED ARCHIVAL SOURCES AND BIBLIOGRAPHY

PRINCIPAL ARCHIVAL SOURCES

Russian and Central Asian Archives

Arkhiv Vneshnei Politiki Rossiiskoi Imperii (AVPRI; Archive of Foreign Policy of the
Russian Empire), Moscow:
Fond 133, Kantseliariia ministra
Fond 137, Otchety Ministerstva inostrannykh del
Fond 138, Sekretnyi archiv ministra inostrannykh del
Fond 143, Kitaiskii stol
Fond 144, Persidkii stol
Fond 147, Sredneasiatskii stol
Fond 154, Asiatskii departament
Fond 184, Posol'stvo v Londone
Fond 188, Missiia v Pekine

Gosudarstvennyi Arkhiv Rossiiskoi Federatsii (GARF; State Archive of the Russian
Federation), Moscow:
Fond 559, A. P. Izvolsky
Fond 568, V. N. Lamsdorf
Fond 601, Nikolas II
Fond 677, Alexander III
Fond 678, Alexander I
Fond 730, N. P. Ignatiev

Rossiiskii Gosudarstvennyi Arkhiv Voenno-Morskogo Flota (RGA VMF; Russian State
Archive of the Navy), Saint Petersburg:
Fond 32, E. I. Alekseev
Fond 410, Kantseliariia Morskogo ministra

Fond 417, Glavnyi Morskoi Shtab
Fond 418, Morskoi General'nyi Shtab

Rossiiskii Gosudarstvennyi Voenno-Istoricheskii Arkhiv (RGVIA; Russian State
Military-Historical Archive), Moscow:
Fond 76, V. A. Kosogovsky
Fond 165, A. N. Kuroptakin
Fond 400, Asiatskaia chast' Glavnogo Shtaba
Fond 401, Voenno-Uchenyi Komitet Glavnogo Shtaba
Fond 431, Great Britain
Fond 447, China
Fond 448, Korea
Fond 451, Japan
Fond 483, Voennye deistviia v Srednei Asii
Fond 846, Voenno-Uchenyi Arkhiv
Fond 970, Voenno-pokhodnaia kantseliariia
Fond 1396, Shtab Turkestanskogo voennogo okruga
Fond 2000, Glavnoe Upravlenie General'nogo Shtaba

Rossiskii Gosudarstvennyi Istoricheskii Arkhiv (RGIA; Russian State Historical
Archive), Saint Petersburg:
Fond 560, Obstchaia kantseliariia ministra finansov
Fond 853, V.V. Grigoriev
Fond 932, A. M. Dondukov-Korsakov
Fond 948, Kaznakovy
Fond 954, Kaufmany
Fond 1622, S.Yu. Witte

Arkhiv Instituta Vostochnykh Rukopisei RAN (AIVR; Archive of the Institute of
Oriental Manuscripts), Saint Petersburg:
Fond 115, A. E. Snesarev

Arkhiv Rossiiskogo Geographicheskogo Obtschestva (ARGO; Archive of the Russian
Geographical Society), Saint Petersburg:
Fond 13, N. M. Przhevalsky
Fond 18, P. K. Kozlov
Fond 32, G. E. Grumm-Grzhimailo
Fond 45, B. L. Grombchevsky

Otdel Pis'mennykh Istochnikov Gosudarstvennogo Istoricheskogo Muzeia (OPI GIM;
Division of Written Sources of the State Historical Museum), Moscow:
Fond 208, M. G. Cherniaev
Fond 307, N. I. Grodekov

Otdel Rukopisei Rossiiskoi Gosudarstvennoi Biblioteki (OR RGB; Manuscript

Division of the Russian State Library), Moscow:
Fond 169, Miliutiny
Fond 363, M. N.Veniukov

Otdel Rukopisei Natsional'noi Biblioteki (OR NB; Manuscript Division of the
National Library), Saint Petersburg: Fond 856, I.A. Shestakov

Tsentral'nyi Gosudarstvennyi Arkhiv Respubliki Uzbekistan (TGA RUZ; Central State
Archive of the Republic of Uzbekistan), Tashkent:
Fond 1-I, Kantseliariia Turkestanskogo General-Gubernatora
Fond 715-I, A. G. Serebrennikov, Podgotovitel'nye materially k sborniku
'Turkestanskii krai'

British and Indian Archives

British Library (London)

India Office Library and Records (IOLR), London:
Military:
MIL 5, Compilations and Miscellaneous
MIL 7, Military Collections
MIL 17, Military Department Library
Political and Secret Department:
PS 5, Secret Letters Received from Bengal and India
PS 7, Abstracts of Political and Secret Letters from India
PS 10, Political and Secret Subject Files
PS 18, Political and Secret Memoranda
PS 20, Political and Secret Library Collections, 1800–1947: Russia, China,
Turkestan, Central Asia
Manuscript Division:
Add. 49683–962, Balfour Papers
Add. 44086–835, Gladstone Papers
Private Papers:
Mss Eur B 380, Earl of Mayo–Duke of Argyll Correspondence
Mss Eur C 144, Northbrook Collection
Mss Eur D 558, Lansdowne Collection
Mss Eur D 573, John Morley Papers
Mss Eur E 218, Lytton Papers
Mss Eur F 86, Temple Collection
Mss Eur F. 90, John Lawrence Collection
Mss Eur F 111–12, Curzon Collection
Mss Eur F 123, C 125–26, Hamilton Collection
Mss Eur F 132, Lyall Collection

Microfilms:
  Reels 311–25, *Argyll Papers*
  Reels 490–535, *Dufferin Papers*
  Reels 794, 944–45, *Hartington Papers*
  Reels 805–22, *Salisbury Papers*

National Archives of India (NAI), New Delhi: Foreign Department, 1878–79

National Archives of the United Kingdom—Public Record Office (PRO), Kew,
  London:
Admiralty:
  ADM 231, Naval Intelligence Department Reports
Cabinet Office:
  CAB 1, Miscellaneous Records, 1866–1949
  CAB 2, Committee of Imperial Defence (CID), Meetings and Minutes
  CAB 3, CID, Memoranda (A Series)
  CAB 4, CID, Memoranda (B Series)
  CAB 6, CID, Memoranda (D Series)
  CAB 8, Colonial Defence Committee
  CAB 17, CID, Miscellaneous Records
Foreign Office:
  FO 17, China
  FO 65, Russia
  FO 106, General Correspondence: Central Asia, Afghanistan, India
  FO 181, Embassy and Consular, General Correspondence
  FO 405, China and Taiwan: Confidential Printing
  FO 410, Japan: Confidential Printing
  FO 418, Russia and the Soviet Union: Confidential Printing
  FO 535, Tibet and Mongolia: Confidential Printing
  FO 539, Central Asia: Confidential Printing
  FO 800, Foreign Office Private Offices: Various Ministers' and Officials' Papers
  FO 899, Cabinet Papers: Memoranda and Press Summaries
War Office:
  WO 30, Miscellaneous Papers
  WO 33, Reports, Memoranda and Papers
  WO 106, Directorate of Military Operations and Military Intelligence, and
  Predecessors: Correspondence and Papers
  WO 110, W. H. Smith Papers

PUBLISHED PRIMARY SOURCES

Aitchinson, C. U., comp. *A Collection of Treaties, Engagements, and Sanads Relating to India and Neighboring Countries.* 14 vols. Calcutta: Government of India Central Publication Branch, 1929–33.

Gooch, G., and H. Temperley, eds. *British Documents on the Origins of the War 1898–1914.* vols. 1–5, 8, 10. London: His Majesty's Stationery Office, 1929.

Great Britain, War Office. *Russian Advance in Asia, 1873.* London: Her Majesty's Stationery Office, 1873.

———. *Memorandum on the Military Forces in the United Kingdom,* London: Her Majesty's Stationery Office, 1907.

Ilyasov, A., ed. *Prisoedinenie Turkmenii k Rossii: Sbornik dokumentov.* Ashgabad: Izdatel'stvo AN Turkmenskoi SSR, 1960.

Lansdowne, H. *The Marquess of Lansdowne Correspondence with the Secretary of State for India, 1888–1894.* 5 vols. Calcutta: Indian Government Office, 1894.

Lieven, D., ed. *British Documents on Foreign Affairs: Reports and Papers from the Foreign Office Confidential Print—Russia, 1859–1914.* Washington, D.C.: University Press of America, 1983–89.

Popov, A., comp. "Angliiskaia politika v Indii i russko-indiiskie otnosheniia v 1897–1905 gg." *Krasnyi Arkhiv* 6, no. 19 (1926): 53–63.

———. "Anglo-russkoe soglashenie o razdele Kitaia 1899 g." *Krasnyi Arkhiv* 6, no. 25 (1927): 111–34.

———. "Anglo-russkoe sopernichestvo v Persii v 1890–1906 gg." *Krasnyi Arkhiv* 1, no. 56 (1933): 33–64.

———. "Pervye shagi russkogo imperialisma na Dal'nem Vostoke." *Krasnyi Arhiv* 3, no. 52 (1932): 34–124.

———. "Tsarskaia diplomatiia o zadachakh Rossii na Dal'nem Vostoke." *Krasnyi Arkhiv* 5, no. 16 (1926): 3–29.

Reisner, I., comp. "Anglo-russkaia konventsiia i razdel Afghanistana." *Krasnyi Arkhiv* 3, no. 10 (1925): 54–66.

Rezvan, E., comp. *Russian Ships in the Gulf 1899–1903.* Reading, U.K.: Ithaka Press, 1993.

Russia, Foreign Ministry. *Afganskoe razgranichenie: Peregovory mezhdu Rossiei i Velikobritaniei 1872–1885 gg.* Saint Petersburg: Tipografiia Ministerstava inostrannykh del, 1886.

———. *Dokumenty, kasaiutschiesia zakliucheniia mezhdu Rossiei i Iaponiei obstchepoliticheskogo soglasheniia 17 (30) July 1907.* Saint Petersburg: Tipografiia Ministerstava inostrannykh del, 1907.

Russia, Ministry of Trade and Industry. *Obzor vneshnei torgovli po evropeiskoi i asiatskoi granitsam.* Saint Petersburg: Tipografiia Departamenta tamozhennykh sborov, 1857–1907.

Russia, War Ministry. *Rossiia i Velikobritaniia v Tsentral'noi Asii.* Tashkent: Tipografiia Shtaba Turkestanskogo voennogo okruga, 1908.

———. *Sbornik geograficheskikh, topograficheskikh i statisticheskikh materialov po Asii.* 87 vols. Saint Petersburg: Voennaia tipografiia, 1883–1914.

Russia, War Ministry, Turkestan Military District. *Svedeniia, kasaiutschiesia stran, sopredel'nykh s Turkestanskim voennym okrugom.* 85 vols. Tashkent: Tipografiia Shtaba Turkestanskogo voennogo okruga, 1898–1906.

Serebrennikov, A. G., comp. *Sbornik materialov po zavoevaniiu Turkestanskogo kraia.* Vol. 17, 2 pts.; vol. 19, pt. 1; vol. 20, pt. 2; vol. 21, pt. 1; vol. 22, pt. 2. Tashkent: Tipografiia Shtaba Turkestanskogo voennogo okruga, 1914–15.

Sergeev, E., comp. "Zadachi Anglii na Vostoke: Doneseniia russkogo voennogo attashe v Londone N. S. Yermolova, 1902." *Istoricheskii arkhiv,* no. 1 (1995): 168–74.

Shastitko, P., ed. *Russko-indiiskie otnosheniia v XIX v. Sbornik arkhivnykh dokumentov i materialov.* Moscow: Vostochnaia literatura, 1997.

Struve, V.V., ed. *Materialy po istorii Turkmen i Turkmenii: Iranskie, bukharskie i khivinskie istochniki XVI–XIX vv.,* vol. 2. Moscow: Izdatel'stvo AN SSSR, 1938.

Trotsky, V. N., ed. *Materialy dlia opisaniia Khivinskogo pokhoda 1873 g.* 2 pts. Tashkent: Tipografiia Shtaba Turkestanskogo voennogo okruga, 1881–82.

Zagorodnikova, T. N., comp. *"Bol'shaia" igra' v Tsentral'noi Asii: "Indiiskii pokhod" russkoi armii—Sbornik arkhibnykh dokumentov.* Moscow: Institut vostokovedeniia RAN, 2005. RAN, 2005.

PARLIAMENTARY PAPERS

Anglo-Russian Convention Signed on August 31, 1907, between Great Britain and Russia, Containing Arrangements on the Subject of Persia, Afghanistan, and Tibet (Russia No. 1). London: His Majesty's Stationery Office, 1908.

Convention between the United Kingdom and China Respecting Tibet, Signed at Peking, April 27, 1906 (Treaty Ser. No. 9). London: His Majesty's Stationery Office, 1906.

Correspondence between Her Majesty's Government and the Russian Government with Regard to Their Respective Interests in China (China No. 2). London: Her Majesty's Stationery Office, 1899.

Correspondence in Regard to the Pamir Frontier, 1890–1891. London: Her Majesty's Stationery Office, 1891.

Correspondence Relating to the Affairs of Afghanistan (Afghanistan No. 1). London: Her Majesty's Stationery Office, 1880.

Correspondence Relating to Chitral. London: Her Majesty's Stationery Office, 1895.

Correspondence Relating to the Occupation of Chitral. London: Her Majesty's Stationery Office, 1896.

Correspondence Respecting the Affairs of Asia (Central Asia No. 1). London: Her Majesty's Stationery Office, 1884.

Correspondence Respecting Affairs in Central Asia (Central Asia No. 1). London: Her

Majesty's Stationery Office, 1881.

Correspondence Respecting Affairs in Central Asia (Central Asia No. 1). London: Her Majesty's Stationery Office, 1882.

Correspondence Respecting the Affairs of Central Asia (Central Asia No. 1). London: Her Majesty's Stationery Office, 1887.

Correspondence Respecting Central Asia (Central Asia No. 1). London: Her Majesty's Stationery Office, 1878.

Correspondence Respecting Central Asia (Russia No. 2). London: Her Majesty's Stationery Office, 1874.

Correspondence Respecting the Imperial Railways of North China (China No. 7). London: His Majesty's Stationery Office, 1901.

Correspondence Respecting the Insurrection Movement in China (China No. 3). London: Her Majesty's Stationery Office, 1900.

Correspondence Respecting the Relations between the British Government and That of Afghanistan, since the Accession of Ameer Sher Ali Khan (1863–1878), London: Her Majesty's Stationery Office, 1878.

Correspondence Respecting the Russian Occupation of Manchuria and Newchwang (China No. 2). London: His Majesty's Stationery Office, 1904.

Correspondence with Russia Respecting Central Asia (Oct. 1872–Jan. 1873). London: Her Majesty's Stationery Office, 1873.

Dispatches from His Majesty's Ambassador at St Petersburg Respecting the Russo-Chinese Agreement as to Manchuria (China No. 2). London: His Majesty's Stationery Office, 1901.

Extracts of Correspondence Relating to the Mission of Mr. Douglas Forsyth to Yarkand. London: Her Majesty's Stationery Office, 1871.

Further Correspondence (Central Asia No 1). London: Her Majesty's Stationery Office, 1888.

Further Correspondence (Central Asia No. 2). London: Her Majesty's Stationery Office, 1887.

Further Correspondence (Central Asia No. 2). London: Her Majesty's Stationery Office, 1888.

Further Correspondence (Dec. 1878–Jan. 1879). (Central Asia No. 1). London: Her Majesty's Stationery Office, 1879.

Further Correspondence (Dec. 1879–Mar. 1881) (Central Asia No. 3). London: Her Majesty's Stationery Office, 1881.

Further Correspondence (Mar. 1869–Febr. 1873) (Central Asia No. 2). London: Her Majesty's Stationery Office, 1873.

Further Correspondence (Mar.–Oct. 1881) (Central Asia No. 4). London: Her Majesty's Stationery Office, 1881.

Further Correspondence Respecting Affairs in Central Asia, 1879 (Central Asia No. 1). London: Her Majesty's Stationery Office, 1880.

Further Correspondence Respecting Central Asia (Central Asia No. 2). London: Her Majesty's Stationery Office, 1885.

Further Correspondence Respecting Central Asia (Central Asia No. 4). London: Her Majesty's Stationery Office, 1885.

Further Correspondence Respecting Central Asia (Sept.–Nov. 1878) (Central Asia No. 2).

London: Her Majesty's Stationery Office, 1878.

Further Dispatch Respecting Affairs in Central Asia (Central Asia No. 2). London: Her Majesty's Stationery Office, 1881.

Further Papers Relating to the Affairs of Afghanistan (Afghanistan No. 2). London: Her Majesty's Stationery Office, 1878.

Further Papers Relating to the Affairs of Afghanistan (Afghanistan No. 3). London: Her Majesty's Stationery Office, 1879.

Further Papers Relating to Tibet. London: His Majesty's Stationery Office, 1904.

The Hansard Parliamentary Debates. London: C. Buck, 1908.

Maps (Central Asia No. 3). London: Her Majesty's Stationery Office, 1885.

Pamirs: Agreement between the Government of Great Britain and Russia with Regard to the Spheres of Influence of the Two Countries in the Region of the Pamirs (Treaty Ser. No. 8). London: Her Majesty's Stationery Office, 1895.

Papers Regarding British Relations with the Neighboring Tribes on the North-West Frontier of India and the Military Operations Undertaken against Them during the Years 1897–1898. 2 vols. London: Her Majesty's Stationery Office, 1898.

Papers Relating to Tibet. London: His Majesty's Stationery Office, 1904.

Telegram from Lieutenant-General Sir Peter Lumsden relative to the Fight between the Russians and the Afghans at Ak Tepe (Central Asia No. 1). London: Her Majesty's Stationery Office, 1885.

DIARIES, MEMOIRS, CORRESPONDENCE, AND REVIEWS

Alikhanov-Avarsky, M.V. *V gostiakh u Shaha: Ocherki Persii.* Tiflis: Ya. Liberman, 1898.

Argyll, Duchess, ed. *George Douglas, Eighth Duke of Argyll: Autobiography and Memoirs,* 2 vols. London: John Murray, 1906.

Babkov, I. F. *Vospominaniia o moei sluzhbe v Zapadnoi Sibiri, 1859–1875 gg. (razgranichenie s Zapadnym Kitaem 1869 g.).* Saint Petersburg: V. Kirshbaum, 1912.

Barnes, W. "Colonel Grombchevsky's Expeditions in Central Asia, and the Recent Events on the Pamirs." *Imperial and Asiatic Quarterly Review* 3, no. 5 (1892): 17–52.

Basily, N. *Diplomat of Imperial Russia, 1903–1917: Memoirs.* Stanford, Calif.: Hoover Institution Press, 1973.

Bellew, H. *Kashmir and Kashgar: A Narrative of the Journey of the Embassy to Kashgar in 1873–7.* London: Truebner, 1875.

Benkendorff, C. *Half a Life: The Reminiscences of a Russian Gentleman.* London: Richards Press, 1954.

Blacker, L. *On Secret Patrol in High Asia.* London: John Murray, 1922.

Blaramberg, Ivan Fedorovich. *Vospominaniia.* Moscow: Nauka, 1978.

Blunt, W. *India under Ripon: A Private Diary.* London: T. Fisher Unwin, 1909.

Bogdanov, R. K. "Vospominaniia amurskogo kazaka o proshlom, s 1849 po 1880 g."

Priamurskie vedomosti, nos. 340–44 (1900): 348–49.

Bower, H. *Diary of a Journey across Tibet*. Kathmandu: Ratna Pustak Bhandar, 1976.

Brackenbury, H. *Some Memories of My Spare Time*. Edinburgh: W. Blackwood & Sons, 1909.

Bradley, J., ed. *Lady Curzon's India: Letters of a Vicereine*. New York: Beaufort Books, 1985.

Brett, M., ed. *Journals and Letters of Reginald Viscount Esher*. 2 vols. London: Ivor Nicholson and Watson, 1934.

Burnaby, F. *A Ride to Khiva: Travels and Adventures in Central Asia*. London, 1877.

Burnes, A. *Travels into Bokhara*. 2 vols. New Delhi: Asian Educational Services, 1992 (orig. pub. 1834).

Chamberlain, A. *Politics from Inside: An Epistolary Chronicle 1906–1914*. London: Cassell, 1936.

Chirkin, S. V. *Dvadtsat' let sluzhby na Vostoke: Zapiski tsarskogo diplomata*. Moscow: Russkii put', 2006.

Chirol, V. *Fifty Years in a Changing World*. London: Jonathan Cape, 1927.

Churchill, W. *Great Contemporaries*. London: Fontana Books, 1937.

Cockerill, G. *A Few Notes on the Possible Lines of Advance from the Russian Base upon Chitral and Gilgit*. Simla: Government Central Printing Office, 1894.

Connoly, A. *Journey to the North of India*. 2 vols. London: R. Bentley, 1834.

Cotton, S. *Nine Years on the North-West Frontier of India, from 1854 to 1863*. London: R. Bentley, 1868.

Curzon, G. "A Visit to Bokhara, the Noble." *Fortnightly Review* 51 (1889): 122–43.

Das, S. *Indian Pundits in the Land of Snow*. Calcutta: Baptist Mission Press, 1893.

Deasy, H. *In Tibet and Chinese Turkestan; Being the Record of Three Years' Exploration*. London: T. Fisher Unwin, 1901.

Dlusskaia, N. N., comp. "Zapiski N. G. Zalesova." *Russkaia starina* 115 (1903): 21–37, 321–40.

Dobson, G. *Russia's Railway Advance into Central Asia: Notes of a Journey from St Petersburg to Samarkand*. Calcutta: W. Allen, 1890.

Dorzhiev, A. *Predanie o krugosvetnom puteshestvii' ili povestvovanie o zhizni Agvana Dorzhieva*. Ulan-Ude: Buriatskii institut obtschestvennykh nauk SO RAN, 1994.

———. *Zanimatel'nye zametki: Opisanie puteshestviia vokrug sveta*. Moscow: Vostochnaia literatura, 2003.

Durand, A. *The Making of a Frontier: Five Years' Experience and Adventures in Gilgit, Hunza, Nagar, Chitral, and the Eastern Hindukush*. London: John Murray, 1899.

Elles, E., comp. *History of Our Relations with Hunza and Nagar from 1886 to June, 1, 1892, and of the Military Operations against Those States in December 1891*. Simla: Government Central Printing Office, 1892.

Evans, M., ed. *The Great Game: Britain and Russia in Central Asia*, London: RoutledgeCurzon, 2004.

Fairbank, J., ed. *The I. G. in Peking: Letters of Robert Hart—Chinese Maritime Customs 1868–1907*. Cambridge, Mass.: Harvard University Press, 1975.

Filchner, W. *Sturm ueber Asien: Erlebnisse eines diplomatischen Geheimagenten*. Berlin:

Verlag Neufeld and Henius, 1924.

Forsyth, D. *Autobiography and Reminiscences.* London: R. Bentley, 1887.

———. *Report of a Mission to Yarkand in 1873.* Calcutta: Foreign Department Press, 1875.

Gordon, T. *The Roof of the World.* Edinburgh: Edmonton and Douglas, 1876.

Grey, E. *Speeches on Foreign Affairs, 1904–1914.* London: George Allen & Unwin, 1931.

———. *Twenty Five Years: 1892–1916,* 2 vols. London: Hodder & Stoughton, 1926.

Grodekov, N. I. *Cherez Afghanistan: Putevye zapiski.* Saint Petersburg: Novoe Vremya, 1880.

Grombchevsky, B. L. *Otchet o poezdke v Kashgar i Yuzhnuiu Kashgariiu v 1885 g.* Novyi Margelan: Tipografiia Shtaba Turkestanskogo voennogo okruga, 1886.

Gwynn, S., ed. *The Letters and Friendships of Sir Cecil Spring Rice.* 2 vols. London: Archibald Constable, 1929.

Haldane, R. *An Autobiography.* London: Hodder & Stoughton, 1929.

———. *Before the War.* London: Cassell, 1920.

Hamilton, G. *Parliamentary Reminiscences and Reflections, 1886–1906.* New York: E. P. Dutton, 1917.

Hardinge, C. *Old Diplomacy: The Reminiscences of Lord Hardinge of Penshurst.* London: John Murray, 1947.

Hedin, S. *Central Asia and Tibet: Towards the Holy City of Lhasa.* 2 vols. London: Hurst and Blackett, 1903.

Henderson, G., and O. Allan, comps. *Lahore to Yarkand: Incidents of the Route and Natural History of the Countries Traversed by the Expedition of 1870 under D. Forsyth, Esq.* Lahore: Niaz Ahmad Sang-E-Meell, 1981.

Hosie, A. *Report on a Journey to the Eastern Frontier of Tibet.* London: His Majesty's Stationery Office, 1905.

———. *Three Years in Western China.* London: G. Philip and Son, 1897.

Ignatiev, N.P., *Missiia v Khivu i Bukharu v 1858 g. fligel-adjutanta polkovnika N. Ignatieva.* Saint Petersburg: Gosudarstvennaia tipogragiia, 1897.

Ioffe, E., comp. *Linii Mannergeima: Pis'ma i dokumenty—Tainy i otkrytiia.* Saint Petersburg: Zvezda, 2005.

Izvolsky, A. *Au service de la Russie: Correspondance diplomatique 1906–1911,* vol. 1. Paris: Les Editions Internationales, 1937.

———. *Vospominaniia.* Moscow: Mezhdunarodnye otnosheniia, 1989.

Kalmykov, A. *Memoirs of a Russian Diplomat: Outposts of the Empire, 1893–1917,* New Haven, Conn.: Yale University Press, 1971.

Kaul'bars, A. V. "Zametki o Kul'dzhinskom krae." In *Materialy dlia statistiki Turkestanskogo kraia,* vol. 3. Saint Petersburg: K. Trubnikov, 1874.

Kawaguchi, E. *Three Years in Tibet.* Madras: Theosophical Publishing Society, 1909.

Khrulev, S. A. "Zapiska o pokhode v Indiu." *Russkii Arkhiv* 3, no. 5 (1882): 42–66.

Kilbracken, Lord. *Reminiscences of Lord Kilbracken.* London: Macmillan, 1931.

King, P., ed. *Curzon's Persia.* London: Sidgwick and Jackson, 1986.

———. *A Viceroy's India: Leaves from Lord Curzon's Note-Book.* London: Sidgwick and Jackson, 1984.

Kliashtornyi, S. G., and A. A. Kolesnikov, comps. *Vostochnyi Turkestan glazami russkikh puteshestvennikov (vtoraia polovina XIX v.)*. Alma-Ata: Tipografiia AN Kazakhskoi SSR, 1988.

Kliashtornyi, S. G., et al., comps. *Vostochnyi Turkestan glazami evropeiskikh puteshestvennikov*. Alma-Ata: Gylym, 1991.

Kornilov, L. G. *Kashgariia ili Vostochnyi Turkestan: Opyt voenno-statisticheskogo opisaniia*. Tashkent: Tipogragiia Shtaba Turkestanskogo voennogo okruga, 1903.

Korostovets, I. Ya. *Stranitsa iz istorii russkoi diplomatii: Russko-iaponskie peregovory v Portsmute v 1905 g.* Peking: Tipografiia Rossiiskoi Dukhovnoi missii, 1923.

Kosogovsky, V. A. *Iz tegeranskogo dnevnika polkovnika V.A. Kosogovskogo*, edited by G. M. Petrov and G. L. Bondarevskii, Moscow: Vostochnaia literatura, 1960.

———. "Ocherk razvitiia persidskoi kazachiei brigady." *Novyi Vostok* 4 (1923): 390–402.

———. "Persiia v kontse XIX v. (dnevnik generala Kosogovskogo)." *Novyi Vostok* 3 (1923): 446–69.

Krestovsky, V. "V gostiakh u Emira Bukharskogo. Putevoi dnevnik." *Russkii vestnik* 159, no. 2 (1884): 469–532; 170, no. 3: 113–54; 171, no. 5: 5–75; 171, no. 6: 608–59; 172, no. 7: 49–110; no. 8, 478–559.

Kuropatkin, A. *Kashgaria: Historical and Geographical Sketch of the Country—Its Military Strength, Industries and Trade*. Calcutta: Thacker, Spink, 1882.

———. *Vsepoddanneishii otchet o poezdke v Teheran v 1895 g.* Saint Petersburg: Tipografiia Shtaba Peterburgskogo voennogo okruga, 1895.

Lamsdorf, V. N. *Dnevnik, 1886–1890*. Moscow: Gosudarstvennoe izdatel'stvo, 1926.

———. *Dnevnik, 1891–1892*. Moscow: Akademiia, 1934.

———. *Dnevnik, 1894–1896*. Moscow: Mezhdunarodnye otnosheniia, 1991.

Lawrence, W. *The India We Served*. London: Cassell, 1928.

Lensen, G., ed. *Revelations of a Russian Diplomat: The Memoirs of Dimitry I. Abrikossov*. Seattle: University of Washington Press, 1964.

Lockhart, B. *British Agent*. New York: G. P. Putnam's Sons, 1933.

Loftus, A. *The Diplomatic Reminiscences, 1837–1862*. 2 vols. London: Cassell, 1892.

Logofet, D. N. *Na granitsakh Srednei Asii: Putevye ocherki*. 3 vols. Saint Petersburg: V. Berezovsky, 1909.

———. *Po Kaspiiskomu moriu i persidskoi granitse: Putevye ocherki po Srednei Asii*. Saint Petersburg: Tipografiia Glavnogo upravleniia udelov, 1903.

Mannerheim, K. *Memoirs*. Moscow: Vagrius, 1999.

———. "Predvaritel'nyi otchet o poezdke, predpriniatoi po Vysochaishemu poveleniiu cherez Kitaiskii Turkestan i severnye provintsii Kitaia v g. Pekin v 1906–1907 i 1908 gg." *Sbornik geograficheskokh, topograficheskikh i statisticheskikh materialov po Asii* 81 (1909): 1–173.

Markov, E. L. *Rossiia v Srednei Asii: Ocherki puteshestviia po Zakavkaziu, Turkmenii, Bukhare, Samarkandskoi, Tashkentskoi i Ferganskoi oblastiam, Kaspiskomu moriu i Volge*. 2 vols. Saint Petersburg: Wolf, 1901.

Matveev. "Poezdka General'nogo Shtaba polkovnika Matveeva po bukharskim i afganskim vladeniiam v fevrale 1877 g." *Sbornik geograficheskokh, topograficheskikh i statisticheskikh materialov po Asii* 5 (1883): 1–57.

Maxwell, H. *The Life and Letters of George William Frederick Fourth Earl of Clarendon.* 2 vols. New York: Longman, Green; London: E. Arnold, 1913.

Metschersky, V. P. *Moi vospominaniia.* 3 vols. Saint Petersburg: V. Metschersky, 1897–1912.

Meyendorff, A., ed. *Correspondence diplomatique du Baron de Staal (1884–1900).* 2 vols. Paris: Libraire des Sciences Politiques et Sociales, 1929.

Michell, J., and R. Michell, eds. *The Russians in Central Asia.* London: E. Stanford, 1865.

Michie, A. *The Englishman in China during the Victorian Era.* 2 vols. Edinburgh: W. Blackwood and Sons, 1900.

Midleton, Earl. *Records and Reactions: 1856–1939.* London: John Murray, 1939.

Miliutin, D. A. *Dnevnik.* 4 vols. Moscow: OR RGB, 1947–50.

———. *Vospominaniia: 1843–1856.* Vol. 2. Moscow: Rossiiskii Arkhiv, 2000.

———. *Vospominaniia: 1856–1860.* Vol. 3. Moscow: Rosspen, 2004.

———. *Vospominaniia: 1860–1862.* Vol. 4. Moscow: Rossiiskii Arkhiv, 1999.

———. *Vospominaniia: 1863–1864.* Vol. 5. Moscow: Rosspen, 2003.

———. *Vospominaniia: 1865–1867.* Vol. 6. Moscow: Rosspen, 2005.

———. *Vospominaniia: 1868–1873.* Vol. 7. Moscow: Rosspen, 2006.

Minaev, I. P. *Dnevniki puteshestvii v Indiiu i Birme.* Moscow: Izdate'stvo AN SSSR, 1955.

Moorcroft, W. *Travels in the Himalayan Provinces of Hindustan and the Panjab.* 2 vols. Lahore: Faran Academy, 1976 (orig. pub. London: John Murray, 1837).

Morley, J. *Recollections.* 2 vols. London: Macmillan, 1921.

Muir, W. *Records of the Intelligence Department of the Government of the North-West Provinces of India during the Mutiny of 1857.* 2 vols. Edinburgh: T. Clark, 1902.

Narzounof, O. "Trois voyages à Lhasa (1898–1901)." *Tour de Monde* 10 (1904): 217–40.

Nidermiller, A. G. *Ot Sevastopolia do Tsusimy: Vospominaniia—Russkii flot za vremia s 1866 po 1906 gg.* Riga: M. Didkovsky, 1930.

Norman H. *The Peoples and Politics of the Far East: Travels and Studies in the British, French, Spanish and Portuguese Colonies, Siberia, China, Japan, Korea, Siam and Malaya.* New York: Charles Scribner's Sons, 1895.

Obruchev, V. A. *Ot Kiakhty do Kul'dzhi: Puteshestvie v Tsentral'nuiu Asiiu i Kitai.* Moscow: Izdatel'stvo AN SSSR, 1950.

O'Connor, F. *On the Frontier and Beyond: A Record of Thirty Years' Service.* London: John Murray, 1931.

O'Donovan, E. *The Merv Oasis: Travels and Adventures East of the Caspian during the Years 1879–80–81, Including Five Months' Residence among the Tekke of Merv.* London, 1882.

Ogorodnikov, P. *Na puti v Persiiu i prikaspiiskie provintsii eio.* Saint Petersburg: M. Popov, 1878.

Pallmer, R., ed. *Earl of Selborne, Lord High Chancellor: Memorials Personal and Political, 1865–1895,* pt. 2, vol. 1. London: Macmillan, 1898.

Pares, B. *My Russian Memoirs.* London: Jonathan Cape, 1931.

Pashino, P. I. *Turkestanskii krai v 1866 g. Putevye zametki.* Saint Petersburg: Tiblen, 1868.

————. *Vokrug sveta. Po Indii: Putevye vpechatleniia.* 2 vols. Saint Petersburg: A. Suvorin, 1885.

Pearse, H., ed. *Soldier and Traveler: Memoirs [Chiefly in His Own Words] of Alexander Gardner, Colonel of Artillery in the Service of Maharaja Ranjit Singh.* Edinburgh: W. Blackwood and Sons, 1898.

Pervyshev, I., comp. "Resale-i-Yakubi: Vospominaniia o Yakub-beke kashgarskom Kamil'-Khana-Ishana." *Istorik-Marxist* 3 (1940): 127–35.

Peterov, G. M., comp. *Iz tegeranskogo dnevnika polkovnika V. A. Kosogovskogo.* Moscow: Vostochnaia literatura, 1960.

Ramm, A., ed. *The Political Correspondence of Mr. Gladstone and Lord Granville, 1868–1876.* 2 vols. London: Royal Historical Society, 1952.

Rediger, A. F. *Istoriia moei zhizni: Vospominaniia voennogo ministra.* 2 vols. Moscow: Kanon-Press–Kuchkovo Pole, 1999.

Reed, S. *The India I Knew, 1897–1947.* London: Long Acre, 1952.

Roberts, F. *Forty-One Years in India from Subaltern to Commander-in-Chief.* 2 vols. London: Macmillan, 1897.

Robertson, W. *From Private to Field-Marshal.* London: Archibald Constable, 1921.

Roborovsky, V. I. *Ekskursii po Tibetu i Kashgarii.* Saint Petersburg: A. Suvorin, 1892.

Ronaldshay, Earl. *On the Outskirts of Empire in Asia.* Edinburgh: W. Blackwood and Sons, 1904.

Rosen, R. *Forty Years of Diplomacy.* 2 vols. London: George Allen & Unwin, 1922.

Schuyler, E. *Turkistan,* vol. 2. London: S. Low, M. Searle, and Rivington, 1876.

Semennikov, V. P. *Za kulisami tsarisma (arkhiv tibetskogo vracha Badmaeva).* Leningrad: Gosudarstvennoe izdatel'stvo, 1925.

Sergeev, E., and I. Karpeev, eds. "Yaponskie dnevniki A. N. Kuropatkina." *Rossiiskii arkhiv* 6 (1995): 393–444.

Shastitko, P. M., ed. *Rossiiskie puteshestvenniki v Indii XIX–nachala XX veka: Dokumenty i materially.* Moscow: Nauka, 1990.

Skobelev, M. D. "Posmertnye bumagi." *Istoricheskii vestnik* 10, no. 10 (1882): 109–38; no. 11: 275–94.

————. "Proekt M. D. Skobeleva o pokhode na Indiiu." *Istoricheskii vestnik* 14, no. 12 (1883): 543–55.

Stead, W., ed. *The M.P. for Russia: Reminiscences and Correspondence of Madame Olga Novikoff.* 2 vols. London: A. Melrose, 1909.

Stein, A. *On Ancient Central Asian Tracks: Brief Narrative of Three Expeditions in Innermost Asia and North-Western China.* London: Macmillan, 1933.

Soloviev, Yu. Ya. *Vospominaniia diplomata: 1893–1922.* Moscow: Izdatel'stvo sotsial'no-ekonomicheskoi literatury, 1959.

Sykes, P. *Ten Thousands Miles in Persia or Eight Years in Iran.* London: John Murray, 1902.

Tcharykov, N. *Glimpses of Higher Politics through War and Peace, 1855–1929.* London: George Allen & Unwin, 1931.

Temple, R. *Men and Events of My Time in India.* London: John Murray, 1882.

Tsybikov, G. *O tsenral'nom Tibete.* Saint Petersburg: IRGO, 1903.

Ukhtomsky, E. E. *Iz kitaiskikh pisem.* Saint Petersburg: Vostok, 1901.

———. *Iz proshlogo.* Saint Petersburg: Vostok, 1902.

Valikhanov, C. C. "O sostoianii Altyshara ili shesti vostochnykh gorodov kitaiskoi provintsii Nanlu (Maloi Bukharii) v 1858–1859 gg." In *Sobranie sochinenii*, vol. 2, by C. C. Valikhanov. Alma-Ata: Izdatel'stvo AN Kazakhskoi SSR, 1962.

Vambery, A. *His Life and Adventures.* London: T. Fisher Unwin, 1914.

Vansittart, R. *The Mist Procession: The Autobiography of Lord Vansittart.* London: Hutchinson, 1958.

Veniukov, M. I. *Iz vospominanii.* 3 vols. Amsterdam, 1895–1901.

Vonliarliarsky, V. M. *Moi vospominaniia 1852–1939 gg.* Berlin: Russkoe natsional'noe izdatel'stvo, 1939.

Voropaev, N. G., et al., comps. *Anglo-Burskaia voina 1899–1902.* Moscow: Vostochnaia literatura, 2001.

Waddell, L. *Lhasa and Its Mysteries: With a Record of the British Tibetan Expedition of 1903–1904.* London: John Murray, 1905.

Waters, W. *"Private and Personal": Further Experience of a Military Attaché.* London: John Murray, 1928.

———. *"Secret and Confidential": The Experiences of a Military Attaché.* London: John Murray, 1926.

Witte, S. Yu. *Vospominaniia.* 3 vols. Berlin: Slovo, 1922.

Wolff, J. *Narrative of a Mission to Bokhara in the Years 1843–1845, to Ascertain the Fate of Colonel Stoddart and Captain Conolly.* 2 vols. London: J. Parker, 1845.

Yate, A. *England and Russia Face to Face in Asia: Travels with the Afghan Boundary Commission.* Edinburgh: W. Blackwood and Sons, 1887.

Yavorsky, I. L. *Puteshestvie russkogo posol'stva po Afghanistanu i Bukharskomu khanstvu v 1878–1879 gg.* 2 vols. Saint Petersburg: M. Khan, 1882.

Younghusband, F. *The Heart of a Continent.* London, John Murray, 1904.

———. *India and Tibet.* London: John Murray, 1910.

———. *The Light of Experience.* London: Archibald Constable, 1927.

———. "Lord Curzon. A Personal Recollection." *The Nineteenth Century and After* 97, no. 579 (1925): 621–33.

Zeland, N. L. *Kashgariia i perevaly Tian-Shania: Putevye zametki.* Omsk: Tipografiia Shtaba Sibirskogo voennogo okruga, 1887.

CONTEMPORARY ESSAYS

Abaza, K. K. *Zavoevanie Turkestana: Rasskazy iz voennoi istorii, byta i nravov tuzemtsev v onstchestvennom izlozhenii.* Saint Petersburg: M. Stasiulevich, 1902.

Aberigh-Mackay, G. R. *[Some] Notes on [the Situation in] Western Turkistan.* Calcutta:

Thacker, Spink, 1875.

Adye, J. *Russia in Central Asia.* Gibraltar, 1885.

Andogsky, A. I. *Voenno-geograficheskoe opisanie Afghanistana kak raiona nastupatel'nykh operatsii russkoi armii.* Saint Petersburg: A. Suvorin, 1908.

Annenkov, M. N. *Akhaltekinskii oasis i puti v Indiiu.* Saint Petersburg: Tipografiia Shtaba Peterburgskogo voennogo okruga, 1881.

Anonymous. *Russia and England in Central Asia: A Problem.* New York: American Church Press, 1873.

Anonymous (A British Subject). *The Great Game: A Plea for a British Imperial Policy.* London: Simpkin, Marshall, 1875.

Argyll, Duke. *The Afghan Question, from 1841 to 1878.* London: Strahan, 1879.

Barker, E. "The Anti-British Policy of Germany." *The Nineteenth Century and After* 61, no. 367 (1907): 345–64.

———. "The Triple Entente and the Triple Alliance." *The Nineteenth Century and After* 63, no. 377 (1908): 1–17.

Batorsky, A. "Opyt voenno-statisticheskogo ocherka Mongolii." *Sbornik geograficheskikh, topograficheskikh i statisticheskikh materialov po Asii* 37 (1889): 1–285.

Baxter, W. E. *England and Russia.* London: S. Sonnenschein, 1885.

Beaufort, F. *Russian Advances in Asia.* London: Ministry of Defence, 1884.

Beresford, C. *The Break-Up of China.* London: Harper & Brothers, 1899.

———. *Russian Railways towards India.* London: Central Asian Society, 1906.

Beveridge, A. *The Russian Advance.* New York: Harper & Brothers, 1903.

Bland, J. *Li Hung- hang.* London: Archibald Constable, 1917.

Bogdanovich, E. V. *Rossiia na Dal'nem Vostoke.* Saint Petersburg: Russian Red Cross Society, 1901.

Bogdanovich, L. A. "Angliia i Rossiia v Srednei Asii." *Russkaia mysl'* 2 (1900): 139–61; 3: 19–29.

Boulger, D. *Central Asian Questions: Essays on Afghanistan, China, and Central Asia.* London: T. Fisher Unwin, 1885.

———. *England and Russia in Central Asia.* 2 vols. London: W. Allen, 1879.

———. *The Life of Sir Halliday Macartney.* London: John Lane, 1908.

———. *The Life of Yakoob Beg, Athalik Ghazi and Badaulet, Amir of Kashgar.* London: W. Allen, 1878.

———. "Why Not a Treaty with Russia?" *Fortnightly Review* 68, no. 406 (1900): 677–86.

Brodovsky, M. *Kolonial'noe znachenie nashikh sredneasiatskikh vladenii dlia vnutrennikh gubernii.* Moscow: D. Inosemtsev, 1891.

Bruce, R. *The Forward Policy and Its Results.* London: Longmans, Green, 1900.

Brunnhofer, H. *Russlands Hand ueber Asien: Historisch-Geographische Essays zur Entwicklungsgeschichte des russischen Reichsgedankens.* Saint Petersburg: Typographie der Allerhöhsten bestaetigten Typographie-Aktien-Gesellschaft, 1897.

Buksgevden, A. O. *Russkii Kitai: Ocherki diplomaticheskikh snoshenii Rossii s Kitaem.* Port Arthur: Novyi Krai, 1902.

Calchas. "The Anglo-Russian Agreement." *Fortnightly Review* 88, no. 490 (1907): 535–50.

Callwell, C. *Instructions for Intelligence Officers Abroad.* London: War Office, 1889.

Cazalet, E. *England's Policy in the East: Our Relations with Russia and the Future of Syria.* London: E. Stanford, 1879.

Cecil, G. *Life of Robert, Marquis of Salisbury.* 4 vols. London: Hodder & Stoughton, 1921–32.

Chirol, V. *The Far Eastern Question.* London-New York: Macmillan, 1896.

———. *The Middle Eastern Question, or Some Political Problems of Indian Defense.* London: John Murray, 1903.

Clarke, G. *Imperial Defense.* London: Imperial Press, 1897.

———. *Russia's Sea Power Past and Present, or the Rise of the Russian Navy.* London: John Murray, 1898.

Cobbold, R. *Innermost Asia: Travel and Sport in the Pamirs.* London: William Heinemann, 1900.

Collen, E. *The Defense of India.* London: Harrison and Sons, 1906.

Colquhoun, A. *Russia against India: The Struggle for Asia.* London: Harper & Brothers, 1900.

Colquhoun, J. A. S. "Essay on the Formation of an Intelligence Department for India." *Proceedings of the United Service Institution of India* 4, no. 18 (1875): 1–73.

Cory, A. *Shadows of Coming Events, or the Eastern Menace.* London: Henry S. King, 1876.

Cotton, S. *A Prophecy Fulfilled, 1869: The Central Asian Question.* Dublin and London: W. MacGee and Simpkin, Marshall, 1878.

Curzon, G. *British Government in India: The Story of Viceroys and Government Houses.* 2 vols. London: Cassell, 1925.

———. "The Fluctuating Frontier of Russia in Asia." *The Nineteenth Century* 144 (1889): 267–83.

———. *Frontiers.* Oxford: Clarendon Press, 1907.

———. *The Pamirs and the Source of the Oxus.* London: Royal Geographical Society, 1897.

———. *Persia and the Persian Question.* 2 vols. London: Longmans, Green, 1892.

———. *The Place of India in the Empire.* London: John Murray, 1909.

———. *Problems of the Far East: Japan-Korea-China.* London: Archibald Constable, 1896.

———. *Russia in Central Asia in 1889.* London: Frank Cass, 1967 (orig. pub. 1889).

———. "Russian and British Competition in Central Asia." *Asiatic Quarterly Review* 8 (1889): 438–57.

———. "The 'Scientific Frontier' an Accomplished Fact." *The Nineteenth Century* 136 (1888): 901–17.

———. *Speeches by Lord Curzon of Kedleston as Viceroy of India, 1898–1905.* London: Macmillan, 1906.

———. *Subjects of the Day.* London: George Allen & Unwin, 1915.

———. *Tales of Travel.* New York: George H. Doran, 1923.

———. "The True Imperialism." *The Nineteenth Century and After* 63, no. 371 (1908): 151–65.

David, C. *Is Russian Invasion of India Feasible?* London: E. Stanford, 1877.

Denikin, A. I. *Russko-kitaiskii vopros.* Warsaw: Tipografiia Shtaba Varshavskogo voennogo okruga, 1908.

Dilke, C., and S. Wilkinson. *Imperial Defense*. London: Macmillan, 1892.

Dillon, E. "The Anglo-Russian Agreement." *Contemporary Review* 92, no. 503 (1907): 690–700.

Dubrovin, N. F. *Nikolai Mikhailovich Przhevalsy: Biograficheskii ocherk*. Saint Petersburg: Voennaia tipografiia, 1890.

Edwards, H. *Russian Projects against India from the Czar Peter to General Skobeleff*. London: Remington, 1885.

Engel'gard, M. N. *M. N. Przhevalsky: Ego zhizn' i puteshestviia*. Saint Petersburg: V. Berezovsky, 1891.

Engels, F. "Persiia i Kitai." In *Sochineniia*, by K. Marx and F. Engels, vol. 12. Moscow: Gosudarstvennoe izdate'stvo politicheskoi literatury, 1958.

———. "Perspektivy anglo-persidskoi voiny." In *Sochineniia*, by K. Marx and F. Engels, vol. 12. Moscow: Gosudarstvennoe izdate'stvo politicheskoi literatury, 1958.

———. "Prodvizhenie Rossii v Srednei Asii." In *Sochineniia*, by K. Marx and F. Engels, vol. 12. Moscow: Gosudarstvennoe izdate'stvo politicheskoi literatury, 1958.

———. "Vneshniia politika russkogo tsarisma" In *Sochineniia*, by K. Marx and F. Engels, vol. 22. Moscow: Gosudarstvennoe izdate'stvo politicheskoi literatury, 1962.

Escott, T. *The Story of British Diplomacy: Its Makers and Movements*. London: T. Fisher Unwin, 1908.

Esher, R. *The Committee of Imperial Defense: Its Functions and Potentialities*. London: John Murray, 1912.

Evans, G. de Lacy. *On the Designs of Russia*. London, 1828.

———. *On the Practicability of an Invasion of British India, and on the Commercial and Financial Prospects and Resources of the Empire*. London, 1829.

Faris, S. *The Decline of British Prestige in the East*. London: T. Fisher Unwin, 1887.

Fedorov, M. P. *Sopernichestvo torgovykh interesov na Vostoke*. Saint Petersburg: Elektro-tipographiia Stoikovoi, 1903.

Forbes, A. *The Afghan Wars 1839–42 and 1878–80*. London: Seeley, 1892.

Frazer, L. *India under Curzon and After*. London: W. Heinemann, 1911.

Geins, A. K. "O vosstanii musul'manskogo naseleniia, ili dunganei, v Zapadnom Kitae." *Voennyi sbornik*, no. 8 (1866): 185–208.

Gerrare, W. *Greater Russia: The Continental Empire of the Old World*. London: W. Heinemann, 1903.

Gertsulin, M. "Dvizhenie letuchego otriada polkovnika Ionova v Rushan v 1893 g." *Voennyi sbornik*, no. 4 (1900): 272–89.

Goldsmid, F. *Central Asia and Its Questions*. London: Macmillan, 1873.

Green, H. *The Defense of the North-West Frontier of India with Reference to the Advance of Russia in Central Asia*. London: Harrison, 1873.

Grenard, F. "L'Angleterre et la Russie au Tibet." *Bulletin du Comité de l'Asie française* 7, no. 79 (1907): 375–83.

Grigoriev, V. V. *Rossiia i Asiia: Sbornik issledovanii i statei po istorii, etnografii*. Saint

Petersburg: Panteleev Brothers, 1876.

———. *Russkaia politika v otnoshenii k Srednei Asii (istoriograficheskii ocherk)*. Saint Petersburg: V. Bezobrazov, 1874.

Grodekov, N. I. *Voina v Turmenii*. 4 vols. Saint Petersburg: V. Balashev, 1883–84.

Grombchevsky, B. L. *Doklad v Nikolaevskoi Akademii General'nogo Shtaba, March 14 (26), 1891*. Tashkent: Tipografiia Shtaba Turkestanskogo voennogo okruga, 1891.

———. *Nashi interesy na Pamire: Voenno-politicheskii ocherk*. Saint Petersburg: Tipografiia Shtaba Peterburgskogo voennogo okruga, 1891.

Grulev, M. *Sopernichestvo Rossii i Anglii v Tsentra'noi Asii*. Saint Petersburg: V. Berezovsky, 1909.

Halliday, A. *The Retention of India*. London: Tinsley Brothers, 1872.

Hamilton, A. "The Anglo-Russian Agreement: the Question of Persia." *Fortnightly Review* 88, no. 491 (1907): 734–43.

———. *Problems of the Middle East*. London: Eveleigh Nash, 1909.

Hanna, H. *Can Russia Invade India?* London: Archibald Constable, 1895.

Haushofer, K. *Geopolitik des Pazifischen ozeans*. Berlin: K. Vowinckel Verlag, 1924.

Hedin, S. *General Prschewalskij in Innerasien*. Leipzig: F. Brockhaus, 1928.

Hellwald, F. *Die Russen in Centralasien: Eine geographisch-historische Studie*. Vienna: Verlag des Verfassers, 1869.

Heumann, A. *Les Russes et les Anglais dans l'Asie Centrale*. Paris: Libraire Militaire, 1885.

Holdich, T. *England's Strength in Asia*. London: Central Asian Society, 1905.

Hunter, W. *Life of the Earl of Mayo, Fourth Viceroy of India*. 2 vols. London: Smith, Elder, 1875.

Idarov, S. A. "Znachenie Indii v politike Rossii s Turtsiei i Angliei." *Russkii vestnik* 171, no. 6 (1884): 487–553.

[An] Indian Army Officer [Frederick Roberts]. *Russia's March towards India*. 2 vols. London: Sampson Low, Marston, 1894.

Jerningham, H. *Russia's Warnings*. London: Chapman & Hall, 1885.

Kadnikov, V. S. "Iz istorii Kul'dzhinskogo voprosa." *Istoricheskii vestnik* 124, no. 6 (1911): 893–909.

Kaye, J. *Lives of Indian Officers: Illustrative of the History of the Civil and Military Services of India*. 2 vols. London: A. Strahan, 1867.

Kent, P. *Railway Enterprise in China: An Account of Its Origin and Development*. London: E. Arnold, 1907.

Kipling, R. *Kim*. London: Macmillan, 1966 (orig. pub. 1901).

Kleinbort, L. M. *Russkii imperialism v Asii*. Saint Petersburg: Znanie, 1906.

Knight, E. *Where Three Empires Meet: A Narrative of Recent Travel in Kashmir, Western Tibet, Gilgit, and the Adjoining Countries*. London: Longmans, 1897.

Korostovets, I. Ya. *Rossiia na Dal'nem Vostoke*. Peking: Vostochnoe Prostvestchenie, 1922.

Kostenko, L. F. "Istoricheskii ocherk rasprostraneniia russkogo vladychestva v Srednei Asii." *Voennyi sbornik*, no. 8 (1887): 145–78; no. 9: 5–37; no. 10: 139–60; no. 11: 5–35.

———. *The Turkistan Region*. 3 vols. Calcutta: Office of the Superintendent of Government Printing, 1882–84.

————. *Zhungaria: Voenno-statisticheskii ocherk*. Saint Petersburg: Voenno-Uchenyi Komitet Glavnogo Shtaba, 1887.

Kovalevsky, M. "Nachalo russko-angliiskogo sblizheniia." *Vestnik Evropy*, no. 3 (1912): 241–64.

Krahmer, G. *Russland in Mittel-Asien*. Leipzig: Zuckschwerdt, 1898.

Krause, A. *Russia in Asia: A Record and Study, 1558–1899*. London and New York: G. Richards and H. Holt, 1900.

Kuropatkin, A. N. *Istoriko-geograficheskii ocherk strany: Eio voennye sily, promyshlennost' i torgovlia*. Saint Petersburg: V. Balashev, 1879.

————. *Russko-kitaiskii vopros*. Saint Petersburg: Novoe Vremya, 1913.

————. *Zavoevanie Turkmenii (pokhod v Akhal-Teke v 1880–1881 gg.): S ocherkom voennykh deistvii v Srednei Asii s 1839 po 1876 g.* Saint Petersburg: V. Berezovsky, 1899.

Lakost, G. *Rossiia i Velikobritaniia v Tsentral'noi Asii*. Tashkent: Tipografiia Shtaba Turkestanskogo voennogo okruga, 1908.

Landon, P. *The Opening of Tibet*. New York: Doubleday Page, 1905.

Langlois, V. *Herat: Dost Mohammed et les influences politiques de la Russie et de l'Angleterre dans l'Asie centrale*. Paris, 1864.

Lansdell, H. *Russian Central Asia*. 2 vols. Boston: Houghton Mifflin, 1885.

Lebedev, V. T. *V Indiu! Voenno-statisticheskii i strategicheskii ocherk—Proekt budustchego pokhoda*. Saint Petersburg: A. Porokhovstchikov, 1898.

Lessar, P. M. *La Russie et l'Angleterre en Asie Centrale*. Paris: Libraire Militaire, 1886.

————. "Voennye puti soobstcheniia na indo-afghanskoi granitse." *Sbornik geograficheskikh, topograficheskikh i statisticheskikh materialov po Asii* 41 (1890): 1–69.

————. *Zametki o Zakaspiiskom krae i sopredel'nykh stranakh*. Saint Petersburg: A. Suvorin, 1884.

Levitov, I. S. *Zheltaia Rossiia*. Saint Petersburg: G. Bernstein, 1901.

Lipsett, C. *Lord Curzon in India 1898–1903*. London: R. Everett, 1903.

Lobysevich, F. I. *Postupatel'noe dvizhenie v Sredniuiu Asiiu v torgovom i diplomatichesko-voennom otnoshenii*. Saint Petersburg: Obstchestvennaia pol'za, 1900.

Logofet, D. N. *Bukharskoe khanstvo pod russkim protektoratom*. 2 vols. Saint Petersburg: V. Berezovsky, 1911.

————. *Strana bespraviia: Bukharskoe khanstvo i ego sovremennoe sostoianie*. Saint Petersburg: V. Berezovsky, 1909.

Macgahan, J. *Campaigning on the Oxus and the Fall of Khiva*. New York: Harper & Brothers, 1874.

Macgregor, C. *The Defense of India: A Strategic Study*. Simla: Government Central Branch Press, 1884.

————, ed. *The Life and Opinions of Major General Sir Charles Metcalfe Macgregor*. 2 vols. Edinburgh: W. Blackwood and Sons, 1888.

Mackinder, H. "The Geographical Pivot of History." *Geographical Journal* 23, no. 4 (1904): 421–44.

————. *India*. London: G. Philip and Son, 1910.

Mahan, A. *The Problem of Asia and Its Effect upon International Policy.* London: Sampson Low, Marston, 1900.

Mahfuz Ali. *Truth about Russia and England from a Native's Point of View.* Lucknow: R. Graven, 1886.

Maksheev, A. I. *Istoricheskii obzor Turkestana i nastupatel'nogo dvizheniia v nego russkikh.* Saint Petersburg: Voennaiia tipografiia, 1890.

Maksimov, A. Ya. *Nashi zadachi na Tikhom okeane: Politicheskie etiudy.* Saint Petersburg: P. Babkin, 1894.

Malleson, G. *Herat: The Granary and Garden of Central Asia.* London: W. Allen, 1880.

———. *The Russo-Afghan Question and the Invasion of India.* London: G. Routledge & Sons, 1885.

Martens, F. F. *Russia and England in Central Asia.* London: W. Ridgway, 1879.

Marvin, C. *Reconnoitering Central Asia: Pioneering Adventures in the Region Lying between Russia and India.* London: W. Sonnesheim, 1884.

———. *The Russian Advance towards India: Conversation with Skobeleff, Ignatiev, and Other Distinguished Russian Generals and Statesmen on the Central Asian Question.* London: Sampson Low, Marston, Searle, and Rivington, 1882.

———. *The Russians at Merv and Herat, and Their Power of Invading India.* London: W. Allen, 1883.

Marx, K. "Britanskoe vladychestvo v Indii." In *Sochineniia,* by K. Marx and F. Engels, vol. 9. Moscow: Gosudarstvennoe izdatel'stvo politicheskoi literatury, 1957.

———. "Budustchie resultaty britanskogo vladychestva v Indii." In *Sochineniia,* by K. Marx and F. Engels, vol. 9. Moscow: Gosudarstvennoe izdatel'stvo politicheskoi literatury, 1957.

———. "Ost-Indskaia kampaniia, eio istoriia i resultaty eio deiatel'nosti." In *Sochineniia,* by K. Marx and F. Engels, vol. 9. Moscow: Gosudarstvennoe izdatel'stvo politicheskoi literatury, 1957.

Maslov, A. N. "Rossiia v Srednei Asii (Ocherk noveishikh priobretenii)." *Istoricheskii vestnik* 20 (1885): 372–423.

Michell, R. *Eastern Turkistan and Dzungaria and the Rebellion of Tungans and Taranchis, 1862–1866.* London: E. Stanford, 1871.

Morell, J. *Russia and England: Their Strength and Weakness.* New York: Ricker, Thorne, 1854.

Nalivkin V. P. *Kratkaia istoriia Kokandskogo khanstva.* Kazan: Kazanskii universitet, 1886.

Nebol'sin, P. *Ocherki torgovli Rossii so stranami Srednei Asii, Khivoi, Bukharoi i Kokandom (so storony Orenburgskoi linii).* Saint Petersburg: IRGO, 1856.

Nedzvetsky, V. "Inostrannoe voennoe obozrenie." *Voennyi sbornik,* no. 6 (1885): 203–28.

Newwall, D. *The Highlands of India Strategically Considered.* 2 vols. London: Harrison and Sons, 1882–87.

Nixon, J. *Notes for Staff Officers on Indian Field Service.* Lahore: Civil and Military Gazette Press, 1897.

Notovich, N. A. *Rossiia i Angliia: Istoriko-politicheskii etiud.* Saint Petersburg: Gosudarstvennaia tipografiia, 1907.

Pantusov, N. N. *Voina musul'man protiv kitaitsev.* 2 vols. Kazan': Kazan University, 1881.

Peterov, A. *Kak zastchistchaiut svoi interesy v Asii Angliia i Rossiia.* Saint Petersburg: Alexander Popov, 1910.

Pirbright, H. *England's Policy in the East.* London: Chapman and Hall, 1877.

Popowski, J. *The Rival Powers in Central Asia, or the Struggle between England and Russia in the East.* London: Archibald Constable, 1893. (Orig. pub. in German: Joseph Popowski. *Antagonismus der Englishen und Russischen Interessen in Asien: Eine Militaerpolitische Studie.* Vienna: Wilhelm Frick, 1890.)

Prioux, A. *Les Russes dans l'Asie Centrale, la dernière campagne de Skobelev (1880–1881).* Paris: Libraire Militaire, 1886.

Probyn-Nevins, W. *Apologia for Russia.* London: Simpkin, 1895.

Przhevalsky, N. M. "Sovremennoe polozhenie Tsentral'noi Asii." *Russkii vestnik* 186 (1886): 473–524.

Putiata, D. V. *Ocherki geografii, ekonomicheskogo sostoianiia, administrativnogo i voennogo ustroistva Sredinnoi imperii.* Saint Petersburg: Voennaia tipografiia, 1893.

Putnam-Weale, B. *The Reshaping of the Far East.* 2 vols. London: Macmillan, 1905.

Pyasetskii, P. *Russian Travelers in Mongolia and China.* 2 vols. London: Chapman and Hall, 1884.

Raaben, L. R. "Kratkii ocherk Tibeta." *Sbornik geografichskikh, topograficheskikh i statisticheskikh materialov po Asii* 78 (1905): 40–70.

Rawlinson, H. *England and Russia in the East.* London: John Murray, 1875.

Roberts, F. *Notes on the Central Asian Question and the Coast and Frontier Defenses of India, 1877–1893.* London: War Office, 1902.

Romanovsky, D. I. *Zametki po sredneasiatskomu voprosu.* Saint Petersburg: Tipografiia Vtorogo otdeleniia sobstvennoi kantseliiarii Ego Imperatorskogo Velichestva, 1868.

Rouire, A. *La rivalité anglo-russe au XIXe siècle en Asie: Golfe Persique—Frontière de l'Inde.* Paris: Libraire A. Colin, 1908.

Russel, R. *India's Danger and England's Duty.* London: Ward, Lock, 1885.

Rybachenok, I. S., comp. *Korennye interesy Rossii glazami eio gosudarstvennykh deiatelei, diplomatov, voennykh i publitsistov.* Moscow: Institut Rossiiskoi istorii RAN, 2004.

Seely, J. *Expansion of England.* London: Macmillan, 1883.

Semenov Tien-Shansky, A. P. *Nashi blizhaishie zadachi na Dal'nem Vostoke.* Saint Petersburg: Saint Peterburgskie Vedomosti, 1908.

Shepelev, A. A. *Ocherk voennykh i diplomaticheskikh snoshenii Rossii so Srednei Asiei.* Tashkent: Tipografiia Voenno—narodnogo upravleniia, 1879.

Shipov, N. N. *Rossiia i Angliia.* Saint Petersburg: Otechestvennaia tipografiia, 1908.

Showers, C. *The Cossack at the Gate of India.* London: Simpkin, Marshall, 1885.

Siarkovsy, G. "O turkestanskikh pokhodakh 1864–1865." *Voennyi sbornik* 197, no. 2 (1891): 357–81; 198, no. 3: 157–64.

Simansky, P. M. *Sobytiia na Dal'nem Vostoke, predshestvovavshie russko-iaponskoi voine, 1891–1903 gg.* 2 vols. Saint Petersburg: Voennaia tipografiia, 1910.

Skal'kovsky, K. A. *Vneshniaia politika Rossii i polozhenie inostrannykh derzhav.* Saint

Petersburg: A. Suvorin, 1897.

Skif. *Persidskii vopros: Anglo-russkoe soglashenie, ego osnovnye printsipy i tseli, i piatiletnie itogi.* Moscow: A. Srel'tsov, 1912.

Skrine, F., and E. Ross. *The Heart of Asia: A History of Russian Turkestan and the Central Asian Khanates from the Earliest Times.* London: Methuen, 1999.

Snesarev, A. E. *Afghanistan.* 2 vols. Moscow: Gosudarstvennoe izdate'stvo, 1921.

———. *Anglo-russkaia konventsiia 1907 g.* Saint Petersburg: Obschestvo revnitelei voennykhznanii, 1908.

———. *Indiia kak glavnyi factor v sredneasiatskom voprose.* Saint Petersburg: A. Suvorin, 1906.

———. *Pamiry (voenno-statisticheskoe opisanie).* Tashkent: Tipografiia Shtaba Turkestanskogo voennogo okruga, 1903.

———. "Vostochbaia Bukhara (voenno-geograficheskii ocherk)." *Sbornik geograficheskikh, topograficheskikh i statisticheskikh materialov po Asii* 79 (1905): 1–148.

Sobolev, L. N. *Anglo-afghanskaia raspria (ocherk voiny 1879–1880 gg.).* 4 vols., 8 bks. Saint Petersburg: M. Khan, 1880–85.

———. *Vozmozhen li pokhod russkikh v Indiiu?* Moscow: Tipografiia Shtaba Moskovskogo voennogo okruga, 1901.

Staryi diplomat. "Angliia i Rossiia v Srednei Asii." *Russkaia mysl',* no. 2 (1900): 139–61; no. 3, 19–29.

Stetsenko, V. *Kreisery i Tikhii okean.* Saint Petersburg: Tipogragiia Morskogo ministerstva, 1893.

Subbotin, A. P. *Rossiia i Angliia na sredneasiatskikh rynkakh.* Saint Petersburg: Ekonomicheskii zhurnal, 1885.

Sykes, H. *Our Recent Progress in Southern Persia and Its Possibilities.* London: Central Asian Society, 1905.

Tageev (Rustam-Beg), B. L. *Pamirskie pokhody 1892–1895 gg.: Desiatiletie prisoedineniia Pamira k Rossii.* Warsaw: Tipografiia Gubernskogo pravleniia, 1902.

Teplov, V. A. *Angliiskaia ekspeditsiia v Tibet.* Saint Petersburg: V. Komarov, 1904.

Terentiev, M. A. *Istoriia zavoevaniia Srednei Asii.* 3 vols. Saint Petersburg: V. Komarov, 1906.

———. *Rossiia i Angliia v bor'be za rynki.* Saint Petersburg: P. Merkuriev, 1876.

———. *Rossiia i Angliia v Srednei Asii.* Saint Petersburg: P. Merkuriev, 1875.

Towle, G. *England and Russia in Asia.* Boston: J. Osgood, 1885.

Trench, F. *The Russo-Indian Question, Historically, Strategically, and Politically Considered.* London: Macmillan, 1869.

Ukhtomsky, E. E. *Iz oblasti lamaizma. K pokhodu anglichan v Tibet.* Saint Petersburg: Vostok, 1904.

Ular, A. *A Russo-Chinese Empire.* London: Archibald Constable, 1904.

Urquart, D. *The Progress of Russia in the West, North and South.* London: Truebner, 1853.

Vambery, A. "The Anglo-Russian Convention." *The Nineteenth Century and After* 62, no. 370 (1907): 895–904.

———. *Central Asia and the Anglo-Russian Frontier Question.* London: E. Smith, 1874.

———. *The Coming Struggle for India.* London: Cassell, 1885.

————. *Rivalry between Russia and England in Central Asia*. London: W. Allen, 1868.

————. *Sketches of Central Asia: Additional Chapters on my Travels, Adventures and on the Ethnology of Central Asia*. London: W. Allen, 1868.

————. *Western Culture in Eastern Lands: A Comparison of the Methods Adopted by England and Russia in the Middle East*. London: John Murray, 1906.

Veniukov, M. I. *Kratkii ocherk angliiskikh vladenii v Asii*. Saint Petersburg: V. Bezobrazov, 1875.

————. *Opyt voennogo obozreniia russkikh granits v Asii*. 2 vols. Saint Petersburg: V. Bezobrazov, 1873–76.

————. *Rossiia i Vostok*. Saint Petersburg: V. Bezobrazov, 1877.

Vernadsky, I. V. *Politicheskoe ravnovesie i Angliia*. Moscow: Moscow University, 1855.

Verney, F. P. "Six Generations of Czars." *The Nineteenth Century*, no. 148 (1889): 827–37.

Wellesley, F. *With the Russians in Peace and War: Recollections of a Military Attaché*. London: Eveleigh Nash, 1905.

Whigham, H. *The Persian Problem*. London: Isbister, 1903.

White, A. "Anglo-Russian Relations." *Fortnightly Review* 82, no. 456 (1904): 960–68.

Wolfe, M. *Military Operations in the Event of a War with Russia*. London: Her Majesty's Stationery Office, 1885.

Yanchevetsky, D. G. *Groza s Vostoka: Zadachi Rossii i zadachi Yaponii na Dal'nem Vostoke. Ocherki*. Reval: Reval'skie Izvestiia, 1908.

Yuzhakov, S. N. *Anglo-russkaia rspria: Nebol'shoe predislovie k bol'shim sobytiiam—Politicheskii etiud*. Saint Petersburg: Obtschaia pol'za, 1885.

Zaichenko. *Pamiry i Sarikol: Ocherk vozniknoveniia, posledovatel'nogo razvitiia i sovremennogo polozheniia Pamirskogo voprosa*. Tashkent: Tipografiia Shtaba Turkestanskogo voennogo okruga, 1903.

Zhukovsky, S. V. *Snosheniia Rossii s Bukharoi i Khivoi za poslednie 300 let*. Saint Petersburg: A. Suvorin, 1913.

Zinoviev, I. A. *Angliia i Persiia*. Saint Petersburg: A. Suvorin, 1912.

Zykov, S. "Ocherk utverzhdeniia russkogo vladychestva na Aral'skom more i reke Syr Daria s 1847 po 1862 g." *Morskoi sbornik* 59, no. 6 (1862): 298–348.

REFERENCE BOOKS, ENCYCLOPEDIAS, AND BIBLIOGRAPHICAL GUIDEBOOKS

Bence-Jones, M. *The Viceroys of India*. London: Archibald Constable, 1982.

Blake, D. *Catalogue of the European Manuscripts in the Oriental and India Office Collections of the British Library*. London: British Library, 1998.

Cecil, A. *British Foreign Secretaries, 1807–1916: Studies in Personality and Policy*. London: G. Bell and Sons, 1927.

Dmitrovsky, N. V. "Bibliograficheskii ukazatel' sochinenii o Srednei Asii, napechatannykh v Rossii na russkom yazyke s 1692." *Materialy dlia statistiki Turkestanskogo kraia* 3 (1874): 181–250.

Guralnik, D., ed. *Webster's New World Dictionary.* Oxford: Oxford and IBH, 1974.

Hartley, J., ed. *Guide to Documents and Manuscripts in the United Kingdom Relating to Russia and the Soviet Union.* London: Mansell, 1987.

Marshall, J. *Britain and Tibet, 1765–1947: The Background to the India-China Border Dispute. A Select Annotated Bibliography of Printed Material in European Languages.* Bundoora: La Trobe University Library, 1977.

Mersey, Viscount. *The Viceroys and Governor-Generals of India, 1757–1947.* London: John Murray, 1949.

Mezhov, V. I. *Bibliogragiia Asii.* Saint Petersburg: V. Bezobrazov, 1891.

Porter, A., ed. *Bibliography of Imperial, Colonial, and Commonwealth History since 1600.* Oxford: Oxford University Press, 2002.

Raugh, H., comp. *The Victorians at War, 1815–1914: An Encyclopedia of British Military History.* Santa-Barbara, Calif.: ABC-CLIO, 2004.

Sokolov, V. S., and S.M. Vimogradova. *Periodicheskaia pechat' Velikobritanii.* Saint Petersburg: Saint Petersburg State University, 2000.

Temperley, H., and L. Penson. *A Century of Diplomatic Blue Books, 1914–1914.* New York: Barnes & Noble, 1966.

Vitkind, N. Ya. *Bibliografiia po Srednei Asii.* Moscow: KUTV, 1929.

Woodraft, P. *The Men Who Ruled India.* 2 vols. London: Jonathan Cape, 1953–54.

PERIODICALS

Note: The materials from those periodicals whose names are followed by an asterisk (★) are from the India Office Library and Records, London, Mss Eur E 218/163, Cuttings from Indian Newspapers, 1876–69.

Bombay Gazette★
British Mail
Bulletin du Comite de l'Asie francaise
Cabul News★
China Gazette
Civil and Military Gazette
Contemporary Review
Daily News
Daily Telegraph
Delhi Gazette★
Economic Journal

Edinburgh Review
Englishman★
Fortnightly Review
Gazette of India★
Geographical Journal
Golos
Hindoo Patriot★
Imperial and Asiatic Quarterly Review
Indian Christian Herald★
Indian Daily News★
Indian Statesman★
Istoricheskii Arkhiv
Istoricheskii Vestnik
Journal de Saint Petersbourg
Lucknow Times★
Madras Mail★
Madras Times★
Manchester Guardian
Morning Post
Morskoi Sbornik
Moscow Gazette
Nineteenth Century and After
Novoe Vremya
Pall Mall Gazette
Pioneer Mail★
Priamurskie Vedomosti
Quarterly Review
Proceedings of the United Service Institution of India
Punch
Rossiiskii Arkhiv
Russkaia Mysl'
Russkaia Starina
Russkii Arkhiv
Russkii Invalid
Russkii Mir
Russkii Vestnik
Simla News
Spectator
Statesman★
Times
Times of India
Tour de Monde

Turkestan Gazette
Turkestanski Vedomosti
Vestnik Evropy
Voennyi Sbornik

SECONDARY SOURCES

Abashin, S. N., et al. *Tsentral'naia Asiia v sostave Rossiiskoi imperii*. Moscow, 2008.

Abdurakhimova, N. A. "Stanovlenie i osobennosti ekonomicheskoi politiki Rossii v Turkestane vo vtoroi polovine XIX–nachale XX vv." *Istoricheskoe prostranstvo: Problemy istorii stran SNG*, nos. 1–4 (2008): 62–88.

Abdurakhimova, N. A., and G. K. Rustamova. *Kolonial'naia sistema vlasti v Turkestane vo vtoroi polovine XIX–pervoi chetverti XX vv.* Tashkent: Tashkentskii gosudarstvennyi universitet, 1999.

Addy, P. "Imperial Prophet or Scaremonger? Curzon's Tibetan Policy Reconsidered." *Asian Affairs* 14, pt. 1 (1983): 54–67.

———. *Tibet on the Imperial Chessboard: The Making of British Policy towards Lhasa, 1899–1905*. Calcutta: Academic Publishers, 1984.

Airapetov, O. R. *Vneshniia politika Rossii, 1801–1914*. Moscow: Evropa, 2006.

———. *Zabytaia kariera "russkogo Mol'tke": Nikolai Nikolaevich Obruchev (1830–1904)*. Saint Petersburg: Aleteia, 1998.

Aisenshtat, M. P., and T. N. Gella. *Angliiskie partii i kolonial'naia imperiia Velikobritanii v XIX v. (1815–seredina 1870-kh gg.)*. Moscow: Institute of World History RAN, 1999.

Akhmedova, L. Sh. *Politika Anglii v zone Persidskogo zaliva v poslednei treti XIX–nachale XX v. (1870–1914 gg.)*. Saint Petersburg: Saint Petersburg State University, 2006.

Akhmedzhanov, G. A. *Rossiiskaia imperiia v Tsentral'noi Asii (istoriia i istoriografiia kolonial'noi politiki tsarisma v Turkestane)*. Tashkent: Fan, 1995.

———. *Sovetskaia istoriografiia prisoedinenie Srednei Asii k Rossii*. Tashkent: Fan, 1989.

Akhmetzhanov, A. "Agressivnye ustremleniia angliiskogo kapitalisma v Zapadnom Kitae v 60-e–70-e gg. XIX v." *Alma-Atinskii pedagogicheskii institut im. Abaia: Uchenye zapiski* 11, no. 1 (1956): 141–54.

———. "Vozvratschenie Rossiei Kul'dzhinskogo raiona Kitaiu." *Alma-Atinskii pedagogicheskii institut im. Abaia: Uchenye zapiski* 14, no. 2 (1957): 69–90.

Alder, G. *British India's Northern Frontier, 1865–95: A Study in Imperial Policy*. London: Longmans, 1963.

Alder, L., and R. Dalby. *The Dervish of Windsor Castle: The Life of Arminius Vambery*. London: Bachman and Turner, 1979.

Alekseev, M. *Voennaia razvedka Rossii or Riurika do Nikolaia II*. Moscow: Russkaia razvedka, 1998.

Allen, C. *Duel in the Snows: The True Story of the Younghusband Mission to Lhasa*. London:

John Murray, 2004.

———. *Soldier Sahibs: The Men Who Made the North-West Frontier.* London: John Murray, 2000.

Allworth, E., ed. *Central Asia, 120 Years of Russian Rule.* Durham, N.C.: Duke University Press, 1989.

———. *Central Asia, 130 Years of Russian Dominance: A Historical Overview.* Durham, N.C.: Duke University Press, 1994.

Aminov, A. M., and A. Kh. Babakhodzhaev. *Ekonomicheskie i politicheskie posledstviia prisoedineniia Srednei Asii k Rossii.* Tashkent: Uzbekistan, 1966.

Anderson, M. *The Eastern Question, 1774–1923: A Study in International Relations.* London and New York: Macmillan and St. Martin's Press, 1966.

Andreev, A. I. "Indian Pundits and the Russian Exploration of Tibet: An Unknown Story." *Central Asiatic Journal* 45 (2001): 163–80.

———. "Soviet Russia and Tibet: A Debacle of Secret Diplomacy." In *The History of Tibet,* vol. 3, edited by A. Mckay. London: RoutledgeCurzon, 2003.

———. *Tibet v politike tsarskoi, sovetskoi i postsovetskoi Rossii.* Saint Petersburg: Saint Peterburg State University–Nartang, 2006.

Andreev, O. E. "K voprosu o razvitii anglo-rossiiskikh otnoshenii vtoroi poloviny XIX veka v osvetschenii ofitsial'noi dvrianskoi istoriografii." In *Politicheskaia zhizn' Zapadnoi Evropy: Antichnost', srednie veka, novoe i noveishee vremia,* edited by E.V. Kuznetsov. Arzamas: Arzamasskii gosudarstvennyi pedagogocheskii institute, 2010.

Andreeva, E. *Russia and Iran in the Great Game: Travelogues and Orientalism.* London: Routledge, 2007.

Andrew, C. *Secret Service: The Making of the British Intelligence Community.* London: Heinemann, 1985.

Andrew, C. "Secret Intelligence and British Foreign Policy, 1900–1939." In *Intelligence and International Relations, 1900–45,* edited by C. Andrew and J. Noakes. Exeter: University of Exeter, 1987.

Anwar Khan, M. *England, Russia and Central Asia: A Study in Diplomacy, 1857–1878.* Peshawar: University Book Agency, 1963.

Armitage, D. *The Ideological Origins of the British Empire.* Cambridge: Cambridge University Press, 2002.

Arthur, G. *Life of Lord Kitchener.* 2 vols. London: Macmillan, 1920.

Avdeev, V. E. "Alexander Petrovich Izvolsky." *Voprosy istorii,* no. 5 (2008): 65–79.

Barrow, I. *Making History, Drawing Territory: British Mapping in India, c. 1756–1905.* New Delhi: Oxford University Press, 2003.

Bartol'd, V.V. *Istoriia izucheniia Vostoka v Evrope i Rossii.* Leningrad: Leningradskii institut zhivykh vostochnykh yazykov, 1925.

Basin, V.Ya., and K. R. Nesipbaeva. "Vneshniaia torgovlia Rossii so stranami Vostoka na rubezhe XIX–XX vv." In *Iz istorii mezhdunarodnykh otnoshenii v Tsentral'noi Asii (srednie veka i novoe vremya),* edited by G. Iskhakov. Alma-Ata: Gylym, 1990.

Baskhanov, M. "Politika Anglii v otnoshenii gosudarstva Yakub-Bega." In *Iz istorii mezhdunarodnykh otnoshenii v Tsentral'noi Asii (srednie veka i novoe vremya)*, edited by G. Iskhakov. Alma-Ata: Gylym, 1990.

Bassin, M. "Russia between Europe and Asia: The Ideological Construction of Geographical Space." *Slavic Review* 50, no 1 (1991): 1–17.

Bayly, C. *Empire and Information: Intelligence Gathering and Social Communication in India, 1780–1870*. Cambridge: Cambridge University Press, 1996.

Becker, S. "The Russian Conquest of Central Asia and Kazakhstan: Motives, Methods, Consequences." In *Central Asia: Its Strategic Importance and Future Prospects*, edited by H. Malik. New York: St. Martin's Press, 1994.

———. "Russia's Central Asian Empire, 1885–1917." In *Russian Colonial Expansion to 1917*, edited by M. Rywkin. London: Manswell, 1988.

———. *Russia's Protectorates in Central Asia: Bokhara and Khiva, 1865–1924*. Cambridge, Mass.: Harvard University Press, 1968.

Beckett, I., and J. Gooch, eds. *Politicians and Defense: Studies in the Formulation of British Defense Policy, 1845–1970*. Manchester: Manchester University Press, 1981.

Bell, P. "Review of M. Dockrill and B. Mackercher (eds.), *Diplomacy and World Power: Studies in British Foreign Policy, 1830–1950*." *Diplomacy and Statecraft* 8, no. 2 (1997): 196–97.

Beloff, M. *Imperial Sunset, Volume 1: Britain's Liberal Empire, 1897–1921*. London: Methuen, 1969.

Belov, E. A. *Rossiia i Kitai v nachale XX v.* Moscow: Vostochnaia literatura, 1997.

Benians, E., J. Butler, and C. E. Carrington, eds. *The Cambridge History of the British Empire*. 8 vols. Cambridge: Cambridge University Press, 1959.

Berlin, L. E. "Angliia i Tibet." *Novyi Vostok* 2 (1922): 355–66.

———. "Khambo Agvan Dorzhiev (k bor'be Tibeta za vezavisimost')." *Novyi Vostok* 3 (1923): 139–56.

Bilof, E. "China in Imperial Russian Military Planning, 1881–1887." *Military Affairs* 46 (1982): no. 2, 69–75.

Blake, R. *Disraeli*. London: Eyre and Spottiswoode, 1966.

Bogomolov, S. A. "Strategicheskie osnovy politiki Britanskoi Indii na severo-zapadnom frontier (poslednyaia tret' XIX v.)" *Vostok*, no. 4 (2010): 34–44.

Boikova, E. V. "Rossiiskie voennye ekspeditsii v Mongolii v kontse XIX v." In *Altaica*, edited by V. M. Alpatov. Moscow: Institut vostokovedeniia, 1997.

Bokiev, O. B. "Anglo-russkoe sopernichestvo v Srednei Asii v sviasi s prisoedineniem territorii Tadzhikistana k Rossii." In *Aktual'nye problemy istorii i istoriografii Srednei Asii (vtoraia polovina XIX–nachalo XX v.)*, edited by M. B. Babakhanov. Dushanbe: Tadzhikskii gosudarstvennyi universistet, 1990.

———. *Zavoevanie i prisoedinenie Severnogo Tadzhikistana, Pamira i Gornogo Badakhshana k Rossii*. Dushanbe: Tadzhikskii gosudarstvennyi universitet, 1994.

Bondarevskaia, L. G. "Anglo-russkie otnosheniia v Persii nakanune Pervoi mirovoi voiny." In *Rossia na rubezhe XIX–XX vv.*, edited by A. G. Golikov and A. P. Karelin. Moscow: Rosspen, 1999.

Bondarevskii, G. L. *Angliiskaia politika i mezhdunarodnye otnosheniia v basseine Persidskogo zaliva (konets XIX–nachalo XX v.)*. Moscow: Nauka, 1968.

Bourne, K. *The Foreign Policy of Victorian England, 1830–1902*. Oxford: Clarendon Press, 1970.

Braun, P. *Die Verteidigung Indiens, 1800–1907: Das Problem der Vorwaertsstrategie.* Cologne: Boehlau Verlag, 1968.

Broadbent, T. *On the Younghusband's Path Peking to Pindi.* King's Lynn: Head-Hunter Books, 2005.

Brobst, P. *The Future of the Great Game: Sir Olaf Caroe, India's Independence and the Defense of Asia.* Akron: University of Akron Press, 2005.

Brower, D. *Turkestan and the Fate of the Russian Empire.* London: RoutledgeCurzon, 2003.

Brown, J., and W. Louis, eds. *The Oxford History of the British Empire, Volume III: The Nineteenth Century.* Oxford: Oxford University Press, 1999.

Bugrova, M. S. "Britanskie ekspedirsii v Kitai i sosednie raiony (70-e-90-e gg. XIX v.)." *Oriens*, no. 1 (2008): 116–27.

Burroughs, P. "Imperial Defense and the Victorian Army." *Journal of Imperial and Commonwealth History* 15, no. 1 (1986): 55–72.

Buzynina, N. K., and K. B. Vinogradov. "Lord Curzon." *Novaia i noveishaia istoriia*, no. 5 (1973): 102–11; no. 6: 116–27.

Bunakov, E. V. "K voprosu o politicheskikh sviasiakh Rossii s Vostochnym Turkestanom v pravlenie Yakub-Bega (1865–1877)." *Akademiia nauk Uzbekskoi SSR. Bulletin*, no. 5 (1945): 21–24.

Bushev, P. P. *Herat i anglo-iranskaia voina 1856–1857 gg.* Moscow: Vostochnaia literatura, 1959.

Caroe, O. *The Pathans: 500 B.C.–A.D. 1957.* Oxford: Oxford University Press, 1984.

Chamberlain, M. *"Pax Britannica"? 1789–1914*, London: Longman, 1988.

Chang, Sungkwan. "Russian Designs on the Far East." In *Russian Imperialism from Ivan the Great to the Revolution*, edited by T. Hunczak. New Brunswick, N.J.: Rutgers University Press, 1974.

Charmley, J. *Splendid Isolation? Britain, the Balance of Power, and the Origins of the First World War.* London: Hodder & Stoughton, 1999.

Chavda, V. K. *India, Britain, Russia: A Study in British Opinion, 1838–1878.* Delhi: Sterling, 1967.

Chicherin, G. V. *Rechi i stat'i po voprosam mezhdunarodnoi politiki.* Moscow: Izdatel'stvo sotsial'no-ekonomicheskoi literatury, 1961.

Cho, Myung Hyun. *Korea and the Major Powers: An Analysis of Power Structure in East Asia.* Seoul: Research Center for Peace and Unification of Korea, 1989.

Chu, Wendjang. *The Moslem Rebellion in North West China, 1862–1878. A Study of Government Minority Policy.* The Hague: Mouton, 1966.

Churchill, R. *Anglo-Russian Convention of 1907.* Cedar Rapids, Iowa: Torch Press, 1939.

Clubb, E. *China and Russia: The "Great Game."* New York: Columbia University Press, 1971.

Clyde, P. *International Rivalries in Manchuria, 1689–1922*. Columbus: Ohio State University Press, 1928.

Dabbs, J. *History of the Discovery and Exploration of Chinese Turkistan*. The Hague: Mouton, 1963.

Dallin, D. *The Rise of Russia in Asia*. New Haven, Conn.: Yale University Press, 1950.

Dankov, A. G. "Britanskai istoriografiia vtoroi poloviny XIX v. ob anglo-russkikh protivorechiiakh v Tsentral'noi Asii." *Vestnik Tomskogo gosudarstvennogo universiteta* 300, no. 1 (2007): 87–90.

Darby, P. *Three Faces of Imperialism: British and American Approaches to Asia and Africa, 1870–1970*. New Haven, Conn.: Yale University Press, 1987.

Das, D. *India from Curzon to Nehru and After*. New York: J. Day, 1970.

Davidson, A. B. "O roli kul'turnykh sviazei v mezhdunarodnykh otnosheniiakh: Anglo-rossiiskoe literaturnoe obtschestvo (1892–1930 gg.)." *Novaia i noveishaia istoriia*, no. 4 (2009): 85–98.

Davies, C. "Lord Curzon's Frontier Policy and the Formation of the North-West Frontier Province, 1901." *Army Quarterly* 13 (1927): 261–73.

Davis, C. "Railway Imperialism in China." In *Railway Imperialism*, edited by C. Davis and Kenneth Wilburn. New York: Greenwood Press, 1991.

Davis, H. *The Great Game in Asia, 1800–1844*. London and Oxford: H. Milford and Oxford University Press, 1927.

Davis, L., and R. Huttenback. *Mammon and the Pursuit of Empire*. Cambridge: Cambridge University Press, 1986.

Davletov, D., and A. Ilyasov. *Prisoedinenie Turkmenii k Rossii*. Ashgabad: Ylym, 1972.

Deacon, R. *A History of the British Secret Service*. New York: Taplinger, 1970.

———. *A History of the Russian Secret Service*. London: F. Muller, 1972.

Degoev, V. V. *Bol'shaia igra na Kavkaze: istoriia i sovremennost'*. Moscow: Russkaia panorama, 2003.

———. *Vneshniaia politika Rossii i mezhdunarodnye sistemy: 1700–1918*. Moscow: Rosspen, 2004.

Dilks, D. *Curzon in India*. 2 vols. London: Rupert Hart-Davis, 1969.

D'Ombrain, N. *War Machinery and High Policy: Defense Administration in Peacetime Britain 1902–1914*. Oxford: Oxford University Press, 1973.

Dubovistky, V. V. *Nikolai Leopol'dovitch Korzhenevsky: Imia ma karte Pamira*. Available at www.ferghana.ru.

Dubrovskaia, D. V. *Sud'ba Sinkianga: Obretenie Kitaem novoi granitsy v kontse XIX v.* Moscow: Institut vostokovedeniia RAN, 1998.

Dugdale, B. *Arthur James Balfour*. 2 vols. London: Hutchinson, 1939.

Duthie, J. "Some Further Insights into the Working of Mid-Victorian Imperialism: Lord Salisbury and Anglo-Afghan Relations: 1874–78." *Journal of Imperial and Commonwealth History* 8, no. 3 (1980): 181–208.

Duthie, J. "Pragmatic Diplomacy of Imperial Encroachment? British Policy towards Afghanistan, 1874–79." *History Review* 5, no. 4 (1983): 475–95.

Dzhamgerchinov, B. D. *Prisoedinenie Kirgizii k Rossii*. Moscow: Sotsial'no-ekonomicheskoe gosudarstvennoe izdatel'stvo, 1959.

Edwardes, M. *High Noon of Empire: India under Curzon*. London: Eyre and Spottiswood, 1965.

———. *Playing the Great Game*. London: Hamish Hamilton, 1975.

Eldridge, C. *England's Mission: The Imperial Idea in the Age of Gladstone and Disrael*. Chapel Hill: University of North Carolina Press, 1974.

———. *Victorian Imperialism*. London: Hodder & Stoughton, 1978.

Elliott, G. *The Frontier: The Story of the North-West Frontier of India*. London: Cassell, 1968.

Evans, J. *Russian Expansion on the Amur, 1848–1860: The Push to the Pacific*. 2 vols. New York: E. Mellen Press, 1999.

Fairbank, J., ed. *The Chinese World Order: Traditional China's Foreign Relations*. Cambridge, Mass.: Harvard University Press, 1968.

Farrington, A., ed. *Lord Curzon's Japan Diaries*. Nagoya: Richard Cocks Society, 1985.

Fergusson, T. *British Military Intelligence, 1870–1914: The Development of a Modern Intelligence Organization*. Frederick, Md.: University Publications of America, 1984.

Fesenko, P. I. *Istoriia Sinkianga*. Moscow: Institut vostokovedeniia AN SSSR, 1935.

Fleming, P. *Bayonets to Lhasa: The First Full Account of the British Invasion of Tibet in 1904*. London: Rupert Hart-Davis, 1961.

Fletcher, J. "China and Central Asia, 1368–1884." In *The Chinese World Order: Traditional China's Foreign Relations*, edited by J. Fairbank. Cambridge, Mass.: Harvard University Press, 1968.

Ford, B., ed. *The Cambridge Cultural History of Britain, Volume 8: Early Twentieth-Century Century Britain*. Cambridge: Cambridge University Press, 1992.

Fraser-Tytler, W. K. *Afghanistan: A Study of Political Developments in Central and Southern Asia*. London: Oxford University Press, 1967.

Frechtling, L. "Anglo-Russian Rivalry in Eastern Turkistan, 1863–1881." *Journal of the Royal Central Asian Society* 26, pt. 3 (1939): 471–89.

French, D., and B. Reid, eds. *The British General Staff: Reform and Innovation c. 1890–1939*. London: Frank Cass, 2002.

French, P. *Younghusband: The Last Great Imperial Adventurer*. London: HarperCollins, 1994.

Friedberg, A. *The Weary Titan: Britain and the Experience of Relative Decline, 1895–1905*. Princeton, N.J.: Princeton University Press, 1988.

Fromkin, D. "The Great Game in Asia." *Foreign Affairs* 58, no. 4 (1980): 936–51.

Galton, D. "The Anglo-Russian Literary Society." *Slavonic and East European Review* 46, no. 107 (1968): 19–38.

Garthoff, R. "Military Influences and Instruments." In *Russian Foreign Policy: Essays in Historical Perspective*, edited by I. Lederer. New Haven, Conn.: Yale University Press, 1962.

Gella, T. N. "Liberalism i 'novyi imperialism' v Velikobritanii v 80–90-kh gg. XIX v." *Novaia i noveishaia istoriia*, no. 2 (2001): 52–65.

———. *Liberal'naia partiia Velikobritanii i imperiia v kontse XIX–nachale XX vv*. Orel:

Orlovskii gosudarstvennyi pedagogicheskii institute, 1992.

———. "Politicheskie krugi Velikobritanii o russko-angliiskom sopernichestve na Srednem Vostoke (60-e–nachalo 70-kh gg. XIX v.)." In *Rossiia i Evropa: Diplomatiia i kul'tura*, edited by A. Chubarian. Moscow: Nauka, 1995.

Geyer, D. *Der Russische Imperialismus: Studien ueber den Zusammenhang von innerer und auswaertiger Politik 1860–1914*. Goettingen: Vandenhoeck and Ruprecht, 1977.

Gibbs, N. *The Origins of Imperial Defense*. Oxford: Clarendon Press, 1955.

Gillard, D. "Salisbury and the Indian Defense Problem, 1885–1902." In *Studies in International History*, edited by K. Bourne and D. Watt. London: Longman, 1967.

———. *The Struggle for Asia 1828–1914: A Study in British and Russian Imperialism*. London: Methuen, 1977.

Gilmour, D. *Curzon*. London: Papermac, 1994.

Glatfelter, R. "Russia, the Soviet Union, and the Chinese Eastern Railway." In *Railway Imperialism*, edited by C. Davis and K. Wilburn. New York: Greenwood Press, 1991.

Gleason, J. *The Genesis of Russophobia in Great Britain: A Study in the Interaction of Policy and Opinion*. Cambridge, Mass.: Harvard University Press, 1950.

Glutschenko, E. A. *Geroi Imperii: Portrety rossiiskikh kolonial'nykh deiatelei*. Moscow: XXI v.–Soglasie, 2001.

Gnevusheva, E. I. *Zabytyi puteshestvennik: Zhizn' i puteshestviia Petera Ivanovicha Pashino*. Moscow: Gosudarstvennoe geograficheskoe izdatel'stvo, 1958.

Goldfrank, D. "Crimea Redux? On the Origins of the War." In *The Russo-Japanese War in Global Perspective: World War Zero*, edited by J. Steinberg et al. Leiden: Brill, 2005.

Goodlad, G. *British Foreign and Imperial Policy, 1865–1919*. London: Routledge, 2000.

Gopal, S. *British Policy in India, 1858–1905*. Cambridge: Cambridge University Press, 1965.

Goradia, N. *Lord Curzon: The Last of the British Moguls*. New Delhi: Oxford University Press, 1993.

Greaves, R. *Persia and the Defense of India, 1884–1892: A Study in the Foreign Policy of the Third Marquis of Salisbury*. London: Athlone Press, 1959.

Grenville, J. A. S. *Lord Salisbury and Foreign Policy: The Close of the Nineteenth Century*. London: Athlone Press, 1964.

Grudzinsky, V. V. *Na povorote sud'by: Velikaia Britaniia i imperskii federalism (posledniaia tret' XIX–pervaia chetvert' XX v.)*. Cheliabinsk: Cheliabinsk State University, 1996.

Gruening, I. *Die Russische oeffentliche Meinung und ihre Stellung zu den Grossmaechte vom Berliner Kongress bis zum Abschluss des franko-russischen Buendnis*. Berlin: F. W. Universitaet zu Berlin, 1927.

Guedalla, P. *Palmerston,* London: Hodder & Stoughton, 1926.

Guillen, P. *L'Expansion 1881–1898*. Paris: Imprimerie Nationale, 1984.

Gurevich, B. P. *Mezhdunarodnye otnosheniia v Tsentral'noi Asii v XVII–pervoi polovine XIX v.* Moscow: Nauka, 1983.

Habberton, W. *Anglo-Russian Relations Concerning Afghanistan, 1837–1907*. Urbana: University of Illinois Press, 1937.

Handel, M. *Intelligence and Military Operations*. London: Frank Cass, 1990.

————. *War, Strategy and Intelligence.* London: Frank Cass, 1989.

Hargreaves, J. "Entente Manquée: Anglo-Russian Relations 1895–1896." *Cambridge Historical Journal* 1 (1953): 65–92.

Hassnain, F. *British Policy towards Kashmir (1846–1921): Kashmir in Anglo-Russian Politics.* New Delhi: Sterling, 1974.

Hauner, M. "The Last Great Game." *Middle East Journal* 38, no. 1 (1984): 72–84.

————. *What Is Asia to Us? Russia's Asian Heartland Yesterday and Today.* Boston: Unwin Hyman, 1990.

Henze, P. "The Great Game in Kashgaria: British and Russian Missions to Yakub Bek." *Central Asia Survey*, no. 2 (1989): 61–95.

The History of the Times, vol. 3. London: Office of the Times, 1947.

Holdsworth, M. *Turkistan in the Nineteenth Century: A Brief History of the Khanates of Bukhara, Kokand and Khiva.* Oxford: Central Asian Research Institute, 1959.

Hopkins, B. *The Myth of the "Great Game": The Anglo-Sikh Alliance and Rivalry.* Occasional Paper 5. Cambridge: Centre of South Asian Studies, University of Cambridge, 2004.

Hopkirk, P. *The Great Game: On Secret Service in High Asia.* London: John Murray, 1990.

————. *On Secret Service East of Constantinople: The Plot to Bring Down the British Empire.* London: John Murray, 1994.

————. *The Quest for Kim.* Oxford: Oxford University Press, 1996.

————. *Trespassers on the Roof of the World: The Race for Lhasa.* London: John Murray, 1982.

Hou, Chiming. *Foreign Investment and Economic Development in China, 1840–1937.* Cambridge, Mass.: Harvard University Press, 1965.

Howard, C. *Splendid Isolation: A Study of Ideas Concerning Britain's International Position and Foreign Policy during the Latter Years of the Third Marquis of Salisbury.* London: Macmillan, 1967.

Hsu, I. *The Ili Crisis: A Study of Sino-Russian Diplomacy, 1871–1881.* Oxford: Clarendon Press, 1965.

Huggler, J., and C. Coonan. "China Reopens a Passage to India." *The Independent*, June 20, 2006.

Hughes, M. "Bernard Pares, Russian Studies and the Promotion of Anglo-Russian Friendship, 1907–1914." *Slavonic and East European Review* 78, no. 3 (2000): 510–35.

————. *Diplomacy before the Russian Revolution: Britain, Russia and the Old Diplomacy, 1894–1917.* London: Macmillan, 2000.

Hunczak, T., ed. *Russian Imperialism from Ivan the Great to the Revolution.* New Brunswick, N.J.: Rutgers University Press, 1974.

Hundley, H. "Tibet's Part in the 'Great Game.'" *History Today* 43 (1993): 45–50.

Huttenback, R. "The 'Great Game' in the Pamirs and Hindu Kush: The British Conquest of Hunza and Nagar." *Modern Asian Studies* 9, no. 1 (1975): 1–29.

Hyam, R. "The Primacy of Geopolitics: The Dynamics of British Imperial Policy, 1763–1963." In *The Statecraft of British Imperialism*, edited by R. King and R. Kilson. London: Frank Cass, 1999.

Ignatiev, A. V. "The Foreign Policy of Russia in the Far East at the Turn of the Nineteenth and Twentieth Centuries." In *Imperial Russian Foreign Policy*, edited by H. Ragsdale. Cambridge: Cambridge University Press, 1993.

———. *Russko-angliiskie otnosheniia nakanune Pervoi mirovoi voiny (1908–1914 gg.)*. Moscow: Izdatelstvo sotsial'no-ekonomicheskoi literatury, 1962.

———, ed. *Istoriia vneshnei politiki Rossii: Konets XIX–nachalo XX v. (ot russko-frantsusskogo soiuza do Oktiabr'skoi revolutsii)*. Moscow: Mezhdunarodnye otnosheniia, 1997.

Ingle, H. *Nesselrode and the Russian Rapprochement with Britain, 1836–1844*. Berkeley: University of California Press, 1976.

Ingram, E. *The Beginning of the Great Game in Asia, 1828–1834*. Oxford: Clarendon Press, 1979.

———. *Commitment to Empire: Prophesies of the Great Game in Asia, 1797–1800*. Oxford: Clarendon Press, 1981.

———. *In Defense of British India: Great Britain in the Middle East, 1775–1842*. London: Frank Cass, 1984.

Isachenko, A. G., ed. *Russkoe geograficheskoe obstchestvo: 150 let*. Moscow: Progress-Pangeia, 1995.

Isiev, D. A. *Uigurskoe gosudarstvo Yettishar (1864–1877)*. Moscow: Nauka, 1981.

Iskandarov, B. I. *Sotsial'no-ekonomicheskie i politicheskie aspekty istorii pamirskikh kniazhestv (X–pervaia polovina XIX v.)*. Dushanbe: Donish, 1983.

Jackson, J. *The Committee of Imperial Defense, the Foreign Office and the Drift to a Continental Commitment: A Study in British Policy Making, 1902–1914*. Tors Park, U.K.: A. Stockwell, 2002.

James, L. *The Rise and Fall of the British Empire*. London: Little, Brown, 1994.

James, R. R. *Rosebery: A Biography of Archibald Philip, Fifth Earl of Rosebery*. London: Weidenfeld & Nicolson, 1963.

Jeffrey, K. "The Eastern Arc of Empire: A Strategic View, 1850–1950." *Journal of Strategic Studies* 5, no. 4 (1982): 531–45.

Jelavich, B. "British Means of Offence against Russia in the Nineteenth Century." *Russian History* 1, pt. 2 (1974): 119–35.

———. *St Petersburg and Moscow: Tsarist and Soviet Foreign Policy, 1814–1974*. Bloomington: Indiana University Press, 1974.

Jenkins, R. *Gladstone: A Biography*. New York: Random House, 1995.

Johnson, F. *Defense by Committee: The British Committee of Imperial Defence, 1885–1959*. London: Oxford University Press, 1960.

Johnson, R. *British Imperialism*. Houndmills, U.K.: Palgrave Macmillan, 2003.

———. "Review of Peter John Brobst, *The Future of the Great Game: Sir Olaf Caroe, India's Independence and the Defence of Asia*, Akron: University of Akron Press, 2005." *Journal of British Studies* 45, no. 2 (2007): 486–87.

———. "Russians at the Gates of India? Planning the Defense of India, 1884–1899." *Journal of Military History* 67, no. 3 (2003): 697–743.

———. *Spying for Empire: The Great Game in Central and South Asia, 1757–1947*.

London: Greenhill Books, 2006.

Judd, D. *Balfour and the British Empire: A Study in Imperial Evolution 1874–1932.* London: Macmillan, 1968.

Kabuzan, V. M. *Dal'nevostochnyi krai v XVII–nachale XX v.* Moscow: Nauka, 1985.

Kalinin, A. I. "O nekotorykh aspektakh sredneaziatskoi politiki Rossii v 40–80-kh XIX v." *Vostochnyi arkhiv,* nos. 4–5 (2000): 49–54.

Kaminsky, A. *The India Office, 1880–1910.* London: Mansell, 1986.

Kastel'skaia, Z. D. *Iz istorii Turkestanskogo kraia (1865–1917).* Moscow: Nauka, 1980.

Kazemzadeh, F. *Russia and Britain in Persia, 1864–1914.* New Haven, Conn.: Yale University Press, 1968.

———. "Russia and the Middle East." In *Russian Foreign Policy: Essays in Historical Perspective,* edited by I. Lederer. New Haven, Conn.: Yale University Press, 1962.

Keay, J. *The Gilgit Game: The Explorers of the Western Himalayas, 1865–1895.* Hamden, Conn.: Archon Books, 1979.

———. *Where Men and Mountains Meet: The Explorers of the Western Himalayas, 1820–1875.* London: John Murray, 1977.

Kelly, J. B. *Britain and the Persian Gulf, 1795–1880.* Oxford: Clarendon Press, 1968.

———. "Salisbury, Curzon and the Kuwait Agreement of 1899." In *Studies in International History,* edited by K. Bourne and D. Watt. London: Longmans, 1967.

Kennedy, A. *Salisbury, 1830–1903: Portrait of a Statesman.* London: John Murray, 1971.

Kennedy, P. *The Realities Behind Diplomacy: Background Influences on British External Policy, 1865–1900.* London: George Allen & Unwin, 1981.

———. *Strategy and Diplomacy, 1870–1945.* London: George Allen & Unwin, 1983.

Kertman, L. E. "O politicheskikh raznoglasiiakh v Anglii po voprosu o sblizhenii s tsarskoi Rossii v period i posle revolutsii 1905–1907 gg." *Nauchnye doklady vysshei shkoly: Istoricheskie nauki,* no. 1 (1961): 115–31.

Khalfin, N. A. *Angliiskaia kolonial'naia politika na Srednem Vostoke (70-e gg. XIX v.).* Tashkent: Sredneasiatskii gosudarstvennyi universitet, 1957.

———. "Drama v spal'ne otelia." *Voprosy istorii,* no. 10 (1966): 216–20.

———. "G. N. Curzon v rossiiskoi Srednei Asii." *Voprosy istorii,* no. 3 (1988): 106–15.

———. "Lord Curzon: Ideolog i politik britanskogo imperializma." *Novaia i noveishaia istoriia,* no. 1 (1983): 120–40.

———. *Missii iz Indii v Rossiiu vo vtoroi polovine XIX v.* Moscow: Vostochnaia literatura, 1963.

———. *Politika Rossii v Tsentral'noi Asii.* Moscow: Nauka, 1960.

———. *Prisoedinenie Srednei Asii k Rossii (60–90-e gg. XIX v.).* Moscow: Nauka, 1965.

———. *Proval britanskoi agressii v Afghanistane (XIX–nachalo XX v.).* Moscow: Sotsial'no-ekonomicheskoe gosudarstvennoe izdatel'stvo, 1959.

———. *Rossiia i Bukharskii Emirat na Zapadnom Pamire (konets XIX–nachalo XX v.).* Moscow: Vostochnaia literatura, 1975.

———. *Rossiia i khanstva Srednei Asii (pervaia polovina XIX v.).* Moscow: Nauka, 1974.

Khalfin, N. A., and E. F. Rassadina. *N. V. Khanykov: Vostokoved i diplomat.* Moscow:

Nauka, 1977.

Khariukov, L. N. *Anglo-russkoe sopernichestvo v Tsentral'noi Asii i ismailism.* Moscow: Moscow State University, 1995.

Khevrolina, V. M. *Rossiiskii diplomat graf N.P. Ignatiev.* Moscow: Institut rossiiskoi istorii RAN, 2004.

Khidoiatov, G. A. *Britanskaia ekspansiia v Srednei Asii (Penjdeh, March 1885).* Tashkent: Fan, 1981.

——. *Iz istorii anglo-russkikh otnoshenii v Srednei Asii v kontse XIX v. (60–70-e gg.).* Tashkent: Fan, 1969.

——. "Rossiia i Sredniaia Asiia vo vtoroi polovine XIX v." *Tashkentskii gosudarstvennyi universitet: Nauchnye trudy* 343, pt. 1 (1969): 11–30.

Khokhlov, A. N. "Voennaia pomotsch Kitaiu v kontse 50-kh–nachale 60-kh gg. XIX v." In *Strany Dal'nego Vostoka i Yugo-Vostochnoi Asii (istoriia i ekonomika),* edited by I. S. Kazakevich. Moscow: Vostochnaia literatura, 1967.

Khudzievkaia, Y., and I. Yaster. *Ludi velikoi otvagi: Rasskazy o pol'skikh puteshestvennikakh.* Moscow: Geografgiz, 1957.

Khvostov, V. M., ed. *Istoriia diplomatii,* vol. 2. Moscow: Gosudarstvennoe izdatel'stvo politicheskoi literatury, 1963.

Kiernan, E. *British Diplomacy in China, 1880 to 1885.* Cambridge: Cambridge University Press, 1939.

Kim, E., and H. Kim. *Korea and the Politics of Imperialism, 1876–1910.* Berkeley: University of California Press, 1967.

Kim, H. *Holy War in China: The Muslim Rebellion and State in Chinese Central Asia, 1864–1877.* Stanford, Calif.: Hoover Institution Press, 2004.

King, P. *The Viceroy's Fall: How Kitchener Destroyed Curzon.* London: Sidgwick and Jackson, 1986.

Kiniapina, N. S. "General D. A. Miliutin i prisoedinenie Srednei Asii." In *Rossiiskaia diplomatia v portretakh,* edited by A. V. Ignatiev et al. Moscow: Mezhdunarodnye otnosheniia, 1992.

——. "Sredniaia Asiia vo vneshnepoliticheskikh planakh tsarisma (50-e–80-e gg. XIX v.)." *Voprosy istorii,* no. 2 (1974): 36–51.

——. "Sredniaia Asiia v planakh i deistviakh Rossii v 60-e–80-e gg. XIX v." In *Rossiia i strany blizhnego zarubezhiia: istoriia i sovremennost',* edited by S. L. Tikhvinsky. Moscow: Institut rossiiskoi istorii RAN, 1995.

——, ed. *Vostochnui vopros vo vneshnei politike Rossii, konets XVIII–nachalo XX v.* Moscow: Nauka, 1978.

Kiniapina, N. S., et al. *Kavkaz i Sredniaia Asiia vo vneshnei politike Rossii (vtoraia polovina XVIII–80-e gg. XIX v.).* Moscow: Moscow State University, 1984.

Klein, I. "The Anglo-Russian Convention and the Problem of Central Asia, 1907–1914." *Journal of British Studies* 11, no. 1 (1971): 126–47.

Klimenko, N. P. *Kolonial'naia politika Anglii na Dal'nem Vostoke v seredine XIX v.* Moscow: nauka, 1976.

Knaplund, P. *Gladstone's Foreign Policy,* London: Frank Cass, 1970.

Knorring, N. N. *General Mikhail Dmitrievich Skobelev: Istoricheskii etiud.* Parizh: Illustrirovannaia Rossiia, 1939.

Kolesnikov, A. A. *Russkie v Kashgarii (vtoraia polovina XIX–nachalo XX v.): Missii, ekspeditsii, puteshestviia.* Pishpek: Raritet, 2006.

Korff, S. A. *Russia's Foreign Relations during the Last Half-Century.* London: Macmillan, 1922.

Korneev, V. V. "Tsentral'noaziatskii region v voennoi politike Rossii (XVIII–nachalo XX v.)." *Oriens,* no. 4 (2004): 5–16.

Koskikallio, P., and A. Lehmuuskallio, eds. *K. G. Mannerheim in Central Asia, 1906– 1908.* Helsinki: National Board of Antiquities, 1999.

Kotliar, P. S. "Russko-afghanskie otnosheniia v seredine XIX–nachale XX v. i anglo-russkoe sopernichestvo na Srednem Vostoke." *Tashkentskii gosudarstvennyi pedagogicheskii institute: Uchenye zapiski. Istoriia* 33, no. 2 (1962): 57–249.

Kowner, R. "'Lighter Than Yellow, but Not Enough': Western Discourse on the Japanese Race." *Historical Journal* 43, no. 1 (2000): 103–31.

Kowner, R., ed. *The Impact of the Russo-Japanese War.* London: RoutledgeCurzon, 2006.

Kozhekina, M. T. "Forpost Rossii na Indostane: K 100-letiyu rossiskogo konsul'stva v Indii." *Vostochnyi arkhiv,* nos. 6–7 (2001): 35–46.

———. "Missiia generala N. S. Yermolova v Indiyu (1911 g.)." *Vostochnyi arkhiv,* nos. 2–3 (1999): 72–85.

Kozhekina, M. T., and I. E. Fedorova. *Politika Velikobritanii i SShA na Srednem Vostoke v angliiskoi i amerikanskoi istoriografii.* Moscow: Nauka, 1989.

Kuleshov, N. "Agvan Dorjiev, the Dalai Lama's Ambassador." In *The History of Tibet,* vol. 3, edited by A. Mackay. London: RoutledgeCurzon, 2003.

———. *Rossiia i Tibet.* Moscow: Vostochnaia literatura, 1992.

Lamb, A. *Asian Frontiers: Studies in a Continuing Problem.* London: Pall Mall Press, 1968.

———. *Britain and Chinese Central Asia: The Road to Lhasa, 1767–1905,* London: Routledge & Kegan Paul, 1960.

———. *British India and Tibet, 1766–1910.* London: Routledge & Kegan Paul, 1986.

Langer, W. *The Diplomacy of Imperialism, 1890–1902.* 2 vols. New York: Alfred A. Knopf, 1935.

Latham, A. J. H. *The International Economy and the Underdeveloped World, 1865–1914.* London: Croom Helm, 1978.

Lattimore, O. *Inner Asian Frontiers of China.* London: Oxford University Press, 1940.

Lederer, I., ed. *Russian Foreign Policy: Essays in Historical Perspective.* New Haven, Conn.: Yale University Press, 1962.

Le Donne, J. *The Russian Empire and the World, 1700–1917.* New York: Oxford University Press, 1997.

Lensen, G., ed. *Russia's Eastward Expansion.* Englewood Cliffs, N.J.: Prentice Hall, 1964.

Leontiev, M. *Bol'shaia Igra.* Moscow: AST-Astrel', 2008.

Leontiev, V. P. *Inostrannaia ekspansiia v Tibete v 1888–1919 gg.* Moscow: Izdatel'stvo AN SSSR, 1956.

Levine, P. *The British Empire: Sunrise to Sunset.* London: Longman, 2007.

Lieven, D. *Empire: The Russian Empire and Its Rivals.* London: John Murray, 2000.

Lisitsyna, N. N. "Pendinskoe srazhenie 1885 goda: Novye dokumenty." *Vostochnyi arkhiv*, nos. 11–12 (2004): 66–72.

Liska, G. *Russia and the Road to Appeasement: Cycles of East-West Conflict in War and Peace.* Baltimore: Johns Hopkins University Press, 1982.

Litvinov, P. P. "Britanskaia Indiia i russkii Turkestan vo vtoroi polovine XIX–nachale XX v." In *Rossiia–Indiia: perspektivy regional'nogo sotrudnichestva*, edited by G. I. Kuznetsov. Moscow: Institut vostokovedeniia RAN, 2001.

Lobanov-Rostovskii, A. *Russia and Asia.* Ann Arbor: George Wahr, 1951.

Lowe, C. *The Reluctant Imperialists: British Foreign Policy, 1878–1902.* 2 vols. London: Routledge & Kegan Paul, 1967.

Lowe, C., and M. Dockrill. *The Mirage of Power: British Foreign Policy 1902–1922.* 3 vols. London: Routledge & Kegan Paul, 1972.

Lowe, P. *Britain in the Far East: A Survey from 1819 to the Present.* London: Longman, 1981.

Luneva, Yu. V. "Lord Edward Grey: Master angliiskoi tainoi diplomatii nachala XX v." *Novaia i noveishaia istoriia*, no. 5 (2009): 182–200.

Luzhetskaia, N. L. *Ocherki istorii Vostochnogo Hindukusha vo vtoroi polovine XIX v.* Moscow: Nauka, 1986.

Macarthy, M. "Anglo-Russian Rivalry in Persia." *University of Buffalo Studies* 4, no. 2 (1925): 27–67.

Maccordock, R. *British Far Eastern Policy, 1894–1900.* New York: Octagon Books, 1931.

Macdermott, W. "The Immediate Origins of the Committee of Imperial Defense: A Reappraisal." *Canadian Journal of History* 7 (1972): 253–72.

Macdonald, D. "Tsushima's Echoes: Asian Defeat and Tsarist Foreign Policy." In *The Russo-Japanese War in Global Perspective: World War Zero*, vol. 1, edited by J. Steinberg et al. Leiden: Brill, 2005.

Macdonald, R. *The Language of Empire: Myths and Metaphors of Popular Imperialism, 1880–1980.* Manchester: Manchester University Press, 1994.

Macgregor, J. *Tibet, a Chronicle of Exploration.* London: Routledge & Kegan Paul, 1970.

Mackay, A. *Tibet and the British Raj: The Frontier Cadre, 1904–1907.* Richmond, U.K.: Curzon Press, 1997.

———, ed. *The History of Tibet*, vol. 3. London: RoutledgeCurzon, 2003.

Mackenzie, D. "The Conquest and Administration of Turkestan, 1860–1885." In *Russian Colonial Expansion to 1917*, edited by M. Rywkin. London: Manswell, 1988.

———. "Expansion in Central Asia: St Petersburg vs. the Turkistan Generals (1863–1866)." *Canadian Slavic Studies* 3, no. 2 (1969): 286–311.

———. *Imperial Dreams, Harsh Realities: Tsarist Russian Foreign Policy, 1815–1917.* Fort Worth: Harcourt Brace College Publishers, 1994.

———. *The Lion of Tashkent: The Career of General M. G. Cherniaev.* Athens: University of Georgia Press, 1974.

———. *Propaganda and Empire: The Manipulation of British Public Opinion, 1880–1960.*

Manchester: Manchester University Press, 1985.

———. "Turkistan's Significance to Russia (1850–1917)." *Russian Review* 33, no. 2 (1974): 167–88.

Mackintosh, J. "The Role of the Committee of Imperial Defense before 1914." *English Historical Review* 77, no. 304 (1962): 490–503.

Maclean, D. *Britain and Her Buffer State: The Collapse of the Persian Empire, 1890–1914.* London: Royal Historical Society, 1979.

Macrae, M. *In Search of Shangri-La: The Extraordinary True Story of the Quest for the Lost Horizon.* London: M. Joseph, 2003.

Madan, P. *Tibet: Saga of Indian Explorers (1864–1894).* New Delhi: Manohar, 2004.

Magnus, P. *Gladstone: A Biography.* London: John Murray, 1954.

———. *Kitchener: Portrait of an Imperialist.* London: John Murray, 1958.

Mahajan, S. "The Defense of India and the End of Isolation: A Study in the Foreign Policy of the Conservative Government, 1900–1905." *Journal of Imperial and Commonwealth History* 10, no. 2 (1982): 168–93.

Mahajan, S. *British Foreign Policy, 1874–1914: The Role of India.* London: Routledge, 2002.

Malozemoff, A. *Russian Far-Eastern Policy, 1881-1905.* Berkeley: University of California Press, 1958.

Mancall, M. "The Ch'ing Tribute System: An Interpretive Essay." In *The Chinese World Order: Traditional China's Foreign Relations,* edited by J. Fairbank. Cambridge, Mass.: Harvard University Press, 1968.

Mannanov, B. S. "Sovremennaia burzhuaznaia istoriografiia o nekotorykh aspektakh istoriografii anglo-russkikh otnoshenii na Srednem Vostoke (iz istorii 'Bol'shoi igry')." In *Fal'sifikatory istorii (kritika burzhuaznoi istoriografii Srednei Asii i stran zarubezhnogo Vostoka),* edited by M. M. Khairullaev and N. A. Khalfin. Tashkent: Fan, 1985.

Marriott, J. *Anglo-Russian Relations 1689–1943.* London: Methuen, 1944.

———. *The English in India: A Problem of Politics.* Oxford: Clarendon Press, 1932.

Marks, S. "'Bravo, Brave Tiger of the East!' The War and the Rise of Nationalism in British Egypt and India." In *The Russo-Japanese War in Global Perspective: World War Zero,* vol. 1, edited by J. Steinberg et al. Leiden: Brill, 2005.

———. *Road to Power: The Trans-Siberian Railroad and the Colonization of Asian Russia, 1850–1917.* London: I. B. Tauris, 1991.

Marshall, A. *The Russian General Staff and Asia, 1800–1917.* London: RoutledgeCurzon, 2005.

Martirosov, S. Z. *Anglo-russkie protivorechiia v Srednei Asii v dorevoliutsionnoi i sovetskoi istoricheskoi literature.* Chardzhou: Turkmenskii gosudarstvennyi pedagogicheskii institute, 1962.

———. *Iz istorii anglo-russkogo sopernichestva v Srednei Asii v sviazi c prisoedineniem Turkmenii k Rossii.* Ashgabad: Izdatel'stvo AN Turkmenskoi SSR, 1966.

Masal'sky, V. I. *Skobelev: Istoricheskii portret.* Moscow: Andreevskii flag, 1998.

Matthew, C. *Gladstone: 1809–1874.* Oxford: Clarendon Press, 1986.

Mediakov, A. S. *Istoriia mezhdunarodnykh otnoshenii v novoe vremya.* Moscow:

Prosvestchenie, 2007.

Mehra, P. *The Younghusband Expedition: An Interpretation.* London: Asia Public House, 1968.

Mendel'son, V. I. "Anglo-russkoe soglashenie 1907 g. v osvestchenii sovetskikh istorikov." *Istoricheskie zapiski* 104 (1979): 268–81.

Menon, K. *The "Russian Bogey" and British Aggression in India and Beyond.* Calcutta: Priyadarshi Banerji, Eastern Trading Company, 1957.

Meyer, K., and S. Brysac. *Tournament of Shadows: The Great Game and the Race for Empire in Central Asia.* London: Abacus, 1999.

Mezin, S. A. "'Zavetschanie Petera Velikogo': Evropeiskie mify i rossiiskaia real'nost." *Rossiiskaia Istoriia*, no. 5 (2010): 18–27.

Miasnikov, V. S. *Dogovornymi statiami utverdili: Diplomaticheskaia istoriia russko-kitaiskoi granitsy XVII–XIX vv.* Moscow: Institut Dal'nego Vostoka RAN, 1996.

Moiseev, V. A. *Rossiiai i Kitai v Tsentral'noi Asii (vroraia polovina XIX v.–1917 g.).* Barnaul: Az Buka, 2003.

Mojtahed-Zadeh, P. *The Small Players of the Great Game: The Settlement of Iran's Eastern Borderlands and the Creation of Afghanistan.* London: RoutledgeCurzon, 2004.

Moreman, T. *The Army in India and the Development of Frontier Warfare, 1849–1947.* London and New York: Macmillan and St. Martin's Press, 1998.

Morgan, G. *Anglo-Russian Rivalry in Central Asia: 1810–1895.* London: Frank Cass, 1981.

———. "Myth and Reality in the Great Game." *Asian Affairs* 60 (new ser. 4), pt. I (1973): 55–65.

Morris, A. *The Scaremongers: The Advocacy of War and Rearmament, 1896–1914.* London: Routledge & Kegan Paul, 1984.

Morris, J. *Pax Britannica: The Climax of an Empire.* London: Faber & Faber, 1968.

Morris, L. "British Secret Service Activity in Khorassan, 1887–1908." *Historical Journal* 27, no. 3 (1984): 657–75.

Mosley, L. *Curzon: The End of an Epoch.* London: Longmans, 1960.

———. *The Glorious Fault: The Life of Lord Curzon.* New York: Harcourt, Brace, 1960.

Mukhanov, V. M. "Mikhail Dmitrievich Skobelev." *Voprosy istorii*, no. 10 (2004): 57–81.

Mulligan, W. *The Origins of the First World War.* Cambridge: Cambridge University Press, 2010.

Narochnitsky, A. L. "Angliia, Rossiia i koreiskii vopros nakanune napadeniia Yaponii na Kitai letom 1894 g." *Istoricheskie zapiski* 24 (1947): 160–83.

———. *Kolonial'naia politika kapitalisticheskikh derzhav na Dal'nem Vostoke, 1860–1895.* Moscow: Gosudarstvennoe politicheskoe izdatel'stvo, 1956.

Nazem, H. *Russia and Great Britain in Iran (1900–1914).* Tehran: Sherkat Iran Chap, 1975.

Neilson, K. *Britain and the Last Tsar: British Policy and Russia 1894–1917.* Oxford: Oxford University Press, 1995.

———. "'Control the Whirlwind': Sir Edward Grey as Foreign Secretary, 1906–16." In *The Makers of British Foreign Policy*, edited by T. Otte. Basingstoke, U.K.: Palgrave, 2002.

———. "Wishful Thinking: The Foreign Office and Russia 1907–1917." In *Shadow and Substance in British Foreign Policy 1895–1939*, edited by B. Mackercher and D.

Moss. Edmonton: University of Alberta Press, 1984.

Newton, Lord. *Lord Lansdowne: A Biography*. London: Macmillan, 1929.

Nicolson, H. *Sir Arthur Nicolson, Bart., First Lord Carnock: A Study in the Old Diplomacy*. London: Archibald Constable, 1930.

Nish, I. *The Anglo-Japanese Alliance: The Diplomacy of Two Island Empires, 1897–1907*. London: Athlone Press, 1966.

———. "British Foreign Secretaries and Japan, 1892–1905." In *Shadow and Substance in British Foreign Policy 1895–1939*, edited by B. Mackercher and D. Moss. Edmonton: University of Alberta Press, 1984.

———. "Great Britain, Japan and North-East Asia, 1905–1911." In *British Foreign Policy under Sir Edward Grey*, edited by F. Hinsley. Cambridge: Cambridge University Press, 1977.

Noelle, C. *State and Tribe in Nineteenth-Century Afghanistan: The Reign of Amir Dost Muhammad Khan (1826–1863)*. Richmond, U.K.: Curzon Press, 1997.

Nuriddinov, Z. R. "Angliia i afghano-russkoe razgranichenie v 80-3 gg. XIX v." *Tashkentskii gosudarstvennyi pedagogicheskii institute: Uchenye zapiski—Istoriia* 33, no. 2 (1962): 250–329.

Nyman, L. "The Great Game: A Comment." *Asian Affairs* 60 (new ser. 4), pt. 3 (1973): 299–301.

Obukhov, V. G. *Skhvatka shesti imperii: Bitva za Sinkiang*. Moscow: Veche, 2007.

Orlov, A. A. *Soiuz Peterburga i Londona: Rossiiskobritanskie otnosheniia v epokhu napoleonovskikh voin*. Moscow: Progress-Traditsiia, 2005.

———. *"Teper" vizhu anglichan vblizi': Britaniia i britantsy v predstavleniiakh rossiian o mire i o sebe (vtoraia polovina XVIII–pervaia polovina XIX vv.)—Ocherki*. Moscow: Giperboreia, Kuchkovo Pole, 2008.

Orlov, E. A. "Vopros ob 'oborone Indii' ot 'russkoi ugrozy' v istoriografii." In *Protiv kolonializma i neokolonializma*, edited by V. I. Danilov. Moscow: Nauka, 1975.

Ostal'tseva, A. F. *Anglo-russkoe soglasheniia 1907 g.: Vliianie russko-iaponskoi voiny i revolutsii 1905–1907 gg.—Na vneshnyuyu politiku tsarisma i na peregruppirovku evropeiskikh derzhav*. Saratov: Saratovskii gosudarstvennyi universitet, 1977.

Ostrikov, P. I. "Angliiskaia pomotsch Yaponii vo vremia russko-yaponskoi voiny 1904–1905 gg." *Kurskii pedagogicheskii institut: Uchenye zapiski* 13 (1961): 91–116.

———. "K istorii imperialisticheskoi ekspansii Anglii v Irane v nachale XX v." In *Protiv falk'sifikatsii istorii kolonializma*, edited by K. Popov. Moscow: Vostochnaia literatura, 1962.

Otte, T. "'Almost a Law of Nature?' Sir Edward Grey, the Foreign Office and the Balance of Power in Europe, 1905–1912." In *Power and Stability: British Foreign Policy, 1865–1965*, edited by E. Goldstein and B. Mackercher. London: Frank Cass, 2003.

———. *The China Question: Great Power Rivalry and British Isolation, 1894–1905*. Oxford: Oxford University Press, 2007.

———. "'Floating Downstream?' Lord Salisbury and British Foreign Policy, 1878–1902." In *The Makers of British Foreign Policy*, edited by T. Otte. Basingstoke, U.K.: Palgrave, 2002.

———. "Great Britain, Germany, and the Far Eastern Crisis of 1897/98." *English Historical Review* 110, no. 5 (1995): 1157–79.

———. "'It's What Made Britain Great': Reflections on British Foreign Policy from Malplaquet to Maastricht." In *The Makers of British Foreign Policy*, edited by T. Otte. Basingstoke, U.K.: Palgrave, 2002.

———. "Old Diplomacy: Reflections on the Foreign Office Before 1914." In *The Foreign Office and British Diplomacy in the Twentieth Century*, edited by G. Johnson. London: Routledge, 2005.

Page, S. "The Creation of a Sphere of Influence: Russia and Central Asia." *International Journal* 49, no. 4 (1994): 788–813.

Paine, S. *Imperial Rivals: Russia, China and Their Disputed Frontier, 1858–1924*. Armonk, N.Y.: M. E. Sharpe, 1996.

Pak, B. D. *Rossiia i Koreia*. Moscow: Vostochnaia literatura, 1979.

Palace, W. *The British Empire and Tibet 1900–1922*. London: RoutledgeCurzon, 2005.

Palmer, A. "Lord Salisbury's Approach to Russia." *Oxford Slavonic Papers* 6 (1955): 102–14.

Panin, S. B. "'Sovetskaia ugroza' Britanskoi Indii: afghanskii platzdarm (20-e gg. XX v.)." *Oriens*, no. 6 (2001): 24–35.

Parfenov, I. D. *Kolonial'naia ekspansiia Velikobritanii v poslednei treti XIX v. (dvizhustchie sily, formy i metody)*. Moscow: Nauka, 1991.

Parker, G. *Western Geopolitical Thought in the Twentieth Century*. London: Croom Helm, 1985.

Parker, I. *Liberal Government and Politics, 1905–15*. London: Palgrave, 2006.

Parritt, B. *The Intelligencers: The History of British Military Intelligence up to 1914*. Ashford, U.K.: Intelligence Corps Association, 1971.

Pashukanis, S. "K istorii anglo-russkogo soglasheniia 1907 g." *Krasnyi Arkhiv*, nos. 2–3 (69–70) (1935): 3–39.

Pavlov, D. B. *Russko-iaponskaia voina 1904–1905 gg.: Sekretnye operatsii na sushe i na more*. Moscow: Materik, 2004.

Pelcovits, N. *Old China Hands and the Foreign Office*. New York: King's Crown Press, 1948.

Penson, L. "The New Course in British Foreign Policy, 1892–1902." In *Essays in Modern History*, edited by I. Christie. London and New York: Macmillan and St. Martin's Press, 1968.

Pethybridge, R. "British Imperialists in the Russian Empire." *Russian Review* 30, no. 4 (1971): 346–55.

Petrov, V. I. *Miateznoe "serdtse" Asii: Sinkiang—kratkaia istoriia narodnykh dvizhenii i vospominanii*. Moscow: Kraft Plius, 2003.

Pierce, R. *Russian Central Asia, 1867–1917: A Study in Colonial Rule*. Berkeley: University of California Press, 1960.

Pokrovsky, M. N. *Diplomatiiia i voiny tsarskoi Rossii v XIX stoletii*. Moscow: Gosudarstvennoe izdatel'stvo, 1923.

Polinov, I. G. "Proiski angliiskikh i iaponskikh imperialistov v Sinkiange (konets XIX–nachalo XX vv.)." *Institut vostokovedeniia AN Uzbekskoi SSR, Trudy* 2 (1954): 80–90.

Popov, A. "Anglo-russkoe sopernichestvo na putiakh Irana." *Novyi Vostok* 12 (1926): 127–48.

————. "Bor'ba za sredneasiatskii platzdarm." *Istoricheskie zapiski* 7 (1940): 182–235.

————. "Iz istorii zavoevaniia Srednei Asii." *Istoricheskie zapiski* 9 (1940): 198–242.

————. "Rossiia i Tibet." *Novyi Vostok* 18 (1927): 101–19; 20 (1928): 33–54.

Popplewell, R. *Intelligence and Imperial Defense: British Intelligence and the Defense of the Indian Empire, 1904–1924.* London: Frank Cass, 1995.

Porokhov, S. Yu. *Bitva imperiiz; Angliia protiv Rossii,* Moscow: AST-Astrel', 2008.

Porter, B. *The Lion's Share: A Short History of British Imperialism 1850–1970.* London: Longman, 1975.

Postnikov, A. V. *Skhvatka na "kryshe mira": Politiki, razvedchiki, generally v bor'be za Pamir v XIX v.* Moscow: Ripol-Klassik, 2005.

Preston, A. "Sir Charles Macgregor and the Defense of India, 1857–1887." *Historical Journal* 12, no. 1 (1969): 58–77.

Primakov, E. M., ed. *Ocherki istorii vneshnei razvedki,* vol. 1. Moscow: Mezhdunarodnye otnosheniia, 1995.

Quested, R. *The Expansion of Russia in East Asia, 1857–1860.* Kuala Lumpur: University of Malaysia Press, 1968.

Ragsdale, H., ed. *Imperial Russian Foreign Policy.* Cambridge: Cambridge University Press, 1993.

Ramm, A. "Lord Salisbury and the Foreign Office." In *The Foreign Office, 1782–1982,* edited by R. Bullen. Frederick, Md.: University Publications of America, 1984.

Raskol'nikov, F. "Rossiia i Afghanistan: Istoricheskii ocherk." *Novyi Vostok* 4 (1923): 12–48.

Rayfield, D. *The Dream of Lhasa: The Life of Nikolay Przhevalsky, Explorer of Central Asia.* London: P. Elek, 1976.

Remnev, A. V. "Kak obustroit' Rossiiu: Geopoliticheskie prognosy byvshego ministra Kuropatkina." *Rodina,* 2004, 32–34.

————. *Rossiia Dal'nego Vostoka: Imperskaia geografiia vlasti XIX–nachala XX vv.* Omsk: Omsk State University, 2004.

————. "U istokov rossiiskoi imperskoi geopolitiki: Asiatskoe 'pogranichnoe prostranstvo' v issledovaniiakh M. I. Veniukova." *Istoricheskie zapiski* 4, no. 122 (2001): 344–69.

Renouvin, P. *La question d'Extrême Orient, 1840–1940.* Paris: Libraire Hachette, 1946.

Reviakin, A. V. *Istoriia mezhdunarodnykh otnoshenii v novoe vremya.* Moscow: Rosspen, 2004.

Riasanovsky, N. "Asia through Russian Eyes." In *Russia and Asia: Essays on the Influence of Russia on the Asian Peoples,* edited by W. S. Vucinich. Stanford, Calif.: Hoover Institution Press, 1972.

Rich, D. "Building Foundations for Effective Intelligence: Military Geography and Statistics in Russian Perspective, 1845–1905." In *Reforming the Tsar's Army: Military Innovation in Imperial Russia from Peter the Great to the Revolution,* edited by D. Schimmelpenninck van der Oye and B. Menning. Washington, D.C., and New York: Woodrow Wilson Center Press and Cambridge University Press, 2004.

Richards, D. S. *The Savage Frontier: A History of the Anglo-Afghan Wars.* London: Macmillan, 1990.

Rieber, A. "Persistent Factors in Russian Foreign Policy: An Interpretive Essay." In

Imperial Russian Foreign Policy, edited by H. Ragsdale. Cambridge: Cambridge University Press, 1993.

———. "Sravnivaia kontinental'nye imperii." In *Rossiiskaia imperiia v sravnitel'noi perspektive*, edited by A. I. Miller. Moscow: Novoe izdatel'stvo, 2004.

Robbins, K. *Sir Edward Grey: A Biography of Lord Grey of Fallodon*. London: Cassell, 1971.

Robbins, R. *The Tsar's Viceroys: Russian Provisional Governors in the Last Years of the Empire*. Ithaca, N.Y.: Cornell University Press, 1987.

Roberts, A. *Salisbury: Victorian Titan*. London, 1999.

Robinson, R. "Railways and Informal Empire." In *Railway Imperialism*, edited by C. Davis and Kenneth Wilburn. New York: Greenwood Press, 1991.

Robinson, R., and J. Gallagher. *Africa and the Victorians: The Climax of Imperialism*. New York: Anchor Books, 1968.

———. *Africa and the Victorians: The Official Mind of Imperialism*. London: Macmillan, 1981.

Robson, B. *The Road to Kabul: The Second Afghan War, 1878–1881*. London: Arms and Armour Press, 1986.

Romanov, B. A. *Rossiia v Man'chzhurii (1892–1906)*. Leningrad: Gosudarstvennoe politicheskoe izdatel'stvo, 1928.

Romanova, E. V. *Put' k voine: Razvitie anglo-germanskogo konflikta, 1898–1914*. Moscow: Maks Press, 2008.

Romanova, G. N. *Ekonomicheskie otnosheniia Rossii i Kitaia na dal'nem Vostoke XIX– nachalo XX v.* Moscow: Nauka, 1987.

Romanova, M. I. "Anglo-russkoe morskoe sopernichestvo na Dal'nem Vostoke v seredine XIX v. i otnoshenie k nemu liberal'nykh krugov Velikobritanii." *Rossiiskii flot na Tikhom okeane: Istoriia i sovremennost'*, no. 2 (1996): 11–15.

Ronaldshay, Earl. *The Life of Lord Curzon*. 3 vols. London: Ernest Benn, 1928.

Rose, K. *Superior Person: A Portrait of Curzon and His Circle in Late Victorian England*. London: Weidenfeld & Nicolson, 1969.

Rosenbaum, A. "The Manchurian Bridgehead: Anglo-Russian Rivalry and the Imperial Russian Railways of North China, 1897–1902." *Modern Asian Studies* 10, no. 1 (1976): 41–64.

Rostovsky, S. N. "Tsarskaia Rossiia i Sinkiang v XIX–XX vv." *Istorik-Marxist* 3, no. 155 (1936): 36–53.

Rozhkova, M. K. *Ekonomicheskie sviazi Rossii so Srednei Aziei v 40-e–60-e gg. XIX v.* Moscow: Izdatel'stvo AN SSSR, 1963.

Rustamov, U. "Iz istorii angliiskoi agressii na granitsakh Pamira v kontse 80-kh gg. i v nachale 90-kh gg. XIX v." *Institut vostokovedeniia An Uzbekskoi SSR, Trudy* 2 (1954): 70–79.

Rywkin, M., ed. *Russian Colonial Expansion to 1917*. London: Manswell, 1988.

Sahadeo, J. *Russian Colonial Society in Tashkent, 1865–1923*. Bloomington: Indiana University Press, 2007.

Said, E. *Orientalism: Western Conceptions of the Orient*. New York: Vintage Books, 1979.

Sareen, T. "India and the War." In *The Impact of the Russo-Japanese War*, edited by R.

Kowner. London: RoutledgeCurzon, 2006.

Sarila, Narendra Singh. *The Shadow of the Great Game: The Untold Story of India's Partition*. London: Archibald Constable, 2006.

Sarkisyanz, M. "Russian Conquest in Central Asia: Transformation and Acculturation." In *Russia and Asia: Essays on the Influence of Russia on the Asian Peoples*, edited by W. S. Vucinich. Stanford, Calif.: Hoover Institution Press, 1972.

Schimmelpenninck van der Oye, D. "Reforming Military Intelligence." In *Reforming the Tsar's Army: Military Innovation in Imperial Russia from Peter the Great to the Revolution*, edited by D. Schimmelpenninck van der Oye and B. Menning. Washington, D.C., and New York: Woodrow Wilson Center Press and Cambridge University Press, 2004.

———. "Tournament of Shadows: Russia's Great Game in Tibet." *Tibetan Review* 29, no. 1 (1994): 13–20.

———. *Toward the Rising Sun: Russian Ideologies of Empire and the Path to War with Japan*. DeKalb: Northern Illinois University Press, 2001.

Searle, G. *A New England? Peace and War 1886–1918*. Oxford: Clarendon Press, 2004.

Seaver, G. *Francis Younghusband: Explorer and Mystic*. London: John Murray, 1952.

Semenov, L. S. *Rossiia i Angliia: Ekonomicheskie otnosheniia serediny XIX v.* Leningrad: Leningrad State University, 1975.

———. *Rossiia i mezhdunarodnye otnosheniia na Srednem Vostoke v 20-e gg. XIX v.* Leningrad: Leningrad State University, 1963.

Senokosov, A. G. "Evolutsiia Antanty kak voenno-politicheskogo soiuza (1891–1923)." *Vestnik RGGU*, no. 14/09 (2009): 72–81.

Sergeev, E. "Anglo-rossiiskaia Antanta 1907 g. Novye aspekty." *Novaia i noveishaia istoriia*, no. 5 (2007): 50–65.

———. "Diplomaticheskaia revoliuysiia' 1907 g. v otnosheniiakh Rossii i Velikobritanii." *Oriens*, no. 2 (2008): 80–93.

———. "Imperskie voennye elity Rossii i Velikobritanii v kontse XIX–nachale XX vv.: Opyt sravnitel'nogo analiza." In *Rossiia i Britaniia: Sviazi i vzaimnye predstavleniia, XIX–XX vv.*, vol. 4, edited by A. Davidson. Moscow: Nauka, 2006.

———. "Obraz Velikobritanii v predstavleniiakh possiiskikh diplomatov i voennykh v kontse XIX–nachale XX vv." In *Rossiia i Evropa v XIX–XX vv. Problemy vzaimovospriiatiia narodov, sotsiumov, kul'tur*, edited by A. Golubev. Moscow: Institut rossiiskoi istorii RAN, 1996.

———. *Politika Velikobritanii i Germanii na Dal'nem Vostoke, 1897–1903 gg.* Moscow: Institute of World History RAN, 1998.

———. "Russian Military Intelligence." In *The Russo-Japanese War in Global Perspective: World War Zero*, vol. 1, edited by J. Steinberg et al. Leiden: Brill, 2005.

———. *Russian Military Intelligence in the War with Japan, 1904–05: Secret Operations on Land and at Sea*. London: Routledge, 2007.

Shalina, A. V. "Politika Velikobritanii v Srednei Asii i na Dal'nem Vostoke v 1904–1906 gg.: Ot protivostoiania s Rossiei k anglo-russkoi konvetsii (po doneseniiam rossiiskikh voennykh agentov)." In *Problemy vseobstchei istorii: sobytiia, liudi, fakty*, edited by I. Zhiriakov. Moscow: Moskovskii gosudarstvennyi oblastnoi pedagogicheskii universitet, 2000.

Sharma, A. "India's Foreign Problem and Lord Curzon (1899–1905)." *Journal of Historical Research* (Ranchi, India) 12, no. 1 (1969): 81–92.

———. "The Russian Menace to India and Lord Curzon (1899–1905)." *Proceedings of the Indian History Congress*, no. 31 (1969): 476–81.

Shastitko, P. M. "K voprosu o mificheskoi 'russkoi ugroze' Indii." In *Protiv falk'sifikatsii istorii kolonialisma*, edited by K. Popov. Moscow: Vostochnaia literatura, 1962.

Shaumian, T. L. *Tibet: The Great Game and Tsarist Russia*. New Delhi: Oxford University Press, 2000.

———. *Tibet v mezhdunarodnykh otnosheniiakh v nachale XX v.* Moscow: Nauka, 1977.

Shirokoriad, A. B. *Rossiia–Angliia: Neizvestnaia voina, 1857–1907*. Moscow: AST, 2003.

Shkunov, V. N. "Bukharskie evrei i torgovye sviazi Rossii s khanstvami Srednei Asii vo vtoroi povine XVIII–XIX v." *Vostok*, no. 4 (2010): 129–33.

Shkvarov, A. G. *General-Lieutenant Mannerheim: Rozhden dlia sluzhby tsarskoi.* Saint Petersburg: Russkaia voennaia zhizn', 2005.

Sholokhov, A. B. *Polkovodets, Suvorovu ravnyi, ili minskii korsikanets Mikhail Skobelev.* Moscow: UniWestMedia, 2008.

Siegel, J. *Endgame: Britain, Russia and the Final Struggle for Central Asia, 1907–1914.* London: I. B. Tauris, 2002.

Sinclair, A. *The Other Victoria: The Princess Royal and the Great Game of Europe.* London: Weidenfeld & Nicolson, 1981.

Skachkov, P. E. *Ocherki istorii russkogo kitaedeniia.* Moscow: Nauka, 1977.

Skrine, C., and Pamela Nightingale. *Macartney at Kashgar: New Light on British, Chinese, and Russian Activities in Sinkiang, 1890–1918.* London: Methuen, 1979.

Smirnov, A. "U sten Indii: Pamirskie pokhody pri Alexandere III." *Rodina*, no. 8 (2001): 67–70.

Snelling, J. *Buddhism in Russia: The Story of Agvan Dorzhiev, Lhasa's Emissary to the Tsar.* Shaftsbury, U.K.: Element, 1993.

Soothill, W. *China and the West: A Sketch of Their Intercourses.* London: Curzon Press, 1974.

Spence, J. *The Chan's Great Continent: China in Western Minds.* New York: W. W. Norton, 1998.

Steele, D. *Lord Salisbury: A Political Biography.* London: University College London Press, 1999.

———. "Salisbury at the India Office." In *Salisbury: The Man and His Policies*, edited by R. Blake and H. Cecil. New York: St. Martin's Press, 1987.

Steinberg, E. L. "Angliiskaia versiia o 'russkoi ugroze' Indii v XIX–XX vv." *Istoricheskie zapiski* 33 (1950): 47–66.

———. "Angliiskaia versiia o 'russkoi ugroze' Indii v XIX–XX vv." In *Problemy metodologii i istochnikovedeniia vneshnei politiki Rossii*, edited by A. Ignatiev. Moscow: Istitut rossiiskoi istorii RAN, 1986.

———. *Istoriia britanskoi agressii na Srednem Vostoke.* Moscow: Voennoe izdatel'stvo, 1951.

Steiner, Z., and K. Neilson. *Britain and the Origins of the First World War.* Basingstoke, U.K.: Palgrave Macmillan 2003.

Stewart, J. *Spying for the Raj: The Pundits and the Mapping of the Himalaya.* Phoenix Mill, U.K.: Sutton, 2006.

Storry, R. *Japan and the Decline of the West in Asia, 1894–1943.* London: Macmillan, 1979.

Strebelsky, I. "The Frontier in Central Asia." In *Studies in Russian Historical Geography,* vol. 1, edited by J. Bates and R. French. London: Academic Press, 1983.

Strong, J. "The Ignatiev Mission to Khiva and Bokhara in 1858." *Canadian Slavonic Papers* 17, nos. 2–3 (1975): 236–69.

Sukash, C. *Afghanistan and the Great Game.* Delhi: New Century, 2002.

Sukhorukov, S. A. *Iran mezhdu Britaniei i Rossiei: Ot politiki do ekonomiki.* Saint Petersburg: Aleteia, 2009.

Sumner, B. H. "Tsardom and Imperialism in the Far East and Middle East, 1880–1914." *Proceedings of the British Academy* 27 (1940): 25–65.

Suteeva, K. "Russkie voennye istoriki XIX v. o prichinakh i motivakh dvizheniia Rossii na Vostok (v Sredniuyu Asiyu i Yuzhnyi Kazakhstan)." http://www.kungrad. com/history/st/rushis/.

Sweet, D., and R. Langhorne. "Great Britain and Russia, 1907–1914." In *British Foreign Policy under Sir Edward Grey,* edited by F. Hinsley. Cambridge: Cambridge University Press, 1977.

Sykes, P. *The Right Honourable Sir Mortimer Durand: A Biography.* London: Cassell, 1926.

Tada, T. *The Thirteenth Dalai Lama.* Tokyo: Centre for East Asian Cultural Studies, 1965.

Tatsuo, N. "Qing China Northeast Crescent: The Great Game Revisited." In *The Russo-Japanese War in Global Perspective: World War Zero,* vol. 2, edited by David Wolff et al. Leiden: Brill, 2007.

Taylor, R. *Lord Salisbury.* London: Allen Lane, 1975.

Tchalenko, J. *Images from the Endgame: Persia through a Russian Lens, 1901–1914.* London: Al-Saqi Press, 2006.

Telepina, G. "Russkaia pechat' o politike Anglii v Tibete v nachale XX v." *Institut Dal'nego Vostoka: Informatsionnyi bulletin,* no. 120, pt. 2 (1983): 62–71.

Ter-Egisarova, R. M. "Turkestanskoe general-gubernatorstvo i anglo-russkoe soglashenie 1907 g." *Tashkentskii gosudarstvennyi universitet: Nauchnye trudy* 343, pt. 1 (1969): 93–99.

Ter-Oganov, N. K. "Persidskaia kazachya brigada: Period transformatsii (1894–1903)." *Vostok,* no. 3 (2010): 69–79.

Terenzio, P.-C. *La Rivalité Anglo-Russe en Perse et en Afghanistan jusqu'aux accords de 1907.* Paris: Rousseau, 1947.

Thornton, A. "British Policy in Persia, 1858–1890." *English Historical Review* 64, no. 273 (1954): 554–79.

———. *Doctrines of Imperialism.* New York: John Wiley & Sons, 1965.

———. "The Reopening of the 'Central Asian Question,' 1864–1869." *History,* 41, nos. 141–43 (1956): 122–36.

Tikhomirov, M. N. *Prisoedinenie Merva k Rossii*. Moscow:Vostochnaia literatura, 1960.

Tikhonov, D. I. "Vosstanie 1864 g. vVostochnom Turkestane." *Sovetskoe vostokovedenie* 5 (1948): 155–72.

Tikhonov, N. S. *Vambery*. Moscow: Mysl', 1974.

Tikhonov,Yu. N. "Novyi istochnik po istorii 'Bol'shoi Igry' v Afghanistane v period dvukh mirovykh voin." *Vostochnyi arkhiv*, no. 13 (2005): 102–11.

Towle, P. "The Russo-Japanese War and the Defense of India." *Military Affairs* 44, no. 3 (1980): 111–17.

Trench, C. *The Frontier Scouts*. London: Jonathan Cape, 1985.

Trevelyan, G. *Grey of Fallodon: The Life and Letters of Sir Edward Grey, Aftermath Viscount Grey of Fallodon*. Boston: Houghton Mifflin, 1937.

Trukhanovsky,V. G. *Bendjamin Disraeli, ili istoriia odnoi neveroiatnoi kariery*. Moscow: Nauka, 1993.

Ulunian, A. A. "Britanskii konzept 'etnopoliticheskogo prostranstva' v 'Bol'shoi Igre' i ego krushenie (70-e–80-e gg. XIX v.)." *Istoricheskoe prostranstvo: Problemy istorii stran SNG*, no. 1 (2009): 175–90.

———. "Magistralisatsiia prostranstva:Tsentral'no-asiatskii vector v otsenkakh i prognosakh imperskikh voennykh i grazhdanskikh chinovnikov (konets XIX– nachalo XX v.)." *Irano-Slavika*, nos. 3–4 (2004): 16–23.

———. *Novaia politicheskaia geografiia*. Moscow: Institute of World History, 2009.

———. "Tsentral'no-Asiatskaia igra' rossiiskoi biurokratii (konets XIX–nachalo XX v.)." *Istoricheskoe prostranstvo: Problemy istorii stran SNG*, nos. 1–4 (2008): 89–107.

Usmanov, K. "Uigurskie istochniki o vosstanii v Sinkiange 1864 g." *Voprosy istorii*, no. 2 (1947): 87–89.

Val'skaia, B. A. *Puteshestvie Yegora Peterovicha Kovalevskogo*. Moscow: Gosudarstvennoe geograficheskoe izdate'stvo, 1956.

Verrier, A. *Francis Younghusband and the Great Game*. London: Jonathan Cape, 1991.

Vigasin, A. A., et al., eds. *Istoriia otechestvennogo vostokovedeniia s serediny XIX v. do 1917 g.* Moscow:Vostochnaia literatura, 1997.

Vinogradov, K. B., and N. K. Buzynina. "Lord Curzon: rekordy tsheslaviia." In *Monarkhi, ministry, diplomaty XIX–nachala XX v.*, edited by K.Vinogradov. Saint Petersburg: Saint Petersburg State University, 2002.

Vinogradov, K. B., and O. A. Naumenkov. "Marquis Salisbury: Poslednii arkhitektor Pax Britannica." In *Monarkhi, ministry, diplomaty XIX–nachala XX v.*, edited by K. Vinogradov. Saint Petersburg: Saint Petersburg State University, 2002.

Vinogradov,V. N. "Russko-tutetskaia voina 1877–1878 gg. i evropeiskie derzhavy." *Novaia i Noveishaia istoriia*, no. 1 (2009): 127–43.

Vitukhnovsky, A. L. "Iz istorii anglo-russkikh otnoshenii na srednem Vostoke v nachal'nyi period anglo-burskoi voiny." *Peterozavodskii gosudarstvennyi universitet: Uchenye zapiski* 1, no. 7 (1958): 115–30.

Voskresensky, A. D. *Diplomaticheskaia istoriia russko-kitaiskogo Sankt-Peterburgskogo dogovora 1881 g.* Moscow: Pamiatniki istoricheskoi mysli, 1995.

———. *Kitai i Rossiia v Evrasii*. Moscow: Muravei, 2004.

Vucinich, W., ed. *Russia and Asia: Essays on the Influence of Russia on the Asian Peoples*. Stanford, Calif.: Hoover Institution Press, 1972.

Waldron, P. *The End of Imperial Russia, 1855–1917*. Houndmills, U.K.: Macmillan, 1997.

Waller, D. *The Pundits: British Exploration of Tibet and Central Asia*. Lexington: University Press of Kentucky, 1990.

Walsh, W. "The Imperial Russian General Staff and India: A Footnote to Diplomatic History." *Russian Review* 16, no. 2 (1957): 53–58.

Wang Furen and Suo Wenting. *Highlights of Tibetan Policy*. Peking: New World Press, 1984.

Ward, A. W., and G. P. Gooch, eds. *The Cambridge History of British Foreign Policy, 1783–1919*, vol. 3. Cambridge: Cambridge University Press, 1923.

Warikoo, K. *Central Asia and Kashmir: A Study in the Context of Anglo-Russian Rivalry*. Delhi: Gian, 1989.

———, ed. *Himalayan Frontiers of India: Historical, Geo-Political and Strategic Perspectives*. London: Routledge, 2009.

Weale, A. *Secret Warfare: Special Operations Forces from the Great Game to the SAS*. London: Hodder & Stoughton, 1997.

Wheeler, G. "Russian Conquest and Colonization of Central Asia." In *Russian Imperialism from Ivan the Great to the Revolution*, edited by T. Hunczak. New Brunswick, N.J.: Rutgers University Press, 1974.

Whitteridge, G. *Charles Masson of Afghanistan: Explorer, Archaeologist and Intelligence Agent*. Warminster, U.K.: Aris and Phillips, 1986.

Wilgus, M. *Sir Claude MacDonald, the Open Door, and British Informal Empire in China, 1895–1900*. New York: Garland, 1987.

Williams, B. "Great Britain and Russia, 1905 to the 1907 Convention." In *British Foreign Policy under Sir Edward Grey*, edited by F. Hinsley. Cambridge: Cambridge University Press, 1977.

———. *The Politics of Entente: Essays on the Determinants of British Foreign Policy, 1904–1914*. Cambridge: Cambridge University Press, 1985.

———. "The Strategic Background to the Anglo-Russian Entente of August 1907." *Historical Journal* 9, no. 3 (1966): 360–73.

Williams, R. *Defending the Empire: Conservatives and Defense Policy, 1899–1915*. New Haven, Conn.: Yale University Press, 1991.

Wilson, K. "The Anglo-Japanese Alliance of August 1905 and the Defence of India: A Case of the Worst Case Scenario." *Journal of Imperial and Commonwealth History*, no. 21 (1993): 334–56.

———. *Empire and Continent: Studies in British Foreign Policy from the 1880s to the First World War*. London: Mansell, 1987.

———. *The Policy of Entente: Essays on the Developments of British Foreign Policy, 1904–1914*. Cambridge: Cambridge University Press, 1985.

Winstone, V. *The Illicit Adventure: The Story of Political and Military Intelligence in the Middle East from 1898 to 1926*. London: Jonathan Cape, 1982.

Wint, G. *The British in Asia*. London: Faber & Faber, 1947.

Wolf, L. *The Life of the First Marquees of Ripon*. 2 vols. London: John Murray, 1921.

Woodcock, G. *The British in the Far East*. New York: Atheneum, 1969.

Woodman, D. *Himalayan Frontiers: A Political Review of British, Chinese, and Russian Rivalries*. London: Barrie and Rockliff, Cresset Press, 1969.

Wren, M. *The Western Impact upon Tsarist Russia*. New York: Holt, Rinehart & Winston, 1971.

Wright, D. *The English amongst the Persians During the Qajar Period, 1787–1921*. London: Heinemann, 1977.

Wynn, A. *Persia in the Great Game: Sir Percy Sykes—Explorer, Consul, Soldier, Spy*. London: John Murray, 2003.

Yakhontoff, V. *Russia and the Soviet Union in the Far East*. New York: Coward-MacCann, 1931.

Yang, L. "Historical Notes on the Chinese World Order." In *The Chinese World Order: Traditional China's Foreign Relations*, edited by J. Fairbank. Cambridge, Mass.: Harvard University Press, 1968.

Yapp, M. *Strategies of British India: Britain, Iran and Afghanistan, 1798–1850*. Oxford: Clarendon Press, 1980.

Yegorov, K. B. "Armeiskii ofitserskii korpus i imperskaia politika Velikobritanii vo vtoroi polovine XIX v." In *Diplomatiia i voina: Voprosy istorii mezhdunarodnykh otnoshenii v novoe i noveishee vremia*, edited by A. B. Sokolov. Yaroslavl': Yaroslavskii gosudarstvennyi pedagogicheskii universitet, 1998.

Yemets, V. A. "A. P. Izvolsky i perestroika vneshnei politiki Rossii (soglasheniia 1907 g.)." In *Rossiiskaia diplomatiia v portretakh*, edited by A. V. Ignatiev et al. Moscow: Mezhdunarodnye otnosheniia, 1992.

Yerofeev, N. A. *Angliiskii kolonialism v seredine XIX v*. Moscow: Nauka, 1977.

———. *Tumannyi Al'bion: Angliia i anglichane glazami russkikh, 1825–1853 gg*. Moscow: Nauka, 1982.

Young, L. *British Policy in China, 1895–1902*. Oxford: Clarendon Press, 1970.

Yuldasheva, F. *Iz istorii angliiskoi kolonial'noi politiki v Afghanistane i Srednei Asii (70-e–80-e gg. XIX v.)*. Tashkent: Fan, 1963.

Zaionchkovsky, A. M. *Podgotovka Rossii k mirovoi voine v mezhdunarodnom otnoshenii*. Leningrad: Nrakomvoenmor i RVS SSSR, 1926.

Zakharova, A. "Alexander II i mesto Rossii v mire." *Novaia i noveishaia istoriia*, no. 2 (2005): 164–93.

Zashikhin, A. N. *Gliadia iz Londona: Rossiia v obstchestvennom mnenii Britanii—Vtoraia polovina XIX– nachalo XX v*. Archangelsk: Pomorskii mezhdunarodnyi pedagogicheskii universitet, 1994.

Zhigalina, O. I. *Velikobritaniia na Srednem Vostoke (XIX–nachalo XX v.): Analiz vneshnepoliticheskikh kontseptsii*. Moscow: Nauka, 1990.

Zhukovsky, S. V. *Snosheniia Rossii s Bohkaroi i Khivoi za poslednee trekhsotletie*. Peterograd: Trudy Obscshestva russkikh orientalistov, 1915.

Zvavich, A. I. "Russko-angliiskie otnosheniia, 1909–1914." *Moskovskii oblastnoi pedagogicheskii institute: Uchenye zapiski* 105, no. 6 (1961): 73–103.
Zyrianov, A.V. *Velikobritaniia: Vzgliad iz Rossii.* Ekaterinburg: Ural'skii rabochii, 2005.

UNPUBLISHED THESES AND MANUSCRIPTS

Alymbaeva, Zh. B. "Istoriografiia zavoevaniia Turkestana Rossiei v XIX–nachale XX v." Kand. diss., Tashkentskii gosudarstvennyi universitet, 2002.
Ananich, B.V. "Angliia i Rossiia v Persii nakanune soglasheniia 1907 g." Kand. diss., Leningradskii gosudarstvennyi universitet, 1960.
Avdeev, V. E. "A. P. Izvolsky: Glava vneshnepoliticheskogo vedomstva Rossii (1906–1910)." Kand. diss., Moskovskii gosudarstvennyi universitet, 2006.
Beaver, W. "The Development of the Intelligence Division, and Its Role in Aspects of Imperial Policy Making, 1854–1901: The Military Mind of Imperialism." Ph.D. diss., University of Oxford, 1976.
Bushev, P. P. "Angliiskaia agressiia v Irane v 1855–1857 gg." Kand. diss., Institut vostokovedeniia AN SSSR, 1952.
Damdinov, A.V. "Agvan Dorzhiev: Diplomat, politicheskii, obstchestvennyi i religioznyi deiatel.'" Kand. diss., Irkutskii gosudarstvennyi universitet, 1996.
Dankov, A. G. "Otechestvennaia i britanskaia istoriografiia o sopernichestve Rossii i Velikobritanii v Tsentral'noi Azii (XIX–nachalo XXI vv.)." Kand. diss., Tomskii gosudarstvennyi universitet, 2009.
Demichev, K. A. "Politika Velikobritanii v Pandzhabe v XIX v.: Sutschnost', osnovnye napravleniia i regional'nye osobennosti." Kand. diss., Nizhegorodskii gosudarstvennyi pedagogicheskii universitet, 2007.
Gal'kov, Ch.V. "Turkestanskii voenno-topograficheskii otdel i ego raboty po kartografirovaniiu Srednei Azii (1867–1914)." Kand. diss., Sredneasiatskii gosudarstvennyi universitet, 1958.
Gleb, M.V. "Evolutsiia imperskoi idei v Velikobritanii vo vtoroi polovine XIX v." Kand. diss., Belorusskii gosudarstvennyi universitet, 2003.
Gopov, O. A. "Rol' ofitserov General'nogo shtaba v osutschestvlenii vneshnei politiki Rossiiskoi imperii na musul'manskom Vostoke vo vtoroi polovine XIX v." Kand. diss., Institut vostokovedeniia RAN, 2004.
Harris, L. "British Policy on the North-West Frontier of India, 1889–1901." Ph.D. diss., University of London, 1960.
Ignatiev, R. N. "Vliianie politicheskikh granits na etnicheskoe samosoznanie." Kand. diss., Institut etnologii i antropologii RAN, 2002.
Ivanov, K.Ye. "Tamozhennaia politika Rossiiskoi imperii v kontse XIX–nachale XX vv.: Perekhod k sisteme konvetsional'nykh torgovykh soglashenii." Kand. diss., Sankt-Peterburgskii gosudarstvennyi universitet, 2006.

Kalandarova, M. S. "Geopolitika Anglii v Tsentral'noi Asii v 20-e–30-e gg. XIX v. (po materialam ekspeditsii A. Bernsa v Bukharu v 1831 g.). Kand. diss., Institut vostokovedeniia RAN, 1995.

Kalmykova, M. V. "Politika Velikobritanii v bor'be velikikh derzhav za neftianye istochniki Blizhnego i Srednego Vostoka v period s 1901 po 1920 gg." Kand. diss., Vladimirskii gosudarstvennyi pedagogicheskii universitet, 2006.

Kasparian, K. V. "Rossiisko-britanskie vneshnepoliticheskie otnosheniia i dinasticheskie sviazi, 1837–1907 gg." Kand. diss., Piatigorskii gosudarstvennyi lingvisticheskii universitet, 2006.

Kazarian, E. E. "Russkii Dal'nii Vostok v sisteme rossiiskoi i mirovoi torgovli ma rubezhe XIX–XX vv." Kand. diss., Nizhegorodskii gosudarstvennyi universitet, 2006.

Khalfin, N. A. "Politika Rossii v Srednei Asii i anglo-russkoe sopernichestvo (1857–1876)." Doct. diss., Moskovskii gosudarstvennyi pedagogicheskii institut, 1962.

Koot, J. "The Asiatic Department of the Russian Foreign Ministry and the Formation of Policy toward the Non-Western World, 1881–1894." Ph.D. diss., Harvard University, 1980.

Kruchinin, N. A. "Politicheskaia elita Velikobritanii v period sotsial'nykh reform liberal'nykh kabinetov G. Campbell-Banerman i H. Asquith (1905–1914)." Kand. diss., Ural'skii gosudarstvennyi universitet, Ekaterinburg, 2004.

Kubanov, K. G. "Pokhody v Indiiu v proektakh rossiiskikh voennykh i politicheskikh deiatelei XVIII–nachala XX v." Kand. diss., Nizhnevartovskii gosudarstvennyi gumanitarnyi universitet, 2007.

Likharev, D. V. "Morskaia politika Velikobritanii v 1900–1930 gg." Doct. diss, Sankt-Peterburgskii gosudarstvennyi universitet, 1995.

Lisitsyna, N. N. "Zakaspiiskii krai v anglo-russkikh otnosheniiakh (1880–1917)." Kand. diss., Moskovskii otkrytyi pedagogicheskii universitet, 2006.

Lunieva, Iu. V. "Chernomorskie prolivy v anglo-rossiiskikh otnosheniakh (1907–1914)." Kand. diss., Institut vseobtschei istorii RAN, 2003.

Lurie, S. V. "Rossiiskaia i Britanskaia imperii na Srednem Vostoke v XIX–nachale XX vv.: Ideologiia i praktika." Kand. diss., Institut vostokovedeniia RAN, 1996.

Lydgate, J. "Curzon and Kitchener and the Problem of Indian Army Administration 1899–1909." Ph.D. diss., University of London, 1965.

Martirosov, S. Z. "Anglo-russkoe sopernichestvo v period prisoedineniia Turkmenii k Rossii." Kand. diss., Moskovskii gosudarstvennyi pedagogicheskii institut, 1966.

Masalieva, O. I. "Istoriia Bukharskogo, Khivinskogo, Kokandskogo khanstv v anglo-amerikanskoi istoriografii." Kand. diss., Tashkentskii gosudarstvennyi universitet, 1999.

Mirzaeva, L. R. "Sbornik 'Turkestanskii krai' A. G. Serebrennikova i ego znachenie dlia sredneasiatskoi istoriografii." Kand. diss., Institut istorii i arkheologii AN Uzbekskoi SSR, 1963.

Morris, L. "Anglo-Russian Relations in Central Asia, 1873–1887." Ph.D. diss., University of London, 1968.

Nishanova, D. A. "Anglo-russkii konflikt v Srednei Asii v kontse XIX v. v sovremennoi zarubezhnoi literature." Kand. diss., Tashkentskii gosudarstvennyi universitet, 1994.

Osipova, I. N. "Diskussiia po probleme 'imperialisma' v angliiskoi obtschestvennoi mysli v XIX–nachale XX v." Kand. diss., Saratovskii gosudarstvennyi universitet, 1998.

Pak, B. B. "Rossiiskaia diplomatiia i Koreia (1876–1898)." Doct. diss., Institut vostokovedeniia RAN, 2007.

Petukhov, L. A. "Obraz Velikobritanii v rossiiskom obstchestvennom mnenii v period anglo-burskoi voiny (1899–1902 gg.)." Kand. diss., Gosudarstvennyi akademicheskii universitet gumanitarnykh nauk, 2008.

Piaskovsky, A. V. "Revolutsiia 1905–1907 gg. v Turkestane." Kand. diss., Institut istorii AN SSSR, 1956.

Plekhanov, A. E. "Anglo-russkie politicheskie otnosheniia v 1907–1914 gg." Kand. diss., Vladimirskii gosudarstvennyi universitet, 2006.

Poltz, L. "Die Anglo-Russische Entente, 1903–1907." Ph.D. diss., Universitaet Winsen (Luhe), 1938.

Preston, A. "British Military Policy and the Defense of India, 1876–1880." Ph.D. diss., University of London, 1966.

Pubaev, R. E. "Ekspansia Anglii v Tibete i bor'ba tibetskogo naroda protiv angliiskikh zakhvatchikov (konets XIX–nachalo XX vv.)." Kand. diss., Leningradskii gosudarstvennyi universitet, 1955.

Ritchie, G. "The Asiatic Department during the Reign of Alexander II, 1855–1881." Ph.D. diss., Columbia University, 1970.

Ryzhenkov, M. R. "Rol' voennogo vedomstva Rossii v razvitii otechestvennogo vostokovedeniia v XIX–nachale XX vv." Kand. diss., Institut vostokovedeniia AN SSSR, 1991.

Schimmelpenninck van der Oye, D. "Ex Oriente Lux: Ideologies of Empire and Russia's Far East, 1895–1904." Ph.D. diss., Yale University, 1997.

Senokosov, A. G. "Angliia i Antanta: Na puti k voenno-politicheskomu soiuzu (1907–1914 gg.)." Moskovskii gosudarstvennyi universitet, 2005.

Shevchenko, D. V. "Basmacheskoe dvizhenie: Politicheskie protsesy i vooruzhennaia bor'ba v Srednei Asii, 1917–1931 gg." Kand. diss., Irkustkii gosudarstvennyi pedagogicheskii universitet, 2006.

Stepanov, I. V. "Ideologiia i politika britanskogo militarisma v kontse XIX–nachale XX v." Kand. diss., Samarskii gosudarstvennyi universitet, 2006.

Sukhorukov, S. A. "Anglo-persidskie otnosheniia v seredine XIX v." Kand. diss., Sankt-Peterburgskii gosudarstvennyi universitet, 2003.

Sushanlo, M. "Dunganskoe vosstanie vtoroi poviny XIX v. i rol' v nem Bai Yanhu." Kand. diss., Institut vostokovedeniia AN SSSR, 1953.

Terentieva, N. V. "Sovetskaia istoriografiia anglo-russkogo sopernichestva v Srednei Asii v pervoi polovine XIX v." Kand. diss., Barnaul'skii gosudarstvennyi universitet, 2003.

Vasiliev, A. D. "Vzaimootnosheniia Osmanskoi imperii i gosudarstv Tsentral'noi Asii v seredine XIX–nachale XX v." Kand. diss., Rossiiskaia akademiia gosudarstvennoi sluzhby, 2007.

Vinokur, A. V. "Ot konfrontatsii k soglasovannomu kursu: politika Velikobritanii i Rossii v Irane (1900–1914)." Kand. diss., Sankt-Peterburgskii gosudarstvennyi universitet, 2004.

Vul', N. A. "Politicheskaia istoriia Tibeta vo vremia pravleniia Dalai-Lamy XIII (1895–1933)." Kand. diss., Sankt-Peterburgskii gosudarstvennyi universitet, 2007.

Yegorenko, O. A. "Bukharskii Emirat v period protektorata Rossii (1868–1920 gg.): Istoriografiia problemy." Kand. diss., Rossiiskii gosudarstvennyi universitet turizma i servisa, 2008.

Yetisgin, M. "How the *Times* of London Covered and Interpreted Russian Expansion into Central Asia in the Second Half of the 19th Century." Ph.D. diss., Texas Technological University, 2000.

Zhdanov, Yu. V. "Diplomatiia Edwarda Greya i osnovnye napravleniia vneshnei politiki Velikobritanii v 1905–1916 gg." Kand. diss., Leningradskii gosudarstvennyi universitet, 1986.

INDEX